SchNEWS
OF THE WORLD

...book 2002 Issues 301-350

CAUTION

BREAKING NEWS
WHITE HOUSE DENIES BUSH ORDERED
ATTACK AGAINST AFGHANISTAN
CNN LIVE

WEAPONS OF MASS
DISTRACTION

CONFERENCE 2001

"There is no compromise possible with such
people... Defeat it or be defeated by it."

Seen Bristol www.bristle.co.uk

SchNEWS Of The World

published by Justice? July 2002.

ISBN: 09529748 6 X

Printed by Calverts Press, London

British Library Cataloguing in Publication Data; a catalogue record for this book is available from the British Library.

Cover

Graphics wizardry by Joe Plant www.joeplant.com

Photos used

Front

Top left: 'You Make Plans, We Make History' - graffiti at Genoa. Pic: John Hodge.

Middle left: 'We Are Zapatistas' at London Mayday, 2001. Pic: Guy Smallman.

Bottom left: Man going mad in green suit at Anti-war demo. Pic: Guy Smallman.

Top right: Revellers at EU Summit protests, Brussels, December 13, 2001. Pic: Guy Smallman

Middle right: Palestinian boys catapaulting stones at the walls of an Israeli army bunker, September 2001. Pic: Alec Smart.

Bottom right: Tripod blockading entrance to Crymlyn Burrows Incinerator, south Wales.

Back

'Ridin High' - cyclist at critical mass, London, Mayday 2001. Pic: Simon Chapman.

'Top Cop Breaks Ranks' - at Disarm DSEI, Docklands, London, September 11, 2001. Pic: John Hodge.

'Woomera Breakout' - protesters break into Woomera asylum seekers' detention centre in central Australia, moments later to help 50 asylum seekers escape. 29th March 2002. Pic: Melbourne Indymedia.

SchNEWS is a free weekly information sheet written, printed and published by volunteers in Brighton. It is obtainable by sending first class stamps (ten for nine issues) or donations (in UK pounds, payable to "Justice?") to SchNEWS, c/o On The Fiddle, P.O. Box 2600, Brighton, East Sussex, BN2 0EF, UK Phone 44 (0)1273 685 913

SchNEWS is also online www.schnews.org.uk. The website is updated each week with the latest issue of SchNEWS as well as the weekly update of the Party & Protest listings: a guide to parties, festivals, demos and actions happening in Britain and elsewhere. (If you would like to put an event in the SchNEWS Party & Protest listing then contact us...)

You can subscribe to SchNEWS electronically and receive the news sheet each week free in either PDF or text file version in an email - see 'Subscribe' on the website.

Also on our arse-kicking banana yellow website:
* search facility
* back issues of SchNEWS from issue 100 onwards
* DIY guide - direct action how-to guides
* Yellow Pages - regularly updated contacts list featuring around 800 direct action, community, alternative media, etc etc groups, campaigns & centres in Britain and abroad (a shortened version updated to June 2002 is in the back of this book).
* Prisoner support page
* Other bits & bobs.

Your turn now: As Indymedia say - 'don't hate the media, become the media' - keep SchNEWS (and all other alternative media) up to date with the news of your actions - big & small - global & local - to help inspire others and keep us all informed.

We are also looking for material for next year's book - so - if you've got articles about events, actions, UK & abroad, or articles exploring the issues of how we're gonna save the planet and all that - then get in contact. And if you've got photos of events, subverted billboards, cartoons, subvertisements etc send em in! We are open to suggestions....

(Send pics as photos - or preferably email tifs/jpg files - at 300 dpi 12x10cm if possible - oh and accompanied by brief blurbs.)

SchNEWS of the World Contents

SchNEWS
www.schnews.org.uk

You make plans, we make history

Welcome to the seventh SchNEWS annual. As usual it's built around another fifty issues of our free weekly newssheet - this book covering the year between April 2001 and April 2002.

SchNEWS was born in a squatted Courthouse in Brighton in 1994 as part of the campaign against the Criminal Justice Act. From the anti road protests at the M11 in London to the Newbury Bypass to the big Reclaim The Streets events of the nineties SchNEWS was there. From worker struggles such as the Liverpool Dockers, fights against the privatisation of public services, racism, genetic engineering, to reporting on positive solutions - week in week out SchNEWS reported the news from the direct action frontline.

Then in February 1998 some of the SchNEWS crew went to Geneva to the first ever Peoples Global Action conference. Here we met people involved in grassroots protests from across the world, swapped stories, made friendships and began to see the bigger picture; that most problems everywhere had the same root cause - it was that 'c' word [capitalism]. We also became aware of the globalised and institutionalised nature of this international economic exploitation - namely the World Bank, IMF (International Monetary Fund), WTO (World Trade Organisation) etc, and like many others who had been involved in localised direct action campaigns, much of our attention now turned to also attacking the corporate carve-up of the entire planet. The first signs of this new shift was in May 1998 when mass demonstrations were held world wide simultaneously against the G7 Summit in Birmingham, then again on June 18th 1999 (J18). It was the mass protests against the WTO in Seattle in November 1999 which really brought this 'movement' to the world's attention. These days no meeting or summit of the rich and powerful happens without mass demonstrations.

SchNEWS prides itself in publishing the news the mainstream media ignores [wonder why], and as the mainstream media becomes ever more controlled by the hands of fewer people, the alternative media becomes ever more important. The internet has enabled independent voices to reach every corner of the planet, instantly, which is key to the international nature of our resistance. We have seen the emergence of the many alternative news websites, most significantly the worldwide Indymedia network- where anyone can post a story on the web instantly. We update our website weekly and also reach a wide audience that way, but that's not to say that the paper copy isn't still the primary version of SchNEWS. In this cyber-age let's not forget the importance of the print media in the counter-propaganda war going back to Calvert and the pamphlet makers of the 1600's, right through to the independent zines and newsletters of today.

So - this book is the collection of the SchNEWS issues of the year, in addition to another 200 pages of articles which expand on the stories which SchNEWS, being just two sides of A4, may have only briefly reported at the time. These stories are mostly contributed by activists actually involved with the issues, not journalists or academics; SchNEWS writers and our mates have done the rest. We have used material from Indymedia, Corporate Watch, A-infos, Allsorts, Bristle, The Paper, Squall, Loombreaker and other trusted sources - writers for whom positive change and saving the planet is more important than their journalist career.

Added to this is a newly updated contacts list - this time shortened and put in easier-to-use categories. If you want the full 'yellow pages' contact list of 800 plus campaign groups - or the last 250 back issues of SchNEWS - or our massive party and protest section listing festivals, demos, meetings etc. as well as radical contact points around the country - or our DIY section with useful tips on everything from setting up your own newsletter to making your own bio-diesel - then check out our website.

And Finally, the book is called 'SchNEWS of the World' because of its obvious focus on global issues. Despite September 11, we wanted to make sure the book wasn't dominated by it, and focus on other stories from everywhere else. But while we avoided overdoing the 9-11 stuff, there was no getting away from discussing the global impact of the United States, the tentacles of the IMF, the Bush cabal and the US oil lobby, who are at the core of every other article in the book. Argentina, Congo, Chechnya, Colombia, Afghanistan, you name 'em - it's going to be about oil or extorting other resources for the West, and people starving because of 'structural adjustment'.

Our bottom line remains - 'Information For Action' - which means this book is not to stick on your shelf with your other right-on literature, or to help you write that essay - but to give you the kick up the arse - and the facts - to go out and...

DO SOMETHING ABOUT IT.

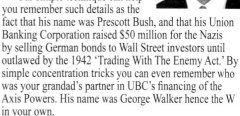

Trotskyites
With the earth drifting off to the right, you feel that your goals will be even harder to attain - and for the first time in your life you may be right about something. Lucky colour - red.

Situationists
You may never match the sun-moon conjunction of May 1968, but the writing's on the wall that something wonderful may happen again - and you're holding the spray can. Spend some time recuperating. Lucky number - 68

Druids
There is a new dawn coming in your life, if you move in the right stone circles. There will be many sacrifices that you'll need to make. Visit an old friend at the lodge - you might be up for a promotion.

Luddites
Just when you think the world has gone crazy things turn out smashing. You have much inner conflict when you find out that your new mobile phone can go on the internet. Lucky number - 1649.

Nihilist
Something revolutionary will happen at the bus stop. But eventually it will come to nothing. This is a good time to write that novel you always talk about. Lucky number - 0. Lucky colour - grey.

Anarcho-Syndicalists
Mercury is in opposition to Mars - so pay special attention to what you say to the splinter groups. You may find yourself in a love triangle with a Luddite who won't like your sex toys, and a Liberal Reformist who will fake their orgasms.

Postmodernists
All the cheap irony and kitsch rubbish you surround yourself is no substitute for a meaningful life. Stop laughing at luddites. Your idea that there is no grand narrative is the biggest grand narrative of them all.

Thatcherites
You privatised your health, and opened your lovelife up to a free market. But your children are the 'have nots' you always hated and sponge off you - because that's the world you've left them. Famous Thatcherite - Tony Blair. Lucky colour - gold.

Squatters
With the moon entering pisces watch out for water leaks in the makeshift plumbing. Tell that hippy who never does the washing up that the equinox would be a good time for him to go. Lucky number - section 6.

Liberal Reformists
You're on the cusp - always trying to please both sides - and end up pleasing nobody. Realise that can't paper over the cracks forever. You lack ambition and only ever fight for titbits. Favourite colour - blue-ish red.

Hunt Sabs
You've had your fair share of false dawns in recent times, but you've got many more years of being hounded for your beliefs. Try to not be so ranty - your preaching about vegetarianism is getting as bland as a lentil flapjack. Lucky colour - dark green.

New Age Travellers
Your moon is in transit - but you will need a new vehicle for your ideas. You will meet a tall dark stranger - who will arrest you. An abrupt change of scenery at the end of the month will be unsettling. Get rid of unwanted baggage before then.

Existentialists
Now is the time to espresso yourself. Constant nausea is a trait of this sign and the only way to deal with it is to say 'what the hell', watch some TV, go out and have a laugh with that jokey situationist. Lucky number - infinity.

To find out about your week in the stars visit party & protest at www.schnews.org.uk

6

WAKE UP! WAKE UP! IT'S YER BURNT OUT

'Anyone got a light?'

Weekly SchNEWS

Printed and Published in Brighton by Justice?

Friday 20th April 2001   www.schnews.org.uk   Issue 301   Warning: Incinerators cause cancer

WASTED!

"Why should others make the effort to think about and change what they are doing when the Government cannot be bothered to put their own house in order?" - House of Commons Environment Select Commitee Report.

In case it hasn't caught your attention SchNEWS likes to slag off the Government. Well, now a "respectable" body of MPs, the House of Commons Environment Select Committee, has joined us in sticking an authoritative boot into the knackers of the Government's policy on waste.

They make many semi-radical recommendations for sorting out the waste problems in this country. Reducing the amount of waste you produce in the first place is the best solution. Providing decent recycling facilities to increase recycling rates also helps. Simple stuff, really. Their report slags off the government for failing to properly educate the public, recycling targets are "depressingly unambitious", "lip-service" is paid to waste minimisation, and the government has simply accepted the growth of waste produced. They say "The Government must set a target for reducing the rate of growth of waste and consider with some urgency precisely how it can drive waste growth down and ultimately reverse it".

Of course, all this is pissing in the wind. In response, the Government will probably come out with a load of crap about how great it is doing and how it is meeting its targets. As the report says, the government "risks succeeding in its own narrow terms whilst failing to provide a foundation for a more sustainable system". Meaning that if your targets are totally pisspoor then it's easy to meet them, isn't it? Well, what did we expect- a state-sponsored no shopping week? Depressingly, the report will presumably end up gathering dust on a shelf or in the bin-they'll probably even forget to recycle it!

UP IN SMOKE

"We believe that incineration will never play a major role in truly sustainable waste management and cannot, and should not, be classified as producing renewable energy." – From that report, again.

To deal with the waste mountain the government's approach is to push ahead with incineration. They want to build up to 160 over the next 20 years, despite the fact that incineration produces lots of nasty chemicals like dioxins that cause cancer (SchNEWS 260). The report reckons there should be an incineration tax and that landfill tax should be increased. Can you see New Labour upsetting its new business friends by whacking up their tax? Most businesses aren't interested in reducing their waste. The report says, "We are extremely disappointed with the inertia and negative attitude of the Confederation of British Industry to changing the way the UK deals with its waste. Rarely has the old phrase 'if you are not part of the solution, then you are part of the problem' been more apt."

So with the Government and businesses not caring about waste or our health we may just have to rely on what poor regulation we've got and keep our fingers crossed we don't die of cancer. Those MPs from the Select Committee reckon "Where recurrent breaches of limit values are found to occur, the operator should be fined. If breaches continue to occur, the plant should be closed down." Have any incinerators closed? Have they bog roll. Since 1996 there have been 899 breaches of emission limits (on average each incinerator has at least one breach every month) but there hasn't been a single prosecution!

Until now. One prosecution *is* at last happening, against the Byker Incinerator in Newcastle. The City Council has kindly spread 2,000 tonnes of by-product toxic ash on allotments, footpaths and bridleways around Newcastle. Concerned locals had to hassle the relevant authorities into doing something rather than the evildoing being discovered through the regulatory action (SchNEWS 293) designed to stop it. The new Food Standards Authority did a report into the pollution, but cleverly failed to study children under 10- the most vulnerable group- and haven't even considered testing breast milk to look for effects on babies. Meanwhile, 2000 hens are going to be slaughtered as they are contaminated with toxic ash, while the 'experts' assure us that there is no risk to humans, just like they said with BSE. While the ash has been removed from 40 allotment sites, there are apparently 20 other sites, and it 's on park flowerbeds, too. Similar practices to those in Byker have occurred in London with toxic ash being "recycled" into streets and paths by wise and generous local councils. We at SchNEWS reckon the only 'wastes' we wanna see incinerated are beaureaucrats and politicians. Trust you agree!

* Communities Against Toxics (CATS) PO Box 29, Ellesmere Port, CH66 3TX. 0151-339-5473. cats@recycle-it.org.uk.

CATS Waste Conference. 11th May, Holiday Inn, Lower Mersey Street Ellesmere Port. 12th May, Stephenson Hall, 85c Highbury Place, London N5.

POSITIVE SCHNEWS

A new Centre made out of 'a load of rubbish' opened in Manchester this month. Bridge 5 Mill Centre has shredded polystrene packaging as insulation, with window frames and doors made from reclaimed timber. The reception has been made from straw bales, mud and an old snooker table. The centre is located in one of the most deprived inner-city areas in the country, and the majority of the work has been carried out by local people, many of whom joined the project as unskilled labourers and have now gained nationally-recognised NVQ qualifications. The Centre includes an exhibition on environmental issues and a resource centre full of infor and advice. Contact MERCi on 0161 273 1736

Not Very Ryton

Ryton Organic Gardens, the long established headquarters of HDRA, the organic organisation, is under threat of losing its organic status – thanks to a nearby genetic test site. The GM maize trial proposed at Wolston in Warwickshire is less than two miles from the gardens.

Not only is organic food grown at the gardens to be sold in their shop and restaurant, but there are trial areas used to develop improved organic methods mainly funded by the Ministry of Agriculture.

So what sort of genetically modified idiot came up with the idea to put the trials at Wolston? Who decides where GM farm trials go? In theory it should be the government appointed Scientific Steering Committee, but in reality it's SCIMAC an industry body who have taken on the job of finding farms, which the Steering Committee then rubber stamp.

The industry then provides the seed and pays farmers a 'compensation package', thought to be around £1,000 per hectare, while the taxpayer stump up the rest. In the case of the 32 maize trials that's £4.4 million.

According to a spokesman from Aventis, the 'life-science' corporation behind the maize trials, they knew of the existence of the HDRA site but they reckon there's no risk from the GM crop so they didn't bother to tell them. The first HDRA heard was through a local radio station.

Fodder maize is grown specifically to be fed to cattle – but it can cross-pollinate with sweetcorn, and bees – which HDRA have on site – could move the pollen several miles from the crop each day. And that sort of contamination could lose the biggest organic organisation in Europe its organic status.

* There's a rally in Wolston Village this Saturday (21) 11am, followed by public meeting at the Village Hall on Thursday (26) April 7.30 pm

* HDRA, Ryton Organic Gardens, Coventry, CV8 3LG Tel: 02476 639229 www.hdra.org.uk

Breaking the Silence

British Sign Language (BSL) is the first or only language for over 70,000 people in this country, yet it's not recognised as an official language. Many deaf children are forced to learn in English in mainstream schools, and denied their own language many leave with an average reading age of 8 or 9 years. Deaf people and their supporters have had enough and are stepping up their campaign to get their language recognised. Following on from their 9,000 strong demonstration in London last year, they have organised demos across the country. Last month in Manchester100 people blocked a road and couldn't be moved, because the cops couldn't get their message across. This month people were in Wolverhampton, and this Saturday (21st) there's a BSL march in Brighton, meet 12 noon, Brighton Railway Car park, contact 0870 4063716 march@sudp.fsnet.co.uk Contact Federation of Deaf People, PO Box 11, Darwen, Lancs BB3 3GH www.fdp.org.uk

SchNEWS in brief

Protesters in **South Africa** are celebrating a victory after 39 drug companies dropped legal action against the South African Government for importing "cheap" generic drugs to treat Aids. Zackie Ahmet from the Treatment Action Group said, "one of the main reasons for their [drug companies] withdrawal was the size of the local and international mobilisation of protest" ** After 3 years of fighting, the **"No Tarmac Quarries At Bestwood"** campaign has stopped the company getting planning permission for two quarries between Bestwood Village and Bestwood Country Park in Nottingham. Tarmac have handed the land over to the Country Park, increasing it's size by a third. ** Former **Crap Arrestee of the Week** Jon Neil has just won £1,200 in compensation after being nicked at last year's Smokey Bear's picnic. The cheeky Mr. Neil was arrested for the heinous offence of laughing at a humourless Hampshire police officer's wig ** After a three and a half year campaign by Newcastle Animal Rights Coalition against **Cornyhaugh Mink Farm**, the Farm announced last week that it was also closing. Protestors in the campaign were some of the first people to be charged under the Protection from Harassment Act, originally designed to protect woman from stalkers ** A 30 second **TV "uncommercial"** showing a blank screen aimed to black out CNN starts next week's TV Turnoff week. Check out www.adbusters.org.

That's enough of the good news.

Nine Ladies Anti-Quarry Campaign, set up to defend the historic and beautiful wildlife site on Stanton Moor Hillside (SchNEWS 258) could be facing eviction soon. People are urgently needed to defend the camp. A big Beltane party is planned so get down there for a party and stay for the eviction! 0797 404 9369 http//pages.zoom.co.uk/-nineladies ** **Fluoride** is an extremely toxic chemical, yet the Labour gov't is racing ahead with plans to change water laws to force water companies to add it to our water. On the continent fluoride is almost entirely banned. The National Pure Water Association is giving a talk this Sat (21) 5.30pm at Hanover Community Centre, HanoverSt, Brighton www.npwa.freeserve.co.uk ** At least 2,500 **Israeli** reserve troops have gone AWOL and thousands more have become conscientious objectors. In a bizarre twist Israel has recently jailed 600 soldiers to stop further rebellion! Meanwhile 3 Israelis were arrested after driving around Tel Aviv broadcasting "A curfew has been imposed ... residents must enter their homes. People seen on the street after 7:30 p.m. risk responses according to the usual procedures." They have been charged with "terrorising the public" unlike the Israeli politicians currently waging a terror campaign against Palestinians ** Take action against **Plan Columbia** (SchNEWS 273), the US's so-called war on drugs. April 30th sees the Columbian Government begging for money from EU governments in Brussels to fund this terror campaign. Demonstrations are planned 07950 923 448 lasocollective@hotmail.com

---

Oh, and if any of you 'orrible lot wanna write for SchNEWS come to our training day next Wednesday 12 noon onwards. Call the office to book yer place quick sharp as places are going like hot pants. And we're really short of writers as you can probably tell.

Inside SchNEWS

Veteran peace campaigner Lindis Percy is in Harrogate magistrate's court next Wednesday (25) to face charges of "abusive or insulting or disorderly behaviour" motivated by hostility towards an ethnic group, the said persecuted ethnic group being - US service personnel! Ms. Percy was nicked after she dragged the sacred Stars and Stripes in front of cars driven by Americans at the US Spy Base Menwith Hill. The crown has accused Ms. Percy of "racial harassment" on the grounds that she most certainly hurt the feelings of the US Servicemen, who broke down in tears as the bully Ms. Percy was hauled off to jail.

* Rosie James and Rachel Wenham are in Manchester Crown Court on Monday, April 30 for a re-trial. The two are accused of boarding and then smashing up a British Trident Submarine at Barrow . Contact Trident Ploughshares at 42-46 Bethel St, Norwich NR2 1NR Tel: 01324 880 744 www.gn.apc.org/tp2000/

* The Trial date for Catholic Priest Martin Newell and Susan van der Hijden has been moved to May 21. They've been on remand since before Christmas after disabling 2 convoy trucks used to carry Trident nuclear war-heads. Write to them at: Susan van der Hijden, EN 5880, HMP Highpoint, Stradishall, Newmarket, Suffolk, CB4 9YG. Fr. Martin Newell, EM 6780, HMP Belmarsh, Western Way, Thamesmead, London, SE28 0EB. A week of activities in support of Susan and Martin is happening from April 19-26, including the "Give Peace a Dance" next Thursday (26) 7:30pm in Camden Irish Centre, Murray St. 07947-569577 www.geocities.com/londoncatholicworker

* Mass fax & phone-in for Mark Barnsley on Wednesday 25th April to governor David Shaw at HMP Wakefield. Fax: 01924 299 315 or telephone: 01924 378282 to demand that Mark be moved from Wakefield Prison.

...and finally...

As the temperature rises in the run up to this year's Mayday protests, the mainstream press have been printing such extravagant lies it's hard to know what's actually going on. Crusties yesterday revealed to SchNEWS their devastating new organic biological weapons, as they finally managed to split the pea. "Why should the police have a monopoly on violence?" a spokesperson told us from the anarchists' new HQ, a squatted postbox in South London. Actions include:

* 'Operation Dessert Storm' will see police lines covered in gloopy custard dropped from marauding helicopters.

* Reclaim the Streets have forged links with Japanese whalers to stockpile harpoon guns, while their millionaire leader is thought to be bribing police to stay off duty on May 1st.

* Carrier pigeons are being used to get around email monitoring. They will be fed raw couscous, as it expands in their stomachs they'll explode all over central London. And unwashed dogs on hemp strings will attack police alsatians.

* Top direct action stylist Anita Roddick will massage police to death with peppermint foot cream.

* Protesters will liberate gorillas from London Zoo so they can do a bit of, er, gorilla gardening.

* The WOMBLES are organising a litter pick of Wimbledon Common.

* In a shocking parody of Blue Peter, the police will produce a riot they prepared earlier.

disclaimer

Subscribe!

Keep SchNEWS FREE! Send 1st Class stamps (e.g. 10 for next 9 issues) or donations (payable to Justice?) Ask for "Originals" if you can make copies. Post *free* to all prisoners. SchNEWS, c/o on-the-fiddle, P.O. Box 2600, Brighton, East Sussex, BN2 2DX.

Tel/Autofax +44 (0)1273 685913 *Email* **schnews@brighton.co.uk** *Download a PDF* of this issue or subscribe at **www.schnews.org.uk**

Twyford Down +10

The tenth anniversary of the first road protest campaign at Twyford Down has us casting our minds back to see how far things have or haven't come since then. Alex – who we may call a er 'veteran' of this campaign reflects on her experience of it...

There is such a thing as a movement whose time has come and Twyford was one of those movements, those moments. Looking back, ten years (!) down the line, from inside this fluid, diverse, complex and sparky movement, it is quite obvious to me (and to all of my political generation who have stayed with it), that waves of action like the roads protest movement are all part of a wider sea, the legacy of radical action... more on that later. So, whilst we - those of us living on the Down and coming down for days of action - were mostly all new to direct action, to the whole scene, blithely unaware of our political heritage as we geared up for the next round, there were other networks of activists and experience and local opposition who in more subtle ways had created the conditions for this moment.

Pic: Alec Smart

These included previous mobilisations like Stop The City demo's in the 80s and Greenham Common; activists from earlier actions like these, with tactical and strategic experience, helped trigger and sustain action on Twyford Down. Greenham women told me what to do with the pallets they brought down as the weather got colder and our benders more scrotty. 'Straighter' groups like Alarm UK! and the Twyford Down Association fought the road at another level, providing us with information and support. It is from people like these that I first learned about roads and how shit they were on so many levels. The whole free festy and traveller scene was very full-on then too, another way people heard about stuff happening- there were so many people out and about in the landscape those first few summers at the start of the 90's.

Not that I - or any of us much, I guess - thought about that much at the time, and we were too busy doing it to analyse it. And there was, on top of the 'mulch' of these other, established networks, so much that was new and innovative, lots of energy and - like with every new wave of mobilisation - lots of amazing people emerging and meeting each other and buzzing off each other and staying up late and going 'and did you know about this....' And 'hey why don't we do that'... There was something in the air, maybe.

The Earth First! networks were also being 'born' in the year leading up to the 92/3 Twyford protests and EF! and the Twyford campaign symbiotically grew, each learning and drawing strength from the other. I clearly remember sitting on the Down and some EF! folk having a workshop on what to do when the police came to carry us down the hill. I was naïve enough to think that it couldn't possibly happen - but none of us knew exactly how full-on things were going to be (a workshop on 'how to kick a security guard in the shins when he tries to grope your tits and pressure – point you, whilst trying to hurl yourself under a bulldozer' would have been more use... a steep learning curve for all of us...) though, if any of us had bothered with a bit of radical history, or listened to any of those 'old fart' peace activists, we might have sussed things a bit more from examples like the peace camp eviction at Molesworth.

It was just such a beautiful place, but quite small really, no impressive 500- year old forests or anything like that, just the hard cleanness of chalk and flint, a place where the Down met the sky, the sense of space, and where the footprints of past generations who'd lived in the landscape were literally visible - the barrows, the field systems and dewponds, and the worn-deep iron-age trackways locally known as 'dongas' where by mid '92 a small camp had been established. Of course it's a fucking great hole now, the heart of the Down carved out and taking a chunk of mine with it (and other peoples' too, I know). Your first campaign, whatever it is, tends to be your real political education, when the penny really drops - and one of the best things about it is that lots of other people are going through it too - that feeling of solidarity, of (often) unspoken understanding, love and rage. And yeah, alienation and resentment and personality clashes too... all totally necessary if painful...

For the first time I heard people ranting about stuff I'd thought for years, about the way society related to nature, value systems, gender politics, and then we had new stuff to put together with this: power relations, state control, roads roads roads... but lets' not forget, we had so much *fun* running around the Down on full moon nights, tripping on mushrooms, stumbling down to the worksite at the water-meadows and giggling, distracting the security guards whilst the pixies slipped about in the shadows. We were doing something about it all, and if, post-Newbury, it all seems a tad unto-gether, well it was, comparatively, but we had to start somewhere - tactics we now take for granted had to be thought up in the field - a legacy of knowledge we have hopefully passed on (though, sorry, everyone will have to learn the hard way about what to do about the pissed nutter whose major contribution to camplife is to fall into the fire, knocking off the just-about-to-boil kettle).

The numbers involved at that point in time- the Autumn/ Winter of 1992 - were tiny. Across the country, new networks of EF! activists were getting established, getting together, blatting down to Twyford for a weekend or day of action, spending time networking what was going on - things were starting to wake up again after a lull in activity generally in the ongoing history (+ her story) of the direct action movement.

Twyford was to catalyse this process and kick things off big styley. Of course none of us at the time knew any of this was going to happen- we were simply 15- odd (very, very odd) people on a hill, with a goat, running out to stop two old bulldozers and a few site officials and cops who'd come up to try and catch us unawares... their goal - to rip off the species- rich turf of the donga trackways. Ours - to stop them. For a few months, all it took to keep them at bay was us on the case, there, and erm, a significant amount of face paint and hippy chants. At the same time the forces of darkness were starting to get their shit together, what with Bray's detective agency lurking in the bushes, police complicity in providing names for injunctions, eviction notices, etc. We were all getting jumpy, there were more frequent, increasingly serious attempts to trash the Down, work on other parts of the site was kicking off and our early attempts at site invasion were not going too well, and we'd long since geared up into nightwatches and all of that.

Still no-one expected the Spanish Inquisition (aka Group 4) that grey December pre-dawn. Seeing that blurred mass of yellow jackets and massive machines it was obvious, running along the edge of our boundary toward the lookout post, that this was it, this was really fucking it. You know the score, whatever you've been up to - when you look over at the machinery and the manpower of *the enemy* lined up against you, coming churning towards you ripping up the trees, or banging their shields... urrgggghhh... aaarrghhh!!!! here we go! It was mental. It was fucked - up and it went on for days. No almost ritualised procedure of 'you know the score chaps' and media circuses, just absolute chaos, violence, pain, loss, instinct, bravery, fear, blinding rage...well, you know how it is.

The shockwaves of 'Yellow Wednesday' had precisely the opposite effect to that intended by our glorious leaders- they increased resistance. The second stage of the Twyford campaign is probably the one most people remember, because numbers kicked off exponentially. People who read about it in green mags came down with their mates to the new camp. People who'd been there beforehand got stuck into networking and strategising with a vengeance. Meanwhile the contractors (Tarmac + Mott McDonald) were getting torn into the cutting with their diggers. For me, and many others, this became a war of attrition, and one we did fucking well at.

Sometimes there'd be dozens of us charging onto the vast, moonscaped site from different angles, painted –up, screaming and yelling and generally going apeshit, thundering past the security guards, pulling out of vice - like hand grips, dodging past the buckets of diggers (driven by psychopaths) swinging viciously at you, leaping up with a desperate scramble on the oily, dirty surface of the machine and up and up... sometimes it ended in tears with bruised bones, others in all-day parties with entire machines disabled, draped in banners and tat and covered in people, kids, old ladies, the sound of drumming and whooping covering up any noises of machinery breaking down. Actions like these, like the bailey bridge, were the result of a lot of hard work and group effort.

By this time the anti- roads movement had a life of its own, with new campaigns urgently needing numbers, people getting more strategic in how to fight and what it was we were actually fighting, using our experience in other situations...Cradlewell, the M11, Solsbury Hill... and increasingly, our actions diversifying into related areas as we adapted tactics we'd learned worked at Twyford (office occupations, for example) for other enemies, other targets. Roads protest was never, ever, a 'single issue' thing but it was a starting point for lots of us to look at the wider picture (the dominant paradigm, modernity, the structure of power, blah de blah) and go, oh yeah... so arms sales and oil extraction and genetic engineering and all the rest of it just followed on 'naturally' as issues we needed to address, as we as individuals and symbiotically as the movement as a whole have grown into a much more complex deconstruction of 'life, the universe and everything' (aka "anti-capitalism and that"), which is where we are now, and how our movement has built up capacity.

Just to wind up with some thoughts about Rio+10: I am angry at the moment- fucking angry. It's all well and good to waffle on about the 'success' of our campaigns, of our movement, its effects on society's values... but let's face it – it's ten years since Rio - and in that time we have fought roads, human rights abuses, business-as-usual-behind-greenwash bullshit summits, about loss of habitats and species and the ozone layer and oil and war and the death of the innocent and power relations and all of it, all of it - and guess what? It's all still happening. This is why activists burnout, when they give their all and their original 'enemy' is not only still there, but you also realise that there's a many- headed hydra out there showing no signs of stopping - sooo tempting to run away and leave it to the next generation…. but I'm not letting go. I am fucking furious, how dare they, how dare they destroy our world and kill babies and call *us* the terrorists? The farce of Rio+10 is the final straw (how many times has that camel's back been broken?!) and boy do I want to stop some roads…. See ya out and about this summer…   Love, Alex 29.4.02

Claremont

While we're at it... Not quite having its 10th anniversary, but well worth recalling. This is one person's account of the famous protest...

My own involvement in road protest goes back to 1992, when I was living near Oxleas Wood, an 8000 year old ancient woodland in south-east London. Oxleas was then threatened by a vast road scheme called the East London River Crossing (ELRC) and, as a local cycle campaigner, it was clear that this lunacy had to be opposed somehow – but how? Local campaigners at Oxleas had given years of their lives to public inquiries, mortgaged their houses to mount legal challenges, organised rallies and festivals – so far to no avail. Some of them were now formulating plans for a direct action campaign to defend the trees. This was late '92, and the forces of Tarmac were already gathering around the Twyford Down defenders' campsite. So I went there initially to get my head around this direct action stuff, knowing that it might soon be the only option left for Oxleas Wood. Fortunately, my fears proved unfounded, thanks to the phenomenal impact of the Twyford campaign, whose reverberations shook the Department of Transport to its core. The crunch point came in July '93, when several campaigners defied the threat of imprisonment by continuing to protest at Twyford in breach of injunctions taken out against them. It took the government just two more days to announce that they were backing down on Oxleas Wood.

For me, the lesson was clear: direct action was inspiring, exhilarating, and – despite the fact that we hadn't stopped the Twyford motorway – it was incredibly effective. We also knew that the Oxleas decision was merely a tactical retreat; far more of the Government's roads programme had to be defeated before we could claim a genuine, lasting victory. Our problem was that the next big road-scheme on the list, the M11 Link Road, was a very unpromising venue for a rematch! Unlike Twyford or Oxleas, there were no Sites of Special Scientific Interest, no 8000-year-old woodland, no obvious appeal for the green-minded radicals who had been central to the Twyford campaign. Most of the route ran through a run-down area of housing that had been neglected ever since the road's "imminent" construction had first been announced 30 years previously.

From this apparently hopeless starting point, I still marvel at the way this campaign – the Cinderella of the three nationally known road schemes at that time – came to be the longest-lasting environmental direct action campaign of the '90s. At the outset, I'm pretty sure that none of us thought this campaign had any hope of taking off. Still, we pitched ourselves headlong into it, despite the odds.

We had some good fortune: the local myth that George Green - the first stage of construction - would remain unscathed (because there would be a tunnel section under it) was exposed at just the right moment. There was a 250 year old sweet chestnut tree in the middle of the green. When it became clear that the destruction of it was imminent, someone started building a tree-house. Then the contractors started putting up wooden fencing around the tree. The local children started bunking off school to obstruct them, and carried on doing so throughout the week. That Saturday, a few local residents planned a "tree-dressing" ceremony for the children but at the last moment, the security guards broke their earlier promise to allow the event to go ahead. Prevented from reaching their tree, people started tearing down the fences. The

Pic: Gideon Mendel

children joined in, followed by their lollypop lady, and then their parents. An entirely spontaneous action to reclaim their commons had brought radicalism to Wanstead.

Then when someone wrote a letter addressed to "The Tree-house, George Green, Wanstead E11", and the postman delivered it, one of the campaign's friendly solicitors latched onto another opportunity: He took the letter to court, claiming it as proof that the tree-house was a dwelling, which meant that the Department of Transport spent a month sorting out the legalities of a proper eviction. Next thing we knew the tree's new mailbox was flooded with mail from people who wanted to be phoned up when the tree was next under threat. There were four hundred people huddled round the tree in a raging storm at 5.30AM on the December morning, when the massed army of police, security and bailiffs arrived for the sweet chestnut's final execution. Thanks to a combination of popular resistance and thick mud, it took them another 10 hours to cut down that tree. All these years later, it still brings tears to my eyes to write about the sadness and the joy of that day.

The campaign had now fully taken off, and would now last for another whole year as a continuous direct action campaign. Its next major focus was a row of four houses just next to George Green, one of which had been the home of Patsy Braga, probably Wanstead's most ardent anti-road campaigner. Over time, all four houses became squats, indeed Pasty moved back in as a squatter. This was the moment for a Declaration of Independence from the UK, and the foundation of the Independent Free Area of Wanstonia – with our own passports, and a 9-year old as our Minister for Education! Wanstonia also ended in a "tragic-spectacular" eviction in mid February '94.

During "Operation Roadblock", we planned days of action every weekday for a month, with short training sessions at the beginning of each day, to make direct action accessible to as many newcomers as possible. Enormous numbers came, discovering the power they possessed working together to halt the bulldozers. Others – notably Earth First! Groups - would come to stay and were invaluable in maintaining the last remnants of sanity among the now exhausted "old hands" of the campaign!

By mid April our attention turned to defending Claremont Road in Leyton, the last intact street on the route. Gradually the whole street was squatted and, over the course of the summer, an extraordinary scene emerged. The paintings, indoors and outdoors, became crazier and crazier, as did the sculptures in the street. So did the people, the parties and the defences. Bunkers were built beneath the houses and in the roof-spaces. Houses were filled with car-tyres – a barricading technique which was beautifully symbolic - the government would have to dispose of the unsustainable waste product of the car culture it so keenly promoted. Cargo nets were strung up above the street, attached to trees or chimneys; wooden towers started sprouting from the rooftops. One day the bailiffs, police and security guards tried mounting a "guerrilla" eviction of part of the street. The wooden towers worked magnificently – so we started getting really ambitious! Over the next two months, we scavenged enough scaffold poles to create an enormous tower 100 foot high above the Claremont rooftops.

We named the tower after Dolly Watson, a wonderful old lady who had been born at 32 Claremont Road in 1901, and still there almost 93 years later. It was her simple wish that she should be allowed to die there, undisturbed by the road-scheme, but ill health forced her away some months before the bailiffs arrived. She could hardly see or walk, but her handling of the media inter-est she attracted was truly inspirational. Take for instance her forthright response to one journalist's question about her new neighbours on Claremont Road: "They're not dirty hippy squatters", she retorted, "they're the grandchildren I never had. The eviction itself took four days to complete. At one point, the bailiffs were gobsmacked to discover a tunnel under a garden, linking a Claremont bunker to a house on the adjoining street!

If Twyford was the campaign that launched the 1990s road protest movement, M11 was the one that anchored it, providing a platform for others to take off from, such as the campaigns at Solsbury Hill near Bath, the M65 near Preston, and the Pollok Estate in Glasgow. The next phase of road protests – campaigns such as Newbury and Fairmile – brought awareness of the issues to every tabloid reader in the land.

PS Remember Oxleas Wood and the East London River Crossing? Ken Livingstone is poised to give the go-ahead to the "Thames Gateway Bridge" – it's the same old river crossing with a different name. Ken's scheme stops short of Oxleas Wood of course, but it will cause an absolute traffic nightmare on the surrounding local roads. And any child can work out how they will "solve" THAT problem when it arises.

Roger Geffen

To read more about the amazing and inspiring road protests of the nineties see... George McKay's 'Senseless Acts Of Beauty' and 'DIY Culture' (both Verso). Gathering Force (1997, Big Issue), 'Copse' by Kate Evans also visit Tash's website - http://tash.gn.apc.org

11

Taring Padi Art Squat, Indonesia

Everyone's An Artist

Alex Kelly taps into the powerful and positive energy created by the Indonesian political art collective, Taring Padi.

Heading up Jalan Gampingan past the fresh produce stalls, street vendors and warungs I spy some graffiti through an archway and I know I have found the Taring Padi squat. Ducking through the archway I find myself in a large courtyard: pavement cracking, with soccer goals at either end. Dodging vicious geese I follow the murals to what appears to be the main entrance to one of the three-story buildings that used to accommodate the visual arts campus of the Indonesian Institute of Art (ISI).

Most of the current occupants studied on the campus before it was abandoned and classes relocated to a less accessible campus further from the centre of Yogyakarta. Many people suspect this move was an attempt to curb the vibrant dissent and pro-democracy organising that was exploding at the inner-city campus, which was becoming a hub in the campaign against the Suharto regime. When the regime fell in 1998, the campus was occupied.

The former classrooms and studio spaces for the most part continue to be used for such work. Meetings and discussions are held here, cluttered and colourful studios fill the buildings. The space also plays host to events and screenings (like Global Insights) The strains of music often ring through the space, as does laughter and animated chatter.

Taring Padi (meaning: the sharp tip of the rice frond) are an incredibly inspiring and unique arts collective - self-described as an "independent non-profit cultural community, which is based on the concept of peoples' culture" – based in Yogyakarta, Indonesia.

Many of the collective's 35 or so members live at the squat, which is simply known as 'Gampingan'. Most are artists, musicians and performers. There is a steady flow of literature and zines thanks to the hard working Emma. T-shirts, post cards and posters printed using wood-cuts are plastered around the town and sold at the night market. Puppets, patches, canvases, sculptures, and performance art are all created here.

Strongly committed to cultural activism, music and the arts, Taring Padi also have strong connections with grass roots movements such as peasant groups and the urban poor. They are extremely hostile to bourgeois and capitalist notions of art, instead they assert that "everyone is an artist" and aim to make art accessible to the people. They also reject the heavy flood of western pop culture into Indonesia and encourage people to take pride in, learn and play traditional instruments.

Puppets and banners, costumes and performance art are commonly used as propaganda at rallies and protests in Indonesia and Taring Padi has developed a powerful and unique style. They use their art, their grand murals and puppets, banners and posters – depicting the faces of ordinary people resisting – to educate and inspire people. Common themes are militarisation, the IMF, imperialism, corruption and of course, resistance.

Despite the weight of problems that Taring Padi struggle against, including deeply rooted cultural issues such as patriarchy, there is a powerful and positive energy in this sprawling social centre. There are only around six women in the collective - which perhaps reflects Indonesian culture - but this remains another challenge.

www.taringpadi.org

Rainbow Commercial Centre, Chiapas, Mexico

By Penny

El nuevo amanceer del arco iris centro commercia en resistencia.

In Cuxulja, Chiapas, in the mountains of the Mexican South-East, a dismantled military base has been transformed into a co-operative economic space to buy, sell, and exchange products.

Co-ordinated by the people from seven zapatista autonomous municipalities, indigenous tzeltales, tojolabales and tzotziles, the centre has been called the "arco iris centro commercia en resistencia" - "the rainbow commercial centre in resistance." Built to strengthen economic autonomy, the centre was lovingly painted with a mural depicting the history of zapatismo and the collective work of the indigenous campensinos.

On 29th October 2001, the mural was destroyed and the centre was violently taken over by members of ORCAO (Ocosingo Coffee Growers Association) with the help of the state police. Members from the group dumped merchandise onto the road, and verbally and physically attacked zapatista campensinos and an international peace observer. Two weeks later, on the 14th of November, hundreds of zapatista men and women non-violently reclaimed the centre.

Since then, people from the seven municipalities have kept up a vigilant 24-hour human cordon in front of the centre. A huge banner, announcing the new dawn of the rainbow centre in rebellion, has been painted, and a small info booklet has been produced. The campensinos have plans to re-paint the mural. In late February a collective of zapatista women opened 'la cocina zapatista', a small co-operative café. The fight for autonomy continues, under constant surveillance from municipal police and members from ORCAO. -Viva la lucha sigue!

WAKE UP! WAKE UP! IT'S YER FREELY TRADED

Weekly SchNEWS

Printed and Published in Brighton by Justice?

Friday 27th April 2001   www.schnews.org.uk   **Issue 302**   **Free/Donation**

SUMMIT WRONG?

"When laws are unjust, it's criminal not to resist them." - José Bové, the anti-globalisation French farmer who helped demolish a McDonalds.

"The truly violent are those who prepare for the summit by accumulating tear gas, plastic bullets and pepper spray. Those who enact laws and measures that will put hundreds of thousands of poor in the street, those who let pharmaceutical corporations make billions on sickness causing the death of millions of people, those who are copyrighting life and creating dependence and hunger. In a word, those who put their profits before our lives. These are the ones we should fear, not the anarchists"

— Black Bloc communiqué

It was the largest and most expensive police operation in Canadian history. People were turned back at the borders. Ninety people even received the honour of being named on a "preventative detention list" to be rounded up shortly before the Summit began. Six thousand police dressed in thick body armour and heavy shields, with water cannons and guns that fired plastic bullets, tear gas and smoke rounds were protecting a no-go zone. This zone, surrounded by a four kilometre long, ten-foot-high chain-link fence, was unapproachable unless you had special residents ID; otherwise you could expect a tear-gas canister in the face for your trouble. Inside this fence was the Citadel, an actual fortress that was built in 1820 to defend against an American assault. Except this time the Americans with their free trade neo-liberal agenda were the guests of honour.

"Don't worry about the Black Bloc; worry about the Blue Bloc [the police]... These leaders are not committed to non-violence."

Jaggi Singh, CLAC

Last weekend leaders of 34 nation states were in Quebec City for the Summit of the Americas. Amongst other things they hoped to achieve was to put the finishing touches on the Free Trade Area of the Americas (FTAA) which aims to establish a "free trade" zone extending NAFTA (the North American Free Trade Agreement – see SchNEWS 200) to the tip of South America. It's been described as 'NAFTA on steroids'.

Unfortunately every time the world's elite have a corporate knees-up, their meetings are met with resistance. Tens of thousands of people from all walks of life faced the usual barrage of rubber bullets, mass arrests and a thick white blanket of gas. No matter if they were masked-up black bloc trying to pull down the fences or peaceful protesters sitting in the road; the treatment was the same. As one protester pointed out, "The scene looked and felt like war, yet only one side had any real weapons. After the extreme police violence I'd witnessed the past few days, a few broken windows didn't merit a second thought."

But like Professor and author John McMurtry put it, "The corporate media will continue to block out the life-and-death issues at stake, focus on the saleable spectacle of a large public confrontation, blame and trivialise the thousands of opponents who are assaulted for putting themselves on the line, and return to selling other images and distractions once the violence entertainment is over."

TRADING STANDARDS

Free trade accords are the icing on the cake for the globalisation-will-solve-all-the-world's-problems cheerleaders. That's because they eliminate "barriers to trade"-you know, inconvenient little things like environmental protection and worker rights-and push the way for the privatisation of anything that moves, even essential services like health care and education.

So just who benefits from these Free Trade Agreements?

John W. Warnock, a Canadian political economist and author of 'The Other Mexico: The North American Triangle Completed' spells it out: "Mexico has always been characterised by inequality, but this has risen under the neo-liberal regime."

73% of the population live in poverty, 45 million in extreme poverty.

Since NAFTA was signed, wages in

Lots of behind-the-scenes activity happened in the build up to the Summit that you wouldn't have seen reported. CLAC (anti-capitalist convergence), CASA, and affiliated groups travelled across Ontario, Quebec and northeastern US to do countless teach-ins on the demonstrations and what the FTAA will mean. Commite Populaire du St. Jean Baptiste distributed 10,000 copies of a 4 page tabloid in the neighborhood where most of the action would occur and set up an "adopt-an-activist" program which encouraged local families to put up visiting demonstrators (hundreds of demonstrators were housed this way). Wanna know more? Try www.ainfos.ca or Indymedia www.indymedia.org.uk

---

CRAP ARREST OF THE WEEK

For possession of a weapon – a theatrical catapult that shot stuffed animals over the Quebec fence.

For sticking stickers... Police in central London arrested a man on charges of criminal damage last weekend for the heinous crime of pasting up Mayday Monopoly stickers. Tailed by police after leaving a Mayday organising event held in Hyde Park, the dangerous criminal stickerer was then caught in the act of "defacing" the sacred storefronts of several chain stores. It's a fair bet that the stickers' anti-capitalist messages had something to do with the arrest, as police would most likely have rewarded him had the stickers contained slogans such as—"Buy more Big Macs" or "Consume, Consume, Consume."

Mexico have declined by 10%, while labour productivity increased by 45%. This is mainly due to the fact that many workers have increased their hours of work from 8 to 12 hours a day.

In 1980 the average carworker in Mexico earned about one third of the wage of an American car worker. By 2000 this was down to one twelfth.

Warnock continues: "Neoliberalism and NAFTA have been good for the rich in Mexico and the large corporations. The banks, privately owned and robbed by the Mexican rich, have been bailed out of bankruptcy twice by taxpayers. The illicit drug industry flourishes and is now more important than the oil industry, and free trade and cross-border trucking have made marketing much easier. Mexicans know that their country is falling behind the United States and Canada in every area. Aside from incomes, spending is very low on education, health, agriculture and rural development plus research. It is not surprising to find that most people, including academics, do not believe that so-called "free trade" has been good for their country."

And that's without even mentioning the environment. According to the Sierra Club total pollution has doubled in Mexico since NAFTA was introduced. As mentioned above, under NAFTA corporations can sue governments for getting in the way of business with daft stuff like pollution laws and safety regulations. In August 2000, following a NAFTA ruling, US corporation Metalclad won $16.7m compensation and the right to pollute an area in San Luis Potosi after local protests delayed the building of a waste treatment and disposal site which would poison the local water supply.

Which is all rather depressing, isn't it?

MAY BE OR MAY BE NOT

From its origins as a pagan festival, Mayday was a time to eat, drink, reject the control of our rulers and 'ave a laugh. So they banned the May fairs. Then Mayday got adopted by the workers movement as the day to celebrate the general strike by the anarchist Haymarket martyrs, executed in Chicago in 1886, and its now got a new lease of life as a time to party and protest- in case it's escaped your notice! Here's wot's 'appenin in a town near you:

UK...

Newcastle: May Day March to Newcastle Exhibition Park. Great speakers, good beer! Assemble 28th April 11am Forth St. Bring banners, placards etc. Rally begins 1pm @ Exhibition Park.

Hackney: There will be another day of strikes against the council (who have apparently gone bankrupt because of financial incompetence). In a recent ballot, workers rejected management's latest ultimatum, despite threats that rejection would lead to dismissal! Meet May 1st 12 noon at Hackney Downs, Hackney Road. March to Hackney Empire for rally at 2.15pm. Donations to the strike fund please!! Payable to Hackney Unison; send to Unison, 3rd floor Netil House, 1-7 Westgate Street London E8 3RL.

London: A fun filled day of direct action all across the capital. For more info check out the Mayday Monopoly Website: www.maydaymonopoly.org

Mayday Convergence Centre in London A temporary social centre is being set up to put up people participating in both autonomous Mayday Monopoly actions and the main Sale of The Century action in Oxford St. Meeting/crash space, café, library and more. Location to be announced closer to date. Contact: 079609 73847 or email: convergencespace@hotmail.com

Swansea: Giant game of Global Monopoly with huge Chance and Community Chest Cards. Bring Music, Fancy Dress, Street Theatre 12.30 pm, Castle Square, Swansea peabrain@mail.com

Brighton: May Day Memorial mourning the death of nature, more specifically the excessive culling of over 1.5m animals in the name of foot and mouth. Meet Pavillion Gardens Café, Brighton 5.15pm. Please wear black.

Glasgow: Meet 12.30pm Buchanan St Underground, bring music, costumes, and good vibes. www.mayfirst.fsnet.co.uk

Birmingham: Party and Protest against Capitalism.12.30 pm outside Virgin Megastore, Corporation Street, Birmingham. Info: 07980 415577 or email: s26brum@hotmail.com

Manchester 'Exposing the Myth of the Global Economy'. Loadsa groups.10am-4pm, Manchester University Students' Union, Oxford Road M13

Sheffield: Mayday Picket of the Sheffield GAP Store. www.sheffieldmayday.ukf.net

Bristol: A variety of events!: Meet 8.00 am @ Arnolfini for Critical Mass. 12 noon @ The Fountains for Carnival around town: street theatre, stilt walkers, drumming, etc - and some surprise activities.

Dudley: 600 hospital workers are continuing rolling strikes against Private Finance Initiative scheme. (see SchNEWS 278) May Day Rally and Social Thurs 3rd 7.30pm at Pensnett Welfare and Social Club, Commonside, Pensnett. Details: Mark New, Branch Sec. 07970 788873

AND AROUND THE WORLD...

Melbourne, Australia: Go to www.antimedia.net/awol if you wanna know: must we do everything for you?

Bangladesh: Garments Workers Unity Council, campaigning for a May Day holiday in the garments sector. Visit http://www.ainfos.ca

Iran: Co-ordinating Committee of Workers Left Unity Iran. Email: info@etehadchap.com or visit http://www.etehadchap.com Fax 004631 139897 or 00448701257959

SQUAT A LIFE

Contrary to what Louise Casey, the 'Tsar' of homelessness, knows, squatting is still legal. Just to prove it the new 11th Edition of the Squatters Handbook is now out. A definitive guide, even having the diagram of a yale lock!! Fully updated to take account of new Civil Procedure Rules. Great value at an incredibly low price of £1+57p postage. From the Advisory Service for Squatters, St. Pauls Road, London N1 2QN. (For squatting advice call 0207 359 8814 Mon-Fri 2-6pm; and they're always on the lookout for new volunteers)

The saga continues! Manchester's **Okasional Café** is back. After a kickin' launch party last Friday, it's business as usual. Events, workshops, poetry and film nights, 3 course vegan meals, capoeira…all are planned. Now at the old Empire Exchange, 61 Charles St, nr. Oxford Rd train station. Tues-Sun 4-Midnite (or later!) Wanna get involved? 07753 606723/ 07977 760842

Women Squatters in Newcastle have reclaimed a building to delay it being turned into a lap-dancing bar. It's been opened by the women as a Social Centre for the community rather than the proposed sad sordid watering hole that was given approval last Tuesday. Named Eclectic City II after a squat that was set up back in October on the future site of a massive entertainment complex called Electric City, the new squat is located in Carliol Square off Market Street. Eviction is threatened for early next week, so get down there soon to show your support before the poles go up! Events are happening every day with a May Day benefit night this Saturday starting at 7pm (to follow on from the Tyneside May Day march). Squat Hot Line 07833 646228

The squatted Atherden community centre in Hackney is gonna be evicted very, very soon. So get down there this weekend for a final fling of festivities and frolics designed to hold off the bailiffs!

This Sat (28)'Never Mind The bailiffs' spring fete, 1-8pm. Music, stalls, food etc.; Sun 29 café and film night; Mon 30 benefit café for Rhythms of Resistance samba band. Tues May 1st: 7am Mayday brekkie for striking Council workers, then all day open house, folks with kids especially welcome. Get down there!!

* 27 till 12th May 1 in 12 club in Bradford celebrates 20 years of autonomous mayhem and fun, providing cheap food, beer and gig/party space (Sch 296). Program of events: 27th critical mass 5.15 pm from Centenary Square and then 20th anniversary party at the club. 1st: May Day carnival meeting at Infirmary Fields 12.30 pm. 5th-6th: Grand Football Competition, and yet another dance party. Finishing 12th with a day of workshops based on 'Taking Control - Direct Action and Autonomous Social Centres' from 12 pm till 5 pm and then cheesy disco from Leeds Action Group for Environmental Resistance (L.A.G.E.R) crew till late. 1in12 Club, 21-23 Albion St., Bradford, BD1 2LY Tel: 01274 734160 www.1in12.com

Inside SchNEWS

Lee Himlin: charged with damage to digging equipment at Stanton Moor Quarry (Nine Ladies). Lee's pleaded guilty and is on remand. Lee is finding life in Sherwood prison hard and is feeling isolated. Letters of support to: Lee Himlin EX7748, HMP Perry Road, Sherwood, Nottingham, N65 3AG

Harold Thompson: Tennessee Prison Authority has sent back the SchNEWS's that we sent US prisoner Harold, refusing them 'cos we 'promote anarchy and advocate rebellion against authority.' What a plug! Write to Harold W. Thompson, #93992 at: NWCC Site 1, Route 1 Box 660, Tiptonville, TN 38079, USA.

It appears the authorities aren't keen on things former US ALF prisoner Rod Coronado has written for anarcho-rags No Compromise and EF! Journal. His parole board has given him an ultimatum—shut up or go back to jail. Rod's new conditions forbid him from writing or volunteering for activist publications, and ban him from speaking out, publicising or supporting illegal actions.

SchNEWS in brief

J-Day Postponed! 'J-Day' Cannabis Festie in Brockwell Park next Saturday (5) is postponed! The reason?…er, the grass is too wet, man. We kid you not. The park is waterlogged, so the fun has been put back til June 16th ** **The Rising Tide Climate Change Tour** kicks off in Brighton (3-4 May), Farnborough (8), London (11), Hackney (12), Edinburgh (14-16), Newcastle (16-18), Lancaster (22-24), Liverpool (24-25), York (26-29), Hull (tbc), Reading (7-8 June), Oxford (9 June) Each Tour visit will see an evening of 'infotainment', alongside workshops, street theatre and creative actions. 01865 241 097 www.risingtide.org.uk If you can't make any of the Tour events but would like to receive the Tour info booklet, or info on inviting people to do workshops or talks on climate change, email climatechaos@yahoo.com ** **Guilfin's** web address has been sold by their internet provider to an Armenian porn site! Who then demanded $500 for them to buy it back. So the new one is www.guilfin.net ** **Hate George Bush?** Turn up at US Embassy, Grosvenor Sq (Bond St tube), Sat May 5, 11am. Rally in support of Kyoto: tell the Toxic Texan wot yer think! 0208 533 7274; www.goatbyte.net/climatedemo

...and finally...

"Big Hairstyles—How High is Too High?" "Monster Trucks: Trading in the Behemoth for a Family-Sized Model" and "Why Manly Shotguns are Preferable to Wimpy Handguns". Do any of these pressing redneck issues keep you awake at night? If they do, click on to www.michaelchaney.com/TrailerTrash/issue1/ index.html. Trailer trash tips for dealing with trespassers include: "If you're not drunk, act like you are. Unless it's cold out, be sure that you're missing a piece of clothing, probably your shirt. Cuss like a sailor. Squint a lot, regardless of how bright the sun is. And make sure to have a couple of dogs tied up around the yard that will bark incessantly the whole time someone else is around." It's not the revolution, but it's a laugh, especially if you're having trouble "keeping commies, fags, hippies, druggies, tree-huggers, and other undesirables off your land."

disclaimer
SchNEWS warns all Monopoly players off to London to see the Queen not to forget their 'Get Out Of Jail Free' card - have a Beltane time! Honest.

14

QUEBEC A20
Breaking down the barriers

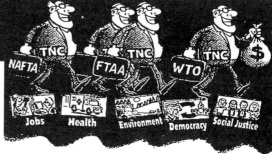

Diversity of Tactics

by Michael DesRoches

The April 2001 Summit of the Americas brought every head of state (north and south), except Castro, to Quebec to discuss the Free Trade Area of the Americas (FTAA) - a hemisphere wide free trade zone similar to the North American Free Trade Agreement (NAFTA) - but this time including Latin America. Trade Unions, authoritarian leftists and direct action groups were invited to join a 'Convergence Table'- organising along strict principles of non-violence - in line with previous North American mobilizations.

However, during an action against police brutality in Montreal in the lead up to the summit, things turned ugly when both police and other activists turned on people engaged in confrontational action, leading to mass arrests. In response to this and the exclusive principles of the Convergence Table, activists in Montreal formed the Convergence des Luttes Anti-Capitalistes - or anti-capitalist convergence - la CLAC. In Quebec City members of the local organizing group broke away to form the Comite d'accueil Summit des Ameriques - or Summit of the Americas Welcoming Committee - CASA. A new alliance between the two was formed which promised to 'respect a diversity of tactics' - a move which got CLAC and CASA speedily excluded from the Convergence Table and excommunicated by the Unions and NGOs. Despite limited resources, CLAC and CASA provided a framework under which people could organise their own actions. Caravans travelled the northeast and networked with other groups, provided educational events, and hosted two regional consultas - giant spokescouncils.

Meanwhile the Canadian security forces erected a 12 foot metal fence around the centre of Quebec City. The Comite Populaire St. Jean Baptiste, a radical community organisation, used the alienation caused by the fence to discuss the Summit with residents - as well as the FTAA and politics in general - all the while plugging their 'adopt an activist' program to provide housing for people during the summit.

The action plan, agreed at the consultas, consisted of providing space around the perimeter for three different degrees of action. A green zone would remain peaceful and creative, a yellow zone disruptive but non-violent and a red zone for more confrontational actions. Everyone was asked to respect the right of others to take whatever colour of action they felt was acceptable. This meant not escalating things where yellow actions were taking place, keeping all direct action out of the green zone and respecting the right of people to be confrontational.

Despite misgivings, the plan actually went off better than expected. The main CLAC and CASA day of action was held on Friday, April 20, the day before the Convergence Table march. Contrary to all expectations the fence didn't last 30 seconds - a problem as most actions had been planned around its destruction. When we broke through, there was no unified response and police managed to push everyone out of the security perimeter fairly quickly. Still, for the next two days Quebec would not be silent for a moment. Actions went on throughout the day and night. The solidarity between protestors was amazing. In the green zone Food Not Bombs provided food non-stop for the entire weekend while a sound system blasted music from bands and DJs to those redecorating the space.

The Convergence Table marched on the Saturday, the organizers having chosen to direct the march away from the security perimeter towards an empty stadium for a rally. The CLAC/CASA contingent turned away from the march and headed for the fence, joined by some union and NGO groups, disgusted with the reformist agenda of their leadership.

Although almost everyone agreed the action had been a success, the links and structures they left behind have proven more important than the street battle. Mutual support has already helped open a squat in Montreal, a campaign of economic disruption in Toronto and is now busy organising for a day of action in Ottawa against the G8 summit. The Quebec actions also set a precedent and anti-capitalist convergences with similar principles have sprung up in Washington D.C, New York City, Denver and Ottawa, making anti-authoritarian organising the base of the movement rather than the exception.

The fence is down, we're in... now what?   Pic: Zoe Mitchell

Coming Off The Fence

On-the-spot reports by Shawn Ewald

A20 Quebec City

A block before the perimeter, people were asked to follow green, yellow or red routes. We went red. It only took a few minutes for the black bloc to take down the fence on l'Amerique-Francaise and not long after that for the first volleys of tear gas to be fired, which were met with rocks and bottles from the protesters.

The Quebec police force has a great deal of experience in crowd control and use extreme violence and terror tactics with skill. In retrospect, everything they did had a degree of strategy which most people were unprepared for.

We didn't bring gas masks because we assumed they would be confiscated at the border. The gas hurt like hell, but when we walked away and faced the wind, it cleared. But after each dose it became harder to recover.

After an hour the police brought in two water cannon trucks behind the protesters, in an attempt to trap them between l'Amerique-Francaise and Turnbull, and lure the black bloc away from the wall. The last part of the plan worked, but not how they expected. The protesters who were now fighting mad after being tear gassed for over an hour, ferociously attacked the water cannon trucks - smashing the windows and attempting to open the doors to drag the drivers out. The trucks made a hasty retreat and from then on stayed safely ensconced behind the perimeter fence.

Later we learnt police - dressed as protesters - kidnapped Jaggi Singh, one of the most visible and effective spokepeople for the actions. They caught him in the green zone, beat the crap out of him, and threw him into an unmarked car.

Police lending atmosphere to the street party with tear gas   Pic: Devin Asch

A21 Quebec City

The next day's assembly point was on Charest at noon. Yesterday we had 15,000 to 20,000 in the streets, today we had 60,000 union marchers according to the organizers and 10,000 to 15,000 protesters and angry locals.

This day we brought goggles, cloth to cover our faces and vinegar to cut the tear gas. A couple of bank windows got broken, no big deal, and sometime before noon, protesters occupied the freeway on and off ramps on Cote d'Abraham and began a massive drum session on the guardrails to disrupt the nearby summit. The drumming started before noon and the marathon did not end until it was viciously dispersed around 4AM. The whole time, these people were under direct attack but the black block came to defend them and draw fire away. The people who took part in that defense (men, women, black, white, asian, First Nations, Quebecquois) showed incredible guts, ferocity and tenacity. Barrages of teargas, plastic bullets, and water cannon blasts were met with storms of bricks and stones, flaming debris, and teargas cannisters flung back in the cops' faces. The "bangers", as we were calling them, on the freeway and the defenders took shifts - it was an informal system: someone got tired or hurt and there would be someone else to take their place. This battle went on for hours.

Vinegar on a piece of cloth will protect you from CS gas pretty well, but not if you're foolish enough to walk into a cloud of it, so we decided to move on down to St. Jean, where we heard the fighting was also getting fierce. On our way over we saw some amazing generosity from the citizens of Quebec City; a lovely middle-aged woman hung a water hose out her window smiling on the crowd below as they rinsed their eyes and filled water bottles; a shopkeeper in the street did the same; a grandfather with his grandchildren sat on his stoop shouting: "Mais oui! Mais oui! C'est Admirable!" as we passed and the black bloc marched down a street to cheers from protesters and locals alike.

There is a long, steep staircase that leads from Cote d'Abraham down to Saint-Vallier, where we sat on the curb to relax and chat, with many locals gathering to mingle with activists. Suddenly, out of nowhere, people came running and screaming down the stairs with a cloud of teargas trailing behind them. The cops had managed to push the line about two blocks down the hill, yet the "bangers" were still going strong.

The locals started throwing bottles and rocks up at the cops and got another round of teargas for their troubles. It took an hour for the cops to back off, but by this time the camel's back has been broken. It was Saturday night, and the bars and streets filled with angry working-class whites, blacks and south asians of St. Jean-Baptiste and Limoilou who had been perpetually gassed the whole day.

The whole intersection of Charest and Couronne belonged to the locals and the activists. A bonfire had been lit and people were drinking hard, smoking dope and the sound system was pumping out hip-hop.

Another amazing street battle occured on Cote d'Abraham, this time with the full resourcefulness of the locals. At one point, they pulled a steel fence seemingly out of thin air and march up Cote d'Abraham to charge the cop line near the top of the hill. The battle raged back and forth until 4AM when the cops finally drove everyone down into the park. We heard there were still battles going on at St. Jean and Rene Levesque, but it was over for us. There was a rumour that the Canadian army may be brought in, provoking people to say there'd be a revolution because Quebecois hate the army: They still remember what the army did in the 70's during the Quebecois civil rights struggles. On Sunday morning, we learned that something like 455 people had been arrested and sources claimed that only approximately 300 were accounted for.
Radio4All http://www.radio4all.org The A-Infos Radio Project

Food not flyovers   Pic: Michael DesRoches

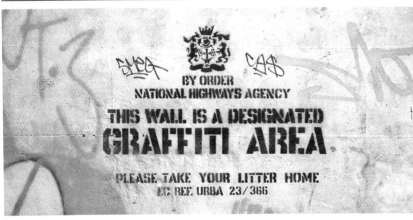

WAKE UP! WAKE UP! IT'S YER UNDERGROUND, OVERGROUND

Weekly SchNEWS

Printed and Published in Brighton by Justice?

Friday 4th May 2001   www.schnews.org.uk   Issue 303   Free/Donation

'...I THINK I'LL PUT A ROW OF COPS ON PICCADILLY...'

THREE THOUSAND CRAP ARRESTS

"The dice reflect the myth of the 'free market' within the Monopoly system… But this is an obvious lie; the dice are loaded from the start."
Mayday Monopoly Game Guide.

After all the media hype and threats of rubber bullets, about 5,000 anti-capitalist protestors turned out to play Mayday Monopoly in London. Police did what they do best, herding people and bashing skulls, but yer suicidal SchNEWS hacks were still there, dodging the video cameras and truncheon blows to bring you the true story.

"I say I've never seen anything like it - I lie. Back home in South Africa, we had something very similar once. It was called the State of Emergency, and that too allowed police total freedom to detain and arrest and harass and intimidate under some draconian "special" anti-terrorist law. In Johannesburg, they used these laws to help people commit suicide out of police station buildings, miraculously losing their fingernails on the flight down - how long will it take for that to happen here?" - Cookie, one of those bloody protestors

Some would say we didn't even need to turn up. Oxford Street had been boarded up and thousands of police replaced the shopaholics, while opinion polls revealed *even* normal people think multinationals have too much power and are uncaring. The Financial Times meanwhile lamented "Business needs to do more to demonstrate the benefits… Governments must defend globalisation more vigorously… Otherwise, [the protesters] may win the battle for public opinion."

Media Circus

"I was led to believe there was going to be absolute chaos and see lots of blood. But this is all very good natured." A bemused Canadian journalist to SchNEWS.

SchNEWS would never suggest that the media build up was over the top, contradictory and, predictably, rubbish. But apparently "Unorganised- but highly trained- anarchists are intent on causing trouble, under the command of 'hardcore anarchist ringleaders'. But they'll be difficult to control, as they haven't got any leaders. Police warned all those intent on criminality to stay away, while 'legitimate' protestors should also stay away because of all the violent thugs. Politicians fear a repeat of last year's violence when *150,000* anti-capitalists rampaged through the streets causing bloodshed. But then, anti-

capitalists are not a threat 'cos there are only a couple of thousand of them." And so the media circus continued until the SchNEWS bullshitometer blew its fuses.

The police fed titbits of so-called intelligence to selected mainstream journalists to scare everyone away. On the day BBC journos had been instructed to search out violence and confrontation; they even had a helicopter up along with the three police choppers. Overseeing it all, was a command bunker in Scotland Yard with 24 screens on one wall, where top police chiefs could control everything in true Big Brother stylee.

"The day started peacefully enough....."

Critical mass cyclists and skaters were up early, picking up free veggie burger breakfasts outside McDonalds and more revellers along the way, with numbers swelling to 1,000 by 10am. Police used a tactic they would repeat all day, namely the 'kettle'. Pen people in for a few hours, and if they try to get out hit 'em over the head. By now actions had sprouted up all over the capital but as 2,000 people converged on Oxford Circus they were detained for nearly eight hours including bemused tourists vainly waving passports at police. Smaller groups met up and a samba procession snaked round, gathering a posse of over 1000, breaking a few police lines, but never quite getting to Oxford Circus. Police eventually hemmed them in too, but thankfully, for once we didn't need to worry too much about pissed idiots throwing bottles from the back of the crowd cos all the off licences were closed.

Wombling Free

More successful at breaking police lines were the Wombles. Using re-inforced banners and kitted out with shields, padding, hard hats and white overalls for protection against the inevitable truncheon blows, they gathered a crowd and the first line of cops retreated in fear. The next police line tried to stop them, but the padding and shields stood up to the onslaught and the cops retreated to the jubilation of the crowd. Two more police lines were broken. These people are not super heroes or martial arts experts and none of them have been trained in guerrilla

warfare in the U.S. but 30 Wombles made a big difference to May Day. Imagine if there was 300 or even 3000 Wombles at the next demo?

Advance to Go

We need to build a mass movement of people to ignore state scare tactics and get out on the streets. To do this we must try to get our message across a lot better. SchNEWS hasn't got any delusions about the mainstream media but our refusal to talk to the press this time mean't that academics and wannabe politicians whinging "We voted for Labour and they let us down" got airtime and are seen to represent us. When Justice? did the Squatters Estate Agents we had up to 10 people talking to the press which meant that no-one could be seen as the 'leader' and we got loads of ordinary people on side.

More importantly behind the media spectaculars, anarchists and and the like are busy working in their communities doing everything from turning empty buildings into social centres, organising kids events, setting up community gardens and co-ops, etc. Not always as sexy and adrenaline filled but essential none the less, and living, breathing anti-corporate examples of how we can show capitalism the door.

*For wombling tips:
www.wombleaction.mrnice.net
* For chants: http://members.tripod.com/~MattWells/womblingsongs.htm
* For a run down of Mayday events around the world: http://uk.indymedia.org/
* Come and hear MayDay report backs next Tuesday (8th) at the 'London Underground.' Arsenal Tavern, Blackstock Rd (Finsbury tube) 7pm

PIG PEN

Section 60 of the Criminal Justice Act '94 gives police blanket powers to stop and search anyone in a certain area where they 'reasonably suspect' there will be incidents of serious violence. They can't read anything of yours (address book, bank cards etc) and you don't have to give a name or address. The police may also detain people to prevent a breach of the peace where they fear one is imminent. The legality of this is questionable and Liberty are compiling reports of people penned up on the day. Email your story to: info@liberty-human-rights.org.uk or write to 21 Tabard St., London, SE1 4LA. If you were arrested, injured or saw arrests/police assaults contact the Legal, Defence and Monitoring Group, 020-82452930, ldmg@altavista.com

Mayday Roundup

Dublin: a very successful and well-attended demonstration forced the Dublin Stock Exchange to shut early.

Bristol: demos took place outside the Army's recruitment centre (a poster 'To kill or to be killed: that's the Army' was pasted up), the ever increasing number of 'employment' agencies, the Job Centre and Mucky D's. Only one arrest was recorded, an activist, trying to stop the coppers filming demonstrators, touched their camera - with a piece of Swiss Roll!

Birmingham: The police stopped any protest of strength occurring. The first arrivals to the protest were immediately surrounded and penned in under Section 60. There were about 40 people in this group, but it was clear that there were more people outside the police lines who could not reach the protest.

Glasgow: Over 1200 people participated in peaceful demos and a very successful recycling system was set up to deal with the copious amounts of empty bottles and cans being produced by the notorious Glasgow thirst!

Throughout the world, hundreds of thousands of people took part in May Day actions, often hindered by police (unless they're fascists!).

Germany: Despite the fact that only fascists had state permission to demonstrate, in six major cities across Germany (Berlin, Frankfurt, Essen, Augsburg, Mannheim, and Dresden), anti-fascist demonstrators still showed their strength. Police throughout sided with fascists, including attacking a family street party at Mariannenplatz, firing a watercannon at the children's merry-go-round.

Greece: Thousands took part to protest against plans by the government to reform social security payments, as well as the threat of globalization.

Poland: In Warsaw over 1200 anarchists took part in a May Day march that lasted over 4 hours, stopping by many government offices and the US embassy to have a chat.

Slovakia: In the capital, Bratislava, hundreds gathered from several revolutionary groups and were visited by many unorganized people who showed interest in ideas of revolutionary anarchism.

Czech Republic: In Prague hundreds of people gathered with anarchist literature, magazines and stickers, as well as music from a soundsystem and free vegan hamburgers. On the demo, nazis came and started shouting nationalist slogans, but cops protected them and then attacked protestors with batons and horses.

Pittsburgh, USA: 200 costumed people, children and pets celebrated mayday with chants, cheers, flags and a mobile maypole. Although starting peacefully enough, the police seemed unsure of what was going on and how to respond to it. Eventually finding their feet, at least 150 cops with dogs, motorcycles, horses, and paddywagons tried to direct the march. 6-10 arrests were made and police used pepper spray and physically beat several other demonstrators.

Long Beach, USA: With cops outnumbering protesters by at least 3 to 1 at times, it is unsurprising that there were over 60 arrests. Cornered demonstrators were shot at close range with rubber bullets. Bystanders who had no idea what Mayday was about were very alarmed at the "cops shooting kids for no reason".

New Zealand: Hundreds of peaceful demonstrators held the Carnival against Capitalism in Wellington, with several well organized groups protesting against privatisation of NZ's water services, free trade and globalisation.

Australia: Thousands took to the streets in Sydney, Melbourne and Brisbane. Protesters three deep linked arms to block the entrance to Australian Stock Exchange (ASX) buildings in Sydney and Melbourne. A McDonalds restaurant near the Melbourne ASX was forced to close after being splashed with paint and slogans such as 'McFilth' and 'Would you like lies with that?'

Kurds Get Dumped On

Whatever next? First lorry drivers, then farmers; now it's the turn of Tornado pilots to get a little miffed with 'inconsistencies' in government policy. Information coming to light about the RAF and USAF's 'humanitarian' role in patrolling the No-Fly zone over Kurdish areas in northern Iraq has set some stiff-upper-lips twitching: Pilots on patrol have been ordered back to base in Turkey- so that Turkish Air Force planes can go bomb the very villages the allies have been protecting!

Pilots have been speaking in confidence to Dr Eric Herring of Bristol Uni, an Iraq sanctions specialist. "They were all very unhappy about what they'd been ordered to do, and what they'd seen", he said. In the US, pilots' dissent has become an open secret. "You'd see Turkish F-14s and F-16s inbound, loaded to the gills with munitions," said one. "Then they'd come out half an hour later with their munitions expended". Upon resuming their patrols, pilots would find "burning villages and lots of smoke and fire". Predictably, no official explanation has been forthcoming, but Dr Herring reckons it's classic 'divide and rule': "They have no desire for the Shi'ite majority to take control or for the Kurds to gain independence. Their policy is to keep them strong enough to cause trouble for Saddam while ensuring that Saddam is strong enough to keep repressing them."

More than 10,000 Turkish troops invaded Iraq in December. Again, air patrols were 'suspended' while the Turks killed masses of civilians and fighters of the Kurdistan Workers' Party, the PKK. In Turkey itself, the government has displaced millions of Kurds, killed thousands more and forbids them to learn their own language.

Blair & co look the other way, 'cos Turkey is a member of NATO. On the other hand, thanks to Jack Straw's Terrorism Act the PKK have become one of the new 21-outlawed' organisations in the UK- despite obeying a cease fire for the past two years.

To make it worse the Home Office has admitted a 'change of practice' in the way it deals with the huge number of Kurdish refugees. 78% (in Feb) are being denied asylum because northern Iraq is now deemed 'safe' for Kurds. Kurdish refugee Ali Namik said "I was tortured psychologically and physically. They're going to kill me, I know what they're like. I won't let them, I'll kill myself." Another man who worked at a power plant and refused to cut off power to Kurdish areas was arrested, beaten and tortured with electric shocks and a mock execution. He escaped to the UK, to find that Jack Straw regarded him as fleeing 'prosecution rather than persecution' and that his arrest was 'valid'!

Fact: In 1999, Britain received one asylum seeker from Turkey for every £47,898 Turkey spent on UK arms.

* There's a demonstration Against the Terrorism Act and the banning of 21 organisations this Tuesday (8) noon at the Home Office, Queen Anne's Gate, SW1. http://go.to/ta2000

* The death toll for hunger strikers protesting the inhumane isolation cells in Turkish prisons has reached 47. Letters of protest to: Prime Minister B. Ecevit 0090 312 418 5743; Justice Minister H.S. Turk 0090 312 417 3854. Contact The Campaign For Human Rights In Turkey 020 7275 8440 www.daymer.org/humanr

* Kurdish shareholders protested at Balfour Beatty AGM this week against the planned Ilisu dam which would flood the ancient city of Hasankeyf and leave 72,000 homeless. The Friends of the Earth motion that they adopt the World Commission on Dams guidelines was rejected - but 40% of shareholders abstained, while BB's Chair whinged "If we had known then how controversial this project would be we could have saved ourselves a lot of trouble by not taking part in it." www.ilisu.org.uk.

SchNEWS in brief

US anti-corporate journalist Greg Palast will be speaking at the Globalisation and its Disontents conference this Sunday (6) at Sallis Benney Theatre, Pavilion Parade, Brighton. Starts 9.30am, cost £5/£2 students www.brighton.ac.uk/globalisation/index.html ** RIP. Ron Stainer had a massive heart attack last week. For years Ron helped Travellers get permission for sites. He was also the owner of Wick Quarry where travellers sought santuary after the Battle of the Bean Field in 1985 ** The fash will be once again trying to march in Bermondsey, London on the 12th May, meeting at South Bermondsey train station at 2pm. There will be a massive counter demo. Anyone for Wombling? Info: noplatform@antifa.net

INSIDE SchNEWS

Editor of Basque magazine 'Ardibeltza', Pepe Rei has been unlawfully imprisoned without charge since the 18th January - under the order of the Spanish Home office. While the publication is not part of ETA - the militant Basque separatist organisation - the government are using 'conspiracy with ETA' as an excuse to nullify a prominent voice of Basque autonomy. Then last Friday (27th April) the office was raided and Judge Garzon ordered the closure of Ardibeltza - a judge who had been exposed in a book by Pepe Rei two years ago for colluding with the Government torture of 200 Basque people suspected of ETA activity. Pepe Rei has suffered two heart attacks since going inside in January, and must be released now – another hearing is due for the 3rd of May. Like many radicals, anarchists and people trying to protect the culture, language and autonomy of the area, Pepe Rei has been lumped together with ETA - even though inevitably there is a large crossover in beliefs, and the magazine did mention them. There have been many arrests in the past two years amongst the squatting and anarchist movement in Basque on suspicion of ETA membership – some just for having copies of 'Ardibeltza'. www.euskalinfo.f2s.com

...and finally...

Among the MayDay communiques, SchNEWS received this anonymous one which we have edited due to space and decency:

'Tired of lock-ons, sit-ins, and street parties? Why not consider a few new ideas for action? How about a fuck-off? Imagine a fuck-off blockade in Shell headquarters. Or perhaps a mass May Day fuck on Oxford Street. The cops wouldn't know what hit 'em if they came across a couple of hippies going at it, let alone a whole pack of perverts humping in the capital. Now one for the vegan police, how about a sustained campaign of cannibalism? Not only is it a solution to over-population and global starvation, but eating the rich frees up much needed resources. Of course the media won't approve, so we say, eat the lying bastards. So it's broil a bureaucrat, roast a republican, pass me a cop-dog and feast on fascist-flambe with capitalist custard and papal source. Of course, sometimes the best action is inaction. Don't participate- watch it on TV! If something gets you worked up, refuse to leave your sofa until your demands are met! Better still, organise you friends to watch TV with you, you could even chain yourselves to the TV. Imagine the effect of millions of people, sitting in front of their TVs, refusing to leave... why the entire economy would crumble.' Honest.

disclaimer

SchNEWS warns all police officers you've made your point and had some fun, now it's time to go home. Please don't take part in any illegal round-ups or criminal activities, in fact just stick your feet up and yer shields up, watch TV, go on endless truncheoning sprees...then you'll feel content.

Subscribe!

Keep SchNEWS FREE! Send 1st Class stamps (e.g. 10 for next 9 issues) or donations (payable to Justice?) Ask for "Originals" if you can make copies. Post *free* to all prisoners. SchNEWS, c/o on-the-fiddle, P.O. Box 2600, Brighton, East Sussex, BN2 2DX.
Tel/Autofax +44 (0)1273 685913 *Email* schnews@brighton.co.uk *Download a PDF* of this issue or subscribe at **www.schnews.org.uk**

MAYDAY MADNESS

Newspaper Hacks make hash of London Mayday

Exclusive Expose
By Chris Hack

Pic: Guy Smallman

IN the build-up to Mayday 2001 in London, rather than report the facts and cover the issues which the protests were focussing on, newspaper journalists showed that they can write the sort of fantasy fiction to rival Lord Of The Rings.

Protestors are used to having the media ignore them, ridicule or demonise them. But Mayday 2001 showed how easily the state can influence the papers, especially with a vacuum created by very few protestors speaking to the media. This article shows how through the mainstream papers the agenda is set early on by the police warning of a sinister plot of a massive "riot". The first to pick-up on the stories are the broadsheets, it is only later that the tabloids - with a shorter attention span - take notice. Many politicians lined up to condemn the protests before they happened, most notably no-longer-Red Ken Livingstone (Mayor of London).

Police got so carried away that they regularly contradicted earlier statements and even warned that rubber bullets may be used for the first time on mainland Britain, this was retracted a day later. The stark warnings from police and politicians served two purposes: to discredit the anti-capitalist movement, and to acclimatise public opinion for a violent police crackdown.

It also meant that most shops in Oxford Street closed on Mayday, losing £20 million trade and many workers got the day off - so in a way the protestors had achieved one of their aims before it had even began. And of course it all began peacefully enough... until the police decided to trap thousands of people for six hours in the rain with no access to food, water or toilets. But with the whole of central London not burnt to the ground as had been predicted some of the reasons behind the protest were given a few column inches.

Calm Before The Storm

The Times led the way on 13th February "ANARCHISTS PLOT MAY PROTESTS TO DISRUPT ELECTION" read the headline followed by how organisers are recruiting support from abroad, all this provided by "intelligence reports". The article indicated that police were going to come down hard on protests. The Sunday Telegraph was quick to follow suit, the fear was that three days of rioting could affect the election on 3rd May (later delayed of course till 7th June due to foot and mouth disease).

Speculation was rife - "the Army could be called in to quell riots", and "Among anarchists who are likely to attend are those from the Black Flag movement and German Terrorists. These are the same people who caused trouble at the meeting of the G8 group of economic powers last year at Seattle in America." Clearly this journalist hadn't done their homework. It was the WTO, not the G8, who met in Seattle and it was Robocops gassing and beating protestors sitting in the road that was the worst violence that occurred. Black Flag isn't a movement it's a journal,

and won't all those nasty Germans be at their own Mayday protests like they are every year? And no pre-riot hype would be complete without a mention of Reclaim the Streets who - said the Telegraph a few days later - according to the police were "planning a repetition of last year's disruption."

Pressing The Button

"200 police officers staged a dawn raid yesterday on a secret training centre for anarchists who are planning to bring chaos to London on May Day." opened the Sunday Telegraph on April Fool's Day, complete with picture of a riot cop kicking down a door. The location they were referring to - the Button Factory - was publicly advertised, hardly a 'secret' and the fact that 200 police were needed to evict the empty building wasn't questioned.

Instead they printed the words of Detective Superintendent Randall "Last year's demonstration was largely organised by Reclaim the Streets, which is a peaceful organisation, although there was trouble. This year the organisation has been taken over by far more violent groups." Er, hang on a minute, the month before the police warned that Reclaim the Streets were "planning a repetition of last year's disruption." Weren't they the naughty anarchists the police told us not to talk to? Curiously a day later The Times reported the Button Factory as a training base used by Reclaim the Streets, clearly they hadn't listened to DS Randall. Obviously they thought, "Anarchists? Mayday?

- Must be Reclaim the Streets!" In the Independent a Scotland Yard spokesman said "We did not anticipate people being on the premises and no arrests were made."

Again the press failed to question why such a large show of force was needed. Maybe the police were scared that once word got out, the black bloc (shipped over from Germany perhaps) were gonna come down in force tooled up for a riot? Or maybe Uncle Bulgaria and the Womble posse were going to get padded up for a bit of push and shove? No, this was done as a symbolic show of police force for the media.

From mid-April the media stepped up a gear following the Met's briefing on the 12th of April about their "zero-tolerance" tactics against those who were out to "hijack" the protest. Assistant Commissioner Mike Todd said "I appeal to anyone who really cares about these issues not to get involved in this protest because it is in danger of being hijacked by a violent minority." or in other words 'If you're nice and fluffy don't come 'cos we might hit you.' However the police still wanted to appear reasonable "We don't want to prevent lawful protest. It's a basic right and we police demonstrations all the time. But we are not going to allow people to commit criminal offences." But the criminal offence the police seemed most concerned about was the 'the organisers' not liaising to the police's liking about the demonstration .

Pic: Simon Chapman

Rioter intimidating police holding a banner inciting violence.

Samurai Ruckus

When British activists allegedly attended the Ruckus Society training camp in California the Times got something right for a change stating that Ruckus teaches people in "the skills of non-violent civil disobedience." But the Daily Mail's headline read "US TRAINING CAMP FOR MAYDAY RIOTERS" and the Evening Standard's "MAY DAY RIOTERS TRAIN AT U.S. CAMPS" and then a few lines later explains that the Ruckus is a non-violent organisation. Er, is it possible to have a non-violent riot? Maybe all those cushions the Wombles were collecting weren't for padding but to give to pissed punks to chuck at the cops instead of an empty beer bottle.

Then things started to get really ridiculous. As if they weren't silly enough already... "Specialist firearms teams are being drafted in to police this year's May Day demonstrations in the City of London over fears that rioters armed with samurai swords and machetes will infiltrate the protests" screamed the oh-so-liberal Observer. In the same article was a good point from Jim Carey of Squall who said "Attempts to reduce anti-capitalism to a menacing monoculture of violence are so wide of the mark as to suggest they are being strategically divisive." Perhaps if the journalists had listened to him instead of the mysterious "senior officer involved in the operation" then they might have printed a more balanced article.

But then balance doesn't make for a good story. Such as printing pictures of 25 people wanted by police from Mayday 2000 and saying "Police fear that they are plotting a violent protest in London next month" (The Times). If these papers actually had any reliable information they'd know that this assertion was implausible.

Reclaim the Womble

Past media reports of anti-capitalist demonstrations demonised the baby-eating anarchist scum Reclaim the Streets. But with RTS taking no part in Mayday 2001s the media hunted for another scapegoat. The Anarchist Federation, Class War, Urban Alliance (or Urban Violence as the Express called them) all sorts of animal rights groups, plus the now defunct S26/Section 28 (journalists seem to confuse the Prague IMF/World Bank meeting with oppressive anti-gay laws) all got a mention, along with the various forms of foreign anarchists and Turkish Communists. The imagined threat of hordes of foreign anarchists descending on London was given new life when the Monopoly guide was translated into different languages: "Until last week, detectives led by Mike Todd, Assistant Commissioner of the Metropolitan Police, believed that foreign activists were being dissuaded from attending." Reported the amnesiac Telegraph, forgetting that a couple of months ago they were warning German terrorists were on their way!

The "hoards of foreign anarchists" fears were further fuelled by the appearance of the Wombles - inspired by Ya Basta! who are almost always referred to as "violent Italian anarchists". Unsurprisingly the Wombles received most media attention. Most of the speculation about the "paramilitary" Wombles was vague and relied on police intelligence (again). Much of the lies stemmed from the raid of the Button Factory (see above), when the Wombles were described by the police as a "radical organisation of anarchists importing a frightening brand of Continental-style violence" - frighteningly silly costumes more like. Just as frightening, the Evening Standard said it is "frighteningly easy to obtain" items such as football shin guards, white overalls and steel capped boots. Isn't it outrageous that it is so easy for footballers and builders to purchase protective equipment? They described the Wombles equipment as "increasingly sophisticated protective clothing" but bubble wrap and duct tape can hardly be described as sophisticated. They also named and shamed the Italian-born "driving force behind the Wombles".

But it was also the Evening Standard that carried one of the best articles about Mayday, in its magazine London Life by Matt Munday. He contacted the Metropolitan Police about the Wombles asking what specifically proved they weren't non-violent. The police spokesperson avoided the question and instead sent a fax saying: "There is intelligence to suggest that a variety of anarchists and other groups are organising a day of anti-capitalist protest on Tuesday 1 May 2001... There are further indications that a sizeable minority is intent on exploiting opportunities for public disorder and violence against a variety of targets which are likely to include the police, commercial institutions and government buildings. We are not prepared to discuss individual groups or their aims." Again we are asked to rely on the police's so-called intelligence (top media tip - put so-called in front of anything to discredit it: so-called anti-capitalists, so-called Mayday protest) to justify a violent crackdown.

Rent-a-Gobs

Sometimes the media didn't need the police to feed them stories, they just got commentators to say a few choice words: "WHY WE MUST STAMP ON THE MAY DAY TERRORISTS" by Richard North in the Express. Ah yes, that emotive word terrorism, and what form does this terrorism take? "...above all, being photographed getting hit by the police." Yes we all like getting knocked unconscious - there is no better way to advance the cause of terrorism.

Such comments from the right-wing Mr North are to be expected. But the Mayday protests were also attacked by some involved in the student protests of the 60s. David Triesman, General secretary of the Association of University Lecturers, wrote in Guardian, starting with all the usual crap about the protestors being simply intent on causing trouble and their ideology not being sufficiently intellectual. His arrogance was astounding "They positively reject any notion that protest or anger occurred before they discovered the Internet. They have "discovered" big business exploits - workers and shareholders are out to make a profit on the investment. Well now, there's a surprise." Er, had he even read the Monopoly game guide? If he had he would have noticed all the references to the history of protest. The first sentence for the first square on the board, Old Kent Road, reads "Always a hotbed of religious and political ideas, the first noted event was that of Wat Tyler who was involved in the poll tax uprising in the 13th century." So much for being a university lecturer, maybe he should do a bit of research before spouting off about something he knows nothing about.

"Nobody outside this coalition has any idea what these demos are about..." said Bryan Appleyard in the Review section of the Sunday Times, who then curiously continues to list all the issues the protests are about, but just dismisses the protests saying "These people just seem to be irritated and hey, are protesting against everything and, therefore, in effect, nothing." But, maybe if the mainstream press printed some intelligent articles about the issues then more people might actually know what the protests are about.

Instead they went for 'lifestyle' articles such as in the Sunday Telegraph about Luke, a middle-class University graduate. His parents explained how he had turned from an animal loving veggie into a lout, ah yes being veggie is obviously a precursor to terrorism. He had apparently gone to "anti-GM crop riots". Er, anti-GM crop riots? Can you call pulling up a few plants a riot?

Mayday!

"The limits if tolerance are past when protestors, in the name of some spurious cause, seek to inflict, fear, terror, violence and criminal damage" - Prime Minister Tony Blair leader of the spuriously named Labour Party.

"ONE NIL TO THE OLD BILL" read the Mirror's headline with a picture of a copper hitting a man over the head, the Mirror took great glee in reporting "Several demonstrators looked seriously injured as they were dragged away. One man was unconscious." The Sun praised the police "It takes real guts to stare down a howling mob with only a baton and shield for protection." - it takes real guts to hit someone only armed with a woolly hat. Most other papers, although not quite as sensationalist still tended to focus on the damage the protestors had caused and the injuries to police. But a look at figures from the ambulance service show police had 3 injured, and the demonstrators 50 - clearly it was the police

Protester gets searched during a Section 60 (See SchNEWS 303 'Pig Pen'). But is he is taking note of events for legal reasons - or - drawing a diagram of an explosive?   Pic: Simon Chapman

who inflicted violence on the protestors. The Daily Mail showed how "balanced" its reporting was by reporting the three injured police officers, but not even mentioning that protestors had been injured.

The media focus was on Oxford Circus and a lot of what happened elsewhere tended to get ignored or pushed further down the article. The first police pen (or kettle) happened near Euston station. NO violence had occurred but the police decided to contain people for a couple of hours - so much for allowing peaceful protest. The numbers of police outraged one local resident who said in the Telegraph "I've lived here all my life and you never see a policeman. They're nowhere to be seen when all the scumbags are selling drugs."

The journalists' attention was focussed on Oxford Circus, but there were other groups around. One of those was a crowd of a thousand with the samba band who nearly got into Oxford Street through Holles Street (by John Lewis). They were viciously beaten back by police in full riot gear, backed up by mounted police resulting in many protestors getting knocked unconscious. This was described by the Telegraph as "large numbers

of brick throwing protestors trying to get into Oxford Street" Large number of protestors, very few bricks. But despite the press always looking for a good story they all failed to mention that protestors did in fact breach police lines at Holles Street, rather than being let out, and it was surprising that they never mentioned the fact that the Wombles did also break through police lines - given the attention the group received in the pre-Mayday buildup.

But in Oxford Circus the protestors were trapped for over six hours including two German tourists who missed their flights home "even though they showed them their passports and airline tickets" and some office workers who had popped out for lunch. If anyone acted provocatively it was the police. The press all seemed to agree the violence occurred after the police had cordoned everyone in Oxford Circus.

It seems that the police tactics backfired on them when civil liberties groups criticised the police's tactics, and more stories of bystanders being

caught in the Oxford Street kettle emerged. The Observer reported that journalists were not allowed to leave cordons and the police "ushered the media away from witnessing the main confrontation with demonstrators outside the John Lewis store in Oxford Street." Once again we have the police stage managing a "riot".

However the Daily Mail remained true to form and totally backed the police and criticised solicitors who advised Mayday protestors as "legal vultures". Yet all the solicitors did was to act professionally and give advice - "Shock-Horror! Solicitor does their job and advises someone of their rights."

Later it emerged that Anna Carteret, more well known as TV cop Juliet Bravo, was caught in Oxford Circus, interviewed in the Guardian she said "We were protesting peacefully, which is every citizen's right, and always has been. Until, suddenly, this country became a police state." But she said she wasn't intimidated "People mustn't feel threatened if they want to speak or protest about something they care about". Another person trapped was Susan Irvine, fashion and beauty writer for the Sunday Telegraph who said she saw very little violence and most of it was borne of frustration. When she asked if she could leave a policeman told her "No. That'll teach you to come to things like this."

All the media hype however did mean that anti-capitalism as a concept got some coverage, even if a lot of it was described in terms such as "anti-capitalism bile", but then what do you expect from the likes of the Daily Mail. Anti-capitalists have to learn to live with the capitalist press, they inform the vast majority of the population, but are fighting against comments like this in the Times "The poorest are not victims of predatory capital but the lack of access to it." With such a large difference of opinion we need our own voice.

To look at some of the pre-Mayday media mania visit - http://uk.indymedia.org/index.php3?resist=mayday&stance=m1coverage

Read Indymedia's reports Mayday Monopoly at http://uk.indymedia.org/index.php3?resist=summer&stance=mayday

'enough apathy'

CRAP/FRAP
Paris resistant and alternative collective

The first two week FRAP - Festival of Resistances and Alternatives in Paris – festival ran in Paris during March 2001. The series of meetings, debates, direct actions, and street protests worked so successfully that a whole new organisation - CRAP (the Collective of Resistances and Alternatives of Paris) was spawned.

CRAP's main activities are publishing the monthly Tohu Bohu newsletter and organising more FRAPs.

The overarching goal is to widen grassroots support for antifascist, antisexist, antiracist, workers, community and ecological (and many more) struggles.

Tohu Bohu is a monthly newsletter listing resistant and alternative events going on around Paris (even though it cannot be exhaustive.) Distributed in bookshops and bars round Paris, it's also available on the web. We encourage people to photocopy and distribute to their friends, families and co-workers, in the desperate hope (!!) it'll spread outside the usual activists, squatters or artists circles.

A second, three week long, FRAP ran from April-May 2002, at the same time as the French presidential elections. The core message was : If you really want to take back your life, everyday action is more important than voting. The main issues raised were labour (expanding workers rights or abolishing labour?), city space (squatting, fighting - or changing - urban development plans, getting politics to the streets...), free things (free transports, free press, free food and clothes...), repressive policies (surveillance cameras, new security laws and other paranoid policies) and minorities (supporting faraway minorities - e.g. Chile's Mapuche - or refugees - e.g. Kurds). There were more participants than last year, and we're hopeful that if we do more CRAP work we'll spark more and more local activism.

As well as FRAP there was a "Forum of Social Disobedience" in March 2002, and in May a week of actions against Securitarian Laws ran alongside another festival, called Charivari. (Though the Charivari fest was coming from a different place - as it was linked to some political parties running for the elections, unlike the other initiatives.) Other FRAP-like festivals around France - like the Festivals of Resistances and Alternatives in Gap and Saint-Etienne, Enrageons-nous (Let's rage) in Brest and FRAKA (Festival of Anticapitalist Resistances) in Grenoble - have us feeling very hopeful. Is this the beginning of a new grassroots uprising?

Web sites to check:

http://letohubohu.free.fr - Tohu Bohu

http://lefrap.free.fr - FRAP 2002 and its program

www.resiste.net - Other festivals of resistance and alternatives

Mayday Prague

Mayday in the Czech Republic began on Strelecky Island, the traditional setting for Mayday demos for over 100 years. Afterwards more than 200 Czech anarchists gathered under the sound systems for a sunny and mostly peaceful day in Palackeho Square, Prague. At midday a march snaked through the town centre, bypassing a nazi demo that was taking place at the same time. Despite a strong police presence - 1000 cops and more secret police – only ten people were reported as having been arrested.

"Sickness of a mad cow"

WAKE UP! WAKE UP! IT'S YER ELECT-TO-STAY-IN-BED

Weekly SchNEWS

Printed and Published in Brighton by Justice?

Friday 11th May 2001   www.schnews.org.uk   **Issue 304**   **Free/Donation**

Oi! Dont!

WOT A LOAD OF BALLOTS!

As election fever grips us at SchNEWS Towers, we spoke to some of our focus groups to see how they will be casting their vote – or not as the case may be...

THE ANARCHISTS

(when they're busy not eating babies)

"Time and again we are asked to trundle down to the polling station and choose between a couple of carbon-copy candidates from the lets-accommodate-big-business party. This June, instead of not voting, why not Vote for Nobody.

If more people go to the ballots and spoil their paper with a Nobody/None of the Above vote than vote for the winning candidate, we will declare the victory illegitimate, and the ward in question an autonomous zone. We will then be free to set up popular local assemblies, overturn central/local government jurisdiction, and start establishing some genuine people-driven, community-centred democracy in Nobody's wards."

http://uk.geocities.com/votenobody/

THE SOCIALISTS

"I'm voting for the Socialist Alliance because, the better it does, the longer that people who hate each other will be forced to work together. There are a number of reasons why those people have come together; frankly, some of them were lonely. But whatever the reasons, being forced to listen to different views about how to change the world has to be good for us. "Why we are right and everybody else is wrong" has never been a very productive pamphlet title for the left.

My hope is that once people in the Alliance have got the hang of respecting one another, they will start to respect people outside it, and earn some respect in return. But I'm glad the RCP has broken up because they were just wankers."

-Jeremy Hardy, Comedian

THE GREENS

"The most important issue in the elections and the biggest threat to the planet today is globalisation and free trade, which really means the takeover of the world by multinational corporations, who will run it for the benefit of the super-rich few, and not for the rest of us. The way to stop globalisation is to vote Green. Voting Labour or Liberal Democrat to keep the Tories out is a sick joke, because Tories, Labour and Liberal Democrats are all corporate-friendly parties who all support globalisation. And not voting at all is like voting for one of them, because it means that one of them will get in instead of a Green. It is quite understandable that people should hate all politicians after having been let down so badly by Blair, but if you are feeling like this, please think again, and go out and vote Green."

And why not? After all, the Greens won't let us down will they? Just look at Germany...

THE FREE PARTY POSSE

"If you're gonna waste your vote, waste it with style!" Yep, Bob Dobbs from the Church of the SubGenius is once again standing in Brighton, this time for The Free Party - who are asking people to come up with a manifesto on their website. "Here any opinion, however ludicrous or wise, may be aired" they say. "As soon as there are ten suggestions for policies, they are placed upon Bob's wheel of misfortune, and the wheel spun by our spin doctors. Whichever policy the fates choose then becomes concrete manifesto. If unchosen suggestions continue to be supported via the web, they can make any number of appearances; unpopular ones will be sold off to the other main parties, being as they are fairly devoid of their own ideas. And like all politicians, our main interest is looking good on television."
www.freeparty.org.uk

THE CLIMATE CHANGERS

"Having consulted our meteorological crystal ball, we can safely predict some severe weather patterns in the run-up to election day, mostly in the form of potentially catastrophic hot air emissions from all parties fielding candidates. What they won't remind you of is that you have 14 more general election votes before 2050. By this time climate change may well have flooded many cities, killed off the Amazon rainforest due to drought, melted the Arctic, brought malaria to the UK and created a billion environmental refugees. Cuts in greenhouse gasses of 60-90% are needed, yet no political party is even willing to discuss cuts of this magnitude. Our sources can also reveal a sinister refusal by parties of all colours to reject the UN-sponsored 'solution', code-named 'Kyoto'. 'Kyoto' seeks to smuggle free market climate change solutions into international law in the guise of a soft and caring environmental treaty. So a June 7th vote is a vote for the end of the world as we know it."

CIVIL LIBERTIES

"With the Terrorism Act and the Regulation of Investigatory Powers Act, the UK has powers that would make any dictator proud. But the pressure on political parties to get ever tougher in crime, fuelled by a public addicted to stories of crime (they now make up 1/3 of your average TV bulletin) is increasing and is turning our criminal justice system into a Orwellian machine.

"What we really need is an end to the fixation on crime in the media, which increases fear of crime and allows police powers to be increased; removal of advertising which creates artificial needs and makes people feel they are only as good as their possessions; rebuilding communities so that they can gradually deal more with crime and offenders rather than leaving it up to an increasingly authoritarian state; viewing crimes with the appropriate level of seriousness: more emphasis on insider dealing, less on hash dealing"

MISCARRIAGE OF JUSTICE

"The election on June the 7th, will witness the second term of the most right wing labour government since the War. When in opposition many within the labour party stood shoulder to shoulder with human right groups protesting the innocence of the wrongfully convicted. Since taken power, not only have they turned their backs on the plight of the innocent, they have introduced more draconian powers than any other government in the past. Which we, in the Miscarriages of Justice Organisation, unfortunately predict will lead to arise in more and more innocent people losing their freedom. New Labour should hold its head in shame."

Miscarriage of Justice Organisation, Tardis Studios, 52-56 Turnmill St, London EC1M 5QR

Tit-Bit

This month is the 20th anniversary of the World Health Organisation International Code of Marketing of Breastmilk Substitutes – the one that Nestle ignores in favour of profit. The way Nestle push their products in poorer countries means many women stop breastfeeding. They are told, sometimes by Nestle-sponsored hospital staff, or by posters on clinic walls, to start bottle-feeding their babies artificial products instead. This means natural antibodies to disease, usually passed from mother to baby, don't get passed on. Mothers who buy and mix the powdered milk themselves (when the free trial supply runs out) put too much water in to make it stretch further, increasing the risk of their baby catching a water-borne disease. The United Nations Childrens Fund estimate that 1.5 million babies worldwide could be saved every year, by stopping the decline in breastfeeding triggered by corporations such as Nestle. For years, people in over 20 countries have been boycotting Nestle Products. and every year loads of people hold a demo on the anniversary of the Code, outside the UK headquarters of Nestlé. Why not join the 20th anniversary one next Saturday, 19th May, between 11-12 noon. Meet outside the Nestlé UK HQ, St. George's House, Park Lane, Croydon Contact: Baby Milk Action 01223 464417 www.babymilkaction.org

Terrorism Act-Up

Last Tuesday, up to 3000 people demonstrated outside the Home Office against the banning of 21 organisations under the Terrorism Act (see SchNews 251). The demonstrators, immediately broke section 13 of the Act by wearing T-shirts emblazoned with logos of the now illegal groups. These include the PKK, the Kurdish workers party that has had a cease fire for more than two years; Tamil Tigers, who have been fighting a bitter war of independence for three decades in Sri Lanka; Sikhs, Kashmiris, and representatives of Muslim groups not to mention a smattering of British activists and assorted trouble makers like the comedian/activist Mark Thomas, John Wadham, the director of Liberty, Louise Christian, a civil rights lawyer and Simon Hughes, Liberal Democrat MP! While the crowd chanted "We are the PKK" speeches were made in support of the now illegal groups, contravening Section 11 and 12 of the act. At one point Mark Thomas and John Wadham went into the Home Office and gave a T-shirt with all of the banned organisations on it to Jack Straw's personal assistant, saying that if it came into his possession he would have to arrest himself as he would also be breaking section 13 of the act! By all accounts this must have been the most multi-cultural demo in recent times with all sorts of people there, the only drawback being that SO 23, the cop photo squad, were there single handedly putting Kodaks share price up by going through loads of film. http://go.to/ta2000

* 'State of Terror' installation performance all about the new Terrorism Act. Friday 25th May 11am Sallis Benney Theatre, Brighton Uni

* US Kansas Governor Bill Graves, with a little help from the Kansas Fertiliser and Chemical Association (KFCA) and the American Crop Protection Association has 'impartially' amended a state law to impose stiffer penalties on people who decontaminate genetic crop sites. The Chairman of KFCA said, "This legislation is a pre-emptive strike and will help deter the growing number of eco-terrorist attacks against crop production".

Positive SchNEWS

The week that was!!...........Compost Awareness Week!!

It may well have slipped us by last week, but now is the time to 'sod' the election and make your garden worms happy. The UK only composts 3% of its total waste. So instead of being an orgasmic, organic pick me up for the garden it produces methane, a potent greenhouse gas that can also pollute ground water supplies. Stop 'couch-potatoing' and start composting, over 40% of household waste can be useful. If you want to find out about making compost contact HDRA, Ryton Organic Gardens, Coventry, CV8 3LG. 024-76303517, www.hdra.org.uk

* Friends of the Earth are running a campaign to save our peat bogs. Peat is used as a compost for gardens, but every time a gardener buys a bag of peat they are directly responsible for destroying some of our most precious wildlife habitats. www.miracle-gone.co.uk

SchNEWS in brief

The **Rising Tide Tour** climate change continues: Edinburgh May 14th, Newcastle 17th, Lancaster 23rd. Tour accompanied by Rising Tide FM (on 87.7, 106.9 in Scotland Details: 078815 435 77 www.risingtide.org.uk **Anyone who knows of any cheap printers or want to put on a benefit gig should get in touch with Eroding Empire, the monthly listings news/music-sheet for London c/o 56a Crampton St., London, SE17 3AE e: erodingempire@888.nu ** **Radio4A** will be on the airwaves across Brighton this weekend on 106.6 FM with a mixture of speech and music programmes with a techno party all Saturday night. Also on the web at www.piratetv.net If you would like to contribute call 07980 168115 or email radio4a@hotmail.com ** **Silbury Hill**, Avebury: a huge hole appeared last year, now it's falling apart 'cos of English Heritage bureaucracy and inaction. Save it! 'Sod Silbury NOW!' demo & talk w/ Terence Meaden. Sat May 19th, 12 noon, village car park, Avebury, Wilts. Bring music, banners, boots and mates. http://www.users.myisp.co.uk/~gtour/ **Anni Rainbow and Lindis Percy have been arrested at the US Spy Base, **Menwith Hill** (yet again). Both when arrested asked for their MPs to be contacted as 'the person interested in their welfare' (surely they are taking the piss). They were protesting against the US 'Star Wars' programme and intend to challenge the byelaws on the base. www.caab.org.uk ** Steward **Community Woodland** low impact project, Dartmoor, Devon, desperately needs letters of support for a planning permission appeal (deadline 28th May). Details www.stewardwood.org **Activists are gathering at **Aldermaston** Atomic Weapons Establishment this weekend. March through Reading, 11.30am from the Station. Vigil on Sunday at the Main Gate of Aldermaston, 2.30pm. Blockade of Aldermaston, from 7 am on Monday. Further details 01324 880744, www.tridentploughshares.org ** www.smut.org.uk is not a **porn website**, but is Spitalfields Market Under Threat which aims to protect the Market from development ** **Earth First! Nigeria** wants to network with other groups, contact them at 20 Dawson Road, By Forestry Junction, Benin City, Nigeria. e-mail environmentalrescue@yahoo.co.uk.

Inside SchNEWS

Polish Anti-Nazi Activist Rafal Rusilowski has been arrested and accused of assaulting a Nazi, despite him not being near the fight when it occurred. Letters of support to Rafal at WARHEAD, PO Box 129, 15-662 Bialystok 26, Poland who will translate your letters and send them to Rafal.

** Mumia Abu-Jamal, ex-Black Panther and journalist, has been on death row in the US since 1982. He was wrongfully imprisoned when police framed him for killing a cop in Philadelphia. There will be a picket in support of Mumia outside the US Embassy on May 12th, 12 pm to 3pm, Grosvenor Square, London W1. Info: Mumia Must Live!, BCM Box 4771, London WC1N 3XX www.callnetuk.com/home/mumia

** Ali Khalid Abdullah is a New African anarchist who has been in jail for over 11 years. He is in prison for assaulting a major drug dealer because one of the sellers sexually molested an eleven year old girl as payment for the girl's mother's drug bill. Since his incarceration, Ali has continued his political struggles. Six years ago he set up the Political Prisoner of War Coalition. For this and other organizing efforts behind the prison walls he has been a target for repression by prison authorities, and was recently denied parole. Write to: Ali Khalid Abdullah, #148130, Thumb Correctional Facility, 3225 John Conley Drive, Lapeer, MI 48446, USA.

Party and Protest

Over 400 revellers partied on the site of a proposed Sainsbury's last Sunday afternoon in Brighton after a carnival parade through the North Laine. Sainsbury's want a brand new 'sustainable supermarket', getting rid of the blatantly unsustainable organic Harvest Forestry next to the train station and increasing traffic. Unfortunately for Sainsbury's, a new store is not most Brightonians' favourite ingredient - the parade and occupation was an opening direct shot against the chain.

Of course the Council still want the supermarket with one councillor saying he "would not be accountable to a public meeting". Police tried to spoil the day by threatening the soundsystem under that old corker the Criminal Justice Act but didn't know what to do with the samba or punk bands.

www.solarcity.co.uk/BUDD_

* Anyone got any pictures of the day? Get in touch with the SchNEWS office and we'll cross yer palm with biscuits.

* Doreen Massey will be talking on the 'urban renaissance', based on her book 'Cities for the Many not the Few'. Tuesday May 22nd 7.30pm, The Lecture Theatre, Brighton College of Technology, Pelham Street. 01273 681166 www.solarcity.co.uk/BUDD

* A new supermarket Code of Practice, meant to protect small suppliers and the public from the damaging practices of big retailers, is in fact to be agreed with the supermarkets with no consumer or public input. www.foe.org.uk

...and finally...

"Foot and mouth- dontcha just love it!" rants the photocopied pages of new hate-rag 'The Bristolian.' "What a class conscious virus! Even Class War couldn't beat this one. Badminton Horse Trials - CANCELLED. Countryside Alliance March - CANCELLED. Queen Mum- DISINFECTED...Meanwhile, footie, darts, boxing and snooker-COMPLETELY UNAFFECTED. Ha! Fucking Ha! Ha! This is germ warfare with a political consciousness. BUBONIC BOLSHEVISM"

disclaimer
SchNEWS warns all voters that we never get cross and are always out for the count. Honest

Nobody wins in Easton

By Jim

BLAIR may have greased a thousand palms to bring his heartland flock of property owning country folk back to the polls, but one corner of Britain didn't give a monkeys what the election outcome was.

Pic: Simon Chapman

The people of Easton in Bristol said a big 'No ta' to every would-be representative and declared their community an autonomous zone, after wreaking havoc on the electoral procedure (of course) - as if the whole fucking charade wasn't laughable enough as it is.

On May 3rd Easton was asked to go to the polls and decide who should run their inner city borough: Nobody or the Council. "Bogus as it is, May 3rd was the day the Council's mandate ran out," said spokeswoman Nora Nobody. "We posted ballots through 5,000 doors and there is enormous local support for ejecting all authority from the community."

Cooked up in the back room of an Easton boozer, the idea was simple. Nobody sticks by election promises; Nobody'll get the next round in... you get the picture. So Nobody was er... born. Ordinary people sick of the system and smarmy parasites, put up their own candidate, ie Nobody. In practice: spoil your ballot paper and elect the community, give the lying politicians the heave ho. If there was more spoiled ballots than the winning candidate then we, the people, could declare Nobody the winner. The politicians would have no authority to rule (under their own rules)- all power to the people.

Stickers and posters declaring; 'Nobody Cares', 'Nobody will make a Difference' and 'Nobody is the Black Candidate' appeared on every lampost and disused shopfront. Posters appeared in a thousand front windows. Billboard graffiti across the community said: 'Vote Nobody'. On May 3rd (the original election date), a righteous Nobody motorcade was mobbed in the streets before the ballot returned 145 votes to Nobody and five to the council. (One extra-staunch anarchist even spoiled their paper in the vote to ban all authority...)

As the result was announced the Autonomous Zone of Free Easton was declared, a stirring rally was held in the Community Building and the first Easton Popular People's Assembly was initiated - it's first task was to give the invasive police presence waiting outside its marching orders. "Your services are no longer required," said one elderly resident as she handed a confused looking officer a large sack. Hopeless Easton Councillors John Kiely and Muriel Cole were also fired in their absence.

The following morning, anyone entering the zone was greeted by the legend 'You are now entering Free Easton'

stencilled across the road at every entry point to the community.

Not waiting for permission from above, residents set up the Easton People's Assembly - everyone welcome. The following week the first assembly meeting began discussing how to address some of the local issues long-time ignored by the old power structures: the lack of youth provision; drug dealing in the local train station; and bringing a stop to the nuclear-waste train that trundles through the community each week on route from Hinkley Point to Sellafield.

"Every spoiled ballot paper is counted and the numbers are announced on polling day" said Nora Nobody. "Today was a victory, but on June 7th we're encouraging people to go to the polls and scrawl Nobody or None of the Above, or er... something more offensive, across their ballot papers again".

As both the ward's councillors were elected on less than 1500 votes (and everyone gets two votes), Nobody campaigners have calculated that if 750 ballots are spoiled then the autonomous zone will even be legitimate under existing procedure. "When the votes are counted central and local government authority in Easton will cease permanently," said Ned (another Nobody). "No more sham democracy. We're taking the power back, and we encourage other communities to do the same."

An openly rattled John Kiely (Lib Dem Councillor for Easton) elected on less than a tenth of possible votes, dismissed the May 3 ballot as "a silly prank". Though he made sure his home had a police guard on the night, in case the community decided to exercise some summary justice on the power thieves in its midst.

While in Eugene Oregon, America, a group of dissident anarchists (eh?-ed) endorsed the re-election of their city's ultra right wing Mayor, Jim Torrey. "Although we don't buy into the scam

of democracy, we encourage others who believe, to vote for the lesser of two evils. If not for pure comedy, at least to make it clear to all what type of fascist system we live under." They believe Torrey's policies of brutal policing and corporate pandering have been instrumental in creating the city's "inevitable and beautiful anarchist backlash", and his re-election can only swell their ranks.

Come June 7 - support for Nobody was community wide. Old Jamaicans would berate door-knocking party canvassers with "I'm voting Nobody - so piss off!" A rambling Nobody support group partied through the streets disrupting polling stations and custard pieing hi-ranking party activists and politicians with glee. Interference FM pirate broadcast to 'voters' for eight hours, until the DTI shut them down. An anticipated punch up with the New Labour massive never materialised, but punk rock legends Conflict baptised the autonomous zone (and celebrated the lowest election turnout since 1918) with a rip-roaring free gig in the Queens Head pub on Easton Road.

The feeble turnout showed, as if it needed showing, that most of the nation think the present electoral system of reshuffling the business party is pretty much a joke. But where do we go from here? Electoral reform is a con trick. Representative democracy has sod all to do with representation and even less to do with democracy. The Nobody Campaign was saying: let's ditch the suits, its time for community power, time to explore the possibilities of setting up alternative structures outside the confines of state control. It was never intended as an end in itself. It was a grass roots, uprising sticking a well-deserved two fingers up at an illegitimate system, ridiculing the 'players' in the process. Nobody is dead, long live Nobody, smash the fucking state. and where's me cup a tea?

25

Rhythms Of Resistance

Rhythms of Resistance samba band - veterans of international actions including Prague and Barcelona. After two years of whirlwind pink and silver action, we're still going strong. So..... here's some thoughts on what motivates us, and why we do it....

Formed in spring 2000 as an open carnival bloc in part from the London based group Reclaim the Streets, Rhythms of Resistance (RoR) has become a way of embracing the changing face of protesting and demonstrations that we have seen in across the world over the last five years.

RoR has been a way of exploring the link between art and politics; between carnival and protest. What we do is part of a long tradition of mixing music and politics. RoR endeavor to continue in this tradition, whilst simultaneously having a bloody good laugh. For us, wearing pink and silver costumes and feather boas is as much political as it is frivolous. We become a subversive version, a circus parody of the uniformed military marching bands that accompany regiments into battle.

To play together in this way is to be doing something that has no hierarchy. We are all dependent on each other for making the rhythms fit together. We are a street guerrilla carnival troupe. Our actions are the very antithesis of capitalism.

When necessary, i.e. Prague during the World Bank/IMF summit in September 2000, with help, we can move large blocks of people quickly and safely with the dual purpose of entertaining as we do so. The police have come to see us as a threatening force, often because they recognise this strength. Playing in Placa de Catalunya at the anti-World Bank demonstrations held in Barcelona in June 2001 highlights this. Towards the end of a long day we headed to another barrio to play in front of the police station where those attending a peaceful demo earlier on in the day had been arrested. RoR hit the streets leading a large crowd down into the metro and off to the site. We had a ball making loads of racket on the tube and generating lots of support. At the time we headed towards the station, it was late, most people had been at demonstrations all day and were cream crackered. However, if we hadn't played, it would have been much more difficult to generate such prisoner support. A couple of hundred people finally arrived in front of the police station along with food, beer and a sound system. Not bad for a random bunch of drummers!

The bright pink and silver colours we wear make it much harder for observers who see us to take offence at our actions, also for the police themselves to take action against us. To try to arrest or assault a frivolously attired musical group when it is such a positive, popular and inclusive force, becomes difficult in the extreme.

RoR shows the possibility of peaceful social change.... sort of like a 'pink' velvet revolution. A type of protest that is accessible to all, anyone can play an instrument, make props, or cover themselves in glitter, and show their feelings that way. The fact that there are now RoR sister bands in Holland, Belgium, Spain and the USA show that there are lots of people looking at alternative ways of participating. We are becoming the McDonalds of Samba! Do it yerself and make some fucking noise!

For more info on us check out our website on: www.rhythmsofresistance.co.uk

If you feel like setting up a radical samba/percussion band, or if you want to join us or another one already in existence, email info@rhythmsofresistance.co.uk

Carnival:

An expression of freedom involving laughter, mockery, dancing, masquerade and revelry.

You cannot just watch carnival, you take part.

An unexpected carnival is revolutionary.

(Taken from a RTS poster for J18)

WAKE UP! WAKE UP! IT'S YER PILL POPPING

Weekly SchNEWS

Printed and Published in Brighton by Justice?

"Your blood pressure's down. But your bill's going up."

Friday 18th May 2001   www.schnews.org.uk   **Issue 305   Free/Donation**

HEALTH CHEQUE-UP

"The government is preaching 'modernisation' of the health service. But New Labour's first term has ended with a law which could dismantle the NHS and take the UK down the US route of healthcare"
- Fiona Campbell, Democratic Health Network

One of the last acts of the Government before setting off on its 'Bore the Nation' election tour was to pass the Health and Social Care Bill. The Act will allow corporations to get an even greater foot in the door of the NHS.

On the surface the Act sounds innocent enough, with its "creation of Care Trusts", and gently-worded intention of "Building on existing health or local authority powers to integrate care". But read between the lines and you witness the beginning of the end of free healthcare.

Healthcare on the NHS is currently free, unlike Social Services, which are means tested. For example, in England at the moment, old or disabled people using council run day centres and residential homes have to pay and are means tested. In 'integrating' NHS and Social Services, the government is paving the way for charges to be levelled for healthcare.

The government has also made charging easier, by guidelines that limit NHS care to six weeks after a hospital stay or acute illness. People who've had a stroke, have Alzheimer's disease or multiple sclerosis could find they are paying for services newly classified as "personal care". As Allyson Pollock, professor of health policy at University College London points out "the idea that the NHS is free will begin to be eroded." There is speculation that ailing train-robber Ronnie Biggs was tipped off and decided to get back before the Bill was passed!

Wealth Service

Health Minister Alan Milburn says he wants to see the Private Finance Initiative extended "beyond the hospital gates to GP surgeries, community pharmacies, health centres, intermediate and long term care facilities." Sure enough, the ironically-named 'Clause 4' of the Act will allow companies to displace the NHS by providing health services for profit, while being underwritten by the government. With the burden of risk shouldered by the tax-payer, corporations should be laughing all the way from the hospital to the bank.

The Patients' Charter has been dumped,

because as Frank Dobson (remember him?) complained it "focused too much on patients' rights". And Clause 67 says that patients' medical records can be handed over to third parties for medical research, without your permission. Info on our DNA, Aids or mental health problems could be used without our consent and don't be surprised if the 'Prescription Fraudbusting Squad' knocks on your door. Fleur Fisher, former head of ethics at the British Medical Association, puts it bluntly "It's the death of medical privacy. It will turn doctors and other health professionals into Government informers. It breaks the bond of trust between doctor and patient".

Meanwhile, Clause 59 gives ministers unprecedented powers to stifle statistics and hamper efforts to show how individual hospitals and health authorities are performing. And if anybody tries to get an independent report, or do spot checks, they could face a fine of up to $5,000

National Stealth

Of course, a vision of huge private healthcare companies taking over the NHS is just scare-mongering by sick SchNEWS hacks. As is the General Agreement on Trade in Services, or GATS, which is being eagerly pursued by our best mates at the World Trade Organisation (see SchNEWS 286). If GATS gets the green light, corporations will get their greedy little mitts on more of our public sector services. As one US health lobbyist grumbled, health in Europe has "largely been the responsibility of the public sector (making it) difficult for US private sector health care providers." Still, thanks to the new Health and Social Care Act those lobbyists and their corporate masters will soon be making their bank balances a whole lot healthier.

* Partnership UK, the main governments players in helping to flog off the nations silver, have themselves been partly privatised. Known by the rather appropriate acronym of P:UK (pronounced puke) buyers include Barclays, Royal Bank of Scotland and Abbey National – all of whom are already involved in the hospital privitisation stitch-ups around the country.

* Find out more about GATS: World Development Movement, 25 Beehive Place, London,SW9 7QR 0800 328 2153 www.wdm.org.uk

In the US, 50 million can't afford access to healthcare, 10 million of these are children. 40% of personal bankruptcies are due to medical bills.

TOTALLY FLUORED

Fluoride is a toxic waste product of the fertiliser industry. The safety information for it reads "Do not let this chemical enter the environment. Dispose of this product as hazardous waste". So it's surprising that the government wants to add it to our drinking water nationwide, supposedly for the benefit of our teeth. But with the added convenience of saving industry the cost of safe disposal of their waste.

Thousands of scientific papers have shown that fluoride is harmful to all life forms. Nearly half the 6 million people that already have fluoride in their water in this country suffer from tooth mottling, caused only by fluoride, and recognised as the first sign of fluoride poisoning. Studies have revealed other problems include cot deaths, mental retardation in children and heart attacks. In India 6 million children are unable to walk because of high levels of fluoride in their environment. Water fluoridation has been banned in all other countries in continental Europe.

Due to concerns the government commissioned research into the issue in 1999 to justify going ahead with their programme. The research was carried out by York University and was called the 'York Review'. Most of the research was, according to research gradings, "poor quality with a risk of bias", and conveniently excluded the fact that there are loads of other sources of fluoride that we all take in apart from in drinking water. The World Health Organisation warned in 1994 "dental and public health authorities should be aware of the total fluoride exposure in the population before introducing any additional fluoride programme".

The National Pure Water Association who've been campaigning against fluoridation for over 40 years have slated the York Review and are calling for a full independent public enquiry. More info 01924 254433 www.npwa.freeserve.co.uk

TEKNO TROUBLE

Last weekend, the hottest of the year, saw the party posse out in full effect with the Hardcore Conspiracy Teknival. Late last summer there was a massive Teknival involving 6000 people in Kingston, Surrey, leaving the cops none too chuffed, so they didn't want to get caught with their pants down again.

Panik, United Systems, Underground Sound, Skirmish, Random Sound, Headfuk, Negusa Negast and other assorted rigs were out entertaining the kids all over the South East. Unfortunately our old sparring partners, the cops, were also out, trying as ever, to spoil the fun. The wacky races started on the Friday night near the Hampshire/Surrey border with an attempted party on old M.O.D. land. This was evicted under the Criminal Justice Act on Saturday morning but the sound system was allowed to leave and the free party people moved onto Guildford, where they tried to set up but again the forces of darkness put a stop to it. The next place people went to was a few miles up the road, near Cobham where about 500 danced until about midnight. This time about 150 tooled up riot cops complete with helicopters and dog units gatecrashed, with one woman beaten unconscious and needing hospital treatment. On the way out all of the systems were confiscated and so people headed towards the coast. But as ever the sound crews are still up for it telling SchNEWS " The struggle continues. They will never kill the music. Expect us back soon."

Meanwhile down in sunny Brighton two big parties were also taking place put on by local sound systems. One was on a legal traveller site and because of the numbers living there already, ie. the travellers, the cops left it alone and the party continued for two nights. The other was at Woodingdean, where up to 1000 people were enjoying a pleasant night on the South Downs. The cops, who didn't even hear about the party till about 4am left two cars on the track leading up to the site. However, they hadn't been paying attention to their own adverts telling people to lock up their valuables and left their car doors unlocked. Unfortunately one of the hand brakes mysteriously released itself and the car slid down into a ditch, while the other flipped itself over and ended up on its roof in the same ditch. The cops weren't best pleased with this and came on to site at about 10am when most people had left and nicked the sound system, the owner, his van and his records.

* Were you at Cobham when the cops steamed on? Witnesses are needed to bring a prosecution against the police for their violent behaviour. Contact Emma on 07774 405368

PARKLIFE

South London residents received a breath of fresh air this week, with news that Crystal Palace Park may be spared the £56 million cinema multiplex development that was planned for it. Left looking like twats, then, are Bromley council, who two years ago waded in to evict the protest camp there at great expense (see SchNEWS 203). It seems the council have fallen out with their firm of developers, London and Regional Properties (L&R), who they say 'have failed to complete the Lease within the prescribed period.' Since 1997, residents and activists have fought a bitter battle against the council's modest proposal. As councillor John Lewis, a keen supporter of the development, observed; "People don't want change and will find any excuse to hinder progress." Apparently people found that taking back the park to resist the development was more exciting and interactive than anything offered by the proposed, soulless wasteland of leisure.

In tandem with numerous legal actions, that campaign of direct action seems to have played a crucial part in the council's downfall, by holding up work in the park for a whole year during a critical period. Still, people at the Crystal Palace Campaign are remaining vigilant, as planning permission for the development lasts until March 2002. And ominously, the council is trying to remove Metropolitan Open Land (akin to Green Belt) status from the site – leaving it unprotected from further development plans. For the moment, as local people celebrate, the frustrated city-planners turn on each other. Bromley are considering legal action against L&R, probably to try and recover some of the money they've thrown down the drain over the last few years. In the meantime, this patch of green space continues to be enclosed by 24-hour guard, though residents are hopeful that the fences will come down in a couple of weeks.

www.crystal.dircon.co.uk

Inside SchNEWS

* Three people with Householders Against The Service Charges (HASC) are currently in Cork Prison for 'littering' outside Cork's City Hall. The offences are bogus and are an attempt by Cork Corporation to intimidate HASC's successful fight against the unfair "Bin Tax". E-mail objections to the Lord Mayor (lord_mayor@corkcorp.ie) and the City Manager (manager@corkcorp.ie). More info: http://struggle.ws/wsm/bins.html

* Garfield Gabbard, nicked during last year's anti World Trade Organisation protests in London, has recently been moved. His new address is: Garfield Marcus Gabbard, Political Prisoner, FT9062, HMP Camp Hill, Newport, Isle of Wight, PO30 5PB. Garfield always likes it when his supporters write "Political Prisoner" on the envelope as it really pisses off the Screws.

* For more details of prisoners check out the Brighton Anarchist Black Cross pages on the SchNEWS website - www.schnews.org.uk/prisoners

SchNEWS in brief

To find out about all corporate lobby groups and their dirty little goings on behind the European Parliament scene check out the latest issue of the excellent **Corporate Europe Observatory** www.xs4all.nl/~ceo ** The **Lamberhurst Bypass** is due to be built this autumn through an area of outstanding natural beauty, alongside a SSSI and through National Trust land at Scotney Castle. www.lamberhurstbypass.com.** The **Earth Liberation Front** has produced a 31 page booklet about the ELF. It costs $6 in the U.S. and $7 elsewhere, cheques and money orders to: "Resistance", c/o North American ELF Press Office, P.O. BOX 4783, Portland, OR 97208, USA. ** **SchWoops!** The website for the free party posse is www.thefreeparty.org.uk. For a simple case for spoiling yer ballot check out www.votenobody.org.uk ** He's had a bucket of water tipped over his head, been hit by water and eggs; All we need now is some flour bombs and some sultanas and **Mr. Prescott** will become a fruitcake. Literally… ** Help build a Hospital in Sheffield, send a brick, at the Labour Party's expense to, Sheffield Labour Party, Freepost SF 1446, S2 1ZZ. Don't delay rummage through your local skips, knock out those dividing walls you've always been meaning to and send yer bricks! ** Dave Morris, one of the **McLibel Two** is facing eviction (which is also the McLibel office) from his home in Haringey. Protest this Saturday (19) 10.15am outside the Council Leaders surgery, George Lansbury House, Progress Way, N22. Or go to an all-day anti-eviction party next Tuesday (22) more info 020-77131269, www.mcspotlight.org ** '**Re-contextualise the fuel protests'**(eh?) Members of Climate Action Direct will try to broaden the British publics understanding of climate change at a fuel protest outside a BP distribution depot. May 23, Coryton, near Basildon. Phone 020-85307577 for more details. Mobile 07930-255233 on the day.

Positive SchNEWS

Permaculture is a word bandied around a lot, but what does it actually mean? A booklet *Permaculture, A Beginner's Guide* has been produced claiming to provide some answers, with loads of information and it encourages you to practice permaculture principles. We're not sure of one of the definitions as "Revolution disguised as organic gardening", but it is full cartoons which makes it an easy read. It costs £5 incl. post from Land and Liberty, 35 Rayleigh Avenue, Westcliff on Sea, Essex, SS0 7DS.

...and finally...

On a recent trip to Australia, the chair of the National Farmers Union Ben Gill, told a Conference 'There's no doubt foot-and-mouth spread to the UK illegally and, unfortunately, we cannot rule out eco-terrorism… The pressures of the green groups are intense in Europe, and what I understand, building here in Australia."

As far back as 1945, Sir Albert Howard who carried out 20 years of research on the disease wrote in his book that foot and mouth comes solely from poor diet and intensive farming methods. But no – it's those bleedin' eco-terrorist animal rights fanatics who are busy bringing the countryside to its knees. Even as we type SchNEWS scientists are busy at our secret urban HQ, ready to unleash egg-on-face disease to afflict all politicians.

disclaimer
SchNEWS warns all coppers attending illegal raves to park up safely with due care and consideration for others and don't be a push-over at the party.

Subscribe!
Keep SchNEWS FREE! Send 1st Class stamps (e.g. 10 for next 9 issues) or donations (payable to Justice?) Ask for "Originals" if you can make copies. Post *free* to all prisoners. SchNEWS, c/o on-the-fiddle, P.O. Box 2600, Brighton, East Sussex, BN2 2DX.
Tel/Autofax +44 (0)1273 685913 *Email* schnews@brighton.co.uk *Download a* **PDF** *of this issue or subscribe at* www.schnews.org.uk

States Of Unrest

THE A to Z of Resistance To The IMF/World Bank in the global 'south'.

The Empire has found that it doesn't always need to pull out the guns to get control of countries and extract their goods when economic 'persuasion' will do, and has intitutionalised this process - with the IMF (International Monetary Fund) and World Bank. Lend money on the pretext of helping the country 'compete in the modern world' - and have them paying the loan off - or at least servicing the interest - for evermore. Chances are anyway that the money went into weapons which are keeping that regime of choice in power, or infrastructure like roads which that multinational corporation needs to do its dirty work. Once you've got that country in debt you can really put the clappers on them: start dictating how far they have to tighten their belt to repay you by imposing wage restrictions and spending cuts. Then enforce privatisation which lets you and your corporate mates come in, own and control vital services like water, prizing a country bit by bit from its people, bumping up the prices up to suit while you're at it. And then get on with the reason you're actually there: to help yourself to that country's natural resources and cheap labour force. Cos these people owe you something and how else are they going to repay the loan?

The IMF acts as a 'gatekeeper' between funding bodies and countries, dictates the conditions of loans, gives its seal of approval to governments who follow the neo-liberal line and lets the international financing community know which countries are 'good-for-business.' Developing countries have few choices - either implement the policies or risk economic isolation, and most governments choose the IMF over their own people. While governments are held responsible for the social and economic upheaval that may result, the IMF and World Bank were escaping largely unscathed - but no longer. People are now making the link between the fact that their water costs ten times more and what the IMF and World Bank is doing in their neighbourhood.

Structural Adjustment Programmes (SAPs) are what get imposed on countries - recently renamed Poverty Reduction Strategy Papers (PRSP) (that's catchy - ed) - and they tend to include these elements:

* Reduced government expenditure, leading to public-sector redundancies, freezing of salaries, and cutbacks in health, education and social welfare services;
* The privatisation of state-run industries, leading to massive lay-offs with no social security provision and the loss of 'inefficient' services to remote or poor areas;
* Currency devaluation and export promotion, leading to the soaring cost of imports, land use changed for cash crops, and reliance on international commodity markets;
* The raising of interest rates to tackle inflation, putting small companies out of business;
* The removal of price controls, leading to rapid price rises for basic goods and services.

To find out more about the wheeler-dealings of the IMF see the interview in this book with Greg Palast 'Four Steps To Heaven'.

For a full copy of this thorough report 'States Of Unrest II', and 'States Of Unrest' - the equivalent report from 2000 - visit www.wdm.org.uk

See also SchNEWS 256, 272, 277, 292, 306, 345, 350

This article gives country reports in two parts - first part is the IMF and Government rhetoric, the second part is what the people of these countries are doing in response.

ANGOLA

Suits You Sir

IMF policy context: The Government of Angola noted that, "governance and transparency of public sector operations; the divestiture of state assets; the strategy for public banks; fuel prices and public utility tariffs" are key economic and structural reforms. The IMF "stressed the importance of adhering to a prudent wage policy, keeping overall public spending in check."

Thanks but no thanks

January 8th 2001: Angolan public sector workers go on general strike, in most provinces, in reaction to Government proposals to lower the minimum monthly salary. The strike continues for at least four days. The state-sponsored media refuse to report the event.

August 2001: Teachers in Angola stage a three-day strike demanding better wages. Their union, SINPROF, say that the Education Ministry has not paid them the agreed wage package. The Ministry denounces the strike as illegal.

ARGENTINA

(see aslo SchNEWS 350 in this book)

Suits US Sir

IMF policy context: Argentina has experienced acute economic crisis over the last three years. After continued crisis talks throughout 2001, the IMF agreed a $21.57 billion loan in September. The loan was granted to, "ensure the sustainability of the public debt" and was made on a variety of conditions. These conditions include making "labour markets more flexible" and that "primary spending will be cut... [including] an across-the board cut of 13 percent in unprotected primary spending, including wages and pensions". The IMF congratulated the Government on, "obtaining limited emergency powers to legislate by decree on tax policy and on the reform of the public sector". In December 2001, Argentina defaulted on its debts, announcing effective national bankruptcy.

We're Not Having It

March 2001: On the 22 March, students and the unemployed join teacher's unions in a two-day strike. Protests spread throughout the country's regions. CTERA, the teachers union say, "the Government is trying to use teachers as hostages to force provincial legislative spending cuts."

June 2001: A series of strikes, roadblocks and clashes with the police spreads through the provinces when the Government announces a rise in taxes. Transport networks are crippled.

In a separate incident, on the 13 June, airline workers block the Buenos Aires airport to protest cut-backs on the Aerolineas Argentinas carrier. Several of the company's aeroplanes are parked across runways and riot police are used to break up protesters in the airport.

July 2001: On the 9 July, in a speech marking Independence Day, President Fernando De La Rue admits that the country has to put in place the IMF-imposed austerity measures because the country's sovereignty is "limited" due to difficulties in servicing its US$128 billion debt.

On the 18-19 July, Argentina's main union, the General Workers Confederation, calls a two-day strike at proposals to cut public salaries by 13 per cent and cut pensions benefits. Tens of thousands of workers take to the streets, blocking roads, shutting banks and Government offices and marching on Congress. Police are deployed on the streets.

July - August 2001: At the end of July, the unemployed and the homeless, in response to the passing of the Governments austerity bill, block over 50 major highways into Buenos Aires. Unemployment is now running at 16.4 per cent. The bill is the seventh attempt since 1999 to bring Argentina out of recession.

Protests and strikes continue into the beginning of August, with the Argentine Workers Confederation (CTA) leading the protests. A CTA spokesperson said: "The future of our country is clearly at stake and, in the face of growing repression, we must mobilise and strike." Another union spokesperson, representing the Argentinean Confederation of Education Workers said: "We are all in the same situation. The people are all affected by these cutbacks and by exclusion, misery and poverty. Nobody escapes."

Late August sees another three-day stoppage, culminating in a rally to the Presidential Palace, which is attended by thousands of people.

November 2001: Angry protesters storm the Buenos Aires stock exchange after the leading stock index (MerVal) falls more than 6 per cent, leading to the resignation of the Finance Minister. Trading is halted for twenty minutes as chanting and drumming protesters take control of the exchange.

December 2001: Several thousand workers, farmers, small business owners and pensioners take to the streets on the 13 December. They protest Government measures limiting cash withdrawals from banks (due to cash shortages) and delays in pension payments. Tens of thousands of pensioners turn up at the banks to collect their pensions and are told that payments cannot be made. Others are unable to withdraw cash from their accounts. The unplanned protest comes days before an official strike organised by the unions. Osvaldo Cornide, a union leader said: "The country is paralysed. There is no money, there is no work." Unions proceed with a general strike two days later.

Argentina's largest and most widespread protests in over ten years erupt across the country on the 19 December. The protests last for two days, leading to the resignation of the President. The main demonstrations occur in the capital, Buenos Aires and are widely reported as a protest of "the middle-classes". Over 6,000 people clash with riot police as they march on the Presidential Palace banging pots and pans. There are incidents of looting and arson to shops. The police use tear gas and rubber bullets to disperse the crowds but eventually retreat "to avoid incidents". On the 20 December, the President declares a state of siege, which is ignored by protesters who remain on the streets. The police continue to try and break up the protests using tear gas and water canons. The President, after failing to secure a political coalition, resigns the next day. Other protests are reported in La Plata, Mar del Plata, Cordoba, Sante Fe, Parana, Salta, Jujuy, Tucuman, Chaco, Santiago del Estero, San Luis, and Catamarca. At least 30 people are killed and many more injured.

A week later, protests erupt against a newly formed Government coalition. On the 30 December, rioters take to the streets and the Parliament buildings are set on fire. One demonstrator said: "The Government has changed but the economic policy is just as bad."

BRAZIL

Fun With Numbers

IMF policy context: The Brazilian Government assured the IMF that: "The policy framework for 2001 aims... at a sustainable improvement in living standards for the majority of the Brazilian people, especially those in the lower income groups." The Government declared that it had passed key legislation, especially the Fiscal Responsibility Law, which "sets out for all levels of Government fiscal rules" to ensure that "fiscal targets are facilitated by... expenditure restraints." The Directors of the IMF agreed, "that the benefits of sustainable economic growth need to be more equitably distributed". The Government also reaffirmed its commitment "to multilateral trade liberalisation in the context of broad-based negotiations to include trade in agricultural products."

Thanks But No Thanks

July 2001: Police in two regional provinces go on strike for 12 days, with six other regions threatening strike action. The strike leads to a breakdown of law and order in which troops are deployed on the streets. The riots end with over 30 people killed, hundreds injured and shops looted. Professor Eduardo Brito is reported saying: "Police are under paid and under trained and are at their wits' ends."

September 2001: Environmental groups protest outside Congress in response to a controversial bill to allow farmers to clear larger areas of the Amazon for agriculture. The new bill stands to increase the proportion of forest that can be cleared for export farming, from 20 per cent to 50 or even 80 per cent. Protesters claim that the powerful landowners lobby, which is well represented in all the main political parties, is pushing for the change, claiming that economic progress depends on it.

COLOMBIA

Getting IMF-ermed

IMF policy context: The Colombian Government reassured the IMF that, "the Government initiated roundtable discussions with the political opposition, the territorial Governments, the business community, the unions, and others on the most important structural reforms. This broad dialogue on issues that affect large segments of the population has been useful, and the views expressed in these fora are being reflected in the structural reform proposals that are being presented to Congress". They went on to announce that the Government had continuing plans for, "restructuring and downsizing... the public sector to strengthen the ongoing effort to increase efficiency and minimise duplications", and, "action will be taken by executive order to merge, close, or downsize a number of entities." They added, "the Government remains committed to a liberal trade regime... agricultural sector protection and import tariff dispersion will be set in accordance with Andean Pact rules and will meet the deadlines set by the agreement with the WTO." The IMF congratulated them in their efforts and, "encouraged the authorities to continue reducing the size of the public sector, including through privatisation of public enterprises."

Farc Off

August 2001: In frustration at trying to persuade the Government to give them financial aid and to end food imports, farmers cause widespread disturbances. Thousands of small farmers, organised by The Movement for Farm Salvation, join rural communities in setting up roadblocks across the country and at least two protesters are killed when police use teargas and armoured vehicles to break them up.

Trade unions in Bogota, Colombia's capital, go on solidarity strike in support of bus and taxi drivers, who are protesting increased taxes. Hector Fajardo, Secretary-General of the United Workers Federation said: "We shall go on to the streets to support Bogota's drivers and protest against the neo-liberal programme emerging in Colombia."

December 2001 - January 2002: Municipal workers from the SINTRAEMCALI Union occupy the 17-storey Central Administration Building of Colombia's water, electricity and telecom companies (EMCALI) (see SchNEWS 339). The workers demand an end to privatisation plans. The union successfully closes the building for a month and negotiates a peaceful settlement, which shelves plans to privatise the company and promises to maintain low prices for the poor. Outside the building, over 800 people support the occupation. Despite police aggression and intimidation they provide food for the people inside. Marches and concerts, organised to support the action, attract thousands more people. The occupation ends over 10 months of 'local action', mainly compromising of mingas, where workers provide services to the poor for free on weekends.

ECUADOR

How Kind Of You

IMF policy context: The Government of Ecuador, in laying out its policies to the IMF, explained that: "In December 2000, the prices of gasoline and diesel were increased by between 20-30 percent; cooking gas prices initially were raised by 100 percent but in February 2001 the increase was rolled-back to 60 percent in the interests of social cohesion." They also set out plans for eighteen privatisations in the electricity sector; an end to state monopoly for telecommunications; and announced that a "foreign company" has "a 30-year concession for the supply of water and sewage services to the city of Guayaquil (the largest city in Ecuador)" and that agreement has been reached for "a consortium of private oil companies to construct a second oil pipeline from the Amazon to the coast."

No Muchas Gracias

January 2001: Almost a year after Ecuador's Government was toppled by popular protest in January 2000, the country erupts into new protests on the 21 January. Indigenous groups led by the Confederation of Indigenous Nations of Ecuador (CONAIE) organise marches, block roads in over half of the country's provinces. Farmers, students and trade unions later join them. The police and army disperse otherwise peaceful demonstrations using teargas, batons and rubber bullets. In response, CONAIE calls for a mass mobilisation to march on the capitol Quito - as many as 10,000 people join the march.

The protesters, mainly indigenous Indians, block roads and set up camp in the main university, declaring that they will not be moved until the Government reverses it plans to impose austerity measures. Domestic heating prices had risen by 100 per cent and gasoline prices had risen by 20 per cent in just two months. Antonio Vargas, leader of CONAIE said: "We do not want to topple this Government. But we will not back down until the Government rescinds measures that are starving the Ecuadorian people."

February 2001: Protesters occupy the IMF offices in Quito on the 1 February. One woman on the protest said: "We want to expose the real culprits. The IMF-imposed policies, carried out by the Ecuadorian Government in exchange for more loans, have resulted in more than 50 per cent of the national budget going to pay foreign debt, have burdened the country with the highest rate of inflation in Latin America, the highest levels of corruption, the most advanced rates of deforestation and the worst example of maldistribution of wealth on the continent."

On the 2 February 2001, the Government responds by calling a state of national emergency, suspending all constitutional rights. Undeterred, the protesters escalate their demonstrations, with some going on hunger strikes at the university campus. Roadblocks are intensified, resulting in around 20 injuries and over 200 arrests.

The protests spread to other cities and regions paralysing the country. In the Amazon region, 300 troops try to disperse a crowd of some 5,000 indigenous people, leading to four deaths, including a 14-year old boy, and over 20 injuries. Elsie Monge, a nun at the protest, comments: "Under no circumstances can bloodshed between brothers and sisters be justified. We firmly reject the use of arms against the people because it violates the most precious right of any human being - the right to life." She adds that if the disproportionate use of force continues then violence may spiral out of control. In similar protests in the highlands at least 25 people are shot and wounded.

Nation-wide protests end on the 7 February 2001, when the Government agrees to lower price hikes and enter into dialogue with leaders of the protest. Protesters in Quito lead a peaceful march through the streets claiming victory, but Antonio Vargas, one of the protest leaders, warns they are, "just one more step along the way, because they will not put an end to the poverty and marginalisation of millions of Ecuadorians."

March 2001: The Government goes ahead with plans to increase VAT to 15 per cent, leading to a strike by transport workers who say that the increase will put them out of business. Business is brought to a standstill in several towns and cities.

April 2001: Talks breakdown between CONAIE and the Government. A spokesperson from CONAIE is reported saying that the Government is not listening to them and they have suspended dialogue until the Government is prepared to change its polices.

June 2001: The Government announces it has approved a controversial oil pipeline, which will be constructed through the Amazon by a consortium of multinational companies. Environmentalists and indigenous Indians protest the project, claiming that it will damage the fragile eco-systems of the 'cloud forests'.

November 2001: Protest groups stage local actions against plans to privatise the electricity company and the introduction of electricity rationing. Trade unions and CONAIE say that the

Government has only introduced electricity rationing in order to win support for the privatisation plans. They also claim that the electricity system was deliberately not boosted to full capacity to deal with the shortages.

EL SALVADOR
Los Gringos

IMF policy context: Although no recent Article IV or Letter of Intent documents were available from the IMF on the country's economic polices, a 1999 Article IV document noted that the "[IMF] Directors welcomed the progress made…in the areas of privatisation, pension reform, and trade liberalisation."

Call A Doctor

November 2000 - March 2001: El Salvador experiences a four month strike by the Social Security Union (ISSS), in opposition to plans to privatise the country's health service. Nearly 12,000 doctors and workers join the strike and demand an end to the privatisation plans, the reinstatement of fired workers and an increase in pay.

GHANA
This'll Hurt Me More Than It'll Hurt You

IMF policy context: While acknowledging that the newly elected 2001 Government, "had inherited a difficult economic situation" the IMF commended the decision to raise prices for petrol and water and recommended "that these [state] enterprises operate in the future at full cost recovery levels, with energy and utility prices being adjusted regularly and automatically". The IMF urged continued, "fiscal tightening [and] the need for restraint in public sector wage negotiations… implement[ing] vigorously the systems…to improve expenditure control."

Learning Lessons The Hard Way

November 2001: Students siege Government buildings and about 300 more blockade the campus of the University of Ghana in protest against non-payment of loans promised to them for their studies. After 10 months of negotiations with the Government, the students decide to take action, claiming that the grants, intended to help students buy learning materials and meet rising living costs, are being withheld against prior agreements.

INDIA
Path Of Least Resistance

IMF policy context: The Indian Government assured the IMF that future reforms would include, "trade liberalisation, the industrial and agricultural sectors, infrastructure, as well as fiscal and social policies". However, the IMF Directors, "cautioned that market forces should be given freer play [to allow for] smoother adjustments". They urged the Government that, "power sector reform was a particular priority [along with] the privatisation of Government enterprises, and liberalisation of labour laws in order to improve competitiveness."

Path Of Greatest Resistance

December 2000 - January 2001: The energy unions call a nationwide strike in response to Government plans to restructure and privatise the energy sector. Widespread disturbances and disruption ensue.

April 2001: India's unions resume strike action. Union leader, Sharad Rao, said, "we are protesting against the Government's economic policies and the impact it will have on the common man." Privatisation polices, he adds, are damaging living standards. Thousands of police are deployed on the streets to ensure the strikes are peaceful.

July 2001: Ten million state employees go on general strike against privatisation plans and call for a halt to IMF, World Bank and WTO policies. A union spokesperson said that the Government policy of backing globalisation is selling the country to the multinational companies and foreign interests, adding that: "This will serve as a warning to the Government against their antiworker polices."

INDONESIA

Viable Options

IMF policy context: The Indonesian Government outlined its commitment to, "reducing and restructuring subsidies [and] to phase out fuel subsidies and restore electricity tariffs to commercially viable levels". The IMF warned, "against additional public sector pay increases unless these were accompanied by significant civil service reform" and hoped the Government would continue with banking sector reforms.

Even More Viable Options

June 2001: At the beginning of June, the Government issues a decree proposing to dilute labour laws and cut severance pay for retiring and resigning workers. The All-Indonesian Trade Union organises a massive strike action, commenting that: "Workers reject the new ministerial decree. It violates their rights and interests." The Government backs down.

On the 18 June, 42,000 military personnel are put on high alert after running battles in the streets of Jakarta over fuel price rises. Police fire rubber bullets and tear gas at students, residents and striking bus drivers, who claim that the removal of fuel subsidies will make it impossible for them to earn their living without putting up bus tariffs. Local authorities agree and bus fares increase by 30 per cent.

KENYA

A Word From The Sponsor

IMF policy context: An IMF loan, granted in July 2000, outlined "macroeconomic and structural reforms; civil service reform [and] privatisation" as key policies. The Government's Interim PRSP stated: "The Government recognises that reforming the public service lies at the heart of tackling poverty... The operational structure of the entire public sector will be rationalized and reduced to reflect perceptions of the functions appropriate to Government. Rationalization across the civil service, defence and security forces, teachers service, local authorities, parastatals and all public institutions will result in cost savings... [and] be reshaped... to more effectively facilitate private sector activities."

You Must Be Joking

May 2001: On the 25 May, state employed air traffic controllers in Mombasa's main airport go on strike demanding better terms of employment and salary increases.

June 2001: Municipal workers, led by the Local Government Workers Union, go on strike in Kakamega to demand payment of their salary arrears. Workers say that without payment of salaries they cannot continue to meet "family obligations" and buy basic necessities.

September 2001: Teachers strike in opposition to a Government housing allowance initiative, which subsidises the rent of some teacher's but not others. The teachers union, KNUT, claims that the initiative unfairly distributes resources to those teachers who have the longest service rather than to those most in need.

Mombasa council workers start dumping municipal rubbish in the streets to protest against continued non-payment of three month's salaries. The strike, which lasts for over a week, ends up with running battles with the police. The workers, however, continue their littering protest until the council promises to pay.

MALAWI

Concerned Parties

IMF policy context: The IMF noted, "with concern", that despite improved economic performance, "a large proportion of the population remains in poverty". They congratulated the Government's, "renewed commitment to implementing a comprehensive stabilisation and reform program", but stressed that success would depend on, "the authorities' determination to resist pressures on wages and salaries and on other recurrent expenditure." They also added, "the pace of privatisation could be accelerated by improving the attractiveness of public sector assets to potential buyers through firmer action to liberalise markets."

Price Of Admission

August 2001: Police, using tear gas, break up two days (28-29) of peaceful demonstrations by over 500 teachers. The teachers claim that the Government has not paid them their promised salaries and benefits. Schools remain closed.

December 2001: On the 18 December, Malawi University is closed because of disturbances by students and citizens. The demonstrations, held in Zomba, are against the increasing cost of living, including soaring maize prices and unemployment. Police, who use live ammunition, rubber bullets and tear gas, break up the demonstrations. One student is killed.

MEXICO

Smooth Operators

IMF policy context: The IMF, "commended the [Mexican] authorities for maintaining prudent fiscal and monetary policies [and] congratulated [them] for achieving a smooth, democratic political transition" during the recent elections. However, the IMF Directors, "attached considerable importance to the authorities' efforts to reform the tax system" and that the current administrations policies, "would be fully effective only if they are accompanied by a comprehensive tax reform."

Ya Basta

September 2001: Roads are brought to a standstill as thousands protest in the streets of Mexico City in response to plans to impose taxes on some foods and medicines. Protesters claim that the taxes will have a disproportionate effect on the poor. Increasing tax revenue is one of the central planks of the newly re-elected President Fox.

MOROCCO

Something To Suit Everybody

IMF policy context: The IMF broadly, "commended the authorities for achieving macroeconomic stability," but warned that, "Morocco faces important remaining challenges in raising growth sufficiently to reduce unemployment and poverty on a sustained basis", that would require further trade liberalisation and structural reforms. They emphasised that, "the highest priority" must be given to "fiscal consolidation [which] will require bold actions...aimed at curbing the growth of the wage bill."

Teachers Pet

November 2001: Education and healthcare trade unions call a general strike to, "prompt the Government to respect its commitments" on the increase of teachers' salaries. The unions claim that the Government has not met its commitments, made in December 2000, to increase the pay of teachers.

MOZAMBIQUE

Robbing Peter To Pay Paul

IMF policy context: The Government of Mozambique outlined, "the reduction of absolute poverty; the attainment of high and sustainable growth through... the private sector" as two of its major economic policies. They continued that these and other objectives would be met through, "the maintenance of a stable macroeconomic environment, public sector reform, and safeguards for freely functioning domestic financial markets."

We Won't Be Railroaded

August 2001: On the 7 August, a strike by the Mozambican Railway Services and workers at Maputo's port brings the south of the country to a standstill. The port and railway company is one of Mozambique's largest, employing over 10,000 people. The workers protest plans to cut the work force by half under a restructuring programme backed by the World Bank. Later in the month workers resume strike action, taking the dispute into its third week. The few trains that continue operating do so under armed guard. Six striking workers are arrested.

NEPAL

A Word In Private

IMF policy context: According to the IMF, "priority should be given to…Wide-ranging reform of the public sector, streamline the civil service, and tackle the problems of inefficient and loss-making enterprises, including through privatisation. Directors were encouraged by the recent policy initiatives to adjust public sector prices and tariffs, and by the authorities' commitment to an open trade and investment regime"

Wire The Fuck Should We?

July 2001: On the 31 July more than 500 protesters denounce a 40 per cent price hike in electricity prices by the Nepalese Government. According to the news report, the Nepal Electricity Authority was put under pressure from the Asian Development Bank and the World Bank to raise prices as a precondition for fresh loans on water resource development.

NIGERIA

Forked Tongue

IMF policy context: "[IMF] Directors understood the desire of the democratic Government to deliver positive results quickly, but cautioned that for most Nigerians, especially the poor, the erosion of living standards from higher inflation could outweigh any gains from increased public spending." They also urged the Government "to control the wage bill [and] welcomed the recent progress in reducing the wage bill." The IMF also stressed the importance of restoring "macroeconomic stability…and to implement market-based reforms that lay the foundations for growth and poverty reduction in the medium term."

Painful Measures

June 2001: Unions at the state-run telecom company, NITEL, go on strike to protest plans to privatise the company. The unions denounce the plans as, "a grand scheme to strip the nation of a most worthy asset, without any consideration of overall national interest."

March 2001: A 1000-strong rally in Lagos protests the Government's continued persistence to phase in the deregulation of fuel supplies. Admas Oshiomole, leader of the Nigerian Labour Congress, said at the rally that: "We can not pay world prices because we do not earn world incomes." Most Nigerians consider that, if nothing else, the Government should provide cheap fuel as Nigeria is Africa's largest oil producer. The unions oppose deregulation and liberalisation because these reforms inevitably lead to a rise in prices on basic necessities. The Financial Times describes the reform package as "painful measures".

October 2001: Students invade the main highway into Lagos, blockading the road and bringing rush-hour traffic to a standstill. The students, from Lagos State University, cite the continued strike of their lecturers as the reason for their actions. The lecturers, who are not being paid and have been on strike for several weeks, reiterate their opposition to the Government's position on salary payments and conditions of work.

PAKISTAN

Rubbish But Well Spoken

IMF policy context: The IMF considered that to, "build a solid foundation for sustained high growth over the medium-term, the authorities will need to pursue further macroeconomic adjustment and implement the structural reform program." They add that some of the country's reform priorities should include "the restructuring of public enterprises [and] accelerated privatisation".

International Monetary Fraud

May 2001: A coalition of Pakistan's Non-Governmental Organisations protest outside the World Bank building in Islamabad on the 26 May. Protesters carry banners saying: "IMF: International Monetary Fraud", and, "World Bank policies: poverty elevation or alleviation?". They call for negotiations on the settlement of foreign debt, a withdrawal of the institutions' demands to end agriculture subsidies and for an independent national commission to investigate IMF/World Bank sponsored programmes. In a press statement the coalition states that the IMF and World Bank have violated Pakistan's national sovereignty by trying to influence the country's budget.

PAPUA NEW GUINEA

Bitter Pills

IMF policy context: The Government of Papua New Guinea stressed that its, "record demonstrates its commitment to implement economic reforms within the broad framework of its structural adjustment program." They added that "public sector reform [and] improving the efficiency of the civil service" have made progress and that, "privatisation is a main pillar of the Government's strategy to improve the efficiency of the public sector."

Private Hell

June 2001: Large numbers of students take to the streets in protest at further austerity measures imposed by the IMF and World Bank. Police use tear gas to disperse a crowd of thousands that congregates outside the Prime Ministers office. Schools, shops and Government offices close, leaving the streets of the capital deserted. The week of peaceful protests ends in the deaths up to six students, with 13 people injured.

Later in the month, Unions threaten to close down the airport and ports and to cut-off electricity supplies in response to privatisation plans.

SOUTH AFRICA

Murky Waters

IMF policy context: IMF Directors, "stressed that reforms to make the labour market more competitive would help ensure that investment increases employment, and that privatisation and continued trade liberalisation would help raise productivity growth and labour demand over time." They continue, "that the public enterprise-restructuring program would enhance productive efficiency and help attract foreign investment, the benefits of which would outweigh possible short-term costs. They welcomed the recently announced policy framework for accelerating the program, which appropriately focused on the four major public enterprises, and encouraged the authorities to transfer majority control of corporatised enterprises to private hands."

Driven To Drink

March: Thousands of protesters descend on Johannesburg to demonstrate against the privatisation of the city's water supply. The municipal water supply was sold to the French multinational, Suez Lyonnaise des Eaux. The South African Municipal Workers Union (SAMWU) claims that the deal, "has not come up with any plan to extend running water to Johannesburg's poor." The union is appalled that the ruling ANC, which came to power in 1994 with promises of providing free basic public services to those who cannot afford them, is inviting profit-driven multinationals to run the city's water.

August: The Congress of South African Trade Unions (COSATU) calls a massive two-day strike (30-31) against the Government's privatisation plans. All major towns and cities are crippled as nearly four million people participate in the strike. A union spokesperson said: "We demand an end to the current programme of privatisation of basic services and national infrastructure. This programme has damaged not only national parastatals but also provincial enterprises, local Government and the public service." COSATU claims that over 200,000 jobs have been lost since 1994 and that the privatisation programme undermines basic service delivery to the poor. Another union spokesperson said: "We want to broaden the public sphere and limit the space in our society that is dominated by un-elected, undemocratic profit-driven forces." Telephone utility Telkom, which is up for privatisation, has shed over 17,000 jobs in the last two years. If privatised, this number is expected to increase.

November 2001: Between 7-9 November, COSATU resumes protests against Government plans to privatise state assets, especially basic services. Protests hit several regions.

(See also 'Down To The Waterline' in this book)

SOUTH KOREA

Rearranging The Deck-chairs

IMF policy context: IMF Directors, "emphasised the critical importance of developing a sufficient social consensus in favour of the needed shift from preserving old jobs in sunset industries to creating new jobs in vibrant growing industries." However, "[they] cautioned that temporary solutions… or further delays in addressing corporate weaknesses could create larger problems that will prove more difficult and costly to resolve later." They added that, "firm action [was needed] to maintain confidence in the restructuring effort."

Go Ahead And Make My Daewoo

May 2001: Protests resume (after massive demonstrations in November 2000) by 20,000 workers from the Korean Trade Unions and Korean Confederation of Trade Unions over restructuring plans and a police crackdown on car workers earlier in April. 15,000 riot police are deployed in Seoul.

June 2001: Demonstrations continue into June, as over 50,000 workers from 126 unions stop work, despite the strike being declared illegal by the Government. All Korean Airlines flights are cancelled and efforts by the police to arrest 14 union leaders of the airline are blocked by workers. Nearly 9,000 hospital workers later join the strike, taking action against Government plans to restructure.

November 2001: Thousands of workers rally in the capital demanding shorter working hours and the release of Dan Byong-Ho, leader of the Korean Confederation of Trade Unions, who was arrested for organising illegal protests in October.

TURKEY

Everything Must Go

IMF policy context: Turkey experienced acute economic problems over the last year and had been in crisis talks with the IMF. The results were, "an ambitious economic reform program" which included the "restructuring the banking sector, improving budget transparency, and preparing the privatisation of state-owned enterprises." Privatisation plans included state-run steel, electricity, airline and telecom companies. The Turkish Government emphasised that "Our economic program respects the need for social consensus and social dialogue."

No Thanks

March 2001: Turkish unions threaten strike action in opposition to their exclusion from crisis talks, sparked off by a financial crisis in 2000 and an austere IMF-bailout package. The Labour Platform, comprising of leading unions and professional groups, declare that: "We will oppose together any programme that does not have our views or our approval." Public sector union leader, Kaya Guvenc, said: "We are determined to leave the programme because the IMF, World Bank and the Government exclude the people. Our problems cannot be solved unless the IMF and World Bank policies are given up." On 31 March the unions and civil society groups organise a protest, with thousands of protesters taking to the streets shouting, "IMF go home!". Bayram Meral, President of Turkeys largest union confederation said: "The policies of the IMF and the World Bank do not aim to help Turkey but to assure that Turkey can pay its debts on time and in full." The union also releases a statement saying that: "In the program that is being prepared there should be a remedy for poverty because as in all economic crisis the price of this crisis is paid most heavily by the workers."

November 2001: A mass rally protesting "the Governments subservience to IMF policies" is organised by trade unions and attended by politicians, local Government officials and thousands of people. Ergin Alsan, chairman of the Kocaeli Syndicates Union said: "The 2002 budget of the Turkish Republic is being submitted to the IMF prior to being submitted to the National Assembly. IMF officials are escorting [Minister] Kamal Dervis to the meetings during which the budget… is being discussed." He added: "They put privatisation on the agenda and they killed the industry sector… [and] they forced us take measures which will exterminate agriculture and textiles sectors… [and] our taxes have been siphoned off… [and] we grew poorer." The protesters disperse quietly.

ZAMBIA

Strings Attached

IMF policy context: The IMF granted Zambia a US$64 million PRGF loan in November 2001 on conditions that included: "Firm control on public wages [and] the privatisation of the National Commercial Bank and liberalisation of the oil sector." The Zambian Government asserted that: "Expenditure pressures during the rest of the year are likely to remain strong, particularly in view of the upcoming elections. The Government recently concluded the lengthy process of reaching wage agreements with the civil service and public workers unions."

Health Warning

April 2001: The Deputy of the Zambia Congress of Trade Unions (ZCTU), President Japhet Moonde, calls on the Government to improve salaries and conditions of service for all public sector workers within the next two months. Briefing the press at Lusaka Hotel, on 3 April, Moonde said that, while the Trade Union Congress welcomed the [new] increment of salaries for health workers, the same should be extended to all public workers: "Government should not be seen to increase salaries only when it is threatened with mass exodus of essential workers."

December 2001: Over 2,000 Lusaka City Council workers go on strike against the non-payment of over 3 months salary arrears. The workers claim that they had reached an agreement and that this was not being honoured.

ZIMBABWE

Adjust Your Set

IMF policy context: The IMF stressed that, "a restoration of macroeconomic stability, which is a prerequisite for recovery, would hinge on the design and implementation of a credible adjustment program". They added that, "the brunt of the fiscal adjustment will have to come from savings in wage and defence outlays" and welcomed the decision to make "periodic adjustments in fuel and electricity tariffs". They concluded that, "structural initiatives such as civil service reform and restructuring or privatisation of public enterprises would also help reduce the fiscal deficit and promote efficiency."

This One's On Us

January 2001: Public servants go on strike to protest against the Government's 15 per cent wage increment. With inflation at 70 per cent, the workers argue that the increment is insufficient and leaves them unable to meet the costs of living. Zimbabwe is going through a difficult socio-economic and political crisis, especially with its costly involvement in the Democratic Republic of Congo conflict. Fuel shortages occur because of lack of foreign exchange. The political situation becomes increasingly unstable.

May 2001: The Government announces a 30 per cent price rise on basic staples such as sugar, milk, corn and bread, provoking widespread uproar. Rioters loot shops and cars, while transport networks, schools and hospitals close. Riot police and the army are put on the streets and use tear gas and batons, in running battles, to control the crowds. At least 60 arrests are made. One rioter said: "We have no jobs. We are hungry. We have nothing to eat. Yes, we are looting."

June 2001: Protesters in Harare block roads in response to a 70 per cent rise in fuel prices. The Congress of Trade Unions renews its threat to call a general strike if the Government does not revoke the price rise.

Excerpts from **STATES OF UNREST II: Resistance to IMF and World Bank policies in poor countries**
By Mark Ellis-Jones April 2002

WAKE UP! WAKE UP! IT'S YER WITHDRAWN

weekly SchNEWS

Printed and Published in Brighton by Justice?

Friday 25th May 2001   www.schnews.org.uk   **Issue 306   Free/Donation**

BANK BONKED

"For the first time in history, they have cancelled one of their meetings because of the prospect of people power rising up against them."

-Barcelona Co-ordination Commission. Anti-capitalists were popping champagne corks last weekend (well, they probably would have if they could afford any) after the World Bank announced it was cancelling its next conference - without a single gas cannister being fired.

The three-day meeting was due to take place next month with thousands of riot police planning to descend on Barcelona and the Spanish borders closed to protestors. The Bank whinged "A conference on poverty reduction should take place in a peaceful atmosphere - free from heckling, violence and intimidation. It is time to take a stand against this kind of threat to free discussion." Which is a bit rich coming from these jokers. One anti World Bank campaigner told SchNEWS, "Whilst these people are demanding the 'freedom' to meet and discuss, millions around the world are being denied basic freedoms, such as to live on our ancestral lands, or to survive without being forced into menial work, by the consequences of these very meetings and discussions."

CASH MACHINE

The Bank was set up after the Second World War, and since then they and their buddies at the International Monetary Fund (IMF) have been handing out generous loans and subsidising projects across the world for decades. Travelling in first class accommodation these people claim to be 'down with the poor' and believe that 'they know what's best for them'. The problem is that not everyone agrees with this. One academic explained, "The IMF and the World Bank have caused more harm to people than any other non-military institutions in human history."

Take the Chad-Cameroon pipeline for instance. With a $225 million price tag, the World Bank's flagship project is set to be 1070 km long, an oil ferry service stretching from Southern Chad through the rainforests of Cameroon to the sea. The Bank claims that the project will transform oil revenues into direct benefits for the poor. Tell that to the nomadic Baka and Bakola people, who face losing their homes and land if the World Bank agrees to foot the project's staggering bill. Or try telling that to the families of the 200 people killed by the corrupt Chad security forces fposing the plan. The pipeline crosses 17 major rivers, meaning the consequences of a leak would be catastrophic,

not least because all communities on the route rely on water for all their needs. A spokesperson from Global Village Cameroon told SchNEWS "This money is supposed to help poor countries improve their situation. But this project will benefit no-one but multi-national companies and local elites." Seems an accurate prediction considering the President of Chad received a $25 million bonus from oil companies for giving the World Bank the go ahead on the project, money which he promptly spent on the purchase of military equipment!

The Bankers, however, are now apparently the victims. "Years ago people used to burn books to try and clamp down on academic freedom. Now they try to prevent academics from reaching debating halls," one Banker moaned. The fact is that the mass mobilisations against these giant institutions have put them under the spotlight like never before with the Chairman of their inspection panel complaining: "The only thing the World Bank is afraid of is publicity. These protestors are creating that." Last year there were mass protests in Washington and their meeting in Prague had to be abandoned (see SchNEWS 277).

But what has really made them cross is that the Barcelona knees-up was part of the Bank's new charm offensive with topics up for discussion like "A Global Economy for All" and the chance for them to push into the 'knowledge-based' economy. Because as one campaigner told SchNEWS "In a way their job has been done in this huge bureaucracy needs something new to do." That something is managing to blag £60 million from Microsoft to set up a "Knowledge Bank" which aims to select and organise all the worlds 'knowledge' about fighting poverty – all from its own unbiased perspective of course.

Still, the Bank is now planning on holding their discussions in cyber-space. Which SchNEWS hopes, for the sake of academic freedom, won't be hacked by pesky protestors.

* This Saturday (26) to mark African Liberation Day there will be a protest outside the World Bank's offices at 80 Haymarket, London SW1 between 11.30 am to 1.30pm. "Africa is still manipulated, robbed and starved. The World Bank and the International Monetary Fund are Africa's new masters. From Sierra Leone to South Africa, governments and elites benefit from their partnership with the IMF and World Bank, while ordinary Africans suffer the consequences." Info 020-87497179.

Forget June 7th here's a couple of more important dates for your diary

* The G8 – the seven richest industrialised countries plus Russia – will be meeting in Genoa from 20-23rd July. SchNEWS has heard rumours that, in an effort to foil the predicted massive protests, delegates will be stuck aboard luxury cruisers anchored in Genoa Bay. www.genoa-g8.org

* The next big European Union meeting takes place in Gothenburg, Sweden 14-16 July, http://motkraft.net/gbg2001/

* 'Crowd Bites Wolf' the unmissable film by Guerrilla vision about last years Prague protests. Copies from SchNEWS HQ £5 + 80p large SAE.

But remember folks, while summit hopping can be exhilarating, inspiring, and make the world sit up and listen, we still have to do all that grass roots stuff in our local communities if we're ever to make a real difference.

SUMMIT STINKS

Eric Laferriere was one of the thousands of protestors who went on the streets of Quebec in April (see SchNEWS 302) to protest against the Summit of the Americas. "It was a beautiful day, and I wanted to be part of something large like that - a once-in-a-lifetime experience." But since the protests, life for Eric has changed forever. Standing with other protestors near the ten foot high fence that surrounded the Conference, riot police started firing tear gas canisters at the protestors. The gas was so thick, he couldn't see the person next to him. He v-signed the cops before one of them, no more than 20 feet away, shot and hit him in the throat with a bullet travelling at 300 feet per second. He now breathes through a small metal hole and speaks in a faint whisper and with difficulty, wincing at the pain from the 6-inch stainless steel pipe stuck in his throat. Every breath burns. "It's like someone is grabbing me by the throat and trying to choke me. How could a cop do this to me?" During the demonstrations the police fired 4,709 tear gas cannisters and 822 plastic bullets, hospitalising lots of other people, some of them seriously. http://quebec.indymedia.org/

1ST CLASS

Thousands of postal workers are back at work after a successful wildcat action. The dispute started in Watford when managers tried to implement a national agreement for more "flexible" working conditions - things like 4am shift starts and 10 hour days on Saturdays, or as one postie told us "more work for less pay." The strike then spread after scab mail was diverted to Liverpool and other sorting centres. A striking postie told SchNEWS "What happened was really impressive, we gave the management a bloody nose and for the moment they have stepped back. They are basically threatening us to accept these conditions otherwise we'll privatise your jobs." Post Office workers have repeatedly ignored anti-strike laws and union leaders who ask them to call their 'illegal' strikes off, so there's nothing for it but to start privitisating the company by stealth.

Recently re-named Consignia, New Labour backed up by the European Union want to open the whole service up to the private sector, with private delivery firms like UPS who, would you believe it, make regular donations to New Labour.

* In a taster of what's to come if New Labour get reelected, Nord Anglia has just been given the contract to run a school in Surrey. They're gonna change Abbeyland into a specialist business school to "turn around it's image and provide a high-quality education for children" under the new name of Runnymede Business and Enterprise College. Nord Anglia are also the company responsible for promoting equality in schools. Which is why their millionaire chairman and former chairman, Kevin McNeany, was brought before a tribunal for racial discrimination. He is alleged to have said amongst other things that he was concerned that the School of Financial Management was "very Indianised."

* The Dudley Group of Hospital strikers, have agreed to go back to work after 10 months of rolling strikes against the transfer of their jobs to a private healthcare company.

* Want to know how big business is getting into bed with Tony Blair? Then check out www.red-star-research.org.uk

FOURTH REICH

Last weekend almost a thousand migrants from across Germany gathered in Berlin for 3 days of action and discussion against the 'Residenzpflicht'. A law which some are proposing be extended to the whole of Europe - which makes it illegal for immigrants in Germany to move outside of a very restricted area. For many immigrants coming to Berlin was itself a 'criminal' offence. An attempt was made to occupy a large church in the city centre, with a number of German citizens burning their passports in solidarity. The immigrant activists have announced that they will no longer respect the law and that they plan to travel to Genoa in July to take part in the resistance to the meeting of the G8. An official proposal for a large convoy of refugees to travel from Germany to Genoa is expected to be released towards the end of June. More info: http://de.indymedia.org

Dedicated crew have opened up some free space in central Brighton for a DIY antidote to corporatisation. Get down to **'Food For Freaks'** at 4 Prince Albert St (between Ship St and all the council crap) for VERY cheap food, vegan ice cream and info for creativity and resistance. Opens this Saturday (26th) and each day from 3pm until whenever.

SchNEWS in brief

After May Day, What Next? - Those loveable rogues the W.O.M.B.L.E.S. are hosting meetings and workshops at Islington Comunity Centre, Sebbon Road, London, 2 June, 1-7pm. Remember you're a womble! www.wombleaction.mrnice.net ** **Moving on From May Day** - Planning meeting for a conference to learn the lessons of May Day. Topics: media strategies, getting organised and tactics for Section 40 traps. June 13, Jubilee Room, Indian YMCA, 41 Fitzroy Square, London W1T 6AQ, Call 07946 687192 or e-mail collective@totalise.co.uk ** **i-Contact**, the Bristol-based video activists, have decided to pull their plug on a program that was going to be shown on Channel Four because, they say, C4 have limited them too much in what they are allowed to show. C4 weren't happy, it seemed, with the program – about subvertising because apparently it would offend the advertisers. Ain't that the point? www.uk.indymedia.org. For more censorship stuff check out **Project Censored** for a list of the top 25 censored stories at www.projectcensored.org ** Check out Brighton Collective's new website to keep up-to-date with things going on in the 'city' www.brightoncollective.org.uk ** There's another fun filled **HAG Cabaret**, Saturday 26th 9pm, Hanbury Arms, St George's Road, Brighton. ** Celebrate the recent victory against the multiplex at **Crystal Palace** this Saturday 2-10pm, at the top of Crystal Palace Park, bring picnics and musical instruments ** There's a meeting about "The proposed **Hastings Bypass** and its link to International Capitalism", 8pm 21 June, Carlisle pub, 24 Pelham Street/Carlisle Parade, Hastings. ** After two weeks and twelve arrests local people are still demonstrating against the burial of **300,000 animal carcasses** at Inkerman, Tow Law. The carcasses are buried in disused mine shafts filled with water that may collapse under the extra weight and will pollute local waterways. The site smells of rotting carcasses, toxic gas hydrogen sulphide may be released and people are starting to suffer from illnesses. More info: Newlittlebighorn@aol.com or phone 01388-731577** Last Saturday about fifty demonstrators broke into **Hackney Town Hall**, giving the place a much-needed redecoration in protest against the Councils cutbacks, as a Samba band played outside. Only three cops were at the scene when it all started, but after about half an hour twenty riot police turned up. Five people have been nicked for burglary, without actually pinching anything.

WASTED! (again)

After three days of occupying the Sheffield incinerator and sucessfully shutting the whole thing down for fifty hours, Greenpeace have ended their anti-incineration action. One of the volunteer climbers said, "Sheffield incinerator has an appalling criminal record and is the worst in England. It has been bombarding the people of Sheffield with toxic chemicals for too long. Enough is enough, this plant must be shut for good." Similar sentiments were echoed outside the Byker incinerator near Newcastle. One of the protesters, a 75-year-old man, handcuffed himself to the gates saying "We are desperate. We want this place shut and we want it shut now!"

Info on the Sheffield actions and a report concerning incinerators can be found at www.greenpeace.com.

There's a Public meeting this Sat (26th) at 2pm, St John's Church, Bernard Street, Sheffield.

Inside SchNEWS

* Helen John and Anne Lee have been given harsh sentances of three and two months for cutting through the security fence at Menwith Hill Spy Base in North Yorkshire which will form part of the US Missile Defence System (aka Star Wars). Messages of support can be sent to them at Low Newton Prison, Brasside, Durham, DH1 5SD. Helen is standing for an MP in Tony Blair's Sedgefield constituency as an independent candidate on a No Star Wars platform. While in prison you can't vote in the election, but you can stand as an MP if yer in prison for less than a year.

* After nearly 6 months on remand, the trial of Susan van der Hijden and Father Martin Newell finally began on Monday (SchNEWS 301). They are charged with two counts of criminal damage, totalling £31,000 for disabling two convoy trucks used to carry nuclear warheads in Wittering. In court an MoD police witness admitted that nuclear weapons were kept in Wittering during transportation. It was also admitted that a Harrier jump jet crashed at the base in 1997, just think what would have happened if it had hit a plutonium transport truck. As SchNEWS went to press the jury were still undecided. Trident Ploughshares 01603 469296, www.tridentploughshares.org

* Celebrate the 19th anniversary of the Faslane Peace Camp, 1st-10th June. There is a week of workshops and actions, beach and road verge clear up and a visit to a community farm. Wind powered film night on the 8th, Saturday 9th is an acoustic party at the camp (bring instruments!) and a 'Rage against the Base' party at the Base. 01436 820901 www.faslanepeacecamp.org

* Love the Planet, Trash Trident Peace Carnival, George Square, Glasgow, June 2, midday-6pm. With music from Shooglenlifty, Scheme and Samba ya Bamba.

* Support May Day Defendants!! - Come to the Drop the Charges march on June 2nd. Meet at 11am in front of the Crown Prosecution Service office in Bressenden Place near Victoria Station.

Positive SchNEWS

Increasingly, people want to know exactly what they are buying, where it comes from and how it's produced. How can they do this? By visiting www.Bigbarn.co.uk. By simply typing in yer postal code in a database, you can instantly discover all organic produce sellers in your area. Wicked!

GM CROPPED

Three proposed GM trials near organic farms have been scrapped. Following a number of protests, two trials in Wales that were within 650m of organic farms were abandoned and this week plans for a trial near the HDRA, the organic research institute near Coventry were shelved. Meanwhile, the Welsh Assembly has passed a resolution for Wales to become GM-free and the Soil Association has called for trials to be planted at least 6 miles away from organic farms. Both requests have been ignored by the government and industry. Meanwhile the nighttime de-contamination of GM crops continues this year. For a list of test sites and other action targets visit www.gm-info.org.uk

...and finally...

Not only did the police cause massive disruption to London on Mayday with their huge presence, but their massive telecom communications caused problems for companies using wireless based networks, resulting in "endless glitches and a generally wasted day". After the police vans went the problem disappeared. www.theregister.co.uk

disclaimer
SchNEWS warns all bankers making a withdrawal not to forget you can bank on more protests. Honest guv'.

Subscribe! Keep SchNEWS FREE! Send 1st Class stamps (e.g. 10 for next 9 issues) or donations (payable to Justice?) Ask for "Originals" if you can make copies. Post *free* to all prisoners. SchNEWS, c/o on-the-fiddle, P.O. Box 2600, Brighton, East Sussex, BN2 2DX.
Tel/Autofax +44 (0)1273 685913 Email schnews@brighton.co.uk Download a PDF of this issue or subscribe at www.schnews.org.uk

The Tide Is High

The Rising Tide Tour, Summer 2001

Coinciding with the COP6.5 UN climate talks in Bonn, climate change group Rising Tide took to the road for an eleven date stop tour of Britain to raise awareness and inspire people to take direct action – a bit like the Earth First! roadshow in the 1990's. The tour looked at questions of what people can do personally and politically to make a difference about impending climate change.

The end of March 2001 marked the wettest twelve month period in the UK since records began – and under the grey skies of a seemingly non-existent spring, the tour set out to spread the word and instill hope that things really can get better, not just wetter...

Time is getting on. We cannot wait any more for politicians to catch up with the changes needed to ensure future survival. This was the message at the heart of the Rising Tide Tour – it's time to leave a monopoly on cynicism with the politicians; it's time to break out of denial over the significance of consistently record-breaking weather events; it's time to stop presuming that it will all be okay if only Bush will put his name to the Kyoto agreement. It's time, quite simply, to do something.

'Do what?' is the million dollar question. People who came to the Tour events often seemed to start from a point of understanding that something needs to happen – but what? It provided a space to develop awareness of the issues and aimed to come up with ideas for resistance beyond purely symbolic activities. In Farnborough, we heard from a campaigner against aviation who started off being concerned about noise, as the planes flew over her house. More information led to her broader concern over the pollution that flying represents. Many Friends of the Earth supporters have heard of the campaign to boycott Esso; the tour broadened the debate to the other oil companies and the dominance of oil in our lives.

While the Tour was going on, a group of families from Hebden Bridge took part in the '90% for 90%' campaign, making the link between accessible and affordable public transport and the need for emission cuts. This campaign calls for 'a 90% cut in public transport fares, to make public transport affordable, to start making changes, that bring the 90% cut in greenhouse gases needed to halt climate change'. Supporters carry the railcard-sized card, distributed through the Rising Tide website, and show it to the guard alongside their ticket, or, as has happened in several group actions, show it and refuse to pay more than 10% of the fare. Of course, greater accessibility to public transport and a properly functioning transport system doesn't equate exactly with the end of climate chaos. But these would be a first step in finding different ways of living and working, ways that are a change from our current relationship to fossil fuels. Ways that are relevant to what makes up peoples' lives, not just what stimulates increased economic growth at the expense of reason.

Many moments during the Tour were quite inspirational, and others plain bizarre, like reading spoof weather reports wearing a tie and a mask and snorkel. Even so, it takes blind hope to hang on to that inspiration, when walking out of a room full of people buzzing with ideas is followed by the route home down a street bursting with corporate chain stores promoting products made in terrible conditions before being flown halfway across the globe; fast food outlets; and corporate chain bars packaging and serving up the 'leisure experience'.

The social context for reversing current damage stands alongside the immediate need to halt environmental degradation. It is not possible to ensure the survival of the planet without addressing power structures which are inherently inequitable and oppressive. Climate change is an issue of social justice: the first to feel the effects are the most vulnerable, the poor. The neighbours of the oil refineries are the poor and those whose voices are already politically marginalised. The people whose lands are destroyed to lay the oil pipelines have no voice at the international negotiations to limit use of fossil fuels. Civil society, like our ecosystem, is not a passive entity. Neither will obligingly accept their own demise.

Neither switching off the lights, nor blaming the social and economic conditions under which we live, is wholly adequate on its own. The scale of action needed to halt, let alone reverse, climate change tempts me to reach for a road map to the nearest Welsh hillside, equipped with a couple of joss sticks and a handful of seed potatoes. But everything has to start from somewhere and doing absolutely nothing about the connections between our own lives and other peoples' cannot be an option.

Climate chaos is not going away, nor are those who are attempting to change the situations which create it. I don't know precisely where the often haphazard ideas which came out of the Rising Tide Tour will go. But I do know that people starting to reduce their own dependence on fossil fuels; and people coming up with ideas which are based in their own lives signals the beginning of broader change. Why is there still a gap between the knowledge that things are going wrong, and the motivation to act to change the situation? Why don't those who hold a tentative grip on the reins of political power begin to engage with the core issues? After all, social and ecological justice aren't just buzzwords: it's time to start picking apart what they could really mean.

Rumble On The Edge Of Europe
- the struggle against the KURDTT rocket engine and fuel reprocessing plant in Votkinsk, Russia.

VOTKINSK, birthplace of famous 19th century composer Pyotr Chaikovsky, is a city of 100,000 inhabitants in Udmurtia, an autonomous republic of the Russian Federation near the Ural mountains. The city, built for the purposes of the huge soviet military-industrial complex, is now the planned site of KURDTT (Complex for Destruction of Heavy Fuel Rocket Engines), a plant for reprocessing discarded fuel and engines from SS-24, SS-24M, SS-25, SS-N-20 ballistic missiles. 70% of Russian ballistic missiles are of these types.

Better if not used, but no good anyway

Each of these missiles is a small-scale environmental disaster. Even if they are not launched, the project to bring 916 of them - altogether 17,500 tons of rocket fuel - to be disembowelled only nine kilometres from the city has rightly met with fierce opposition. An active and unique protest movement has sprung up in what is generally a disillusioned post-Soviet society.

The project was initially to be sited in the Nevada desert USA, but this plan was cancelled due to fears for the safety of the area's endangered tortoises. After being moved to a second site - about 250 kilometres from the nearest settlement, (a small Indian village) in 1996, the US congress had an even better idea: move the entire project to Russia, make it ten times bigger, and pump US$52.4 million into it. Originally Lockheed Martin, one of the biggest military-industrial corporations in the world were the major player, but they withdrew altogether in May 2001, and the project passed to the lesser known American corporation Energotech. Protesters didn't find out about the change of contractors until last August, and it was discovered that the project budget had already swollen to US$150 billion.

The first attempt to build the plant in Western Siberia's Perm area was cancelled thanks to local resistance, so the focus changed to Votkinsk - a city dependent on the military-industrial complex, and under the corrupt government of the Udmurtian republic. Already most modern Russian ballistic Topol-missiles are currently built in Votkinsk. In 1999 the project was put to a referendum in Votkinsk and 99.4% of voters were against the plant's construction - but the highest court of the Udmurtian republic declared the result invalid. Another poll, organised in the neighbouring city of Chaikovsky, gave the highly popular project a paltry 0.042% support.

No Go NGO's

When the old voting route failed, the townsfolk took to the streets with ongoing petitions, mass meetings of crowds of up to 3000, court cases were brought against the Republic's administration. Local ballistic missile specialists and rocket engineers who

had originally backed the project turned against it arguing that it would give little employment to locals, be governed from abroad, and be based on experimental technology. The factory is expected to produce thirteen tons of cyanic natrium NaCN - the stuff of chemical weapons - and they're talking about dumping this stuff in the area surrounding the factory, without any environmental provisions. The 'Ecological Impact Assessment' that green-lighted the project was from the Green Cross, a corrupt business NGO founded by Mikhail Gorbachev, who do a nice line selling certificates to various businesses. It should be called a 'Green Wash'. In March the city elected a new mayor with a pledge to drop the plant, who promptly turned back on that promise once elected.

Protest campaign in the summer of 2001

When the locals were getting nowhere with the fight to stop the plant, along came the direct action group the Rainbow Keepers who, along with the International Socio-Ecological Union, the Union for Chemical Safety, and local ecological activists, had a protest camp for six weeks during the summer of 2001. Daily info-stalls and actions were organised, and 20 000 copies of an anti-plant tabloid paper were distributed. A public meeting in late July drew a crowd of 3,000.

In the early hours of July 29th, the camp came under a surprise attack, when a group of five men broke in, and a tent was set alight, but fortunately no-one was injured. On the 3rd of August 300 inhabitants protested outside Lockheed Martin's city offices, but the crowd was violently dispersed by police and several people were arrested. A resulting solidarity picket for the imprisoned lasted five hours.

On August 13th protesters blockaded several roads in Votkinsk. The following day a court declared July 26th's mass meeting illegal; even though it was called by the city mayor himself! On the 21st of August another mass meeting drew a crowd of 1000. During the week of August 21st to 28th Rainbow Keepers blockaded the main entrance of the Votkinsk administration, with supportive locals protecting activists and giving them food. Federal Inspector S.V. Chikurov, who had steadfastly refused to meet protesters for two weeks, then demanded the city mayor "put an end to the organisation of mass disruptions in Votkinsk". On August 30th thirty masked attackers, supposedly from fascist groups descended on the camp, laying into campers with iron bars, knives, and baseball bats, and leaving five Rainbow Keepers with head wounds and other injuries.

During the summer one Finnish activist got a five year deportation from Russia.

The Future

The Camp ended on the 30th of August, but the campaign has stayed active over winter. In Moscow on the 3rd of November a theatre action was organised outside the Udmurtian HQ: three suited officials from America, Russia, and Udmurtia, pompously opening up the reprocessing factory, after which thick smoke billowed out onto the street and people died painful deaths. On the 12th of March a cartoon cruiser called the "Aurora" bombed the Moscow bases of Energotech, the Ministry of Atomic Energy, and Duma, with firecrackers. The running street revolution that kicked off then lasted five hours, as protesters evaded arrest by dodging from one administrative area to the next.

More protests will be organised in Votkinsk this summer (2002). Not only have officials not reversed the decision to build the plant, but building works have started at the factory's planned site.

- Thanks to Antti
Read more (in Russian): www.goriachiy.narod.ru
Rainbow Keepers online: www.chat.ru/~rk2000
If you are interested in participating this year write to tw@ecoline.ru, rkrzl@ecoline.ru and dikobrazi@lists.tao.ca

WAKE UP! WAKE UP! IT'S YER WATCH THIS SPACE

Weekly SchNEWS

Printed and Published in Brighton by Justice?

THEY GO SOFT IF THEY DON'T SHOOT THEIR LOAD MR PRESIDENT.

Friday 1st June 2001   **www.schnews.org.uk**   **Issue 307   Free/Donation**

LOST IN SPACE

"Space is being opened for business - the war business and commercial business. Will humanity be able to prevent the armed conflict and rampant greed that has marked human history on Earth from extending into the heavens?"

- Karl Grossman, author and professor of journalism at the State University of New York.

"It is time for new consciousness about space - it is not a junkyard or a playground for high-tech toys. It is a place of wonder and life."

- Dr.Caroline Lucas, Green MEP

Star Wars is back – but with a new twist. Back in 1983 under President Ronald Reagan we were told it was the Soviet Union, dubbed the "evil empire", whom the world needed to be defended against. Problem is the Soviet Union is no more, so in order to justify spending billions of dollars the States needs to find a new bogeyman. 'Rogue states' come on down.

The plan is to build a National Missile Defence 'protective shield' against the rogues – to shoot their missiles out of the sky before they ever reach American soil. But this is described in US space documents as merely a "layer" in a broader program.

And that program is part of a cunning plan for the US to continue to militarize space and so dominate the global economy.

STAR CRAZY

Two documents by the US Space Command "Vision For 2020" and "Long Range Plan" - spell out what America have got up their sleeves: "The United States will remain a global power and exert global leadership... Widespread communications will highlight disparities in resources and quality of life - contributing to unrest in developing countries... The global economy will continue to become more interdependent. Economic alliances, as well as the growth and influence of multinational corporations, will blur security agreements... The gap between 'have' and 'have-not' nations will widen - creating regional unrest... One of the commonly understood advantages of space-based platforms is no restriction or country clearances to overfly a nation from space."

Their "Vision for 2020" goes on to compare the U.S. effort to "control space" to centuries ago when "nations built navies to protect and enhance their commercial interests," referring to the great empires of Europe that ruled the waves and thus the Earth to maintain their imperial economies.

COST IN SPACE

"National Missile Defence is not driven by common sense, but by corporate greed. In essence, the Space Command will become the military instrument by which corporations maintain their global control."

- Dr.Caroline Lucas, Green MEP

Working closely behind the scenes with the U.S. military are major aerospace corporations. Four large corporations - Boeing, Lockheed Martin, Raytheon and TRW stand to gain over 60 per-cent of the National Missile Defence contracts. And would you believe it, board members of those companies are on 'independent' advisory councils to help George Bush make up his mind on security issues!

Not that Star Wars, with such powerful backers, ever really went away. Funding at $6 billion-a-year plus continued through the Clinton administration. Last December, Clinton's Department of Defence cleared the way for development of the "Space Based Laser Readiness Demonstrator" that has a "lifecycle budget" of $20 to $30 billion. A second space-based laser weapon on which development continued through the Clinton years is the "Alpha High-Energy Laser," now test-fired more than 20 times. The problem is the weapons the U.S. military wants to deploy in space - especially lasers - will need large amounts of power. And nuclear energy is seen by the U.S. military as the "natural" power source for them.

YANK IT OFF

In their book "The Future of War: Power, Technology and American World Dominance in the 21st Century," George and Meredith Friedman, conclude: "Just as by the year 1500 it was apparent that the European experience of power would be its domination of the global seas, it does not take much to see that the American experience of power will rest on the domination of space... Just as Europe expanded war and its power to the global oceans, the United States is expanding war and its power into space... Just as Europe shaped the world for half a millennium, so too the United States will shape the world for at least that length of time... For better or worse, America has seized hold of the future of war, and with it - for a time - the future of humanity." Surely the USA in starting a new arms race is the real rogue state.

* If the UK gives its approval to Star Wars it would involve upgrading the early warning station at Fylingdales and Menwith Hill Spy Base. Defence Secretary Geoff Hoon has

admitted that doing this would make Britain a target of the so-called 'rogue' states.

* The Campaign for the Accountability of American Bases holds regular pickets outside Menwith Hill Spy Base, near Harrogate every Tuesday 7-9pm Tel 01943 466405 www.caab.org.uk.

* 22 June Stop Star Wars-blockade the Ministry of Defence. ARROW 020 7607 2302

*13 October is International Day of Action against Star Wars and people are being asked to protest outside their nearest American base. In the UK there will also be a demo outside the US Embassy. CND 0207 700 2393 www.cnduk.org/

* Star Wars Returns - new video by EnviroVideo. www.envirovideo.com

* Global Network Against Weapons & Nuclear Power In Space. www.space4peace.org

* Susan van der Hijden and Martin Newell received one year prison sentences for disabling nuclear convoy trucks, but walked free as they'd already spent 6 months on remand.

SchWOOPS!

Couple of mistakes in last week's front page. The World Bank are trying to set up www.developmentgateway.org., sponsored by the Financial Times and other corporations who get to sit on the board and select editors who can tell the poor what they need. It's part of a wider initiative of the Bank to repackage itself as the 'knowledge bank' with tactics like bunging money to think tanks and academics etc. To find out more check out www.realworldbank.org

And just cos the bankers aren't going to Barcelona anymore, doesn't mean the protests won't continue. There'll be a counter conference, actions and occupations from 16-25 June. www.j25.org

FREE PARTY AND PROTEST GUIDE INSIDE

1st- The Rising Tide Climate Change Tour continues in Reading (8), Oxford (9 with Seize The Day playing in the evening) Each visit has an evening of 'infotainment', alongside workshops, street theatre and creative actions. 01865 241097 www.risingtide.org.uk ** **1-10th 19th anniversary of Faslane Peace Camp**. A week of workshops and anti trident actions. There'll also be a beach and road verge clean up locally, and a visit to the local Community Farm for a day's volunteering. 01436 820901 www.faslanepeacecamp.org ** **4th CND** peace walk around Nuclear Weapon States embassies to enquire about what effort has been made for the Nuclear Proliferation Treaty. Dick Sheppard Chapel, St Martin-in-the-Fields Church, Trafalgar Sq, 10.30am. 020 7700 4200 ** **5 Time to go Veggie** - talk by Vivas! Juliet Gellatley 8pm, 42 Marine Parade, Worthing. www.worthing.eco-action.org/porkbolter ** **5 i-Contact video network summer solstice** themed evening of radical grassroots activist films, 7.30 pm. at The Hat & Feather, Walcot St, Bath £3 www.videonetwork.org **7 Low Impact Dwellings** - a slideshow and talk by Selena Merrett, about the growing countrywide low impact movement. SS Mary & John Church Hall, Cowley Rd., Oxford ** **7 Election Day!** Manchester will be home to a daylong fluid colourful festival of anti-government and anti-corporate frivolity. Accommodation can be sorted for a few hundred and there'll be parties . The Carrumba Collective, BOX 23, c/o Bridge 5 Mill, 22a Beswick Street, Ancoats, Manchester M4 7HS TEL: 0161 226 6814 june7@corporatedirtbag.com ** **7 Put Your Cross Against The Politicians** at the Crossroads Womens Centre. If you aren't voting with conviction, or at all, register your views for community and against privatisation. From 10am, 230A Kentish Town Rd, London, NW5. 020 7482 2496. ** **7 Avoid more election bullshit, talk about Genoa instead.** Brighton Collective host a night of video and tunes to raise cash and awareness for the upcoming trip to Genoa. Palmers Bar (Near the ice rink), 7.30 email: brightoncollective@hushmail.com ** **8 World Oceans Day** Walks, talks, exhibitions and events worldwide. Marine Conservation Society 01989 566017 ** **8-10 Brighton Women Speak Out.** Women Speak Out is a gathering for women interested or involved in DIY political, social, environmental activity. Space to sleep, creche, vegan food, bring sleeping stuff, cutlery, yourselves and ideas. 24 ansaphone message from June 1, 01273 298192, or 07900 374015, www.spor.org.uk ** **9 Public Service Announcement Benefit** night featuring ska/samba and punk night with The Restarts, Maroon Town, Rhythms of Resistance, DJ Alex (from Transglobal Underground) 7.30pm-1am, Chat's Palace, 42-44 Brooksby's Walk, Homerton, E9 £5/3.50. Benefit for Reclaim The Streets, PGA, Indy Media UK and No Borders. Tel. 020 85330227 publica@tarakan.demon.co.uk ** **9 Stop The Crop - peaceful protest** against the two farm-scale trials of GM maize and oil seed rape at Hinton Waldrist, Oxfordshire 01865 821198 holly@gn.apc.org ** **9-10 Lampeter Drovers Festival**, Lampeter, Ceredigion, West Wales.FREE 01570 434407 mail spirit@madasafish.com ** **9 i-Contact video network summer solstice** themed evening, 8pm at the Cube Microplex, Kings square, Bristol. £3 www.videonetwork.org ** **9 Homelands**, Aberdeen. £38 ** **9-10 Globalisation: The Good, the Bad and the Alternatives** at The Manchester Conference Centre, UMIST, Manchester (5 minutes walk from Manchester Piccadilly train station). Bookings to Lara Marsh, Events Officer, World Development Movement, FREEPOST (WC4268) London SW9 7BR 0800 3282153 or by email lara@wdm.org.uk ** **10 Stoke Newington Street Festival.** World Music stage at Clissold Park www.stokenewingtonfestival.co.uk ** **10 Mad Pride 2nd Birthday Anniversary Gig.** 3-8pm at the Foundry, Old Street, London EC1. Nikki Sudden, famous 80s New Wave musician and more,free. 0207 7018535 www.madpride.net ** **14 New York's anarcho-arts collective 'The Surveillance Camera Players'** will be at the Okasional Squat Café, Charles Street, Manchester 7.30pm. Tel 07752 287825. www.surveillancecameraplayers.org ** **14-16 European Union meeting in Gothenburg, Sweden.** The next big EU meeting takes place in the pictuesque city of Gothenburg. Anti-EU feelings are running high in both Denmark and Sweden. Events planned so far include a counter conference, a reclaim the city on Friday followed by another big demonstration on Saturday. http://motkraft.net/gbg2001/ www.forumgoteborg.org ** **15 Post Election Skittle Night** at the Coach and Horses pub, Keddlestone Road (Off Evington Road) To raise funds for Leicester Radical Alliance. Tickets £6 (£5 concs) including meal http://radical.membe rs.beeb.net ** **15- 25 The Oerol Festival**, Terschelling Island, Holland. 10 days of amazing location performance, stages and clubs on a beautiful Island off Holland. Island/Festival is completely bicycle led and unique.www.oerol.nl

** **15-17 'Making Global Connections with Local Experience'** conference Liverpool. Eleanor Rathbone Building, Beford St South, Liverpool. £30 (£10 unwaged), includes Saturday lunch and refreshments. Contact Chart s@TranscendingImages.org or fax 0161 224 4985 ** **15-17 Stoke Newington Street Festival** family events and childrens stuff at Clissold Park and Stoke Newington Church St. 0208 3566415 www.stokenewingtonfest ival.co.uk ** **16 Cannabis March and Festival, Brockwell Park, London.** FREE . End the Prohibition march, noon in Kennington Park, departs 1pm sharp to Brockwell Park, Brixton. 2-8 pm Festival in Brockwell Park, Brixton: bands, comedy, sound systems, food and cannabis stuff, etc. www.schmoo.co.uk/may2001.htm ** **16 Summer Tekno Kaos** with Underground Sound and Defcon 1 and United Systems 9pm-6am @ The amazing Stratford Rex Auditorium, 361 High Street, Stratford, London £10 Info:07833 600 459 ** **16 World Smell Day.** Time to put the crustie in the bathtub. Details from the Aroma Foundation, Mellon Charles, Loch Ewe, IV22 2JE ** **16 International Refugee Day** see www.united.non-profit.nl ** **16 Colombia Solidarity Campaign Day School** 10am-5pm. The Cock Tavern, 23 Phoenix Road, junction with Charlton Street, London NW1 (near Eversholt Street) between Euston and King's Cross. £3/1.50 . Call 07950 923 448 ** **16 The Colombia Peace Association** presents a Fundraising Fiesta with a top Colombian Vallenato Band and DJs at Conway Hall, Red Lion Square, London WC1 (Holborn tube) 7pm-midnight £8 on the door £5 concs All proceeds will go to assist displaced families in Colombia liz.atherton@freeuk.com to order tickets ** **16 London Fleadh**, Finsbury Park, London ** **16 Gatecrasher**, Turweston Aerodrome, Brackley, Northants Noon -6am £50 (but it is called Gatecrasher so bring a ladder) **16 - 24 National Bike Week** ** **16-17 Leamington Peace Festival**, Pump Room Gardens, Leamington Spa,Warkwickshire. FREE. There'll be 2 stages and thirty different acts including Seize The Day and le Cod Afrique. Workshops and kids activities and loadsa stalls and stuff. ** **16-17 National Organic Gardening Weekend.** Organic gardeners throughout the country will be opening up their gardens to the general public. Contact HDRA info 024 76303517 www.hdra.org.uk ** **17 Provinssirock Festival**, Finland ** **17 -23 Brithdir Mawr Summer Solstice Camp**, West Wales. Music, dance, permaculture. 01239 820099 ** **18 Actions at Ministry of Defence national purchasing centre in Bristol, Filton Abbey Wood.** As long as it's nonviolent, imagination is the limit. There is an offer of accommodation in Bristol the night before the action info:www.access.lowtech.org/ collectableanorak ** **18 Elephants - Do they have a future?** Coexistence not Conservation. Talk by Bill Jordan, Vice Chair of the RSPCA and founder of Care for the Wild. APE, The Bathouse, Gwydir St. Cambridge, 8pm. ** **19 Resistance at work meeting.** Safety above all - stop so called accidents at work. Speakers include UCATT and Building Worker Group and other safety campaigns. 7.30pm at Wood Green Labour Club, Stuart Crescent, N22. Organised by Haringey Solidarity Group http:// hsg.cupboard.org ** **19 McLibel: Anniversary of 1997 High Court Victory** McLibel Support Campaign.5 Caledonian Rd, London N1. 0207 713 1269. Adopt-A-Store Network: 0115 958 5666 ** **19 Act Together** (A coalition of women opposed to Iraqi sanctions) Drawing attention to the intellectual embargo will be displaying books that were returned by customs. maysoon@oxymoronfilms.demon.co.uk ** **20 Online-demonstration against the deportation business.** On May 28, 1999, Amir Ageeb from Sudan suffocated and died from mistreatment by German border police while being deported on a Lufthansa airplane. This is a call to block website of Lufthansa Airlines, in which flights can be booked; if a lot of people log on at the same time, the entrance to this publicly displayed webpage can be blocked due to overload. contact: online-demo@gmx.net ** **21 Summer Solstice** 8.33am, access to Stonehenge for sunrise. 07748 954954 ** **21 "The proposed Hastings bypass and its link to International Capitalism"** At: The Carlisle pub, 24 Pelham Street/Carlisle Parade, Hastings, 8pm ** **20-24 Healing Field Gathering.** After 15 years of Glastonbury they're stepping out on their own…0177 955 6690 www.healingfield.btinternet.c o.uk ** **21 World Earth Healing Day** linking thousands of people in meditation, prayer, and mindful activity. Hold hands and the world will become a better place..apparently www.worldhealing.co.uk ** **23 Alternative Glastonbury.** 24 hour extravaganza with Firestarter Stage and some of the most amazing festival rumours ever. Still TBC Tel: 0208 509 3353 www.continentaldrifts.uk.com/ ** **23 Public Service Announcement Benefit** night featuring Punky reggae/ska night with P.A.I.N., The Trojans, Headjam and Megabitch DJs 7.30pm till 1am at Chat's Palace, 42-44 Brooksby's Walk, Homerton, Hackney E9 Benefit for Reclaim The Streets, Peoples Global

Action, Indy Media UK and No Borders. Tel. 0208 533 0227 publica@tar akan.demon.co.uk ** **23 National demo against Huntingdon Life Sciences** Meet at Parker's Piece, Cambridge, 12 noon. Contact SHAC 0845 4580630 www.shac.net ** **23 Justice for Jimmy Ingram** - nine years in gaol for a crime he didn't commit. Join the Kent Against Injustice picket 1-2pm outside HMP Maidstone, County Rd. Contact PO Box 781, Canterbury, Kent, CT2 7FB ** **23 March Against Racism and Police Brutality.** Assemble 12 noon, Tottenham police station, march to Wood Green Library. marchagainstracism@yahoo.co.uk ** **24 European Sun Day** www.sundayeurope.com ** **25 Day Of Action Against Novartis** june25@shacusa.net ** **25 -1st July National Vegetarian Week** 0161 9252000 ** **25-26 Starbucks Days of Action** tell 'em to stop using GM products, improve working conditions and to start using fair trade coffee. Everywhere. www.organicconsumers.org/starbucks ** **25-29 Trial of the Broomfield School Three,** Lordship Lane Magistrates Court, 10 am. Last year 20 young men armed with baseball bats, knives etc. entered the grounds of Broomfield school and attacked and hospitalised an innocent 14 year old black boy. Later students from the school spot the perpetrators on a bus and told the police who talked to them, then laid into the school-kids and their teacher. Three of the schoolkids now face criminal charges. Contact 07957 696636 ** **26 Leicester Radical Alliance meeting.** The Secular Hall, Humberstone Gate, Leicester 7.30pm http://radical.membe rs.beeb.net ** **27 LX Cool Festival**, Lisbon, Portugal ** **28-30 Grado Zero 2001** Creative Resistance against G8 summit, Rome a collective effort of various squatting communities in Italy coming together to create a platform to discuss ideas for the G8 summit. Info gradozero@disinfo.net www.ecn.org/forte http://squat.net/cia ** **29-1st July Anti-Sanctions Conference** Featuring Denis Halliday, former UN Humanitarian Coordi-nator for Iraq and Kathy Kelly, co-founder Voices in the Wilderness, Kingsley Hall, Powis Road, London E2. www.viwuk.freeserve.co.uk or www.casi.org.uk ** **29-1ˢᵗ July Winchester Hat Fair**. For all you summer fete massive Tel: 01962 849841 www.hatfair.co.uk ** **29 -1st July Bar-celona meeting of European Noborder Network** www.noborder.org ** **30 Statewatching the new Europe**: international conference on civil liberties, immigration, policing, freedom of information, surveillance etc. at University of London Students Union, Malet St., London. 020 8802 1882 www.statewatch.org ** **30 Mardi Gras**, Finsbury Park, London. 1-10pm £15. Sponsored by Eurostar, Virgin and Ford. www.londonmardigras.com ** **30 Forget Mardi Gras, La Di-Dah!** Piss take of the comercialszation of the Mardi Gras festival. "Come, this year, in the company of: rebellious fags - transgressive dykes - outraged celibates - insurgent faeries - frustrated freaks - queers of all sexualities. 3pm till dusk in Finsbury Park. www.queeruption.com ** **30 Skateboard festival at Clissold Park, London** 0208 3566415 www.stokenewingtonfestival. co.uk ** **30 National Day of Action against the Fur Trade in London** Meet 11am Trafalgar Square. 0845 4584775 ** **30 Mass protest outside Harmondsworth Detention Centre.** To mark the opening of another block to hold 550 refugees. Midday at the Centre, north of Heathrow, on the A4/Colnbrook by-pass. 07931-198501 ** **30 Palestine: the New Apartheid - Building the Solidarity Movement,** 11am-4.30pm at Uni-versity of London Union, Mallet, St, London ** **30 Protest march against GM foods being grown in Wivenhoe.** noon at Wivenhoe station for a march to Sunnymead farm where the crops are being grown for a picnic. mclarkc@essex.ac.uk for more info

* For info on **parties and teknivals** http://www.guilfin.net and http://cobalt.freetekno.org
* For a comprehensive listing of **folk, roots and world music festivals** in the UK and Europe check out www.froots.demon.co.uk/
* For a list of seriously **hippy rainbow gathering** type festivals send an SAE to **Campscene Directory**, Cirenor, Wells in the Field, Whitchurch, Hants, RG28 7NG or http://bobo.realitycom.com/spiritnet
* For more information on **The Animal Right Calendar**, contact Veggies, 180 Mansfield Road, Nottingham NG1 3HW www.veggies.org.uk/calendar.
For information on a wide range of weekend courses on **renewable energy and sustainable development** contact **Centre for Alternative Technology** Machynlleth, Powys, SY10 9AZ Tel: 01654 703743 www.cat.org.uk
* For courses and events about **sustainable lifestyles** (everything from composting to fruit tree grafting to pond building) contact the **Permaculture Association**, London, WC1N 3XX 0845 458 4150 www. permaculture.org.uk

Teknival Hitch

The French free party scene is under attack by the government over there. They're amending the new Public Safety Bill, mirroring our 1994 Criminal Justice Act, which criminalised but didn't crush the UK's scene. One day after the start of April's massive 5 day teknival in Marigny outside Paris, which drew systems and crowds from all over Europe, the amendment to the act was passed and this week put before the senate. Under its powers the authorities will be able to fine and imprison organisers as well as confiscate their sound systems and records. It's not only the big teknivals that have been targetted, small house parties have also experienced the wrath of the law.

Sound familiar? Sound system crews and party goers are not taking it lying down though, and across France demonstrations have taken place in all major cities. Whilst over 2,000 demonstrators organised a silent sit-down protest outside Paris town hall, truncheon happy riot police clashed with people in Toulouse, leaving 2 demonstrators injured. This is not unusual, the right-wing CRS riot police regularly have running battles with party-goers. With teknivals often attracting tens of thousands of people – there were 25,000 at Marigny – the authorities feel threatened by so many people coming together. Unfortunately many of the organisers and party goers don't tidy up after themselves, and farmers' crops and the countryside have been trashed. One teknival goer told SchNEWS, "this [amendment] is totally unacceptable as the principle is free music for all…but it is difficult to defend this movement if they can't be responsible and respect the environment." Like over here, many responsible party people get caught in the crossfire and are often subject to the same over the top laws and the clampdown on autonomous free creative space.

Further simultaneous festivals/demonstrations are planned for June 16 in Paris and Marseille, to urge the retraction of the amendment and the return of confiscated systems.
* Check out the new SchNEWS and Squall Yearbook 2001 for more on teknivals. For (French) reports: www.imaginet.fr/kanyar/ Teknival info: www.defocore.net and www.freetekno.org
* Despite the recent crackdown on parties over here, last week a big party went off outside Bristol with no problems and quite a few rigs (okay, we don't know how many).
* Three evictions later and the [c]ounter [i]nformation [a]gency (CIA) Infocafe has a new location in the heart of Amsterdam. The squatted, open public space aims to counter corporate and government control of information (production, distribution, censorship, copyright, etc.), providing a platform for non-mainstream information and a space for groups to present their projects and information. It can be found at Vijzelstraat 5, 1017 HD, Amsterdam, for forthcoming events check out www.squat.net/cia or phone +31-20-6831021
* In Brighton the 'Food for Freaks' info café has been open for a week, with music and cheap, healthy vegan food served up daily. Juice and smoothies have quenched thirsts while the coffee direct from cooperatives in Chiapas and Ecuador have kept everyone buzzing. There's a library of info for action, and events are planned for next week. Come and check out this antidote to profit making at 4 Prince Albert St (between Ship St and Bartholomew Sq).

POSITIVE SchNEWS

Author and radical farmer Jose Bové is on a UK speaking tour to promote his new book, 'The World is Not For Sale' written with co-author Francois Dufour. Bové is best known for his spectacular dismantling of a McDonalds, but by no means is that all he's done. He's been involved in direct action since the 70's, when he and other student activists squatted a deserted village near the Larzac plateau to protest against the French army's plans to build a huge military base there. After ten-years of almost daily pitched battles with the police, they won their fight - the Larzac is now a national Park. Bové's book is a fascinating and easy to read account of his infamous McDonalds escapade and the issues behind the campaign: the industrialization of agriculture in a global economy, the massive environmental damage this is causing, and the tasteless, unhealthy food that results. The book is £16 in hardbook at the moment (ISBN 1-85984-614-9). Order it from your local library or buy it for only £10 at Bové's London speaking date, June 12ᵗʰ, 7:30pm, Camden Centre, Judd Street, near King's Cross Station. Bové will be in Glasgow on the 13ᵗʰ (Anya Lyngbaek at isecuk@gn.apc.org for more info), and Norwich on the 14ᵗʰ, 6:30pm at University of East Anglia, Lecture Theatre 2, admission free, contact tel: 01953 889100, or email flink@gn.apc.org.

ONE DAY AT A FESTIE...

Oldham Press

"When Oldham erupted on Saturday, it was not a riot. That word does no justice to the desperation and righteousness of young Asians. What happened was an uprising - an intifada against persecution by media, police and fascists, and self-defence is no offence. There will be no peace in Oldham without justice." - Ally Fogg, activist and journalist.

The problems in Oldham go back at least thirty years when Oldham council decided, unlike Manchester, to keep the Pakistani, Bangladeshi and white communities apart, and in ghettos. There's always been a history of conflict between the groups, but guess whose side the local media and police force have usually been on?

The Oldham Evening Chronicle was fire-bombed on the weekend. Random vandalism? Well the paper has always towed the police line about racism in the town, and published bigoted letters from BNP members. In 1998 Chief Superintendent Eric Hewitt gave an interview saying that "the majority" of racist attacks in Oldham were by Asians on whites. Last year they published the figures that 60% of racist attacks, that were reported, were on whites. Asians claim that they have given up reporting attacks because the police either don't arrive, or if they do, the complaints are dismissed.

Recent escalations go back to April when pensioner Walter Chamberlain was severely beaten in Glodwick, and the police told the media that it was a racist attack by Asians, making "a No-Go area for whites". Mr. Chamberlain's family insisted it wasn't race related but police still charged four youths with racially motivated offences (as opposed to the Leeds footballers who attacked an Asian lad some months ago – and the word 'racism' wasn't allowed to be mentioned in court). The attack gave the NF and BNP an excuse to 'reclaim the territory', and there were reports of numerous racist attacks on Asians, but no arrests. Things were getting worse last week when a group of ex-pupils arrived at Breeze Hill school to chant slogans and intimidate Asian pupils, but despite appeals from teachers, the police refused to intervene. The following day a group of Asian pupils fought back and the police arrived immediately, and there were four arrests - all were Asian.

For four weeks police had attempted to keep a lid on the cauldron of anger in Oldham. Despite their claims that they 'had no idea' that anything on the scale of last weekend was likely, they have been throwing around Section 60 stop and search orders like confetti in anticipation of 'serious public disorder.' Furthermore, on four consecutive Saturdays, when fascists have threatened to gather in town, residents of whole estates have been restricted to their ghettoes under public order legislation. A group of 30 anti-Nazi activists travelling from Manchester to leaflet on Saturday 19th were stopped on the outskirts of town, searched, photographed, videoed and then escorted to a back street behind a disused bus station where they were told they could have 'a rally'. Attempts to hand leaflets to members of the public were blocked on the basis that it was 'behaviour liable to cause a breach of the peace.' This was only two weeks after a group of 50-70 fascists were allowed to march unhindered through the town centre in flagrant defiance of a Home Office ban.

Whatever started the violence, the fact is that by Wednesday, 33 whites and 16 Asians had been arrested and given the police bias this speaks for itself. Meanwhile Nick Griffin, is standing as BNP candidate in Oldham West in the coming election.

*No SchNEWS next week cos we'll be busy posting our new books out to you 'orrible lot.

SchNEWS in Brief

Agricultural biotechnology is probably the most contentious food issue facing the UK and Europe today. Despite every effort of industry and their 'scientists' people all around the world continue to resist this threat to the environment. Even before it wipes out biological diversity, it's going to wipe out the lives of millions of small farmers, their land and their independence. A hastily organised counter-conference 'Seeds of Opportunity' has been organised (SchNEWS 225) in response. It's on today (sorry about short notice) 2-8pm ULU, Malet St, Room 3c. 020-76900626 www.geneticsaction.org.uk ** **Percy Schmeiser**, the farmer sued by Monsanto for having his crops contaminated (SchNEWS 300) has raised enough money for an appeal, www.paercyschmeiser.com ** The Polish secret police have shut down the **No-Borders** two-day multicultural festival after initial permission was granted. Camp plans will now be made in top secret and the camp will take on a more confrontational attitude than the peaceful, communitarian one previously adopted. www.noborder.org ** A No Borders Close **Campsfield** Camp has been set up outside the Detention Centre, they hope to be there for a few weeks. Bring camping stuff, food, music, ideas and creativity. Camp mobile - 0781 355 2570.** A website for **African anarchism** has seen massive expansion in response to totalitarian African governments supported and armed by 'developed nations'. Check out the reports of fledgling anarchist movements at www.struggle.ws/africa/ ** The monsoon season in India is approaching and the waters will be rising again behind the Sardar Sarovar Dam on the **Narmada River**. half a million indigenous peasants have resolved to stay in their homes to drown rather than see their livelihoods washed away in return for false promises of nonexistent resettlement. They are calling for international supporters to go to the valley during summer to show solidarity and to relate the struggle to globalisation. www.narmada.org ** **U'wa** families resisting oil drilling by Occidental Petroleum in Colombia have been told they must evacuate their area due to a risk of landslides, which has been increased by oil drilling and road building! www.ran.org ** The Moving on from **MayDay** meeting in London we mentioned last week has been cancelled ** There's a day of action for **Mark Barnsley.** Picket the Home Office, 8 June, 1pm, 50 Queen Anne's Gate . Transport from Brighton courtesy of the ABC, meet at St. Peter's Church at 10am. Donations for petrol will be welcome.

McDEATH

McDonalds once again demonstrated their (lack of) compassion recently in South Africa. Despite regular muggings and rapes, McDonalds employees are not entitled to transport when they finish work late, often after 2am. One waitress was gang raped in February, and is now so terrified of going home after work that she spends her nights hiding in the local mall and leaves after sunrise. Despite an unsuccessful appeal to Mucky D's for help to buy anti-retroviral drugs, the megacorp did offer her a short-term loan. She declined the offer, knowing she wouldn't be able to pay it back, but help finally arrived when she contacted a community-based anti-rape organisation. The woman, who is too afraid to be named, said, "If I do end up getting HIV, McDonald's will have helped sign my death warrant." McDonald's still has not provided the trauma counselling it promises employees, and has not even offered the waitress the option of day shifts.

PILLS THAT KILL

Four thousand people bleed to death each year after being prescribed cheap painkillers such as aspirin and diclofenac, which can cause stomach bleeding that is fatal in extreme cases. This is just one example of pills that kill - medicines supposedly safe following animal testing. To counter vivisection propaganda, Seriously Ill Against Vivisection (SIAV) held their first demo outside the Research Defence Society (a pro-vivisection 'charity' bankrolled by pharmaceutical companies). SIAV are a group of people who are ill or have disabilities and are challenging the vivisection industry over claims that vivisection saves lives and promotes human health. All welcome at the next demo: Animals in Medicine Research Information Centre, 12 Whitehall, noon, 6th June. 0845-4581720. www.siav.org

* Join a march of people dressed as killer drugs through Harrogate as part of the campaign to close down Covance vivisection labs. 23rd June, noon at Harrogate train station: 07960-900401.

*Animal rights campaigners are often portrayed as violent thugs, when in reality it's animal abusers who get their kicks from killing animals and beating up protestors (or just letting the police do that for them). A campaign has been launched to try and shed some light on these facts. www.violenceinanimalrights.co.uk was launched at a press conference with victims of animal abusers, including Steve Christmas (nearly killed by Hunt followers, see SchNEWS 274) and three coffins representing Jill Phipps, Tom Worby and Mike Hill. The website shows what animal rights campaigners suffer on a daily basis from attacks by hunt supporters to assaults and crap arrests by the police. While the state supports violent attacks on animal rights protestors, it introduces more legislation to crack down on protests. The new Police Act gives police powers to stop demonstrations in the vicinity of anyone's dwelling if they (un)reasonably believe harassment may be taking place. This has already affected the Save the Newchurch Guinea Pigs Campaign as at one of the Guinea Pig 'farms' someone lives there (how convenient). Undeterred they're having another demo on 7th July, phone 01902-564734 for details.

POOLING RESOURCES

Glasgow Council owned Govanhill swimming pool has been occupied since the Spring Equinox. A dynamic protest with 24-hour pickets has kept the pressure on. It's the usual Council 'lack of consultation' story all done in the name of saving money. The Council wants to 'bung' a local businessman £500k to get rid of the pool whose last 'community' act was to convert the old Post Office into a 5 star Hotel and sixty luxury apartments that he wants to flog for £0.5 million each. No wonder the community has rebelled, forfeiting the best of the summer to stay indoors to keep their pool. Help needed: 07000-752752.

...and finally...

"...THIS UNIVERSE AIN'T BIG ENUFF FOR THE BOTH OF US."

Subscribe!

Keep SchNEWS FREE! Send 1st Class stamps (e.g. 10 for next 9 issues) or donations (payable to Justice?) Ask for "Originals" if you can make copies. Post *free* to all prisoners. SchNEWS, c/o on-the-fiddle, P.O. Box 2600, Brighton, East Sussex, BN2 2DX. *Tel/Autofax* +44 (0)1273 685913 *Email* schnews@brighton.co.uk *Download a PDF* of this issue or subscribe at www.schnews.org.uk

Democracy

What Democracy?

By Flaco

When Blair finally decided his heartland flock of country landowners were ready to re-elect him, he set the date for his 2001 general election and the tongues of the back room boys at Wapping and Westminster were instantly blistering despite being more than fifty klix from the nearest foot and mouth cull-zone. But, is this really all democracy has cracked up to be?

Somehow, having the infrequent option to 'X' a box in favour of one or other of the almost identical, single-ideology factions on offer has become our accepted input into the democratic process - despite the result having no discernible effect on the economy or social policy.

Have we perhaps become too accustomed to watching our politicians and newsmen laud or condemn other nations' democratic virtue on their ability to emulate Western style elections. The founding of the modern states were met with considerable resistance. People refused to pay taxes, to be conscripted or to obey laws passed by national governments. Yet those who covet power have constantly promoted the concept that a centralised 'representative' government does, or can, serve the people. And even the most sceptical have difficulty shaking the notion that electoral participation equates to some sort of popular control.

"Voters are given the choice between tweedledum and tweedledee, and then bombarded with a variety of techniques to sway them towards one or the other," adds Brian Martin from the University of Wollongong, NSW, Australia. Martin, who has published extensively on the drawbacks of the electoral system, believes: "The problem with voting is that the basic premises of the state are never considered open for debate, much less challenged." He points out that all governments have a monopoly over 'legitimate' violence (with their armies, police, prisons and security services) to wage war or for internal control (anti-capitalists and asylum seekers are the latest in a long old line of truncheon magnets to be condemned as violent criminals). The same goes for taxation and the sacred status of property (under capitalism) or bureaucratic privilege (under state socialism), neither of which are up for debate.

Voting is the antithesis of debate, negotiation or consensus. Votes cannot show if voters are voting for something or against something else. They cannot express preferences between different issues, how strongly people feel about any particular one, or what they are willing to forego or pay in order to get it. Though not trusted with any level of decision making ourselves, as voters we are expected to soundly assess all the major issues of policy and the merits of the competing parties on the back of highly-choreographed, often deliberately-misleading information spun by the doctors and filtered by corporate media. We are then expected to translate that into a multiple choice (of two) answer. We are not invited to enter the (non) debate - just to endorse the outcome.

Even by their own scoring system, the mandate of those in power is at best shaky, and at worst non-existent. Every British government since 1951 has been elected on less than half the votes cast. New Labour's 1997 'landslide' victory polled 13 million votes - less than 44 per cent of those dropped in the box. With only 71 per cent of eligible voters turning out (the lowest for fifty years), Labour - as Thatcher did before them - managed to secure two thirds of parliament's seats backed by less than a third of those allowed to vote. (If the state thinks you are too young, insecure or has decided to jail you - you don't even get a walk on part in the electoral pantomime.)

Local elections are in even shabbier shape when it comes to legitimate mandates. John Kiely, one of the Lib Dem councillors for the Bristol's Easton ward polled 27 per cent of the 33 per cent turnout (even with everyone having two votes). Support from less than a tenth of the ward's electorate was enough to secure his seat.

Then there is Europe. In one Sunderland ward MEPs mobilised an awe inspiring 1.5 per cent turnout for their last election. Across the South West of England less than 28 per cent of voters bothered taking the trip down the community centre to 'choose' their MEP. Under the PR system, the Tories took four of the seven seats with 42 per cent of the vote. That's 11.5 per cent for each seat - 2.8 per cent of the total possible vote for each seat. And they were the winners.

Politicians of all colours say they are keen to see a higher turnout – after all, it makes the voters feel involved in the machinations of government and less likely to question their democratic impotence. Similarly bolstering suffrage - something those in power do occasionally as a 'concession' to their 'subjects' - is a good way to make people feel empowered. Bristol West MP Valerie Davey says we are "taking our votes for granted," and compares current "voter apathy" to the sacrifices of British suffragettes or South Africa's black population. Yet, despite having the hard-won ability to 'X' the ballot, women are still pathetically un-represented in positions of power in Britain, and little has changed in the distribution of land, wealth or opportunity in the universally-enfranchised South Africa.

"Revolutionary movements can enter the electoral arena and sometimes help bring more progressive people into government," says US historian Howard Zinn. "But if they sink all their energy into electoral activity they weaken their real strength, which is organised protest outside the electoral process. Concentrating energy on elections is deadly, because if you lose, it deals a death blow to your movement."

"Time after time," says Brian Martin, "[so-called] radical parties have become chains to hold back the process of radical change." In 1945 Labour sailed into power on a sea of promised reforms. Did they materialise? As if! Again in 1997 Labour managed to diffuse large chunks of support for an increasingly popular environmental movement with promises of eco-friendly policies that have crossed the central reservation and are heading up the other lane of the brand new bypass. It says something about the scope of debate that German Green Party Foreign Minister Josker Fischer's recently-exposed militant credentials have caused more of a stir in the press than the ease with which he sent bombers against civilian targets in Serbia.

UK Green Party candidate Glen Vowels feels his party has gained access to people it otherwise wouldn't have by entering the electoral fray. Though admits it is "the more pragmatic" Greens who secure the top jobs and there "is a fear at the back of my mind that we could become a caricature, as Labour have." No shit Glen!

The Greens presume that it is the individual that corrupts the office of government, whereas advocates of participatory democracy say it is the other way around. As Wendy McElroy said: "You can't change government by electing politicians any more than you can prevent crime by becoming a criminal." Coathangers against car theft anyone?

Russian émigré Mikhail Bakunin believed that every government, regardless of who's in control, is an instrument of repression. He even described Marx's envisioned dictatorship of the proletariat as "the most autocratic of all regimes". However fair majority rule appears, it is to the exclusion of the minorities within society.

When cornered, Lib Dem chief whip and MP for Cornwall Paul

Tyler, admits the party system severs the link between people and politicians. "You just need to keep your nose clean with the party hierarchy, get yourself a safe seat, and you have a career for life."

Voting statistics have enabled the parties to precision target the swing voters whose votes hold the power balance. This has removed most people from the electoral equation altogether. So it's not surprising that the 2001 election saw an all-time low turnout. Speaking before the election, Professor Patrick Dunleavy, chair of policy research at the London School Of Economics predicted, correctly, that over a third of the electorate would choose Corry over Tony, Billy or Charlie. He says that yet again politicians will concentrate on a tiny fraction of voters. "Unemployment is less than one million, and politicians are cynical enough not to bother with groups that won't turn out," he says. "Young people, the jobless and homeless won't get much of a look in. Those in safe Labour seats will be neglected, as will those in the cities." (*See boxout below*).

John Kiely (Easton) and his fellow Councillor Helga Benson (Lab, St Pauls) represent wards containing Bristol's largest Asian and Afro Caribbean communities respectively. Yet, there are no non-white councillors in the chamber - or candidates on the ballot paper. Both politicians balk at the suggestion they step down in favour of a black candidate.

"More and more people are concluding that the ballot box is no longer an instrument that will secure political solutions," says Tony Benn - an unlikely line coming from Britain's most institutionalised parliamentarian. But this is the case, and it's not just those 'shopping' in Oxford Street on Mayday who have ditched the ballot as a tool for change. Most policy is made and implemented by bureaucrats that aren't up for election anyway. Who can remember electing the lobbyists, the corporate bosses, the men from the OECD, OPEC, NATO, NAFTA, the WTO, IMF or any of the rest of the gangsters that steer policy regardless of what colour of curtains hang in the cabinet office. No matter how much of their benefactors' money the politicians throw at the advertisers to convince us to vote one way or the other - we still end up with a smirking, besuited, Stepford-style Whitehouse puppy dog in Downing Street, who'll sit up and beg for anyone with a gold card.

So it is no wonder that recent years have seen a rise in extra-curricular political activity. The months preceding the election saw London grid-locked by both anti-capitalists, seeking to distribute wealth and influence a little wider, and by the ultra-capitalist Countryside Alliance who fear their copious wealth and influence is still not enough.

Once in power, governments are released from any sort of popular control. Manifesto pledges become disposable: Labour promised reduced hospital waiting lists, then gave us waiting lists to go on the waiting lists, reduced class sizes - but then not for secondary schools, a referendum on PR, a hunting ban. The last Tory government said it wouldn't increase taxes and would restore family values, then raised taxes 22 times, while a string of ministers caught with their pants down were forced to cut and run. In 1979, Thatcher famously predicted 'a nation at ease with itself', before embarking on the most divisive government Britain has ever seen. (After sparking the 1981 riots, she went on to run British manufacturing into the ground, the miners out of the ground and the unions into the sea, before capping it off with the poll tax). No matter who you vote for, the government will maintain the stranglehold the rich property owning classes have on the poor, who, in turn, are offered what? New Deal?

No party is suggesting to shelve the defence budget, relinquish international debt repayments, resuscitate the welfare state, redistribute land and resources, or stop giving enormous tax breaks to multinational corporations. Certainly there is no ballot option for doing away with central government altogether and replacing it with a network of autonomous local direct-democracies.

Though elections may prevent any single group seizing power, centralised representative government and democracy - where people are involved in the decisions that affect them - are just not compatible. Most people, and several paid-up politicians, we questioned on the subject agreed that the present system is flawed if not completely fucked. But what, they (very reluctantly) ask, is the alternative?

One thing the politicians don't like but the anarchists have been doing for centuries is - no, no, not white overalls and armchair stuffing - abstaining from voting.

If it's humiliating to be ruled, they say, then how much

Who really elects the government?

In the 1997 General election, the electorate was 43.8 million, the turnout 31.2 million. Labour polled 13.5 million (43% of the vote – 30% of the total electorate - but won 67% of the seats). Despite everyone over 18 supposedly having an input in the outcome, the parties will focus their 2001 general electioneering on just a tiny fraction of voters.

Why?
It has been calculated that only 1 in 5 votes actually count. i.e. the rest are voting for outright losers, or piling 'wasted' votes onto massive majorities.

In a usual close fought election less than 10,000 votes hold the balance of power (out of 43.8 million). Even with Labour's massive lead, this figure is still less than 20,000 - however, these voters don't know who they are, and are not voting as a block.

Where?
Parties target the swinging voters in specific marginal seats - these are the ones who will win you the election. Effectively they are appealing to about 200,000 swinging voters in less than 100 seats whose majorities are under 3,000. These

seats are both rural and city electorates. Currently the vast majority of these seats are of course Labour.

Who?
An all time low turnout of 64/65 per cent is expected for the 2001 election. The 35/36 per cent of no shows will be mainly young and poor people and most of them will be in the cities.

"Unemployment is less than 1 million, and politicians are cynical enough not to bother with groups that won't turn out," says Professor Dunleavy. "Young people, the jobless and homeless won't get much of a look in. Those in safe Labour seats will be neglected too, as will those in the cities."

The target voters are the suburban/ countryside home owners of working age - probably families with children, in those marginal seats. Also, as the turnout falls, pensioners are being courted for the first time.

Over what?
Though the topics are big: families, education and the health service, the debate will be limited to service provision for the targeted middle class voters. Both

main parties will promise the same things (mild and gradual improvement), brought about in slightly different ways.

The Tories are preparing to pull the in-or-out-of Europe card - something that only really concerns people with money (though the issue can be played on a jingoistic level).

Labour will talk up the economy (but again, low inflation is of most interest to people with money. People in debt benefit from inflation). As Dunleavy says: "Labour's help to the poor has been very subtle. You can see it in the statistics, but you'd be hard pushed to see it in daily life." However, for the rich, there is also the spectre of US style economic downturn looming, so the Government may play the economy down.

Pensions and pensioners (in Gordon Brown's last budget, but absent from Labour's 97 manifesto) are featuring for the first time. Old people are more likely to vote.

"There is a danger in the UK," says Professor Dunleavy. "That we'll end up with a system like America, where only the middle classes vote and the poor don't participate at all."

more degrading is it to choose your masters? Abstentionists believe that voting gives elections, and the administrations they produce, a false legitimacy. Nineteenth century French abstentionists described parliamentary action as "a pell-mell of compromise, of corruption, of charlatanism and absurdities which does no constructive work". No change there then. The Italian anarchist Luigi Galleani said: "Abstentionism strips the state of the constitutional fraud with which it presents itself."

A significant minority of libertarian Britons have been skipping ballots and spoiling papers for years, and statisticians admit they are unsure how many of the eligible twelve million people who failed to vote in 1997's general election did so out of apathy or in protest. After all, people who don't want to vote are unlikely to hang round shopping precincts answering questions on voting behaviour.

Wombles spoilt for choice in the election   Pic: Guy Smallman

"Democracy does not exist in practice," says John Burnheim in the opening to his book 'Is Democracy Possible?' "At best," he says, "we have elective oligarchies with strong monarchical elements." Burnheim goes on to explain how elections do little but legitimise the political pantomime where personalities outshine the issues.

Despite achieving full attendance in every incarnation of the national curriculum (taught in schools whose hierarchies are the very antithesis of democracy), elections and democracy are not the same thing.

So what is the alternative?

The Liberal Democrats and a few loose-tongued Labourites are big fans of electoral reform. Proportional Representation (catch it now in a European sub-state of your choice) has several forms. But, be it preferential, transferable or shut-your-eyes-and-jab-em-with-a-pencil, it's still just a choice between pre-selected careerist politicians, resulting in un-recallable, runaway government.

To belay bosses fears of 'subversive' Trade Unions running riot in the workplace, Labour introduced quorums into their 1999 Employment Relations Act. This means, workers can only get recognition as an organised bargaining group if they win a ballot supported by a minimum fifty per cent of the workforce. Needless to say, there is no move to bring quorums into mainstream politics.

Australia, and until recently Holland, get around the turnout trap with compulsory voting. Though politicians from all three main UK parties recoil from this suggestion - preferring the non-attendance of inert voter apathy, to the antagonism of serious disenfranchisement.

The Swiss have taken the referendum route. Any citizen can force a referendum on any issue under government consideration if backed by a petition of 1 per cent of the electorate, or on any issue at all, if backed by 2 per cent. This has led to quarterly referendum days. Though it is the state that sets the question, and it is the state who provide the 'information' supporting, er...'both' sides of the argument.

"It is questionable whether people can know enough to make rational decisions on the very large range of issues that have to be faced," says John Burnheim. "This point has nothing to do with the ignorance of the mob. It applies equally well to professional politicians, social scientists or any other aristocracy. It is an argument against all centralisation of decision making power."

The UK Direct Democracy Campaign back a system of electronic voting for mass referendums either through interactive TV, the internet or cash-point style street machines. Though if people are disinterested enough not to vote, it is unlikely they'll participate in constant button pushing to vote on a host of issues that have no direct impact on their lives. Again Burnheim thinks this is not enough: "People would be reduced to accepting or rejecting proposals from their armchairs. There is no way in which any significant proportion could participate in framing them."

"Rearranging the deck chairs on the Titanic has always seemed a pointless task. I mean, how many different ways can you set up a few dozen chairs; in a circle, a pile, chop them up for life rafts. Whatever you do, sooner or later you're going to end up treading icy water in the dark" says John Jordan, a time-served activist in the British anti-roads movement, who holds little hope for electoral reform.

"The solution to such problems is usually seen as electoral politics with a new content: better candidates, new parties, fairer procedures, a better-educated electorate," says Brian Martin, who has been researching democratic alternatives. "The major complaint is seen not as the electoral system itself, but with the people who are elected and the policies they implement."

"The illusion that democracy can be assured by so-called democratic control of the state is disastrous," argues Burnheim. "The state cannot be controlled democratically. It must be abolished."

At the time of writing, John Jordan had just returned from Chiapas where he was studying the decision making processes used by the Zapatistas, a network of indigenous communities fighting, with some considerable success, for recognition in Southern Mexico. "Though they have an army, decision making is done by collective consensus during village assemblies." Consensus decisions are reached by negotiation, and the discussion only moves forward when nobody feels they need to block the consensus. It is this negotiation (apart from that conducted by the single-ideology politicians within very limited boundaries) that is missing from Western style electoral politics.

Jordan believes a model has been created in the Mexican jungle that we can all learn from. "Zapatismo has an ability to grasp change, to dissolve vertical structures of power and replace them with radical horizontality. It has the courage to demand nothing for us, but everything for everyone."

This 'roots-up' process of consensus decision making - very similar to the workings of a courtroom jury - has been emulated by activist groups for years. Well executed anti globalisation protests of tens of thousands of people, from Seattle to Melbourne to Prague have been organised with consensus reached decisions.

Large numbers of people are often accommodated by creating assemblies of delegates. Groups within the assembly or federation have autonomous control over their actions, though delegates from different groups come together to make 'decisions' that effect everyone. Unlike representatives, delegates are members of the source group (perhaps from a street or village), are beholden to them and can be recalled at any time. The danger, as various trade unions and progressive organisations have discovered, is that 'professional' delegates morph into representatives and it's rule by personality all over again.

Supporters of so-called 'strong government' argue that if decisions were left to consensus, nothing would ever get done. Tory MP Ian Bruce, told SchNews that he thinks that anything short of first-past-the-post, winner-takes-all elections would result in unthinkable outcomes on a par with having a committee installed as managing director of a company (his choice of analogy). Is it too presumptuous to say that had a workers committee been in place at West Lothian's Motorola (which closed in April 2001), Bathgate may not be heading for ghost town status today.

During a recent 'Democracy Day' held by Bristol City Council trying to 'engage' voters, every speaker banged on about 'making people vote' and how democracy started in Athens in the fifth century BC. Strangely they all forgot to mention a couple of key aspects - namely the Greeks' outright rejection of a centralised controlling state, and how they selected their decision making bodies at random.

Demarchy

Randomly selected courtroom juries are one of the few decision making bodies that large numbers of people still have faith in. (A faith not shared by those in government wishing to restrict access to them - judges, after all, are easier to keep on the political track). Considering the pressures put on them by the law, the lawyers and the judges, juries fair pretty well. In his book 'Is Democracy Possible?' John Burnheim proposes a comprehensive alternative to our system of elected representatives that he calls Demarchy.

Anarcho syndicalists have been promoting self organisation through popular workers and community councils for years. Realising the unlikelihood of imminent global revolution, Burnheim has tried to address the question of how to institute direct democracy in our present industrialised, corporatised and shot-between-the-eyes'd society. He suggests we get rid of politicians, bureaucracy and governments altogether, and instead replace them with decision-making groups of randomly selected citizens. "Democracy is possible only if the decision makers are a representative sample of the people concerned," he says.

Each group could address a particular need of the community - such as schooling or rail transport - within a defined locality (perhaps 10,000 perhaps 100,000 people). He calls this a decentralisation of functions. "Where decentralisation simply means centralisation on a smaller scale - bringing as many issues and powers as possible together under a single local authority - is of very dubious value," says Burnheim.

Group members could be chosen randomly from people who volunteered specifically for a group whose function concerns them. The random selection principle could easily be designed so that membership was representative in terms of sex, ethnicity, age, income and so on. There would be no deference to a higher authority, but negotiation with groups whose tasks effect their own.

Demarchy recognises that it is impossible for single bodies to make far-reaching decisions in any kind of informed way on a wide range of issues. So functional groups would have a strictly limited domain.

The legitimacy of random selection lies in regular replacement, rather than experience or popularity in the polls. Group members would serve a limited term in office, perhaps two years, then someone else would have a chance. Political wheeling and dealing would be reduced. Lobbyists would have a harder time applying pressure to decision-makers and there would be no career politics and no culture of playing for re-election. "The demarchist does not believe that there is any group of people whose capacities entitle them to a position of special or wide ranging power in the community," says Burnheim. The motivation would have to be; to be seen to be doing well. Everyone who nominated themselves, but was not selected, would be sure to scrutinise the group's performance, as would ex-members whose decisions were being overturned.

No central state would mean no central police force or army. Demarchic decisions would have to stand on their acceptability by the community. Unpopular decisions would lapse by unobservance. Unlike distant politicians, demarchic bodies would be more likely to address the underlying causes of crime, poverty and social exclusion, as the decision makers and their families are the people being directly affected. Also they aint playing 'quick-fix' for future votes. Maintaining the state's monopoly on 'legitimate' violence would be unnecessary. Burnheim argues such a decentralised state would be impossible to invade (ie no central bureaucracy to conquer would mean each individual body and community would have to be separately subdued - a tricky task, as the Romans discovered during multiple failed attempts to overcome the Welsh Celts and the Scots Picts). Its decentralised nature and internal community focus would also make a demarchic state virtually no threat to its neighbours.

The citizens' juries could call on all the expertise they wanted, and tests suggest people would be quick to grasp the issues. The Institute of Public Policy Research is one of a number of British bodies who have been conducting tests with citizens' juries for some years, using panels of 12-16 randomly selected people to address issues ranging from community safety, health service provision and decency on television. "Members of the public were willing to take part in decision-making and were capable of grasping complex issues," their report concluded. "The juries were a powerful tool for consensus building... helping participants take a wider and more objective perspective."

Similar studies have been conducted in the US, and by the University of Wuppertal, in Germany, for over twenty years, where a 500 strong randomly selected 'planning cell' was used to formulate telecommunications legislation in 1991.

New Labour are not unaware of the ability of citizens' juries, and have been cynically using their ability to address the genuine concerns of communities for "consultation" and "to gain insight" into what people want. (ie find out what people want, then legislate as you originally planned but spin your agenda so it looks like you're following public opinion). A far cry from people making their own decisions.

Burnheim is up front that his theories need to be expanded, questioned and tested. He encourages anyone interested in direct democracy to take his demarchic model, tear it apart and reconstruct it. He sees his proposal as a potential debate opener, not as a stone-set blueprint for a future utopia. Demarchy need not appear overnight and could be introduced in a piecemeal way to begin to tackle all the problems needing to be sorted from radical land redistribution, systems of tax and the rest. Is there any good reason why randomly selected citizens groups should not replace government appointed quangos, addressing such issues as pharmaceutical licensing, planning or police complaints? Surely such a jury would fair better than the bodies presently packed with financially concerned parties and industry bosses.

Electoral representative government is not working. We are coerced into acceptance of our poor democracy through threats of the 'autocratic alternative'. If you don't want Blair you gotta have Xiang Zemin. Yet this is not the case. Of course those in power, those who hold the wealth and the corporate muscle are in no hurry to look for an alternative. Big-business-as-usual is fine by them. Those peddling reform do more harm than good by dissipating any energy that could be spent addressing genuine democratic alternatives.

If we sit on our hands until those in power choose to give even a little bit of it back, we will have a long bloody wait. Maybe we should emulate India's Karnataka State Farmers who have discarded government control in favour of self-organisation. They tie politicians to trees who dare to enter their communities.

If we are to progress surely we must be ready to change, and if we want genuine democracy we must be willing to stand up and take the word back out of the mouths of the Blairs, Bushes and Sharons who have bastardised its very meaning. If we want freedom and want liberty we must be willing to try something better.

"Let us look in silence, let us learn to listen," wrote Subcomandante Marcos about how would-be-leaders must defer to the spirit and wishes of the people. "Perhaps later we'll finally be able to speak."

WOT a Load of Rubbish!

A WILDCAT STRIKE IN SUNNY BRIGHTON – THIS WAS A FUCKING EXCITING THING TO HAPPEN HERE (THOUGH THERE WEREN'T ANY PETROL BOMBS INVOLVED, SORRY). I'M STILL ABUZZ SO LET ME RECOUNT WHAT HAPPENED..

MONDAY, JUNE 11TH

HI!

The Anus
Refuse workers stage sit-in after dispute
SACKED

GUESS WHAT? THE BINMEN HAVE OCCUPIED THEIR DEPOT & WE'VE JUST BEEN DOWN & IT WAS EXCELLENT...

WE SAW THIS, AND THE DEPOT'S JUST UP THE ROAD SO WE WENT TO HAVE A LOOK. BASICALLY, THE MANAGEMENT-SITA-PRESENTED TOTALLY IMPOSSIBLE NEW ROUNDS FOR THE SWEEPERS THIS MORNING. SO THE SWEEPERS COMPLAINED, GOT SACKED, THEN ALL THE OTHER WORKERS PROTESTED & ENDED UP MORE OR LESS DISMISSED – ALL 240 OF THEM! SO THEY WENT AND CHUCKED OUT THE MANAGEMENT AND OCCUPIED THEIR DEPOT! OH WE MADE AN EXECUTIVE TEAPOT* DECISION TO SPEND TEAPOT MONEY ON BUYING THEM FOOD & SUPPLIES.

*ANARCHIST TEAPOT MOBILE KITCHEN – OUR CATERING COLLECTIVE

TUESDAY, JUNE 12TH: WE WENT DOWN TO THE UNEMPLOYED WORKERS CENTRE FIRST

WE'RE OFF TO PRINT UP THIS LEAFLET THE BINMEN WROTE

OKAY – SHALL WE GO GET FOOD?

TROJAN

-YAY

HEY, IT'S THE ANARCHISTS!

OH, IS THAT CHEER MEANT FOR US?

OCCUPIED

FOOD'S REALLY APPRECIATED, TA

THERE ANY DONUTS AGAIN?

HM. I SEEM TO BE THE ONLY YOUNG GIRL HERE

BUT I DIDN'T GET ONE SINGLE SEXIST REMARK.   THOUGH...

HM. WHERE'S THE LADIES'?

GENTS

TALK ABOUT A MALE ENVIRONMENT! (I DID FIND ONE EVENTUALLY - WAY OUT IN THE OFFICE!)

THE BINMEN WE MET WERE FRIENDLY, AND SO UP FOR FIGHTING TO IMPROVE THEIR WORKING CONDITIONS.

WE'LL FUCK SITA UP BIG TIME!

YEP.

S.I.T.A "FREE" WORKER

US OLDER ONES SAW A STRIKE THROUGH IN 1976.

THURSDAY, JUNE 14TH, AFTER A RINGROUND:

THERE'S A RUMOUR SITA GOT 10 EXTRA TRUCKS SO WE'RE GOING TO TRY AND FIND & STOP THEM.

SOMEONE SAW THEM UP AT ST PETERS CHURCH!

SO WE RAN AFTER LORRIES.

HUH. WE'RE TOO LATE.

UNSUCCESSFULLY.

WAIT! WORD IS SITA DIDN'T GET THE EXTRA TRUCKS, AND THE WORKERS AT THE DISPOSAL ARE ON GO-SLOW ANYWAY.

THERE'S A RALLY IN TOWN IN 20 MINUTES WE'VE BEEN ASKED TO COME TO.

SO WE WENT THERE, AND CAME ACROSS THE FIRST VISIBLE LEFTY PARASITES!

DO YOU WANT TO BUY A COPY? IT'LL EXPLAIN WHAT'S BEEN HAPPENING WITH THE STRIKE!

Socialist Wanker — DEFEND THE SOMETHING - WHATEVER'S A TRENDY ISSUE

YOU MUST BE FUCKEN JOKING! I'VE BEEN DOWN THE DEPOT EVERY-DAY, FROM THE START, UNLIKE YOU & YOUR BLOODY TROT PAPER!

THEN WE WENT AND GOT SOME MORE FOOD TO TAKE TO THE DEPOT

(WE COULD REALLY HAVE DONE WITH A CAR OR SOMETHING)

AND SOME PEOPLE WENT & VISITED AN AGENCY IN WORTHING - THE ONLY ONE STILL PROVIDING SCAB LABOUR.

OKAY, OKAY! WE'LL PULL OUT. WILL YOU LEAVE US ALONE THEN?

9 PM AT THE DEPOT:

OKAY - I'VE JUST HEARD THE OUTCOME OF THE SITA + COUNCIL TALKS...

YEAH, WE'LL KEEP IN TOUCH, WHAT-EVER THE RESULT.

YOU'VE GOT OUR PHONE NUMBERS, RIGHT?

WELL - **THEY WON!** **ALL** WORKERS GOT RE-INSTATED - EVEN GETTING PAID FOR THE WEEK ON STRIKE - THE NEW IMPOSSIBLE ROUTES WERE WITH-DRAWN, AND SITA'S **LOSING** ITS CONTRACT IN SEPTEMBER! THE SHOP STEWARDS ARE LOOKING INTO BIDDING FOR THE CONTRACT AS A WORKERS CO-OPERATIVE, TOO. AFTERWARDS, **EVERYONE** SHOOK **EVERYONE'S** HAND, AND LEFT THE OCCUPATION.

OOH - IT'S OVER! WHAT DO WE DO NOW?

>SNIFF< (MOVED)

WELL, WE **ARE** OFF TO BARCELONA ON MON-DAY, AREN'T WE?

Manchester 7th June - Election Day

A festive air prevailed in Manchester on election day, though police fought valiantly to contain outbreaks of grassroots politics. The theme of the day was not so much "don't-vote," as "it's irresponsible to just vote when faced with a problems that can't be dealt with by a corporate-driven parliament." People are already fighting this powerlessness in a world of different ways.

Starting the day was 'There's No Such Thing as a Free Lunch' - as free food was given away. The message was self-reliance, as plants were distributed to say - get away from supermarket food and grown your own. Diners were entertained by music & street theatre - which gave the police a scare when a white-clad group entered the square ("back up! back up!...cancel that sarge, it's street theatre").

To work off some of the food, merry pranksters headed off to banks, supermarkets, bookshops, train stations, coffee shops and fast food merchants, with further uncontrolled outbreaks of popular control over consumer society. In banks that fund dictators and arms deals blood was spilled in the cashiers' trays, stopping any transactions. Cash machines got 'out of order' stickers slapped on them. In a supermarket GM food was left to defrost in trolleys sprouting banners and leaflets. Burma leaflets got inserted into holiday guides, and train ticket counters got besieged by people with 90% for 90% cards claiming their discount. Nestle cafes were leafletted, Starbucks had free vegan drinks and cakes on offer outside, and a rival free veggie burger stall called NotDonalds did a roaring trade outside you-know-where.

Now obviously these threats to the very fabric of democracy had gone too far, and with a Critical Mass bike ride threatening to end car culture as we know it, the police had had enough; it was time to protect the democratic system - pen people in and crack their heads.

After the cops went back on the route they'd promised cyclists, they decided it was a much better ruse to pull people off their bikes, threaten, arrest and then de-arrest after taking people's details, and contain any remaining cyclists for two tense hours.

Moving off at a funereal pace was - the State Funeral. Yes, the State is dead, democracy is dead (but we're alive). Less than half of the voting public turned out to vote on June 7th - maybe they were doing something more useful instead. To the beat of a drum and a New Orleans-style jazz band, the pall-bearers followed the four horses of the Eco-pocalypse and a twelve foot grim reaper, behind a "Call this Apathy?" banner, to the headquarters of the media machine conspiracy...well, the BBC building on Oxford Road. Here, the last will and testament of the state was read out, after which a mighteous samba wake was held, before revellers went to dine in a nearby park. Two arrests (one man for fake blood in bottles found after a Section 60 search, and one woman for indecent exposure), and not a line of press coverage (despite the journos having been fed with an exceedingly large spoon..). It was a good day.

> We are the uninvited, the excluded.
> The political circus doesn't mean anything to us.
> We are the ones who want a policy of full enjoyment, not full employment.
> We are those who care about the trees, the air, the animals, which will all suffer whoever gets elected.
> We are the ones who will get poorer whichever hand is controlling the state's purse.
> We are the ones who are creating a new world.

One of the 160 sacked Brighton refuse workers - now occupying the depot - sees his mates on the front page of the local rag. Main pic: Anthong Howell.

WAKE UP! WAKE UP! IT'S YER TALKIN' RUBBISH!

weekly SchNEWS

Printed and Published in Brighton by Justice?

Friday 15th June 2001   www.schnews.org.uk   Issue 308/309

SITA'S A PARROT

"This unelected, unaccountable multi-national is holding the City to ransom."
Gary Smith, GMB Official

Within a week of Labour winning the election with the promise of privatising our public services, refuse collectors in their flagship city of Brighton are getting a taste of what Blair and co have in store – sackings, attacks on working conditions and profiteering as services get poorer. Or to put it another way...

After one of the largest votes of no confidence in politicians since 1918, Blair, his town-hall-cronies-by-the-sea and their mates in multinational companies are getting a taste of what they can expect when they take on public workers and our basic services – strike action, occupation and direct action in resistance to corporations' slow destruction of our public services.

Brighton's refuse workers went to work this Monday to find that SITA – the French multinational with the contract to clear Brighton's rubbish – had imposed increased workloads, that the workers knew would be impossible to deliver. One typical run would involve one driver and two others sweeping a major part of the sea front, an entire estate and a bit more for luck. As one refuse worker told SchNEWS, *"What would you do if you went into work and were told you had to clean 18 miles of streets a day?"*

What 11 workers did was refuse to do these impossible rounds – and they were promptly suspended. When the rest of the 160-strong GMB workforce protested against this, SITA's management sacked the lot. It was the last straw - the workforce occupied the depot. They demanded that SITA, who have cost local people an extra £1.8m a year since they took over Brighton's street cleaning, get the sack and that they get back to the job of cleaning streets - instead of increasing some company's stock market value.

SITA brought in bin lorries to a nearby industrial park where they tried to get employment agency workers to scab against the strike. It didn't work. In an unusual political alliance, local Green Party councillors emerged as the only politicians in touch with the widespread local disgust at SITA's profiteering, while supporters of the Free Party – fresh from cheerful annihilation at the polls – persuaded employment agency workers that if they scabbed they wouldn't be welcome anymore at Brighton free parties. Party politics, Jim, but not as we know it. One local activist called "Jamie" got up at 5am to lock onto one of the trucks for five hours, preventing the rest from moving. As one striker put it, "This fellow is crazy but what he has done is much appreciated".

Faced with a determined strikeforce occupying its depot with enormous local support, SITA's bullying started to crack. Employment agencies started refusing to have anything to do with them. SITA workers in neighbouring areas suddenly developed strange, short-term illnesses when asked to scab. The local council held hours of secret meetings with SITA but couldn't come up with a way to beat the strike.

By Thursday evening, SITA and the council had caved in. All the workers were reinstated, getting full pay for the time they were on strike. SITA were given 11 weeks notice that their contract was being terminated – and they could forget their new work practices in the meantime.

GMB official Gary Smith told SchNEWS, "SITA deliberately provoked this dispute by trying to lock members out. Unfortunately for them, the workers decided to lock themselves in. We had enormous public support from the local unemployed centre, direct action people and loads of different communities who are fed up with their services being run for profit. We should take inspiration from this fight, because it shows that when people get together we can stop privatisation in its tracks."

SITA on it

We all know that recycling is the only good thing to do with our waste, but currently in this country we only manage a meagre 8 % while other European countries recycle over half. In Canberra, Australia, they're aiming for zero waste production by 2005. Recycling makes not only environmental but also economic sense. It would reduce our greenhouse gas emissions, save energy and creates jobs- in Germany more people are employed in recycling than in steel and telecommunications. But building up a recycling scheme takes time and for short term, quick buck companies like SITA it is a simple inconvenience- cos' time is money.

Luckily not all organisations have the same approach as SITA. There are over 200 community recycling groups in this country who are constantly challenging attitudes to waste. Of the seven Beacon awards for innovation in waste management, 5 were awarded to councils who involved community recyclers. The town with the highest recycling levels in the country – Bath, has (you guessed it) community recyclers involved. Here in Brighton, the Magpie recycling co-operative has been operating for 10 years. From providing Brighton's first recycling bin in the Hanover Centre, they now provide domestic recycling for 5000 homes (using converted milk floats) and 400 businesses and pubs. They also run a furniture recycling scheme.

Bottled it

Despite the excellent record of the co-ops and community groups, they rarely get awarded the big municipal waste contracts. One of the main reasons is the way contracts are awarded – only companies with a large turnover are deemed "responsible" enough to handle a large contract. In Brighton this has meant that SITA won the contract to be in control of everything to do with waste- clean the streets, collect waste, and recycle it. From their short term view recycling doesn't make financial sense. They're bidding to run Sussex's proposed incinerators, and they'll have needed to set aside some rubbish to burn. Companies have sussed that there's no way they can loose with incinerator's cos they can sue the council if they don't get enough waste to burn. This will severely hold back recycling for the lifespan of the incinerator.

SITA on my face

SITA's failure to provide a good service is an important kick in the teeth to the privatisation of public services. The GMB, the union representing the sacked binmen are keen to explore the possibility in setting up a workers co-op to take over Brighton's waste contract. This will be owned by the workers and run for the benefit of the people of Brighton. If this did happen they would be the first co-op running an entire municipal refuse service in this country. As one Magpie worker told SchNEWS "The possibility of a workers' co-op running the contract instead of one big waste company opens up some very exciting opportunities to create a social enterprise with some very different approaches to our waste strategy."

This whole scenario is nothing new. In France when it became evident that multinationals were more interested in recycling taxpayer's money than people's waste, local referendums were held and they were kicked out in favour of the original community companies.

* Magpie 01273 688022

* Community Recycling Network www.crn.org.uk

PARTY & PROTEST - JUNE & JULY

JUNE

18 Actions at Ministry of Defence national purchasing centre in Bristol. North of Bristol, at Filton Abbey Wood. Action called by campaigners against depleted uranium, inviting everyone to picket, climb, lock on, … as long as it's non-violent, imagination is the limit. Poss. accommodation in Bristol info: www.access.lowtech.org/collectableanorak ** **18 Sheffield Environmental Action present a public meeting on the Zapatistas.** With Mexican and British activists. Arthur Anderson Room, Students Union, Red Deer pub, Pitt St. 8pm. www.sheffiel dmayday.ukf.net ** **18 Elephants - Do they have a future? Coexistence not Conservation.** Talk by Bill Jordan, Vice Chair of the RSPCA and founder of Care for the Wild. APE, The Bathouse, Gwydir St. Cambridge, 8pm.** **18 Phone Blockade of Dow Chemicals** - part of the campaign to close down **Huntingdon Life Sciences** (01462 457 272/01235 772 900/01642 374 000/01553 692 100/0208 917 5000) Let them know what you think of this supplier of animals to the vivisection trade. www.shac.net ** **18 Campaign Against Criminalising Communities meeting/** Campaigning for the repeal of the Terrorism Act and for the recognition of the 21 banned groups (SchNEWS 305) 6.45pm, Conway Hall, Red Lion Square, London WC1. 020-72501315 ** **19 Support Political prisoners in Burma.** Room Z229, London School of Economics, Houghton Street, London WC2. 6.30pm Bo Kyi, is an ex-Burmese political prisoner who has set up Assistance Association for Political Prisoners 07931 753138. www.freeburmacoalition.org ** **19 Resistance at work meeting.** Safety above all - stop so called accidents at work. Speakers include UCATT and Building Worker Group. 7.30pm, Wood Green Labour Club, Stuart Cres. N22. Haringey Solidarity Group http://hsg.cupboard.org ** **19 McLibel: Anniversary of 1997 High Court Victory** McLibel Support Campaign. 5 Caledonian Rd, London N1. 020 77131269. Adopt-A-Store Network: 0115 958 5666 ** **19 Act Together** (a coalition of women opposed to Iraqi sanctions), is targeting women in 'decision making' positions and displaying books that were returned by customs. maysoon@oxymo ronfilms.demon.co.uk ** **19 Speak Out Against Racism - Defend Asylum Seekers** and commemorate the anniversary of the deaths of the 58 Chinese people Vigil: 5.30 - 6.30pm Public Meeting: 7-8pm, Upper Hall, Emmanuel Centre, 9-23 Marsham Street, London SW1. 020 72479907 / 07879 612234. ** **20 Online-demonstration against the deportation business.** More than 40,000 people a year are being deported from Germany, most of these by plane, they are often fettered, gagged and drugged. Amir Ageeb from Sudan died from mistreatment by German border police while being deported on a Lufthansa plane in 1999. This is a call to block website of Lufthansa Airlines, in which flights can be booked; enough hits and this webpage can be blocked: online-demo@gmx.net ** **20 Vivisection in the 21st Century** @ University of London Union, Malet St., London WC1. Tickets in advance from the Vivisection Information Network, PO Box 223, Camberley, Surrey, GU16 5ZU 07950 570324 ** **21 "The proposed Hastings bypass and its link to International Capitalism"** The Carlisle Pub, 24 Pelham Street/Carlisle Parade, Hastings, 8pm ** **21 In protest of George W. Bush's energy policies** and lack of emphasis on efficiency, conservation and alternative fuels, there will be a voluntary rolling blackout on the first day of Summer across the planet 7 pm - 10 pm in every time zone. But will it be dark in the UK by 10pm? ** **21 THE WOMBLES present "for your Solstice Special Treat something strange and beautiful"** with The Big Striptease, and more

For all yer latest parties and protests check out the SchNEWS website - updated every week.

- The Swan, Tottenham. 7-11.30pm £3/£2 unwaged. 0789 0360640 www.wombleaction.mrnice.net ** **20-24 Healing Field Gathering.** 0177 955 6690 www.healingfield.btinternet.co.uk ** **21 Summer Solstice** 8.33am, access to Stonehenge for sunrise. 07748 954954 ** **21 Cardiff Drop the Debt** - Meal and info evening. Jubilee Wales 01286 882359 ** **22-8 July. Sussed'n'Able** Permaculture Design Course. email resi@tesco.net or call 01248-490578. ** **23 Alternative Glastonbury.** 24 hour extravaganza with Firestarter Stage TBC. 020 85093353 www.continentaldrifts.uk.com ** **23 Public Service Announcement** Benefit night punk/reggae/ska/djs 7.30pm-1am, Chat's Palace (Arts and Community Centre), 42-44 Brooksby's Walk, Homerton, Hackney E9. Benefit for RTS, PGA, IndyMedia and No Borders. 020 8533 0227 publica@tarakan.demon.co.uk ** **23 Covence Campaign National Summer Demo** in Harrogate. "Pills That Kill" will focus on human casualties of animal tested drugs. Tel: 07960 900401 ** **23 National demo against Huntingdon Life Sciences** Meet Parker's Piece, Cambridge, 12 noon. Contact SHAC 0845 4580630 www.shac.net ** **23 Justice for Jimmy Ingram** – 9 years in gaol for a crime he didn't commit. 1-2pm outside HMP Maidstone, County Rd. Contact PO Box 781, Canterbury, Kent, CT2 7FB ** **23 March Against Racism and Brutality** by Haringey and Hackney police. 12 noon, Tottenham police station, march to Wood Green Library. marchagainstracism@yahoo.co.uk ** **23 – July 9 International conference on 'Nonviolence in the context of war and armed conflict'** at Wustrow, Germany. Info: kurve-wustrow@oln .comlink.apc.org ** **22-24 June 12th National Hazards Conference** at UMIST Sackville Street, Manchester. 0161 953 407. ** **24 European Sun Day** www.sundayeurope.com ** **25-27 Meeting of the World Bank, Barcelona.** CANCELLED (SchNEWS 306) - but actions will still be continuing www.j15.org ** **25 Day Of Action Against Novartis** june25@shacusa.net ** **25 -1 July National Vegetarian Week** 0161 9252000 ** **25-26 Starbucks Days of Action** pressure them to stop using GM and start using fair trade. Everywhere. Contact: www.organicconsumers.org/starbucks ** **26 Leicester Radical Alliance meeting.** The Secular Hall, Humberstone Gate, Leicester 7.30pm http://radical.members.beeb.net ** **26 Mass trespass to protect the peat bogs of Hatfield moor.** www.cornerstone.ukf.net/crc/ ** **27 LX Cool Festival,** Lisbon, Portugal. ** **27 Rock around the blockade will be taking its Boycott Bacardi Campaign** to cities all across Britain - Glasgow Campaign Launch 7.30 pm, Glasgow Caledonian University Hamish Wood Building, Rm.W323. 07899 810735 pmallonfrf@yahoo.co.uk ** **29-1 July Anti-Sanctions Conference** Gathering in

solidarity with the people of Iraq, Fri eve till 3pm Sun, Kingsley Hall, Powis Road, London E2. www .viwuk.freeserve.co.uk or www.casi.org.uk ** **29-1 July Winchester Hat Fair.** For all you summer fete massive Tel: 01962 849841 www.hatfair.co.uk ** **30 Statewatching the new Europe:** Uni of London SU, Malet St., London. Statewatch 020 88021882 www.statewatch.org ** **30 Mardi Gras**, Finsbury Park, London. 1-10pm £15. Sponsored by Eurostar, Virgin and Ford! www.londonmardigras.com ** **30 Forget Mardi Gras, La Di-Dah!** Pisstake of the comercialisation of the Mardi

Gras festival. 3pm till dusk in Finsbury Park. Contact anarquist @chickmailchickmail www.queeruption.com ** **30 Skateboard festival at Clissold Park, London** 0208 3566415 www.stokenewingtonfestival.co.uk ** **30 National Day of Action against the Fur Trade in London** Meet 11am Trafalgar Square. 0845 4584775 ** **30 Palestine: the New Apartheid - Building the Solidarity Movement,** 11am-4.30pm at University of London Union, Mallet St, London.

JULY

1 "Wherever You Are" Action by The Freedom To Be Yourself naked crew, 2pm. www.geocities.com/ thehumanmind ** **1 Falmouth Big Green Fair** 01326 375158 ** **1 Metropolis Festival** - Rotterdam ** **1-3 Protests against the World Economic Forum (WEF) and the Right-Wing-Populist Austrian Government, Salzburg, Austria. www.antiwef.org** ** **2 Red Rambles Cromford Canal to Scarthin Promenade** 0177827513 http: //members.tripod.co.uk/ainema/index-2.html ** **4 Menwith Hill - Independence from America day –at Menwith Hill Spy Base.** (SchNEWS 307) Campaign for the Accountability of American Bases, 01943 466405 www.caab.org.uk ** **6 Dour Festival,** Belgium - sounds fun! ** **6-8 Larmer Tree Festival,** Victorian Gardens, Cranborne Chase. off A354 near Blandford. 40 artists, free campsite 01722 45223 www.larmertree.demo n.co.uk ** **6-8 Organic Food and Wine Festival** West Hall, Alexandra Palace, London. 020 8746 2832 www.organicfoodwinefestival.co.uk ** **6-8 Willow Festival** Six stages and 120 bands - FREE. May be some camping www.willowfestival.co.uk ** **6-9 'Camping is Fun' at Aldermaston atomic weapons establishment.** Contact: 0708 553 778 or email aldermastonwpc@hotmail.com ** **7 March to have British Sign Language recognised as an official language** (SchNEWS 301). 12 noon, Uni of London Union, Malet St, London (Euston Sq tube) www.fdp.org.uk ** **7 WOMBLES Wimbledon Picnic** Bring the whole padded family, food, drink, musical instruments... Meet @ Wimbledon Tube @ 2pm. Call 07960 973 847 www.wombl eaction.mrnice.net ** **7 Peace Messenger Fair** Noon-7pm Hove Lawns, Brighton seafront. 01273 676957 email danny@dharmony.freeserve.co.u k ** **7 Pole Pole Festival,** Ghent, Belgium ** **7 Northern Anarchist Network summer conference,** Hebden Bridge 10.30am -5.30pm. Contact 0161 707 9652 www.perso.libertysurf.co.uk/ northernanarchistnet/index ** **7-8 T in the Park** Tel: 0115 912 9190 www.tinthepark.com ** **8 Ambient Green Picnic, Shalford Park, Guildford.** www.ambientpicnic.co.uk ** **8 Lewisham Peoples Day** www.lewisham.gov.uk ** **9 Mad Pride Day of Action - Bollocks to Compulsory Treatment Orders.** 8am Picket the AGM of Royal College of Psychiatrists and more. Contact 07758-907357 or PO Box, 4144, Worthing BN14 7NZ www.madpride.net ** **9-11 Exploring Cyber Society II - Dissent and Deviance in**

the Information Age. University of Northumbria, Newcastle. www.unn.ac.uk/corporate/cybersociety ** 10 Book launch "Trident on Trial" 7.30pm, Conway Hall, London, with Tony Benn and Roy Bailey www.trident ploughshares.org ** 11 International Day of Action against ExxonMobil (ESSO) - picket their petrol stations, refineries or offices. This lot are President Bush's biggest supporters encouraging him to increase global warming. www.globalwarming.isbad.net ** 12-13 Renewable Energy Fair, Stroud Town Centre, Gloucestershire. Contact Energy 21 on 01453 752277 www.energy21.org.uk ** 13-22 Anti-racist, Anti-sexist Summer Camp Bremen, Germany www.summercamp.squat.net and www.ainfos.ca ** 13-14 Berlin Love Parade ** 13-15 Essential Music Festival. Hackney Marshes, London. Dance Saturday, Roots Sunday. £35 a day. www.essentialfestival.com ** 13-15 Roots, Hoots & Boots Festival at Bradninch, Devon. Tel: 01392 881304DB / 01392 881916JC. Email: dik-banovich@bigfoot.com ** 14 Global Boycott of Procter & Gamble Day. www.uncaged.co.uk/ 0114-253-0020 ** 14-15 Bristol Community Festival, Hengrove Park. Finest free event in the West Country. Tel: 0117 904 2275 www.digitalbristol.org/membrs/bcf/index.htm ** 14-22 Foot and Mouth. A festival of Resistance and Revolution. As in Foot it round Edinburgh on the 14th and Mouth off letting people know about the festival on 21/22. Free. www.mouthoff.org.uk ** 14 Vauxhall Music Festival, Spring Gardens, London. 020 7793 026 email vstphc@aol.com ** 14 London Permaculture Gathering, Islington. Starting 11am with a guided tour of the city's forest gardens. 020 7281 3765 ** 14-15 Tolpuddle Martyrs Festival, nr Dorchester, Dorset. Tel: 0117 947 0521. Email: southwest@tuc.org.uk

14-21 Climate Change Talks, Bonn, Germany. From the 16th delegates from all over the world will converge in Bonn to carry on the farce of the Kyoto 'climate talks'- the most corporate-friendly environmental treaty in history (SchNEWS 285). Some of the events planned: 16 Critical mass bike demonstration, 17-18 workshops and planning, 19 Global day of direct action - if you can't make it to Bonn do something in your area, 21 Friends of the Earth mass action: building of huge lifeboat-Noah's ark 27 Final action. For info about travel to Bonn and accommodation contact Rising tide coalition - 01132629365 www.risingtide.org.uk Friends of the Earth 020 7490 0881 www.foe.co.uk

15 Russian Protest Camp Lockheed Martin, is planning to build a factory to process old heavy rocket fuel in Votkinsk with a population of 100,000, because they were refused a plot in the Nevada desert! Autonomous Action of Moscow, dikobrazi@lists.tao.ca ** 15 Summer Garden Fayre at the HDRA organic gardens, Coventry. Guided tours, kids entertainment, organic advice desk. £3/kids free 024 7630 3517 www.hdra.org.uk ** 16 Torquay Festival ** 16 - August 4 Faslane to Flyingdales CND fund-raising walk with public meetings along the route Tel 020 7700 4524 ** 18 The New Rulers of the World - a special ITV report by John Pilger. ** 18-22 Protest camp against Campsfield Detention Centre and the G8. Contact g8campsfield@hotmail.com or call 07900 653990. www.closecampsfield.org.uk ** 19 "Bollocks to Compulsory Treatment Orders"- Mad Pride Benefit at Freebutt, Richmond Tce, Brighton. Feat. Fish Brothers & more. 8-30pm £3.50/3 Contact 01903-210351 ** 20-22 Sheep Music, Presteigne, Wales. Local music event ** 20-22 Big Chill Festival Larmer Tree Gdns, Wilts (nr Bournemouth & Salisbury), contact 0207 688 8080, www.bigchill.net ** 20-22 Trowbridge Village

Pump Festival, Wilts. Tel: 01225 769132. Email: alan.briars@virgin.net ** 21 'Respect' festival, Finsbury Park, London 12 noon onwards. FREE. Run DMC, Courtney Pine, FM dance stage and lots more. To promote anti racism and celebrate cultural diversity. www.respectfestival.org.uk ** 21 Leicester Lesbian, Gay, Bisexual and Transgender Pride.

IT'S A GOOD JOB WE'VE BEEN ISSUED WITH THESE FOR THE DAY.

From Wellington St to Victoria Park. Dress: if you want. ** 21 Love Parade, Newcastle ** 21-23 Lakeside Festival All night, Rother County Park.

21 - 23 G8 Summit, Genoa. The G8 is a group of the most powerful countries in the world. Their leaders are meeting (again) to discuss economic policies which will create huge gaps between rich and poor countries, threaten the global environment and generally promote nasty things. Of course, no summit would be complete without mass demonstrations. Wild rumours are spreading - all Italian borders will be closed, one part of the city will be cut off from the other, train stations, airports and the main motorways will be shut down, commandos will be 'assisting' police on the streets, marines will be patrolling the water where the delegates will meet aboard luxury cruisers anchored in Genoa bay, and George Bush decoys will be on hand to distract would-be assassins and those pesky anarchists. Yeah sure, more info www.genoa-g8.org brightoncollective@hushmail.com for transport from Brighton.

21-22 Festival of Resistance and Revolution, Studio 24, 24 Carlton Rd, Edinburgh 11am-5pm. To co-incide with the G8 Summit in Genoa. Talks, workshops, films, football etc. www.mouthoff.org.uk ** 21-22 Dartford Free Festival. Feat. Headmix Collective + DJ's & lots more. Tel: 020 8509 3353 www.continentaldrift.uk.com ** 21-22 Bradford Mela Largest Asian event outside of India. Cutting edge of Asian Underground, dance and Alternative. ** 25-29 ACE - African Celtic Experience Festival, Blaennant, Carmathenshire. African drumming; dance the night away in Club Ska; mellow family atmosphere geared towards children. 5 day ticket is £78 (waged), £58 (unwaged) £7 (children) 01994 484708 ** 26 Bladelse festival, Bladel, The Netherlands ** 26-29 Cambridge folk festival Featuring Suzanne Vega, The Levellers, Richard Thomson Band, Bill Wyman's Rhythm Kings and others. £56 (concs available) + camping. 01223 457245 www.cam-folkfest.co.uk ** 27-29 WOMAD Festival, Rivermead, Reading, Berks Tel: 01225 744494 www.womad.org ** 27-August 5 Anti-imperialist Camp 2001, Italy www.antiimperialista.org ** 27- 11 August Trident Ploughshares 4th Annual Summer Disarmament Camp Peaton Wood, Coulport. Info/briefing pack: 01324 880744 or 07775 711054 www.tridentploughshares.org ** 27-29 Renewable Energy Summer School, Wales. The Old College, Uni of Wales, Aberystwyth. Fee: £35 (Concession: £25) Green Dragon Energy: 01974-821564 or dragonrg@talk21.com

** 28 The 16th Sex Maniacs' Fairy Tale Ball, London, UK. www.sex-maniacs-ball.com ** 28 Campaign against Climate Change, March against Bush. www.Stopesso.com ** 28-1 August Tribe of Doris, The Leela Centre, nr Gillingham in Dorset. Global dance/sing/play heaven. £140 /£12.50 kids 0117 907 3118 www.tribeofdoris.com ** 28-5 August Lammas Full Moon Celebration Camp, Herefordshire 07787 190162 ** 29 Festival for the Homeless, Milton Keynes Bowl. £85.00 For the Big Issue Foundation and Drum Housing Project. ** 30-5 August One World Summer Festival, Gaunts House, Dorset. 300+ workshops. 01273 249770 www.macrobios.com 1-5 August Earth First Summer Gathering, for everone involved or interested in ecological direst action. This year's gathering is on a beautiful site in the foothills of the Peak District. Share skills, learn what's been happening, fun activities - rock climbing, nature walks, games. Plus entertainment (sorry, no sound systems!). Cost £10 donation to cover costs. Accommodation is camping only, No dogs, no cameras. Details 0845-4589595.www.eco-action.org/gathering

Party Briefs

*For a complete list of festivals get Festival Eye, now available for £3 (cheques to Festival Eye) + A4 addressed envelope from Distribution @ Festival Eye, BCM 2002, London, WC1N 3XX.

* Brighton sound system Ground Zero were in court this week to face the music after the Woodingdean party on the Downs a couple of weeks back when two cop cars were turned over (SchNEWS 305) In the end they got their system back but were fined £500 with £75 costs - so watch out for benefit gigs and remember to dig deep. Meanwhile Sussex police are reportedly £70,000 out of pocket, for the cost of trial and wrecked cars, while all free parties around the City are paying by having parties stopped.

* Brighton Soundsytems unite and un-plug for the Solstice gathering Burning Of The Rigs on the beach/Madiera Drive, Brighton. 21 June 8pm, with acoustic sounds from Marmoset, members of Headmix plus fire performers, drums and more. All performers welcome. After party in Concorde 2 - free party DJ'S Take Control - 11pm-3am.

*DSG have released the POTWOW EP from the Studio 284 stable. So if you know any POTWOWs (prisoners of the war on weed), you'll be happy to know that a percentage of all sales goes to the cause. Details 01273-572277, studio284@junglelink.co.uk

WHADDA WE WANT?

ER SKINS

HOW MANY DO WE WANT?

ER ABOUT THREE'LL DO

NADTS

LEGALISE IT

FEELING CROSS

The first votes of election day were cast not in a ballot box, but in a field of genetically modified (GM) Oilseed Rape. In the early hours campaigners cut an 'X' shaped swathe through the controversial GM crop currently growing at Munlochy on the Black Isle, Inverness.

All over the country GM crops continue to be mysteriously trashed. Six out of 13 oil seed rape trials have been destroyed by night-time pixies and mother-nature has destroyed another two. The remaining five sites may not provide enough data for pharmaceutical giant Aventis to introduce the crop as a commercial variety, possibly delaying this by a year. SchNEWS spoke to one of the pixies who told us "Opinion polls have shown time and again that the public doesn't want these crops polluting the environment. Government and businesses won't listen, so the only thing to do is destroy the crops". It's not just in Britain that pixies are active, in Belgium three trials have recently been destroyed.

In fact it looks like things may only get worse for Aventis and their mates, as the 'Justice system' appears to be unable to make most charges against GM protesters stick. Many charges are dropped and even if they go to court, juries often find them not guilty of criminal damage. This week seven GM campaigners were cleared by magistrates for aggravated trespass. They successfully argued that as no other people were present in the field the action was not "aggravated". Soon the authorities are gonna run out of laws they can use - hopefully leading to a decriminalisation of crop trashing.

*For a list of all UK test sites including which ones have been destroyed, visit www.geneticsaction.org.uk/testsites. If there's a test site near you, contact GEN on 020 76900626. For a guide to night-time gardening, contact TOGG on 01803 840098

*Protest March against GM crops being grown in Wivenhoe, Essex. Meet noon, 23rd June, Wivenhoe station. mclarke@essex.ac.uk

Inside SchNEWS

This week American environmental activist Jeffrey Luers (a.k.a. Free) was sentenced to 22 years, 8 months in jail in Eugene, Oregon. Accused of attempted arson over a year ago, Free admitted setting fire to several Sport Utility Vehicles at Romania Chevrolet, saying during the trial he did so out of frustration over the environmental destruction that cars (especially gas-guzzling SUVs) wreak. But in his statement to the court, Free also emphasised the care he took to ensure that no one would be injured in the fires, "It cannot be said that I am unfeeling or uncaring. My heart is filled with love and compassion. I fight to protect life... not to take it. Forty-thousand species go extinct each year, yet we continue to pollute and exploit the natural world... All I ask is that you believe the sincerity of my words, and that you believe that my actions, whether or not you believe them to be misguided, stem from the love I have in my heart." An appeal is underway, but activists everywhere are still shocked by the severity of the sentence - 22 years is longer than many murderers and rapists receive. Craig Marshall (a.k.a Critter), who was arrested with Free, accepted a 5 1/2-year sentence for his role in the fire as part of a plea bargain last November. Send letters for both Free and Critter to: c/o the Legal Defense Committee at FCLDC, P.O. Box 50263, Eugene, OR 97404, USA. For more info visit www.efn.org/~eugpeace/freecritter

SchNEWS in brief

The **Wombats** (White Overall Mobile Buffer Against Truncheon Strikes) have arrived! These are the down-under cousins of the Wombles formed in response to police violence at the S11 protests last year. wombats@disinfo.net ** All good Wombles should read **Bodyhammer: Tactics and Self-Defence for the Modern Protester**. 22 pages about shields, helmets, body armour and self-defence tactics for street protests. Download it at www.devo.com/sarin/shieldbook.pdf ** **RIP Old Mick** former resident of Claremont Road. A brave and fierce East End man with a great love of the mother. A teacher, storyteller, schemer and visionary who, when his geezer gave up was ready to go into the next big mission with eyes shining. ** **Slovakian anarchists** held their second street party in Bratislava to protest against the massive road building programme, while the once-impressive public transport network rapidly deteriorates www.streetparty.sk ** **www.ruralfutures.org** is a website for a discussion of rural issues that tries to get away from the "angry farmers and foxhunters" characterisation of the countryside. ** Oldham East Labour MP Phil **Woolas** wants all claimants to sign on the electoral register or lose all benefits, he's also in favour of DNA testing the whole country! To protest at this nine people visited the local Labour Party HQ and eight were nicked to prevent a breach of the peace - making criticisms and asking awkward questions apparently isn't peaceful. ** The **Map of Activities on Transport Europe** is now accompanied by an updated booklet called 'Freeway for a free market?' a guide to 'whatever you would want to know about the European transport situation'. From: Car busters, Kratka 26, 100 00 Praha 10, Czech Republic. email:carbusters@ecn.cz ** **Liberty** has written to the Metropolitan Police threatening legal action on behalf of hundreds of people unlawfully detained by the police at the May Day protests ** In **South Korea** 55,000 workers from 126 unions are on 'indefinite strike' including airline pilots who have stopped most airline's flights, and hospital workers. Protestor blockades managed to stop cops taking 14 union leaders of South Korean Air into custody. Workers are demanding that their 44-hour, six-day week be reduced and that working conditions for temporary workers improve.

Mersey-less Treatment

Ten refugees from Liverpool are on hunger strike in protest over their barbaric treatment within the British asylum system. The protest has been sparked by a combination of delays in the asylum process and appalling conditions in the flats where the group live, owned by a private company contracted by the government - Landmark Liverpool Ltd. Press reports last year showed residents living in damp, overcrowded, filthy accommodation. Residents have reported that the landlady threatened to have them 'sent back' if they complained to the press. "We came to this country to seek refuge from persecution," said one of the refugees, "instead we have been treated like animals." E-mail messages of support to: landmark_hungerstrike@hotmail.com or call 07801 554918 for more details.

* At the end of June, the government will be opening a new asylum-seekers detention centre at Harmondsworth. This new prison will house 550 refugees - how hospitable! Picket 30th June, noon-2pm, Colnbrook bypass (A4 north of Heathrow). Close Down Harmondsworth Campaign 07960 309457.

* In Bedford Yarlswood Detention Centre is about to hold 900 refugees. There's a metting on the 7 July at 22 Chaucer Road,Bedford. Tel 07767-414714 eginn@arrowuk.com

Talk Ain't Cheap

"The police and its thug friends have made a complete mockery of every value and principle that this nation has been struggling to establish in the last three years, along with the sacrifices that have gone with this struggle. With a single stroke, the raid in Sawangan has simply turned back the clock on the nation."

Jakarta Post Editorial.

Last Friday a conference near Jakarta, Indonesia, on "fighting neo-liberalism in the Asia-Pacific region" was violently broken up by 100 armed police plus a posse of machete-wielding right-wing militia thugs. Police took 40 participants into custody for 24 hours without charge, removed passports, and threatened fines and deportation. This left the militia free to attack the remaining Indonesian participants, injuring several and hospitalising two, one critically, as well as stealing conference computers, and personal belongings of delegates.

When the delegates - including many Australians - were released without charge, and passports returned, the Director General for Immigration claimed that the police 'acted on their own', and declared the visas and conference legitimate. The Australian government - maintaining a 32 year 'special relationship' with dodgy Indonesian regimes, fobbed the fiasco off as a "visa misunderstanding".

Budiman Sudjatmiko, organiser of the conference, must have had a sense of deja-vu: the former student radical, sentenced to 13 years jail for subversion in 1996 under the Suharto regime, was only released in 1999. Local police still treat him as a 'communist threat' and last month his parents' home was bombed. The timing of this vicious attack raises the possibility of police collusion with the gangs, and a re-emergence of the sort of alliance between right-wing terror groups and the military which featured in East Timor.

www.asiet.org.au

INTERFERENCE INTERFERED WITH

On Election Day Interference FM broadcast to Bristol for a few hours before being busted. Members of the Radio-communication Agency spotted the transmitter on the roof of a house and arrived with lots of police. This is the second time that Interference has been busted, while other pirate radios have an easier life often broadcasting for many days. The reason Interference was busted was since the morning it was spitting rage on the waves about the election and encouraging citizens not to vote. The confiscation of transmitter and stereo has been a big blow for this collective. Show solidarity and send contributions to Interference FM, Box 6, 82 Colston St, Bristol BS1 5LR.

...and finally...

New York cops bit off a bit more than they bargained for when they raided a medical marijuana club, and arrested two people for selling pot. Feeling a bit chuffed with themselves after a good days work, and finding themselves a bit peckish, they gobbled down 50 cookies that they'd confiscated. "By the end of the evening they were all red eyed and giggly" said one of the defendants. A week later all the charges against the two were dropped - looks like they may have got themselves some new customers. www.hightimes.com

Subscribe! _____
Keep SchNEWS FREE! Send 1st Class stamps (e.g. 10 for next 9 issues) or donations (payable to Justice?) Ask for "Originals" if you can make copies. Post *free* to all prisoners. SchNEWS, c/o on-the-fiddle, P.O. Box 2600, Brighton, East Sussex, BN2 2DX.
Tel/Autofax +44 (0)1273 685913 *Email* schnews@brighton.co.uk *Download a PDF of this issue or subscribe at* www.schnews.org.uk

LIVING AMONGST THE TREES

Fancy living your dreams in a sustainable vegan utopia in the Devon countryside? We need YOU to help continue the passion, the fun, the commitment, dedication, and the sheer delight of living in the woods in a low impact way. We are a bunch of vegan campaigners who set up Steward Community Woodland two years ago to demonstrate the value of integrating conservation woodland management techniques (such as coppicing and natural regeneration) with organic growing, permaculture, traditional skills, and low impact sustainable living.

The Wood

We are now enjoying our third summer in a 32 acre wood on the edge of Dartmoor. It's a mixed former plantation of larch, scots pine, and ash, with much uninvited sycamore. The site is diverse ranging from shady boulder-strewn stream under a close ash canopy to open emergent broadleaf under the well-thinned larch, and a virtual monoculture of rosebay willow herb in an area that was cleared of trees by gales.

Sustainable Woodland Management

We manage the woodland sustainably using hand tools, without use of fossil fuel machinery, employing traditional techniques such as coppicing and charcoal burning. Our aim is to gradually extract the mature conifers (which will be used for building materials, sawing into timber and for firewood) while encouraging natural regeneration of native trees and planting trees where appropriate. In this way, the woodland will slowly revert to a native, deciduous wood. We hope to have a sawmill by next winter, running on wood gas or bio-diesel (made from vegetable oil). We minimise use of fossil fuels and so, for example, we use one van between us when not cycling or using public transport.

Gardens

We are growing food organically in a sheltered area clear of trees near the bottom of the land. Alongside the vegetable beds, we have planted fruit trees to establish our first forest garden. As well as working in the wood and gardening, we spend our time maintaining and improving our dwellings and infrastructure, on outreach work (such as green woodworking displays and cycle-powered workshops), and on working for social change.

Low Impact Dwellings

Because we live on a slope, most of our low impact dwellings comprise timber platforms on stilts with bender roofs topped with green tarpaulins and they're insulated inside with plenty of blankets. All have wood burning stoves and are fitted with windows looking out into the valley. Our communal 'Longhouse' houses an office, library, a large stove and lots of sofas. We have a micro-hydro system and solar panels to generate electricity for our computers, lights and phones. Most of the materials for building our structures and systems are from the wood, reused or recycled. In the future, we hope to build straw bale structures, log cabins, turf roofed dwellings, etc.

Community Life

We often have communal evening meals, cooked on a stove or an open fire, which form the mainstay of the community. Social time spent together, sometimes jamming and singing, also creates a strong bond. We celebrate life and the cycles of nature, especially at the time of full moon and the eight Celtic festivals. We also have our first woodland baby which is a joy. We often work as a group which is a useful way of bringing people together and encourages skill sharing. It's also good for getting large, unappealing jobs done!

We have frequent meetings about permaculture site design and more mundane business matters. We decide everything by consensus. To work well, this requires each person to place the interests of the project and community above their personal interests. On the whole, it has worked really well for us. It usually results in a full discussion of the issues, and suitable adaptation of the proposal to ensure everyone is happy, and feels fully heard and included.

We spent two years planning the project, establishing a shared vision, setting up legal structures, raising zero interest loanstock, and learning to work together before moving on site. We were all involved in environmental and social justice campaigning and we coalesced around the vision of creating something positive rather than just campaigning against the systems and attitudes that cause so much suffering and destruction around the world. One of our main principles (avoiding potential difficulties and conflict about animals often apparent in other communities) is that the project is vegan and we therefore do not have any domesticated animals (apart from three dogs).

Conflict Resolution

One of the biggest challenges we face is living together as a loving cooperative community, working through emotional problems and personal conflict. We have a weekly Talking Circle to help us communicate and come together as a community. Each person in the circle has a chance to say what they like without being interrupted while the others are attentively listening. Often, simply creating the space for people to air their feelings and grievances is enough for them to let go of them and move on.

Local and Global Links

Rather than being an isolated community with links only to other 'alternative' people, it is our vision to be as integrated as possible into the local community. We wish the woodland and the project to be a valuable local resource, providing scope for both voluntary and paid work, and an educational resource. We have established a woodland walk and hope to set up a community composting scheme (when the Environment Agency let us!). We intend to have school visits to the gardens and nature trails, and courses will be run on, for example, permaculture design and green woodworking. The wood is also being used as a venue for Forest School courses and activities.

We produce a quarterly newsletter and have a large, lively website with our latest news and events, alongside 'how to' guides, a photo gallery and much more.

Our Planning Future

On the planning side, we applied for permission for 'change of use' after moving onto the site. Despite an initially favourable response from the Dartmoor National Park (with a lively debate focusing on environmental problems, sustainability, Agenda 21, and so on), our application was refused on the grounds that it's contrary to the Local Plan. This was repeated on Appeal after a public inquiry, despite the fact that many people (including some of those opposing the application) had thought we were going to win. We are now intending to appeal to the High Court on the basis of the Human Rights Act.

Visitors and New Members

People are welcome to come for a short or longer stay. Please contact us first to arrange this. We are currently low in numbers and so are especially in need of people who would like to make a long term commitment, to come and live as part of the community. We are trying to take responsibility for as many areas of our lives as possible. Would you like to too? This is your chance to live out your ideals in a beautiful setting, co-creating a sustainable way of living and working for the present and for the future.

Steward Community Woodland, Moretonhampstead, Newton Abbot, Devon, TQ13 8SD.
Telephone: 01647 440233
Email: affinity@stewardwood.org
Website: www.stewardwood.org

Chile: Mapuche People Take Back Their Land

Text and pics by Richard and Holly

Manuel Maribur looks up from the mammoth fly he has captured between his bulky fingers; "I think we're going to fight for our land. We're reclaiming it because it's in our nature. We're fighters, communists, revolutionaries." Manuel is an indigenous Mapuche farmer from Chile, but also a locally renowned communist activist, who was exiled with his father to Cuba during Pinochet's military rule. His vision of his people as communist revolutionaries may be idealised - but his acknowledgement of them as tireless fighters certainly isn't.

Manuel lives in the Elicura Valley, midway down the length of Chile. A lush mountain landscape surrounds his sunny and well-tended little farm, where he lives along with his 84 year old father, Juan. But it's not all peaceful amidst the hills. Mapuches from some of the nearby communities are staging occupations of the vast, neighbouring estates, reclaiming land that was taken from them a generation or more before. Now, most of the estates are owned by multinational forestry companies, and planted with monocultures of exotic pine or eucalyptus.

"We've been fighting to get our land from the big companies over there", explains Fernando Urbino, another Mapuche *campesino*. "But they still haven't given us a single part." 41% of Fernando's district of Lumaco is covered by tree plantations; native forest is all but vanished. His farm is a dusty plot: the effect is monochrome, with earth, skin, crops, and wooden shack all meeting in a shade of sandy brown. Far ahead, it's possible to see hordes of pine trees, maturing for the chainsaw.

"The forestry companies have a big effect on the communities," he explains. "The plantations are drying up all our water here." The exotic trees' fast-growth, which makes them such a great cash-crop, means that they absorb a lot of water from the

Left - a Machi (Mapuche shaman woman) banging a kultrun, and right, the banner posse on the march at a demonstration in Temuco for the release of the leaders of Mapuche group Consejo de Todas Las Tierrase, who were in prison at the time.

ground. What water there is left is heavily polluted with agrochemicals from the plantations. "We don't even have enough water to give to our animals", says Fernando. The industry provides few jobs, usually contracted to outside companies, while the locals are barely scraping by.

"100 years ago this Elicura Valley belonged completely to the Mapuches", Manuel explains. "Now we've got, I reckon, a quarter of that territory - the other three quarters belong to the forestry companies." The story of how the people of Elicura came to lose and win (and lose and win again) their territory, is illuminating. It is an almost perfect pattern for what happened to the Mapuche people in Chile in the 120 bumpy years since they were conquered.

The Mapuche – who are also in western Argentina - were never colonised by the Spanish, fighting them off at every turn. They were finally subdued in 1881 by a bloodthirsty Chilean army in a mass slaughter tactfully known as the 'Pacification of Araucania'. At this point, a people who had once roamed free, horse trading with European adventurers, were downgraded to subsistence farming on meagre *reducciónes*. Today the situation is so much worse that the Mapuche movement is still fighting to recover even these small parcels of land.

Just what the locals need - a good bit of 'infrastructure' - Pangue Dam, upper Biobio River.

"Our land was usurped through very fraudulent sales", Manuel explains. "It was taken by the landholders with the backing of the government." Stories of illiterate Mapuches being swindled and bullied out of their community lands are as abundant as the horseflies, and it's still going on today. Eventually the *reducciónes* became so shrunken that the Mapuches became more militant.

Inspired by the Land and Freedom movement elsewhere in Latin America, in the 60s and early 70s Mapuches and other *campesinos* began to occupy the large, farming estates. Near Manuel's farm in Elicura, The Las Vertientes and Santa Elmira estates were handed over to Mapuche squatters under the government's Agrarian Reform programme. Juan, Manuel's father, remembers the period with fervent clarity. "Before Agrarian Reform one man would have 60 farms – just one foreign man. And we would have half a hectare." He gestures with his stick towards their tidy wooden house; "We had no water, no light."

While 95% of Mapuche communities recovered at least some of their lands through Agrarian Reform, that was also the time when the government began encouraging people to start the tree plantations. And when Pinochet took the lands back into the hands of private enterprise, he all but paid a few big corporations to plant swathes more. Juan, his voice rising, remembers Allende, Pinochet's leftie predecessor; "That dead president represented the Mapuche; he represented all the people. They killed him."

Of course, flashing forward a few years and into the present era of democratic government, things should have changed. Under the current socialist administration, a government agency – CONADI – buys land back on behalf of indigenous communities. A generous scheme? Oh no it isn't: there is no legal pressure for landowners to sell, and at market prices most of the lands are well beyond CONADI's limited funds. If you're Mapuche, this means that you'll be lucky to get your land in time to use it as a funeral plot.

CONADI's efforts miss the wider picture. Though Pinochet stepped down in 1989, his economic policies (moonlight and candles for the multinationals, a swift screwing for the rest) seem still unassailable. Many Mapuches accuse CONADI of helping divide (and rule) the communities it is supposed to serve. The government buys the co-operation of 'reasonable' Mapuches with occasional fragments of land, while the more rowdy ones are branded terrorists. "At Lago Lleu-Lleu the government used seductive policies", says Manuel. "They declared it an 'Area of Indigenous Development' where there are 'open doors' and 'opportunities' for the communities. But no land."

Beseiged by the forestry companies, as Mapuches have learned the value of the new Chilean model of democracy, they've began to get restless once again. In late 1997 Mapuches torched a couple of forestry trucks belonged to the Mininco company, and things kicked off. Land occupations are multiplying. During a confrontation over a roadblock in May 1999, police fired off tear gas, but were unprepared for the shotgun fire returned by the Mapuches. No-one was killed. It's not the first time Juan has seen his people in revolt. It's unlikely to end soon. "One day we will regain our lands", he says. "We, born here, in the land of our grandfathers."

See also www.mapuche-nation.org

ROLL UP! ROLL UP! IT'S YER TIGHTROPE WALKING

Weekly SchNEWS

"Welcome to Blair's Capitalist Circus."

Printed and Published in Brighton by Justice?

Friday 22nd June 2001 www.schnews.org.uk **Issue 310**

SEND IN THE CLOWNS

"An anarchists' travelling circus that goes from summit to summit with the sole purpose of causing as much mayhem as possible" - Tony Blair.

It's the Euro Big Top and the main attraction is 'mayhem causing anarchists'. Step right up and try your luck at the 'decipher the EU political bullshit' stall. See three protesters shot with live ammo. Applaud European leaders with their 'time to get tough' on protesters announcements. Boo and hiss the anti capitalist critics and ignore the mostly *peaceful* rally on the Saturday. Still, that's the name of the game.

Before the European Union Summit had even begun in Gothenburg police had surrounded one of the Convergence Centres - rented from the local council for people to sleep in, organise actions and take part in 'For Another Europe' Conference. One person who was trapped inside told SchNEWS "They barricaded about 400 activists in by putting up huge freight containers all around the school. They didn't let anyone in or out and said they would arrest everyone in there, which in the end they did." Inge Johansson of the International Noise Conspiracy added "Everybody involved in the protest saw this as something very provocative and it was clear that the police had set the tone for how they wanted the rest of the weekend to be."

After that, anytime people gathered to demonstrate they were either arrested en masse or attacked with police batons, dogs and horses. Some cops threw rocks and some of the angry protestors replied in kind and kicked in stores like McDonalds for good measure. But it was during a Reclaim The City street party that the police fired shots into the crowd - injuring three people, one of them critically. At the last update, the protestor was in 'critical, but stable condition', however there has been a blackout on official information about him. Finally on the Saturday 25,000 people gathered in a peaceful demonstration. But that isn't really newsworthy now is it.

WOT A BIG 'UN

From Stockholm came words that European leaders hoped would be music to environmentalists ears, with them boasting that Europe will become the most sustainable society in the world. There's just one slight problem with this – the EU's over-riding priority remains ever-increasing international trade and competitiveness.

At the Lisbon 'Jobs Summit'in March last year, European leaders talked about "greater regulatory freedom" for corporations, asking the European Commission to find ways of simplifying all those bloody rules and environmental regulations that are burdening business.

Meanwhile, thirteen countries mainly from Central Europe want a piece of the EU action – but joining will come at a price with the Polish Prime Minister talking about selling "difficult measures to the people." That's because the price is all about getting their economies 'harmonised' ; y'know public services slashed and privatised, dismantling social services, removing restrictions on the purchase of land by foreign companies etc… In fact you could call it the European version of the Structural Adjustment Programmes that is forced onto the 'Third World.' (SchNEWS 287).

Pushing for these reforms are powerful business lobby groups. The most powerful of which is the European Roundtable of Industrialists (ERT), made up of 45 'captains of industry'. Its former secretary-general boasted about phoning European leaders whenever he wanted policy changes and its web-site says "every six months the ERT makes contact with the government that holds the EU presidency to discuss priorities." They usually get their way. Take a paper published in the eighties demanding a tunnel under the English Channel, a roadbridge connecting Denmark to Sweden, a European high speed train system, and a new Europe wide roadbuilding programme. Hey presto – they got the lot.

Now they've got all guns blazing for "a minimal regulatory system with the maximum of flexibility." Which roughly translates as sod the environment, sod workers rights, where's the cash.

So when Blair goes on about this 'undemocratic… travelling circus' let's point the finger at big business pulling the strings behind the scenes and going from country to country causing mayhem in their quest for more profits.

* Keep up to date with European Union going's on with the excellent Corporate Europe Observatory, Paulus Potterstraat 20, 1071 DA Amsterdam, Holland Tel +31 20 612 7023 www.xs4all.nl/~ceo
* "From Seattle to Nice - Challenging the Free Trade Agenda at the Heart of Enlargement" by Caroline Lucas Green MEP. A4 SAE to 58 The Hop Exchange, 24 Southwark St., London, SE1 1TY

* To get up-to-date information on the situation in Gothenburg and the status of the wounded protestor, visit sweden.indymedia.org
* To get the latest on what will happen in Genoa check out the Party and Protest section on the SchNEWS website.
* In the biggest action in the city since S26, 700 people partied on the streets of **Prague** to protest against the privatisation of public space, against new repressive laws and in solidarity with the protests in Gothenburg. www.ulicelidem.cz

Globalise This

Well kids, it looks like globalisation is here to stay. SchNEWS got the low down from a few "experts" on the topic, and here's what they had to say: Mike Moore, Director General of the World Trade Organisation reckons that, "Globalisation is with us. It cannot be uninvented." For Bill Clinton, globalisation is "not a policy choice, it's a fact." In the UK, Tony Blair has called it "irreversible and inevitable." And according to Renato Ruggiero, former head of the WTO, trying to stop globalisation is "tantamount to trying to stop the rotation of the earth." Um, excuse us? What is it with these clowns??! It's clear that these descriptions of globalisation are deliberately designed to try to stop us from analysing, criticizing, or finding alternatives to the phenomenon. But alternatives do exist! (gasp!) Globalisation is NOT driven by irrefutable economic laws; it is NOT governed by inevitable market forces. It has NOT happened by accident of nature or divine intervention. (No George Dub'Ya, God didn't invent free trade). To the contrary, globalisation has been driven over the past 3 decades by the world's leading business and government elites. But there are alternatives to environmental degradation, economic exploitation, and all the other "inevitabilities" that come along with the G word. You'll just have to keep reading the Positive SchNEWS column to find out what some of them are.

PLANNING DISSENT

In a week when Tony Blair complained about "undemocratic anarchy" on the streets of Gothenburg his own Government is pressing ahead with changes to the planning system to make it harder to object to things such as motorways, airports and nuclear power stations. Under new proposals ministers will have the right to give the go ahead for controversial projects with little parliamentary debate. At a public enquiry you'll be able to discuss trivial things such as how projects are landscaped, but not to discuss if it's needed. So you can't object to a waste incinerator in your back garden on the grounds that it is bad for your health and an unsustainable approach to waste management, but you can ask them to paint it a nice shade of green!

And who is behind these proposals? SchNEWS is shocked to hear that its Tony Blair's big business friends, the Confederation of British Industry, who have been whinging about the time it takes for projects to be approved. The Campaign for Planning Sanity has promised: "We will fight these proposals at the ballot box, in the courts, on the streets, and in the trees and tunnels." To get involved call 0161-959 0999, www.onlincam.freeserve.co.uk.

* The Government is also thinking about building new nuclear power stations to replace old coal fired power stations. Rather than putting investment into renewables such as solar, wave and wind power it wants to use outdated, polluting technology. The new planning rules would help the government push through the proposals against objections that are bound to surface.

WOMBLES CAMP IT UP

"Corporations cross borders all the time in search of people to exploit for profit and no one stops them. They call this process Globalisation. On the other hand, the victims of corporate domination are told they cannot cross borders in search of better lives."

While the G8 meet in Genoa to discuss expanding free trade and profit, thousands of people are forced to leave their homes and seek asylum just to survive. On arrival they get detained. Campsfield is the UK's flagship Immigration Detention Centre. Its inmates are escaping from oppressive states like Iraq, Turkey and Afghanistan. Opened in 1993, it is privately run by Group 4 for profit. A permanent camp (with the aim of closing the centre down for good) has already been opened near Campsfield and the happy campers have already made several incursions into the centre, but there is still more to be done! During the G8 meeting (20-22 July) Ya Basta! will open a "No Borders" camp in Italy. Here in the UK, The Wombles are calling for actions in solidarity with those in Italy and those locked inside Campsfield. Actions at Campsfield will commence on 18 July and will demand the closure of the centre. Bring your mates, white overalls, helmets, padding, fun, food, banners, tents, ladders, bolt croppers, siege equipment. Site mobile: 0781 3552570 www.closecampsfield.org.uk or www.wombleaction.mrnice.net

* Following on from last years 'Reshape Urban Space' event **Edinburgh** will host The 'Foot & Mouth' festival from 14-22 July which isn't to do with the mild illness animals get. The name comes from the idea they will 'foot it around Edinburgh' in a street party called Reshape Urban Space 2 on July 14th then 'mouth off' about it at Studio 24 for a day of workshops and discussions the following weekend. This coincides with the G8 summit in Genoa and is being held in solidarity with the planned protests there. www.mouthoff.org.uk

SchNEWS in brief

RIP. **Andrew Wayman** (Wez) died recently while working on an organic farm in Costa Rica. Wez helped set up Greenwich Organics, a shop in south London, and was involved in many actions and parties including Claremont Rd and Newbury. ** The protest against **Countryside Residential in Hockley** continues in cyberspace. The campaign and evictions have cost Countryside £3 million and they've been forced to sell some of their land to get some money back. www.plumberow.org.uk ** About 200 people picketed the entrance of the new **MOD** National procurement centre in Bristol in the first national protest against the purchase of depleted uranium and other radioactive weaponry. www.access.lowtech.org/collectableanorak. ** **Calvin Klein** was creamed by pie-throwing anti-fur protestors at the recent American Fashion awards. ** This Saturday (23) 11am-4.30pm **'Open Borders- Is it time?'** Film, discussion, art, story telling and food. @ The Friends meeting house, Brighton followed by the 'Boombastic refugee party' @ The Joint, West street, Brighton. Carnival collective etc. 10pm-2am £5. Free to Asylum seekers ** Our long serving **mail out** crew need a helping hand or two. We also need people to deliver SchNEWS around **Kemptown**. So if you've a couple of spare hours on a Friday afternoon, please get in touch.

FAMILIES & FRIENDS

In 1969 David Oluwale became the first black person to die in police custody in the UK. Little has changed since; hundreds have died in suspicous and often brutal circumstances. Oddly, no police officers involved have ever been convicted. Even when unlawful killing verdicts are returned, charges against the police never seem to follow. The classic 'he fell on my truncheon' must be a tired line now. So The United Families & Friends Campaign, have been set up demanding the police force be made accountable, as well as all deaths to be investigated independently. How can the police investigate the police objectively?

The UFFC are holding a tribunal (11&12 July) where the Government and police will be "on trial" for human rights abuses. The findings will be presented to international bodies, urging intervention and support. Tel: 07770 432 439. www.appleonline.net/justiceuk/jus.html

(I)RANSOM

On Tuesday, workers from Tehran's Chit-e-Rey factory, once called the 'mother of Iran's textile industry', held the manager of their privatised company hostage for 3 hours. They were protesting at non-payment of their wages and the sale of the factory to dodgy private investors who just wanted to sell off the land. Hours later it appeared that their long struggle for $20,000 of unpaid wages and against privatisation had finally succeeded. This was achieved without a union and the right to strike or protest. www.etehadchap.com

* In General Mosconi, north Argentina, police broke up a two-week picket, with tear gas and rubber bullets, two people were killed and many were hospitalised. Demonstrators included the unemployed demanding benefits and construction workers demanding a living wage. The police entered the town and cut services like electricity, gas and water and access to the press, while they battled with civil rights activists. Interior Minister Ramón Mestre said that a "state of siege" could be declared in the area if violence continues. Similar protests were held in May and November last year. On November 10, a police crackdown on pickets in Tartagal unleashed an angry rampage by protestors who set fire to public buildings and looted shops. www.indymedia.org

Inside SchNEWS

* British librarian Paul Robinson was arrested in Gothenburg and has been charged with violent rioting and battery, which carries a maximum 4-year sentence. He's on remand in a Swedish prison pending trial in a few weeks. He'd welcome letters (please be careful what you say), newspapers and magazines would be much appreciated. It's also his birthday on 4th July so send him a card!! Write to: Paul Robinson Goteburg Remand Centre (Haktet), Goteburg Polis Headquaters, (Polis Huset), Box 429, 40126 Goteburg, SWEDEN. Friends of Paul are asking people to email the Swedish ambassador to condemn the shooting of three protestors, and to voice concerns that Paul has not been allowed any telephone calls, has received no medical treatment for injuries sustained by police, and is being denied the right to change his court-appointed solicitor for one of his own choosing. Email the Swedish Ambassador Mats Bergquist about these issues at: ambassaden.london@foreign.ministry.se, or embassy@swednet.org.uk

* In 1992 Eddie Gilfoyle was arrested for the murder of his wife. His case has been covered by Channel 4's 'Trial and Error" programme , and the Cheshire and Lancashire police and the Home Office have all concluded that his wife did in fact tragically commit suicide. But last December he lost his appeal, and he remains behind bars. Things got worse when, as his case was being prepared for the European Court, his solicitor was sent to prison for stealing nearly £70,000 from past clients. His new lawyer Campbell Malone is calling for an overhaul of all the evidence against him. Malone wants to get campaigners and lawyers to unite to fight the injustice of the appeal court system. There's a public meeting, Wednesday 4th July 6pm at Conway Hall, Red Lion Square, London WC1. Speakers include Michael Mansfield QC, and solicitor Jim Nichol who handled cases of the Bridgewater 4. Info: PO Box 1845, Stoke on Trent, ST7 4EG or email: Paul.Caddick@btinternet.com

...and finally...

Last Friday some of the SchNEWS crew picked up the last boxes of our new book from the printer in East London. Just as we entered the 'ring of steel' near Liverpool St Station, police pulled us over saying that surveillance cameras, which check every number plate entering the city, showed that ours had a query. The problem was with the previous owner of the van, but before we knew it seven over-eager cops opened it up. Seeing the book with the word 'terrorist' on the cover and thinking they had uncovered some sinister plot, they asked if we were at Mayday. Getting quite excited they said, 'Did you know that under the Terrorism Act it could be illegal to be carrying such literature?' Urmm… Then they had an even better idea: 'Under the Terrorism Act we can search your van without reason'. The cops told us later that we had fitted the bill as terrorists - two guys, an old white van, boxes in the back, entering the city, and apparently in the four hours our van sat in Bishopsgate looking suspicious, there were 15 calls to the station about it! The City Of London is a security 'ring of steel' best avoided.

PS. A chance to plug our book again – get your copy quick before the office is raided. £8.50 including postage, cheques payable to Justice?. Just don't wave your copy around in the ring of steel.

disclaimer

THE GOTHENBURG ONE

At the EU Summit at Gothenburg 14-16 June 2001, Paul Robinson was pulled from the crowd, beaten, arrested, charged and sentenced to one year for 'violent riot'. He tells his story...

Part of me still smiles at the absurdity of it all – the moments of pure comedy, the initial rage and anger replaced, quite naturally, with exasperation and a grim determination; the other political prisoners and the fearless good will and grace with which we took to our task, sharing, along with phone cards and manic riot memories, an unspoken, instinctive solidarity and fierce loyalty; the quiet friendships and inspired letters (the way the word still managed to get through); the bad English lessons given almost daily across the dinner table along with arguments over the political nature of sci-fi(!), tales of revolutionary activity, football teams supported and universal contempt for all that the Swedish state could throw at us... for a time it was some other kind of existence, dull and distracted, strange and unremarkable, but for all the distance and isolation and time lost, the eight months spent in a foreign prison fills me, even now, with nothing more than an overwhelming sense of the absurd.

For those who went to Gothenburg for the EU demonstrations in the summer of 2001, and watched with horror and disbelief as riot police shot indiscriminately into the crowd almost killing 3 people, it was the starting point of something that would lead, almost inevitably, to the transparent state brutality at Genoa. But for me, around 10.20pm on the evening of Friday June 15th, it was the beginning of a very different journey.

The morning of the 15th was one of the of the most incredible scenes I've ever witnessed - the streets of Gothenburg erupting in spontaneous anger and outrage, activists from all over Europe united in defiance, inspired and unapologetic, attacking wholeheartedly and with absolute joy the might and amoury of the Swedish state. It was a truly magnificent. Later that evening, when it kicked off again, defending ourselves once more against constant police charges the outcome turned out to be very, very different. In a lull in the confrontation I was grabbed by four

Police with guns in the vicinity where Hannes Westberg (below) is shot in the back, nearly being killed. Moments after this Paul was arrested.

riot police, dragged behind police lines and beaten with such force that I had to be prescribed painkillers by the prison doctor for two months after. Having been arrested, thrown in a cell and charged with 'violent riot' I spent the next month in solitary confinement up until my first trial. I saw or spoke to no other person (apart! from my solicitor and the British Consul – who turned out to be best friends with the chief of police!), spent 24 hours locked in my cell, was escorted to and from the toilets/showers, and offered nothing in the way of explanation or information. It was going to be a long, slow summer.

Both my trials turned out to be mundane in their predictability and outcome. One riot cop accused me of being a terrorist (this was on Sept 12th – the day after the twin towers attack!), and later freely admitted to shooting at people as they ran away because he 'feared for his safety'. A prosecutor demanded I should be convicted anyway simply because of the clothes I was wearing! Due to the nature of political show trials the verdict was never really in doubt, what surprised everyone, including the prison staff, was the severity of the sentence.

Police on horses retreat as protesters bowl a few overs at them. (Not everybody's idea of cricket of course)

When I was finally released out of solitary and the restrictions lifted the mail started flooding in. Letters from all manner of people, from all over of the world. Almost on a daily basis guards would come in with a huge bundle of letters and parcels and incredulous looks on their faces 'who the fuck are you, why are all these people writing to you'. One even asked how famous I was back in the UK. The level of solidarity and support, which to be honest even amazed me, was completely lost on them. All restrictions lifted meant I could eat meals and socialise with the other prisoners. Right from the start me and the other three politicals convicted of rioting ("the stone-throwers") formed ourselves into a solid little group. Jesse the autonomist from Berlin – thoughtful, sincere, devouring political ideas with an almost obsessive intensity. The two of us would spend Sunday afternoons in each other's cells discussing tactics, theory, history, he arrived in Gothenburg replete with full body armour that would shame the most well-equipped police force. The evidence against me barely covered two pages; the evidence against Jesse amounted to a small volume.

Sebastian, a nineteen year old from southern Germany, was one of the unfortunate ones who got shot. TV cameras showed him struggling into court on crutches, barely able to walk because of his injuries, next day he was bouncing around the exercise yard like a two-year-old. And Gigi, a middle-aged Italian socialist living in Norway. Out of all of us Gigi was the one who genuinely shouldn't have been there. A small, slight, mild-mannered, incredibly quiet man with various physical ailments, it served absolutely no purpose for him to be imprisoned except to allow the Swedish state to show the rest of Europe how successfully it was dealing with these 'violent thugs'. His detention would remain, through our time together, a source of unspoken resentment we all felt. We secured our own table at mealtimes (our own miniature EU of dodgy radicals) and at one point I became the elder statesman of the remand centre finding myself in the dubious position of being the longest serving remand prisoner ever. This afforded me no particular privileges other than polite nods and general all round acknowledgement and the oddity of hearing everyone saying 'cheers' and 'alright' to each other at mealtimes. Everybody spoke some degree of English and because remand prisoners were mostly foreign nationals it was the universal language most commonly adopted. Made my life a hell of a lot easier.

The remand centre was essentially the eighth floor of the police station (view from my cell window: giant Volvo factory) and like Gothenburg itself clean, modern and practical. The 'exercise yard' was an enclosed concrete cage on the roof so the only time I set foot on solid ground in the six months I was there was my two days in court. Life in prison is about two things: conformity and

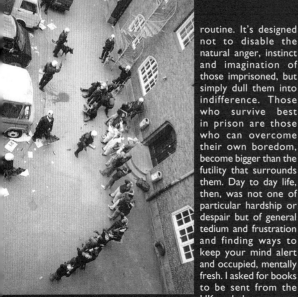
Arrestees are lined up

routine. It's designed not to disable the natural anger, instinct and imagination of those imprisoned, but simply dull them into indifference. Those who survive best in prison are those who can overcome their own boredom, become bigger than the futility that surrounds them. Day to day life, then, was not one of particular hardship or despair but of general tedium and frustration and finding ways to keep your mind alert and occupied, mentally fresh. I asked for books to be sent from the UK and the response was phenomenal! By the time I left for prison at Karlskoga I had accumulated over 93 books, plus pamphlets and journals, pissing off the person who had to count every personal item prisoners had. They'd never seen anything like it, I had more books than the prison library, most were given to the Solidarity Group in Gothenburg who were not only unconditional in their support but were also wonderful, generous people as well. And if books (and tapes) were a godsend then letters were pure emotional sunlight, an absolute necessity. They acted as a barrier, a source of comfort and sense of pride.

It's difficult to describe or explain or convey just how much they meant but every single person who wrote to me while I was inside will forever occupy a tiny part of my soul. As Carole Maso would say, the dark was not so dark.

By the time I got to Karlskoga, a tiny, quiet prison stuck in the middle of the Swedish countryside to serve the last two months of my sentence, I was a fully accepted member of the criminal fraternity. Prisoners there knew exactly who I was and what I was in for. I was afforded a great deal of respect, which took a while to get used to. The armed robbers and gang members were genuinely impressed with my stone throwing abilities and general lack of fear in the face of oncoming riot police. But despite the greater freedom and distractions, it just wasn't the same anymore - I was now just killing time, counting down the days and keeping myself to myself. The other stone-throwers had been moved to other prisons and somehow the fire and focus had shifted from retaining your sense of self to thoughts of home and the London I'd left behind.

As an experience, yes it was unique and no it's not one I'd like to go through again, liberty is not to be taken so lightly or traded so easily. Here is what I am: working class, a revolutionary, anarchist, troublemaker, ex-criminal – all of which I treasure with equal warmth and determination, all of which cannot be taken from me.

Of the 53 arrested, some 40 received sentences on the charge of 'violent riot'. While Paul served eight months and is now out, others – including others mentioned in this article - got longer sentences and are still inside in Sweden. To offer support to these prisoners contact: Gothenburg Solidaritygroup GBG, c/o Syndikalistiskt Forum, Box 7267, 402 35 Gothenburg, Sweden. solidaritetsgruppen@hotmail.com

To follow the progress of the Gothenburg arrestees after the summit see 'Inside SchNEWS' – backpage on issues 318, 322, 326, 329, 334, 347.

UK Genetics Actions Round-up

2001 was a bit of a failure for biotech giants in the UK who seem to be have been experiencing some difficulty with their GM test sites - they keep disappearing. Over thirty trials were damaged or destroyed. A fair few crops failed to grow sufficiently for the tests to be valid and some trials were withdrawn after public pressure. All of the National Seed List Trials for winter oilseed rape were invalidated! Following this wave of actions against GM trials there are reports of increased security measures at previously damaged test sites. At Wivenhoe and Arlesford in Essex, infra-red sensors and video cameras were installed, hidden in bird boxes and placed near the two maize trials, as well as security guards, dogs and car patrols. Despite these measures, 95% of the Arlesford trial has been damaged by protesters, and 10% at Wivenhoe. At Jealotts Hill, Berkshire, high security including barbed wire fences, infra-red cameras and mobile patrols, surrounded the trials of Syngenta GM potatoes. Again, the measures failed to prevent 75% of one of the trials being destroyed. As one protester commented: *"Police claim to lack resources, but when they want to protect a mutant crop that no one wants there's suddenly a bottomless pit of cash."*

Long Marston, 9th March

The Trouble With Genetics

There were more actions at GM test sites in the summer of 2001 than ever before.

30th June Two hundred people joined a lively carnival of protest against two farm scale trials of maize in **Wivenhoe, Essex**. The costumed procession made its way through the town to meet at the farm for a picnic. They tried to place biohazard signs around the edge of the trial but were prevented by police. Seven people were arrested, three charged with criminal damage.

Pulling crops - Long Marston, 9th March

14th July Around one hundred and fifty people gathered for a day of protests against the only trial site in Wales, a farm scale trial in **Flintshire**. The farmer was handed a petition and people began to pull up the maize. About 10% was destroyed, and six people were arrested.

19th August Not one, not two, but three actions took place in England, Scotland and Wales. In **Dorset**, thirty or so locals went for a stroll to highlight their farm scale trial of winter oilseed rape. Three camera crews and assorted media types reported the event. At the **Flintshire** site in Wales, protesters braved the weather and strong police presence (56 police for 15 protesters!) to have an organic picnic at the site. In Scotland 300

STOP NOW BEFORE IT'S TOO LATE! NO GM

Long Marston, 9th March

people gathered in **Munlochy** (see next page).

13th December 10 people with a purple cow banner blockaded the BOCM Pauls (the country's largest animal feed producer) plant in Radstock, Somerset, for two hours. The gates were D-locked together and lorries backed up along the road. A few protesters wandered around inside, chatting to workers while sitting on the conveyer belt, and on their departure the local policeman thanked them and said they could return any time(!).

The next day a group of 22 campaigners staged a protest at the Exeter base of BOCM Pauls Ltd. Two scaled a silo while another eight, including a pregnant woman, chained themselves to a weighbridge using bike D-locks and arm tubes.

By obstructing the weighbridge the group had calculated that they would cause maximum disruption, and as the day progressed a queue of lorries built up, needing to use the weighbridge before leaving the plant.

It was the second time the group had targeted BOCM's premises. In newspaper reports a BOCM spokesperson confirmed that the company does produce feed that incorporates GM ingredients which he said *"they were entitled to do under current laws"*.

13th December, BOCM Pauls plant, Radstock.   Pic: Simon Chapman

9th March 2002 The first rally against GM crops in 2002 took place in **Long Marston** near Stratford-Upon-Avon. After a peaceful rally about 100 people went onto the field of GM crops and in full view of the police proceeded to pull up the crop for half an hour before the police moved in and made 5 arrests.

To keep up-to-date with protests and GM sites check out www.geneticsaction.org.uk and to get the very excellent 'Genetix Update' publication visit www.togg.org.uk

Fighting for a GM free Scotland

An intense anti-GM campaign has been fought against Aventis crop trials in Munlochy, on the Black Isle peninsula in the Scottish Highlands.

Protests have been ongoing since GM crop trials were approved by the Scottish Government early in 2000, and the first GM oil seed rape trial was planted that winter.

400 locals challenged Aventis Crop Science (since sold to Bayer) and the seed company involved on three points at a public meeting in August 2000. They firstly objected to the safety track record of GM crops causing harmful and unpredictable effects on humans and the environment. Secondly, concentrated dosages of herbicides and pesticides involved threaten the livelihood of Highland farmers whose produce has a reputation for coming from an unspoilt natural environment. Lastly they objected to the patenting, and ownership of seed types by GM companies which takes seed control away from the farmers into the hands of corporations. (see SchNEWS 346). Aventis couldn't answer these questions satisfactorily

A few months later, a government-organised meeting drew another 150 concerned locals, many of whom had never been involved in campaigning before. At the event one man turned to face the crowd and asked: "Who in this room would be prepared to destroy this crop with me?" Nearly half the audience raised their hands.

On the day of the general election, the 7th of June, a large x got trampled into a GM oilseed rape trial crop sending the message to politicians that "GM is not welcome in Scotland."

300 people gathered on August the 17th to oppose the farm scale trial of winter oilseed rape there. Following a march through the town with a tractor everyone enjoyed the sunshine with a picnic, music and speakers from around the country.

Then on the 23rd of August 2001, three women from Highlands & Islands GM Concern went to visit a site set for a farm scale trial of winter oilseed rape at Tullich Farm near Munlochy. "As we were standing looking at the field a tractor appeared with drilling equipment. We didn't want to believe that the GM oilseed rape was being planted in front of our very eyes!"

Nancy McAdam is arrested at Tullich Farm, August 24th

The driver tried unsuccessfully to convince them that he was only fertilising, but then the media were called and started arriving, along with police, and then more local protesters. Twelve people – including a mum and her kid then blockaded the tractor, and after discussions the driver went home.

The next morning police called all the protesters together and announced that sowing would be starting again immediately. "Within minutes the tractor appeared on the horizon. Nancy and Rhona walked in to the field and sat in the tractor's path. They were arrested and removed from the field. The driver carried on sowing. At 4:45pm myself, Pete and Gavin decided enough was enough and we sat in the tractor's path."

By late afternoon about fifty protesters had gathered, their numbers matched by police. The protesters set up an information caravan. Thirteen people were arrested for breach of the peace, most of them over 35 and had never done direct action before. For several days a presence was maintained at the field, but despite repeated waves of obstruction the GM oilseed was eventually sown. Following on from this action a permanent camp was built next to field to keep a vigil over the growing GM crop. The vigils petition now has over 4000 signatures. Local people are highly supportive. In a nearby village 92% of people voted against the trial.

Towards the end of September a yurt was built to keep up a constant vigil at the site. In November the protest camp - including two caravans and a toilet - was granted planning permission to remain until the end of August 2002; after the council received 120 letters supporting the application.

300 locals turned out to show their support in March 2002 when Donnie MacLeod, a local organic farmer and one of those arrested on August 24th, appeared in court. Donnie served eight days of a 21 day sentence, after he was charged with criminal damage and refused to name anyone else who was present with him.

Writing from inside Inverness's Porterfield Prison he said:

"It has taken me 53 years of living on this planet to achieve this new experience courtesy of Sheriff James Fraser at Dingwall Sheriff Court. There has just been a very noisy demonstration outside that could be heard through the bars on the window and I wished that I could break open this metal door to thank the 300 or so people showing their support.

But I am not free to do so.

I have received about 200 letters of support from people all over the country and I would like to reply to them.

But I am not free to do so.

For the last week I have not been a free man in the physical sense of the words. But that week has allowed me to reflect on what freedom is all about. There are very few people who are truly free. We all have responsibilities of one kind or another. Freedom itself carries great responsibilities towards others. That is why, when I am released, I fear that I will have a responsibility to continue my direct actions against the deliberate contamination of the Highlands by the biotechnological multinational moguls for their profit.

I ask myself why do I have to do it and not someone else? It simply stems from the fact that I am in the privileged position of being in possession of the facts behind the GM crop trial farce and am aware of the reasons behind it. Couple this with the fact that I am in a position of being able to do it, and you have the reason.

I believe that my imprisonment was a political tactic to try and intimidate other protesters against taking direct action against the iniquitous GM crop trial at Munlochy."

The Munlochy site has evolved into a GM information centre. Towards the end of last year a craft auction was held, and local musicians released 'Oilseed Raped?' - a five-track CD - to raise money for the Vigil.

In early February, a petition with over 5000 signatures, supported by all the main political parties and members of the Scottish, UK and European Parliaments, was presented to the Scottish Parliament.

On the 16th February they held a conference 'Biotechnology, Environment and Health' which was attended by several top scientists in the (eherm) field, with 350 people attending.

The latest action happened in April. Just days after the Scottish executive called for the Munlochy crop trial to be ploughed up because it had come into flower, about 5 acres of the field was mysteriously destroyed.

www.scottishgenetixaction.org www.munlochygmvigil.org.uk
0781 330 7337

WAKE UP! WAKE UP! IT'S AN AIR RAID

Weekly SchNEWS

Printed and Published in Brighton by Justice?

Friday 29th June 2001   www.schnews.org.uk   Issue 311

HOW EMISSIONS TRADING WORKS

I'LL TRADE THAT SPEECH FOR THIS EMISSION

EMISSION: *IMPOSSIBLE*

"The unsigned Kyoto protocol is becoming a carbon trade deal dominated by businessmen desperate for a piece of the new market in trading." - Rising Tide UK

In the lead up to the next month's climate change talks in Bonn, the European Union has published draft plans for an "emissions trading" scheme which they hope will be up and running by 2005. But what we're getting here is not a solution to climate change but essentially a market for buying and selling the right to pollute.

Emissions trading systems are already operating in Britain and Denmark with unofficial trading expanding in Canada and the United States, but what's it all about?

Well, imagine for a moment that you run a gas power plant that, under the Kyoto Protocol, manages to emit less than its allocation of C02 emissions. You will then be rewarded by being allowed to sell your surplus emission credits. If you 'overspend' you'll have to buy 'carbon credits' from other companies - or face a fine.

Direct action group Rising Tide describes this sort of trading system as the "privatisation of the climate". And at the mere mention of the word privatisation the New Labour lapdogs will come running. Forget schools and hospitals – let's sell our hot air! As you would expect this has also got big business in raptures with Carlton Bartels of CO2e.com. (a web-based carbon trading consortium which includes old friends PriceWaterhouseCoopers and mega-brokers Cantor Fitzgerald) describing it as "potentially one of the world's largest markets" and crooning "Regardless of the fate of any particular treaty or proposal, the reality of a carbon-constrained future is upon us. Companies that recognise this and begin their transition now will be the leaders of the new economy."

It's not a new idea. The online exchange has a new take on the old model of trading the rights to pollute. For the past decade - mainly in America - companies have bought and sold pollution credits, which specify how many tons of acid-rain chemicals a smokestack can emit. Under that system, a relatively clean manufacturer can sell unused credits to a refinery that can't meet its limits. And both BP and Shell have been running their own in-house trading systems for some time – after all, where corporations lead, governments love to follow.

So while the United Nations' own scientists talk about the need for a 60% reduction

to reverse climate change, and groups like Rising Tide call for 90%, big business and governments are squabbling over cuts of 5.2% and frothing at the mouth over 'whole new market opportunities'.

CARBON CASINO

New Labour have just announced one of the most far reaching energy reviews for decades and have put the new energy minister Brian Wilson in charge. Just one snag - Wilson is a cheerleader for nuclear power. And in the small print of the announcement on current policies, just 4.5% of our energy use will come from renewables by 2020. This despite wave power being able to supply 40% of the UK's energy needs and wind power being able to supply 20% at less cost than nuclear and without the waste problems or risk of serious accidents.

* The UK's first conference on ecological debt, with a strong climatic focus, is taking place on Tuesday July 10th at the ICA in The Mall, London. Contact New Economics Foundation O20 7407 7447 or ruth.potts@neweconomics.org.

* The Climate Change talks take place in Bonn, Germany from 16-23rd July, with actions and events planned throughout. For info about travelling there and accommodation, see www.risingtide.de or contact Friends of the Earth 26-28 Underwood St. London N1 7JQ 0207 490 0881 www.foe.co.uk

* If you can't get to Germany there's a Week of UK Climate Actions called by Rising Tide UK, from July 14-21st. Details: 16b Cherwell Street, Oxford, OX1 1BG www.risingtide.org.uk info@risingtide.org.uk 01865 241097

* 90% for 90% National Day of Action on the 16th July, which is part of "A call for a 90% cut in public transport fares, to make public transport affordable, to start making changes that bring the 90% cut in greenhouse gases needed to halt climate change…Get the 90% card to show the guard. Get together with a group in your area, speak to local public transport workers, and plan a 90% for 90% trip on the 16th: to the seaside (get there before it gets to you); to the countryside; to view your nearest oil refinery - the possibilities are endless."
Details: climatechaos@yahoo.com Cards are available £3.50 for a pack of 50, cheques payable to 'Rising Tide' c/o Manchester Earth First! Box 29, 22a Beswick Street, Manchester, M4 7HS. Or download from www.risingtide.org.uk

* 11 July International Day of Action against ExxonMobil (ESSO) - picket their petrol

stations, refineries or offices. Dubbed the "Greenhouse Gangsters" this lot are President Bush's biggest supporters encouraging him to ditch Kyoto and drill for oil in Alaska.www.globalwarming.isbad.net

Further reading:

* 'Greenhouse Market Mania – UN climate talks corrupted by corporate pseudo-solutions' from Corporate Europe Observatory, Paulus Potterstraat 20, 1071 Amsterdam, Netherlands www.xs4all.nl/~ceo

* 'The Dyson Effect – Carbon Offset Forestry and the Privatisation of the Atmosphere', from The Corner House, 01258 473795, www.icaap.org/cornerhouse

* 'Collision Course - free trade's free ride on the global climate' (Central books)

POSITIVE SchNEWS

Modern intensive agriculture might be an environmental disaster but if we want to feed the world then there is no alternative. Or so we are told. But this myth has been seriously challenged by the largest ever study of sustainable agriculture, with nearly nine million farmers covering over 3% of agricultural land in the third world studied. The report by Jules Pretty and Rachel Hine of the University of Essex showed significant improvements in food production with cheap, low-cost, sustainable inputs and technologies. They concluded "Were these approaches to be widely adopted, they would make a significant impact on rural people's livelihoods, as well as on local and regional food security."

Not only does sustainable agriculture produce food and other goods, but also improves things such as flood protection, water quality and wildlife biodiversity. Sustainable agriculture also improves social cohesion by keeping the production of food and goods within the local economy. Something that intensive agriculture can never do.

* Check out 'Poverty and Globalisation' by Vandana Shiva in the new SchNEWS and Squall Yearbook 2001, available from SchNEWS for £8.50 inc. p&p. Cheques payable to 'Justice?'

STONE ME!

10,000 people celebrated sunrise on the summer solstice at Stonehenge, the second time this has been allowed since 1984.

No sound systems were allowed in the car park – it being too close to the stones, and despite assurances that no drunk drivers would be made to leave the site before sobering up, within hours an eviction order was produced and riot vans chased vehicles off. Months before, the Stonehenge Campaign had negotiated a party site on military land at Barton Stacey with the police, but the authorities went back on this, leaving people with nowhere to go. A site at Chicklade was taken and a party went off on Thursday night, but was predictably evicted by Wiltshire police, who promised that another venue near Glastonbury had been sorted for the weekend and so passed the buck on to their Avon and Somerset 'colleagues'. Pissed off party heads soon discovered that the site was a healing festival – pay to get in, no drink, drugs or amplified music allowed. So people set off round the countryside looking for a venue, with farmers, worried about last week's new outbreaks of foot and mouth, calling the cops every five seconds.

By Friday night, parties were setting up for the weekend at Daventry (near Northampton) – 10 rigs and a band stage – and at Hinckley Point (near Bridgwater) – 10 rigs and a nuclear power station. All glowed well.

* Stonehenge campaign newsletter: c/o 99 Toriano Av, London NW5 2RX www.dicenews.com/stonehenge For background on Stonehenge and its place in our culture check out Tash's website: www.gn.apc.org/tash

* Rupture is a wicked monthly free party zine. For copies send SAE to P.O. Box 30199, London E17 5FJ or email rupture@headfuk.org

WELSHED ON

Despite everything for the Welsh Green Gathering being sorted, Carmarthenshire County Council have bowed to police pressure and refused permission for the eco-festival at the last minute. The Green Gathering has a reputation for top organisation skills – they were approached by English Heritage for advice on sorting Stonehenge – but police snotted out a tissue of lies about how travellers would descend on the site. Dyfed Powys's police licensing officer ranted "I'm afraid that if the festival went ahead we would be left with 25 acres of land which would be filled with human waste, diesel and cannabis, as well as other matters which I will not go into" (!?). Organisers are now trying to sort a new venue, which is scheduled for August 16th-19th. Welsh Green Gathering: 01267 267500 www.big-green-gathering.com/wales.html

* For a list of festies over the summer, check 'Party and Protest' on the SchNEWS website.

TEKNIVAL HITCH UPDATE

The French Socialist Party has rejected a controversial amendment to the Public Safety Bill, which would have criminalised the massive teknival movement with a law similar to the UK's Criminal Justice Act (SchNEWS 307). Perhaps this came as a response to the thousands who took to the streets of Paris and Marseille in simultaneous peaceful demonstrations a few weekends back as well as gaining support from people like Jean-Michel Jarre and the Green Party deputy. As an alternative, the socialists intend to propose a "charter" of good conduct which Teknival organisers will be invited to sign.

For more info check www.freetekno.org. Email marcgout@imaginet.fr and ask to be subscribed to the Kanyar mailing list for up to date info on parties on the continent.

SchNEWS in brief

The **Somers Town** People's Defense League are organising against the King's Cross Eurolink. Building begins 2nd July, bringing disruption and pollution, and tearing up a whole community. Open meeting with action planning, banner making etc.. on Friday night, actions on Saturday and Monday. Ring 07905 372 480 ** For the latest on the successful **bin strike** in Brighton (SchNEWS 308) go to the Brighton Collective Meeting, with Union reps and Magpie Recycling Co-op. Albert Pub, Trafalgar St. 7.30pm, 3 July. ** The new **Corporate Watch** email list has news, features, book reviews, briefings, dates etc. www.corporatewatch.org.uk ** **AMEC** is due to start construction work this Monday (2 July) on the Bingley Bypass. The Bingley Environmental Transport Association are asking people to join them in a non-violent protest march and picnic on Sunday 1st. Crossflatts Railway station, Bingley, Yorks 12 noon. a.j.plumbe@bradford.ac.uk ** In October last year a gang of youths went into **Broomfield School** and attacked a group of black students, one was hospitalised. Later that day, some of the students saw the attackers on a bus in Bounds Green and called the police. The police let the attackers go and turned on the black students. Three of them were assaulted, arrested, detained in cells and charged. The court case was postponed twice until last week they were finally cleared of all charges. marchagainstracism@yahoo.co.uk ** **Help!** Our phone/fax machine is dying, if anyone's got a spare let the SchNEWS crew know. And we still need help on Friday afternoons with the mail out and distribution round Kemptown. ** Walk to have **East Brighton Downs** included in the South Downs National Park. Meet Garden Centre Car park (by Racecourse). 8 July 10am, 01273-620815.

MAFF MEANZ NAFF

Tow Law is a burial site for a potential 300,000 animal carcasses slaughtered due to foot and mouth. Although it's filled with only 30,000 there have been leaks of deadly hydrogen sulphide gas. The Town Council has declared the site illegal on health and safety grounds, pending a Public Enquiry. Yet MAFF continues to dump regardless. Local people are now taking direct action, chaining themselves to the incoming trucks and so far 9 people including a 13 and 15 Year old face charges. One protestor is in court on the 2nd July and they are desperate for help with daily protest/defence costs. There's a video available about the protests costing £6 (cheques payable to 'Newlittlebighorn Defence Fund') 5 Elm Park Terrace, Tow Law, Co. Durham, DL13 4NH email Newlittlebighorn@aol.com

AVENTIS A BAD TIME

Poor Aventis. They've had all their 11 English National Seed List Trials of genetically engineered (GE) winter oil seed rape destroyed by covert actions or failing naturally, this leaves just two sites in Scotland. Two other Aventis crops in Dorset and Hertfordshire have both been damaged. Poor old Aventis didn't even recover costs from its damaged crops when various courts and judges ruled crop trashers were acting with a "positive purpose." For an updated list of test sites and their status visit www.geneticsaction.org.uk/testsites.

*The only GE crop in Wales is a farm-scale trail of Aventis maize at Sealand in Flintshire. There's a seminar 14th July, 10.30am Connahs Quay Civic Hall off Wepre Drive, Sealand, followed by a Citizens Inspection of the Site - grid reference SJ 697 862 - at 2.30pm. For transport from Camarthen, West Wales, Cardiff and Newport contact Jules 0774 779 2203 or Ken 01792 405887 to book a place ASAP.

* Dutch activists have been targeting Monsanto. Monsanto's only two GE sugar beet fields were destroyed by "Raging Hares".

SPAIN IN THE ASS

After the World Bank chickened out of their planned shindig in Barcelona last weekend (see SchNEWS 306) anti-capitalists decided that cos of all the hard work organising a counter demo and invites sent out it would be a shame not to carry on with the party. The day started with a 20,000 strong march headed by a samba band and dancers. On arrival at the main square, masked up under cover cops started throwing bottles at the assembled riot cops. How did people know they were cops? Well they were seen getting out of police vans and then masking up by a number of witnesses including the leader of the opposition party of Catalan. This gave police an excuse to fire volleys of plastic bullets into the crowd injuring 40 people. After this the real black block went "window shopping" with banks and posh stores getting the usual makeovers. An anarchist demo later in the day was also attacked without any warning leaving more activists needing hospital treatment whilst others spent the night in the cells.

The next day a 4000 strong jail solidarity march headed by the padded-up White Overall crew marched first to the stock exchange for a samba party and then on to the Court where they stayed until the prisoners were let free.

* Were you in the main square on the 24th when the police attacked. Have you any film evidence? Contact IndyMedia who are preparing a court case against the cops. http://barcelona.indymedia.org
* Among those nicked in Gothenburg (SchNEWS 310) was a Russian, Artem Chlenov. His crime was possessing souvenirs from Berlin squats, including the 'Radikal' paper, banned by German authorities way back in 1997! An EU police register, the Schengen Information System (SIS) supplied the info. It stores information about criminals, victims of crimes and possible victims of future crimes. Information includes names, nicknames, physical descriptions, sexual behaviour, friends and politics. The Swedish police saw the entry on Artem Chlenov, made four years before and held him for the sake of 'national security'. Terrorists eh?
* The Schengen agreement removed controls on internal movement between 13 European countries. This doesn't mean free movement because borders are policed by the SIS to "maintain public order and security, including state security".
* More info about the protestor who is critically ill after being shot by police in Gothenburg: Hannes Westberg suffered damage to his liver, spleen and one of his kidneys. He is still on a respirator in hospital although his condition is stable. There are reports that an additional two people were shot, which has been covered up by police and media, they were a journalist and a passer by, both have been released from hospital. E-mail suf_gbg@hotmail.com
* The Swedish authorities are in good company when shooting protestors. On Tuesday the Papua New Guinea government shot dead three students and wounded 17 others who were protesting against the IMF and World Bank, which is forcing a harsh privatisation regime on the country.

...and finally...

With the 4th of July nearly upon us the anti-corporate group Adbusters have come up with a different slant on the Stars and Stripes. The stars have all been changed to corporate logos. So now all you types that would normally be burning the US flag can now download the alternative from http://adbusters.org/ and join in the protest. As the organisers say "The spectacle of these flags snapping in the wind is sure to raise sparks. But many may look and think "dammit if that ain't the truth."

Subscribe!

Keep SchNEWS FREE! Send 1st Class stamps (e.g. 10 for next 9 issues) or donations (payable to Justice?) Ask for "Originals" if you can make copies. Post *free* to all prisoners. SchNEWS, c/o on-the-fiddle, P.O. Box 2600, Brighton, East Sussex, BN2 2DX.
Tel/Autofax +44 (0)1273 685913 *Email* schnews@brighton.co.uk *Download a* **PDF** *of this issue or subscribe at* www.schnews.org.uk

Kyoto Protocol: Money To Burn

Industrial societies have long been releasing excessive amounts of carbon from underground deposits of coal and oil, where it was safely sealed off from the atmosphere, into the air. It's now clear to everyone except the flat earth society that this burning of carbon-based fuels has set us on a collision course for climate chaos. It's also clear that the world's most highly industrialised countries - with the US firmly at the top of the list - have done the bulk of the damage.

Cue the United Nations on its shining white charger, riding into Kyoto to deal justly with this threat to the planet with a 'protocol' that rights all the wrongs. In your dreams…

The Kyoto Protocol is aimed initially only at rich industrialised countries, asking that they make a pathetic 5.2% average reduction of 1990 carbon emission levels by 2012, and, for the time being, countries in the 'global south' don't have to change. This appears like the industrialised countries are taking responsibility for the problems they know they've caused, keeping the onus away from the poorer economies for the moment. Again, sorry to disappoint…

Kyoto is not a positive change towards reducing greenhouse emissions, let alone a redressing of global imbalances, but rather a commodification of the atmosphere, a thriving new market with the same old business interests firmly in charge. For a start, a 5.2% reduction isn't remotely what's needed to halt climate change - try something nearer 60-90%. The Protocol is effectively not just business-as-usual for the energy and financial industries, but actually creates the conditions for them to keep growing.

Carbon Trading is a central part of the deal. This is a system where instead of actually reducing emissions, a system of credits is introduced, where permits to 'emit' can be bought instead of actually reducing emissions. It goes something like this: countries which are either using less than their quota of emissions, or say they can remove carbon dioxide from the atmosphere by planting something called a 'carbon sink' (that's a forest you and me), have credits to sell 'permits' to those who are spewing out more emissions than they should. For example if Russia doesn't need all the permits of greenhouse gas output which it was granted in 1997, it can then sell the surplus to Europe or Japan, who may decide that reducing emissions by 6% was too expensive, and a cheaper option is to buy cheap emissions permits from elsewhere. It won't need to buy permits for the remaining 94%: these it already has "title" to, free of charge - at least until 2008.

This is a key inequality of Kyoto - that from the outset every country is given permits to spew out what it's already spewing (minus the paltry 5.2%). So in this privatisation of the atmosphere, the worst polluters continue to get a vastly disproportionate licence to pollute, as they drag the rest of the world towards climatic catastrophe. The succession of UN conferences (known as COP's, or Conference of the Parties) which have been held since Kyoto have led the protocol firmly towards a new carbon trading market, with oil industry lobbyists weaving in loopholes wherever possible, pushing the fact of this global inequality to one side, and the prevention of climate change on the other. The most recent meeting - November 2001's COP7 in Marrakech - was no different, and it's unlikely that there will be a change at October 2002's COP8 in New Delhi either.

How can you earn these 'carbon credits' in this emerging new market of the carbo-industrial complex? Not only by planting trees, but also rearranging traffic signals (!), 'managing' forests, or even burning more coal - provided you can show that these are resulting in fewer greenhouse gas emissions than "would otherwise be the case".

George W Bush's withdrawal from the climate negotiations means very little at this point because Kyoto isn't even a very small step in the right direction, and essentially the oil lobby have got what they wanted.

On The Rocks

An iceberg 40 miles wide and 53 miles long, covering 2,130 square miles, has broken off Antarctica. The National Ice Centre reports that the berg broke free from an ice tongue in the Amundsen Sea, an area of Antarctica south of the Pacific Ocean. Must be time to rearrange the deckchairs again.

THE CASE AGAINST CARBON TRADING

(From Rising Tide)

CARBON TRADING IS CONTRARY TO SOCIAL JUSTICE

THE LARGEST RESOURCE GRAB IN HISTORY: You can't trade in something unless you own it. When governments and companies "trade" in carbon, they establish de facto property rights over the atmosphere. At no point have these atmospheric property rights been discussed - their ownership is established by stealth with every carbon trade.

THE CARBON TRADE WILL STRENGTHEN EXISTING INE-QUALITIES: Shares in the new carbon market will be allocated on the basis of who is already the largest polluter and who is fastest to exploit the market. The new "carbocrats" will therefore be the global oil, chemical and car corporations and the richest nations; the very groups that created the problem of climate change in the first place. What's more, the richest nations and corporations will be able to further increase their global share of emissions by outbidding poorer interests for carbon credits.

SO-CALLED SOLUTIONS POSE A DIRECT THREAT TO VULNERABLE PEOPLES: Development projects such as nuclear energy, large dams and other large-scale, hi-tech projects - as well as tree planting - have come to be known as Joint Implementation and Clean Development Mechanisms in the Kyoto Protocol and are tradable. But they assert foreign ownership of local resources, consolidate the power of undemocratic elites, oust people from their land and undermine local self sufficient economies and low-carbon cultures.

CLIMATE CHANGE REFUGEES: Displacement of peoples caused by the large scale projects on their land, as well as those who have had to leave land because of climate change effects such as droughts or flooding, are turning millions into refugees.

ECOLOGICAL DEBT TO 'SOUTH' NOT ADDRESSED: Repayment of the ecological debt of the north to the south, which is caused by the extraction, use and destruction of southern resources such as fossil fuels, minerals, forests, marine and genetic resources, is not acknowledged. Neither is the fact that while a small number of highly industrialised countries have caused the damage, all countries suffer the consequences of climate change.

MANY OF THE SOURCES OF CARBON CREDITS ARE SCAMS

TREE PLANTING IS NOT A SOLUTION TO CLIMATE CHANGE: Carbon absorbed by forests is only removed from the carbon cycle for as long as the tree is standing and alive. Industrial forestry will not sequester (breathe in) carbon.

CARBON TRADING ALLOWS COMPANIES TO PROFIT FROM MEASURES THAT WOULD HAVE BEEN INTRODUCED ANYWAY: Because we cannot know the future, we cannot be certain that a project selling carbon credits has really reduced its emissions further than would have occurred without this intervention. Competition and technical innovation, for example, ensure that industry consistently reduces its energy costs. For example, British Airways, an early supporter of the new UK emissions trading system, is claiming financial credits from the government for the cut in emissions caused by the collapse of its business after September 11th last year, (actually it was in trouble long before S11, and simply used it as a convenient hook on which to hang extensive job cuts...)

"HOT AIR" TRADING IS AN ACCOUNTING FRAUD: Russia's economic collapse since 1990 has reduced its emissions by 30%. Russia is intending to sell this incidental windfall (often call "hot air") as international carbon cred-

its - potentially swamping the market. If countries subsidise their emissions with these Russian credits, the final global emissions will end up being exactly the same as they would have been without a carbon market or a Kyoto protocol.

HUGE INCENTIVES FOR CHEATING: There are strong incentives for cheating and creating bogus credits that do not represent any real reduction in emissions. The seller gets the cash without having to change anything and the buyer gets cheap credits. And what's to stop you transferring polluting activities to areas that are not accounted?

CARBON TRADING CANNOT WORK

THE CARBON MARKET CANNOT BE MONITORED OR CONTROLLED: The temptation for all parties to cheat means that every transaction must be scrutinised and every sale certified. Yet there is no global institution or accounting system that can manage the complexity of this market.

THE LEGAL FRAMEWORK WILL NEVER BE STRONG ENOUGH: International legal frameworks are usually very weak. Countries that want to use carbon credits to subsidise their emissions are already arguing for penalties so small they will fail to discourage cheating. The door is open for any country desperate for foreign currency to endorse doctored carbon credits.

CARBON CREDITS FROM DIFFERENT SOURCES ARE NOT EQUIVALENT: The market assumes that carbon credits from different sources will be fully interchangeable. However, carbon sequestered in sinks (that is breathed in by forests) is an entirely different product from the carbon "saved" by a technical innovation, which is different again from the carbon "saved" by changes in social patterns. Add to this the complexity of trading in different greenhouse gases. Each source requires different monitoring rules, different criteria and different agencies. Forcing them to be interchangeable in one market is a recipe for corruption and fraud.

THE REAL REASONS FOR CARBON TRADING

* Governments want to be assured of a cheap way to buy off their failure to meet Kyoto targets that will keep the public and corporations content.

* Brokers, accountants, and financial institutions are extremely excited at the thought of the size of their cut in a new $2.3 trillion speculative market.

* Corporations and other major polluters want "flexible" governments who don't punish them for their emissions and hand over public money to pay for any emissions they are forced to make.

* Oil companies support carbon trading as a way to avoid making any cuts in oil production.

* Academics and financial consultants see rich pickings from becoming "experts" in the new market.

SOLUTIONS TO CLIMATE CHANGE

* Educate the public on the urgency of climate change and the need for dramatic solutions.

* Set a schedule for cutting global fossil fuel consumption by 60%, and 90% within ten years.

* Recognise the moral (and political) imperative for fairness and social justice by allocating targets to every country on the basis of equal per capita emissions.

* Reduce the supply of fossil fuels with an international ban on all new oil, gas and coal development. As a first step, cut the $200 billion per year global subsidies for coal and oil power. Carbon trading is not concerned with the supply of fossil fuels, which is why oil companies support it. As a result, government subsidies are increasing, reducing the price of energy and swamping any attempts at reducing demand.

* Invest heavily in renewable energy to replace all fossil fuel supplies. Right now funding renewables is a far more expensive way to reduce carbon emissions than credits from bogus "hot air", tree planting, or outright fraud. These cheap carbon credits will dictate the market price.

* Involve all people in the achievement of climate justice - particularly those most affected in the 'global south'.

WAKE UP! IT'S YER FORTIFIED AND ENRICHED

Weekly SchNEWS

SIS

Printed and Published in Brighton by Justice?

Friday 6th July 2001 | www.schnews.org.uk | Issue 312 Free/Donation

Big SIS is Watching You

"Everyone was told the Schengen agreement was all about the removal of internal borders. In fact 98% of it was about police co-operation, internal security, public order and securing external borders."   *- - Statewatch.*

As thousands of protestors head to Genoa to demonstrate against the G8 summit later this month, European leaders are putting their heads together to try to stop those pesky anti-capitalist demonstrators in their tracks.

More laws, closed borders and increased police co-operation are all on the agenda with a special meeting being planned later this month for ministers to talk about safety at future EU summits. Not that the authorities don't already have an arsenal of measures at their disposal.

One of these is the Schengen Information System (SIS) first dreamt up in the late eighties by interior ministry officials in secret working parties. A computerised information exchange system whose purpose is "to maintain public order and security" SIS stores peoples names, descriptions, nicknames, sexual behaviour, habits, friends, political opinions and membership of organisations. You don't have to have done anything wrong to have your details stored with much of the SIS info 'intelligence' based on suspicions. Dr Heiner Busch from Germany's Citizens Rights and Policing complained that "The amount of data is growing and growing." By the end of the year it's predicted it will have 14 million pieces of information (much of it false) including details on 1.9 million people. 15 countries have now signed up to SIS.

32 year old Artem Chlenov became a victim of SIS when he was arrested at a peaceful demonstration against police brutality in Gothenburg last month (see SchNEWS 310). After he was nicked he was put in isolation "for the sake of national security" and has been there ever since. Artem's crime was that in 1997 he was with a group of Russians travelling by train from Berlin to Prague when he was stopped at the border and his visa queried. He was eventually let through. However, he had a collection of souvenirs from Berlin squats, including the Radikal newspaper, which was eventually banned by the German authorities, but which Artem couldn't even read as he only speaks Russian. Still, that was enough proof to be labelled a potential terrorist and to be recorded on SIS. A record which Swedish police picked up more than four years later.

In 1998, Stephanie Mills, a Greenpeace activist from New Zealand who had flown into Holland, was denied access to the whole Schengen area because the French government had entered her and other Greenpeace activists names into the SIS.

Europol-axed

The Schengen Agreement promised open borders for "markets, goods, services and people" but a get-out clause says that borders can be closed or controlled "where public policy and national security so require...". There is no time limit for the suspension of borders and countries can inform their neighbours *after* they've been closed. Earlier this year Belgium re-introduced border controls to stop (they claimed) record numbers of Romanian refugees seeking asylum.

At the weekend Austria re-imposed border controls turning people away who were trying to get to the protests against the World Economic Forum. This tactic was also used recently by Czech Republic to stop IMF protestors getting to Prague, and in Slovenia for USA President Bush's meeting with Russian premier Putin. Now Italian officials are promising the same treatment for demonstrators against the G8. They've warned they will halt what's been called dubbed the 'Anarchist Express' long before it reaches Genoa. Italian police have promised to stop and search everybody with British cops on hand to help identify 'troublemakers' who will then immediately be deported.

BOOKED

In the UK the Football (Disorder) Act gives police powers to arrest and detain people they believe *might* commit offences and gives magistrates the power to issue banning-orders where there were "reasonable grounds" that it would "help" prevent disorder. How long before 'emergency legislation' could be extended to anti-capitalist protestors? Stephen Jakobi from Fair Trials Abroad said the "notion of hooliganism is expanding. Anyone who demonstrates will be seen as a hooligan."

This is already happening in Germany. During last weekend's protests in Austria a 20-year-old German student was one of four political activists classified by the German police as 'dangerous troublemakers'. Her passport was taken away and she had to report to a cop station twice a day. If she tried to leave the country she would have faced a year in gaol. She was arrested during anti-globalisation protests in Davos earlier

in the year (see SchNEWS 292). No charges have ever been brought against her but her details were taken and added to the German Federal Crime Office database.

So what does happen to all the names and addresses of people arrested en masse at anti-capitalist protests around Europe but never charged? A spokesman from Statewatch told SchNEWS "Data will certainly be shared and, since there's no enforceable data protection rules for such exchanges, copied into whatever databases or files that the receiving state decides." Which is reassuring. As one of Artem's friends put it "you better not travel in EU with the wrong magazines, wrong company, wrong ideas or wrong outlook. All these are enough reason to record you to SIS, and be the next international terrorist to be locked up."

* For details of how to help Artem go to www.tao.ca/~dikobraz/freeartem (but you'll have to speak Russian).

* Despite 5,000 police who threatened to "shoot at protesters", strict border controls, and most protests being banned there were still demonstrations against the World Economic Forum in Salzburg. To find out what happened check out http://austria.indymedia.org/

* SISNET, is SIS the next generation with plans for it to be up and running in time for European Union enlargement. It will enable the electronic transmission of photos, fingerprints and DNA. Finland wants it to go even further with "real-time video and sound", including that obtained during undercover surveillance operations.

* Police forces from Europe, North America and Australia have all been invited to an international conference "maintaining public order: a democratic approach" in The Hague at the beginning of October.

* To find out more about how big sis' and bro' are watching you contact Statewatch, PO BOX 1516, London, N16 0EW. Tel 020-8802-1882 www.statewatch.org/news

Star Billing

It's been kicking off in Cyprus with 1000 angry locals attacking British Military Police, injuring 40, destroying the police station and burning vehicles at the British Episkopi military base. It happened after the arrest of Cypriot MP Marios Matsakis who was leading a campaign to stop the building of a 190 metre high radio mast which is needed for "the UK military's global communications network" (in other words for spying). It will emit radiation that could cause cancers and will ruin the natural habitat of the lake, home to migratory pink flamingos. The MP also claims the mast will be used in part of the Star Wars programme.

The British high commissioner in Cyprus described Marios as "a medical monkey stuck up a stick", presumably he wants to cut Marios open for medical research.

* On US Independence Day over 100 Greenpeace activists invaded Menwith Hill US spy base in Yorkshire to protest against Britain's impending involvement in Star Wars, which provoke a new arms race (SchNEWS 307).

* Trident Ploughshares are having a direct disarmament camp at Coulport on Loch Long, Scotland (near the Trident nuclear warhead store) from 27 July to 11 August. 0845-4588361 www.tridentploughshares.org/

Bank Of Weapons

Bolivian workers have had enough of being exploited by corrupt, neo-liberal private banks, so last Monday kicked things off with a bang. 1000 Workers occupied the government's bank authority and detained 94 of the institution's top brass and tied bundles of dynamite to them to make the police behave themselves! Gasoline was sprayed outside the superintendent's office meanwhile from the balcony - in between speeches, and singing - dynamite and molotov cocktails exploded onto the la Católica plaza below.

After three months 12,000 workers (and debtors) have converged on La Paz to protest against the private banks' exorbitant interest charges, and the impounding of their meagre goods - many have lost everything and are living on the street, while the banks dish out funds to venture capitalists. A statement from Juventudes Libertarias (Anarchist Youth) read "The Bolivian government is openly fascist. The genocidal President-General Banzer has murdered many social fighters during the four years of his regime. We denounce the human rights clowns, the reactionary Catholic Church and the Bank vultures as makers of a smoke screen to divert attention to the negotiating table while the government prepares its dogs to execute a bloodbath".
* Twelve days ago Aymara farmers blocked highways in the Altiplano region to demand an end to neoliberalism – two were murdered. www.come.to/jlb (in Spanish)

Spill the milk

Nestlé's plans to open a new café in Bristol turned sour this weekend when activists disguised as job seekers 'applied' for work. Interviews went out of the window as the would-be 'employees' asked managers why they should want to work for Nestle. Spawn of East Croydon, Nestlé continues to pressurise the world's poorest mothers into buying powdered milk for their babies. As a result, the mothers' milk, rich in essential antibodies dries up and babies fed on the milk powder and water mix get an often lethal dose of water-borne diseases. More actions are planned and if you'd love to work for Nestlé for £4.20 an hour selling their crap coffee give the New Era recruitment team a ring on 0117-908-1241 or email NEWERA2000LTD@aol.com www.babymilkaction.org

SchNEWS in brief

Pirate Radio 4A is broadcasting across Brighton this weekend (6-8 July) on 106.6FM, its also on www.piratetv.net. To get involved phone 07980168115 or email radio4a@hotmail.com ** **The Other Israel** is a bi-monthly peace movement magazine. Hard copies from pob 2542, Holon 58125, Israel. Email version otherisr@actcom.co.il ** Check out: '**Trading Health Care Away?** GATS, Public Services and Privatisation' by Sarah Sexton. The Corner House, 01258-473795 www.icaap.org/ Cornerhouse ** **Nottingham University** who recently accepted £3.8 million from British American Tobacco to fund the study of ethics in its business school is now holding talks with **Monsanto**, the world's leading producer of GM foods for funding of the Institute for the Study of Genetics, Bio-risks and Society. ** The **Rainforest Action Network** is being targeted by right wing groups in America, supported by the Oil, Timber and Tobacco industries. RAN runs highly visible, aggressive campaigns against corporations destroying old growth forests in North America and around the world. These corporations are trying to fight back by threatening RANS funding. A spokesman for RAN says that despite the threats "the work to protect our forests will not only continue, but escalate." www.ran.org ** Brighton-based **Don't Fuel Climate Change** are organising a demo against Bush and US oil interests this Saturday (7th), 10:30am outside Esso, Lewes Road. ** Local council bigots have bowed to moral objectors and issued this year's **Bournemouth Pride (**3-5 Aug) with a very limited licence. In order that 'normal people' don't have to see gay men and women the event cannot start before 5pm and must end by 9pm! Undeterred by local intolerance/discrimination the event will still take place minus the "party in the park". 09065-666500 www.pridebournmouth.com ** **Pride in Brighton and Hove** will take place in Preston Park, Aug 11th following a carnival procession through town. Dust down yer sequined dresses and join in the fun, www.prideinbrightonandhove.com ** For over two years residents in **Derby** have been fighting plans to demolish their central Bus station and replace it with a smaller less accessible one. The proposals also include destroying the peace and quiet of Riverside Gardens with pubs, nightclubs, and cinema etc. As usual politicians are not listening and the residents are threatening direct action . http://beehive.thisisderbyshire.co.uk/derbyfoe ** **RIP: Sicknote** who tragically drowned last week. He was well known around protest campfires up and down the country from Fairmile to Newbury to Manchester Airport to Nine Ladies.

Positive SchNEWS

After opening up a community centre in Blaenllechau village, a small welsh ex-mining village, in 1996 the Community Blaenllechau Regeneration Programme is celebrating the opening of community allotments this Saturday (7). They already runs a credit union, cafe, chip shop, youth drop-in centre and a 106-acre permaculture farm and is an example of the how the community can take control of its own environment. Info 01443 730749, Ffaldau2000@hotmail.com

Blood Money

"The UK Government support for arms exports and the defence industry has been based for too long on an unchallenged belief that it is good for jobs, the economy and our military." - Dr Ian Davis, Arms and Security Programme Manager at Saferworld.

While the UK government continues to cut subsidies to hospitals and schools by forcing them into Public Private Partnerships (SchNEWS 257& 293) it is reassuring to find that there are no such plans a foot for the UK arms industry! A new report from the Oxford Research Group and Saferworld reveals how the UK government spends around £420 million annually to subsidise the arms trade. Who said New Labour-New Bastards?

At a cost of £69 million to the taxpayer, the Defence Export Services Organisation (DESO) works endlessly to find tin-pot dictators and heavily indebted countries to sell the latest British weapons to. When an arms export deal is struck, SchNEWS faves, the Export Credit Guarantee Department, step in to underwrite any credit agreement, after all heavily indebted countries are by their very nature skint, the last thing they can afford are new tanks and war planes and might just default on repayments. Annual cost to the UK taxpayer £227m. But it gets better, any costs incurred by arms firms in winning export contracts with foreign governments i.e. bribes and other corrupt practices are all of course tax deductible, wonderful! Annual cost to the taxpayer around £64m.

The government claims that arms exports and supporting a UK defence industry are vital for jobs. So vital in fact that the subsidy works out at £4,600 for each of the 90,000 jobs (or just 0.3% of UK employment) reliant on arms exports! The ending of ALL subsidies to the UK arms industry, an industry that continues to prolong poverty and suffering around the world, would save the government a further £4billion! www.oxfordresearchgroup.org.uk/

* Ever wanted to buy some guns, tanks or cluster bombs to kill pesky protestors? If you are a nasty dictator you'll be welcomed with open arms at the Defence Systems and Equipment International arms fair at the Excel Centre, London Docklands, 11-14 September. Maybe you'll be able to pick up some landmines, they're banned under international law but they got away with it last time.

Mind you, if you're a peace protestor please don't turn up on the opening day for A Fiesta for Life Against Death, and don't call 020-72810297 or visit www.disarm-trade.org, to find out how you and your mates can get involved.

...and finally...

The law doesn't just have a long arm… A shame faced Tonbridge custody sergeant with 26 years experience has been fined £500 and could lose his job and pension for flashing at old ladies in a retirement home. The 21 stone copper told magistrates that he had not realised his private parts were on display because he was so fat, and couldn't see beyond his stomach! SchNEWS supposes he'd have been promoted if he'd shot someone with his weapon instead of showing it off.

♪ ♪♪ **Disclaimer** ♪♪ ♪♪
"Ya put yer fatcats in, ya kick yer asylum seeker out, you ban your anti-capitalists, then ya Schengen it all about."

SCREENING INJUSTICE

by Ken Fero (director of 'Injustice') & Tariq Mehmood

Countries where police and paramilitary forces kill with impunity, where the press sings to the rulers tune and journalists who dare to write about what they see are stopped either by force or by threats of legal action are described by the United Kingdoms politicians and media as dictatorships. But in the UK, police officers can kill, safe in the knowledge that they will not be prosecuted for their actions, even if they are found by a jury to have been unlawfully killed.

Since 1969 over 1000 people have died in police custody. No police officer has ever been convicted for any of these deaths. INJUSTICE exposes and opposes this outrage. It is a call for justice by the families of the deceased. It is a voice the police are now trying to stop.

Jasmine Elvie, mother of Brian Douglas who died in police custody in 1995: 'Before this I was shy, I'd never been a public speaker' she tells a crowd in the film.

Voices rising

On 6th July 2001 at 6.30 p.m. INJUSTICE was due to be officially launched at the Metro Cinema in London. In the audience there were many relatives of people who had died in police custody. Some had traveled hundreds of miles for the viewing. The screening was the culmination of seven years of work and was to be the platform for the films national release later in the year. With a run already secured at the Ritzy Cinema and other cinemas to follow, INJUSTICE was breaking ground in putting feature length documentaries on the big screen. Apart from the international press present, there were diplomatic representatives from a number of embassies who were there to find out more about the human rights abuses that the film documents.

Reviews had been strong. The Guardian called it "one of the most despairing and powerful films ever made in this country". The Gleaner called it "moving and militant". On the week of the Metro launch the film received Critics Choice in Time Out which called it a "powerful polemical documentary". The ongoing press and television interest in the launch meant that outside the cinema, news crews from all over the world were holding interviews with the filmmakers and the families of those who had died. Many people were meeting for the first time, for some the evening was bringing back memories of how their brother, mother, sister or husband had died. Some of them would be seeing INJUSTICE for the first time so the atmosphere was charged. This was also to be a celebration, and a declaration to the world that the families would not stop fighting for justice.

Police attack

The mood soon changed. At 6.11 p.m. the director of the Metro Cinema received a fax from the lawyers of two police officers. The solicitors threatened the cinema with a claim for substantial damages should it show INJUSTICE. They represented Police Officer Paul Harrison, who was involved in the death of Brian Douglas and Police Officer Stephen Highton, the custody officer when Ibrahim Sey was unlawfully killed. The letter from Russell, Jones & Walker to the Metro Cinema stated: "You should be aware that should your screening go ahead, our clients will have no hesitation in pursuing their rights against your company for very substantial damages that will be their only means of compensation and vindication." The Metro had to decide within minutes whether they should go ahead with the screening.

The decision was taken. In the cinema Eva Kirkhope, the director of the Metro stood before a stunned audience and read out the police solicitors letter. Some of the family members burst out crying in disbelief. Others in the audience demanded the cinema go ahead with the screening. Many of them had spent years fighting their case and at every step of the way police solicitors, the press office of the Metropolitan Police Service, the Police Complaints Authority and the Crown Prosecution had effectively gagged their voices. Now they were trying to do

it again. The very heart of the film, that the officers responsible should be prosecuted for these deaths, was being threatened. Eva wanted to consult her lawyers but in view of lack of time it was not possible. She was a widow, trying to raise two children and the cinema was her livelihood. As such she could take no risk and pulled INJUSTICE. The film was under attack from the police. As filmmakers we went on national television and spoke about the appalling distress the actions of the police had caused the families that night. We also made the point that no matter how hard they tried the police could never suppress the film which had already gained international interest. As usual the police refused to comment. The next days headlines read: "Film Screening pulled after police legal threat" The Independent and "Death in Custody film halted by police action" The Guardian.

We issued a press statement in which we vowed to fight on. We stated: "In a letter which was sent to the Metro Cinema at 6.11 p.m., only 19 minutes before the scheduled screening, Russell, Jones & Walker Solicitors make inaccurate claims about the content of the film. One of the officers they represent is not even named in the film. Out of the three main cases those of Ibrahim Sey and Shiji Lapite resulted in inquest verdicts of unlawful killing. In the third case, that of Brian Douglas, the film presents overwhelming evidence for the prosecution of the two officers involved, one of whom is represented by the solicitors. We are appalled at the bullying tactics that the police have employed to stop the film being shown."

Active Audience

Over the next few days Migrant Media booked Conway Hall, run by the South Place Ethical Society. It was important to screen the film urgently and not to bow down to the police threats. Conway Hall were well known to have a policy of standing up for freedom of speech. By now we had engaged David Price Solicitors, a firm specialising in media libel, who had provided a legal opinion that could safeguard Conway Hall in the event that the police try to stop the film again.

On Wednesday July 11th families began to gather at the Hall. As the screening time approach people who had come from as far as Manchester, Liverpool and Birmingham arrived. Around 5.45 p.m. Conway Hall started received faxes from Police solicitors threatening legal action against the screening of INJUSTICE. We hoped that they would be able to stand up to police pressure. They didn't. There were around 250 people in the hall at this time. The manager switched on the lights making it impossible to see the film. He informed the audience that he could not show the film because of the legal threats. People were shocked. Many families had been at the Metro the previous Friday and they began to protest, angrily.

The manager refused the requests for allowing the screening to go ahead. For some it was the final straw. A cry went out: "Let's occupy the hall". The audience took control of the projector and started running the film. The manager threatened to turn the power off. Some people rushed to stop this from happening. As the struggle between the manager and the audience intensified, around 50 people drifted away from the screening. INJUSTICE continued to be screened, with many people in the audience shedding tears at the suffering and showing pride at the resistance on the screen.

Conway Hall called the police. On hearing this, the audience barricaded the doors and continued to screen INJUSTICE. Two police officers arrived a few minutes later but after discussing the situation with them they agreed that it was a civil matter and left without taking any action. Some lights were still on and this affected the quality of the projection. Having to watch families of those killed by police watching a film about the death of their loved ones in these conditions was intolerable. But at the same time there was a feeling of strength and power in the audience. They had taken an important stand not just in support of the film but as a group of people prepared to stand up against police threats. It was a night that many of them said they would never forget.

The events of Conway Hall were widely reported: "Audience hijacks hall to see death in custody film" *Evening Standard*. "Injustice goes ahead, despite threats" *Screen International*. "Crowd defies death film legal threats" *The Metro*. The next day we gave television and radio interviews, as always making the struggle of the families central to our arguments. We demanded that the police desist from their actions and allowed people to see INJUSTICE, without intimidation and threats. We have continued to show our film wherever people have asked us to and will continue to do so.

Marking the struggle

Even before the police's attempts to suppress the film it had already been screened in London. On Thursday 5th April 2001, INJUSTICE was shown at the Ritzy Cinema in Brixton. It was fitting that the film had its pre-launch in an area of London in which Brian Douglas, one of the men killed by police and featured in the film, grew up and lived. It was also the 20th anniversary of the Brixton uprisings when Black youth had taken to the street and rebelled against police that had been harassing them. INJUSTICE was being screened as the closing night film for the US based Human Rights Watch International Film Festival. There were two showings of both to packed houses. The audience included the families and friends of those who died in police custody. They sat in an emotionally charged first screening. Some of the audience wept, others were angry at the brutality of the police officers and the inhumanity of the judicial system. Throughout there was pin drop silence, broken by cries of disbelief or shouts encouraging the struggles on screen. Many people were shocked at the deaths but they were also impressed by the courage and resilience shown by the families portrayed so powerfully in the film.

At the end of the film the audience sat in a momentary contemplative silence and then participated in a lively debate featuring the families of Joy Gardner, Brian Douglas, Christopher Alder and Harry Stanley. Each family gave an update on what was happening in their cases and also on the coalition they had formed, the United Families and Friend Campaign, which the film had captured the birth of. People wanted to know how they could help. The families urged the audience to come and join the campaigns and gave dates of the next few major events. Many wanted to know how they could get the film shown in colleges and community centres across London, nationally and internationally.

Keeping the spirit

After Conway Hall the police strategy had become clear when they began to threaten every organisation, cinema or venue that wanted to show INJUSTICE with libel actions. They were trying to ban the film using intimidation. The film exposes human rights abuses which they believed they had covered up. It depicts the frustrations that families had experienced as every door they opened in their search for justice was slammed in their faces. The police were trying to use the same technique to try and gag the film. Our response has been to out manoeuvre their 'legal terrorism' and make sure the film lives on. In some senses INJUSTICE has taken on the spirit of the dead people who we are trying to help get justice for.

Even as we struggle to show the film in cinemas, on the streets the deaths continue. On Thursday 12th July Andrew Kernan, was shot dead in Liverpool. On Monday 16th July Derek Bennett, was shot six times by police in Brixton. He was taken to King's College Hospital where he was pronounced dead. On the 17th July we arranged a press screening of INJUSTICE at the Cornerhouse Cinema in Manchester. The police solicitors wrote to us demanding the names of those who had been in attendance. We refused to give them the names in order to protect the journalists present. The number of officers they were representing had also increased and now included police officer Mark Tuffey, who had hit Brian Douglas with such force on his head that he fractured his skull causing his death and police officer Jackie Cannon who had sprayed CS gas in Ibrahim Sey's face as he was restrained by at least four other officers.

The controversy over the film was increasing. On the 24th July the film was screened by the Metropolitan Police Authority, the body meant to oversee the police in London. The solicitors wrote to the MPA wanting them to stop the screening but it went ahead. After the screening the Police Federation, the organisation that was backing the officers in their legal action was told to "grow up" by Lord Harris the Chair of the MPA. Apart from Channel 4 News, television crews from Iran, France and Japan covered the story.

Two days later, on the 26th July INJUSTICE was pulled hours before a public screening at the Cornerhouse Cinema in Manchester after legal threats but an alternative venue has been arranged so the film still filled the hearts of over 150 people in Manchester that night and many vowed to arrange other screenings. For us every person that sees the film is a victory. Now it is hundreds, soon it will be thousands. Then it will be millions.

As the battle intensified we challenged the police to sue us and by the end of August they had gone quiet. Over the last few months Injustice has been screened in Vienna, Derry, Belfast, New York and Tehran. International Film Festivals have selected the film for 2002 and it has begun a cinema run in central London and across the UK. All these screenings have raised the issue of deaths in police custody to an international level and the families are also beginning to organise at an international level.

The power of the film is in the words of the families. Towards the end of the film Brenda Weinberg, the sister of Brian Douglas, reflects the burning feelings felt in many audiences: "Dead is dead it's permanent, it's forever and wanting justice for that death is also forever. It's a forever wanting. I will always want it and will never rest until it's achieved. If it's meeting MPs, if it's joining groups or campaigning or fighting or making a damned nuisance of myself. That wanting of justice and eventually getting it is my goal because I can't grieve, I can't put Brian to rest, ever, if I know someone's walking around out there responsible for his death and they haven't been taken to justice. The only thing that does happen is that as the time gets longer it's any kind of justice. It can be legal justice or street justice. I don't really care anymore."

INJUSTICE is a film that the world needs to see. It is as much a film about family love as it is about resistance. It is at the forefront of the struggles of the families who want to see the police officers responsible for the deaths of their loved ones prosecuted and convicted for their crimes. It is just a matter of time.

www.injusticefilm.co.uk

WAKE UP! WAKE UP! IT'S YER REALLY COLOURFUL!

Weekly SchNEWS

Printed and Published in Brighton by Justice?

Friday 13th July 2001   www.schnews.org.uk   Issue 313

Burnley Bradford
Oldham
NO RIGHT TURN

Race Against Time

"We took direct action ourselves, never again will we be pushed off our own streets, forced into hiding in our houses, keeping our heads down. 'Community leaders' have always sold us out. We're fighting back and won't be betrayed. This is 'anti-capitalism' at its most vocal, a community in revolt." **Anon, posted on Indymedia website**

Last weekend Bradford became the fourth northern town this summer to erupt into rioting, with the spark once again the threat of the British National Party (BNP) marching in a town with a large ethnic population. But with all the major political parties using issues like asylum as a cheap political football, backed up by the media fascists have been rubbing their hands with glee. BNP party leader Nick Griffin commented "The asylum seeker issue has been great for us. We have had phenomenal growth in membership. It's been quite fun to watch government ministers and the Tories play the race card in far cruder terms than we would ever use, but pretend not to. This issue legitimises us." As a recent report to the UN Human Rights Committee concludes "Negative presentation of asylum seekers has not only led to direct attacks on asylum seekers but also an underlying greater hostility towards all those from ethnic minority communities, and heightened racial tensions. In our view, the recent riots in Oldham and Bradford are to an extent directly linked to the above."

Even before the general election the BNP have been helping to whip up the resentment felt by many whites who feel their own needs are being ignored in favour of people of other racial backgrounds. Of course, the Asian people of Bradford, Oldham and Burnley are not the cause of unemployment and poor housing, but in the eyes of some, egged on by the BNP, they remain the most immediate and plausible target for their anger.

In Britain such talk helped Griffin poll 16.4% of the vote in the Oldham West, the largest ever for a fascist party in a parliamentary election. Now the fascists are eyeing up next year's local elections with the hope of winning council seats around the country.

As one anti-racist put it, "We must engage in a real debate with those who voted BNP. They are not nazis and their grievances, many of them real, must not be dismissed out of hand."

Or as Rev Kenneth Leech wrote in the foreword to 'Brick Lane 1978': "The battle against racism and fascism cannot be won by outsiders who march into an area, chant slogans, and then march out again; it can only be won by the most dedicated, rooted and persistent commitment to undermine and destroy the injustice and neglect on which such movements thrive".

But the riot was not just about the BNP. It might have been an initial spur, to ignite the massive anger but the explosion was a long time coming. One person commented "The people of Bradford had had enough, from a political and economic system that is based on exploitation and discrimination". One Asian added "Look mate, this is a high unemployment area, a fucking BMW garage in here is an insult to this community, why shouldn't we burn it?"

Getting Shirty

The tactics of stirring up race hatred, of blaming other ethnic minorities for the problems such as bad housing are not new. A look into the past shows how diverse groups from churches and communists to Jewish ex-servicemans groups stopped the spread of fascism by offering concrete support in improving peoples living conditions.

During the 1930s and 40s Oswald Mosley's British Union of Fascists was trying to get a stronghold targetting the East End of London. Solley Kaye was one of those involved in fighting them. "You had massive unemployment, immense poverty, social services nowhere near what they are today, terrible slums. The fascists had their strongholds in places like Bethnal Green, Shoreditch, South Hackney, parts of Poplar, all of which were on the edge of Stepney where the large Jewish population lived. So that they could involve people on the basis of envy, fear, or whatever, they said 'the Jews, they've got your houses, the Jews, they've got your jobs.' Even though we were all living in bloody poverty with bugs crawling all over us in the night.

"At the time the Communist Party together with some very courageous Church people, organised the Stepney Tenants Defence League, and all the tenants living in bad houses were being involved in a fight to get the repairs done and the rents reduced. There were some people being evicted from a block of flats called Paragon Mansions, Phil Piratin (later to become a Communist M.P.) heard about it. He went there and got the rest of the tenants to organise barricades to stop the bailiffs coming in." Some of the tenants were members of the British Union of Fascists, but they didn't want anything to do with them after they saw who their real allies were.

The turning point came in 1936 when a quarter of a million people stopped Mosley's party marching through the East End. His party never recovered with another

veteran anti-fascist Mick Mindel recalling, "The victory on 4 October 1936 was very sweet. Of course the fascists did not stop their attacks in the East End but it made many young Jews recognise the need to stand up and fight and realise that together with non-Jews they could defeat the racists and fascists. Our experience was like that of many young Asians today who learn the lessons of struggle through direct experience: they see their families attacked and some decide to stand up and be counted."

This country has had a wake up call - if we don't get our act together then racism and fascism will continue to grow. On the other hand, as journalist and activist Ally Fogg told SchNEWS, "The British Asian uprising of 2001 could be a healthy, momentous occurrence IF the people involved keep sight of their targets - racist police, racist system, racist state. If they get sucked into thinking that it is Asian v. White, then it could be disastrous for race relations and for the wider struggle for justice and equality."

As for New Labour… Well they, like the police, are blaming the riots on a hardcore of 'mindless hooligans' and 'outside agitators' (now where have we heard those phrases before?). While places like Oldham and Bradford are crying out for greater integration between the different communities, New Labour have got something else in mind: tear gas, water cannons and other new toys to help riot cops crush anyone who dares to fight back.

* Recommended reading: 'Keep the Red Flag Flying' by Phil Piratin (one time councillor and Communist MP who helped ** 'Out of the Ghetto' by Joe Jacobs ** 'The 43 Group' by Morris Beckman. Excellent account of how fascists were kicked off the streets of East London in the 40's. A pilot film about the group should be out soon, and the producers are currently looking for funding to make a longer version. Any rich benefactors out there who'd like to help make this happen get in touch via SchNEWS.

71

ONE IN THE EYE

Yesterday the government finally rejected plans for Hastings' bypass, but as usual the debate is between either jobs or the environment. However, earlier this month Friends of the Earth published a report, "New Jobs Without New Roads", showing that a sustainable regeneration strategy for the town could create up to 2,570 jobs for local people for significantly less than the £130 million cost of the bypass.

Tony Bosworth, Friends of the Earth's Transport Campaigner, said: "The last prop supporting the case for the Hastings bypasses has been kicked away. We knew they wouldn't solve the town's traffic problems. We knew they would be environmentally destructive. And now we know they aren't needed to bring new jobs."
* 21st July East Sussex Transport 2000 celebratory walk. Meet at Bexhill Station at 10.20 a.m or Hastings Station at 1pm. Tel 01323 646866
* Critical Mass in Brighton this Monday (16) 4.30 pm, outside St. Peter's church. Bring wheels (connected together in bike form, we presume), whistles, water, etc.

FTSE4what?

The London Stock Exchange is launching a new index of 'ethical companies', called FTSE4Good. Companies involved in gambling, tobacco-manufacturing, porn, nuclear power or arms manufacturing are excluded. But the index includes corporations like BP which has investments in Tibet, Shell - involved in human rights abuses in Nigeria, and GlaxoSmithKline which tried to prevent South African Government getting cheap anti-AIDS drugs. SchNEWS wonders where they looked up the definition of ethical...a corporate bullshit dictionary?

Terminalator 5: I'll Be Back

Across London and the Thames Valley aircraft noise affects people's lives, in London alone one million people live under the flight path to Heathrow. The number of planes in the UK is increasing at a rate of 4% each year and aviation is a major contributor to global warming. HACAN ClearSkies is opposing the 5th Heathrow Terminal, which will increase the number of aircraft and hence noise. The extra terminal will also attract more traffic on top of the colossal 3,750,000 cars already visiting daily. There's a '12 Steps to Terminal Britain' rally of the BAA (British Airports Authority) AGM at 10am, July 24th outside QE2 Conference Centre, Westminster. www.hacan.org.uk or 020 8876 8332.

Peatiful

The peat works on Hatfield Moor near Doncaster, run by Scotts, was occupied for the day by activists recently. Peat mining is a seasonal activity, so if work is stopped during the summer it sets their targets back quite a bit. If Scotts carry on at their current rate there will be no peat left in the area within three years. The area supports a great diversity of wildlife (around 5,000 species). After pixieing for the day and seriously affecting the peat harvesting everyone left the site, no arrests were made. More info from leedsef@ukf.net **SchNEWS gardening tip: Stop using compost that contains peat, it's destroying an irreparable habitat, and leaf mould works loads better anyway.

Positive SchNEWS

The "Gardening Industry" is now worth £2.6 billion a year, spurred on by programs such as Ground Force encouraging suburban conformity of decking, water features and ornamental plants. But gardens can become a haven for wildlife, so rather than spend a fortune on the latest garden design trend why not grow useful and attractive native plants, which are easy to grow. Get a list of plants native to your area at www.nhm.ac.uk/science/projects/fff.

SchNEWS in brief

Hold the front page – it's the **World Pea Shooting Championships** in Cambridgeshire this Saturday. About 100 competitors will be blowing peas at a target 12 feet away! ** Don't miss 'The New Rulers of the World' - A Special Report by **John Pilger**, ITV Weds 18th 10.30pm. "...examines the real meaning of the 'global economy', the latest phase of colonial domination of the weak by the powerful inc. the virtually unknown and bloody history of how globalisation took root in Indonesia." ** The **Welsh Green Gathering is off** following the decision of Carmarthenshire Council to refuse the use of the Llanelli site, on the advice/smear campaign of Dyfed Powys Police. It might still go ahead in May or August 2002. 01267 267500 ** Memorial plaque ceremony for **Ricky Reel** this Saturday (14) victim of racist attack and flawed police investigation. Kingston Bridge, Kingston Upon Thames, 11.45 am. 07956 410773 sukhdevreel@hotmail.com ** **Roger Bloxam is currently inside** for dancing on a Jaguar car in Oxford Circus on Mayday. Write to him at HMP Bullingdon, PO Box 50, Bicester, OX25 1WD. ** In **Iran**, mother of two Maryam Ayoobi was imprisoned a year ago and sentenced to death by stoning, for committing adultery. The International Committee against Stoning had organised a wide scale campaign to save her. Despite 1000's of protest letters, Maryam Ayoobi was killed. www.hambastegi.org.

Farm trials

At a "citizens' jury" in Medak District, Andhra Pradesh, India, 19 small farmers, inc. 13 from the untouchable (dalit) caste, called for a halt to foreign funding of their Govt's Vision 2020 by the World Bank and the UK Govt. They oppose a reduction of farmers in the area, land consolidation and displacement of rural people, forced mechanisation of farming, and contract farming, and want control of their land back, with no interference and forced 'development'.

Let Them Eat Cake

The Guinness Trust – a registered social landlord busy buying up council housing round the country, recently had another slice of the cake trying to squeeze the Homes For Change housing co-op. The HFC are wanting to buy the building they have spent years maintaining, but their 'partners' Guinness want far more money than the co-op's independent valuers suggest for the place, and are threatening to pull the plug on them. A decision was to be made at a Guinness Trust do at Apsley House, the Marchioness of Douro's gaff on Wednesday, when the co-op sweetened things up by giving them a scale model of the building – as a cake!!! It's won them a 6 month reprieve. charlie@cch-uk.org

Bordered Up

Globalisation makes it easier for money and capital to move around, but harder for people to move – unless they are cheap labour. Fortress Europe keeps the EU economic zone free from 'unwanted aliens' (ie people without money). **No Borders** resists borders worldwide, and fights deportation of asylum seekers [www.deportation-alliance.com]. This summer they are holding camps on the frontiers of Fortress Europe:

Last week a camp was held on the eastern edge of Europe, at Krynki, Poland - where campers were greeted by scenes reminiscent of the martial law days: not only border guards and police turned up but also water cannons, a helicopter and a tank! Other camps held last week were: Tarifa in Spain - a frontier between Europe and Africa where 1,000 Africans are arrested by the border police every month; and Lendeva Slovenia – a border soon to become a new militarised EU frontier. Next camps are at Genoa – 21-24th July, Frankfurt 28th July-5th Aug and Tijuana [Mexico] 24-26th August (borderaction@aol.com). Visit www.noborders.org

GENOA WHAT I MEAN?

Its yer no-nonsense SchNEWS guide to Genoa:
Any problems crossing the Italian border hang around and email talpaeorlogio@tiscalinet.it or tel +39-333460372 coming from France, coming from Switzerland tel.:+41-763302443, coming from Austria tel +39-3480345857. Try to get to Genoa by the 18th as then the real crackdown starts. In the west of Genoa is the "red zone" where, only G8 delegates, cops and residents are allowed. Police are apparently making 1,200 ID checks a day, so don't look dodgy, although it seems gas masks are not forbidden to carry, (but they are hard to get hold of).

The **Convergence Point** has space for 20,000 people, lots of info, and the venue for the public forum. Get to it from Stazione Brignole and walk down Via le Brig. Partigiane towards the coast until you reach the parking lot. A few hundred metres away in Via Cesare Battista are 2 schools (press centre, independent media centre, computer access and meeting space). Bring a tent and sleeping bag for **accommodation** as hotels are limited, Carlini Stadium (in the east) can hold at least 1,200 people where the White Overalls are converging, more places to be announced. The **social centre** Terra di Nosuno has some resources and camping area. But it is in the west of the city and so may be easily isolated, but it could be useful for staging entry to the Red Zone, get to it by Bus 35 (not 35/ to the mountains!) from the principal square in front of the pharmacy to stadium Lagacchio. **English speakers** are wanted in Genoa for helping out in the legal support office, if you wish to help call 0039 0118178142. This number can also be used as a contact for English speakers going to Genoa.

Dates: 18th Concert at Convergence point, 19th Migrants international march, 5pm, Principe Square, 20th Direct actions to surround and enter the Red Zone, 21st International March, 4pm, Corso Europa. **More info:** www.genoa-g8.org and italy.indymedia.org.

Convergence from 16th at **Bologna Social Centre TPO** www.ecn.org/tpo/ with a mass bloc of people leaving for Genoa on the 18th at 6pm from Bologna central station. If people are interested they should email wombles@libero.it with the subject line 'GENOA'.
* If you can't get to Genoa, there are actions at **Campsfield** Detention Centre (nr Oxford) 19-22 July. Join refugee groups and the Wombles in solidarity with G8 protestors and refugees at a protest camp. Also Critical Mass from Oxford Station on 21st, see www.wombleaction.mrnice.net/camp.htm or call 07900 653990 for more info.
* **Genoa solidarity action Birmingham**- 'defending the right to protest' outside McDonalds off Corporation Street, 21st 1pm 07980415577 S26brum@hotmail.com

...and finally...

Forget about live ammunition, plastic bullets, water cannon, and Genoa's missile defence system, cops in the U.S. might soon have a new weapon to use on demonstrators: stink bombs! Yep, those playground novelties are making a comeback albeit more souped-up and on the side of the establishment rather than a bunch of naughty kids. Pam Dalton of the Monell Chemical Senses Centre in Philadelphia has come up with right whiffy substance which she says "smells like shit only stronger. It's very powerful." SchNEWS reckons the cops have always acted like shit, and we're sure this latest offensive will get right up the noses of anti-capitalist protesters, but being dirty unwashed anarchists they ain't gonna notice any difference anyway! We wonder how long it will be before clothes pegs, like gas masks, will be banned?

Subscribe!

Noborder Camps 2001

"The exploitation of the world's multitudes, is only made possible by our restriction behind borders. Capital derives its profit and power from the theft and plundering of the land and the exploitation of labour. Once this was organised by the colonial powers of Europe, now they are joined, by the International Monetary Fund (IMF) the World Bank, and Washington with their structural adjustment programs and free trade treaties. This means massive impoverishment of the global South, displacing millions from their homes and making the survival of billions harder and harder. Some countries are economically devastated, in others there is war and genocide. As the world is homogenised, the laws we live by are increasingly the values of the market place. And while there are few borders for trade and the movement of capital, restrictions on the movement of people are tightened.

So we are faced with a choice. A global society organised as a Great Confinement or one in which people are

No Border Camp at Petisovci, Slovenia July 2001

free to move. One in which people are trapped, free for capitalism to exploit them, without rights, without freedom. Or one in which our diversity, communication and creativity is unbounded. Any discussion of refugees must at its core be an examination of this choice, of capitalism."
- Noborder Network's declaration.

Kein mensch ist illegal - Ninguna persona es ilegal - No-one is illegal

The UN High Commission on Refugees estimates that there are 12.1 million refugees world-wide. An estimated 3 million people live in Europe *sans-papiers* (illegally without visa papers). The rhetoric of globalisation calls for the removal of economic borders and free trade, meanwhile freedom of movement for people is another story. Governments are playing on nationalism and racism, promoting fear of 'the other' and scapegoating refugees to justify greater border protection, while in the mean time benefiting from the cheap labour that those without legal status provide.

The economic entities of the global north are constructing the harshest border regimes (take for instance Fortress Europe) and while their affluent lifestyles rely on the cheap resources of the 'south' flooding in, the masses of poor from these countries are locked out. One major consequence of this transnational resource grab is traditional peoples in the south are being displaced from their ancestral land, turned into refugees who *have to* move. It has been standard practice for governments and corporations to install regimes and set off wars if it suits them and they certainly don't mind kicking people off their land - to put up that refinery, road or mine - or seeing them starve – because they've lost farm land or water supply - to get oil, timber or gold. The majority of refugees move around the continents in which they are, but some take the risk of attempting to break through the security of 'Fortress Europe', or cross the Mexican border into the US, or reach the north coast of Australia by boat or reach other so-called democratic countries which they believe will be a safe haven. Those that enter undetected take low paid work and live a clandestine existence, while others find themselves locked up in detention centres for years while their application for asylum is processed.

Noborder Network
The European Noborder Network banded together to form an international movement after a series of grassroots demos and direct actions against the 1999 EU heads of Government meeting in Tampere, Finland, a meeting which ushered in an agreement that formally transferred responsibility for immigration policies away from nation states to the European level. This came after the Rothenburg German-Polish-Czech border camp in 1998 and there have been camps all over Europe each summer since. In 1999 a camp in Zittau, Germany saw a parade and festival crossing the border between Germany, Poland and the Czech Republic. In 2000 Forst, Germany, Ustrzyki Gorne, Poland, Marzamemi, Italy and Tijuana, Mexico played host to Noborder camps.

"Freedom of movement" Bordercamps Summer 2001
Tarifa, Spain
The biggest flow of African migrants that arrive in Europe pass through the Straits of Gibraltar. They arrive every night in "pateras", little wooden boats. Tarifa is the first European town that they find, only 14 km across the water from Africa. A local network is supporting migrants to make their way into Europe.

About 300 people participated in a bordercamp organised by the Spanish network "ninguna es illegal". The camp involved workshops on issues of self-organisation, civil disobedience, gender and globalisation, and actions – the most dramatic of which was a public nude action where tourists and locals were treated to the sight of more than 50 naked people appearing on the beach, dancing and singing. In front of a no-doubt captive audience, the nudists turned round to flash their backs – each with a big letter painted on it which spelt the message: Ninguna Persona Es Ilegal - Racismo No - Ya Basta! (No Human Being Is Illegal - No Racism – Enough Is Enough!). Behind them a huge "Frontera de Europa - Peligro de Muerte" (European Border - Danger of Death) banner was unfurled, and passers-by were leafleted.

Over the days of the border camp 300 asylum seekers from Morocco were caught by the Guardia Civil and taken to a detention centre. In Tarifa's beaches, you can often find shoes or clothes from the migrants who risk their lives to get here, and more than 1,500 people have already died at sea and around one thousand are arrested a month trying to make their way across.
See www.sindominio.net/ninguna

Lendava, Slovenia
From 4th - 8th July about 100 people participated in a camp in the village of Petisovci near Lendava, 1km from Slovenia's border with Croatia, and 2km from the Hungarian border. The key action was a borderwalk between the three countries, ending up in a carnival procession and street party with the locals of Lendava listening to Italian and Slovenian bands performing. Slovenia has recently become a key transit country for people seeking to enter Germany, with an estimated 36,000 clandestine migrants crossing the Slovene border in 2000 - up 91% from the previous year. For Slovenia to join the EU – and fit in with the Schengen Agreement

We're lost - has anyone got a proper map?

Streaming Over The Border

On July 7th there was a web linkup between the camps at Tarifa, Lendava, Krynki and Campsfield. Initial plans for live web video streaming between the camps was thwarted, but the pre-recorded material that all the camps could see still established a sense of a common identity, making the events less isolated.

Publix Theatre Caravan Get Nicked After Genoa

After Slovenia the Publix Theatre Caravan took its theatrical resistance to the Genoa anti-G8 demonstrations, but on the way out of Genoa the entire caravan – twenty five people – were arrested and detained for a month before being deported back to Austria. They were initially charged with vandalism, endangerment of public safety and 'membership of a criminal organization' - this last, most serious charge, was pressed under Italy's anti-mafia laws. Even the Italian public prosecutor's office has questioned the amount of force used by the police.

(see SchNEWS 312) it must increase the 1000 police currently patrolling the border by 3000. The Siska Detention Centre in the Slovenian capital Ljubljana holding 300 asylum seekers also saw a demonstration in front of its gates including a performance by the Publix Theatre Caravan.

Bialystok and Krynki, Poland

The Noborder camp at the Polish-Belorussian camp was held between the 5th and the 12th July.

Starting off with a demonstration of 250 people in the town of Bialystok featuring activists from Poland, Ukrainia, Belarus, Russia, Finland, and Germany, the group then set off to Krynki, a border town between Poland and Belarus, and setting up an info tent in the town square.

The police/military response was extreme with a dozen police vans, trucks with water cannons, two army transporters and even a tank (!) turning up for the party - the largest display of military force since martial law days. Four people were arrested and police tried to provoke a riot. At one point campers were surrounded in a park by police cars circling with sirens on, and when some of them shouted at police, the police attacked the crowd but support from locals helped tone down the tense atmosphere.

The significance of Poland in 'Fortress Europe' is that the country is applying to join the EU, but in the meantime it's western border with Germany forms part of the perimeter of the European superstate, and movement of people and trade mostly exists – as it has done since Soviet times and before – with its neighbours to the east. When it joins the EU its eastern border with Belorus will become the new edge of Europe, heavily militarised, and suddenly movement of people and trade with its eastern neighbours will be closed down or made illegal. (See SchNEWS 320)

Campsfield

The Wombles called for a No Border camp to coincide with immigration day during the G8 protest in Genoa on July 19th, but a week before the day a media and police campaign warning the public of "dangerous" protestors, was in full swing. The small town near the detention centre was turned into a Genoa-like no-go area, with a massive police presence, closed pubs and empty streets. About 80 detainees were moved out of Campsfield. Although a proper border camp was not possible, protestors took to the streets of nearby Oxford in a solidarity march.

Orchestra performs at Frankfurt Airport, 2nd August.

Frankfurt Airport

Almost all German deportations of asylum seekers are carried out by airlines under the escort of migration police, and Frankfurt Airport is responsible for most of them – around 10,000 a year. The past decade has seen tumultuous changes for the country's immigration situation – with "illegalisation" becoming a mass phenomenon after the escalation of the war in Yugoslavia led to rapid rises in the number of people seeking asylum during the 90's. The policies of detention camps, direct deportation of rejected asylum-seekers and withdrawal of social benefits from others have seen ever increasing numbers of people kicked out. In 1988 there were barely 3,000 deportations, which rose to more than 50,000 by 1994, and more recently the figure is around 35,000 a year.

On Sunday August 2nd, Frankfurt airport was inaccessible. Fraport, the private company running the airport, allowed only ticket-holders in – those who wanted to pick up friends or family had no access. As a result, travellers had plenty of time to discuss "free movement for everyone", and enjoy the classical live music of the orchestra "Lebenslaute" which was also part of the border camp.

Tijuana, Mexico

August 24-26 saw the last of the summer's bordercamp actions taking place along the US/Mexico border. Border activists and hactivists descended on Tijuana for the second borderhack festival.

Fence In Space: US-Mexican border

http://www.no-racism.net/nobordertour

"Tijuana and San Diego are one city - that like Berlin - got divided by accidents and things of destiny" and now signify the north-south divide: the vast gulf between rich/poor, educated/uneducated, and developed/under-developed. To the south, cardboard shantytowns in the dust, to the north, skyscrapers sparkling in the sun. Between them a 2000-mile wall running alongside a strip of no-mans land.

Camped on the beach where the tall metal fence trails off into the Pacific Ocean, the wired-up three day event brought 100 US and Mexican activists together. By day the tent beside a light-house hosted a series of workshops on immigration, ecology, vegan cooking and independent radio and by night technoheads turned the scene into a giant rave before crashing out on the beach.

Woomera, Australia

Easter 2002 saw more than 1000 people help about 50 asylum seekers escape from a remote desert detention centre. (See article in this book) http://woomera2002.com/

Get Involved 2002
Strasbourg, France

From the 19th to 28th July 2002 there will be a ten day international noborder action camp bringing activists together from all round the world to a 'laboratory of civil disobedience and creative resistance', featuring actions and discussions. http://strasbourg.noborder.org

A series of European camps are also scheduled to run through July and August 2002. www.noborder.org/camps/02/

For more info about fighting asylum seeker deportation: www.deportation-alliance.com

No nation under a groove, getting down just for the...

"NATURE ALWAYS WINS IN THE END"

lappersfort stays !!

A beautiful forest, less than two kilometres from the centre of Bruges, abandoned by homo sapiens for many years that now has to be partly cut down for a new road, new industry and a place for coaches. When we heard of these plans, we immediately thought: "No fucking way".

It was in the beginning of 2001 that a local called Peter showed our anarchist collective 'uitgezonderd' the unknown forest 'the lappersfort'. He told us about the plans of the local government and about the action group he had started, Axiegroep Zuidelijke Ontsluiting. They had put up a petition and organised an event in May where 300 people enjoyed a biking tour, a walk in the forest and live music. The next month we organised a vegan barbeque, climbing workshop, and a botanical walk. On the 27th of July we took it to the streets, held a critical mass with a hundred people (which is quit big for the small city of Bruges), climbed in the flag poles , hung a big banner and put on some political theatre for the locals. The plans for an action-camp were put upon the indymedia-website, and a week later we started occupying the protest camp that has become our home.

The Lappersfort is situated south of Bruges, by the canal to Ghent. While it is land with a history of human intervention, it has been fallow for many years and has become wild again, turning back into a forest. It contains seven different biotopes, being situated by a canal and next to a swamp where many birds breed including three different kinds of owls, robins, tits, and woodpeckers. There are also a lot of squirrels and bats and a huge amount of midges! It is wooded with old oak, chestnut and beech trees. Now it is owned by Fabricom , a big enterprise in the steel industry, who want to sell it. Once Belguim was a land of forests and moors; now it is agriculture, industry, and the densest road network in the world!

The Plans

The forest is currently threatened by three different projects, which would leave very little natural land intact:

They want to build a road connecting the motorway with the Bruges ring road, and next to that a big cinema complex. Through the publicity of our actions and camp, they have toned down this project and now only want to widen an existing 'local traffic' street; but this still would take out a part of the forest.

On the site of a munitions factory which burned down many years ago - but which nature has since reclaimed - the city council wants to build a coach car-park, claiming that the current spot is 'inefficient'. The local wildlife are going to love the stench of the buses on top of losing their homes.

The biggest part of the swamp has been reserved for small industry. Although the City Council has been put under enough pressure to say that they will negotiate with the land owner to change the course of the new road, the most beautiful part of the swamp could still end up as parking space. Possibly only a quarter of the whole site will remain as nature.

Action Stations

As Lappersfort is Belgium's first direct action camp, we had to learn a lot of things - legal issues as well as practical. A week after we started occupying the site we informed the press, the police and the owner. The local press was interested, but the national press weren't bothered. The plod came after a week to inform us that we were doing an illegal action. The city council declared that our action was too early as their plans were only in the preparation stage.

The owner was quite friendly in the beginning. Even when the police asked permission to evict us because they believed the forest was going to be used as a base for violent protesters at the anti-globalisation-demo in September the owners said 'no', because they wanted to negotiate with us. These negotiations stalled when the owner worked out that we in fact planned to save the whole fucking lot - at that point they asked us to leave.

Soon after publications came out people began to visit. Locals were amazed by the beauty of this unknown location, and people from all over came to help. Some Dutch activists helped to build treehouses and repair the old house. A crew from the 'Nine Ladies protest site' built a tower on the house and people came by with food, building material, and climbing material. In the beginning we had a meeting every night (called fire moment). But after eight months of occupation this has gone down to weekly meetings. When winter came things grew a bit silent around the camp; so we made our own entertainment getting in speakers, a slideshow, and vegan pancakes which was a raging success.

At the time of writing (April 2002) we're having lots of press attention. Last week we held a press conference together with some conservationist groups because we wanted to publicize another place that is threatened by industry. One national newspaper picked up on the fact that we were into the 250th day of our occupation, and other national press followed. Suddenly we were giving interviews for the seven o'clock news, getting the front page of a French paper, being made into a documentary and invited to chat with the mayor on a political programme on national tellie. But if we have learned one thing on this camp it's about the hypocrisy of the press, because most are more interested in lifestyle matters than in the real issues - the nature that has to be saved from destruction. Having said that we haven't had any negative press so far...

Coming Up

In one newspaper the city council declared that they want to start building the place for the coaches at the end of the year and evict us then (when Bruges stops being the cultural capital of Europe). Just in case this is true (not that we believe anything in this particular paper) we are building a fort on this area and help is welcome.

In August 2002 we will celebrate the first anniversary of our occupation by having a big feast. This summer will be more actions on this land which holds ecological as well as archeological value (aerial photos show signs of Bronze Age burial sites). Anyway we are not giving up our fight to save precious nature.

Contact address: PB 715 8000 Brugge Belgium (don't mention Lappersfort)
Site-phone:
(0032) 0494591467

How to get there: standing with your back at the main entrance of the station, you turn right and just before the high bridge, you turn right again (Vaartdijkstraat), follow the canal and pass some industry, follow it some more and you see a path with willows. Now follow this into the forest where you'll soon meet some pixies.

NOT COPPING OUT

Reports from Rising Tide inspired actions inside and outside the UN climate conference COP 6.5 in Bonn, July 2001

Critical Mass

July 16th: The Rising Tide series of actions against the climate summit began with a 300-strong critical mass bike ride around Bonn. Everything was in good humour, and the bike ride culminates in the main square of Bonn City where they are met by the samba band. Food was provided for the occasion by Rampenplan, and the day ended at Rheinaue Park for a dance.

Crashing The Party

Wednesday July 18th: This evening, a group of initially about 50 activists congregated outside of the Deutsche Telecom building (near the conference centre) where delegates from various NGO's and renewable energy representatives were meeting with the German Minister for the Environment. Under the spell of the rhythmically irresistibly combined forces of London and Amsterdam samba band members, protestors danced in front of the building, handed out copies of the spoof conference paper 'The Earth Crimes' and Carbon Credits (detailing the immorality of emissions trading) to the attendees. We had banners galore reading '60% reductions now', 'profiting from pollution is not the solution' and another which read, 'NGO's, Do your job! Reject Flex Mex', (flex mex = flexible mechanisms, or the piece of jargon that sums up Kyoto's many scams.) The samba band launched into a fresh onslaught of deep latin grooves, while the party attendees were bombarded with propaganda from us as they entered.

Then a truck containing a sound system pulled up in front of the building but after only five minutes the police shut it down, despite the efforts of the samba band who clustered round the truck. In the ensuing melee and with little apparent provocation, one woman was dragged out from underneath the truck, had her hands cuffed tightly behind her back and was driven off.

Whilst all this joyful protest happened outside the party, activists had infiltrated the party disguised as suited delegates. Underneath these innocuous-looking suits were climate super heroines who took their uninvited display to the stage. To the applause and cheers of watching delegates the climate super heroines were chased round the stage by keystone-cop style security who insisted they not have the chance to speak. However they did manage to read off a few of their 'Principles for a Better Protocol' before being roughly dragged out into the street.

Reclaim The Rain

Thursday 19th July: A reclaim the streets action today was dramatically turned into a road blockade by activists from the Rising Tide Network and other groups. Demanding that their twelve-point manifesto be read out in the COP 6.5 conference halls, approximately 90 activists from the 500 strong parade locked arms around a central ring of people chained together for what turned into a four hour clash with police. All sides acted peacefully and although many demonstrators were forcefully carried away the situation was quite calm for most of the afternoon.

Members of the world's press, cameras wrapped against the rain, reporting from close quarters throughout the tense afternoon. Spokespeople for the demonstrators hailed the action as a success in an upbeat discussion this evening, after the police barricades had finally been pulled away and the evening traffic blocked for miles by the action on one of Bonn's main streets, had started moving again.

Banner In The Sky

Sunday 22nd July: Rising Tide people climbed to the top of a 50 metre crane outside the conference centre and unfurled the "60%-80% CO2 reductions here and now" banner from it.

Beaming In

Friday 27th July: In the final session of the latest round of climate talks, climate justice activists occupied a beam in the conference centre hall and unfurled a banner which read 'Trading in Pollution is not the Solution'.

One of the activists explained, 'We are here to bring some common sense back to these negotiations. The US pull-out made everyone so desperate to get any agreement that we've ended up with a deal which is a step in the wrong direction. The current loopholes will mean that the already pitiful 5.2% CO2 reductions could now only be 0.3%*. The trade in emissions lays a foundation for inaction rather than building a framework for the necessary emission reductions. This deal can only serve the interests of big business and reinforce global inequality.'

The welcome that this deal has received from media, governments and the big environmental NGO's masks the real story of the talks. The myth that any deal - no matter how weak - is a step in the right direction should be challenged. One activist who had Article 19 of the UN Convention of Human Rights, freedom of speech, written on her naked body stated 'Not only is this treaty going nowhere for the climate, any public concern or

Rising Tide taking the high ground inside the conference centre.   Pic: Leila Mead

voice about this has been completely repressed by corporate and political interests. As citizens who will be adversely affected by climate change and have not been able to participate in the decisions made about it, we have a right to be heard here and have been forced to take such drastic measures in order to do so.'

After occupying the beam in the conference centre entrance hall for around 45 minutes, the four activists came to an agreement with the UN security (who were unable to get them down safely) that they would come down of their own accord on the condition that they could proceed to the media room and speak to any journalists who were interested in hearing the reasons why they had been forced to take such drastic measures for dissenting voices to be heard within the proceedings.

However, in a sneaky, underhand twist, as soon as the protestors had come off the beam, they were led directly outside to a waiting van of very edgy riot cops, had plastic cuffs put on them and were made to sit in stifling heat in the van for some time to the point where one of the protestors passed out. The UN security chief was heard telling the police that they needed to be severely punished.

The relationship between the police and the protestors has been on the whole very respectful and calm, and these final arrests were no exception once they had been delivered into the hands of the normal police. They were duly processed and then sat in front of the police station having a picnic and drinking cold beer with the prison support crew who had come to greet them.

For more information visit: www.risingtide.de

The rising tide network www.unfccc.int/cop6_2

Official website for Bonn COP6.5 www.climateconference.org

*As stated by Greenpeace in their press release July 23

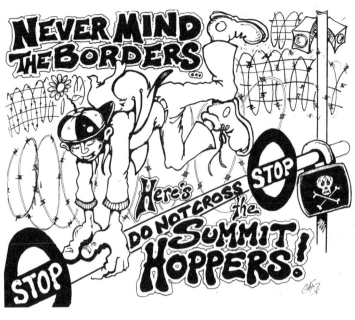

Going Swimmingly: an action by DAAMDU (Direct Action Against Militarism and Depleted Uranium) at Ministry Of Defence offices at Abbeywood, Filton, Bristol on the 18th of June. About 200 people picketed the entrance, and four went for a swim in the lake on the MoD complex with a banner (below), in protest against the purchase of depleted uranium and other radioactive weaponry. Pics: Simon Chapman.

Tony Blair goes up a tripod blocking the entrance to the UK headquarters of Esso (Exxon-Mobil), Leatherhead, Surrey, 24th July.   Pic: Stan Kujawa

WAKE UP! WAKE UP! IT'S YER PIZZA THE ACTION

Weekly SchNEWS

Printed and Published in Brighton by Justice?

Friday 27th July 2001   www.schnews.org.uk   Issue 314/315   Free/Donation

WELCOME TO G-HATE

"It was just endless, I really thought I was dying. It's a horrible thing when you feel your bones breaking inside you. And after a while I just tried to keep one eye open, trying to stay alive. I finally blacked out and couldn't remember anything else till I woke up in hospital."
– Markus Cavell (Sky).

"After all the people had been brought out either to the hospital or jail everyone flooded in. The cops had sent in cleaning teams, but it was still a mess. Blood was smeared on walls and the floor, the gear of everyone was torn open and thrown everywhere. Doors and windows were smashed. The computer terminals were lying on the ground in pieces. Absolute chaos." – Eyewitness.

This isn't a description of the actions of police in some tinpot dictatorship, but first hand accounts of the scenes in Italy late last Saturday night when the Carabinieri, Italy's conscript military police, attacked the centre where the Genoa Social Forum (GSF) and the Independent Media Centre (IMC) were based. Some of the people were asleep when they were attacked, others eating. 93 were arrested, 31 of these taken straight to hospital. The police destroyed computers and took hard drives and documents belonging to lawyers of the Genoa Social Forum - evidence of illegal police activity that could be used as legal defence. One man, IMC UK reporter Markus "Sky" Covell, will be in hospital for another week after suffering two broken ribs and a punctured lung. Yet what happened to people in Genoa last week is often the norm for protesters outside the EU. When they demonstrate against policies of global political elites like the G8, they expect state violence. In Brazil recently, members of the landless workers union, Movimiento Sem Terra, were travelling in a five bus convoy to Curitiba to protest about logging, mining and abusive landlords stealing their land. The army stopped the convoy, forced everyone from the buses at gunpoint and made to lie on the road. One man was shot in the stomach and a local police chief who admitted that the violence had taken place, was silenced by govt officials. In Papua New Guinea, three students protesting against World Bank privatisation have been killed during the last few months. On June Severo Mamani, was shot dead for being part of a Bolivian peasant workers protest. They blocked roads to demand better services, land rights and an end to exploitation. The army replied by killing him.

MASSIVE ATTACK

"It was inevitable that the centre would come under attack. The night before, we'd discussed this and there was a strategy to stash all the videotapes gathered by IMC. We had known that the raw footage may contain incriminating evidence, with people saying that the cops "know that we have evidence of police presence in the black bloc." – SchNEWS correspondent.

The attack on the centres was launched at midnight by the Mobile Operative Squad, claiming that the School and Indymedia Centre were 'harbouring black bloc'. One witness said "We could see them taking laptops, minidisc players, other recording equipment and... some salad knives." The salad knives would later form part of the display the police would show to the world to show how violent the protesters were. They would also display construction equipment, hammers, bricks and scaffold bars – but fail to mention that one of the schools was a building site!

One copper from the Squad has broken ranks comparing the operation to a nightmare under Pinochet's Chilean dictatorship accusing some colleagues of behaving like fascists. He told the centre-Left daily La Republicca what happened when people got to a holding center "They lined them up and banged their heads against the walls. They urinated on one person. They beat people if they didn't sing Facetta Nera [A Fascist hymn]…One girl was vomiting blood but the chief of the squad just looked on. They threatened to rape girls with their batons."

Despite the raid, Indymedia kept going. There were continual multilingual updates and a web radio broadcast throughout the protests, with millions of hits on Italian Indymedia throughout the protests.

RIOT ON?

"I have never seen so many wounded people at a demo (over 500 in the hospital), and the level of shock in some people is unbelievable. Some people are talking to themselves and spacing out. Some are going through some really tough times mentally and we seem very unprepared to deal with it. It's a weird feeling though to sort through

---

Earth First Summer Gathering
1-5 August

Being held on a beautiful site in the foothills of the Peak District. Over 100 workshops sharing skills, campaigning and networking. National and international campaign round ups, as well as rock climbing, nature walks, games. £10 donation to cover costs. Accommodation is camping only.

Details 0845-4589595
www.eco-action.org/gathering

---

all the feelings of rage and trauma over what has happened (and wanting it to just go away) and know that it happens to people all over the world in non-western countries, who are resisting and have been resisting for ages." Brian, protester

The umbrella group the Genoa Social Forum set up a huge convergence centre - a massive operation to cope with the expected 100,000 protestors. But, like at festivals burger bars charging high prices angered many while different shades of red mixed uncomfortably with greens and anarchos. At one end Jubilee and Drop the Debt on the other end the militant Tute Bianche and Cobas (a coalition of street-fighting anarcho-syndicalist and marxist trade unions).

Before the G8 had even started, blue-collar workers had brought the country to a standstill. At the heart of the dispute were employers' attempts to break up national bargaining and force the unions to accept a plant-by-plant system, which would immensely weaken them. Many of the demonstrations were addressed by the GSF who persuaded some of the strikers to come to Genoa.

Thursday's march against the racism of Fortress Europe's immigration controls was peaceful - no immigrants could risk arrest otherwise they would face deportation back to the countries they were fleeing from. Still, the police showed their intentions filling side streets with riot cops and pointing CS gas launchers at protestors from the tops of their armoured vans.

The next day was never going to be peaceful. The "White Overalls"- who wore helmets and padding behind big shields- had already declared that they would march straight up the main avenue to enter the red zone. And of course there was the anarchist "black bloc", regarded as public enemy number one. Sure enough the streets soon became a war zone, a mix of white, black and red blocks facing cops who used extreme force - tear gas, water cannons, tanks and lethal bullets for Carlo Giuliani.

Late in the day one massive crowd developed chanting "Assassini!" at the cops as endless tear gas volleys rained down injuring many. This tactic didn't work as planned when protestors in gas masks and leather gloves threw the canisters onto the railway line. Eventually police dispersed the crowd by driving tanks at high speed into it. The only thing to do was run. SchNEWS hacks have been on many demos but this was worse than anything we've experienced before. One woman whose son disappeared in fascist Argentina was shaken at what she had seen, saying it was uncomfortably close to Argentina during the dictatorship – and you thought Europe was a nice safe place.

THE G8 - PASTA CARING

"They are in a position of all ruling elites, who must preside over the flow of wealth from poor to rich, without appearing to do so." - Jeremy Seabrook, Author

The G7, which has been meeting since 1975, is made up of the leaders of the world's seven richest countries (USA, Japan, Germany, France, Britain, Italy, and Canada). In 1994 Russia was admitted, turning the G7 into the G8. The G8 have annual summits where they decide what sort of world you and your children will live in. As well as making decisions on ruining our environment and privatising public services, they also plan directives to the International Monetary Fund and World Bank for their structural adjustment programmes.

The current G8 are probably some of the dodgiest capitalist cronies around. Here are some of their credentials: Bush illegally seized the US Presidency by getting his brother to stop thousands of black people in Florida from voting in the presidential election… Putin is pursuing a genocidal war in Chechnya… Chirac is facing allegations of corruption… Berlusconi, the summit's host, has a such a massive personal fortune that he could pay off the debt of several African countries with his spare change; he owns most of Italy's media, and has been convicted of illegal party financing, bribery and false accounting. Meanwhile his right hand man is on trial for consorting with the Mafia. No wonder the African Monitor described them as "opulent idlers hiding inside a steel cage".

The reality of the system the G8 head up is truly frightening for the majority of the planet. While some people, mainly in a handful of rich countries, live in relative comfort, the majority of the world's people face worsening poverty as a direct result of capitalist control of their economies. The 'third world debt' is not a debt in any real sense - it is the mechanism for keeping the majority of the world under the thumb of international capital.

Between 1980 and 1996 the countries of sub-Saharan Africa paid the amount borrowed by their ruling elites twice over, only to be left owing three times what they owed in 1980. Every day, £28 million flows from the poorest countries in the world to the banks of the rich countries. 19,000 children die every day as a result of the debt.

The problem isn't what the G8 decides – it's the fact that a tiny group of politicians are taking life and death decisions affecting the whole of the world on behalf of a few hundred corporations and banks.

FORTRESS ROCHER

While the carabinieri were busy arresting and assaulting people in the Indymedia centre it was a very different story across town in the official press centre inside the red zone. The divide between life inside the red zone fortress, with its well-defended borders, and life outside, was a pretty neat metaphor for the world the G8 were in Genoa to sustain. Inside, the Ferrero Rocher was piled up on the tables (just like the crap adverts) getting guzzled by corporate journos, delegates and other hangers-on whose every need was catered for by an army of local servants (no doubt chucked out of the zone at the end of their shift). Hundreds of metres of computers laid on for the world's press along with books, CDs DVDs and everything else you'd need to explain how sane, rational and useful the G8 are. There were luxury boats, cheese and wine receptions, free rides on Genoa's tourist attractions, not open to the riff-raff outside. There was even an official joke book.

The port area was eerily silent - in the middle, like in some science fiction film, there was a big glass dome with three trees in it ("look, son, these used to be everywhere!"). Sure, there seemed to be police checks every few yards, but as long as you had your papers you could soon move along - and, as press reception told us, "You will be safer inside here on Friday".

And if you think the journos were having it good seven of the leaders (all except Bush) slept on the spanking new cruise liner European Vision (sic), a $250 million floating holiday resort that offers almost every luxury imagination can devise. With a golf range, a gym, Turkish baths, a Givenchy shop, an English pub and a cigar and brandy room. There's also a basketball court, mini golf, climbing wall and Internet café. And if the leaders drop their currency at the roulette wheel, there's always the ATM machine. Cor we really feel sorry for old Tory Blair who said, "We are here to work. I suppose most of us would have preferred to have spent a weekend with our families rather than in meetings from morning to night."- yeah, right…

PUTIN HIS FOOT IN IT

With the battle of Genoa raging outside and the G8 looking less and less democratic as time went on the powers that be started the P.R. war. "Saint Bob", otherwise known as has-been pop star gob shite and businessman millionaire Bob Geldof, was flown in on Tony Blair's private jet to tell people that the G8 was *really* a force for good and not the un-elected power crazy cabal that everybody knows they are. Interviewed on T.V. this celebrity made out that one third of debt had been cancelled. The actual figure is 1%. The poorest 40 countries in the world owe $218 billion and of this $2.16 billion has been cancelled. Like me owing you 99p instead of £1.

Geldof gave a bearhug to Vladimir Putin, the Russian President, otherwise known as the Butcher of Chechnya. Since the war started again in 1999 nothing short of genocide has taken place. In the first war between 1994 and 1996, when Putin was Boris Yeltsin's number two, up to 100,000 were killed by Russian artillery but the war continuing at the moment is even more sinister. Concentration camps have been set up all around Russian controlled Chechnya with tens of thousands of civilians being tortured and killed.

Rozita, a grandmother, was detained in January of this year and held in a death camp outside the village of Khottuni. On arrival she was thrown into a 4-ft deep pit with heavy logs as a roof so she couldn't stand up and made to stay there for 12 days, pissing and shitting where she sat. After this she was taken out to be interrogated and tortured which entailed attaching electrodes to her body and turning the current on. "Yes I screamed something terrible", she said. "It hurt a lot when they turned on the current. The FSB (Russian secret police) people said 'You aren't dancing well enough. Lets add some more voltage.' And so they did." Rozita screamed louder and louder. All this for the charge of "sheltering terrorists" something she denies. After a while the FSB sussed out that she wasn't the militant that they thought she was and so Rozita's relatives were told they had to pay a ransom to them to secure her release. This was done with the help of her fellow villagers and she was let go.

But its not just grannies that have been held in these death/torture camps. In Grozny, the capital, most of the visible population is female, all with tales of mass round-ups of men between the ages of 16 and 50. Isa was one of these men. He was also taken to the Khottuni camp and was kept in a pit measuring 3m by 3m half filled with water with five other men. While being 'interrogated' he had cigarettes stubbed out on his body, his fingernails pulled out, his feet beaten with clubs and then gang raped. Like Rozita, Isa was also released after a ransom was paid, but the five others, along with thousands of others, were tortured and then killed.

Anna Politkovskaya, a respected Moscow journalist, also fell foul of the FSB when she went to Chechnya to find out about the human rights abuses going on there. After she had seen the 'pits' for herself she was arrested and tortured, all the while her captors reminding her that the FSB take their orders direct from Putin himself. Which kind of puts the G8 statement that he signed condemning the street violence in Genoa in perspective.

BLACK PROPAGANDA

The black bloc is a tactic used by people who believe that physical confrontation is an important way of showing that peaceful opposition to the state and capital is not enough. In Seattle, the black bloc physically attacked banks and multinationals guilty of human rights abuse such as McDonalds and Nike. In Prague they worked with other groups in physically confronting the police's defence of the summit. In Genoa, however, some people dressed in black went on a spree of destruction in working class areas, smashing phone boxes, emptying recycling bins, burning cars and looting corner shops. Although the police were nearby, they did not intervene. There is no doubt that plain clothes police were pretending to be protesters in Genoa – a familiar tactic of the Italian state – an hour before the IMC center was raided la7 an Italian TV company showed 'black bloc' climbing in and out of police vans in the red zone.

Many Black Bloc were refusing to have anything to do with the people wrecking neighbourhoods far from the red zone. As a statement from some Black Bloc involved in Genoa read, "Day by day, the capitalist world order produces a diversity of violence. Poverty, hunger, expulsion, exclusion, the death of millions of people and the destruction of living spaces is part for their policy. This is exactly what we reject. Smashed windows of banks and multinational companies are symbolic actions. Nevertheless, we do not agree with the destruction and looting of small shops and cars. This is not our policy. However, we also do not let us be divided. To divide resistance is a usual way to weaken resistance. We appreciate and count on solidarity criticism."

GENOA SOLIDARITY

* There have been solidarity demonstrations against the killing of Carlo across the world. In Manchester activists got into the Italian consulate on Monday, graffitied walls and set-off fire alarms and extinguishers in solidarity with those who suffered at the hands of police in Genoa. The Italian consulate in Edinburgh had 'murder' written across it. In London a mobile demo started at the Italian embassy then went to the Italian Tourist Board and Italian Chamber of Commerce.

* The Indymedia Centre UK has set up a legal fund to help with the legal work for the Genoa prisoners. Cheques or Postal Order can be sent to: The Independent Media Centre (IMC) UK, P.O. Box 587, London, SW2 4HA, UK. Please write LEGAL FUND to distinguish between donations to IMC UK and to the legal fund.

* To keep up to date with the Genoa Protests visit www.indymedia.org

FLUFFY TERRORISTS

On arrival six British activists were deported from Genoa before the protests even began. They all had one thing in common, they were all arrested (but not charged and convicted - whatever happened to innocent till proven guilty) at the peaceful Trident Ploughshares blockades at Britain's Faslane nuclear submarine base. Hardly riot tourists part of an anarchist travelling circus intent on mayhem and destruction.

The following morning, three of the deportees went to London's Italian consulate and constructed a shrine to Carlo Giuliani. They were watched by two armed police and around 30 riot cops in attendance. Later that evening, one person was dropped at a train station by his son, who was then surrounded by 30 police officers, four pointing automatic weapons at him, they ordered him from his van, which was then thoroughly searched. The police claim they were acting under the Terrorism Act, and kindly left him a note "thanking him for his co-operation". Nice to know they care.

* There's a public meeting next Tuesday (31) organised by the Campaign Against Criminalising Communities (part of a coalition of groups against Terrorism Act 2000) at Camden Town Hall, Judd St, London NW1 7pm. The meeting will bring together representatives of some of the groups banned under the new Terrorism Act such as the Kurds, Tamils, Sikhs, Kashmiris, and Algerians as well as journalists, trade unionists lawyers and campaigners Tel 020 7250 1315

* Protesting against the Terrorism Act this weekend is Ralph Smyth cycling 170 miles from Lindholme Detention Centre, Doncaster, to Oakington Detention Centre, Cambridge. He'll be wearing an illegal T-shirt and riding a 'terrorist' bike (i.e. showing support for organisations which are banned under the Act.). Sponsorship money will go to Liberty and the Medical Foundation for the Care of Victims of Torture. To sponsor him call 0709 203376, www.blagged.freeserve.co.uk/ride4ref.htm

---

NOISE DEMO

*This Saturday (28th July) there will be a National Noise Demonstration at the Italian embassy, bring lots of banners, drums, whistles, pots & pans, and anything else that can make a lot of noise! Meet 2pm, Italian Embassy, Three King's Yard, W1 London (nearest tube Bond St.)

Stop Press: Paul Robinson has been given a year for 'violent rioting' at the Gothenburg EU demo in Sweden in June. Please write to him at: Goteburg Remand Centre (Haktet), Goteburg Polis Headquarters (Polis Huset), Box 429, 40129 Goteburg, Sweden.

BONN VOYAGE!

While the cops were beating shit out of protesters in Italy this week, delegates in Bonn, attending the COP 6.5 meeting on climate change were busy selling the environment down the drain.

As NGO's, the so-called defenders of the environment were quickly celebrating the agreements reached in Bonn as a "a major political victory" others with a better understanding of the games being played inside the conference centre took a more direct course of action. Nine activists from Rising Tide climbed a 50 metre crane outside the congress centre on Godesberger Allee and dropped a banner which read, "60% CO2 Reductions HERE and NOW." After four hours the cops finally managed to get the activists off the crane. All nine were released without charges at noon yesterday.

What the activists were aware of, and something that the NGO's had completely overlooked, was that the new watered-down version of the Kyoto agreement 'with added loopholes' looks more like a concession to the interests of big corporate business and political harmony than anything concerned about preserving the environment. The deal reached behind closed doors contains no environmental integrity at all. Delegates inside the talks forgot that they were negotiating a treaty for the future of humanity and settled down to their usual game of political brinkmanship. The inadequacies of the deal struck starkly demonstrate that governments are not prioritising for the destruction that climate change is bringing.

COP-Out 6.5

The Kyoto protocol if implemented will see the beginning of a new form of colonialism, as carbon becomes the new currency of the rich. The treaty allows countries to use 'carbon sinks' and gain carbon credits for managing its forests and agricultural land, which absorbs carbon from the atmosphere (SchNEWS 311). Ironically it is forests that were originally cut down and used to fuel the industrial revolution and colonise the world creating the West's consumer nightmare. Now we have a technology economy we have no use for our forests we can get highly tradable carbon credits for managing these forests.

Rich countries will not use carbon sinks to reduce domestic Greenhouse gas emissions, instead it will provide industrialised countries with a loophole to avoid reducing their emissions at source. There is no such thing as a market-based solution to a market-based problem. 'Free' trade will not provide a solution to the climate crisis.

In order to stabilise Carbon Dioxide at a safe level it will require a 60 to 80 per cent cut in carbon emissions from 1990 levels. Some of the "flexible mechanisms" or loopholes depending on yer perspective which have been introduced into the Kyoto Protocol reduce the cut in CO2 emissions between 1990 and 2010 from 5.2% to between 0-3%. In reality this may actually lead to a 14% increase in carbon emissions as rich countries simply buy their way out of real changes heavily relying on carbon sinks and carbon trading.

Sinking Low

About the only piece of good news to come out of the Bonn agreement is that there are no nukes in the Clean Development Mechanisms (CDM).

If ratified at the next climate talks, in Marrakech, Morocco, (COP7, Oct 29-Nov 9) this agreement will be legally binding and will open up a financial aid fund of $520 million per year for developing countries to cope with climate change. This agreement will also give some strength to fight the WTO on a few of their environmental issues.

The Kyoto Protocol is clearly a political move and not a true agreement to address all issues of climate change. The heavy use of Sinks and Carbon Trading will create yet another market-based system in which the already rich developed countries of the North will profit from the poor countries of the South. Rather than tackle the fundamental causes of climate change, dependency on fossil fuels and an unwillingness to switch to alternative sources of energy, the delegates have disregarded the environment and created yet another system of neo-liberal trading in the new global market economy. It is clear that Kyoto is a sell-out. "The chilling reality is that the climate summit agreement in Bonn enables northern governments and their corporations to escape their promised CO2 reductions, but allow them to significantly increase their emissions." Corporate Europe Observatory. www.xs4all.nl/~ceo

A simple and far more effective method of reducing carbon emissions by 90% and stabilising climate change is to reduce public transport fares by 90%. This is more than just a nice idea it's essential for our survival. For a 90% for 90% info pack and more info on climate change contact; Rising Tide c/o Manchester Earth First!, Box 29, 22a Beswick St., Manchester, M4 7HS. www.risingtide.org.uk

Essoholes

On Wednesday Greenpeace shut down the Esso (Exxon Mobil to our US readers) fuel distribution centre in Purfleet, Essex. People blocked the gates to the depot with two big customised shipping containers bolted to the road. Two volunteers chained themselves to the inside of each container that were covered with posters of George W Bush and Esso. A second team shut down the fuel supply to the petrol tankers and then occupied the rest of the site. Greenpeace climate campaigner Rob Gueterbock explains the action, "Because of Esso, Bush has stuck two fingers up to the world and is refusing to abide by the Kyoto Global Warming Treaty. Bush does what Esso tells him. To get the US, the world's biggest polluter to sign up to the agreement, we have to stop Esso." According to The Economist "Exxon Mobil, the biggest oil company, is also the worlds most powerful climate change sceptic" it also made record profits of over $17 billion last year. During the same period the company spent $7.9 billion on oil exploration and nothing on renewable energy or green fuels. Greenpeace are encouraging everyone to boycott Esso in protest at their profits before the planet policy. www.greenpeace.org.uk

CHOKER-COLA

So, not only is it bad for your teeth, it appears that the world dominating mega-corp Coca-Cola is responsible for the "systematic intimidation, kidnapping, detention and murder" of workers in an outsourced bottling plant in Columbia, according to the US union, United Steelworkers, on behalf of Sinatrainal, the Columbian union. Since 1994 it is claimed that five workers have been killed by paramilitary organisations on behalf of the bottling company. Coca-Cola naturally deny any responsibility, as the company operates under contract, but union lawyers claim they tightly control operations and are well aware of intimidation tactics to scupper unions within the plant. In the 1980's, Coca-Cola wielded it's mighty fist to curb human rights abuse in Guatemala, after three union members were killed.

SAB CASE

Following last year's running over of hunt sab Steve Christmas by a hunt supporter, a demo was held at kennels in Felbridge. Police arrested loads of protestors in a series of dawn raids after the demo. Those arrested are currently awaiting trial, faced with transport costs to and from court every day for up to six weeks. Please send donations if you possibly can, payable to Burstow Defendants Fund, c/o 6 Tilbury Place, Brighton, BN2 2GY.

...and finally...

After the Genoan people had been so nice to us in the days preceding the conference the SchNEWS crew were a bit confused when the local residents waved pants and random bits of washing out of their windows during protest marches. Were they telling us we were pants? No, this was their way of showing support. The pants thing was related to the fact that Mr Belusconi doesn't wear any pants (just a G8-string!). The dirty washing was put out in defiance of the local mayor who had asked residents to help keep the city tidy. He obviously hadn't considered the fact that his city might get trashed anyway!

disclaimer

FORGET THE DEBT DROP YOUR PANTS

Dedication
This issue of SchNEWS is dedicated to Carlo Giuliani and all those who have died fighting for a better world.

GENOA EYEWITNESS ACCOUNTS

G8 SUMMIT GENOA JULY 19-21

You make plans, we make history

By Wednesday, 18th July - the day before the first mass demonstration - the convergence centre in Piazza Kennedy was teeming with activity. The sports grounds, parks and schools made available by the city council - needed to accommodate the tens of thousands flooding into the city - were filling up. The Genoa Social Forum (GSF - the umbrella group who were overall organisers of the Anti-G8 event) was in full swing: welcoming newcomers by handing out food, bottled water and maps from under marquees; the schools on Via Cesare Battista were buzzing with GSF volunteers - many holding legal or medical passes - as well as Indymedia people who had one floor of the building.

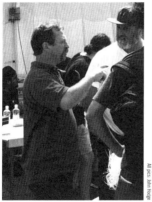

All pics: John Hodge

Arriving at Genoa were a spectrum of the usual suspects - lefty, anarchist, green, liberals and the rest from around Europe plus Kurdish activists, Indians, Africans and many others. Also jetting in were some high profile 'anti-capitalists' such as José Bové, the McDonalds smashing French farmer (right), who was speaking in the public forum talks around the topic of 'Another World Is Possible' which had been running since Monday.

Wednesday night saw a big free concert by Manu Chao at the convergence centre (below, right). But the stage, the food stalls (and prices they were charging) and the white marquees gave the whole thing the feel of a corporate beer festival rather than an anti-capitalist protest. However it wasn't like this for long: by the end of the summit, the centre was the scene of a police sweep involving tear gas and truncheons. The road to the right was to have burning car bodies and banks and other glass fronted shops smashed and burned. The police conveniently had their depot next door, behind the row of shipping containers.

Carlini Stadium, 2PM Thursday July 19th: The huge marquee houses thousands of mostly regional Italian activist groups getting ready to pad-up and become Tute Bianche on Friday. At this moment all over the stadium, - immediately prior to the migrants march - mass production of padding is underway. In the early hours of this morning Carlini was raided and searched by police, getting the three day event off to a flying start.

THURSDAY JULY 19TH
MIGRANTS MARCH

I'VE BEEN COUNTING: TWENTY SEVEN THOUSAND, THREE HUNDRED AND FIFTY SIX.

WHAT - PEOPLE ON THIS MARCH?

NO - IMAGES OF CHE GUEVARA

Genoa? She's Like A Sister To Me

By Flaco & Gibby

GENOA July 19: The sun ain't shining, but 100,000 well-tooled lunatics are gearing up for some heated exchanges on the streets of Genoa.

The shakers and breakers of the G8 nations may have hand picked the Ligurian capital for its winding streets and an old-skool trading port, but Bush, Blair and Berlusconi hadn't counted on 100,000 uninvited guests (literally) gate crashing their party.

Today, July 19, kicked off proceedings with a 70,000 strong march through the town in solidarity with the millions of asylum seekers getting universally-stiffed across fortress Europe. An international soup of banner-waving, wall-tagging, trumpet-blaring, cop-taunting anti-imperialistas meandered through the streets, giving Genoa's multi-faceted police response the chance to air their newly painted firepower.

Meanwhile, as the Japanese PM touched down at Genoa airport, all was quiet inside the forbidden Zona Rossa. Dark-windowed motorcades monopolised the roadways save only for cop cars and camera crews. Every entrance point is stalked by a sneering lynch-mob of gun toting cops in Gucci shades and goatees. A four metre high steel fence - set in concrete and nailed to the tarmac (listen up Mr Eavis) - blocks all access points to the sacred sqaure mile where the world's most powerful justice-dodgers plan to trough on marinari and the misery of millions. Spooks stop and search those sneaky enough to blag security passes like it's Derby day in Glasgow. No one walks ten metres without getting a spin. Armoured cars, bulldozers and scores of horses line the Via 20th Septembre, the main artery heading straight for the Ducalo Palace (the conference centre). This is the spot where every fucker in town knows the cardboard-covered army of the Tute Bianche intend to make their entrance.

Meet The Players...

Unlike the Czechs faced with the World Bank meeting in Prague in September 2000, the Italian resistance is more than ready for the G8. But, outside the pages of the British mainstream press, don't expect to get your head easily around the breakdown of the blockade. The Genoa Social Forum, who sparked off the mobilisation for this meeting, is a loose coalition of surprisingly varied forces. At one end of the scale is the Jubilee, Drop the Debt reformist lobby and at the other end is the militant Tute Bianche and COBAS (themselves a coalition of street-fighting anarcho-syndicalist and marxist trade unions). Despite all parties signing up (crossed fingers behind backs stylee) to the GSF "No sticks, no stones, no fire," manifesto - it's well accepted that once the old bill start cracking heads - anything goes.

12PM July 19: SWP/Global Resistance warm up the tonsils for the Migrants March back at the convergence centre (left)

Pics: John Hodge

Needless to say the organised anarchist groups massing in Genoa have more self respect than to get involved with dubious liberal coalitions and have stayed well clear of the GSF. Having said that, unlike previous incarnations of similar coalitions, the GSF are not dissing anyone else's tactical or ideological approach and everyone on the streets seems happy enough to co-exist (so long as no one's attack infringes on anyone elses). Of course, the SWP - here in force to paint their name all over proceedings - are tolerated by nobody except their French and Italian opposite numbers in the comically titled 'Globalise Resistance'...

The White Overalls - or Tute Bianche - (remember Milan's Muppetmen Ya Basta) who include well-padded crews from all over Italy have decided er... not to wear the white overalls afterall - this is because they've linked up with Social Center activists from Naples and the COBAS militants to form a single attacking block. Having said that, other COBAS contingents are linking with the anarchist black blocks tomorrow (who have fallen out with the Tute Bianche because of the hierarchical make-up and insistence in adherence to the leadership's plans). They, the anarchists, are in turn joining the not provocatively-violent-but-willing-to-defend-themselves-pink-block (no relation to their Prague colour campeneros) for another fence breach elsewhere. Confused? Well, let's hope the fucking beasts are too.

As it happens though, the old bill's break down is equally mashed. The local (municipal) police - answerable to the local left wing government - are on the streets dressed identical to the state police - answerable to the national fascist government. They are joined by the paramilitary style Carabinieri, who's numbers include national servicemen (no need to explain what kind of asshole becomes a cop for a year to aid their country's well being). The Carabineri are cruising round town in armoured cars completely sealed, but for little holes to shoot people out of.

Hanging out with friends at the School A. Diaz

The normal police have got Brinks Matt style caged vans, and they've all got helicopters and guns galore. Alongside them are the soldiers, the navy personnel, the financial police, the forest (eh? - ed) police and the secret servicemen - who, incidentally, spent the last week posting letter bombs around the town in order to pump up the air of tension. Milling in the crowd are badly disguised undercover policemen carrying (get this) police issue crash helmets... doh!

However, despite the forces lined up against them, and the daunting task of busting down the barricades - beyond which undoubtedly lie the world's most sophisticated personnel protection systems - the liberators gathered in Genoa are in positive spirits. Despite the cynics questioning their support, the 70,000 who marched tonight are being continually joined by trainload after trainload of equally dedicated comrades. The Italian authorities chose not to shut the borders after all. A decision they may well live to regret. There is a storm coming and this time it aint heading for bankers or bureaucrats, this time it's the shot-callers on the slab. No more fucking around. Leaders, it is time to meet your world.

Pic: Guy Smallman

The Red Zone - boot boys and bolly

85

The Point Of No Return

EYEWITNESS ACCOUNTS

This was the day of 'civil disobedience'. Time for Tute Bianche (or Ya Basta or White Overalls), Black Block. Pink Block, COBAS and everyone else to try their hand at attempting to breach the Red Zone, and stop this bloody summit!

"Protesters awoke on Friday morning to find that the red zone leapt four blocks east overnight. Despite 70,000 marching on Thursday, once the tear gas filled the streets Friday morning, tens of thousands of protesters had miraculously (or not) disappeared.

An anarchist block assembling in Piazza Paolo di Novi had barely started filling their bins with cobblestones when the state police volleyed in the first CS rounds. A street battle ensued pushing us eastwards - away from the target zone."

Pic: Guy Smallman

Pic: Alec Smart

"A black flag waving marching band managed to regroup the four thousand strong unit, who then crossed the railway and headed to the northern limits of the red zone, stopping on the way to rearrange some banks and feed the masses thanks to a helpful supermarket (on the return journey the shutters were still off and local residents were taking shopping trolleys full of free groceries home).

However, it is true that the focus of the siege was lost for a while beneath the youthful excitement of trashing the banks. It was unfortunate that the post office, bus stops and a few local traders got trashed, and several times the block stopped moving towards it's goal due to a window breaking frenzy. It may be inspiring that several thousands of young people are prepared to don crash helmets and gas masks to forward the anarchist cause - but the more focussed elements of the block were saying 'If we are here to bust the G8, let's bust the G8, if we're here to fight the police, let's fight the police - but let's not fart around trashing people's communities coz it's 'black block style to hoof bricks at windows'. Having said this, mass disobedience and the element of chaos is not to be underestimated, on top of that, many of the block were highly focussed on why they were here, and pushed the police advances back."

"In a beautiful old barrio, the battle raged. Protesters charged up tightstreets flinging stones at police lines. The police, protected head to toe, amassed behind shields and flanked by armoured vehicles, responded with tear gas and by flinging back the rocks. The ferocious spirit of the protesters more than the paltry stones pushed back the police lines. Barricades were built with dumpsters, cars, anything at hand. The front lines would retreat nursing wounds and poisoned eyes. The more seriously injured were carried to ambulances. New people rushed to the front, while others tore up the pavement for ammunition."

"Another surge, everyone rushed forward on 2 or 3 different streets. Some riot cops got stranded in their retreat and hand-to-hand fighting ensued. Those fighting are not necessarily in black, though they are masked. Some have helmets. It is not the Black Bloc, and there are no agent provocateurs. This is a militant energy driven by people who have said - Ya Basta!, Fuck the police! rage! energy! resolve!"

Pic: Hamish

You're only supposed to blow the bloody doors off

"They move forward. Tear gas is everywhere. The police are retreating. An armoured carabinieri truck is captured and the occupants flee. It is smashed up and set ablaze. This symbol of the hated oppressive state is burning and everyone is cheering, filled with rebel joy. Someone sprays 'We Are Winning!' on the side of the carcass of the armoured beast. Now they are almost in Piazza Alimondo. They are pushing the police back, two blocks, then three, further and further. Protesters are euphoric, storming forward, overwhelming the despised carabinieri. Approaching the wall of the G8; 'Here we are,' they chant, 'we resist!'"

"Hundreds strong, they poured into the expansive Piazza Alimondo. Two armoured police Land Rovers drive recklessly into the crowd, one drives away, the other stalls; obviously it didn't want to scratch its paintwork by ramming the wheelie-bin out of the way. It was attacked, the cop at the back began waving his gun around, deliberately pointing it at different people. Some saw it and retreated. Some didn't. Carlo walked across the back of the van and picked up a red fire extinguisher lying on the ground. He turned and advanced on the van and was shot in the head."

NO MORE MO

POSTAMAT

Pic: Alec Smart

Tute Bianche: What A Gas

Preparations began early at Carlini Stadium - Ya Basta HQ - with talks followed by training sessions. Resembling an army preparing for war, the 10,000 of them spent all morning taping up their bodies with foam and padding. The atmosphere was tense, the mood defiant. Anything was possible. There was an ecstatic mood of celebration when we finally set off on the 4 km march to the city centre. An endless sea of bopping helmets interspersed with a vast array of flags of every hue and color. At the front a long line of Ya Basta militants pressed forward behind a wall of plastic shields.

Despite all the ominous reports, we swept down the wide boulevard confidently - we were so many! So many people prepared to use their bodies to break through, to defend themselves, to struggle. 'El Pueblo Unido, Jamas Sera Vencido' they chanted. 'Genova Libera!' 'E-Z-L-N!' Rage Against The Machine blasted from the mobile P.A. It was momentarily powerful and wonderful.

Two kilometres from the Red Zone, the police attacked us. First a barrage of tear-gas canisters were lobbed over the front lines, deep into the heart of the demonstration. Nobody had gas masks (doh! - ed). The people, packed in tightly, panicked and surged backwards. 500 heavily armed riot squad stormed the front lines. In brutal scenes, the Ya Basta militants crumbled despite brave resistance. All were battered. People screamed, turned, fled, falling over each other.

We retreated up the road. The sky was heavy with gas and helicopters hovered overhead. A water cannon blasted away, throwing bodies around like paper bags. What now? People looked to the Ya Basta leadership in all this disarray but there was no Plan B - the microphone that issued commands during the march was now silent. People retreated further and further, meanwhile the front lines struggled to hold on, and the fighting was intense, the tear gas volleys raining down, the police hitting out viciously as the plastic shields shattered and the helmets cracked. Bleeding people were rushed to the back with head injuries including some inflicted when they had been shot in the face with tear gas canisters.

We were defeated before even beginning. The non-violent, active defence tactic crushed in the face of decisively brutal police tactics. As the majority of the march sat down further up the road, thousands of others streamed off into the side streets. The north side was blocked by the railway track, to the south lay small enclosed streets. "Open new fronts! Break through police lines at 2, 3, 4 different points!" Spontaneous and enraged, thousands ran into the sidestreets. Meanwhile, the Ya Basta loudspeaker requested people to stay put on the road, far from the Red Zone.

Carabinieri snuff out the last resistance of the Tute Bianche as they charge at protesters with armoured vehicles, water cannons and tear gas volleys.

Pic: John Hodge

Pink Block

Pic: Guy Smallman

"On the day the pink block wove through the Genoa streets, singing and dancing and exchanging waves and smiles with people in their houses. It was a vibrant atmostphere. The pink march breached police lines and attacked the fence – the first tear gas of the day scattered us, but we regrouped and tried agian - more tear gas. Behind the fence were armoured tanks with machine guns on top. We have no doubt that if we had succeeded in getting over we would have been shot.

We regouped further off to decide what to do next, then were caught up in a maelstrom of black block and police, scattering us like leaves. More tear gas, so much we couldn't breathe, but this time savage beatings for the people who couldn't run fast enough. We were all in shock and traumatised by this point.

After winding back through more streets, we found Ya Basta! massed in thousands trying to breach the fence. The amount of tear gas being used was unbelieveable, but there was order – the canisters were quickly thrown back at them. The police suddenly charged with tanks and we scattered again, fleeing into side streets. The police blocked everywhere – someone told us that there had been a death nearby. Eventually we managed to get round and back to where we had started from – passing random groups of traumatised, injured and angry people as we went.

We ended the day in shock and pain, watching slow motion shots of the death of Carlo Guiliani repeated over and over again, interspersed with Bush, Blair, etc looking grey and distant and somehow irrelevant, and wondered where we would go from here."

Five minutes behind the black block, the police wade through with tear gas canisters ablaze (above) only to run into the pink block, who they violently attack.

NB From all accounts people moved around a lot between blocks, and the make-up of individual blocks was varied. For instance many COBAS people - an anarchist union group - ran with the black block. Many people were still deciding who to go with at the last minute, and the pink block was only announced on the Thursday. Many started with Tute Bianche but left due to its authoritarian and ineffectual tactics to join the black block or others; numbers would have left the black block because they were tired or getting paranoid.

Sight For Sore Eyes

On the third day was the 'International March'. This march was to be the big, non-confrontational event. Big it was - 200,000 - but with the police having assassinated a protester the day before, it was bound to be a bit edgy...

Pic: Alec Smart

Pic: Alec Smart

For SWP/GR and co. this march started out like the real McCoy - banners, chants, more banners, walking - the sort of things which really bring governments down. On the Friday they had been really effective as the 'Headless Chickens' Block.

"Although this march was supposed to be completely non-confrontational, and in spite of the relaxed mood of the morning, there was a lot of tension on the march. As well as the sizable numbers of people with white-painted hands, there were a lot of people carrying sticks (and thousands more carrying red flags). Every time a police helicopter flew overhead (at least every five minutes), the chant of 'Assassini' would go up from hundreds of voices, and a wave of arms would go up to give the police the finger.

Really though, the most memorable thing about the march was its sheer size (around 200,000). There was just no end to it. We watched the march pass for almost two hours before we joined in, and even then we were far from the end. It was impossibly big, with all sorts of people, from all over the world.

Eventually a several-hundred strong anarchist section turned up. It contained a fair mix of people - some had their sticks and gas masks ready, and were obviously prepared for a fight, others were equally obviously (and I think deliberately) unprepared - it looked like a lot of people had already left town.

The next mile or so was fairly uneventful. Then, but still a good distance from the GSF convergence centre, the march stopped, and then surged backward for a second. Nobody was sure what was happening, but all around us the goggles and bandannas started coming out. There was the possibility that the helicopters were dropping gas on top of us. It was another few minutes before we found out what was going on. The march was supposed to continue west along the coast until it reached the city centre, and would then turn up one of the main streets and continue to the north (staying well away from the red zone). Down at the GSF convergence centre the carabinieri were out in force, making sure that the march turned where it should, instead of carrying on towards the zone. But as the march turned into the city, a pitch battle between hundreds of people and police erupted, with teargas filling the street as more and more people joined the attack (though the largest section of the march continued away from the GSF, away from the fighting)."

"Maybe they [the cops] had watched the crowd go past in their numbers, and had picked their moment to wade in. Most of the those on the peaceful march had gone past them and it was as though the cops waited for the rear section of the march (where they expected black block numbers to be) and as soon as they thought it had arrived, broken the march in two at that point, letting all the flag wavers continue on, and attacking that last bit of the march. Why else would they split the march like that?"

"The militants stream through the crowd to the front. There they attempt to build barricades and hold back the advancing cops. The sky fills with stones. They hold the police and those behind them have a few moments more to retreat. Those who needed to get away from the zone could. Communist party stewards directed people away, but many people stayed, indignant that the demonstration could be so brutally dispersed even before it could get to the piazza. All afternoon the streets were mad with tear-gas, with stones, with burning banks, burning cars, barricades. The air was shrill with screams, of beatings, violence and fear.

Tourists and holiday makers have gone for the day from this tourist beach, and the ice cream shops and bars have shut so this lot can play war games. It'd be a bit like seeing a tank and a load of bootboys charging past the Brighton Palace Pier.

The next bit of news in the Indymedia rooms at around dusk was the raid at Carlini: "At the Carlini Stadium, base of the Ya Basta (Tute Bianche) movement, the officials ordered an immediate evacuation. "Like Saigon" reported one eye-witness. Hundreds of other activists not present at the time were left stranded. Plain clothes police swarmed in, and criminals were allowed in to rummage through peoples' belongings. That night, all over Genoa people fled from camping sites to roam the streets and alleys and back lanes of the city in fear, hunted like escaped convicts. It was the longest night. Eventually dawn came, but everything had changed."

Many of these people sought refuge that evening at School A. Diaz...

All pics: Alec Smart

Eventually the barricades were overrun. The police advanced ferociously, beating people indiscriminately. In a most surreal scene, cops in gray overalls beat up people on the beach, the Italian Riviera, while bathers looked on. Police in small boats launched tear-gas onto the beach. A helicopter overhead fired gas into the fleeing hordes. Further up, people jumped off the rocks into the sea. The huge march ended in absolute mayhem. Let it be recorded - 200,000 overtly peaceful protesters were not allowed to demonstrate."

"The police took over the convergence centre – and did this sweep, extending their line right across the convergence centre to the beach, and forced us eastward with constant tear gas. When they'd got to the eastern end of the

centre, I was with people trapped between the road – which had armoured vehicles and carabinieri on it – and the beach. It was a matter of running eastward to get outside this trap. Eventually a group of us were cornered. People put their hands up, and with this gesture cops let you walk through a gap between them. One guy's hands fell, and he said something to a cop. Straight away the cop started smashing his face – instantly he was on the pavement with a pool of blood quickly forming, then paramedics came out of nowhere. (normally a spot where tourists eat icecreams, today, a warzone). Once past this, we were still being pushed east by armoured vehicles and constant gas, into the flow of the march, which was still coming. You almost got used to the gas, kicking the canisters as they fizzed around your feet. By this stage any thoughts of lingering to take pictures were gone, and we were really running. Eventually some locals led a group of us into an enclave which they said we would be safe. After an hour or so we had the all clear, and I walked back to Indymedia rooms – by this stage the big raid was only hours away".

All pics on this page: Hamish

Dark Night
GSF Building Raid
EYEWITNESS ACCOUNTS

"After the violence of Saturday, and news that the Carlini stadium - where most of the Tute Bianche were staying - was under the control of plain clothes cops it was on the cards that this centre would become under attack. There was a strategy to stash all the video tapes gathered by Indymedia, knowing that the raw footage may contain incriminating evidence (and people were saying that the cops 'know that we have video evidence of police presence in the black block').

"At about 10PM some police vehicles drove past the two buildings (on one side the school used by the GSF including their legal and medical offices, with one floor housing Indymedia; and on the other side of the street School A. Diaz which was more of an accommodation centre). Somebody threw an object at the police car. Helicopters were buzzing. There was that feeling of 'this is gonna kick off'. I thought 'er time to go round the corner for a pizza' – and when I got there a few of the other Indymedia people had the same idea. We were having food when suddenly there was a convoy of police vehicles, riot vans, then marching troops. People began nervously dialling mobiles.

The first sign of the worst was when we rang the legal office in the GSF building - the phone answered and someone said 'it's OK', but voices in the background shouted "don't say anything – it's police".

We had to convince the pizza bar manager that we were in danger if he kicked us out, and he let us hide there until it was all clear at 3:30AM."

"We had just finished our meeting when we heard shouts and sirens and the roar of people yelling, objects breaking. The cops had come and they were raiding the centre. We couldn't get out of the building because there were too many people at the entrance. We went up, running up the five flights of stairs, to the very top. We found an empty room, a couple of tables, grabbed some sleeping bags to cover our heads if we got beaten. And waited. We could hear doors being slammed and voices shouting below, then quiet. Someone came in, walked around, left. The light went on. Through a crack between the tables, I could see a helmet, a face. A big Italian cop with a huge paunch loomed over us. He told us to come out. He didn't seem in beating mode, but we stayed where we were, tried to talk to him in English and Spanish and the few Italian words I know: "paura" "fear"and "pacifisti". He took us down to the third floor, where a whole lot of people were sitting, lined up against the walls. We waited. Someone came in, demanding to know whether there was someone there from Irish Indymedia. We waited. Lawyers arrived. The police left."

From the vantage point of the 4th floor of the GSF building looking across the street to the School A. Diaz: "I could see at least 100 cops kick the door in of the school, and we could see through the windows police truncheoning people sleeping. I saw one man held down while two bashed him. Tear gas was used. Nobody was getting out. We stood in total fear, then after watching this, at 12:10AM news came up that they were now breaking through into our building."

"At 12:20 I climbed up to the roof of the building and and lay face down for 1 1/2 hours, with a helicopter spotlight scanning around, and sound of screaming coming from the school. At some point we found out the Carabinieri had left our building, and we went back to looking at the scene across the street. At least fifteen people were being stretchered out, and the crowd screamed when police came out with what looked like a body bag - but I think this was a stunt to upset people (no death has been confirmed)."

"They had come in to the rooms where people were sleeping. Everyone had raised up their hands, calling out 'pacifisti! pacifist!' And they beat the shit out of every person there."

"Police vans were passing all the time, and ambulances racing with sirens every 5-10 minutes. This was a chilling sign that a lot of people were getting badly hurt. A Carabinieri came to the entrance of the pizza bar which was our refuge. He asked if there were protesters inside, and evidently he was convinced that there weren't, and went."

"In the school A. Diaz was the sound of screaming. Out of a group of 400 people which arrived from the Carlini Stadium, thinking that it was going to be safer here (numbers were too small by now at Carlini), a group of 20 year old Spanish pacifists were hurt badly, eight of them were hospitalised, and eight-nine arrested. The Spanish legal team feared the worst about police beatings."

From the Indymedia Rooms: "At first we tried to have a barricade, but then realised that this would antagonise the cops. From the second floor we heard banging. Then they came through here. There was a group of plain clothes cops - with batons. We had our hands up, then we (about 30) were put facing the wall spreadeagle while the police went around the computers. Then they let us sit down. One of the police was a woman in a high fashion outfit and a truncheon. We could see them taking some laptops, and minidisc players, other recording equipment and... some salad knives. They wouldn't let us answer phones."

"A crowd had gathered and were shouting 'Assassini! Assasini!' They brought out the waking wounded, arrested them and took them away. The crowd below was challenging the cops and the cops were challenging the crowd and suddenly a huge circle of media gathered, bright camera lights."

A photographer outside: "I was taking pictures of the injured. I thought some of them were dead. Then I got a truncheon in the stomach. The cop took the camera, another held my arms behind my back, pinning me to a wall. I had him thinking that my Indymedia pass was actually an official media pass and he let me go." "I heard a policeman say 'there's too much media.'"

The GSF legal office on the 2nd floor was the only room in this building trashed - computers and phones badly damaged.

A woman with a badge with an EU symbol finally came to the building, and this was the moment when the violence stopped. Evidently she had the power to stop them. Then the police retreated, but still occupied the street."

From Indymedia: "As soon as they were gone we immediately shut down all computers, and removed any sensitive phone numbers in the rooms. We found that despite the gear which had been taken - all the images saved on the files were still there, and the tapes safe." (most of the footage had already been uploaded anyway). "We then got on with emailing news outside."

Pic: Hamish

Carabinieri haven't worked out that there's better ways to get information out of a computer than a good 'ol beating.

"At 4AM we were back at the GSF. We immediately found out about the horrendous injuries to British media activist Sky (See SchNEWS 316). In the aftermath I walked around the school - large pools of blood along the corridor, smears on the walls, and personal objects, clothing and bandages bloodied. Peoples' possessions just thrown around the room on the ground floor where they were sleeping. Some people were still weeping and trembling. All the computers in the foyer had smashed

Pic: Gday

Pools of blood: School A. Diaz would have needed a heavy scrubbing before children returned after the summer break.

screens (as though the dickhead cops thought the screen held the memory). At this point there was an emergency meeting to plan support for those hospitalised and arrested – work out who was missing, who had transport etc."

Later we got stories back from arrestees: "We know that they have arrested everyone they hospitalised, taken people to jail and tortured them. One young French man had his head badly beaten on Friday in the street. In jail, they took him into a room, twisted his arms behind his back and banged his head on the table. Another man was taken into a room covered with pictures of Mussolini and pornography, and alternately slapped around and then stroked with affection in a weird psychological torture. Others were forced to shout, "Viva El Duce"!! Just in case it wasn't clear that this is fascism, Italian style."

"The next morning – as a final insult – we watched on a café TV the police laying out tables of weapons, sledgehammers, molotovs, knives, etc, which they claimed to have confiscated from the buildings, justifying the raids. But what would a Spanish pacificist walking three miles at night to safety be doing carting a sledgehammer?"

"Back at the GSF building at lunchtime, everybody was in a panic saying that the place would be raided again, and all people could think about was getting out of town. There were furiously packing down roomfuls of computers. There were scare stories that once you'd left Genoa, and on your own, regional police would attack you. I took a bus out of town, and boarded a train south. I sunk into the seat in the carriage feeling lucky to have escaped with my life."

A DEATH IN THE FAMILY
...BUT WILL IT BREATHE NEW LIFE INTO THE MOVEMENT?

By Flaco

Seattle may be touted as some sort of watershed, but Carlo's killing in Genoa is a turning point for the anti-capitalist movement (if such a thing really exists). How we play it from here will have repercussions far beyond the blood-stained streets of Northern Italy. It was no freak cub-cop overreaction that left one mother mourning and several others preparing to, as the sun hit the sea on July 20th, but a deliberate act of terror - in the most basic sense of the word.

The snowball that's been gaining weight and speed as it rolled through Geneva, Prague and Gothenburg has become far too jagged a spike in the side of those steering the planetary carve up. Young people are shot dead for daring to think there can be another way. The message from the world's authorities is clear: go back to your homes, do not meddle in what doesn't concern you, return to your televisions, to smoking dope and stealing traffic cones and leave the intricacies of global economics alone - because if you don't we will kill you. The same way we killed Carlo Giuliani.

For decades, the poorest of the planet's families from Asia, Africa and Latin America have been burying the fathers, the sisters and the first born sons who have dared to confront the forces of global capitalism. But Carlo's death spells something different. For the first time the global elite has begun to kill the children of its own people. Dissent will no longer be tolerated. The whip of economic dictatorship is finally cracking at home.

But where we go from here is still up for grabs. The globalisers would dearly love to see us run scared, or split our ranks with paranoid accusations of 'whose side are you on?'. Tactical difference should not be confused with police-collusion and counter-revolutionary activity... or vice-versa.

True enough, there were cops in ski-masks leading the more excitable and naive among Genoa's young bloods on attacks on corner shops, bus stops and post offices. But the agitators can be addressed. If everyone who takes any action knows why they are taking it and what sort of action they think is necessary to achieve their goal, then the police will not be able to steer the crowds, the meetings, the discussion groups or 'the movement' as a whole. The problem is less one of infiltration, more one of focus.

The more liberal elements of groups such as the Genoa Social Forum (GSF) or Prague's INPEG, need to understand, that just because they have the ear of the newspapers, it doesn't mean they speak with the voice of the people. The reformist agenda of these groups, who call for more legislation, more institutions and stronger government control over the runaway capitalist train, is an entire philosophy away from the genuine participatory democracy sought by many.

Instead of calling for the deployment of "non-violent methods of restraining and defusing violent behaviour" for those who fail to adhere to "the political and ethical parameters of our mass actions" (Walden Bello I expected so much more from you), perhaps the up-in-arms brigade should be questioning their own attempted coup of the global resistance movement. Both INPEG and the GSF produced documents laying down "rules" for "participation" in what were illegal blockades of international meetings. The GSF tactical manifesto was insulting to the resistance history of many of it's signatory groups. The anarchists were perhaps the only people (police included) who took to the streets with honest intentions, both about their goals and what they were prepared to do to achieve them. The anarchists have long been aware that power (be it economic or governmental) is the problem - not who holds it - and needs, therefore, to be removed altogether. The Black Bloc do not "detract from 'the message'"- they have a different message. And unlike the liberals

and the hierarchical groups of the organised left who would, at best, replace those in power with their own institutions manned by their own people, and at worst, settle for a seat at the G-8 table, the anarchist's message is not a lunge for the throne shrouded in the smoke screen language of 'justice' and 'liberty'. The anarchists recognise that a power wielding state is no better than a power wielding corporation, and they are well aware that the police are the front-line defence for both.

This is not to dispel organisation. Organisation is imperative. Co-operation and communication between the disparate groups involved in the resistance is key. But an insurrectionary pseudo-government (complete with pseudo-police if Walden gets his way)? Hmmm... four legs good, two legs bad time already.

The strength of this movement/loose-amalgamation-of-people-who-ain't-taking-any-more-shit, has always been its leaderless fluidity, its constantly changing strategy, its unpredictable tactics and targets. This is why the authorities (until now) have found it so hard to get a handle on what we were up to - we weren't following patterns or playing by any discernible rules. Now, as we witnessed in Genoa, the Man has caught up. Infiltration is the price of protesting-by-numbers. Though Italy was an ideal venue for us to mobilise an unprecedented number of insurrectionaries, it was also a touch for the global authorities who could mobilise one of the West's most corrupt, right wing and violent state security forces. Recent history has shown the Italian security services are prepared to stoop to anything in order to undermine subversive movements. Genoa proved they haven't lost their touch.

James Anon made the point on Indymedia.org that if the non violent protesters came up with something that worked maybe more people would adopt their tactics. (http://www.indymedia.org/front.php3?article_id=55463&group=webcast) However, non violence should not be confused with not rocking the boat - as often appears to be the case. Those who feel the 'violent anarchists' are curbing their successes should maybe look at how successful their own tactics are. It is no coincidence that Tony Blair "welcomes" peaceful calls for debt reform - the communiques are duly issued, the lip service paid, and then..... nothing changes, and the global carve up getting mapped in the Oval Office doesn't miss a step.

Maybe time within the 'movement' would be better spent skipping the anarchist witch-hunt and focusing on our common enemies.

One of the more eye opening moments in Genoa came when the non-violent protesters and the Black Bloc crossed paths. At around three o'clock on July 20th, an anarchist bloc had tried to cross the Piazza Manin en route to the red zone, the non-violent white handed pacifists in the square, refused

to let them pass. Discussions between the two groups were interrupted by a vicious police attack during which the white hand protesters sat down hands aloft and took a severe beating without fighting back (as is their prerogative). However an hour later when three masked youths walked back through the square the (understandably upset) pacifists threw first a stick, then a bottle, then a rock at them. They saw the Black Bloc as the cause for their pain. No violence had been directed at the police wielding the boots, the clubs and the teargas, but strict pacifist adherence could be suspended in order to attack anyone (without authority) who had not stuck to "their" tactical code. Perhaps this pacifist submission to authority says more about the the authoritarian nature of the society they seek, than about their abhorrence of the Black Bloc's tactics.

The more reasoned voices of Italy's Ya Basta collective are already admitting the error of attacking the brick throwers (there is something twisted about an elite Tute Bianche hit squad in Subcommandante Marcos t-shirts beating people with crash helmets for wearing bandannas over their faces). However, the security services will no doubt be fuelling the fire of division and will embrace the peace-policers (as they did in the US during the anti-Vietnam protests of the 1960s) who, they hope in turn, will return the anti-capitalist front-line to the letters pages of the Washington Post.

The rats inside the global red zone want us to crawl back to our workplaces, to the fear of unemployment and to the gratitude for an irregular playtime. But we can say no. We can say: we do not care how well protected you are with your armies, your police, your banks or your brands, because we have had enough and we will not run from your guns.

These would-be leaders can scuttle off to Qatar or cruise ships or Rocky Mountain retreats, but we know their meetings have little impact on the real decisions made elsewhere. Perhaps we in the West should follow the example of India's farmers who removed Monsanto's headquarters brick by brick and took it away. If we don't like Bush's missile defence plans, we could go to Flyingdales and take it away... brick by brick, bullet by bullet.

We could pick a company, say Balfour Beatty, and put them out of business. A thousand actions at a thousand sites dismantling every facet of their insidious business. Would their shareholders bail them out? Unlikely. Then we could move on and up. When we can co-ordinate our actions as millions of people, then maybe we can dismantle the oil industry, the arms industry, the jail industry... the government industry?

The mass street actions we have been able to mount and the dedication, planning and application of those on the streets has shown us that we have the wherewithal to make decisions and carry them out regardless of what the state may think or threaten. If we put this dynamic to work away from the mega-summits we can become a threat again. But we need to be imaginative and we need to stay ahead of the beast. Where we choose to go from here is crucial to whether we are in the process of sparking serious global change or whether we are merely in the death throes of another cycle of resistance.

If we don't want corporate activity in our neighbourhoods, let's chuck the corporations out. If we don't want the police or the government flexing their muscle in our neighbourhoods, let's stop recognising their bogus authority and encourage others to do the same. Let's link our communities together - not through state or business initiatives - but through people who share a common struggle. If we believe in making changes and creating something better, and if we are prepared to take the risks and put in the time, then lets do it. Let's not let Carlo's death be in vain. Because when one of us catches a bullet, a club or jail sentence, a little bit of all of us dies. But together we are alive and together we can, and we will, win.

See also The Case for Confrontation, by the same author: http://uk.indymedia.org/display.php3?article_id=673

AND AT THE END OF THE DAY...

Recommended Reading
ON FIRE

Featuring accounts and reflections on the events in Genoa by a range of contributors who were out on the street and part of it.

Available (unless it's sold out) for only £3.00 from AK Distribution or Active Distribution.

One Off Press

ISBN 1 902593 54 5

The battle of Genoa and the anti-capitalist movement

"Genoa was gutted. No city will host the G8 for a while. 34 banks burnt. 83 vehicles both police and civilian destroyed, 41 businesses torched or looted, 6 supermarkets, 12 government offices - illustrating the belief which some protesters have that targeting the economic organs of the enemy is the most effective tactic. (No buses were burnt, apparently because the bus drivers union was in solidarity with the protesters, ferrying everyone around for free the whole week). With Genoa in ruins, the G8 left quietly with a few empty promises to give some money to Africa.

The truth about agent provocateurs and what actually happened on the night of terror at the schools is coming out. During the whole event some 200 people were arrested, and 600 injured. In the jails, the protesters were tortured while police mocked them with pictures of Mussolini and Nazis. They tortured them, as they have done in Seattle, Prague and Quebec; as they did in Pinochet's Chile. They attempt to destroy the movement by spreading panic and fear. To break the back of the militants of this totally unarmed global protest movement."

Eyewitness Accounts: Ramor Ryan, Starhawk, Alec Smart, el Flaco, Gday John, http://struggle.ws/wsm/, Rachel, Dave and others from UK Indymedia.

CARA GO 1-0 UP

Burlo: It's the best Cara squad ever

European political football had a big weekend in Genoa this week, with the Carabinieri stunning everybody by going 1-0 up against the Black Block during the second half of Friday's tie.

By Tony R Green

CARA MANAGER SILVIO BURLESCONI went into the weekend round of fixtures with one aim in mind - to defend, defend, defend. He put together a rock-solid backline unit which kept on top of all visiting attacks: Instead of opting for a five man backline - he brought on about 20,000 - all in the familiar dark blue strip, with 1000's of other roaming strikers disguised in opposition strip.

"The last thing I was expecting at five o'clock on Friday was to be one nil ahead, but then many of my young squad were clearly up for it. I told them 'a draw will do', but my boys were more ambitious than that." said a proud Burlo. This is all the more remarkable considering the visiting teams came packed with many players already on international records.

Packed Out

The earlier part of the week saw coachloads of supporters draped in team colours come in from all over Europe hoping their teams could make an impact on this difficult Italian side. Some found themselves in Europe for the second time in twelve months after Prague - with many of their European counterparts crossing Europe all the time in recent seasons to play in what is essentially a dark-blues-versus-the-rest league. Locals batoned down the hatches in the Italian port city as the streams of coaches came into town for the match.

Kick Off

On the Thursday at 10AM the first game kicked off. The Cara stood their ground as 70,000 players streamed through the streets, in the familiar red strip of Workers United. Essentially an uneventful game, both teams were keeping to their own halves and by 5PM the game edged towards an inconclusive draw. Many recollected the heroics of the Argentinian striker Che Guevara in the 1966 final and supporters had him on t-shirts.

Black Block striker loses boot trying to kick a tear gas canister

On Friday the teams got down to business: By lunchtime the Black Block streamed out onto the pitch and managed to avoid the red flags as they ran riot around the east of the zona rosa goalmouth, scoring many banks and shops along the way, and alluding the Cara around the flanks.

The Pink Block - in their familiar colour with their samba band and latin American passing game - made the most of a couple of chances but didn't fair so well when they found themselves exposed to Cara tear gas attacks which might have been aimed at the Black Block, who had been in the area only minutes earlier.

That morning the coaches and trains hired for the event brought supporters of Globalise Resistance who were seen in the customary red bandanas, and their chant rung out through the Genoa terraces - 'The world is not for sale, but our paper is'. The club was on its perpetual membership drive.

In the second half, Burlesconi's Cara were leaving gaping holes in their defence which the Blacks exploited, and the Cara found themselves playing catch-up.

The Tute Bianche team came out of their homeground at Carlini Stadium in the white strip, and were initially full of promise to make a mark on the game. But they disappointed once outside their half and struggled to put anything together all day. All the Cara had to do was give them a whiff of tear gas, and the Bianche's tactics were badly exposed.

Breakthrough

Eventually the Cara made a breakthrough at 4PM when - using a fairly unorthodox move - they shot dead a Black Block striker, then ran over him in a landrover. Again they were very lucky that the red card stayed in the ref's pocket. It's all part of the flair and unpredictability of Italian football that Burlo not only manages the Caras, but also owns the refs as well as the commentary box, and can use this to get an advantage on the scoreboard.

Sitting comfortably up in the sponsor's box during all the action was other guest managers who were meeting to talk about the new international 'Champions of Capitalism Cup' super-league, which is to feature teams from the top eight football countries. George W Bush - coach of the All American Rednecks, and Tony Blair - manager of the Neo Labour Lapdogs were keen to swap notes about the state of the game, and buying up top players cheaply from football mad South America and Africa.

Third strike

In the third game on the Saturday morning, the visitors didn't really have any new players waiting on the bench - while the Cara showed the depth of their national Italian squad. The schedule for the last day was a non violent march with the United Reds along the seafront, but after the Cara's shooting the day before both sides wanted to get ahead early.

At the convergence centre - where the international squad had been training - the Cara came in and split the reds defence into two, and the group caught at the back were on the receiving end of some top attacking moves in the style the Italian dark blues have developed. After trying to get a stamp on the game by setting fire to some car showrooms and banks, the visitors were shown about life in the big league when the Cara brought on armoured vehicles, constant tear gas volleys and baton charges, which drew first - second - and third blood from players hemmed in by the tanks.

Extra Time

By the end of the third day the visiting players retreated to their dressing rooms - but as they ate cut up oranges and the pundits discussed what might have been, nobody realised that the final whistle had not been blown. Burlo, the master tactician, sent on some strikers - this time no longer in the blue strip - into the Carlini Stadium, and many of the Bianche players were forced up the road to have their showers at School A. Diaz.

Then - deep into extra time and close to midnight, the Cara made their last real attempt to go two nil up. In another highly innovative bit of fascist football, the Cara really caught the visitors with their pants down by actually entering their changerooms wielding batons, just when everyone thought the game had finished. With a bit more Burlo magic the off-side flags stayed down. Many of the visitors were sleeping which made them vulnerable to the Cara boot-work. About 100 found themselves hospitalised and arrested - with the Cara showing that they were no strangers to night-time football.

In the morning Burlo talked down calls for bookings of his players from video evidence, saying 'it's the best job in the world managing the current Cara squad. Musso would have been proud.'

Weekly **SchNEWS**

WAKE UP! WAKE UP! IT'S YER BULLSHIT BUSTIN'

Printed and Published in Brighton by Justice?

"It's the sharp end of globalisa-tion."

Friday 3rd August 2001   www.schnews.org.uk   Issue 316

BLAIR-FACED LIAR

A week after the massive protests in Genoa, the free-trade-is-good-for-you brigade are on the offensive. In the New Labour corner Prime Minister Blair and Chancellor Gordon Brown went on a tour of Brazil and Argentina with an official government spokesman saying, "The Prime Minister believes people at the sharp end of the globalisation debate have a much more realistic view of the benefits of globalisation."

Maybe the 12,000 people attending the World Social Forum in Porto Alegre, Brazil earlier this year just weren't listening. The Forum was set up to counter Davos – another one of those corporate shingdigs where the ruling elite decide how to carve up the planet – and to declare that "another world is possible." Francois Houtart from the World Forum of Alternatives certainly hasn't got Blair's message. In Porto Alegre he described globalisation as "a fragmenting and destructive process; destroying communities, cultures, economies and the environment."

Meanwhile in Argentina this week, thousands of jobless people and state employees set up roadblocks in more than 40 cities, protesting at the government's austerity plan and demanding jobs. Argentina has been in recession for the past four years and the government's answer to this economic hiccup is the usual one of slashing wages, pensions, deep spending cuts and increasing privatisation. This is in order to save about a billion quid, and to assure creditors that it won't default on its debt which, currently stands at a staggering £91.5 billion.

Blair reckons the spending cuts were "a very significant step forward" but for who? The banks maybe, but certainly not for ordinary Argentinans. In a ruling last year a federal judge concluded "Since 1976 our country has been put under the rule of foreign creditors and under the supervision of the International Monetary Fund by means of a vulgar and offensive economic policy that forced Argentina to go down on its knees in order to benefit national and foreign private firms."

Moore of the Same

Over in the World Trade Organisation corner, Director General Mike Moore has been seriously getting his neo-liberal knickers in a twist. At a two-day meeting in Geneva this week he told negotiators to pull their fingers out or there won't be a new global trade round in Qatar in November. Moore is scared that the WTO will become irrelevant if a new trade round isn't launched after the kicking it got in Seattle (see SchNEWS

240). Along with his pals in the European Commission and some of the world's richest countries, he's been threatening developing countries by telling them that "a[nother] round would help the poor and weak countries more than anyone else. The big guys can fend for themselves. But without multilateral rules, the poor are subject to the law of the jungle."

Like Blair, Moore doesn't take too kindly to the "stuff-capitalism posse", telling anyone that will listen 'If you oppose the WTO, you are opposing lifting the poor out of poverty.'

But it's not only protestors who oppose a new round. India's Ambassador to the WTO, Srinivasan Narayanan, said just a few weeks ago, "We're not ready for it [a new round]. We'll lose more than we'll gain."

While one delegate from Lesotho added "What has the WTO and market liberalisation brought for Lesotho? Up till now, I haven't seen anything. The only thing I have seen is the opposite. The agreement on agriculture has almost wiped out our domestic industry." Federico Cuello Camilo the Dominican Republic's Trade Ambassador added "The WTO was supposed to have been an impartial referee of common rules, where countries could learn to play the game...It hasn't turned out like that. The rules are biased against the weak, and nothing has changed since Seattle."

As Aileen Kwa from Focus on the Global South points out, "Negotiations at the WTO institutionalise the law of the jungle. Arm-twisting is commonplace and weak countries are constantly threatened that their food aid would be cut off, or their loan suspended, if they do not tow-the-line." She adds, "While the majority of developing countries are refusing to back down, their positions could easily collapse without massive civil society backing."

The real problem for Blair, Moore and cronies is the growing movement opposed to the way the world is being run. At its most spectacular you've see it on the streets and TV screens when the global elite meet up to plan further carving up of the planet. But every day across the world people are fighting for a better, fairer world.

* Trade Union leaders worldwide have declared a Global Day of Action on November 9th on the opening day of the WTO Conference in Qatar. www.global-unions.org

* For more information on next year's World Social Forum and a full summary of this year's meeting check out www.forumsocialmundial.org.

* That global loan shark the International Monetary Fund (IMF) have slapped

Ghana with a $39 million fine "for misrepresenting the state of the economy", something the IMF should know all about. The fine comes just a few days after giving the same government $46 million in new loans! As Soren Ambrose from the 50 Years Is Enough Network points out, "Is the most appropriate punishment for failure on this score to take away 85% of the money lent to a struggling economy a few days before? The fine must be paid now, but the people will be paying that $39m back for years. The IMF's priority is not development, nor people. It's obedience. To the neo-liberal model, and to the IMF itself." www.50years.org

* For a detailed analysis of the Argentina debt go to www.personal.umich.edu/~russoj/debt/argentiniandebt.htm

Bare Faced Facts

In 1969 David Oluwale was the first recorded black person to die in police custody, today one person dies in police custody a week, without a single police officer being convicted. 'Injustice', a documentary film, has taken 7 years to make and follows the struggle and resistance of the families that have been campaigning for justice. Brian Douglas, for example, was buried with his brain missing. Due to the nature of the film, 6 police officers with the assistance of the Police Federation's lawyers are threatening any organisation that tries to screen it, because it 'accuses them of murder'. Commercial cinemas have been intimidated and only a sit-in at Conway Hall in London forced the venue organisers to show it. In Manchester, the 'arts' cinema Cornerhouse pulled out, but in a last minute change of venue, the Okasional (squat) Café managed to screen it to 150 people. Venues - not the film - have been served with threats because an injunction would bring the film to court and those 6 police officers would have to go on trial. If you want to arrange a screening contact Migrant Media on 0207 254 9701 www.injusticefilm.co.uk. Watch this space for details of a Brighton screening.

GENOA GOOD LAWYER?

In the aftermath news which is coming back is mostly in the 'verification' stage – but certain things are confirmed:

* Still at San Martino hospital: a German woman with a punctured lung, one person with head injuries, and another still in a coma. Meanwhile Sky – who is bringing a case against the police - was ordered by a Judge (higher than the Carabinieri) to perform a 'reconstruction' at the scene of the crime, but just before this was to happen the Carabinieri rushed in with a Deportation Order, which the medical staff at the hospital repelled by refusing to discharge him – and he still got to do the reconstruction. Sky will be home soon.

* 25 people from a theatre group moving around the no borders camps during the summer are still banged up in Italy. They were arrested on the Monday after Genoa as they tried to travel onto Frankfurt. They are currently in an 'investigative prison' – which they could be held theoretically for 6 months. The weapons they were found with included fireshow and juggling stuff, and the orange overalls and helmets with No Border No Nation stickers on them. Actions are being held at the Italian Embassy in Austria. www.no-racism.net/nobordertour/index_uk.html

* Meanwhile the body of an English person – believed to have been dead a week – was washed up on the beach at Genoa.

* On Weds August 1st 50 activists from the "Ya Pasta! Collective" occupied the Italian consulate in Amsterdam in protest against the violence, as well as a noisy demo outside the Italian Embassy in London last Saturday.

* Renato Ruggerio – the ex-director general of the WTO – is to lead the investigation into the police violence. Well that's in safe hands. And while all police chiefs are still in power, the head of the Genoa Social Forum, (also the head of the Italian AIDS association) has been forced to resign.

* Around 47 people are still being held with charges – and money is needed to pay lawyers. Contact the legal support office in Torino - 0039-0115806888 blackout@ecn.org

* A whip round is being made to help six British residents who were arrested, to pay for expenses including the £230 air fare, phone bills, lost money and possessions, and funds to mount a legal campaign. Contact Genoa Bust Fund, MelanieC@theseed.net

WALK THE PLANK

A couple of weeks ago animal rights activists visited the home of the President of Capital Markets to the Bank of New York (BNY), the one that bailed out animal torturers and murderers Huntingdon Life Sciences (HLS). Hardcore pirates fucked up the twat's 30 foot yacht in fine style, drilling holes in the side, tampering with equipment, and when it began to take on water they cut the moorings and pushing it out to sea. The boat and dock were tagged up, and as a final touch the Amerikkkan flag on the money man's estate was replaced with a skull and crossbones. Nice one!

* Meanwhile, an animal rights sympathiser at BNY leaked internal documents listing codes to confidential info on the accounts of high profile BNY clients and put the info on the web.

* Over here, at the beginning of July campaigners blockaded the gates of HLS by driving up cars, letting down the tyres and then locking on just as staff were due to end work for the day. Blue crew in six cars, three riot vans and a helicopter faffed around for an hour before security cut a gap in the hedge so that humiliated workers could finally leave. Eight activists were arrested after unlocking themselves three hours later and released without charge.

Stop Huntingdon Animal Cruelty (SHAC) 0845 458 0630 www.shac.net

SchNEWS in brief

RIP Steve Coward, father of Rowan and Heather, a former activist at Menwith Hill, Molesworth and many other places, who died on July 14th, a few days after the birth of his grandson Joe. More giggles than frowns ** Sick of biased and ignorant reporting on the TV? Then head to the Cinematheque in Middle St, Brighton, 8pm, Aug 9th for a premiere of the **Indymedia Newsreal**. Focussing on ordinary people taking action. Only 50p in ** The **'Red, White and Blue Festival'** happening next weekend (11-12) in Powis, North Wales is in reality a training school for Nazi thugs. Anti-fascists are meeting next Saturday (11) 10 am Welshpool Railway Station. More info 020 7924 0333 ** SchNEWS desperately needs people with a couple of spare hours on a Friday afternoon to **help with the mailout** and get paper SchNEWS out to activists, info shops and armchair anarchists. Call the office for directions.

WRIGHT IS WRONG

Earlier this month Mr. Justice Wright ruled in a court case that the Government was not liable for anything that happens to inmates in the privatised immigration detention centre at Campsfield, near Oxford. In August 1997 Group 4 security guards, who run the place, physically attacked inmates after they protested about conditions in the jail. This lead to nine asylum seekers being charged with violent disorder and riot. The trial, however, collapsed when the court was shown CCTV evidence which totally contradicted the guards' statements - basically it was the screws who caused the damage and started the violence (See SchNEWS 172/173). John Quaquah, one of the 9 defendants, sued the Home Office over his injuries and after a long case the judge decided that the government was absolved of any blame for the violence because the jail was privatised. This could set a dangerous precedent given New Labour's privatisation policy – not only prisons but schools and hospitals soon won't be the state's responsiblity, especially if things go wrong.

** On 26th July 100 asylum seekers held in HMP Liverpool refused lunch and so started a hunger strike in protest at their inhumane conditions. They're locked up for 23 hours a day, denied education and forced to wear prison clothes. All this and their only crime was to leave their homeland because of either extreme poverty or state oppression. No court has sentenced them to serve time - it's only on the say of an immigration officer and it's often an indefinite amount of time they have to stay. Contact gregd@gn.apc.org

** Free Liverpool Detainees Demo Saturday 4th August 1-2pm HMP Liverpool, Hornby Road (nr Walton Merseyrail Station) Tel. 0161 7408206.

Inside SchNEWS

* A member of Solidari@s con Itoiz – who are resisting the building of the Itoiz dam in Spain – has been arrested and is awaiting transfer to another prison. Inaki Garcia Koch was sentenced to nearly 5 years for cutting cables on the dam construction site. The other 7 activists sentenced remain free and on the run. Show Inaki your support by writing to him: Iñaki Garcia Koch, Centro Penitenciario, "Villa Hieros", Mansilla de Mulas, 24210, Léon, Spain

* Mumia Abu-Jamal, a renowned African-American journalist framed for murder (see SchNEWS 228), is in court on Friday, August 17th in Philadelphia. This is a hearing to take the appeal back to the state courts. Back in 1995, international demonstrations showed the US legal system that we are watching and will not tolerate their racist actions. Mumia has now been on death row for 18 years, it's time he was released to carry on the good work he was doing in his community. In the US, call 215-476-8812/5416 or www.mumia.org, Mumia Must Live! BM Haven, London WC1N 3XX.

RANK OUTSIDERS

Four years down the line (and up the trees), the West Wood of Lyminge Forest (near Canterbury) is finally safe from the developers. The Rank Organisation had wanted to build a leisure centre on over 1,000 acres of the North Downs Area of Outstanding Natural Beauty (SchNEWS 114). Protesters have made camp on the site since 1997. After Rank lost interest two years ago, other developers initially looked as if they might build some middle class holiday crap, but planning permission expired this April and no renewal has been submitted. Wahey! To celebrate this great victory, there's a De-tatting Party next weekend (10-12 August). Walkways and platforms will be taken down, if we don't do it, the Forestry Commission will use heavy machinery and damage the trees. Bring climbing gear and other useful stuff for a clean-up and party. Directions and more info: 07803 173805 / 07767 604409 http://westwood.enviroweb.org There are concerns that protesters will stay on in Lyminge, but don't bother, there are at least two other camps in need of support:

* Faslane Peace Camp (Scotland): monitoring and taking action against the naval base and the Trident nuclear submarine program. Tel: 01426 820901, or Trident Ploughshares 01324 880744 www.tridentploughshares.org for details of other peace camps.

* Nine Ladies (Derbyshire): a 4,000 year old stone circle in a Bronze Age burial ground, with abundant wildlife. Blockstone UK want to re-open two quarries last mined in 1942. 0797 404 9369 http://pages.zoom.co.uk/nineladies

* SchNEWS is planning a Protest Camp section on our website, so if you're involved in frontline resistance up a tree or down a tunnel let us know.

* Meanwhile, ten years after Twyford Down, Winchester council has gone back on its word and is planning a car park on part of an Area of Outstanding Natural Beauty. The site was originally part of the old A33, which was dug up and returned to meadowland to make up for some of the damage caused by the M3 extension. 200 species of flowering plants and 27 species of butterfly are already established. The car park – part of a Park and Ride scheme – will reduce traffic to the city centre by a highly significant ½ percent. But now the Council are going to set aside yet another wildlife area. So that's alright then. Local residents are resisting the development.

POSITIVE SchNEWS

Based in Wales, Green Dragon Energy have designed and installed renewable energy systems in the UK and Africa. Their aim is to make renewable energy accessible to as many people as possible, as it's the only way towards sustainability. They design and assemble user friendly small to medium-sized solar and wind systems, which can be custom-made for personal requirements, as well as larger units which can be used with a battery bank or connected directly to the electricity grid to sell surplus energy. Green Dragon also offers training courses and a consultation service. Check out their new website: www.greendragonenergy.co.uk

...and finally...

The internet has its very own Oscars now, 'The Webbys'. The star of this year's ceremony was a gas mask clad raider who took home the 'News award'. The winner was announced but it was the raider who grabbed the award, running off stage after a brief acceptance speech: 'Fuck corporate media'. The flummoxed host's come-back was the classic 'Someone just took off with the award' line, while a masked up Indymedia reporter took pictures from the side of the stage. Rumours of the after party erupting in a cloud of teargas remain unconfirmed.

Disclaimer
SchNEWS warns all readers that the only round of talks we're interested in is 'whose round is it anyway?'

Subscribe! ─
Keep SchNEWS FREE! Send 1st Class stamps (e.g. 10 for next 9 issues) or donations (payable to Justice?) Ask for "Originals" if you can make copies. Post *free* to all prisoners. SchNEWS, c/o on-the-fiddle, P.O. Box 2600, Brighton, East Sussex, BN2 2DX.
Tel/Autofax +44 (0)1273 685913 *Email* schnews@brighton.co.uk *Download a PDF of this issue or subscribe at* www.schnews.org.uk

Iraq Sanctions BustingTour

By Jo Wilding

"Hello Officer. We've come to hand ourselves in for breaking the law. We've broken the sanctions against Iraq by taking supplies into Iraq without a licence from the foreign secretary, contrary to article 3 of Statutory Instrument 1768 of 1990. We've also broken Article 2 of the same law by buying things in Iraq and importing them into this country for sale here without a licence."

The copper in reception at Charing Cross nick looks a bit bewildered and scuffles off to ask his sergeant what to do. "I don't think we can arrest you," is his verdict when he comes back. "Oh, yeah, you can. It's an arrestable offence under the Police and Criminal Evidence Act." He looks at the relevant bit of the printout of the legislation and scuffles off again. "Um. Can you come back in a couple of hours? We haven't got enough officers here at the moment to arrest you."

It's never this hard to get arrested when you're not trying.

The five of us crash out in the corner of reception to sleep off the night flight and the sergeant comes out eventually to tell us it's a customs matter. He takes our names and addresses, promises to pass them on to the relevant authorities and ushers us out of his station. And no we bloody can't use their loo.

I'm not generally in favour of accountability to a corrupt state system, but the amount of useful tat you can carry into Iraq in a suitcase is limited. The civil disobedience of sanction breaking is more significant than the token amount of aid you can take in. Global capitalism is responsible for poverty and death around the world but the difference in Iraq is it's so blatant and on such a massive scale. 4000-6000 children under five die every month as a result of sanctions. The total death toll may be as high as 1.5 million people - roughly 6% of the population. We've returned to the place where civilisation began to destroy an entire nation of people for the oil under their desert.

Sanctions were imposed on August 6th 1990, days after Iraq invaded Kuwait, having been told that the US would take no action if it did so. In 1996 the Oil For Food programme began, whereby Iraq can sell oil and the revenue goes into a bank account administered by the Sanctions Committee (less 25% for administration of the programme, compensation for Kuwait, one of the richest countries in the world, and miscellaneous other expenses). Credit notes can be issued against this account and supply contracts applied for.

The Sanctions Committee can put holds on contracts it doesn't approve of - to date this has included a consignment of pencils for the Ministry of Education, because they contain graphite. Quite right too, otherwise they'd only have the kids peeling the wood off the pencils and turning them into nuclear reactor cores. As of February 2002, there were $5.25 billion of holds on humanitarian items and oil industry spare parts.

Driving into Iraq from Jordan the desert highway was littered with torn tyres which didn't mean much to us till August 6th, the day of the 11th anniversary protest at the UN HQ in Baghdad. We were across a busy road from the UN and, in six or seven hours, we saw three cars completely wrecked in accidents caused by bald tyres blowing out. Two of them were taxis - their drivers' entire livelihoods. Safe tyres, even if available, are unaffordable for most Iraqis.

We met a woman called Fadma who runs a money exchange. Before sanctions one Iraqi dinar was equivalent to £2. Now it's about 0.02 pence - a fiftieth of a penny, 3650 to the pound. If, before 1990, you had £5000 in savings, it'd be worth around 75p

Omran, a 13 year old boy was killed during US bombing in May 2000 while shepherding cattle and goats in this village. His father is on the right.

now. There's no insurance because the currency's worthless and the only social welfare is the monthly food ration, because there isn't any cash to give to people. Unemployment is rampant -jobs, even whole industries, have disappeared because there's no public money to pay public sector workers and most people have no money for private spending.

The ration consists of flour, beans, rice, oil, tea, sugar and powdered milk - there's no fresh food, fruit or veg because it can't be stored and distributed on a monthly basis. For a lot of people the food ration is their main or only income, so some of it has to be sold to buy things like medicine, transport to hospital, shoes and clothing, just basic essentials.

The doctors we met told us that over the last year their wages have gone up from 5000D to 30000D a month. The increase comes from the proceeds of illicit border trading with Iraq's neighbours, bypassing the Oil For Food programme. It's still only about £10 a month and a packet of aspirin costs £2, a pair of women's shoes about £8, but it's a lifeline. It's also evidence that the money from the smuggling is going into the economy and the population where it's so desperately needed, and not being used to get weapons. This lifeline is what the British and American governments are trying to cut off with their so-called "Smart Sanctions" proposal.

The smart bit of "Smart Sanctions" is the humanitarian veneer they put on what's really a tightening of the sanctions. Instead of everything being embargoed and certain items being allowed through, as things are now, everything would be allowed through apart from certain items. Obviously there needn't be any practical difference at all in the range of items let into Iraq, but the trade off is the sealing of the borders, severing the only source of desperately needed cash.

We made friends with Ahined and Saif, two fourteen year old shoeshine boys who hung out outside our hotel. Hazim, a shopkeeper we met, told us that before sanctions, it was unthinkable that there would be children working on the streets. There were a few shoeshiners but they were unemployed adult men. Education was compulsory to sixteen and free through university.

A lot of kids are too malnourished to go to school or else they have to work to help support the family or their parents can't afford shoes and transport to school. Even those who do go face lack of sanitation facilities in the schools, lack of electricity, books, desks, chairs, pencils, everything. UN observers rated 90% of primary and 75% of secondary schools as unsafe in the Secretary General's report m March 2001. Some materials have been distributed for repairs, but without cash, it's impossible to pay for installation.

Similarly the water, power and sewage plants are operating well below demand and can't be repaired under sanctions. Damaged water pipes run alongside damaged sewage pipes, so the drinking water gets contaminated, reaching families unsafe for consumption. Doctors told us that gastro-enteritis is the biggest killer of children. The power goes off for about six hours a day in Baghdad and up to twenty hours a day in Basra, in the south. That means no air conditioning, which causes heat related illnesses. It means people use cheap kerosene lamps which blow up and cause serious burns and lots of deaths. Public and private poverty combine to fill the hospitals with children.

The thalassaemia unit at Mosul Paediatric Hospital in the north was filled with children receiving blood transfusions. Thalassaemia's an extreme form of anaemia. It's congenital and patients can be kept alive with monthly blood transfusions, but they need bone marrow transplants. Without transplants, the doctor said, they wouldn't make it past sixteen.

There were two toddlers sitting on the first bed, giggling at us and putting the medical instruments into their mouths, and their mothers were taking them out again. And as you looked around the room the children got older and sicker, less animated, thinner, their skin yellower, more translucent, their heads on one side, the necks too limp and fragile to hold them. It was like looking through the years of those two babies' lives, watching them die young.

The Oil For Food system is so cumbersome that quality control just doesn't happen and suppliers feel able to offload any old shit onto Iraq. One of the doctors showed us damaged transfusion bags that are no use. As a result there aren't enough bags to treat all the patients. We cuddled a woman as her eleven year old son went into a coma which the doctor said he wouldn't recover from because there weren't enough platelet bags to treat him.

There was a young woman called Alia - she was 17. She had leukaemia, went into remission, had a relapse. She was in tears when we met her because she wanted to go home and hang out with her friends, go back to school and go to teaching college. Its' worse for the teenagers than for the little ones, because they know what's happening to them. There's been a twelvefold increase in cancers since the Gulf War. The cure rate for leukaemia before sanctions was 70%, similar to the rate in Britain, using the same treatment protocol. Here, eleven years on, the cure rate is 90%. In Iraq now it's zero. Children who get leukaemia die.

We went to the mental hospital in Baghdad to deliver some occupational therapy journals. The chief resident told us that since 1990 Iraq has experienced a vast increase in neurotic disorders: schizophrenia, manic depressiveness, depression, anxiety, post-traumatic stress. He said sometimes there aren't the drugs to treat the patients properly - they stabilise on one form of medication and then its not available anymore and they're back to where they started from. The hospital's stretched to its capacity of 1200 in-patients and they're forced to discharge even homeless patients too soon as more acute cases come in.

The war hasn't ended for anyone there. There were at least two US/UK bombings a week while we were there. We heard the air raid sirens go off in Mosul but no one else even seemed to hear them: "So what? They bomb all the time."

We met a man in the southern marshlands whose 13-year-old son Omran was killed by a US bomb in May 2000. He was herding goats in a field at the beginning of the school holidays. He was no kind of target. He was a boy in a field near a mudbrick village with some skinny cattle and skinny goats and the water drying up in the drought.

We went to the Ameriyah Shelter where 409 women, children and old people were killed in 1991. The first missile made a hole in the roof, took out the power supply so the doors couldn't be opened and burst the boiler pipes so the lower level flooded. The second one was a thermobaric weapon dropped through the hole made by the first one. A thermobaric weapon is a fireball which sucks out all the oxygen, sucks the eyeballs out of their sockets, melts bodies together. It also made the steel doors swell with the heat so they couldn't be opened manually, and it boiled the water flooding the lower level, flaying the skin from the bodies of the people trapped in there. It's still stuck to the walls now.

Now Bush and Blair are plotting a new bombardment as part of their War of Terror. Watch this space for yet more violations of international law and human rights. The "Smart Sanctions" resolution comes up for debate in May so be ready to counter bullshit humanitarian propaganda.

Check out www.viwuk.freeserve.co.uk for more info.

Break the sanctions without leaving the country: send vitamins, painkillers, kids' clothes, toothbrushes, medical and other academic journals, etc, by post, either to Iraqi Red Crescent Society, Al Mansoor, Baghdad or University Library, Baghdad. If you write "Iraq" under the address, the parcel will probably be returned to you, but it's worth doing because the authorities will know people are opposing the sanctions. If you write "Jordan" underneath there's a much better chance of the items getting through to Iraq. Alternatively, find someone who can write Arabic and write "Jordan" in English at the bottom. It's a really useful, practical thing that everyone can do. Not to resist is to collaborate.

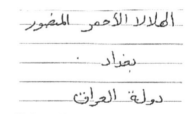

الهلال الأحمر المصور

بغداد

دولة العراق

This is the address of the Iraqi Red Cresent in Arabic

IF OWNING MORE THAN ONE BILLION DOLLARS OF PERSONAL WEALTH WHILE OVER HALF THE WORLD'S CHILDREN GO HUNGRY ISN'T IMMORAL... THEN WHAT IS?

STEALING FROM SHOPS

WELFARE FRAUD

SINGLE MOTHERS

MEN KISSING MEN

KICKING PUPPIES

Polyp

WAKE UP! WAKE UP! IT'S YER NO HOLDS BARRED

Weekly SchNEWS

Printed and Published in Brighton by Justice?

Friday 10th August 2001   www.schnews.org.uk   Issue 317   Free/Donation

HER MAJESTY'S PROFIT

"We are currently seeing the growing exploitation of prisoners' labour by private companies and by the state... compulsory work is nothing less than slavery." - Prisoners Mark Barnsley and John Bowden.

Last Friday saw the first action against forced prison labour in Britain, when supporters of wrongfully jailed anarchist Mark Barnsley invaded and shut down Hepworth Building Products in Edlington, South Yorkshire. Hepworth uses prisoners at Wakefield Prison to carry out tedious work packaging their products. In return the prisoners receive a whopping £8 a week, which for a 25 hour week works out at a pocket bulging 32p an hour. Wakefield has no educational programme and the prison labour is compulsory. Mark has refused to do the work and as a result he's now being held in the notorious isolation block.

About 30 supporters invaded the site - locking the main gates and disrupting the lunchtime shift-change - quickly knocking up some leaflets on Hepworth's copier to distribute to workers with details of the company's exploits. The action disrupted the warehouse and offices for about 2 hours. The fire brigade were called to cut through the locks on the gates but turned around and departed to cheers after it was explained to them what the protest was about.

One of those involved told SchNEWS "It was only a small action, but considering it was relatively spontaneous it was a great success. There were no arrests, the workers were mostly pretty supportive (including one who actually knew Mark Barnsley from being involved in anarchist politics back in 1980s!) and seemed to know nothing of their company's involvement in prison labour." A delighted Mark Barnsley said "This is brilliant! I really hope actions against companies like this carry on; they are so easy to target on the outside and it is so inspiring to those on the inside. Prisons themselves can stand up to pressure, but the companies that profit from them can't. This is what I call real solidarity."

But it's not just Hepworth who are involved in prison labour. Companies like Virgin, who get prisoners in Lewes to untangle headphones for use in its planes; Joe Bloggs who get Strangeways inmates to stitch its clothes and Age Concern who have their donation bags printed and folded.

JAILHOUSE STOCK

"We are talking about the creation of a Prison-Industrial Complex, wherein the government and corporations change the entire focus of prisons from mere punishment to profits, where private industry exploits prison labour, and where a prison corporate support industry makes millions of dollars to provide security products like gun towers, fences, motion detectors, guns, and so on. In addition to all this, the economy of the government is distorted from social spending to create jobs, housing or community development to that of prison building alone. The poor are thus incarcerated, but not employed in decent jobs, while the state creates concentration camps for social control and to make a dollar" - Lorenzo Komboa Ervin, former Black Panther and ex-political prisoner

In America – the country that leads the world in jailing its population - half a million prisoners are involved in forced labour. One person from the Anarchist Black Cross told SchNEWS that it should be compared with "human rights abuses" in China. Still, it's not hard to see why companies are climbing on board the gravy train.

In 1995, Lockhart Technologies Inc. laid off 150 workers in Austin and transferred the jobs to a prison. Their former president boasted that the company enjoys having "a captive work force." "They're here every day, their cars don't break down, they're rarely ill, and they don't have family problems.... They're delightful to work with."

In search of lower wages, San Francisco-based Data Processing Accounting Services moved U.S. assembly jobs to a maquiladora in Tecate, Mexico. But increased competition sent the company back to the United States in 1992—to San Quentin State Prison. "Some of the work went to China and some of the work we sent to San Quentin," The company left San Quentin in 1996 because of high prisoner turnover, but it's looking for an alternative site, ideally at another prison.

In 1986 prisoners were used during a flight-attendant strike at TWA. The company made its check in staff become flight attendants and then used prisoners to work on the phone paying them $5 an hour as opposed to the usual union rate of $18.

* Mark Barnsley was sentenced to 12 years in prison back in 1994 after being convicted of GBH for defending himself against a gang of drunken students. Mark has been systematically victimised by the Prison Service for his anarchist beliefs and

for continuing to maintain his innocence. For the full story read 'Beaten up, Fitted Up, Locked Up' £2 from Justice for Mark Barnsley. Cheques/Postal Orders payable to 'Justice for Mark Barnsley', PO Box 381, Huddersfield HD1 3XX. Tel: 07944 522001 www.freemarkbarnsley.com

CHAIN LETTER

Mark and another prisoner John Bowden have issued a statement calling for UK prisoners to show solidarity action with Turkish Hunger strikers. The Turkish prisoners are continuing their protest against the new isolation cells. So far nearly 60 have died including 28 prisoners either shot or burnt alive by the authorities while on hunger strike.

The solidarity action, which is also being taken by prisoners in France, Greece and by Basque and Kurdish prisoners, is in the form of a hunger protest on the first Saturday of each month. Mark and John then go on to list three demands for British prisoners – a minimum of one hour's daily exercise in the open air, the right of all prisoners to wear their own clothes and the abolition of compulsory prison work. "There has been a concerted attempt to crush the British prison struggle once and for all. By making this simple act of solidarity we are taking the first step towards renewing the struggle and asserting our humanity and our defiance."

Write to Mark Barnsley WA2897 HMP Wakefield, 5 Love Lane, Wakefield, West Yorkshire, WF2 9AG & John Bowden B41173, HMP Bristol, 19 Cambridge Road, Bristol, BS7 8PS

* Next Thursday (16) there's a solidarity meeting in support of political prisoners. with speakers representing Turkish hunger strikers and the Mark Barnsley Campaign. 7.30pm, Conway Hall, Red Lion Square, London

* A Prison Abolition Conference is being organised for Saturday 26th January 2002 at Conway Hall, For more info or to help out send SAE to Prison Abolition Conference, c/o BM Hurricane, London WC1N 3XX.

Copstrop

"A peaceful protest outside the baths was hijacked by a minority of violent youths whose sole intent was to intimidate and injure police officers." - Colin McKerracher, Assistant Chief Constable, Strathclyde Police.

SchNEWS is fed up of hearing this sort of bullshit from the cops, whenever there is 'violence' at a demo it's always blamed on outside agitators, never the fact that people are pissed-off with what's going on in their local communities or that the police can get heavy.

For five months residents in Govanhill have been fighting the closure of their local swimming pool by Glasgow Council who say it isn't economical to run, the council haven't met with locals despite a 12,000 strong petition (SchNEWS 307). On Tuesday they sent in sheriffs backed up by the boys in blue to evict protestors occupying the swimming pool, quickly a crowd gathered and by the evening more than 200 had assembled. When shutters on the pool were put up the police pushed into the crowd and some people, including police got hurt. One local Karen Fisher said, "The decision to put shutters up on this building has inflamed people. The people of this area are very angry." Another local described police behaviour as "disgraceful and shameful". Hardly outside agitators.

http://crowd.to/saveourpool/

Cop Shop

Last week people demonstrated against Avon and Somerset Constabulary's recruitment drive for people from ethnic minorities. A bus from outside Easton Job Centre took candidates for a tour around constabulary facilities (Better there than inside a vacuum van handcuffed and with a coppers knee on your back as activists and black people have experienced). While protestors unfurled banners deploring police brutality and racism, the coppers left with just 4 possible recruits.

* Vigil this Monday (13th) in memory of Firsat Yildiz, an asylum seeker stabbed to death in Glasgow. 4 - 6pm at The Home Office, 50 Queen Anne's Gate, London. National Assembly Against Racism 020 7247 9907.

* The Red, White and Blue festival is happening this weekend but SchNEWS won't be having a stall. The event is being organised by Nick Griffin's British National Party at Llechwedd-du farm, Welshpool, Powys. Anti-fascists are gonna try and stop it. Meet either Llanerfyl car park (on A458) or Talerddig (on A470) 9am. Contact No Platform 079670 771571.

* Mike Taylor has an appeal against his conviction for organising a demonstration at Heathrow Airport to stop the deportation flight to Iraq of Amanj Gafor, a mentally-ill Kurdish refugee. He has support of BA pilots and air traffic control workers. Picket Isleworth Crown Court, 9am, 24th August, 36 Ridgeway Road, Isleworth. Bristol Defend Asylum Seekers. 0117-965-1803, bdasc@hotmail.com

* 'Injustice' the film the Police Federation don't want you to see (SchNEWS 316) - London showing Aug 17th, ring 07770-432439 for details. Liverpool showing 6.30pm, Aug. 18th at Masque, 90 Seel St. It's part of a benefit night to start the campaign for justice for Jimmy Ashley who was shot dead in his bed in Hastings by armed cops. Paddy Hill of Miscarriage of Justice Organisation. will be the main speaker.

SchNEWS in brief

Reclaim the Beach - Your radio is the sound system. Bring a radio and tune into Radio 4A (106.6FM) on Brighton beach this Saturday (11th), near Gemini's 8-10pm, for a live broadcast. Radio 4A is Brighton's premier pirate station and will be on the air all weekend. If you're not in Brighton tune into www.piratetv.net. ** London has a new **Vegan Organic Rawfood Space** at Unit K4 Arena Business Centre, 71 Ashfield Road London N4 1NY. 020-88004849.** 6 Russian activists from a **Rainbow Keepers** camp in Udmurtia, against the building of a Lockheed Martin rocket fuel factory are on trial for a variety of offences, more info (in Russian) can be found at www.goryachiy.narod.ru. ** The 8th Annual Portsmouth **Smokey Bear's Picnic,** is happening this Sunday (12th), 2pm at Southsea Common. One man ill be giving away £100 worth of munchies, part of the cash he received from the cops after being arrested for taking the mickey out of one of their wigs at last years festie. www.smokeybearspicnic.com

Plane Speaking

On Thursday the offices of British Airports Authority (BAA) were occupied by London Rising Tide, in protest at the way the company profits from climate change. BAA is planning massive expansion of its airports, including a controversial 5th Terminal at Heathrow. Despite the noise and pollution etc, £250 million has already been spent on infrastructure for Terminal 5, while £2.5 billion will be spent on it the next 10 years. If that wasn't enough, in order to provide for the predicted growth of air traffic, the equivalent of 4 new Heathrows will need to be built by 2020. So it's a good job the plan for extending Stansted airport got the go ahead a couple of weeks ago.

Aviation is the world's fastest growing source of CO2 emissions, while the oil industry that supplies the untaxed kerosene is guilty of untold human rights abuses from Alaska to Indonesia.

SchNEWS recommends that the government concretes over everything, that way we'll be able to get around quicker. And while they're at it, why not make the places where we live so fucking horrible we all need to escape for two weeks every year. Then we can destroy all of those places too. Sorted. www.risingtide.org.uk

* SchNEWS is having a whip round for poor old BP who this week announced record profits of 1.3 million an hour.

Sinteltown

Spain's longest strike ended in a good result for 1000 workers of the defunct telecommunications Company, Sintel. They had set up a squatter 'Camp of Hope' on the pavement outside the finance ministry over 6 months ago in the middle of Madrid's icy winter. This was in protest at being laid off by Sintel, which is alleged to have been asset stripped by American investors. Sintel was privatised 5 years ago after being part of the state-owned Telefonica and sold to the Miami based anti-Castro leader Jorge Mas Canosa. The workers used their skills and tools to illegally tap into overhead cables, build home-made cabins with fully equipped kitchen ranges. Running toilets were created by plumbing pipes into local sewers and there were even 3 portable swimming pools. All of this came from donated or scavenged street junk. A deal was struck with the social and finance Ministries to get 11 months back pay and early pensions. 6 former directors of Sintel are being investigated for illegal asset stripping.

* Not the usual suspects for strike action, but Scottish Medical secretaries are on a 3 day strike in protest at the crap money they receive for their present grade, £12.000.

Genoa another venue?

The fallout from the massive protests in Genoa continues unabated (see SchNEWS 314/5). While more than 250 cities across the world mobilised against the actions of the cops and three Italian police chiefs were 're-assigned', the German Interior Minister has suggested setting up a European riot police force of "specially-trained police forces to…help defuse and, if necessary, combat violence with appropriate force". Forget about the issues just kick the protestors heads in. Still, they better be quick because the Italian No-global network have promised to mobilise 30,000 people and invade security zones at next months NATO summit in Naples in revenge for what happened in Genoa. The Mayor of Naples wants the meeting cancelled complaining "It is too risky. The climate in the country is too hot and I don't want to militarise the city." Which probably isn't the best choice of words for a NATO summit that will be discussing amongst other things America's son of star wars plans. Meanwhile Italian President Berlusconi has asked if the United Nations could move the world food summit planned for Rome to Africa.

* Three weeks after Genoa and not only are 48 people still in prison, but even more worryingly 80 are still missing. If you have info email: supportolegaleto@disinfo.net.

* John Lawrie is accused of affray at the MayDay protests and will go to prison if convicted. He urgently needs witness's. John is 55 years of age, 5ft 4" tall and was wearing a light blue fleece top coat over a black fleece with grey lining around the neck, a black woolly hat, a t-shirt, black tracksuit bottoms and a pair of black boots. He also had a 12" black plastic horn which he blew occasionally. He was standing on the roof of a ladies toilet by the entrance to the underground at Oxford Circus. If you saw him call Andrew Katzen at Moss & Co, Tel 020 8986 8336, email: andrew@mosslaw.co.uk

...and finally...

"An angry mob gathered around a train station, passing out photocopied flyers and shouting protests against another dodgy company. Scrappy stickers were slapped on billboards, directing passers-by to a crudely designed website. The company they were railing against was a frequent target of grassroots activism: Nike. And the group running this guerilla-style anti-advertising campaign? None other than Nike itself." What the fuck is going on?

Nike like other corporations are hijacking the techniques of activists. Creating their own subverted billboards by Fans Fighting for Fairer Football (FFFF), but this group of "actorvists" are complaining that wearers of Nike shoes have an unfair advantage. Other corporations have tried to cash in on activist chic, The Gap have dressed their windows in fake black spray paint reading 'Freedom' and 'We the People.' They've even hung anarchist flags alongside their sweatshop-produced jeans. IBM has even taken to spraying stencils of Peace, Love and their Linux Penguin logo on city sidewalks, they've been fined thousands of dollars reinforcing their hip, anti-establishment image!?

But the last laugh goes to activists who took no time to properly subvert the fake subverted billboards, rallies were held outside Nike stores and the Melbourne megastore had to be boarded up and two days after the FFFF website was mentioned in the mainstream news, it was taken down!

www.alternet.org

disclaimer

Subscribe!

SINTELATING

SPAIN'S most successful industrial dispute ended victoriously for a group of telecommunications workers on the 5th August 2001. Champagne and a night of singing, dancing, and fireworks marked the end of El Campamento de Esperanza "The Camp of Hope", built in the centre of Madrid by 1,000 protesting telephone technicians. The workers' defiant six month occupation of one of Madrid's poshest streets earned them the respect of the nation and forced the transnational politicing that shafted them to be held accountable.

In 1996 Sintel, the company these people had worked for was sold by its owner Telefonica (the Spanish equivalent of British Telecom) to Mastec, a US cable installation firm. In December 2000, after months of non-payment of wages, everybody in the firm was laid off with no financial compensation and no new jobs on offer. Most blamed mismanagement and Mastec's aggressive policy of asset stripping and knew they had good grounds to refuse their forced resignations and a claim to around $10 million in unpaid wages between them. Normally such cases might work their way through the courts, perhaps supported by a lobby group and a few noisy demonstrations: Sintel's ex-employees chose an altogether more direct and radical approach.

The action started in the middle of winter, when the disgruntled workers set up a ramshackle collection of tents and blue tarpaulin shelters outside the Ministry of Finance. The smell of breakfast and wood-burning stoves mingled with traffic fumes as the techies quickly made themselves at home on Castellana Boulevard. Putting their redundant skills to good use they improvised along with the best of sorted squatters to set up their village with all mod cons: Using the boulevard's underground road-sensing equipment and overhead cables they pirated leccy; water was blagged from underground pipes and they connected up to public sewerage pipes for their waste.

As the months went by their dwellings became more permanent, as they got more cosy bringing in televisions, washing machines and the rest. By late spring the improvised and self-sufficient community became a settlement stretching a kilometre long of nearly 1,800 people, with a meeting hall, library, museum and three small swimming pools (sounds like luxury) - and even a barbershop!

Although the squatters had taken limited defensive precautions against forced eviction - collecting rocks and other missiles in shopping trolleys - an attack from the city's police force never came. The camp enjoyed active support from some local companies, workers and churches who supplied the community with food, building materials and moral support. Real Madrid football club gave away hundreds of free tickets to their home matches. Even the nation's media seemed to take a largely favourable view of the Sintel workers' defiance.

By March, there was the first news of real progress: anti-corruption prosecutors opened a case against six of Sintel's senior managers and board members, with charges of driving the company into punishable insolvency. At the same time Rodrigo Rato, the finance minister who walked past the camp every day on his way to work, set out to broker a deal: the workers could receive the money due to them and be given the choice to take early retirement or new employment with the firm's old owner, Telefonica.

As the issue climbed its way up the national agenda, Prime Minister Jose Maria Aznar became personally involved. In August, the government offered to finance early retirement for some of the workers and to find jobs for most of the others. Aznar also promised that the government would guarantee a 2.5 billion peseta loan, which would cover the 11 months of unpaid salary due to the ex-Sintel employees. Payment would come from liquidation of the company's remaining assets in bankruptcy

pic: www.manifestacionvirtual.com

proceedings (though it was an earlier bid to avoid bankruptcy which precipitated the lay-offs in the first place). With this deal struck the workers claimed a victory, and packed up the camp disconnecting the illegal electric and water connections.

Residents said they would miss the technicians. "At first we were outraged that they had been allowed to camp here, but then we heard how they had been sold out and we began to see them in a different light," an elderly lady walking her dog said.

As they packed up and prepared to head back to homes in 35 different provinces, the campers were digesting the lessons of their protest. "One thing is sure, and that is we are all better people now than [when] we arrived here," Aniceto Diaz said. "There were times when we thought we were not going to achieve anything. No back pay, no jobs and no future.'" Mr Diaz added. Some were not quite sure how they would re-adapt to normal family life. Some could not wait saying "Now I am just going to devote my time to the wife and kids."

The Sintel saga demonstrates the power of imaginative self-sufficiency, resourcefulness, determination - and of course solidarity.

pic: www.manifestacionvirtual.com

The People 6 - Glasgow City Council 0

In March 2001, Glasgow City Council's plan to close the Govanhill Pool complex, which lies in the one of the poorest and least healthy parts of Western Europe, was thwarted when members of the local community occupied the building, maintaining a 24 hour picket for over 6 months.

In addition to the pool occupation, direct action has been a hallmark of the campaign, including "egging" council leader Charles Gordon; closing off the road outside the pool to hold numerous street events; holding a campaign meeting inside a Police Station to protest at the alleged surveillance of campaign members; occupying GOMA [The Gallery of Modern Art]; demonstrating outside events at the City Chambers and serving an 'eviction order' on the firm of sheriff officers [bailiffs] charged with carrying out the eviction of the occupation.

The occupation ended on August 7th 2001, when sheriff officers, supported by over 250 Police, horses, dogs and a helicopter confronted hundreds of local people who had spontaneously come out onto the streets to fight for a facility at the heart of their community. Next day, the spirits of even the most ardent car hater would have been lifted by the sound of drivers sounding their horns as they crawled past the pool. Local people who had not previously been involved in the Campaign, stopped to chat to those of us who were sweeping up the debris, before pausing to shout comments such as "You should be ashamed of yourselves!" at the Police on duty. A concerted attempt to crush the spirit of resistance in a Glasgow community had become an own goal for those in remote authority, one beamed to TV screens around the world.

This Campaign, the most diverse and imaginative that many people have experienced, now has a permanent hut outside the pool and continues to fight for the re-opening and development of this facility, as well as opposing other attacks on the community. The effects of the campaign have been far reaching in terms of politicising people who would not have described themselves as 'political'. Similarly it has enabled people to make the links between the fight in our our community and the war in Afghanistan for instance and to question the system of electoral democracy [sic]. We have heard that the Campaign inspired local people in a neighbouring area to occupy a hole in the ground destined to take a mobile phone mast, with the result that it has now not been installed.

The Campaign has not been without it's difficulties, and people on the libertarian left have been at the forefront of raising questions about how decisions are made within the campaign. It has, however, been one of the most vibrant and inclusive campaigns that has happened for years in Glasgow. If we believe that people can self organise, spontaneously take collective action and be politicised by doing so, we should be encouraged by what has happened in Govanhill and despite the campaign's difficulties and challenges it presents, I have no doubt that the community in Govanhill deserves our continued support.

- Mwasafu. Visit: www.saveourpool.co.uk

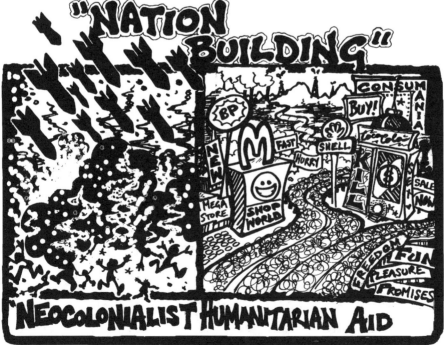

Fisch

WAKE UP! WAKE UP! IT'S YER INCREDIBLE

Weekly SchNEWS

Printed and Published in Brighton by Justice?

UK PLC SPECIAL OFFER

This voucher entitles you to a third off all weaponary.
ACCEPTED BY ALL MAJOR ARMS DEALERS

Friday 17th August 2001   www.schnews.org.uk   **Issue 318**

DSEi International Arms Exhibition
Excel Centre, Docklands, London, 11th Sept

CREDIT TO THE NATION

"In 1988 Tanzania's per-capita income was $280. Then, in 1998, it was $140. So I asked the World Bank people what went wrong. Because for the last ten years Tanzania has been signing on the dotted line and doing everything the IMF and the World Bank wanted. Enrolment in school has plummeted to 63 per cent and conditions in health and other social services have deteriorated." – Julius Nyerere, former leader of Tanzania.

Tory Blair left last month's G8 Summit in Genoa blabbering something about making Africa his priority. True to his word he is currently deciding whether or not to grease the wheels for a British company to go in and make a quick buck in Tanzania – one of the poorest countries in the world.

The decision is whether to give an Export Credit Guarantee- and hence the green light - for UK arms company BAE Systems to install a new £28 million air-traffic system (with military potential) in Tanzania, further adding to that country's current crippling foreign debt of £5 billion. This is a deal that even the IMF/World Bank won't support, and are even threatening to stop any more loans if the deal goes ahead.

As well as the debt, Tanzania suffers the ravages of AIDS, a 1 in 10 child mortality rate, land degradation and half the population living on less than $1 a day. So what everyone is really crying out for is an 'over the top' air-traffic system.

The behind-closed-doors machinations which underlie this deal we will never know. Oxfam told SchNEWS that the new air traffic system would include military radar equipment needed to scour the region for gun-smugglers in small aircraft – a big problem in an area which includes The Congo, Rwanda and Burundi. As an OXFAM report points out "In N.E.Kenya, the barter rate for an AK-47 has dropped from 10 cows in '86 to its present level of 2 cows. Wars in the developing world which only decades ago were fought with spears, bows and arrows are now waged with automatic and semi-automatic weapons and the victims are usually civilians. According to the UN Secretary General, the death toll from small arms 'in most years greatly exceeds the toll from the atomic bombs that devastated Hiroshima and Nagasaki'."

But if such noble anti-smuggling work were the prime motive for investment, then why haven't BAE Systems and Tanzania been announcing it as such? We were starting to get a whiff of that familiar old smell…

DEBT TO THE WORLD

A search through East Africa news services reveals page after page of stories about land disputes, factional disputes, privatisation, buy-outs, and companies and governments setting up 'strings attached' deals and aid packages. But on the subject of this air-traffic story you will find nothing definite, apart from these few things we stumbled on. Could they, perhaps, be linked?:

* The Bush Administration is 'committed to helping nations of Africa improve their aviation safety record' and 'seeking an 'open skies' agreement'. Tanzania is one of the African countries singled out to be part of the 'Safe Skies for Africa' programme.

* Swissport International Ltd, a major aviation 'ground handling company' are a big part of the ongoing privatisation of airports in Tanzania, and recently acquired a majority stake in Dar Es Salaam airport, where the new system is to be installed.

* BAE Systems has long been a big privatisation and arms sales player in Africa - coming in with war jets and communications.

* Governments like Tanzania's are surrounded by agencies such as 'Mindworks', who, in their words 'develop executive agencies to assume responsibility for a range of operational functions which were formerly carried out by government departments' – er, sounds like a privatisation broker.

SchNEWS invites readers to make your own mind up – money well spent to fight arms smuggling, or a company earning a fortune from a country who desperately needs its meagre funds to deal with AIDS, starvation, and environmental degradation?

Ethicing 'ell

The Export Credits Guarantee Department (ECGD) is backing the BAE project in Tanzania. This Dept acts as insurance for companies and banks involved in export deals. If the receiving country doesn't cough up the cash the ECGD steps in and foots the bill - funded by us the taxpayer!

In theory the Department supports projects in poor countries so that the population can benefit from improved infrastructure. In reality, of course, the ECGD doesn't take social, human or environmental rights into consideration, and has funded a whole load of dodgy schemes. Over the past decade a third of guarantees have gone to cover arms exports, others have gone to schemes like nuclear power stations and copper mines, with more of the same in the pipeline - like the backing of the notorious Ilisu Dam in Turkey (SchNEWS 259 & 266).

But don't worry dear reader: the UK government has had a review of the ECGD to make it more ethically accountable, and is planning a toothless 'Arms Export Bill'. We can all sleep soundly in our beds knowing that weapons exported to regions of conflict will be used ethically. Especially as BAE Systems - with more export credit guarantees than any other company - boasts on its website of being a 'global citizen', which must mean they don't care who their weapons kill - black, brown, white or yellow, everyone's a winner!

We've heard all this ethics stuff before when 'New-improved' Labour was first elected in 1997. For years, India and Pakistan have been in dispute over the province of Kashmir. In the late 90's tensions increased and border skirmishes became a regular occurrence – and UK arms exporters profited as both countries increased their arms imports. Similarly, the UK cashed in on the bloody civil war in the Democratic Republic of Congo - training Zimbabwean soldiers (who made up two-thirds of the Congo's military force) and selling weapons and military hardware to Uganda, Angola, Rwanda and Burundi, all of whom were involved in the fighting. The International Institute for Security Studies expressed it in no uncertain terms: "Britain is inflaming the situation by arming both sides.

Going For A Bomb

Where can you buy good ol' British weapons then? One such place is the Defence Systems Equipment international (DSEi) arms fair. Where military generals hob-nob with ministers as they buy weapons from BAE Systems and all their ethical arms dealing mates. As Baroness Symons, Minister of State for Defence Procurement, said at the last DSEi "[Defence exports] enable us to spread and bolster enlightened concepts of democracy and freewill." You might even be able to pick up an illegal anti-personnel mine, openly on sale at the last one – not that anyone got prosecuted for the oversight.

If all this stuff sounds really dodgy to you, why not bomb on down to the opening day of DSEi on the 11th September for a Fiesta for Life Against Death. To get involved call 020-7281-4621. www.disarm-trade.org

Free/Donation   **@ANTI-COPYRIGHT - INFORMATION FOR ACTION**

Inside SchNEWS

URGENT - Today (Friday 17) Philadelphia Court has ordered that Mumia Abu-Jamal should not appear in court for his appeal- because there is apparently not enough room in local prisons 'to house him'!! An international fax and phone blitz campaign is being launched to demand his constitutional rights not be violated once again. Mumia, an ex-Black Panther, has been on Death Row for 18 years, pleading innocence to the crime of shooting a policeman. Bearing in mind that in England we're 5 hours ahead, there's still plenty of time to phone or fax the demand that Mumia gets a trial that he can actually attend!! Court administrator Phone: (215) 686-2547 Fax: (215) 686-7485 City Hall, Room 336. Mayor of Philadelphia, Phone: (215) 686-2181 Fax: (215) 686-2180 City Hall, Room 215

www.mumia2000.org

* Demonstrate outside the US Embassy (Grosvenor Square, London W1) this Saturday (18) 12noon - 2pm. Organised by Mumia Must Live! BM Haven, London WC1N 3XX

e: mumia@callnet.uk.com

GOTHENBURG - 23 people have so far been found guilty of rioting during the EU Summit in Gothenburg (see SchNEWS 310) with sentences from eight months to four years. 8 others are still in prison awaiting trial. Hannes Westberg, the man who was shot by the police is out of hospital and working with the prisoner solidarity group. Despite his injuries he still faces a trial. If you wish to send publications, letters, money etc. to pass onto the prisoners send them to Solidarity group GBG, c/o Syndikalistiskt Forum, Box 7267, 402 35 Gothenburg, Sweden. Tel + 0046 733 16 42 96.

* One UK person found guilty of 'violent rioting' at the Summit is appealing against his one year sentence. Send letters of support to Paul Robinson, Goteburg Remand Centre (Haktet), Gotebug Polis Headquarters (Polis Huset), Box 429, 40129, Goteburg, Sweden.

GENOA - This coming Monday is an international solidarity day for those still imprisoned in Genoa and in remembrance of Carlo Giuliani. If you're in Liverpool meet 10.30am central station to go to Italian consulate, or 12 noon by the horse statue, Church Street.

www.peoplesnotprofit.co.uk. Other actions around the world see http://g8solidarity.protest.net/

* The newly formed Genoa Justice Campaign are holding a public meeting for people "who were at Genoa to discuss strategies for supporting each other and developing the campaign for Justice." It's on Wednesday 29th August at Conway Hall, Red Lion Square, London. (nearest tube Holborn) 7.30pm. Solicitors are available for legal advice

* Loz O'Reily, doing a life sentence, is a Pagan who because of his religious beliefs is refusing to take mandatory drug tests, with the consequence that he will not be put on a release plan. His case is going to the European Court and he would really appreciate letters from any Pagans out there. Write to him at R13613, F Wing, HMP Long Lartin, Worcs, WR11 STZ.

Subscribe!

SchNEWS in brief

Banner Theatre, community theatre with 'disenfranchised' groups are producing their latest play 'Local Stories/Global Times'. To see the play or their book 'Workers' Playtime', call 0121-4400460 or e-mail voices@btinternet.com ** The new **Rainbow Centre in Nottingham** (activist and community offices, social centre, etc) have released two benefit CDs: Moving On Vol. 1 – Sing Songs & Moving On Vol. 2 – Electronica Exotica. £6 each, inc. p&p from Moving On, Rooted Media, 145-149 Cardigan Rd, Leeds L56 1LJ www.movingonmusic.org.uk ** Mass trespass on **Hatfield Moor** in Yorkshire Sat 25 Aug to stop US company Scotts extracting the peat (bogs). Campaigners want the digging suspended and the place declared a 'special area for conservation,' otherwise Scotts will carry on digging for the next two years. This is a family friendly event - meet at Tyrham Hall Motel fishing lake 10:30-11am. Tel 07971-073282 ** If anarchy is your black hooded wet dream, then get a copy of the **Re-Pressed catalogue**. SAE to CRC, 16 Sholebroke Av, Leeds LS7 3HB. www.re-pressed.org.uk ** The Buckmaster Institute is planning to publish a book **"Traffic Life"** dealing with the problems of traffic and the nuisance of cars. www.buckmaster.ca/trafficlife ** You've heard them on the streets of Prague, Barcelona, London, The Hague and Slough, now check out the London samba band **Rhythms of Resistance** new website www.rhythmsofresistance.co.uk ** And why not join the **Reclaim The Streets** congo on the 15th September, as a protest against the meeting of European transport ministers in Leuven, Belgium. reclaimthetop@hotmail.com ** If any musical people out there are interested in being part of an **'anarchist travelling circus'** band at next months arms fair in the docklands (see front page) get in touch with jess@km551818.demon.co.uk ** **Squatters in Montreal**, Canada have recently claimed a resounding victory. At the end of July they squatted a building that had been empty for 13 years. But instead of evicting, the council they gave them an old council building, five times bigger than their squatted one, for long term use! The new squat will have workshops, crèche, cafe, living space as well as organic allotments. ** **Esso Boycotting action** this Saturday, 12 noon till 2pm at the Esso station on Dyke Road (near the Dyke Tavern). Watch out for people in tiger suits doing unmentionable things to George Bush. ** 3rd Sept - **Cardiff Social Forum**. Discussion about Genoa, global capital etc. Grassroots Cafe, Charles St Cardiff, 6:30PM. 02920 707102.

Brighton Call To Arms

Find out more about the Arms Trade at a **Public Meeting**, 7.30pm, 4 Sept @ Friends Meeting House, Ship Street.

* Brighton will be hosting an anti-arms fair **Spors not Wars** with street theatre, music, films, food, kids activities. 8 Sept. Venue TBC. sporganism@spor.org.uk

* There's a couple of benefit gigs: Folk Music, Videos, **Ragga-Dub Disco and Techno Shenanigans**. 8pm-late, 29 Aug @ The Volks. £Donations. and **Headmix** with Marmoset, 10pm, 5 Sept @ Concorde2, £5/£4.

* The **Rebel Alliance** returns after a summer break. Brighton's meeting of local direct action groups. 7pm, 2nd Sept @ Hannover Centre, Southover Street.

* **Transport to the Fiesta For Life Against Death**. Tickets £4 from the Peace and Environment Centre, Gardner Street. Please buy your ticket in advance.

For up to the minute info 01273-298192.

Big Blue Gathering

So lets get this straight, the Welsh Big Green Gathering was cancelled because the police licensing officer said that if the festie went ahead they "would be left with 25 acres of land…filled with human waste, diesel and cannabis."

On the other hand last weekends "Red White and Blue" BNP fascist festie was allowed to go ahead with the cops thoughtfully placing a "Section 14 Banning Order" 15 miles around the site. They then used roadblocks, surveillance units, mounted police, dogs and about 200 riot cops to stop anti-fascist protestors getting anywhere near. One demonstrator told SchNEWS "Anyone wanting to get anywhere near the festival, including residents, had to stop at a police road block and show a pass provided by the BNP. Anyone suspected of heading for the demo was stopped, searched and given an escort to the Gorsedd Stones on the outskirts of Welshpool where they were cordoned in by riot police and kept there for 5 hours." One of those protesting was Brig Oubridge who helps organise the Welsh Green Gathering. He complained "The police went out of the way to stop the Welsh Green Gathering, a peaceful event, yet here they are working hand in hand with the forces of darkness." www.thecopshavespoiledoursummer.org

* There's a counter demonstration this Saturday against the National Front - meet 1pm at Sunderland train station. Tel 0777 967 5284

Positive SchNEWS

While we in the rich north worry about computers, e-mail and mobile phones it is easy to forget that four fifths of the worlds population don't have access to a telephone. Radios, on the other hand, are to be found in even the poorest communities off the beaten development track. As an example Tanzania, a country with a population of over 35 million, has only 103,000 TV's and 127,000 telephones- but 8.8 million radios. The Developing Countries Farm Radio Network, set up in 1979, is a not-for-profit organisation providing radio scripts to local radio stations in more than 100 countries covering topics on health, micro-credit schemes and low-cost farming practices. The scripts are sent free to a network of over 1500 radio stations whose only obligation is to comment on the content while sharing information with millions of farmers around the world. Info www.farmradio.org. Developing Countries Farm Radio Network, 416 Moore Avenue, Suite 101, Toronto, Canada M4G 1C9.

Negative SchNEWS

Pirates Beware! After many futile years of trying to catch pirate radio stations, the DTI has decided to hassle local authorities into doing their dirty work for them. The DTI recently sent a letter to councils reminding them that it is THEIR responsibility to ensure that council properties are not used for illegal broadcasts.

...and finally...

Ever wondered why sometimes yer past convictions have done a Lord Lucan leaving you without a criminal record? Well if you live in Longido, in the Monduli district of Tanzania, the answer is simple - termites! Yep those class-conscious invertebrates have been busily munching through case files held at the Longido Primary Court, leaving the court in chaos and bringing most trials to a standstill. SchNEWS reckons we should import some of these insurgent insects to the next summit of paper treaty mountains and let 'em do the business. But why stop at termites? We could get all sorts of creepy crawlies to deal with the real parasites and their travelling flea circus - redback spiders, army ants, killer bees, the list is endless. If you can't beat 'em- eat 'em!

disclaimer

Keep SchNEWS FREE! Send 1st Class stamps (e.g. 10 for next 9 issues) or donations (payable to Justice?) Ask for "Originals" if you can make copies. Post *free* to all prisoners. SchNEWS, c/o on-the-fiddle, P.O. Box 2600, Brighton, East Sussex, BN2 2DX.

Tel/Autofax +44 (0)1273 685913 *Email* schnews@brighton.co.uk *Download a* **PDF** *of this issue or subscribe at* www.schnews.org.uk

Native Resistance to "Canada"

In the past two years, indigenous people have taken back their land from the control of government and industry, in the area known as western "Canada." These land re-occupations are the latest actions in a history of resistance to genocide and oppression by the Canadian government. Below are updates and background on four re-occupations that are continuing now (April 24th, 2002).

Sutikalh, St'at'imc Territory - "British Columbia"

The snow is almost melting at Sutikalh, and the mountains have been spared from Ski Resort development for another season. Sutikalh, the St'at'imc community at Melvin Creek, north of Mt. Currie (approximately 4 hours north of Vancouver) has been growing over the past two years. The St'at'imc have remained strong in their stand for sovereignty and against the $550 million ski resort that Al Raine and Nancy Greene-Raine want to build at Melvin Creek. On May 2, 2000, St'at'imc women and grassroots traditionalists began the community at Sutikalh by lighting the sacred fire at the access road to the planned resort. The camp has grown into a community of people, youth and elders, defending their territory from the hands of the ski industry and the government.

Over the summer of 2001, Sutikalh had numerous incidents of RCMP (Royal Canadian Mounted Police) harrasment. On July 5th, a roadblock which was set up to stop logging trucks on Highway 97 was met with 40 RCMP officers, including snipers. Six people were arrested and are facing charges of mischief and were given conditions that they can't return to Melvin Creek and can't wear camouflage (!! - ed). The RCMP tore down a lean-to that was a welcome and information center for visitors to the camp (in November 2000, racist rednecks burned down the previous welcome center, now the RCMP have replaced them). The RCMP continued to harrass various members of the Sutikalh community both at Sutikalh and in neighbouring towns, but the St'at'imc have not backed down and given up. They continue to build permanent dwellings at Sutikalh and welcome supportive visitors to the community. They need financial support and people to spread the word.

Skwelkwek'welt, Secwepemc Territory

Since November 2000, the Secwepemc people have been reoccupying their traditional territory at Skwelkwek'welt, known by the colonizers as the Sun Peaks Ski Resort, near Kamloops, BC. They are reasserting their title to their land, in face of the genocide that the BC and Canadian governments continue to commit against them. The Sun Peaks Ski Resort, with the blessings of the BC government, wants to expand and build more lodges and ski runs, increasing their profits at the expense of the Secwepemc.

On Monday, December 10, 2001, on International Human Rights Day, Sun Peaks and the BC Government demolished two homes in the Skwelkwekwelt and McGillivray Lake area. "We received a court injunction to leave those areas. We agreed to leave peacefully." says spokeswoman Janice Billy of the Skwelkwek'welt Protection Center. There was to be a court hearing on the morning of Tuesday, December 11 to test the legality of the BC Government's removal of the house at McGillivray Lake, but then that night, the BC Government and Sun Peaks Resort went into McGillivray Lake while no one was there and used 3 big machines to totally demolish the house.

Graphic: Tania Willard

They bulldozed the sacred sweatlodges, traditional cedar bark lodge, removed sacred tobacco ties, and left no trace that the Secwepemc had ever been there. The demolished house had been built by a young Secwepemc woman with the help of many volunteers who had re-connected with the land and learned many traditional teachings from the Elders. A family with young children had just moved into the house and upon returning to the site on Tuesday, found the house and sweatlodges bulldozed to the ground to make way for groomed ski trails.

Despite the destruction and devastation felt by the Secwepemc Elders and youth, their spirit is not broken and they are more determined than ever to seek justice for the Secwepemc.

On December 28th, 2001, two Secwepemc elders, Irene Billy, 73 years old, and Winnifred McNab-Lulu, 75 years old, were arrested and charged for blocking the road near the Sun Peaks resort. The road was blocked in response to their outrage at the destruction of the cord wood home and sweatlodges at McGillivray Lake.

One month later, on January 28th, the Skwelkwek'welt Protection Center was re-established near McGillivray Lake in the Skwelkwek'welt (Sun Peaks) area by twenty five people from the Neskonlith band of the Secwepemc, and their supporters. The Secwepemc continue to maintain the Protection Center and are rebuilding the homes and sweatlodges.

"We want the world to know that genocide and ethnic cleansing is not something that happens in other countries, but right here in British Columbia, Canada. We seek your support to obtain recognition of us as Secwepemc Peoples and for a fair and just settlement of our lands. We ask you to express your indignation and horror to these genocidal actions by the Government of British Columbia and Sun Peaks Ski Resort Corporation."

www.skwelkwekwelt.org

Cold Lake Dene Suline Territory - "Alberta"

The Primrose Lake Air Weapons Range (PLAWR) in Northern Alberta, Canada is a favored NATO playground, where they test missiles, bombs, weapons and aircraft that are currently being used in the 'War against Terrorism.' Since June 2001, the Dene Suline of Cold Lake have maintained a camp at the main entrance of the weapons range in opposition to the theft and destruction of their traditional territory to feed the war machine and the oil industry. This land was stolen away from the Dene Suline in 1952, under the pretense of national security. After harassment and heavy coercion a 20 year lease was granted by the Dene Suline.

Fifty years have passed and the government and military have not moved. PLAWR has increased in importance as the NATO combat simulation program, known as Operation Maple Leaf, brings 18 NATO countries to Dene Suline territory every year to drop bombs and test out the new weapons they use in their wars in Iraq, Yugoslavia, Afghanistan and everywhere else. Depleted Uranium missiles are tested at PLAWR, leading to disproportionate cancer and sickness rates amongst the Dene Suline. The oil industry has also descended upon PLAWR, extracting billions of dollars annually from Dene Territory.

On June 3rd, 2001 Dene traditionalists erected their camp and continue to maintain this occupation. On December 12th, the government passed their next stage of land by working with the Band Council government to pass a referendum which forced a deal onto the Dene to take $25.5 million and a measly 5,000 acres of land in exchange for the 4,500 square miles of Dene territory, encompassing the weapons range. This works out to only $35 an acre and $2,500 for each Cold Lake band member. This deal is genocide and legitamised theft of Native land. The Dene continue to fight and in March and April, they occupied the Band Council offices, calling for the resignation of the corrupt chief.

"Saskatchewan" Dene Suline of La Loche

The wheels of colonization and genocide continue to roll into the 21st century and communities like La Loche in Northern Saskatchewan are in their path. The Dene Suline of La Loche have been fighting against the mining and theft of their land. In 2001 their struggle erupted in blockades and direct action.

In 1974, the Cluff Lake Uranium Mine began operating 64 km outside of La Loche and since then people in the community have been getting sick and over 60% of all deaths have been related to the mine. On top of that wild animals, plants, trees, fish and berries - the lifeblood of the community - have also died from it.

In 1984, the Saskatchewan government and the Ministry of Environment decided to make a provincial park in the traditional hunting and trapping grounds of the Montgrand family, who are Dene Suline. They said they consulted the family and the Dene, but as is usual went over their head and stole 890 sq. miles to make the Clearwater Wilderness Pronvincial Park. Since that time, the Montgrands have lobbied the government in an attempt to regain control over their lands.

In 2000, the Montgrands made repeated demands on the government to produce the documents to prove they had legally taken the land - but after none were forthcoming in another meeting on May 1st 2001 the Montgrand family and other Dene Suline established a blockade on the road leading into the park and the access road for the Cluff Lake mine. They blocked all vehicles from preceding and faced intense persecution as the RCMP came in with SWAT/sniper teams in attempt to kill the people at the camp and leave no trace. Despite this, the Dene stood their ground and continue to assert their title to their lands.

The Dene Suline of La Loche are calling on all supporters to come join them this summer and support their struggles to regain control and access over their traditional territory. There will be another meeting with the government on May 24th, 2002, after which the Montgrands and Dene Suline are planning to obstruct the mining and tourism industry.

"Our leaders are doing nothing for nobody, so we're not going to depend on our leaders," says Skip Montrgand. "We fight for the people. If we stop right away, what's the worth in living? We have to fight for freedom from the government."

For more information about these struggles email tintin@tao.ca

For radical indigenous anarchist publications from western "Canada" write to zig_zag48@hotmail.com or Redwire, a Native youth magazine, www.redwiremag.com.

Congratulations UK Arms Industry

The UK arms industry is the second biggest in the world, worth £5 billion per annum, selling to over 130 countries. But this industry wouldn't be such a success if it wasn't for the generous £1 billion in subsidies from the British government each year - including £420m going into research and development, £260m being shelled out to cover Export Credit Guarantees (See SchNEWS 318) and then there's the Defence Export Services Organisation (DESO):

DESO is a government group specifically to promote UK arms sales, providing marketing assistance to exporters, as well as organising arms fairs and promotions, employing over 600 in London and abroad. Heads of DESO, past and present, come from major military exporters, giving it a nice impartiality.

British Aerospace (BAe) is the the third largest arms company in the world.

What other UK industry can boast these figures:
* Sales to Pakistan have risen to £14m up from £6m in 2000.
- combat aircraft components, combat helicopter components, large calibre artillery production equipment, components for torpedo launching.
* Sales to India - level since last year at £62.5m.
- components for combat aircraft and helicopters, aircraft canons components and targeting equipment.
NB - the UK arms industry has been able to capitalise on arming both sides of the Kashmir conflict (See SchNEWS 357).
* Sales to Israel - doubled from last year up to £22.5m.
- components for air-to-air missiles and surface-to-air missiles, components for bombs, components for combat helicopters and aircraft, general purpose machine guns and submachine guns.

Other UK arms sales to key human rights champions include:
* Sales to Turkey up from £34m in 2000 to £179m in 2001 - to be used in the war against er terrorism (AKA the Kurds).
* Saudi Arabia upped their UK arms purchases from £13m in 2000 to £20.5m in 2001.
* Indonesia took their's from £2m last year to £15.5m in 2001.

Campaign Against Arms Trade www.caat.org.uk

WAKE UP! WAKE UP! IT'S YER LET'S BE 'AVIN YOU!

weekly SchNEWS

Printed and Published in Brighton by Justice?

Friday 24th August 2001   www.schnews.org.uk   Issue 319

Bruised & Bartered

"The country doesn't belong to the people, it belongs to the puppetmasters of the dictatorship in bed with the United States...The universal cry in the streets of Argentina, that the country is returned to the people, will never be fulfilled while every politician, policeman and army officer are corrupt to the core and of an immovable tendancy to fascism."
- *Alexis Daunaravicius, whose family fled Argentina years ago in desperation.*

"It would be tragic, not only for Argentina but for the global economy if it were concluded that Argentina's experience was useless and did not work." - *Domingo Cavallo, Argentinian Finance minister*

With the Argentinian economy in free fall, the International Monetary Fund (IMF) yesterday decided to bail the country out with yet another loan - this time $8 billion. Not that this will help a country drowning under debts of $128 billion (£88.4 billion), three years of recession and the prospects of defaulting on its 'debt'.

Yet this so called debt has been payed off by the Argentinian people many times over. In a ruling last year a federal judge concluded "since 1976 our country has been put under the rule of foreign creditors and under the supervision of the IMF by means of a vulgar and offensive economic policy that forced Argentina to go down on its knees in order to benefit national and foreign private firms."

Financial whizz kids and corporate loan sharks call Argentina the 'teachers pet' of the financial world. It's sold off everything it ever owned, with foreign firms taking over key sectors of the economy. (A French company for example picked up chunks of the water system and raised charges in places by 400%)

It's deregulated its markets and tried to make its workforce more 'flexible' (meaning you work longer for less pay) yet in the last couple of months has had to introduce *more* IMF-imposed austerity measures which will save about a billion quid and hardly put a dent in the debt. For public sector workers and pensionsers however these measures will mean cuts of 13% and increased taxes. Unemployment meanwhile is booming and a third of the population live under the poverty line.

BARTERING RAM

"We are creating something new. Argentines of all classes are coming together to say enough is enough. The government keeps telling us that there is no alternative to the recession they are imposing to free up money for the servicing of the foreign debt, yet they are doing nothing to stop the rich from taking their money out."
- *Victor de Gennaro, one of the protestors.*

The new austerity package has sparked demonstrations and direct action across the country. Meanwhile the authorities are slipping back into the bad old days of the miltary dictatorship with torture and worse for protestors. Anibal Veron, a 37 year old father of five, who lost his job as a bus driver with his company still owing him nine months' wages, joined the 'piqueros', the angry unemployed who blockade roads. When police cleared one of these blockades last November, the military police killed him with a bullet to the head.

Don't Buy For Me Argentina

Remember 'Bartertown' in Mad Max – where people came out from the hinterland to the market settlement which had sprung up in a post-apocalypse world? Well it's coming to that in Argentina. This is an story of survival, and the ability of people to adapt, and create workable and sustainable solutions to the problems their government and the international money markets have imposed on them.

Bartering in Buenos Aires started in 1995 with just 20 people trading in food, textiles and handcrafts. With the signing up of a dentist the system developed into a goods and services trading scheme, and now every profession, and type of goods is available for barter. By 1999 it was handling the equivalent of $400 million a year with the idea spreading throughout Argentina, and now there are 1200 clubs with over one million people involved.

As the system rapidly grew, and went from cashbooks to computer databases, a system of 'slips' was brought in, and the barter currency was born. Anti-fraud measures were introduced and now the system is kept highly regulated, avoiding the influence of existing power bases in Argentina such as political parties, NGOs or syndicates. Regular weekly meetings of barter clubs bring trust amongst the participants, and exchange across clubs increases diversity of the markets.

Swap Shop

"We should underscore the concept of **"prosumer"** in the Argentinian Global Barter (RGT) Network: it's a word coined by tying together "producer" and "consumer", meaning that RGT members are individuals who are producers and consumers at the same time." - RGT Statement.

As globalisation destroys local markets, alternative economies are one way of opposing this. The barter system is helping Argentinian people take back control from the corporations and keep the money in their local area. Trading with your neighbour and buying local produce keeps the wealth in the community,

as opposed to buying from the local branch of a supermarket or chain where the profit goes back to head office - and into the pockets of shareholders. In other words drink at your local café, not Starbucks. Alternative economies make sense everywhere, and other significant examples include the "Other" Stock Exchange in Mexico, Ithaca Hours in New York State, USA, the SELs in France and LETS Systems in Canada, Europe and Australia. These systems are not just short-term solutions, they are an essential part of a sustainable world.

For many this scheme is more than just survival – it is being used as a base for social as well as economic change. The system may offer a new lease of empowerment and freedom for participants, but, just as out goes the old style of retailing as they know it, in comes many challenges: Professor Heloisa Primavera of Buenos Aeries says "Freedom, autonomy and equity have been the issues; building trust and reciprocity in the network, learning how to deal with power and to accept the legitimacy of different others."

One protestor said "Argentina has sunk into 'Latin Americanisation'. It used to be the jewel in the crown, but now has all the same problems of poverty as the rest of the continent."

You wonder what Tory Blair saw from his car window when he visited Argentina proclaiming that globalisation was working. Argentina has jumped through all the capitalist hoops with promises of prosperity, yet has now hit bottom of its 'sell off' barrow and it's either default the debt, or tighten the belt even further and accept another handout. For the moment other countries are finding another forest or water company to flog, but they are sure to arrive at this point. Argentina was the seventh richest country in the world before it had contact with the IMF and World Bank.

* To find out more about what's happening in Argentina go to (it's in Spanish) argentina.indymedia.org/. For more on the barter system www3.plala.or.jp/mig/econ-uk.html
* Protests against the IMF/World Bank in Washington 29-30th September www.globalizethis.org/s30

GENE JUNKIES

Genetically engineered "terminator" technology makes seeds sterile so farmers can't re-use harvested seed. The biotech companies responsible claimed they developed it to help prevent the escape of genes from GM crops to related plants. In reality though all they care about is money and masssive profits they would make as many of the 1.4 billion people who rely on saving seeds would have to start returning to them each year to buy new seed.

Back in 1998 there was worldwide protest and two of the largest companies Monsanto and AstraZeneca vowed never to commercialise the terminator technology. Predictably though the prize was too high and many biotech companies have continued to develop the technology regardless. It is likely within a few years the first "suicide seeds" will be available after the US government announced that it has allowed the licensing of first terminator technology to Delta and Pine Land.

Biotech companies are now developing 'Genetic Use Restriction Technology' (GURTs) which includes various 'traitor' technologies that control more sophisticated traits than just fertility of the seeds. For example experiments are now being carried out that would inhibit the ability of plants to flower and ripen fruit unless certain chemicals are applied. The plants become 'junkies'- unable to survive unless they get their regular chemical fix - good news for the corporations who provide the junkie seeds and the necessary chemicals.

Syngenta the world's largest agribusiness firm formed last year after a merger between AstraZeneca and Novartis are hooked on serious mega-profits and control 6 Terminator patents. They've just got the green light to test traitor oil seed rape in an open field trial at Jealotts Hill near Bracknell, Berkshire. The seeds will be planted soon, a local group Green Watch oppose the plans. Vigil Monday 10th Sept, 4.30pm outside the main gate, Jealotts Hill. Genetics Education Conference, 7th October with talks by scientists and campaigners £8/£4. More info 01344 452893.

*More info on terminators, traitors and junkie genes can be seen at www.rafi.org

* In Canada scientists have found strong evidence of GM superweeds. Escaped rapeseed is now Canada's 13th worst weed – "We set a gap of 800 metres between GM rapeseed and other crops but our research has shown this is not enough" says John Culley, Research Director, Ag Canada. Of serious concern for the environment in Britain is not only do we have more wild relatives of rapeseed than Canada, but GM crops are only separated by a mere 200 metres at most from other non GM crops.

* Sri Lanka has banned the import of all genetically modified foods. But the US has taken offence and is threatening to challenge the ban before the World Trade Organisation. The Sri Lankan government is now reconsidering their position www.poptel.org.uk/panap/caravan.htm

* Basmati rice is a traditional variety grown for centuries in India, but this didn't stop American Company Ricetec attempting to register Basmati as a trademark four years ago, it later withdrew due to massive opposition. But now they've got the patent on three hybrids: texmati, jasmati and kasmati, and also have permission to claim that its brands are "superior to basmati". GM coffee beans are being developed that can be mechanically harvested. This will give no benefits to coffee drinkers, but could mean disaster for up to 7 million small holders who'll find it increasingly harder to compete with the big plantations. www.actionaid.org

* Crop Trials around the country continue to be trashed by alien spacecraft. For a list of sites see www.geneticsaction.org.uk/testsites

Positive SchNEWS

Why not get with the majority of the world's gardeners and save your own seed? Around the world seed companies are being gobbled up by the very same biotech giants that are trying to get us all to eat their genetically modified greens. The Henry Doubleday Research Association has set up the Heritage Seed Library. The deal is you join the library and they 'lend' you seeds that aren't available in the shops any more thanks to the National Seed List. More info 01203-303517 www.hdra.org.uk Or get a copy of 'Back Garden Seed Saving – keeping our vegetable heritage alive' by Sue Stickland (Eco-logic Books 2001).

* Find out more about outlawed vegetables, seed saving, terminator genes etc. at a talk "The Fascination of Vegetable Seeds" by Harold Dunning. Sat 22nd Sept, 2pm 2Moulsecoomb Library, Lewes Road, Brighton.

SchNEWS in brief

A **treehouse camp** in **Lappersfort**, Belgium has been set up to stop a motorway and an industrial area going through a city green area. 0032 498 19 36 54. PO box 715, 8000 Brugge, Belgium. ** **Media Lens** is an alt media site with interviews and articles. Download 'media alerts' by subscription. www.MediaLens.org **Uncut** independent film forum at the Institute of Contemporary Arts, London. Palestinian filmmakers will be talking about their work before the films 1-4pm 25th August. 020-7930-3647 www.ica.org.uk/ ** **Reclaim the Streets** have meetings every Monday night in London. **CItY** ('Change It Yourself' formerly London Underground) meetings every Tuesday night in London. Come and hear report-backs from diverse ant-capitalist direct action groups throughout the capital. Venue for both meetings: 020-7281-4621. ** SchNEWS recommends the book **'Restructuring and Resistance - Diverse Voices of Struggle in Western Europe'**. It's 566 pages about the bureaucratic shenanigans going on in Europe, and the resistance to these new re-jigs of capitalism. From Poland to Portugal, written by grassroots activists involved in the countries themselves. Very inspiring, get yerself a copy for £11 from: AK Distribution 0131-555-5165 www.akuk.com. ** **Environmental Racism** produced by greenpepper looks at issues like power inequality created by colonialism, and the blinkered focus on 'corruption' and 'poor management' in the Third World. Contact greenpepper at www.risingtide.nl/greenpepper ** Uncaged are having a **Diaries of Despair** "Die In" on 21st September. 500 primates that died at Huntingdon Life Sciences in xenotransplantation experiments (SchNEWS 279) so bring monkey masks, face paints, costumes, banner, horns and whistles for monkey buisness etc. 12 noon, Parliament Sq, followed by a 'die in' at the Home Office. www.xenodiaries.org ** Benefit for **Rokpa & children** of the **Tibetan** homeland. With folk music and **SchINEMA** followed by Technoshenanigans and Raggadubdisco at the Volks, Brighton next Wednesday (29) 8pm-3am. ** The **IMF & World Bank Wanted for Fraud** Campaign is having a demo against UK govt's refusal to recognise slavery and colonialism as crimes against humanity at the UN Conference Against Racism in Durban, South Africa. 12-2pm, 1st September, Downing Street, Whitehall. 020-8749-7179. ** **SchWOOPS** In last week's Tanzanian air traffic story, we thought BAE Systems needed an Export Credit Guarantee (ECG) but they need an Export LICENCE. Schwoops! However – the info about both Tanzania and Export Credit (Yawn) Guarantees is correct, and one pleasant little Department backed scheme we'll be having a lot more about is the Yusefeli Dam. UK company AMEC is lining up for an ECG of £68 million which could displace 15,000 Georgians from their homeland. Contact Ilisu Dam Campaign 01865-200550.

Inside SchNEWS

* **Jeffrey Luers** (aka Free) sentenced to an outrageous 22 years for setting fire to several jeeps in a car lot (SchNEWS 308/309) recently received a 42-day sentence in solitary after being attacked by two other inmates. While in solitary he can only receive letters, so get scribbling. Jeffrey Luers #13797671, TRCI, 82911 Beach Access Rd, Umatilla, OR. 97882, USA

* In a desperate attempt to get SchNEWS free **Sean Creagan** (first ever Inside SchNEWS prisoner) is in jail again. This time for violent disorder at Mayday 2000. Write to Sean Creagan - FR8832, HMP Wandsworth, P.O.Box 757, Heathfield Road, London, SW18 3HS.

* **Mark Barnsley** has been moved yet again. From Wakefield Prison to HMP Leeds segregation unit for refusing to do prison work for private companies (SchNEWS 317). Mark Barnsley WA 2897, HMP Leeds, 2 Gloucester Terrace, Armley, Leeds, LS12 2TJ

* **Mark Cullinane** has been in a Moroccan jail for 5 years for smuggling cannabis. If £2,000 can be raised before the end of the year Mark will be released a year early and rejoin his family. Benefit gig 5th November at the Concorde2, Brighton. Donations are welcome http://potwow.20m.com. Write to: Mark Cullinane 21486,Chambre 7, Cartier C, Prison Civil, Tangiers, Morocco

Witnesses Needed: 20th May Hackney Town Hall was stormed by 50 angry residents protesting about council cuts (SchNEWS 306). Stephen Doyle (a drummer with Rhythms of Resistance who were outside the hall) was assaulted, sprayed with CS gas and arrested by police. He now faces a charge of threatening and assaulting a cop. And May Day this year, Nick Gray was arrested on the Critical Mass bike ride for wearing a baseball cap and sunglasses about 2pm on Malton Street, Euston.

Witnesses for either case contact Andy Katzen at Moss & Co solicitors 020-8986-8336, andrew@mosslaw.co.uk

Pool The Other One

We've received more info about the Govanhill swimming pool protest (SchNEWS 317). We've received reports of how a woman was taken to hospital with a suspected broken leg and an 11 year old boy was kicked by the police. Another woman was beaten up by police in a lane. When she made a formal complaint the police visited her at 3 in the morning in a blatant show of intimidation. Police on the demo were racist calling Asians "black bastards" and four officers beat an Asian man unconscious who was running away from a police horse charge. A daytime picket outside the swimming pool continues along with a police presence.
More info: 07000 752752 www.saveourpool.co.uk.

...and finally...

If you've ever been confused by all the jargon surrounding the global capitalist system here's a few definitions from The Devil's Dictionary of Free-Trade:

conquest: The means by which wealthy, powerful nations formerly subjugated weak, impoverished nations; since replaced by *debt*.

debt: A form of subjugation, formerly achieved by *conquest*.

fair trade: A soft-headed neo-socialist fancy.

International Monetary Fund: (IMF) The Third World's primary creditor and owner.

level playing field: Conditions favouring our exporters

See it in full at:www.seattleweekly.com/features/9947/features-beers.shtml
disclaimer
Would you credit it but we're bankrupt of warnings. Gotcha!

Down To The Waterline
Privatisation In South Africa

In 1994 the first 'free elections' were held in South Africa, the ANC were swept to power, Nelson Mandela became president and apartheid was dead. Nice one. But as soon as they were in power the ANC were visited by the big boys of global capital (World Bank, IMF etc) to be told that they had inherited a $25 billion debt from the apartheid days (it was money used to prop up that regime). The new ANC government were also told to adapt to the 'realities of the global economy', paving the way for the country to start 'modernising' with new infrastructure (read: new loans needed for new roads and power etc to attract more transnational companies to come in and extract more resources). The gist of this is that South Africa is another country in debt with the IMF, and paying this money off on the IMF's terms – which includes mass privatisation of its public utilities. These policies get results alright – the standard of living in South Africa is lower than during the apartheid days.

Water

In September 2001 when something happening in the US was taking all the headlines 1800 houses in Tafelsig, South Africa had their water cut off because they couldn't afford to pay the bills the recently privatised water company was demanding. People who resisted the cut offs were shot with live ammunition. Plumbers disconnected the pipes under the guard of riot cops. After the cut-offs the Unicity Council installed taps in the middle of some of Tafelsig's streets as an emergency water supply. More than 40 houses were forced to share each tap. The mayor of Western Cape Province, Gerald Morkel, went on radio to say that the people of Tafelsig don't pay for water because they spend all their money in casinos! The real situation is that most families of seven or more people in Tafelsig survive off a pension or disability grant from one family member - little more than R500 (£32) per month, and after the privatisation of the water system some families got water bills of more than R800 (£51). In a country with 45% unemployment these bills simply could not be paid. The communities formed the Anti-Privatisation Forum (APF) to make their voice heard.

Electricity

Meanwhile the recently privatised electricity company Eskom started cutting off the electricity of people who couldn't pay their massively increased bills. Poor communities in South Africa organised a boycott of their Eskom payments and the Soweto Electricity Crisis Committee (SECC) began illegally reconnecting the power of families who were left in the dark. For nine months, it organised a boycott of electricity payments to Eskom, with around eighty per cent of Sowetans taking part. Then there was the SECC's Operation Khanyisa – a campaign to illegally reconnect peoples' power. All this has worked and last October Eskom announced it would no longer disconnect those who couldn't pay:

"Peoples' Power was responsible for Eskom's U-turn. We mobilized tens of thousands of Sowetans in active protests over the past year. We established professional and intellectual credibility for our critique of Eskom, even collaborating on a major Wits University study. We demonstrated at the houses of the mayor, Amos Masondo, and local councillors, and in the spirit of non-violent civil disobedience, we went so far as to disconnect the electricity supplies of the mayor and councillors to give them a taste of their own medicine." (Trevor Ngawane SECC)

The success of the campaign inspired a similar boycott of water payments, and thousands of Sowetans took to the streets since SECC and the APF merged to form a joint political front. Trevor Ngwane said: "We decided to broaden our struggle to include a demand that all basic services in South Africa should be free - water, housing, electricity, healthcare, education and transport."

Telecommunications

And the privatisation fun doesn't stop there. The South African telephone system has also recently been privatised and now 40 percent of the new phone lines that the company Telkom has delivered have been disconnected because the people can't afford the new rates. While the company is rolling out new phones, basic rentals and local call costs have gone up by 35% pushing telephones beyond the reach of many South Africans. In contrast, the price of domestic long-distance and international calls, used more by the richer population who can afford to pay the new rates, became cheaper by 40 per cent. To stay competitive and make a profit the phone company is weeding out the people who can't pay, and making calls cheaper for the people who can.

Housing

Communities are being shafted as their housing get subjected to privatisation. On the 8th of November 2001 Cape Town Unicity tried to evict people from houses they own, for non-payment of rent?! Residents who own houses in Mitchell's Plain, specifically Tafelsig, Montrose Park, Lost City and Silver City, were understandably shocked to receive final demands for rental arrears. They were given one week to pay or face eviction. These 'arrears' goes back to money owed from the apartheid days, debts which were supposed to be annulled by a 1994 law. As well as fighting this, the Western Cape Anti-Eviction Campaign and National Housing Department are investigating the way Unicity pockets the R7500 (£485) government cheques meant for each household.

On the 6th of March 2002 over 1000 People living in the semi-privatised GEMS scheme houses in Hanover Park, Woodlands, Portlands, and Mitchell's Plain marched on parliament, to the Provincial MEC of Housing and then to the Unicity council offices. The families were angered that they were moved into so-called starter homes on the basis that they would pay bonds of between R150 - R350 (£10-22) per month. They found the homes to be substandard and their bonds rapidly increased up to R1000 (£64) per month. They have been boycotting further payments since November and are currently involved in legal action with the GEMS scheme directors over breaches of contract. "These are supposed to be starter houses for the poorest of the poor and we hear that GEMS receives R25 million from government every year to help the poor get homes, but all we are getting is corruption. These privatised homes are no good," (Ishmael Petersen - Western Cape Anti-Eviction Campaign.)

Private Hell

On the 21st of March The Kathorus Concerned Residents group led a march with the Anti-Privatisation Forum to the Ekurhuleni mayor and on the same day in Soweto, the SECC and the APF marched to the UBC council offices in Jabulani.

On the April 9th, after hundreds of residents were issued with eviction and water cut-off notices people in the communities of Mandela Park and Lingelethu West in Khayelitsha, CapeTown took their protests against evictions water cut-offs and privatisation directly to the council. A new magistrate's court has been built in Mandela Park. Although it is not yet open, the cleaning services have already been privatised! The community has marched to the court and protested outside three times to stop the privatisation and keep the few jobs in the area within the community. Other residents occupied the municipal offices to demand an affordable flat rate basic payment for services.

On the 12th of April after months of resisting privatisation the Western Cape Anti-Eviction Campaign (AEC) received a memo from mayor Gerald Morkel which claimed that nobody will be evicted or face water or electricity cut offs if they make arrangements to pay. What was all the fuss about eh? Maybe the mayor forgot that the reason so many people are being turfed out of their homes is because they CAN'T AFFORD TO PAY. This is the same mayor who took out a full page advert in the newspaper, using public money to announce that the disconnected water supplies in Tafelsig had been reconnected – a blatant lie as revealed in the press the next day.

The AEC and the Cape Town APF picketed the parliament on the 16th April in support of the 50 people from the SECC who were jailed for disconnecting the mayor Morkel's water, just to let him know how the community feels.

And again on the 23rd of April anti-eviction activists disrupted traffic on a main road going into Cape Town demanding a meeting with mayor Morkel, to try and resolve the issues around the ongoing evictions and water cut-offs. Police had to form a human chain to prevent the protesters from entering the highway. They delayed traffic on the highway and vowed not to leave until their grievances were addressed by Morkel. They were told that the mayor was not in his office and that no one from the council would speak to them.

Rio + 10

Since all the recent community mobilisations, Soweto, the township of two million outside Johannesburg (known for its 'Spirit of '76' when 1,000 students protesting Afrikaans-language education were killed in the 1976 uprising against apartheid) has become very politicised. In August the 'Rio+10' summit will happen in Sandton, Johannesburg, and the area will be the scene of an international anti-capitalist convergence. In the media spotlight of this, already the Anti-Privatisation Forum (APF) and the Soweto Electricity Crisis Committee (SECC) have been labelled 'criminals' by the ANC government.

The South African government would be hoping to avoid a repeat of the international embarrassment of last year's United Nations World Conference Against Racism in Durban when five million workers spoiled the party by going on a two day strike – and 20,000 marched through Durban - against the privatisation of electricity, telecommunications and transport. Although they expect a tight crack-down on public dissent, anti-privatisation fighters in South Africa are promising similar humiliation for Rio+10. www.johannesburgsummit.org

Ulice patri lidem
- Streets belong to the people

On September 1st last year around 150 people gathered for a reclaim the streets party in the small Czech town of Vysoke Myto in East Bohemia.

Organised by local social-ecology collective Ulice patri lidem - 'Streets belong to the people' – the party started in the town-square at 12:30. Forty-five minutes later people headed off to set up on international auto-route I/35.

Two activists, masked up as Czech president Vaclav Havel and Vaclav

Klaus, the leader of the biggest right-wing party, lead banner-waving protesters carrying red-black and green-black flags.

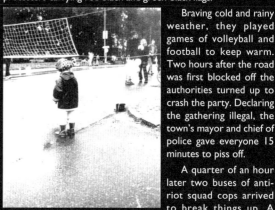

Braving cold and rainy weather, they played games of volleyball and football to keep warm. Two hours after the road was first blocked off the authorities turned up to crash the party. Declaring the gathering illegal, the town's mayor and chief of police gave everyone 15 minutes to piss off.

A quarter of an hour later two buses of anti-riot squad cops arrived to break things up. A few people wandered off, leaving others to go on with the blocking. 15 of the people who stayed were then accused of having caused a "traffic disorder." After being abused and threatened they were arrested and taken down to the local police station. The rest of the crowd followed them to the station and stood outside chanting for their release. During this solidarity party one more girl was arrested for having "broken the police line" – by standing too close to the police station. After three hours everyone was released and the demo was over.

Ulice patri lidem/Streets belong to the people

Pics: Pavel Dosoudil

WAKE UP! WAKE UP! IT'S YER VODKA HELL'S GOING ON!

Weekly SchNEWS

Printed and Published in Brighton by Justice?

Friday 31st August 2001   www.schnews.org.uk   **Issue 320**

EUROTRASH

"In numerous important votes European Parliamentarians have bowed to industry pressure… In its campaigning for international trade and investment deregulation, the EC works very closely with large European corporations and their lobby groups." -*Olivier Hoedeman of Corporate Europe Observatory.*

Yesterday the European Central Bank unveiled the shiny new Euro coin in Brussels. The Euro is set to replace the existing currencies of eleven EU countries (excluding Sweden and Britain) at the beginning of next year. Baron Daniel Janssen, a member of the powerful corporate lobbyists, the European Roundtable of Industrialists (ERT), describes what is taking place as a "double revolution." First you've got sweeping privatization and deregulation, second is the transfer of decision-making "to a more modern and internationally minded" structure. That's business-friendly to the rest of us. This is a business 'revolution'. Good for the shareholders but not so good for the people who are living in countries banging on the EU door. For these countries, entry into the single market and the Euro is already creating massive upheaval. For starters aspiring countries must incorporate more than 20,000 directives and regulations, unchanged, into their legal frameworks (yawn). Once they've joined, their businesses must compete with Western European firms so it's likely that large redundancies will follow.

In Poland 27% of the population still work on farms, the majority of which are small family set ups. Joining the EU could spell disaster for them, as the country is flooded with cheap, heavily subsidised and mechanised agricultural imports from Western Europe. The entry of Poland to the EU will undoubtedly "favour large conventional farms and methods" says Jadwiga Lopata from the European Centre for Ecological Agriculture and Tourism. Lopata feels this would also "uproot small farmers and create further unemployment, migration to unhealthy overcrowded cities, and to the destruction of the rural culture and way of life."

POLEAXED

Borders are politically drawn, and the shape of Poland itself is a clear example of this. At the end of WW2, borders in Eastern Europe were moved according to reparations and other factors: areas which were once Germany are now within Poland,

and bits of old Poland are now the Ukraine. Poland was part of the former Soviet bloc and so its trading was orientated towards its eastern neighbours. The natural movement of people meant that many Ukranian, Russian and Belorussians made their homes there. But now because the militarised Fortress Europe frontier has moved east, Poland must switch its ties to the West.

Once, citizens from all ex-Soviet countries had free access to Poland but now they must fit the regulations of the draconian Valid Foreigners Law. These new 'aliens' must now show that they have the funds to visit, or have a 'sponsor' - or they must apply for asylum. The trade that has gone on freely over these borders for generations will now become a 'black market', and won't to be tolerated by border authorities. Traders from Belorussia have begun throwing stones at Polish cars at the border, in protest against the blockade.

You'd think that there was something in this for Poland wouldn't you? All this hard work on Polands part – such as devoting considerable amounts of money militarising their eastern border (and extending their military budget if they want to be part of NATO) – and bugger-all support from the EU for the social problems it's creating. As mass intensive farming obliterates small scale farming structures and small businesses are closed off from the markets they have historically been dealing with to the east, employment options will dwindle. In May the EU member states decided on a seven year ban on work permits for workers of 'candidate states.' Meaning many won't even have a chance to 'get on their bikes' to get work. This will leave Polish workers just as the EU wants 'em - on their knees-sitting targets for the imposition of EU infrastructure. As an anti-EU campaigner commented, "They are becoming 'colonies' of western European interests, having to open up land tenure and natural and productive resources to market dynamics."

* Recommended reading 'Diverse Voices of Struggle in Western Europe - Restructuring and Resistance' edited by Kolya Abramsky. For more details email resresrev@yahoo.com, or get copies for £11 from AK Distribution 0131 555 5166 www.akuk.com

Rebel Alliance
Meeting of local direct action groups 7pm, 2nd Sept. Hannover Centre, Southover Street.

CRAPSKI ARREST OF THE WEEK
For handing out a newspaper. A Polish man was nicked for 'inciting people to criminal acts' after he handed out copies of radical paper "Shipyard worker". The paper attacked the rich financiers who run the shipyard with articles about workers rights.

POSITIVE SCHNEWS
The European Centre for Ecological Agriculture and Tourism-Poland are coming up with some of the solutions to the threats their rural economy faces in the next few years. The Centre doesn't want Poland to go down the road of unsustainable large-scale agribusiness, what spokesperson Jadwiga Lopata describes as a "sunset industry." Instead, "Poland has a unique opportunity to become a world leader in the 'sunrise industry' of organic farming."

One way of helping and encouraging farmers to go organic is through eco-tourism, which helps farmers earn an income when they are converting to organic. As Jadwiga says, "Unlike agribusiness and its spin-offs, eco-farming and eco-tourism are broadly-based and overwhelmingly positive for society and the environment." Due to poverty, most small Polish farms use relatively little chemical pesticides and fertilizers, so the transition to organic isn't even that difficult. "People in Poland, both consumers and farmers can decide not to follow the EU development model and not to make the same mistakes of over-specialisation and over-intensification, Instead they can skip the EU phase and try to look for a model of sustainable development of the country."

European Centre for Ecological Agriculture and Tourism—Poland, 34-146 Stryszow 156, woj. Malopolskie, Poland Tel +48 33 8797114 www.sunflowerfarm.com.pl/eceat/
* The TransAtlantic Business Dialogue (TABD) is having their annual corporate knees up in Stockholm, Sweden, 11-12 October. TABD is made up of the 100 most powerful chief executives whose mission is to "remove obstacles to trade" between the EU and US. According to US officials up to 80 per cent of TABD's recommendations have been turned into official policy. For details of protests planned: www.tabd.nu

No Borders Camps
Last weekend a No Border camp was held at the US–Mexico border – a fence which divides the cities of Tijuana and San Diego. www.de-lete.tv/borderhack This comes after a summer of No Border camps protesting against Fortress Europe – including Bialystok in Poland, Tarifa South Spain, Frankfurt Airport, Petisovci Slovenia, and Genoa. www.noborder.org

---

Free/Donation   **@ANTI-COPYRIGHT - INFORMATION FOR ACTION**

CAMP FIRE STORY

In what may be a first in this country, a protest camp has been set up against the Crymlyn Burrows incinerator due to be built near Swansea. Local people from Stop The Incinerator Campaign (StIC) have occupied the site in protest against the dangerous health effects that the incinerator will have on the area.

We currently produce 28 million tonnes of waste a year in this country, an amount which is constantly rising. Of this we only recycle a measly 9% (compared to over 50% in other European countries). The government is giving lip service to reducing and recycling waste whilst giving out private contracts to companies to burn waste in incinerators. Over 70 new incinerators are currently on the burner.

In Swansea the local council has used Blair type spin and have renamed the incinerator a "materials recovery and energy centre". An artist's impression of the site didn't even include the 40m high chimney! When asked about this, the chief executive of the council came over all Mr.Magoo* like saying "It's an artist's impression"; maybe he's under the impression that cancer causing dioxins that will emerge from the chimney will only have "microscopic" health implications (another quality council quote). The council's arrogance has been astounding, not even consulting residents of Swansea Eastside a few hundred yards from the proposed site, locals responded with demonstrations, lobbying, direct action and a month ago the setting up of the camp. The campaign group have now managed to persuade Sue Essex , the environment minister at the Welsh Assembly to consider revoking the planning permission.

They'd appreciate support, so visit them or send postcards to Crowleys Campsite, The Incinerator protest, Fabian Way, Swansea. www.stic.org.uk

For more info on incinerators contact Communities Against Toxics, PO Box 29, Ellesmere Port, Cheshire CH66 3TX. 0151 339 5473. ralph.ryder@communities-against-toxics.org.uk.

*SchNEWS Vocab watch: Mr.Magoo – a particularly blind cartoon chararcter who older readers will remember.

STONEDPORT

Next month sees another attempt at opening a Marijuana coffee shop in this country in 'the Amsterdam of the North', a.k.a. Stockport. Lets hope it lasts longer than the '73' cafe that opened a few years back in Brighton. Nicknamed 73, cos that's how many minutes it lasted!! The imaginatively named "The Dutch Experience" is being opened by weed activists, Colin Davies and Ol Van Schaik. Colin is famous for giving a weed bouquet to the Queen and allegedly 'sharing a spliff with a HRH'. Colin, who has severe back injuries has set up the British Medical Marijuana Cooperative, which provides pot to a growing number of patients and hopes to provide low-cost marijuana to medical users, subsidised by sales to recreational users. To register with the co-operative you need a letter of diagnosis from a Doctor/Consultant. After verification patients are asked to agree to a code of conduct. The drug must not be resold and must be used in private. www.mmco.org.uk

Inside SchNEWS

Lee Himlin has been sentenced to 15 months in prison for sabotaging quarrying equipment at the 9 Ladies Quarry. Due to time Lee has spent on remand he is expected out in October. Drop him a line Lee Himlin EX7748, HMP Perry Road, Sherwood, N65 3AG.

SchNEWS in brief

Norwich street Carnival 8th September. Details 0794487393. **Norwich Direct Action Forum** meet on the 1st Wednesday of every month 8pm. To find out where they meet call the same number as above. ** If you're interested in Serbo-Croat counterculture (and aren't we all) then check out **Kontrapunkt** www.kontrapunkt-online.org ** Trial date for 9 people arrested at **Birmingham Mayday** is 15-19th October. Support and donations to help the defence are urgently needed. Cheques to BMDDC c/o PO Box 9417, Birmingham B13 9WA tel: 07980 416346 ** **Bellow** is a new newsletter by Women Speak Out. Copies from Box 35, c/o Green Leaf Bookshop, 82 Colston Street, Bristol BS1 5BB, e-mail bellow1@bigfoot.com ** **Year Zero** is an excellent anarchaic tabloid, out now. From Dulwich Hamlet FC to Genoa via John Pilger and the Nobody republic of Easton. It's £1:50 from PO Box 26276, London, W3 7GQ www.yearzero.org ** **Genoa eyewitness account** and discussion in Worthing, 7.45pm Tuesday 4th, Downview pub near West Worthing station worthing@eco-action.org ** **FLAN** (Flintshire Action Network) is a new nonviolent direct action network in Wales. flandoobie@yahoo.com ** Find out what's happening in **Scotland** join directactionscotland@yahoogroups.com ** Regular protests outside **Esso** in Brighton during September. Noon 1st, 15th and 29th outside Esso on Dyke Road. ** All budding video activists can attend a free **Undercurrents** Weekend Video Activism Course at Ruskin College (21-23 Sept), as long as you're a UK resident over 20 and don't have a degree. Interested? email: underc@gn.apc.org

OFF OUR HATCH

A group of Roma gypsies are facing eviction from a caravan site they own at Hatch in Bedfordshire. The council are spending a whooping £230,000 on evictions, which would more than pay for the modifications required for the site to get planning permission. This is not an isolated example, Romas have repeatedly been subject to this sort of abuse in this country. There's a rally and barbecue against the intended closure of the caravan park, meet 11am, Tuesday 4th Sept at the site. Info Friends and Family of Travellers 01273 234777 www.romaniworld.com/camwood.htm

UP IN ARMS

The assembly point for the 'Fiesta of Life Against Death' against the DSEi Arms Fair is 12 noon on the 11th September, Tidal Basin Road, London E16. "Come in costumes. Think pink and silver. Bring drums, instruments, food and water to share, props, puppets, banners, circus skills, your blue suede shoes and your love of life." New flyer and booklet avaliable to download at www.disarm-trade.org

DSEi training day: Legal briefing, non-violence training and Wombles workshop for anyone going to DSEi actions. Sunday 2nd , 12-4pm, St Ann's Church Hall, Berwick Rd, Newham. Info: 020 7281 0297.

In Brighton there's a whole feast of activities against the arms trade.

Public Meeting: Films, speakers and discussions about the arms trade 7.30pm, 4th Sept. Friends Meeting House, Ship Street. **Benefit Gig with Headmix and Marmoset** From 9pm, 5th Sept. Concorde2, £5/£4. **Spors not Wars** Occupation and street theatre, music, films, food, kids activities. 8th Sept. Venue TBC. email: sporganism@spor.org.uk. **Transport to the Fiesta For Life Against Death** Leave 9am 11th Sept. from St. Peter's Church. Tickets £4 in advance from the Peace Centre. Latest info 01273-298192.

Timber Wars

On 24th May 1990 two Earth First! activists involved in a campaign to protect Pacific forests from unsustainable logging practices, were blown up by a car bomb. The driver Judi Bari suffered a broken spine, smashed pelvis and a paralysed foot, Darryl Cherney in the passenger seat received lesser injuries. The FBI claimed the two activists blew themselves up with their own bomb, lied about where the bomb was placed, conducted a media smear campaign and ignored the fact that Judi and other Earth First! activists had received anonymous death threats – apparently from logging supporters. Judi and Darryl were never prosecuted. A year after the bombing they filed civil charges against the FBI for conspiracy to interfere with the right to organise politically, false arrest, unlawful search and seizure, and denying equal protection of the law. For ten years the FBI have stalled the case, during which time Judi died of breast cancer, but the case will finally come to court on October 1st. Details of the bombing, attempted frame up, the trail and how to help can be seen at www.judibari.org/ Check out Bari's 1994 book *Timber Wars*. A compilation of her articles, essays and speeches, including her first person account of the car bombing and its aftermath. Available in most bookshops, published by Common Courage Press, ISBN 1-56751-026-4.

26 of the Best

A rally this Sunday commerates the longest ever strike in history - 26 years!!

In 1914 Tom and Kitty Higdon were sacked for sticking up for rights of agricultural workers, in response they set up their own Strike school on the Village Green!! Rejecting the notion that education was just about knowing your place in society and respecting 'the betters', they preached radical themes of freedom and justice. 66 kids attended lessons on the green, leaving only 6 kids behind in the council school. The authorities were none too pleased and took the Victorian attitude, 'if you can't beat them, flog'em'. Parents were fined and even had land taken off them. In response Trade Unionists came to the Strike school to show their support. The school continued until 1939 when Tom died. The site is now an educational Museum. www.pastonroot.co.uk/gdownes/index.htm

...and finally...

It was certaintly not yer usual football entertainment. Three men and a woman dance naked on stage holding onto sparklers in an unusual fashion. Next up is Timmy the hypnotist who using his 'sexual prowess' persuades a woman to chop off her leg with an electric angle grinder. Luckily for her she's wearing metal knickers. Welcome to the alternative world cup. And at least at this World Cup, England came out on top. In fact England couldn't lose as in 12 (Bradford) beat Easton Cowboys (Bristol) 2-1.

In a field in Dorset, 2000 people had gathered with invitations to teams across the world. Champons of the first tournament, Diepkloof FC from South Africa couldn't take part this time as they've gone all professional.

The Alternative vision aims to promote camaradie, fair play, creche facilities, and socialising by getting the team players to perform at the above mentioned Saturday night Cabaret. Past ventures for the Easton Cowboys include touring the Zapista held zones, playing Cricket against the infamous Compton Homies in Califorina and creating the 'Nobody Republic in the last Council election.

Next years venue is Antwerp so get fit for your booze, fags, football and creche www.hemalimodha.co.uk/eastoncowboys/index.htm

Subscribe!

BURNING ISSUE
Crymlyn Burrows Incinerator

A small village in south Wales is next to the site of a planned waste incinerator, but the members of the community - Crymlyn Burrows - think the whole idea is complete rubbish...

In 1998 the Neath Port Talbot County Borough Council held meetings with local residents of Crymlyn Burrows to tell them about this 'recycling facility' project which was to be built in the neighbourhood, that would recycle everything possible, and 'produce energy from the tiny bit which could not be recycled'. Sounds great but the council artist's impression of the facility failed to feature one rather important aspect of the plant: incinerator stacks. They were planning to build an incinerator but when we found out about the dangers of this we formed a local resistance campaign.

In January 2001, we found out that there was a chance to stop the incinerator, if we all pulled together. Stop the Incinerator Campaign (StIC) was formed, with Mike Ryan 43, a resident of Crymlyn Burrows and father of two, elected as Chairperson. Objections from every house in Crymlyn Burrows had been made to the council (though now with hindsight we realise that no matter what our objections, the council were determined to do it). We organised a protest march to raise public awareness, and the community led campaign began. There was loads of press coverage, and much public support with people protesting against the incinerator ranging from the elderly to young parents with babies.

The IPPC (Integrated Pollution Prevention and Control - the licence necessary to allow the Waste Management Facility to operate - we call it a 'Insidious Permit to Poison Children') was applied for on 1st March 2001, giving residents one month to make their observations. Information tables were set up in Swansea and Neath with leaflets and petitions, protests were held outside the Civic Centre, Environment Agency and Health Authority; and marches through the streets of Neath and Swansea were held. One of our protests involved a tripod set up at the plant gates, with a campaign member suspended from the centre: this prevented traffic flow to the plant, and workers were sent home. On another occasion, campaign members were outside the plant gates, handing out leaflets to the contractors advising them of the severe ground contamination in which they were working. One of our boys handcuffed himself to the steps of a large crane entering the facility and his refusal to unlock himself resulted in the driver getting out his toolkit, unbolting the steps and calmly driving into work, leaving 'Thomas Tree' outside, still handcuffed to the steps…!

BBC Wales' "Week In Week Out" covered the story, and they looked at the Portuguese company HLC who were to operate the incineration plant. We heard about dodgy HLC dealings in Portugal and France and their (a little bit worrying) lack of experience in incineration. The managing director stated that 'dioxins do not cause cancer', and that the company had 'no track record in incineration' (well that's in safe hands then - ed). Teresa Brzoza, founder member of PAIN (Parents Against INcinerators), a group who worked alongside StIC, was interviewed on behalf of the two campaign groups.

The famous protest camp, set up by Vince and Mike has received a removal notice (pending the 22nd May 2002) from Swansea Council. It has served as a constant reminder to everyone passing by on the busy dual carriageway, that the incinerator was here,

but there are already plans to replace it in the very near future - watch this space.

I initially became involved in the campaign due to concerns regarding the impact of the facility on the health of my children. After searching the internet the report 'Incineration - The British Government Ignores the Danger to Health' found on www.cqs.com made me realise that the Government could not be trusted. I have now seen for myself that none of the associated local authorities really represent the needs of the public. I am disgusted that the authorities are allowing this monstrosity to be built at all, let alone where little children live, play and go to school. I am disillusioned by the attitudes of the Borough Council, the Health Authority and the Environment Agency, who are all refusing to acknowledge sound scientific evidence that incineration is dangerous. The Authorities will not acknowledge the health effects of PM2.5s - the tiny dust particles emitted during industrial processes such as incineration, which can be inhaled deep into the lungs where your body's own defence mechanism cannot remove them, thus causing permanent lung problems. They insist that monitoring and abating PM10s is sufficient, as this complies with the European Waste Incineration Directive. (PM10s are much larger dust particles, which get caught in the upper respiratory tract, but can be removed by coughing or sneezing, apparently).

And as for that 'recycling scheme' the council talked about in the first place? They introduced the scheme a couple of years ago and then stated that it did not work because 'people couldn't be bothered' to recycle.

An Offer You Can't Refuse

The plant will take 166,000 tonnes of refuse per year. 31,700 tonnes of this will be sorted to go for recycling - a paltry 19.1%. 53,490 tonnes per year will be composted, that's 32.2% (even though the compost will have to be landfilled because it's sub-standard and contains animal matter). The rejects, which will go straight to landfill will constitute 17% of the refuse at 28,310 tonnes. The remaining 52,500 tonnes, or 31.6%, will be incinerated. If we total everything up, we will see that, apart from the miniscule amount of recyclate, the waste has not been reduced at all. It has, in actual fact simply changed into toxic emissions, toxic ashes and toxic landfill. In simple terms, out of the total 166,000 tonnes of waste accepted by the plant each year, 31,700 tonnes will be recycled; 63,460 tonnes will go to landfill; and 70,840 tonnes will be released into the air.

Update

On Thursday the 9th May 2002, the Environment Agency announced its decision to grant the IPPC operating licence to HLC, even though no health risk assessment has been carried out on another unsavoury aspect of the refuse plant: the composting activity. The composter will release a bio aerosol of tiny particles, containing fungal spores and human pathogens into the environment - as if the incinerator emissions alone weren't enough to worry about! Those most at risk? According to the Environment Agency, the people living within 250 metres of the plant - the residents of Crymlyn Burrows. Particles from incinerators have the potential to travel airborn for great distances depending on prevailing winds - up to 50 miles according to one pollution expert.

For every planned and operating incinerator in Britain, there is a campaign, but in general the public are not made aware of the extreme dangers of this form of waste disposal.

Visit StIC website www.stic.org.uk

Where were you on September 11 2001?

POLICE AGAINST THE ARMS TRADE

Fiesta For Life Against Death
Dis-arm DSEI Arms Fair

Most Pics: Guy Smallman

WAKE UP! WAKE UP! IT'S YER THREE-TWO-ONE-FIRE

ALL THE FUN OF THE ARMS FAIR

Weekly SchNEWS

Printed and Published in Brighton by Justice?

Friday 7th September 2001   www.schnews.org.uk   Issue 321

ALL THE GUN OF THE FAIR

"The price of one British Aerospace Hawk is roughly the amount needed to provide 1.5 million people in the third world with fresh water for life." - Campaign Against the Arms Trade.

"It is the trade in weapons that allows exploitation and murder to continue around the world ... On the 11th we are setting our sights on the arms trade." - Disarm DSEi.

Every second the arms industry and global war machine continues to kill people and destroy lives around the world. 2,000 children are killed or disabled by weaponry every day – without counting those left without parents or homes. According to the UN Human Development Report, in 1999 the world's governments spent an estimated £450 billion to run their military machines. This is 14 times more than is needed to eradicate 'absolute' poverty from the world.

Robin Cook - now about as trustworthy as a snake in a cage of hamsters - said back in 1978 (when he was a lowly MP on the up): "Wherever weapons are sold there is a conspiracy to conceal the reality of war… It is a truism that every war for the past two decades has been fought by poor countries with weapons supplied by rich countries." Any hint of integrity he may have had was soon wiped out when Neo-Labour came to power in 1997 - Cook and his cronies lied about their 'ethical foreign policy', but then signed papers to export weapons in every class banned by European legislation.

UK arms companies thrive upon deliberately supplying opposing states, stirring up conflict and making a killing. For example, in 1997 under the pretext of setting up an aid programme to stabilise conditions in Lebanon, British firm Alvis sold the Lebanese 3,500 rifles for £300,000. This after the rifles had been sold as surplus to Alvis for £195,000 by the MoD, who suggested giving the first 500 rifles free of charge as a sweetener! At the same time Israel, who occupied large parts of Lebanon - were also buying weapons from British firms. Or take the Iran-Iraq war, which saw 1million deaths, again Britain armed both sides. The same thing is happening now in the escalating conflict between India and Pakistan.

Bombs R Us

"In no other export sector is Britain so successful as in the arms business, which is cosseted like no other industry" - John Pilger, 'Hidden Agendas'

While 1 in 4 children in the UK grows up in poverty, arms exports are subsidised to the tune of £420m, and the industry as a whole for as much as £4.25 billion. British weaponry companies employ loads of Research and Development (R&D) scientists to make their nasty machinery.

SchNEWS wonders if these boffins could do something more constructive instead.

In 1976, 13 unions in Lucas Aerospace put their heads together and composed a "Combine Plan." They proposed that instead of military hardware they could make useful products like kidney machines. The plan was ignored. We are now in the ridiculous situation where there is a subsidy of £4,600 per arms export job. If the R&D of £570m is included, this would rise to £11,000 a year. So you are paying the salaries of defence workers. And what are the effects of this work?

"The boy near me died and I was thrown a metre in the air. The boy who died was 14 – he had his head cut off." - A 13 year old boy, who lost both legs, describing the effects of playing with an unexploded cluster bomb, dropped as part of NATO's 'humanitarian' bombing campaign in Kosovo.

Cluster bombs are one of the most indiscriminate weapons around, forget all the 'precision bombing' bullshit you see on the telly. Cluster bombs disperse a whole load of 'bomblets' over an area up to three football pitches in size. These bomblets can be anti-armour weapons, incendiary devices or fragmentation bombs (effectively nail bombs) designed to maim rather than kill. The sale of anti-personnel landmines is banned, but to get round it anti-vehicle landmines with anti-handling devices are produced - sensitive enough to be detonated by a human. And who ensured this loophole was included? No prize for guessing it was UK plc.

Excel in Death

You might have missed the news (maybe cos there's been none), but the UK govt is holding an arms fair in London next week. The Defence Systems and Equipment international (DSEi) is the largest arms fair in Europe, and attracts arms dealers from oppressive regimes such as Indonesia, Burma and even the US. Guns of all deadly shapes and sizes, Hawk jets, warships, tanks, etc will be on sale, making that boring old job of keeping peasants in line that little bit easier. Kick-off with a neighbouring state over borders, religion or water? This is the place to get seriously tooled up. Britain is the world's second largest arms exporter, after the US of course.

CRAP ARREST OF THE WEEK

For wearing a purple hairband!! Pamela Smith was in Edinburgh Sheriffs Court supporting a fellow Trident Ploughshares banner dropper, when she was told 'the sheriff wants your hairband off.' Pamela claimed her right to wear it, but the Sheriff disagreed and had her locked up for two hours before charging her with Breach of the Peace!

DSEi is taking over the entire EXCEL Centre in London's Docklands.

* Since WW2 there have been more than 250 major wars in which over 23 million people have been killed.
* There are an estimated 500million small arms and light weapons around the world, responsible for 500,000 deaths a year.

Breach the Peace

So what can we do about it? Well there's a Fiesta of Life and Against Death on the first day of the arms fair (Tues). Thousands are expected to pour into Docklands for some serious fun. Samba, carnival, pink and silver costumes, props, direct action and whatever you can make happen.

At the last DSEi arms fair two years ago, people seriously harangued delegates, locking onto trains, blocking roads, launching water-borne sorties, breaching the conference centre, generally being creative and making a positive impact. Make this year bigger and better. While the profits of doom puff on about doing it for peace, let's breach the carefully police orchestrated peace where they do business, break down the barriers surrounding the EXCEL Centre, and make some fuckin' noise about their dodgy exploits. So get a group of mates together or just turn up and let's see what we can do…

* 'Critical mass' bike ride meets at 10am by Waterloo Bridge on September 11th. Bring yer wheels.
* The Fiesta for Life Against Death will assemble at 12 noon on Tuesday 11th at Canning Town Station, Silvertown Way/Newham Way (A13). Bring drums and noisy stuff, get Wombled up… Disarm DSEi office/ London Reclaim the Streets!: 020 7281 4621 for maps and tactics etc. Wombles www.wombleaction.mrnice.net
* Campaign Against the Arms Trade are also organising a procession on the 11th starting at 10am in the recreation ground, Appleby Rd, Canning Town and holding a peace vigil outside the EXCEL Centre by Tidal Basin Rd, London, Docklands. Actions are planned for the rest of the week, and there'll be a camp, café and legal support too. CAAT 020 7281 0297 www.caat.org.uk
* Check www.uk.indymedia.org for reports on the day and afterwards.

Talk Show

"Colonialism is dead but new overlords impose themselves. The World Bank, WEF, G8, IMF and WTO. They are supported not only by lackey governments like our own but also by a legion of other forked-tongue abbreviations: NGO's, UNO's, USAIDs and WCAR's; of which we are all deeply suspicious, despite their pretense at caring for us." - Durban Social Forum statement.

While the Americans and Israelis were busy storming out of the UN's World Conference Against Racism (WCAR), South Africa was in the grip of a national strike. Over five million workers took part in the two day strike against privatisation in which "most industrial areas were effectively closed down." Following this 20,000 people marched last Friday against the conference.

Thabo Mbeki, the President of South Africa, opened proceedings at the WCAR, with observer Heidi Bachram commenting "Mbeki spoke of fighting global apartheid but failed to mention that he was embracing an economic programme that increased poverty and homelessness. While Mbeki spoke of the present world order built on slavery and colonialism, his government is busy privatising the water and electricity in South Africa, which is resulting in a 'pay or die' scenario for people here. As he spoke about the successes of the anti-apartheid struggles, local people are being forced to drink water from toilets and since the water was privatised, 200 people in Durban have died from cholera. This is the brave new world of post-apartheid, neo-liberal South Africa."

After the first free elections in South Africa in 1994, the new ANC government was visited by the big boys of global capital (IMF etc) – who told them to adapt to the 'realities of the global economy'. The message was that if they wanted money to raise the standard of living for the black majority they had to, er… lower their standard of living. The ANC inherited a \$25 billion foreign debt – funds used to support apartheid, and on top of that the IMF imposed their usual conditions for loans – wholesale privatisation. Initially people were patient through the compromises to western demands, but now they see their leaders hobnobbing with world leaders while their water and electricity get turned off. Inequality in society has actually increased after seven years of an ANC government in South Africa.

But these people - who have the anti-apartheid struggle still fresh in their minds - aren't taking this lying down. Battles have been fought against evictions and water cut-offs, and over 3000 of the Landless Peoples' Movement are camping to protest against being used as farm labour on their ancestral land. In Soweto, people are reconnecting electricity and water themselves, occupying the offices of the service companies, and setting up anti-privatisation groups.
* IndyMedia South Africa were refused press entry into the Conference, because it was thought they might be 'one sided' - which of course the mainstream media never are. Visit http://southafrica.indymedia.org/
* Check out South African anarchist/libertarian paper 'Zabalaza' http://www.struggle.ws/africa/safrica/zabamag.html

FOX THIS

The Crown Prosecution Service have decided to drop charges against Martin Maynard, the 'psychopathic' hunt supporter, who drove over and almost killed hunt saboteur Steve Christmas. Steve who had to be airlifted to hospital, had two foot of bowel removed and spent four weeks in intensive care. Whilst Maynard walks free, 18 anti-hunt protestors still remain on charges relating to broken windows at the hunt kennels during a demo the next day held in protest against the attack. Donations needed for their bust fund. 01273 622827 www.huntsabs.org.uk

SchNEWS in brief

800 protesters in the **Philippines** stormed one of **Monsanto's GM fields** last week uprooting all the Bt corn plants http://ens-news.com/ens/aug2001/2001L-08-29-03.html ** Meanwhile in **France** the **Militant Peasants Confederation** have vowed to continue openly trashing GM crops despite presence of riot cops at their demos ** Good news for those living in **Bristol** the **Bristolian** alternative newsletter will now be hitting the streets every week. Get it by e-mail: localnews4us@yahoo.co.uk or pick it up locally ** There's now a **Bristol WOMBLES group**, bristolwombles@hushmail.com contact 07904 097065 ** **A Reclaim the Streets Party** in the small **Czech** town of Vysoke Myto was scattered by police after a two hour occupation of a street ** **Healing UK** is a forum to discuss and plan medical support for demos and actions. If you want to get involved healinguksubscribe@yahoogroups.com ** Campaigners at the proposed **Crymlun Burrows incinerator site** (see SchNEWS 320) in Swansea successfully closed down work for the day by erecting a tripod at the entrance gates. More people are needed on the protest camp. www.stic.org.uk ** **Samba Carnival Procession** in **Canning Town** this Saturday (8th) in the build up to the Fiesta for Life Against Death. Costume: pink and silver, meet 10.30am Rathbone Market, Barking Rd., London E16 (Nearest Tube Canning Town DLR) ** Scottish football fans bought 20 asylum seekers tickets to watch Scotland play Croatia in last Saturday's World Cup qualifier. Hamish Husband, chairman of the West of Scotland branch of the **Tartan Army**, said: "We decided it would be a good way of showing some solidarity with these people. They've suffered persecution in their own countries and after the trouble here recently we thought we'd do this one small thing to show them support."

Foundation Block

Strathclyde Police are promising that they will be mounting their largest police operation for this October's big blockade at Faslane naval base, Scotland. Their strategy Code-named 'Operation Foundation' includes plans to draft in hundreds of extra police and to use cells across the region to hold those arrested. Special Branch and other services have recently returned from Gorleben in Germany (site of regular nuclear train protests) where they drooled over their German mates beating up protesters.

Protesters though aren't fazed and are vowing to make this year's Faslane blockade massive, it's taking place on 22 October so get up there and help block up the police cells. A detailed 10-page briefing with maps, photos, legal details and tactics is now available. Action Line: 0141 423 1222 www.cndscot.dial.pipex.com

Inside SchNEWS

Avia Atai, a female Israeli teacher, was sentenced on Monday to 28 days in prison for refusing to transfer to the Gilo settlement in the occupied territory, where she was due to instruct children on how to avoid the shelling/gunfire from the neighbouring Beit-Jalla (whose land Gilo was built). She stated: "I do not believe in brutality and use of force. I feel the Military and the Politicians have brought this war upon our heads. I will not enter the territories occupied in 1967. I do not believe in the expansion of Israel". Conscientious objectors are often sent to prison in Israel. Find out about other prisoners, visit www.newprofile.org

Positive SchNEWS

Fed up with paying extortionate rents? Then joining or setting up a housing co-op is a great alternative. In a co-op you not only get cheap rents you're also your own landlord. The Housing Co-op Head-to-Head on the 15 Sept has been arranged for those who live in co-ops in Sussex or those who want to find out more about the movement. It's a free event but booking is essential. 11am at The Old Market Arts Centre, Upper Market Street, Hove. Send your contact details to Housing Co-op Head-to-Head, c/o Brighton Rock Housing Co-op, 397 Kingsway, Hove BN3 4QE www.co-op.org/mutualaid/

Stanmer Organics a community food project in Brighton is having an open day this Saturday (8) 12noon till 5pm. Veg for sale, food by spiralbean, earth kiln demo, music, storytelling etc. More details 01273 261811

Oi! Gerroff Yer Land

Inhabitants of the Stewart Wood have unfortunately lost their planning appeal against a decision by the Planning Inspectorate to refuse them permission to live on the woodland that they own, and are managing as a permaculture garden and low intervention wildlife zone. The group are considering an appeal against the decision in the High Courts. They desperately need help to cover their legal costs. Steward Community Woodland, Morehampstead, Newton Abbot, Devon TQ13 8SD Tel: 07050 674464 www.stewardwood.org

Hackneyed Story

Roll up! Roll up! For two days only get down to the squatters estate agents at 52 Stoke Newington High Street, and view over 50 community properties that, thanks to Hackney Council going bankrupt, are in danger of being sold, privatised, or suffering serious cuts that threaten their very survival.

The estate agents with a conscience have recently got hold of 'exempt' minutes from a recent council meeting. It lists over 130 Council owned properties to be assessed for sale as part of their 'disposals programme'. These includes everything from community centres, adventure playgrounds, allotments, nurseries and shops, as well as 100's of houses.

One of the properties reads "Formerly a nursery, but we got rid of the kids + their whining parents. We even fibbed in court, to get rid of the squatters who had reopened it as a community centre of all things. We told the master that we were not going to sell this building but, Ha! - It is now freed up to give lots of potential for profit as a yuppie wine bar or a private health club for city workers.

Price: Don't bother enquiring, you couldn't afford it. In fact why don't you just move to another borough so that we can speed up the process of gentrification here in Hackney."

Hurry readers – doors close on Friday evening. If you can't make it, get down to a Noise Demo outside Hackney Town Hall next Thursday (13th) 6pm, where the councillors are meeting to discuss the next round of cuts and sell offs. Tel 07752 592 740 hackney4sale@yahoo.co.uk

...and finally...

Cunning scientists have developed the ultimate pointless object - a 'green grenade'- it will blow yer average person to smithereens but won't pollute the environment. Professor Thomas Klaptoke of the University in Munich has been working on the new greenies said, "It's a very important issue …You don't want to pollute your own environment nor do you want to put your own policemen and soldiers at risk." Well that's alright then.

COMING SOON TO A TOWN NEAR YOU

FROM THE MAKERS OF 'THE THOMAS ENRON AFFAIR' AND 'GOOD MORNING KOSOVO'

BASED ON A TRUE STORY

GROUND ZERO

THIS TIME IT'S PERSONAL

BEN KINGSLEY as OSAMA BIN LADEN   CHEVY CHASE as GEORGE W BUSH   MORGAN FREEMAN as COLIN POWELL

BILL MURRAY as RUDY GIULIANI   HUGH GRANT as TONY BLAIR   CHARLTON HESTON as DONALD RUMSFELD   Directed by DICK CHENEY   Executive Producer GEORGE BUSH snr   Screenplay by the CIA

 WARNING: This film may contain scenes of genocide

'I love the smell of depleted uranium in the morning ... smells like ... a darn good war film. ' - Infotainment Weekly

'You either think this film is completely unbiased - or else you're against us.' - White House Press Secretary

'We have uncovered a brilliant new scriptwriting talent - the CIA.' - CNN News

'Hollywood takes on the news channels - and wins' - The Mammon Spectacle

THE DAY THE WORLD CHANGED

The day the towers came down most of the SchNEWS crew and our mates were in London at the DSEI demo in the Docklands. Early in the afternoon, before the news broke, most of us who were with the main group found ourselves in a bit of carpark hemmed in by police, a long way from the actual Excel Centre where the arms & torture fair was being held. We were just getting used to the fact that for us the demo was basically scuppered and we were stuck there for a few hours at least. Then people started talking out loud that the World Trade Centre in New York and Pentagon had been hit with hijacked planes. Initially it was like 'yeah right'. When it was clear that this wasn't just random nutters, the demo went into disarray and lot of people disappeared, and many of us went to a pub round the corner to watch TV, leaving the row of cops still holding the line along the road. It was a case of 'see you later, we're all off to the pub' as the cops stood arms folded.

As we sat stunned watching continual re-runs of the fresh footage it was a case of trying to get your head around the reality that this was one of those enormous historical moments which would be with us forever, endlessly gone over like the Kennedy shooting - and in many ways bigger than any of them. But for the Dis-arm DSEI crowd in that hushed pub, the question of what the US were going to do in response to this was possibly more frightening than the sight of the towers falling themselves.

The first thing to expect was even-greater-than Diana levels of rubbish coming out of peoples' mouths and newspapers, and all the tedious memorials and pretense that nations had been united by the grief etc.

The worry was what Bush was going to do. It was clear before this that he'd been dying to spend money on the military, pushing the missile defense system. You just knew that innocent people were about to be killed (colateral they call it) by a rampant, revengeful US.

In the weeks after, the way people were whipped up into a mushy frenzy of blind patriotism showed the way the US/western media/propaganda machine is as monstrous as its military. Many had the feeling that the US 'had it coming', but there was an apparent media ban on that line of thinking.

The other way of looking at it was - fuck the spectacle of the towers: sure, look at what's behind the attacks, and see the broader context, but don't join in on the mass distraction. Other events were big news at the same time - such as the impending economic collapse of Argentina for instance. In the following weeks other stories were made to look 'trivial' compared to 9-11 - then there was the small matter that most of the crises in other countries were caused by either the US, its IMF/WB/WTO /etc bogey men or western corporations - but you couldn't be caught slagging America off could you.

Some thought that this was the end of the 'anti-capitalist movement' - which was blatant rubbish as the problems hadn't gone away, neither had the protesters. What we had was a whole new set of factors to mix into the landscape of global capitalism - not the least being the possibility of the US 'bombing for peace' again. The only people who thought that the 'movement' was over were either conservatives willing it to finish, or intellectual trendies pre-empting that Seattle/Prague/Genoa etc was suddenly last year's shirt. There was never any doubt that it would be back - even if it was in the shadows for a few months.

For SchNEWS and others the weeks after September 11 were a time of saying the things that needed to be said, and concentrating on the right sources of information, but in an environment of swimming against tidal waves of propaganda; and writers and public voices disappointing us badly by coming out with unforgivable wet nonsense in the aftermath of the attacks.

In these pages we have included articles from a range of people - to try give a bit more of an even perspective - keeping the self indulgent emotive waffle to a minimum of course...

OSAMA BIN BUSH VS GEORGE W LADEN

* is the spoiled son of a powerful businessman, from extremely wealthy construction family
* has declared a holy war ("Jihad") against his "enemies"; believes any nation not with him is against him; believes God is on his side, and that any means are justified
* supported by extreme fundamentalist religious leaders who preach hatred, intolerance, subjugation of women, mistreatment and worse of gay, lesbian, bisexual and transgendered people, and persecution of non-believers
* was not elected by a majority of people in a free and fair democratic election
* operates through clandestine organisation (CIA) with agents in many countries; uses bombing, assassination, other terrorist tactics
* using war as pretext to clamp down on dissent and undermine civil liberties

* is the spoiled son of a powerful politician, from extremely wealthy oil family
* has declared a holy war ("crusade") against his "enemies"; believes any nation not with him is against him, believes God is on his side, and that any means are justified
* supported by extreme fundamentalist religious leaders who preach hatred, intolerance, subjugation of women, mistreatment and worse of gay, lesbian, bisexual and transgendered people and persecution of non-believers
* was not elected by a majority of people in a free and fair democratic election
* operates through clandestine organisation (al Qaeda) with agents in many countries; uses bombing assassination, other terrorist tactics
* using war as pretext to clamp down on dissent and undermine civil liberties

WAKE UP! WAKE UP! THE WORLD IS UNDER ATTACK

Weekly SchNEWS

Printed and Published in Brighton by Justice?

Friday 14th September 2001   www.schnews.org.uk   Issue 322

VICIOUS CIRCLE

"**What is the alternative? More bombs? More security? More cameras in the streets? More phone taps? More subsidy to the arms industry? … Is that where we're going? On a race to the bottom trapped between GW Bush and the CIA-created Osama Bin Laden? Because it seems that's what is wanted." Adam Porter, Year Zero magazine**

While the SchNEWS crew with hundreds of other protestors were being hemmed in by police for the bare faced cheek of wanting to shut down an arms fair, news came filtering through of the attacks on the World Trade Centre towers and the Pentagon.

As always, the deaths of innocent people are terrible and harrowing but carnage happens around the world every day of the year. The difference this time is that for once it is happening in the US, on the doorstep of corporate and military power. The Archbishop of Wales, only a few blocks away when the World Trade Centre were hit said, "It's given me a vivid sense of what people around the world live with daily."

Adam Porter, the editor of Year Zero magazine explained the tragedy most clearly, "The loss of innocent lives is more disgusting than words can express. The office workers, the cleaners, the lift repair men, the people who jumped to their deaths perhaps hoping against hope that they would somehow survive … those incinerated in the building by thousands of gallons of aircraft fuel … ordinary US citizens … just like ordinary people in Paris, Amsterdam, Bangkok, Tripoli and Baghdad. But look, and look hard, this is what men of violence do to cities, what British and American planes did to Basra in Iraq, what British and American planes did to parts of Belgrade. When I spout on about missiles slamming into the side of escaping Kosovan women, children and pensioners packed into a train I mean it. They died terrible, flesh-ripping deaths. When you fire cruise missiles into packed shelters full of women and kids in Baghdad they too died terrible deaths. When you kill 5.8 million Vietnamese, carpet bombing their rudimentary homes whilst leaving the centre of Hanoi and Saigon clear so you had somewhere nice to stay when you invaded they too died terrible deaths. When you rounded up every socialist and liberal in Indonesia and had them killed and tortured they too died terrible deaths. We can add Panama, Honduras, Guatemala, Colombia, Ecuador, Nicaragua, Laos,

Cambodia, Israel…" he wrote. (Go to www.yearzero.org for the full article).

And if the superpowers' expensive bullets and bombs don't get you, then their economic policies will. Just think - the income of the richest 20% of the world's population is at least 75 times greater than the income of the poorest 20% (it was 'only' 30 times greater forty years ago). Third world debt, enforced by the military might of the United States, Britain and other rich countries, is simply a racket to keep this inequality entrenched. Every day £28 million flows from the poorest countries in the world to the banks of the rich countries. These are the economies of the winner-takes-all capitalist mentality where millions die in a world of plenty through hunger and disease.

> America are pointing the finger at Osama Bin Laden, forgetting to mention that it was the CIA who recruited Bin Laden and other Islamic zealots from middle eastern refugee camps, gave them weapons, money and the knowledge of how to run a war of attrition that was violent and well-organized enough to help destroy Afghanistan. To do this they used the Pakistani Inter-Services Intelligence Agency to create a front organisation Maktab al-Khidamar (MAK). This motley crew of tooled-up CIA sponsored fanatics helped to lay Afghanistan to waste, and create one of the most repressive regimes in the world. Bin Laden split from MAK in 1988 and established a new group, al-Qaida, which included many of the more extreme MAK members he'd met in Afghanistan.

Linking Arms

We were protesting about an arms fair where a brand new Trimaran warship is docked for show, and where the latest hi-tech weaponry is being flogged to any country with a big enough national bank account or International Monetary Fund loan – and bugger the human rights record. But straight away, the police violently pushed us into a cordon and completely surrounded us, confiscating water pistols and searching people for ammo to 'prevent a breach of the peace', even trying to snatch musical instruments as potential weapons! Er, excuse us officer, but maybe you should take a look inside the Excel building - we're sure a section 60 weapons search in there would result in a satisfying 'nick'. But of course the delegates and salesmen of flesh-ripping devices are not only creating breaches of the peace for profit, they are doing it with the endorsement of governments the world over.

Change of Tactics

The police weren't going to let us get away with trying to shut down the arms fair. They'd even raided two squats in south London the Friday before where they smashed up props for the demo and nicked four people for 'conspiracy to commit violent disorder'. The 'evidence'? A stick with a nail in it!

Individuals and affinity groups that broke away from the main demo had slightly more success. Some valiantly tried time and again to get through security whilst wandering delegates were told just how much their work was really appreciated. Local support was excellent - people lapped up SchNEWS and slagged off the rozzers: some, once aware of the arms fair, also decided to join in with hounding delegates. Later, kids picked up all the discarded white overalls and pink accessories and had a pop at the old bill themselves!

But we need to seriously reassess our tactics. Firstly, why didn't *thousands* of people want to come and protest about the arms trade? – do people think, after Mayday, that big London demos aren't worth it, or was the publicity poor? Secondly, if we can't get the numbers and if we continue with the same tactics we'll become increasingly demoralised as we find ourselves in 'the kettle', surrounded by the police. The cops are now used to this style of protest: they can see how events will unfold so they act swiftly and crush them. Thirdly, don't expect a single group or organisation to take the lead. The more successful actions on September 11th seemed to be by smaller affinity groups who used their initiative, and seized opportunities. It's a lot harder for the cops to keep track of lots of small groups, and they're a lot more mobile, so even if one group gets surrounded there are still plenty more on the loose. Get together, use your imagination and creativity, and - most importantly - take responsibility for yourselves.

* Just what sort of a disgusting world these arms companies live in showed itself pointedly the next day, after the bombing when BAE systems shares went up at the prospect of America tooling up even more. While in true capitalist style computer company Cisco Systems said "This is a good opportunity to sell kit to accommodate these financial institutions needs."

Copwatch

The Police now have new guidelines for dealing with the threat of animal rights protesters, nuclear protests and Reclaim The Streets type actions. SchNEWS hacks have read snippets of the reports, which contain ground-breaking comments like "Animal rights protesters are different from other groups as their sole interest is to prevent testing on animals." They also worryingly link nuisance faxes in the same league of terrorism as letter bombs! Copies of the guidelines are available from the National Operations Faculty helpline on 01256 602777.www.training.police.uk/news/insider/insider_12/police.html

*The Dutch police are organising an international police knees-up to swap methods used to combat activism at global summits. It will take place from 3 to 5 October 2001 in The Hague. The official program can be found at: www.burojansen.nl/orde/engels/ineng.htm

* Scotland Yard's detection rate fell to 15% last year (Evening Standard, 19th July 2001). Police are only succeeding in prosecuting 1 in 20 muggers and fewer than 1 in 10 burglary suspects. Hardly surprising given how much effort they put into hassling anti-arms trade activists!

Inside SchNEWS

This week sees the start of the last trials for activists involved in actions in Gothenburg in July. In all, 37 activists have been labelled the 'communications group' and are charged with being the 'leaders' of all the actions/demos in Gothenberg, (the idea of 'DIY' still seems to be escaping those that can't live without someone telling them what to do). Most of the accused are appealing against sentences of up to 4 years for 'rioting', with some non-Norwegians, including German, Italian and English citizens, facing expulsions of up to 10 years. Local prison support is being provided through solidaritetsgruppen@hotmail.com, and they still need help to provide money for those awaiting trial. Please contact the group first and they will advise you of the best way to do this. They also need books, mostly in Swedish but also in German, Danish and English, to take in to prisoners to relieve that terminal boredom. Books etc can be sent to Solidaritygroup GBG, c/o Syndikalistiskt Forum, Box 7267, 402 35 Gothenburg , Sweden. For more info see www.motkraft.net.

Positive SchNEWS

The reforestation action group Treesponsibility have been up and planting for only four years, and have already had a positive impact on their local area. They reforested the hills of Calderdale, built their own tree nursery and have pledged to plant 20,000 more trees in the near future. They are plotting various projects and actions such as a boycott Esso tree week. "Lets plant trees in our communities, while getting the word out about who really cares for the planet and who is paying lip service while raking in profits made from destroying our planet." And they want to see people planting trees in BP and Shell forecourts too cos they're just as bad as Esso.If you're interested in tree planting, debating climate issues and organising local actions then there's a Treesponsibility gathering happening at Hebden Bridge, Yorkshire, on the 5th-7th Oct. There will be workshops on wild food, ecology, and woodland economy as well as plenty of kids stuff, food, fire & party, cost £8/£5 low/unwaged per day. Contact 01422 843222, 10 Broughton Street, Hebden Bridge, HX7 8JY. Pick up provided from Hebden train station. Childcare available if requested. No dogs.

Unsound Asylum

"I was tortured psychologically and physically. I was beaten up, sometimes with cables, sometimes for an hour they would beat me. They're going to kill me, I know what they're like. I won't let them kill me, I'll kill myself." - Ali Namik, Kurdish asylum seeker persecuted before coming to Britain for owning a video shop stocking western films

As SchNEWS goes to press there are over 40 armed conflicts happening around the world. The arms traders and western governments who subsidise some of the dodgiest regimes around help them to maintain these conflicts and dish out human rights abuses. Countries invited to this years arms fair included Saudi Arabia, Sri Lanka, Lebanon, Pakistan and Israel who are all at war to some degree. The governments of rich countries such as ours promote the arms trade, yet turn their backs on those fleeing the wars that they helped to create. And the more weapons that are sold, the more unstable the world becomes- good if you're a fat-cat arms trader who makes money from conflict generation. Given this, it's unsurprising that 1 out of every 115 people alive today is a refugee or displaced person.

In April last year New Labour's Asylum Bill came into force. It paved the way for the locking up and dispersal of asylum seekers and for benefits (a mere 70 percent of the pittance everyone else receives) to be paid in vouchers rather than cash. New arrivals in this country now have a 1 in 8 chance of being detained on arrival and locked up in a detention centre. They've commited no crime, have never been tried, and there is no limit to the time they can be held.

Last week a high court judge agreed that this policy was completely dodgy when he ruled that four Iraqi Kurds held at Oakington detention centre were detained illegally. This could seriously affect government plans - and they could now face bills for damages running into millions, as more than 11,000 people have been held in the camp since it was opened.

Inspired by the high court ruling, asylum seekers have been on hunger strikes and sit-ins at Haslar and Campsfield detention centres. They're demanding immediate release and an end to no-time-limit detention. The protest at Haslar, near Portsmouth, was brought to an end on Monday when prison staff dressed in riot gear raided the compound and shifted many of the protesters to Winchester prison (so no change in conditions, then). A similar protest at Campsfield, where 100 detainees had been refusing food, ended peacefully on Wednesday night.

* National weekend of action against detention Sept.22nd-23rd Info: www.closecampsfield.org.uk
* 'Barbed Wire Europe' report on asylum/detention £5 inc. p&p from 40 Richmond Terrace, Oxford OX1 2JJ. (Cheques to Campaign Against Immigration Detention.) www.barbedwirebritain.org.uk
* In Iraq, new tortures and punishments- including amputation of the tongue and beheading-have been introduced and reportedly used on scores of political prisoners. Iraqi Kurds constitute the largest percentage of asylum seekers in the UK, but they're routinely booted out cos, as Jack Straw pointed out, they've nothing to fear and nothing to complain about back home.

SchNEWS in brief

September 25th, fifteen Greenpeace volunteers and two freelance journalists are on trial in Los Angeles for conspiracy after delaying the **Star Wars** missile test launch at Vandenberg Air Force Base in California. www.greenpeace.org ** The **Brazilian Commission** recently overturned a Brazilian law protecting the country's forest, mangrove, and grasslands ecosystems. But it still has to pass through the full Congress and be approved by the president. More info and a protest email at www.codigoflorestal.com.br/english/ ** **Sri Lanka** has cancelled its ban on genetically engineered food designed to protect human health, after pressure from the World Trade Organisation who say it is against trade rules. ** Cyberactions for **Satpal Ram's** release are being co-ordinated over the next few weeks by **Miscarriages of Justice UK** -see www.appleonline.net/justiceuk/jus or 0121-554-6947 ** FLAN (Flintshire Action Network) will be holding a non-violent protest outside **The GAP** in **Chester,** 12 noon, Saturday 22 September, flandoobie@yahoo.com ** Those pleasant people at the **National Front** have set up a website www.redwatch.org.uk putting up pictures, names etc of people who gone to Anti-fascist demo's. Sabotage the site if you know how, or give false information to debunk the site (do it through www.safeweb.com and/or hotmail address to avoid comeback) ** 27 activists were arrested at a successful blockade of **Shell**'s Stanlow refinery in Cheshire in protest at its links with **Huntingdon Life Sciences.** ** The public were excluded from a **'Public' inquiry** into a greenfield development in **Coleridge** near Rushmoor. One villager decided to go anyway and stopped the enquiry after threatening action under the Human Rights Acts. The government are pressing ahead with changes to the planning system to make it harder to make objections to controversial projects at public enquiries. www.onlincam.freeserve.co.uk

Not so sMart

Wal-Mart (owners of Asda in this Country) are now the world's largest retailer and the largest employer in the USA, and they surely ain't got to that position by being nice. They've now officially earned themselves the title of the world's most sued corporation, with a new lawsuit being filed against them every 2 hours. You name it and they've been found guilty of it - that's if they haven't destroyed the evidence first. In three states in the US judges have found Wal-Mart guilty of destroying and withholding evidence. www.sprawl-busters.com, www.walmartsucks.com

...and finally...

The advertising game is all about doing what ever it takes – gimmicks and pulling the wool – to get us all to go out and spend, spend, spend. But marketing brand consultants Lambie-Nairn – whose approach is 'creative strategies and strategic creativity' have been pulling the wool on the advertisers themselves, charging big money for virtually the same logo.

Their logo for the renaming of BT Cellnet as O2 is a circle with a two next to it. Which must have used up a lot of brainpower because their new logo for Digital TV channel Music Choice is the words Music Choice next to a large circle. Phew! And for BAE System's the logo is... a circle with their name next to it. And for Friends of the Earth...you get the picture. Let's just say they're paying money for a big fat zero …

disclaimer

"People almost feel guilty to want to trade for profit in circumstances like these."
A right London banker. Almost…

AFTER MATH

By Adam Porter

Speech bubble: AH...IT'S A TERRORIST!

GHASTLY, EVIL UNCIVILIZED FANATICS FLYING IN PLANES AND CAUSING MASS DESTRUCTION ALL OVER THE WORLD

- London, 12th September 2001 -

And you think to yourself, is this it? Is this all we did? Is this the end of the world? Two passenger aeroplanes slam into the side of the World Trade Centre's so-called Twin Towers. They are twin towers no more. Like millions of others before them ordinary citizens die horrific deaths as a result of American foreign policy. But this time the deaths are American and in America.

The level of hyperbole drives through the ceiling, fear and sanctimony are everywhere, uncertainty rules. Tony Blair can't talk to the Unions at the TUC Conference as he is too moved. The TV and the media, unsurprisingly are over majoring on it. The U.S.-Mexican border is sealed. All flights over the US are cancelled. The internet service providers get bogged down under the weight of the news junkies desperate for knowledge of what had happened. Mobile use in the USA imploded. All flights over London are cancelled. The creator of Frasier dies. Like the White House, Disneyworld in Orlando was evacuated. And after all that, who did it? And why?

Well, listen, you can take your pick. America has been rocked not only by the explosions themselves but by the fact that Americans may have died at the hands of a deliberate audacious extraordinary attack. They seem shocked that anyone would want to make their political point through such destruction. They are bemused, yes really, that America should be the target of such ruthless, bloody anger. They are amazed that someone could kill innocent people in order to make itself known.

The news rampaged around the world. Flicking across Europe's channels every one bar MTV had the images of the smoking stacks blazing out across the airwaves. It was like a Manga movie, a disaster epic. Every stunning, shocking minute that went by you were battling with reality, sure they would announce that a giant green lizard had been spotted off the coast of NY, NY. They didn't but still it doesn't seem completely real. Four planes? At once? Destroying three huge buildings in the heart of New York and roughing up the Pentagon? Are we awake?

But this is reality. The loss of innocent lives is more disgusting than words can express. The murder of men, women and kids to get a political point across is outrageous. The office workers, the cleaners, the lift repair men from Ace Lifts who worked in the World Trade Centre. People gossiping, drinking a coffee from a foam cup, avoiding the first bit of work of the day. The people who jumped to their deaths perhaps hoping against hope that they would somehow survive, wracked with unimaginable fear. Those incinerated in the building by thousands of gallons of aircraft fuel. Ordinary U.S. citizens just like you and me, just like ordinary people in Paris, Amsterdam, Bangkok, Tripoli and Baghdad. But look, and look hard, this is what men of violence do to cities, what British and American planes did to Basra in Iraq, what British and American planes did to parts of Belgrade.

When I spout on about missiles slamming into the side of escaping Kossovan women, children and pensioners packed into a train I mean it. They died terrible, flesh ripping deaths. When you fire cruise missiles into packed shelters full of women and kids in Bahgdad they too died terrible deaths. When you kill 5.8 million Vietnamese, carpet bombing their rudimentary homes whilst leaving the centre of Hanoi and Saigon clear so you had somewhere nice to stay when you invaded (a tactic the Nazis employed on London) they too died terrible deaths. When you rounded up every socialist and liberal in Indonesia, Algeria, Iran, Malaysia, Greece, Turkey and more and had them killed and tortured they too died terrible deaths. We can add Panama, Honduras, Guatemala, Colombia, Ecuador, Nicaragua, Laos, Cambodia, Israel. The American death machine. Ordained by God.

So ask yourself something. Do you object to violence? Really? Or do you object to "their" violence. Will you object to the American military striking back? Bombing Kabul or Khartoum or Tripoli. A tactical nuke on northern Afganistan? Will you object if the Israelis open up on the Palestinians? Will you?

Because what is the alternative? More bombs? More security? More cameras in the streets? More phone taps? More subsidy to the arms industry? More dead foreigners whose minute of lives are never reported on CNN they way the Trade Centre's demise has been. Is that where we are going? On a race to the bottom trapped between GW Bush and the CIA-created Osama Bin Laden? Because it seems that what is wanted.

James Rubin, former White House playboy and spokesman said, "They have attacked every civilised country in the world," Tony Blair said that we must "eradicate this evil completely" and that the perpetrators of the attacks were "indifferent to the sanctity of human life". Within hours General Wesley Clark of the Kosovo campaign said it was "only one" group who could have done this, of course, "it's Osama Bin Laden." But remember that James Rubin also said that "Tibet is part of China, that's settled. Tibet is part of China" (Radio 5 Live), Tony Blair ordered British involvement in a major war without any recourse to international law and General Wesley Clark carried out that war in the full knowledge that the commencement of that war would lead to an increase in Kosovan deaths, as he put it that "was entirely predictable."

Then Tom Clancy on CNN tried to be a bit liberal and balanced. Islamic people he informed us "were not all madmen." Of course he meant that men who commit this kind of violence must be mad. Try telling George W Bush who mimicked his first woman victim on TV. "Please save me Mr Bush," he squealed in a 'white trash' high pitched voice, giggling at her imminent death. Try telling Clinton, the cruise missile king or the 'great statesman' Henry '1-800 Bomb Cambodia' Kissinger who declared it "an act of war" before he even knew who he was at war with. Because they will be too busy scheming, plotting, advising "the great democracies" (James Rubin) how to strike back.

One furious senator on CNN busted his spleen. "We are at war," said the completely-not-madman. "The priority of this country isn't healthcare or nurses, it is security, defence."

So much killing, so many men of war, so few men of peace.

And you think to yourself? Is this it?

Capitalism's Final Solution - what took so long...?

By FLACO

Though isolated from the thoughts of the majority of the planet, George Bush is not crusading alone. Last week, pollsters at ICM and Gallop jostled to tell us exactly how big a majority of Britons are clamouring for blood in the Afghan hills. The phrasing of the Daily Telegraph-sponsored questions, or the persuasions of the target poll group, are not important. After all, pressmen and broadcasters have spent the last week valiantly enforcing the illusion that leaders speak for people and governments speak for nations.

Yet outside of Texas and Kandahar, this is not necessarily the case. Many people, though sympathetic with the innocent victims of the Manhattan attack, are saying: "Well, they [America] had it coming."

Perhaps a debate on the levels of innocence between Deutche Bank Fund Managers and Iraqi babies killed by American pilots is inappropriate right now, but greater TV coverage and more expensive real estate does not make their deaths more 'important'.

Unlike American Airlines Flight11, and the subsequent baffled response of the media, the motivation for Tuesday's attack did not 'come out of the blue'.

"The idea that we've done something to provoke them is repellent," one ex-US government employee come expert commentator told the BBC's Radio 5Live. The saturation bombing of Vietnam, Laos, Cambodia never happened of course. Neither did the bloodletting in Guatemala, Chile or Nicaragua. Invasions and incursions in Egypt, Lebanon, Palestine, Syria, Libya, Iran, Iraq and the Balkans were all carried out in the name of 'stability', as was the manufacturing of state terror by Turkey, Israel, Iraq and Indonesia. For fifty years or more US banditry has left a global trail of dead and landless in its quest for control.

Liberal voices in the Guardian newspaper have described Bush's crusade as heralding a "reversal" of globalisation. I don't agree. Globalisation - or more accurately the securing of global control of resources, wealth and power by the West - has never been about market freedom and has always been steered and supported by Western governments. If George W Bush and Tony W Blair have their way, we may be about to witness 100 years worth of global capitalist power expansion in as many days. This is globalisation in fast forward. Whitehall is threatening a "lengthy" campaign against "terrorism" that could last ten years. A decade to complete world domination? Sounds like fast work to me. No more squeezing, no more loans, no more gerrymandered puppet governments, threats or sanctions - just, give us the keys and shut the fuck up! Job done. - and what a result.

Democracy (remember democracy - it's the thing Osama bin Laden and the rest of the terrorist demons are out to destroy) well that'll just have to be put on hold (you mean it wasn't - ed). The language says it all. Blair goes to the US to be BRIEFED, Blair TELLS Parliament (Channel 4 News 14.9.01) how far Britain will tag along with America's battle plan. And George W stomps around the oval office like some charicature DC-Comics despot President plotting his mythical 'war on terrorism'. "You're either with us or you're against us!" There is no complexity, there is no history. Either you support the messaniacal lunacy and imminent bloodbath of 'Operation Infinite Justice' (read Operation Infinite Control) or you're a scumbag dancing on the graves of New York's finest. Taliban or Texan, Turban or Stetson - there ain't no third way now!

America, we are told (in every UK Newspaper, every day since 11.9.01) has 'every right' to avenge itself for an attack on its homeland. Yet - nobody else no right to avenge themselves for America's rolling genocide against their lands and people. Despite cursing the 'terrorists' "cowardly" tactics the "allies" are out to "defeat the enemy at it's own game" (The Times 20.9.01). Why weren't the CIA out assassinating these foreigners - how could it possibly be the other way round? The Taliban's jihad/holy war is the strategy of killers and madmen, yet Bush's jihad is a reasonable response by a nation under siege. Similarly, fundamentalists are okay if they're on your side. The Osama bin Laden/Mullah Omar - a man so deranged he refuses to be photographed - double act, draws gasps of 'how can we let them live?' Yet when Bush appears in a New York Cathedral alongside reactionary-TV evangelist-nutter Billy Graham, all is well with the western world.

One arsehole's holy crusade is another's act of provocation. You can tell who's in the right by asking for receipts. If you've given billions of dollars to multinational arms manufacturers in order to equip your army - then you're the good guys. If you dared to nick your missiles and machine guns from the last invader - then you're gonna get whats comin! If this is to be the valley of death - how fitting that we are shepherded into it by a couple of minted oil barons who soared to the crest of their respective waves of bogus legitimacy on daddy's ill-gotten gains, greasing palms and executing their own people along the way. Bush's village-idiot status is tempered by the constant 'reminder' that Colin Powell and Dick Cheney are a couple of steady hands pulling his strings. Well that's okay then - what the fuck are we worrying about?

So America is off to central asia - to where empire's go to die - a holy war in a dusty minefield against a people living on grass and animal feed. Donald Rumsfeld tells us Amerikkka has the stomach for a long fight - just as they did during Vietnam (ahh - the luxury of rewriting history). The catch is, we're all coming too.

Meanwhile, back in the belly of the beast, assimilated Muslims are being cornered into apologising for Islam's excesses. The BBC's Newsnight produces a London Afghan who says: "America has every right to invade my country," (19.9.01) while upstanding UK Muslims "disown the lunatic fringe" (Daily Telegraph 20.9.01). The Muslim Council of Britain dutifully disown any dissenters as "clowns". We all defer to our leaders.

In a posting to YearZero.org's message board, Rachel from Yorkshire summed it up quite nicely: "I know that most folk will carry on with their three minute silences and ignorance - not for the folk who jumped out of the WTC towers, not for the ordinary people who have lost friends and family... but because the US is the most powerful country in the world and, like when royalty dies, the world has to join in showing fealty."

Then we had the cheering Palestinians. Pre-teen kids who have spent their short lives watching their friends and fathers gunned down by American armed troops with US supplied M16s and Apache helicopters. Children whose homes have been bulldozed by American tanks at the whim of an American crutched oppressor. Kids whose only direct experience of Uncle Sam is when he strafes arabs with bombs and fire and depleted uranium - how dare these young upstarts feel anything but sorrow and remorse when America takes a direct hit in the seat of its financial and military powerbase.

There is an ongoing debate over when these images were taken - but that is to deny these feelings exist. Okay it suits the rabble rousing agenda of the press to whip up enough anti Islamic fervour to back the new crusade - but America is hated and feared throughout the planet. But, as long as the cellphone calls from the World Trade Tower keep getting played on our radios and the aircraft carriers keep gliding across our screens no-one will ask why. After all, a result is about to be had - A few days after the towers fell, the brother of one of the victims, said he thought war was not a legitimate response to the attacks and that Bush "should be caged". Unfortunately Bush's crusade is less a response to the attack, and more an escalation of America's existing imperialist agenda that caused it in the first place. US Defense Secretary, Donald Rumsfeld shed some light at the end of the tunnel last week when he told the Pentagon faithful of his government's plan to "end" non-compliant states. The world has just subjugated itself to American supremacy - and despite the implied transience of a 'war coalition', this is not intended to be a temporary state of affairs - all that remains to be done is sweep up a few dissenting arabs - and who said capitalism's days were numbered?

Fighting terrorism of all brands

By Vandana Shiva

September 18 was the day for solidarity with victims of the terrorist attacks on the U.S. on September 11. I joined the millions of people to observe two minutes silence at 10:30 a.m. for those who lost their lives in the assault on the World Trade Center and the Pentagon. But I also thought of the millions who are victims of other terrorist actions and other forms of violence. And I renewed my commitment to resist violence in all its forms.

At 10:30 a.m. on September 18, I was with Laxmi, Raibari and Suranam in Jhodia Sahi village in Kashipur district of Orissa. Laxmi's husband Ghabi Jhodia was among the 20 tribals who recently died of starvation. In the same village, Subarna Jhodia had also died. Later, we met Singari in Bilamal village who had lost her husband Sadha, elder son Surat, younger son Paila and daughter-in-law Sulami.

The deliberate denial of food to the hungry is at the core of the World Bank Structural Adjustment programmes. Dismantling the Public Distribution System (PDS) was a World Bank conditionality. It was justified on grounds of reducing expenditure. But the food subsidy budget has exploded from Rs. 2,800 crores in 1991 to Rs. 14,000 crores in 2001. More money is being spent to store grain because the Bank wanted food subsidies to be withdrawn. This led to increase in food prices, lowering of purchase from PDS and build up of stocks. The food security of the nation is collapsing.

Starvation deaths in Maharashtra, Rajasthan and Orissa are symptoms of the breakdown of our food systems. Kashipur was gifted with abundance of nature. Starvation is the result of waves of violence against nature and the tribal communities, of ecological plunder of the resources of the region, the dismantling of the food security system under economic reform policies and the impact of climate change which caused crop failures.

Twenty years ago, the pulp and paper industry raped the forests of Kashipur. Today, the herbs stand naked and the paper mills are bringing eucalyptus from neighbouring Andhra Pradesh. Now the giant mining companies - Hydro of Norway, Alcan of Canada, Indico, Balco/Sterlite of India have unleashed a new wave of terror. They are eyeing the bauxite in the majestic hills of Kashipur as it is used for aluminium that will go to make Coca Cola cans and fighter planes.

Imagine each mountain to be a World Trade Center built by nature over millennia. Think of how many tragedies bigger than what the world experienced on September 11 are taking place to provide raw material for insatiable industry and markets. The Aluminium companies want the homelands of the Kashipur tribals. But the tribals refuse to leave. They are defending the land and earth through a non-violent movement. This forced apportioning of resources from people too is a form of terrorism - corporate terrorism.

The 50 million tribals who have been flooded out of their homes by dams over the past four decades are also victims of terrorism - they have faced the terror of technology and destructive development. For the 30,000 people who died in the Orissa supercyclone, and the millions who will die when flood and drought and cyclones become more severe because of climate change and fossil fuel pollution, the U.S. President, Mr. George W. Bush, is an ecological terrorist.

The WTO was named the World Terrorist Organisation by citizens in Seattle because its rules denied millions the right to life and livelihood. Terrorism can only be stopped by cultures of peace, democracy, and people's security. It is wrong to define the post-September 11 world as a war between "civilisation and barbarism" or "democracy and terrorism." As we remember the victims of Black Tuesday, let us also strengthen our solidarity with the millions of invisible victims of other forms of terrorism and violence which are threatening the very possibility of our future on this planet. We can turn this tragic brutal historical moment into building cultures of peace.

RAWA: The people of Afghanistan have nothing to do with Osama and his accomplices

A statement from the Revolutionary Association of the Women of Afghanistan (RAWA) - September 14, 2001

On September 11, 2001 the world was stunned with the horrific terrorist attacks on the United States. RAWA stands with the rest of the world in expressing our sorrow and condemnation for this barbaric act of violence and terror. RAWA had already warned that the United States should not support the most treacherous, most criminal, most anti-democracy and anti-women Islamic fundamentalist parties because both the Jehadi and the Taliban have committed every possible type of heinous crimes against our people. In order to gain and maintain their power, these barbaric criminals are ready to turn easily to any criminal force.

But unfortunately we must say that it was the government of the United States who supported Pakistani dictator Gen. Zia-ul Haq in creating thousands of religious schools from which the germs of Taliban emerged. In the similar way, as is clear to all, Osama Bin Laden has been the blue-eyed boy of CIA. But what is more painful is that American politicians have not drawn a lesson from their pro-fundamentalist policies in our country and are still supporting this or that fundamentalist band or leader. In our opinion any kind of support to the fundamentalist Taliban and Jehadies is actually trampling democratic, women's rights and human rights values.

If it is established that the suspects of the terrorist attacks are outside the US, our constant claim that fundamentalist terrorists would devour their creators, is proved once more. The US government should consider the root cause of this terrible event, which has not been the first and will not be the last one too. The US should stop supporting Afghan terrorists and their supporters once and for all.

Now that the Taliban and Osama are the prime suspects by the US officials after the criminal attacks, will the US subject Afghanistan to a military attack similar to the one in 1998 and kill thousands of innocent Afghans for the crimes committed by the Taliban and Osama? Does the US think that through such attacks, with thousands of deprived, poor and innocent people of Afghanistan as its victims, will be able to wipe out the root-cause of terrorism, or will it spread terrorism even to a larger scale?

From our point of view a vast and indiscriminate military attacks on a country that has been facing permanent disasters for more than two decades will not be a matter of pride. We don't think such an attack would be the expression of the will of the American people.

The US government and people should know that there is a vast difference between the poor and devastated people of Afghanistan and the terrorist Jehadi and Taliban criminals.

While we once again announce our solidarity and deep sorrow with the people of the US, we also believe that attacking Afghanistan and killing its most ruined and destitute people will not in any way decrease the grief of the American people. We sincerely hope that the great American people could DIFFERENTIATE between the people of Afghanistan and a handful of fundamentalist terrorists. Our hearts go out to the people of the US.

Down with terrorism!

CABAL RULES U$A

from **BRISTLE**

THESE DAYS ARE an echo of a previous age when collective hysteria drove the U$ into the most absurd militarism and brutal repression (including imprisonment, death and execution) inside its borders. The McCarthy era and Nixon governments are remembered for the 'witch-hunts' against communists and anarchists. What Muslims, ethnic minorities and dissidents have experienced recently closely resembles this. Some 6000 Arab residents between the ages of 18 and 33 have been summoned for interrogation by the FBI in the U$A and more than 1,000 in the UK. The British media have stated that there are over 1000 Al-Qa'ida activists operating in the UK, though so far only 13 have been arrested on allegations. The majority of the 6000 detainees in the U$A are held incommunicado and denied access to their families or lawyers. This secret detention is edging towards the practice of 'disappearing people' in Latin America and elsewhere.

In the U$A, Bush and his attorney John Ashcroft have introduced the Patriotic Act, violating Amendments 1, 4 and 6 of their own constitution. Under section 213 of this Act (also called 'sneak and peek' by legal analysts), police can enter a home and search through belongings without a warrant and without informing the owner. If you disagree with such imposition, persecution and repression, then according to Ashcroft, "Your tactics only aid terrorists". As Jack Straw said of the 2000 Anti Terrorist Act: "Those who are innocent have nothing to fear...."

Bypassing the American congress, Ashcroft has also introduced the Military Commission. Headed by the military and without solicitors or juries, these tribunals can put on trial any suspect, whether or not they are a US citizen. There are some 20 million non-citizens living and working in the U$A right now. These military commissions are a gross transgression of international law to which the U$ government and over 140 other governments have subscribed and that the U$ has used to condemn other countries like Peru, Nigeria and Russia. According to Bush however, these tribunals are "full and fair trials".

124

Pentagon Calls In Hollywood's Finest Brains

By Robert Newtown

THE PENTAGON WILL TODAY announce a series of national security measures resulting from emergency summit meetings with Hollywood scriptwriters. After September the 11th, the best brains in Hollywood were called into the Pentagon to predict what tactics the terrorists will take next and to envisage possible terrorist scenarios.

The Pentagon announcement is expected to echo the Hollywood strategists' suggestion that, following their attack on the World Trade Centre, Al Qa'ida may, in an effort to gain funds for their terror campaign, turn their sights onto other major sources of US capital. In particular the Pentagon communique warns of a daring, carefully-orchestrated night-time heist of not one but three Las Vegas casinos. This attack, it is thought, would involve short-circuiting the city's electricity supply and getting a Chinese acrobat to somersault past the infra-red detectors in the safe-deposit vaults.

Sources close to the Pentagon claim that particular attention was also given to another possibility: that of bombs being placed on buses and triggered to go off if the speed falls below fifty miles per hour. Citizens are advised that in these situations all newly-qualified female drivers should give the wheel to any cute-looking young slacker male who happens to be onboard. The briefing also urges US public works departments to signpost more clearly those bits of uncompleted motorway flyover which stop in mid-air half-way.

Success

There have already been successes as a result of film-industry assistance in security matters. Following a tip-off from leading Hollywood producers, Camp X-ray guards in Guantanemo Bay immediately took down one Al Qa'ida prisoner's Britney Spears poster and discovered it to conceal a long tunnel which had been scooped out by a spoon (hidden inside a Koran). The tunnel led to a boat being repaired by Tim Robbins and Samuel L Jackson.

Concerns

The meeting has, however, left Defence staff with a sense of the full magnitude of the task they now face. Of single greatest concern following the brainstorming conference is that Saudi-trained scientists, loyal to Al Qa'ida but resident in the United States, may develop the capability of using a Delorean car or old steam-train (powered by lightning hitting a small-town church steeple) to go back in time. This would enable Al Qa'ida to replace Thomas Jefferson with Mullah Mohammed Omar. The terrorists plan is then to re-write the US Declaration of Independence to read 'Death to the infidels, Allah achbar.' Most chillingly of all is that, were this plan to succeed, the first that most US citizens will know about it, will be when they find themselves surrounded by religious fundamentalists in a terrorist rogue state led by the unelected son of an oil billionaire..... yet think this state of affairs COMPLETELY NORMAL!!!!

The American Official Secrets Act is also due to be reviewed. Bush and the CIA want to include the leaking of administration information to the media as a crime. This means that any scandals exposing corruption that have struck American politics in the past (Watergate or Iran-Contra) will be prevented therefore Bush would be free of any shit from such current scandals as Enron. Without transparency, fascism consolidates. Ashcroft has admitted that none of this anti-terror package would have prevented September 11s attacks.

As we know, Bush is the fucker who executed one person every two weeks in five years when governor of Texas, and is an anti-abortion extremist. His background

is as a businessman in the oil industry exploiting his family connections, and has strong links with a number of multinationals such as Exxon-Mobil and Enron.

Bush's 'team' includes Ashcroft, who is a Christian fundamentalist, an active anti-abortionist and a fervent defender of the death penalty; Colin Powell, the made-up hero in the war against Iraq; and Tom Ridge, who re-established the death penalty in Philadelphia after 23 years and signed Mumia Abu Jamal's death warrant.

So the ingredients are there: a U$ administration fully involved in multinational business interests, and prepared to ruthlessly use their legislative powers to disable oppositional forces, and protect themselves from accountability.

A Time to Question

Fareena Alam speaks out on BBC Question Time, 13th September

Fareena Alam, 22, is a news editor of Q News, Britain's leading Muslim magazine. *(www.q-news.com)* She spoke from the audience on the now-notorious live Question Time debate on the night of September 13. BBC director general Greg Dyke publicly apologised the next week after receiving over 2,000 complaints from viewers over the expression of "anti-US sentiment."

"A friend suggested I should join her in the audience. I thought we could just watch the show, I didn't expect to get on TV. I didn't plan to say anything.

"I told them one of the reasons the world despises America is because it sees Israel as a terrorist and America as one who harbours Israel as a terrorist. The former American ambassador on the panel, Phil Lader, said he couldn't believe I was talking about this two days after the attack on the World Trade Centre.

"The whole point of the show was to discuss what America was going to do next. I think I got picked on in the papers because I had tanned skin, I'm a Muslim, a woman and I was wearing a headscarf. I was the perfect symbol of anti-Americanism. I was portrayed as an Arab, automatically lumping me together with the people accused of the attack. But I was born and educated in London to Bangladeshi parents. I am a British citizen. Judgments were made purely on appearance. No one bothered to find out.

"Two tabloids put my picture on their pages, one with the caption 'Angry Middle-Eastern woman'. It seems I have been made a symbol of anti-Americanism, which is totally inaccurate. A lot of Muslim women I know are being insulted in the street, being spat at and having their head-scarves pulled off.

"After Question Time, lots of people in the audience came up to me and said, 'Good on you'. I was surprised at what a positive reaction I got.

"I don't think the BBC should have apologised. It is stifling good, balanced debate, which is what we need at the moment, not rhetoric - that is dangerous.

"I wept when I heard about the terrorist actions in New York. I was absolutely horrified. But I think one of the reasons why I spoke out during the debate is because I find the nationalism, vengeful rhetoric and talk of war on CNN and other media very worrying. I think this kind of talk is an exploitation of US grief.

"I think it strange that America refers to the West as the civilised world, the free world, implying that the rest of the world is not. "I worry that the US public isn't seeing what it needs to see. CNN is not giving the American people the whole story. The events in New York were a big insult to the US government. It is meant to have the best intelligence organisation in the world, but it obviously isn't that intelligent." *- Interviewed by Max Daly.*

Fareena wrote these post-Sept 11 thoughts for SchNEWS:

They say that in war, truth is the first casualty. I look back on the day I chose to be a Muslim journalist; I could never have fathomed my choice would undergo such trials. Our first war. Prisoners of faith. Prisoners of war. Not a day has passed since September 11th that I have not wondered how loyal I, and others in this profession, will be to truth and justice in what has proven to be a tumultuous time.

Within minutes of the terrorist attacks of September 11th, our political leaders informed us that these were attacks on the 'free and civilised' world. As a British citizen, I assumed that one of those key values was the freedom of speech. Question Time was an epitome of this right, giving ordinary members of the public the opportunity to put their questions to the country's key thinkers.

For days after the show, the Muslim woman who brought the ex-American ambassador to tears, was transformed into a emblem of anti-American sentiments. Her question, after 30 minutes of heated discussion about American foreign policy, was: "When Bush speaks of a war against terrorists and the countries that harbour them, does he consider that the reason why so many people despise America is because they consider Israel a terrorist and America a nation that harbours Israel?"

It was 'the day the BBC shamed Britain' according to the Daily Mail who described her, inaccurately, as an 'angry middle-eastern woman' while the Sun referred to her as an 'Arab' woman. That woman happens to be me.

In a nation that spends millions of taxpayers' pounds protecting Salman Rushdie and claims to wage a war for the sake of 'freedom', the BBC apologising says political correctness is the new censorship.

Despite audience and panel members being equally, if not more critical of American foreign policies than myself, I had been made the target. Naturally, I was the only one with the audacity to mention the words terrorist state and Israel in the same breath in front of Question Time's 5.6 million viewers. I am a "brownie" like most immigrants to this country. I wear a scarf on my head, which for many translates as an oppressed Muslim woman covering her mind as well as her head. Coat all of the above with the accusation that I am supposedly anti-American and I was suddenly the alien spokesperson for those suspected as responsible for Tuesday's attack.

Contrary to popular belief, the terror of September 11th led to a great deal of grief and introspection within the Muslim community. More than ever before, Muslims are looking inward for answers to a thousand painful questions: how did these fringe elements take refuge in our community? What could we have done to stop this? Where do we go from here? Will we ever feel at home in these nations where we were born and raised?

Bush's threat that 'you are either with us or against us' has radicalised a number of Muslims who feel they've been pushed into a corner. To many, this is a war against Islam and Muslim interests. In a Newsweek interview shortly after September 11th, I expressed the fear that the impulsive war mongering was creating adverse currents in society. People who ordinarily wouldn't have been involved are getting more and more involved. Muslims who aren't normally devout feel a formerly dormant loyalty to the Muslim struggle. British Muslims who were already considered militant, are pushed towards terrorism. Barring extreme cases, I have always believed that a little Islamophobia is good for the Muslim community. There is nothing more dangerous for a faith-based community than apathy!

A large majority of Muslims, however, have found renewed belief in the importance of building grassroot alliances. A fresh, new identity of British-Muslim-ness is emerging. It is exciting because it overrides over a hundred languages and ethnicities of its members. Before September 11th, non-faith based left-wing movements were far more reticent about engaging with faith-based communities – let's face it, many are very uncomfortable with Islam. This is changing because it cannot be ignored that as a community, Muslims in Britain suffer the most acute levels of economic, political and social marginalisation. This has led to a paradigm shift within mainstream left-wing movements: if they are to continue to ostracise the Muslim community, while claiming to stand for social equality and justice, they have always been and will continue to be just as racist as right-wing movements.

Muslims are also beginning to internalise the realisation that we must break out of this dangerous victim mentality. We must slowly stop leaning on our marginalised status in society as some sort of sad crutch. It is time to wake up and recognise that despite all our differences - gay and abortion rights being two sore spots - there is a myriad of issues that are of common interest with non-faith based groups: the anti-war movement, protection of the environment and anti-globalisation are prime examples.

Blue Stream in the Black Sea

The Black Sea and the region around it is one of the key areas in the world for the transport of oil and gas, and it has paid the price. NATO wouldn't have been as eager to bomb Yugoslavia, if there was no pipeline through the Balkans. Russia may not have been as ruthless in Chechnya, if the most important transfer route of Baku oil didn't go through this small piece of land.

The Construction of a huge gas pipeline 2150m deep in a seismically active (risk of earthquakes) area sounds pretty stupid but this is exactly what's being built from Nadym-Pur-Tazovsko in Russia to Ankara in Turkey. Oil and gas are obviously important enough to take such a huge chance with the environment. The pipeline called 'Blue Stream' is a project of the Russian government and the formerly state owned Gazprom, now a multinational with access rights to a larger amount of natural resources than any other corporation on the planet. Construction work on the 390 kilometre part of the pipeline below sea level is being done by Saipem, a branch of Italian trans-national ENI. The plan is to transfer some two billion cubic metres through Blue Stream by the end of 2002, and up to 16 billion in 2007.

The original deadline of the project was the end of the year 2000, but Gazprom has missed several deadlines already announcing different reasons each time. The financial and infrastructure requirements of the project are huge even for Gazprom who are on the brink of financial collapse because of the huge fines it will have to pay the Turkish government if the project misses its final deadline in October 2002.

In the early 1980s an earthquake completely destroyed an undersea cable in the Indokopas marine area as close as 30 kilometres away from the proposed route for the pipeline. The Black Sea also has a high concentration of hydrogen sulphide 150-200 metres below the surface. According to the Russian state committee of environmental specialists, it is possible that a leak would allow gas to combine with the hydrogen sulphide at enormous pressure causing a huge explosion and destroying much of the sensitive marine ecosystem.

During the summer of 2001, the folk of the city of Smolensk blockaded the main road which Gazprom used in construction work twice. Police were in the process of charging the people arrested at these blockades with 'disobeying the police orders to disperse', when they tortured one of them, Andrei Rudomaha, at the police station. This led to those who had been arrested going on a hunger strike, and due to wide pressure were eventually released without charges.

Between the 6th and the 15th of August grassroots activists - mostly from the Rainbow Keepers network and Autonomous Action - organised "a caravan of peace for a clean Black Sea". They began from the point where the Blue Stream pipeline goes under the Black Sea at Cherkesskoy Schel, finishing at the endpoint of the CPC (Caspian Pipeline Consortium) oil pipeline in Yuzhnoe Ozereyka.

On September 20, four activists from the Socio-Ecological Union of Western Caucasus, Autonomous Action and Rainbow Keepers movement blocked the ship which was used to lay piping for Blue Stream. They locked on to gangways in the middle of working area and dropped a banner reading "No Blue Stream!" until being captured Russian border guards. However because of attention from the media and NGOs about the activists' arrests and the controversy of the Blue Stream project, it was hushed up and they were also released without charge.

www.potok.hotmail.ru (yes there's bits in English)

GAT LOST WTO

BANGALORE, 2nd October: A convention of world farmers organised by the Karnataka Rajya Raitha Sangha (KRRS) has urged the Indian government to opt out of the WTO. An international group of farmers agreed to refuse to be hoodwinked by the agendas of multinational corporations. The KRRS President, Prof. M.D.Nanjundaswamy, who referred to several issues involving trade, agriculture and economic policies of the US, the Centre and the State Government, said GATS (See SchNEWS 327) was the root of all "evils". He called upon people to understand the political purposes of the parties and sever their relationship with them and gain a new political perspective. Politicians and business are trying to enforce the use of Bt Cotton (genetically modified) on the KRRS farmers, who are vowing to fight this and the propaganda that perpetuates it. swamy.krrs@vsnl.com

Karnataka Farmers (KRRS) and friends meet in Bangalore to agree that they don't want the WTO and GATS, October 2nd 2001

WAKE UP! WAKE UP! IT'S YER UNCIVILISED

"This here world ain't big enough for the two of us."

Weekly SchNEWS

Printed and Published in Brighton by Justice?

Friday 21st September 2001   www.schnews.org.uk   Issue 323   Free/Donation

BUSH-WHACKED

"The response to this unimaginable 21st-century Pearl Harbor should be as simple as it is swift - kill the bastards. A gunshot between the eyes, blow them to smithereens, poison them if you have to. As for cities or countries that host these worms, bomb them into basketball courts." Steve Dunleavy (New York Post, 9/12/01).

As the world edges closer to war, a poll in America finds that 75% of those asked agree that military action should be taken against those responsible for last week's bombing – even if it leads to the deaths of more innocent people. So, let's get this straight, a country is mourning innocent victims of a terrorist attack – and in revenge wants more innocent victims to be killed? But isn't that terrorism? And just who will be the victims of this revenge bombing?

Even before aid workers started leaving the country in anticipation of air strikes, there were dire warnings that Afghanistan was heading for disaster. A three year drought on top of two decades of war and Soviet occupation has left more than 5m people - a quarter of the population - threatened by starvation. As Tamim Ansary, an Afghan writer and columnist who now lives in San Francisco, says, "We come now to the question of bombing Afghanistan back to the Stone Age. Trouble is, that's been done. The Soviets took care of it already. Make the Afghans suffer? They're already suffering. Level their houses? Done. Turn their schools into piles of rubble? Done. Eradicate their hospitals? Done. Destroy their infrastructure? Cut them off from medicine and health care? Too late. Someone already did all that." After last week, the US government is painting the Taliban as evil without realizing that its main victims are the Afghan people themselves. "Some say, why don't the Afghans rise up and overthrow the Taliban?," says Ansary. "The answer is, they're starved, exhausted, hurt, incapacitated, suffering. A few years ago, the United Nations estimated that there are 500,000 disabled orphans in Afghanistan - a country with no economy, no food. There are millions of widows. And the Taliban has been burying those widows alive in mass graves. The soil is littered with land mines, the farms were all destroyed by the Soviets. These are a few of the reasons why the Afghan people have not overthrown the Taliban."

Chris Buckley, Christian Aid Programme Officer for Afghanistan explained that "The real Afghanistan is one where 85 per cent of the population are subsistence farmers. Most Afghans don't have newspapers, television sets or radios. They will not have heard of the World Trade Centre or the Pentagon...There isn't even a postal service. Now, in these isolated villages, families are down to their last few weeks of food and already men, women and children in the bulging refugee camps are dying of cholera and malnutrition. And that was before the aid agencies were forced to withdraw."

In a remote village, Dominic Nutt, an emergency officer for Christian Aid, was told by the inhabitants that they had got through almost all their food supplies and had even eaten seeds which should have been planted for next year's crop. Large families were sharing one piece of bread a day. And these are the people who are to be held responsible for last week's tragedy? As the corporate media wags and government figureheads attempt to disguise their bloodthirsty desire for revenge under the guise of justice, it becomes more and more obvious that the punishment America seeks to inflict will only affect people who have spent their whole lives suffering under the worst excesses of war and totalitarian government.

> While the West quibbles over a few hundred refugees reaching our shores to try to seek out a better life, countries neighbouring Afghanistan are being swamped. A million refugees are expected to arrive in Pakistan, 400,000 into Iran and the remainder into Tajikistan and Turkmenistan.

SMACK ON THE WRIST

As last week's SchNEWS pointed out, America's most recent public enemy number one, Osama Bin Laden, was actually funded and trained by the CIA themselves back in the 80's in an effort to keep the big bad Soviets (a previous US public enemy number one) out of Afghanistan. As recently as this Spring, the US government was also surprisingly cosy with another newly declared enemy—the Taliban. In May 2001, the US presented the Taliban with a $43 million gift, making America the leading sponsor of one of the world's most repressive regimes. The reason for this gift? A reward to the Taliban for declaring that opium growing was against the will of God. So how does this reasoning go again? 'Help us in the Sacred War on Drugs and we'll overlook your record of atrocious human rights abuses, but only until you piss us off by not immediately handing over the terrorist we ourselves trained, at which point we'll declare war on you and bomb the fuck out of your country'. Brilliant.

TAKING LIBERTIES

"This attack will benefit the militarists in this country far more than it will benefit anyone else… This unforgivable act of inhumanity will be used as an excuse to crack down on dissent here, to engage in military aggression against other peoples, and to whip up an already more-than-latent anti-Muslim xenophobia." Stan Goff, retired US Army Veteran-cum-radical

In the wake of Bush's preparation for a long and drawn out "war against evil," an American anti-war movement has sprung into life, urging that last weeks attacks should not lead to more civilian casualties. With the IMF/World Bank meeting that was due to take place in Washington later this month now cancelled, the anti-globalisation rally on the 29th will now become an anti-war protest. As Goff points out, "There is quite simply no security system in the world that can not be bypassed, and there is no way to protect absolutely against these kinds of attacks. When we accept this premise, we have to conclude that overwhelming violence in retaliation for these kinds of acts will not bring such acts to an end, but escalate the levels of overall violence."

And while America's military machine cranks up - and the US military budget is about $9,000 a second - around the globe governments are planning new anti-terrorist laws. But what is the true aim of these laws? Many fear that instead of preventing repetitions of last week's events, new anti-terrorism legislation will only serve to restrict basic freedoms and stifle any resistance against the war-mongering, money-hungry governments that pass them. As one American Earth First! activist told SchNEWS, "There's been so much flag-waving patriotism in America after what's happened, but what people don't realise is that the military and legislative response the US government is planning proves just how empty and meaningless these symbols of American "freedom" and "justice" really are."

Bypass the corporate media www.alternet.org www.indymedia.org www.michaelmoore.com

Plane Failing

After last weeks hijack attacks, the atmosphere looks set to get a breather as people begin to reconsider how they travel and are choosing to keep their feet firmly on the ground- SchNEWS just wishes this was for a better reason than fear!

Air travel, the most polluting form of transport, chucks out loads of carbon dioxide and other nasty pollutants, emitting a lot of this stuff directly into the upper atmosphere where it does the most harm. Despite this, aircraft emissions are not considered for reduction under the Kyoto Protocol.

Now, if you've ever wondered why it's almost as cheap to fly from London to New York, as it is to get a train from London to York then here's a few interesting facts. No VAT is paid on air travel and aviation fuel isn't taxed; if VAT was charged and the fuel taxed at the same level as petrol it'd pull in £6.8 billion a year. Chuck in all the other tax breaks and concession then this rises to the equivalent of every person in the UK donating £182.45 to the aviation industry every year.

The airlines, already in financial trouble before last week's attacks, saw their shares take massive nosedives. Their response has been to give thousands of staff the push and grovel to governments for subsidies. British Airways and Virgin Atlantic begged the DTI for help so that they could operate on a "level playing field" with the rest of the world. Er, perhaps the World Trade Organisation might be interested in investigating…

*Rising Tide, a grassroots network taking action to tackle climate change, have organised a weekend gathering 13-14th October. The aim is to bring together those campaigning on climate issues to share ideas, tactics and plan for next year. The gathering is at Bridge 5 Mill, a new environmental center in Manchester. More info and bookings: 01865-241097 or RTgathering-subscribe@topica.com www.risingtide.org.uk

* For an in-depth report on the environmental and economic costs of air travel check out www.greenparty.org.uk/reports

Tub-thumping!

Despite a petition of 4,500 signatures, two fun days, a blockade of the Commonwealth Games Stadium and disrupted council meetings Manchester City Council still decided to close Gorton Tub swimming pool to save a mere £70,000. But still managed to fork out £45 million on their egos building the Commonwealth Stadium! More info: meet 7pm, 1st Oct., St. Jame's Church Hall, Wellington Street, Gorton, Manchester.

www.savegortontub.freeserve.co.uk
* 3 Govanhill Pool protestors were nicked for a 'breach of the peace' for the riotous act of sitting on chairs! They occupied The Lighthouse Gallery in Glasgow as part of the campaign to get Glasgow City Council to reverse its decision. www.saveourpool.co.uk

Gatecrashers

The Neo-Labour Party is coming to Brighton for its annual shallow, war mongering, privatising, media orientated Mc-conference. SchNEWS is none too pleased about this, but we welcome the anarchist-travelling circus who plan to Gatecrash Labour's Party. The fun starts Sunday 30th September, 1pm on The Level in Brighton. To find out more there's a public meeting at St.Peter's Church, Brighton, 7pm next Tuesday (25th). And a meeting next Wednesday 8-10.30pm at Islington Community Centre, Sebbon Street, Islington, London. More info: 01273-298192 or gatecrashing2001@yahoo.com

SchNEWS in brief

Brighton Peace & Environment Centre wants local arts and crafts, made from recycled/ sustainable source materials, to exhibit/sell in their shop. Interested? Call Dinky 01273-570378 ** SchNEWS warns people to NOT join **Smash-TheNazis** e-mail group on Yahoo, as it appears to be a fascist trap to get details of anti-nazis. When checking fascist websites use a web utility like Safe Web to mask your computer's identity www.safeweb.com ** URGENT: Ancient woodland is being cut down in **Snowdonia National Park** for the A470 road widening, more info 07812-429947.

Genoa Headline?

The Parliamentary Commission in Italy has predictably totally exonerated the police actions at the Genoa G8 SummiT. Meanwhile recriminations still continue for Italian activists. Last Saturday night the Genoan Pinelli social centre used for planning demos was firebombed, no-one was hurt but the interior was gutted. The following night a memorial dedicated to Carlo Guiliani who was shot dead by police was damaged in a similar attack.

On Tuesday there were about 100 police raids all over Italy with 60 arrests to investigate "Solidarieta Internazionale" which actively supports prisoners in Spain and Greece, and is accused of a number of bombings in Milan. The 'Villa Occupata' squat in Milan was raided, the place trashed and computer equipment confiscated and arrests made, similar events occurred in 20 Italian Cities. All those arrested were released, but 17 are still under investigation under Italy's severe Subversive Association and Subversive Organizations law (anti-'terror' laws).

The raids and intimidation has made planning for the NATO Summit in Naples and a mass mobilization for Genoa on 20th October very difficult. Global solidarity actions are planned. www.genoaresistance.org

* One Italian identified from photos around Carlo Guiliani´s murder has had his charges reduced from accessory to attempted murder of a policeman to resisting a policeman. Three Germans arrested at the Genoa protests are still in prison. Money for the Genoa Indymedia Legal Fund can be sent to The Independent Media Centre (IMC) UK, P.O. Box 587, London, SW2 4HA. Cheques made payable to The Independent Media Centre (UK).

Off the Warpath

The newly formed PAW (Peace and Anti-War) collective had a demo on Tuesday with over 300 people outside the Houses of Parliament. Activities around the country include:

Friday 21st: Queen Victoria Statue, Town Hall Square, **Reading** 7pm. 0118-9546430 peacegroup@gn.apc.org * Public meeting 'Which way now for peace?' 8pm Friends Meeting House, Ship St., **Brighton.** (Every **Tues** vigil, 12-2pm, MOD recruitment office, Queens Rd) * Public meeting Friends Meeting House, Euston Rd, **London,** 7pm * Vigil, St.Giles Cathedral, **Edinburgh** 5-6pm 0131 6695591 jane@gn.apc.org

Saturday 22nd * George Square, **Glasgow** 11am 0141-4231222 * Peace Gardens, St.Peters Square, **Manchester** 2pm 0161-2738283 * Hippodrome, **Bristol** 2.30-6.30pm * Reform Street, **Dundee** 1pm-2pm, 07761104609 http://wib.matriz.net/. * Whitehall, **London** 2pm Wear black, no banners, no placards, no chanting. CND 020-77002350 www.cnduk.org.

For stuff in your area call CND or check their website * What's happening in **Wales** 01286-882359

* E-mail list to co-ordinate activities. Subscribe by sending email to : aftermath-11-September-2001-subscribe@yahoogroups.co.uk

Propaganja

Surprise national news of the weekend was the bust of the Dutch Experience Cafe in 'The Amsterdam of the North', aka Stockport (SCHNEWS 320). They didn't manage to beat the Brighton record of staying open 73 minutes, in fact after the ribbon was put up, it was a matter of seconds before the police unofficially tore thru' the tape, took away the goodies and nicked Colin Davies and his Dutch friends. They were detained for 18 hours before being released on police bail. Good news is that the cafe is still open for Ganja-less business as an informal social centre.

* Campaigning continues with the renamed Cannabis Peace March on September 29th. Meet noon Speakers Corner, Hyde Park for march to Trafalgar Square. Stewards and funding is needed for the March. 020 7636 0951, www.cannabiscoalition.org/

Positive SchNEWS

Set up in response to increasing class sizes and the inflexibility of the state education system Human Scale Education promotes small schools and small classes, and there are currently fifteen small alternative schools associated with them. 'Small class size can bring many educational benefits – children are treated as individuals with human scale interactions, their energy and creativity is channeled into positive actions and encouraged to make a full contribution to the communities to which they belong.' Education is aimed to extend the pupils range of their understanding of the world rather than deliver the pre-packaged state curriculum to prepare you for the rat race of work.

If you want to learn more they are having an Alternatives In Education Fair at Conway Hall, Red Lion Square, London. 10.30am -5pm. More info Human Scale Education, 96 Carlingcott, nr.Bath, BA2 8AW. 01275-332516 www.hse.org.uk

...and finally...

So why was America bombed last week? Maybe it was because of their continued support for Israel's occupation of Palestine and their arrogant foreign policy.

Osama Bin Laden may be the number one suspect, but what about those cheeky lesbians? Religious fruitcake Rev. Jerry Falwell, an American TV evangelist, reckons the terrorist attacks occurred because God was angry that the U.S. had become a nation full of abortionists, homosexuality, secular schools and the American Civil Liberties Union!

But maybe it was those hell-raising eco-terrorists? Alaskan Congressman Don Young thinks there's a possibility the attacks are linked to the protests against the World Trade Organization. His reasoning being "If you watched what happened in Genoa, in Italy, and even in Seattle, there's some expertise in that field" Er, when was the last time you saw Earth First! types hijack 737's at demos?

And what about those nasty animal rights activists? Janet George, a big cheese in the Countryside Alliance, reckons that hunt sabs are the same as the people who hijacked four planes and killed up to 5000 people. "Scale is the only fundamental difference between Tuesdays atrocities and the regular behaviour of animal rights extremists in this country and abroad" says the barmy bumpkin. Excuse us but ask Steve Christmas, a hunt sab who was nearly killed last year by hunt supporters,(see SchNEWS 274) about terror and intimidation and while you're at it ask the families of Mike Hill and Tom Worby, two sabs who were killed in 1991 by hunt supporters, about violence.

Subscribe!

Keep SchNEWS FREE! Send 1st Class stamps (e.g. 10 for next 9 issues) or donations (payable to Justice?) Ask for "Originals" if you can make copies. Post *free* to all prisoners. SchNEWS, c/o on-the-fiddle, P.O. Box 2600, Brighton, East Sussex, BN2 0EF.
Tel/Autofax +44 (0)1273 685913 *Email* schnews@brighton.co.uk *Download a **PDF** of this issue or subscribe at* www.schnews.org.uk

Report: 3rd
Peoples Global
Action (PGA)
Conference
Cochabamba,
Bolivia,
September
19th-22nd 2001.

By Hazel (with Alex)

Tribulations and Inspirations

Peoples Global Action is a network which links and creates a space for direct and unmediated contact between people's struggles and grassroots movements from around the world.

Growing out of the two international Zapatista encuentros against neo-liberalism, the PGA had its first conference at Geneva, Switzerland in February 1998 (see SchNEWS 156), where representatives and members of movements from every continent launched a worldwide co-ordination of resistance against the common enemies of globalised capital. This led to the international actions held during the WTO ministerial conference in Geneva in May 1998 where many different demonstrations, actions and street parties took place across the globe. The second international PGA conference took place in Bangalore, India in 1999 (see report in SchQUALL), and now this third September 2001 get-together in Cochabamba, Bolivia. In addition to these, there have been two PGA caravans (Europe 1999 and South America 2001), and a number of regional conferences. As well as these events the PGA has played its part in the wave of global days of action we have seen since 1998 (J18, N30 et al), aiming to establish networks of horizontal solidarity between disparate and geographically distant movements in common struggle. The PGA initially focused on free trade agreements, but have since developed to encompass a much broader critique, and aims to spread information and coordinate actions between autonomous groups with a commitment to direct action and civil disobedience. PGA is often associated with the phrases "We are everywhere" and "our resistance is as transnational as capital".

PGA is not an organisation and has no members. Different groups volunteer to act as contact points in each region and are responsible for disseminating information and convening regional and international conferences.

(see PGA website www.agp.org for history and manifesto in full)

The Place

Cochabamba, Bolivia was an apt location for an international gathering of grassroots movements. The streets are filled with poems and murals depicting peoples uprising and social justice, symbols of indigenous resistance like the coca leaf ("long live the coca leaf, death to the yanquis"), indigenous heroes and the inspiring graffiti of the anarcho-feminist group "Mujeres Creando". This city is famed for the "Water Wars" which took place in 2000 when a triumphant people's uprising reversed the privatization of their water by Canadian multinational Bechtel. Since the Government de-privatised the water supply the multi- sectored coalition which coordinated the protests cooperatively administer their local water resources.

"We have been the object of a great robbery, we are owners of nothing... We occupied the streets and highways because we are their true owners. We did it counting only on ourselves. For us, this is the true meaning of democracy: we decide and do, we discuss and carry out. We risked our lives to do what we consider just. Democracy is sovereignty of the people and that is what we achieved" - 6th February 2000. Declaration of the Water Coordination.

The People

The conference was hosted by the Six Federations of the Tropics (the coca-growers peasant federation) and the Domestic Workers Union. Other Bolivian movements present included Mujeres Creando, peasant unions, coca growers, anarcho-punks zinesters, cultural art collectives – responsible for much of the fantastic street art – and youth groups. About 230 delegates from 170 countries were in attendance. This included UK's Reclaim the Streets, South African Soweto Electricty Crisis Commision, an anti-Apartheid group, Italy's Ya Basta!, womens groups from Mexico, Nepalese and Indian peasant federations, landless peasant movements, indigenous peoples, radical trade unionists, Indymedia activists, ecological direct activists, members of autonomous networks and more …..!! Full list of delegates on the PGA website, suffice to say that it was an amazingly diverse and inspiring range of groups and movements!

The Conference

These are some of the points discussed at the roundtable discussion.[For a minutes of these discussions plus analysis of the whole event and the new hallmarks and manifesto visit the website]

* Free trade agreements in Latin America – FTAA, Plan Dignity, Plan Colombia, Plan Puebla Panama and the Andean Initiative for example.

* Water – with the Bolivian experience as a case study. The same issue is arising globally and emphasis was placed on coordinated resistance through the PGA.

* Land – The take over of land continues to threaten traditional communal lands of the indigenous and of the black communities of Africa. This is increasingly linked to World Bank/IMF policies.

* Indigenous – representatives from a variety of indigenous groups present met to discuss parallels between their struggles and ideas for coordinating campaigns

* Gender – Gender was a major focus of the conference with the first round table discussions focusing on gender equity and sexism within social movements. It was conceded that gender issues need to be part of all PGA work.

* Communications – The small round table on communications discussed the importance of enacting strong communications structures between movements, emphasising the need for adequate translation etc. There was strong feeling to support existing structures such as IndyMedia rather than re-invent the wheel, but some discussion around internet access raises more questions to be discussed!!

Conference outcomes include...

* A call for a Global Day of Action was issued for November 9th 2001 coinciding with the WTO ministerial summit in Qatar. (see SchNEWS 332)

* A call to mobilise the Americas against the March 2002 meeting of the Free Trade Area of the Americas (FTAA) in Quito, Ecuador. (www.camp-ecuador.de.vu)

Conflicts / Challenges

Given the diversity of groups represented, differing political positions, lack of resources (meetings were run on butchers paper), linguistic barriers, huge meeting size and limited time there were obviously many tensions and challenges stopping the conference running smoothly. Cultural misunderstandings, varying ideas of meeting facilitation, lack of clarity over themes for discussion - and the role of the PGA itself! - generated further frustrations and obstacles for the delegates.

At previous PGA conferences some people have contended that delegates from the North, with greater mobility and access to resources, had tended to turn up as individuals, not linked to organisations. To offset this a ratio of 70% Southern and 30% Northern was established for the conference – but given the location it was naturally dominated by South Americans anyway. While many Southern delegates represented groups such as the All Nepalese Peasants Association (ANPA) – a movement of millions – those from Northern autonomous networks such as AWOL,

Australia or CLAC, Canada were coming from groups who are non-hierarchical and have no membership as such, making it difficult to be 'spokesperson' for 'the group'. This distinction between speaking only for oneself or for millions raises the issue of the weight that each delegate may have in making decisions and the need for some to confer with their networks/members before taking a position in a discussion.

The functions of the PGA network and notions of solidarity were also contested terrain, with different understandings and expectations from each group present: some saw solidarity as being largely related to resource sharing, others were hostile to this, seeing it as perpetuating a paternalistic role between North and South. Other groups sought out research assistance from outside groups, international peacekeeping roles or actions of political pressure. Still others advocated horizontal skill sharing and information exchange. Some Northern delegates were defensive when confronted with the role of solidarity – feeling that this ignored the importance of their own local struggles and expecting them to focus on Southern campaigns.

These tensions and many more questions remained unresolved, an impossible task in one week. What is important to remember, however, is that a network is simply that: a network – and groups are autonomous to organise and act as they see fit. What does need to be decided upon however, is how the groups involved in such a network should communicate, make decisions and coordinate actions! And in spite of these big obstacles energy was generally

Communiques From PGA Tour

The PGA conference in Cochabamba, Bolivia was followed by an 18-day people's caravan through Peru, Ecuador and Colombia. Twenty-five delegates who had attended the conference continued on the caravan, which met with people from social movements during its journey north. These accounts illustrate starkly what activists in these countries are up against...

Fighting same with same

Quito, Ecuador: Sitting looking at my friend, I feel my insides fall away and my head swim. I'm unable to comprehend what he is telling me. Two of his friends were murdered by the paramilitary today. It was only three days ago that he told me one of his old housemates was killed while we were in Cochabamba [at the PGA conference]. I am so out of my depth. I flounder and look at him trying to gauge his feelings. He is not crying, but he is not stoic either. He looks tired and heavy, but still carries his daggy, light energy.

We are having a day off the [PGA] caravan and are in a 'campasino' building in Quito. The day before, I visited the border province of Ecuador and listened to horrible stories about the refugees, fumigations and Plan Colombia violence there. Someone is playing guitar and there are innumerable bottles of alcohol scattered around the backpacks and mattresses. It seems so incongruous to the stories Marco* is telling me. But then, I can't imagine where his stories would make sense to me; given my background and the comfort zone I inhabit most of the time.

I have my arm around him. I am wondering if I will see him again after I leave Colombia. I shyly ask him, knowing that it's a stupid question, but nonetheless needing to fathom: how they continue in spite of the risks, assassinations, kidnappings, massacres and tortures. He looks at me with the same heaviness in his face and tells me flatly that they don't choose to struggle, that they are forced to by the political situation in Colombia.

But, despite what I could have let myself think after travelling with activists and meeting amazing radical social movements across the country, not all Colombians are politicised. Many look no deeper than the media spin: that Plan Colombia means helicopters and drug eradication. Although they realise a war is going on they prefer to go about their lives without engaging deeply with politics. I resolve that it takes a special strength to resist in Colombia.

Last week the American government declared that the 'war on terrorism' will extend to Colombia, and announced that both FARC and ELN - two of the strongest guerrilla organisations in the country - were terrorist groups, and vowed to destroy them. Extending the 'war on terrorism' to Colombia will justify an even more brutal persecution of activists and social movements here.

The stories of torture are limitless. Over 3000 unionists have been killed or disappeared in the last year, not to mention teachers, cultural leaders, nuns, priests and often, entire communities and villages. One activist we met described Plan Colombia as a scorched earth policy on social movements, he told us they don't even talk about human rights any more, but ask 'at least let us live'. Most organisations spend the majority of their energy just surviving - to fight is another step.

As an activist, I find it's necessary to seek as much inspiration as information, so you don't stumble under the weight of the atrocities you discover. But although I drew from the spirited resistance of people I met in Colombia and across South America I still carry a heavy weight of confusion and helplessness. When you know something is wrong, wrong beyond debate - so intrinsically evil and short sighted that it is unfathomable - what do you do? I don't know how to help. I know that our struggle is their struggle, as Marco says: 'same with same'. I wish I could adequately convey the emotion of what I have seen. I wish could express the magnitude of the problem in Colombia: the extent of the violence driven by the state, greed, the USA and corporations at the cost of between 11,000 - 40,000 lives a year and the displacement of over 2.6 million people.

November 1st will see a national strike, which has been planned for two years. It is with much anticipation and fear that I will follow the events.

My time in Colombia was full of contrast: I would dance with Marco to cheesy salsa, share a joint and laugh as he teased me about Australian English, (which he insists consists of 'fuck' and not much more), and forget that there was even a war. Then as we walked through the streets of Bogota, five young soldiers would walk past with machine guns slung over their shoulder and all the statistics and horror stories would come flooding back. At these moments, Marco would look at me and say, 'We don't need your sympathy'. Making fists and placing his hand together knuckle to knuckle he would look up: 'we need to fight same with same'.

high and patience quite remarkable… and consensus was reached on many occasions.

Responses to September 11th

Delegates faced a lot of hassle at borders: some were stranded at Geneva airport for a number of days, others were held up at the La Paz airport, and an entire bus load were stranded on the Peru/Bolivia border for the duration of the conference. The Bolivian government denounced the PGA as a 'terrorist summit' and Interpol paid a friendly visit. The Executive Intelligence Review published the article 'Terrorism Central: People's Global Action' which is typical of efforts to depict activists as terrorists. During a press conferences held by the PGA, journalists questioned the relationship between the PGA and the terrorist attacks. This line of questioning was met with a calm answer of "We are against human genocide and state terrorism". The fact that the conference occurred just over a week after September 11th did not interfere with the agenda, and the predicted repressive response only serving to reinforce the need for a global campaigns against militarism.

Overall

Despite the aforementioned tensions and challenges the conference was an invaluable space for inspiration, the exchange of information and ideas, and expansion of networks and campaigns. The bewilderment and frustration were outweighed by the value of meeting people face to face, of sharing meals and chicha (fermented corn alcohol) and spontaneous dancing and bursts of revolutionary songs.

The sheer diversity and energy of so many movements and hearing the tales of such incredible actions world wide was awe inspiring, and a good reminder that we truly are "everywhere".

The PGA is young and developing, and although there are tensions we should not be disheartened. It is a unique network for the unmediated contact it provides grassroots activists. Its existence fosters international resistance to economic globalisation and environmental destruction and gives us the chance to not only deepen our analysis, by learning about a variety of perspectives, but also to coordinate actions to create the kind of world we want to live in – right across the planet.

GET INVOLVED: There will be a European PGA conference on the 31st of August - 4th of September 2002 in Leiden, Holland. www.pgaconference.org

OUT SOON A book featuring interviews from Cochabamba with women activists covering the topics of… ways of organising, children and political choices, gender issues in social movements, culture jamming, an inside tale of the women who helped orchestrate the water wars and more! Contact: hazel@redbricks.org.uk

The corridors of the university will have a scar...

Bogota, Colombia: 'We are very sad and worried, it's too hard to understand that another 'compañero' is dead...'

The National University of Colombia, in Bogota, is a colourful and lively place. Almost every available space on buildings, in class rooms and corridors is covered in murals, graffiti, posters and stencils decrying Plan Colombia, protesting the war in Afghanistan and celebrating resistance.

Over 80% of universities in Colombia are private. There are 32 public universities, which have long been recognised as a hotbed of activist and leftist activity. The National University of Colombia is the largest public university and a vibrant centre for a range of critical projects. Students have renamed all of the landmarks, squares and buildings on campus and there is strong sense of radicalism thoughout the university. There are hundreds of active affinity groups on campus from Virus, a media and mural collective, to anarco-feminists and political musical groups. In addition to the diverse groups, the teach in-style meetings and discussions held daily around the campus, there are regular tropels - literally 'bustles' - when students directly confront police, taking over streets surrounding the university or blockading the main university entrance. When there is a tropel the hazy smoke of tear gas fills the campus, the constant noise of rallying cries and molotovs and tear gas canisters exploding fills the air.

At a tropel last week students protested the privatisation of health and education, and world wide American imperialism. A group of students were protesting the bombings in Afghanistan when police responded to the demonstration with violence. Police fired tear gas on the crowd and over 15 students were injured, two seriously, and one died. Police denied responsibility for the shooting, but a number of witnesses confirm the shot came from behind police lines. Carlos Giovanny Blanco Leguizamo a twenty-two year old medical student was shot at around noon, he died ten minutes later, still on the university campus.

Emilie*, a student from the National University, said, "the media and the autopsy report says it was a shot from a .22 gun and that he was shot from less than 10 metres. They want people to think that there was someone from inside the university who killed Giovanny, but people who saw say that it was the police, they used a gun that isn't like the guns they officially use so there aren't many proofs, but many people saw the act."

The following day two more students were murdered at the National University in Medellin. Reports suggest that they were playing chess in an education centre when two gunmen entered and shot them. Protests were been held simultaneously at universities across Colombia. Protesters were demanding respect for their anti-war sentiments and their right to protest and were marching in defiance of the murder of the medical student.

In the past two years, students, professors and university union leaders have been killed at four universities. Three students and six professors have been slain in the last year at the University of Antioquia in Medellin alone. The fact that universities provide a space for resistance activity means that they are also extremely dangerous places for activists, with many plants and right wing groups on campus. The United Auto-Defence groups of Colombia (AUC), which represents some 20 far right-wing paramilitary groups, announced its arrival, through a campaign of bathroom graffiti in student and professor lounges, at the University of Cartagena. There has been precious little reported about these latest killings, as is the case with many of the devastating attacks on civil liberties and human rights in Colombia. Morale is low, people are afraid, but resistance continues.

By this time the National University will be covered in the tents of students staying on campus in protest and new graffiti will mark the walls; 'asesinos' - assassins. In spite of the almost complete blind eye the media has turned on this event, the denial of responsibility by police, and the fear and confusion that people feel, 'many students will stay at the university discussing things and making decisions'. With heaviness Emile finishes her mail, "the situation is very difficult, many people are too scared... but we have to go on. This isn't the end of the story, we hope and believe that there is another possible story for this country, so we go on..."

*names changed for security reasons
By Alex Kelly 'The Paper' www.thepaper.org.au

Monopolise Resistance

The SWP try to hijack anti-war protests

Schnews published a pamphlet **Monopolise Resistance – how Globalise Resistance would hijack revolt** in early September last year, just before the attacks on New York and Washington. We published it in response to the Socialist Workers Party (SWP)'s sudden involvement in the anti-capitalist movement through its wholly-owned subsidiary Globalise Resistance. We warned that the Labour-voting-slogan-shouting-anti-direct-action politics of the SWP posed a real danger to the vitality and independence of the anti-capitalist movement. We also argued that we would only be able to stand up to this attack if we became better organised, more open to new people and more grounded in our communities. All this still stands, despite the attacks.

September 11th saw a monster that the US state had created come back to bite its maker. The gangsters who carried out the attacks on the Twin Towers and Pentagon were established, nurtured, pay-rolled, trained and supported by the US government, much like the death squads in South America and puppet regimes in south east Asia, installed to carry out its fight against 'world communism'. All this is denied of course, as the attack is used by the more powerful and heavily armed gangsters in the White House to launch a 'war against terrorism' that marks a significant escalation of the war that is constantly waged by the rich countries against the peoples of the majority of the world. War, racism, economic domination and, increasingly, the threat of nuclear first strikes against people the US or UK government don't like is on the agenda. Capitalism was never nice, but recently it has turned decidedly nastier.

The only response to this baring of capitalism's teeth is to broaden and deepen anti-capitalism. It's a sick system and, more than ever, people are questioning its existence – we should be building serious opposition to get rid of it altogether. Unfortunately, the problems we discussed in *Monopolise Resistance* have become even starker than before.

In Britain, where a Labour government sends troops to Afghanistan to turn rocks into rubble, the only reasonable response is to sabotage the war effort and support those attacked by it. Much activity has taken place – blockades of the British invasion force's HQ at Northwood, lock-ons at Downing Street, civil disobedience and occupations, sit-down protests. But at every turn the SWP has been there to calm things down and make it all acceptable to the Labour Party.

Since the start of the war against Afghanistan, the SWP has switched its resources from building Globalise Resistance to building another front organisation the Stop the War Coalition which they say "...unites Labour MPs, Asian community organisations and the Socialist Workers Party". As ever, their aim is to make an organisation acceptable to Labour Party members, not one that will effectively challenge the war-drive. Meetings of the coalition would refuse to discuss direct action, despite pleas from activists to do so. SWP stewards on a march organised by the coalition tried to get 600 people staging a sit-down protest in Whitehall to stand up and "go and listen to the speakers" – Labour MPs.

These aren't isolated examples – they flow from the SWP's view that there are millions of Labour Party members just gagging to join the SWP if they are argued with enough. As an internal instruction put it soon after the war against Afghanistan started,

"There are many people who are very critical of Bush and American imperialism's interventions and attacks over the last decade. We should go big on recruiting these people. We are likely to have long conversations with people over this but we could also get some very big sales".

So we can't do anything that might upset these potential recruits - even sit down protests are too hardcore for these 'revolutionaries'. In Dublin on Mayday – *our day*, for christ sake - Globalise Resistance even went as far as apologising to a trade union leader for getting heckled –

"Globalise Resistance regrets the inappropriate behaviour of some of its members on Mayday, and would like to assure you that most of those involved were not GR members. As you know we are a diverse group and some of our members have strong views concerning the trade union leadership. We would like you to know that the behaviour of these members does not reflect the views of Globalise Resistance as a group".

Hand in hand with this pathetic brown-nosing of pro-capitalist politicians goes the denial that it is possible to be involved in anti-capitalism without being in the SWP – or, at the very least, one of its many subsidiaries like Globalise Resistance or Stop The War Coalition. In order to portray themselves as revolutionary, they play down the day-in, day-out activities of thousands of anti-capitalists involved in campaigns, groups and collectives that have nothing to do with their sect.

Recently SWP leader Alex Callinicos described the fight against the Criminal Justice Bill in the mid 1990s as "reflect(ing) a broad anti-Tory consciousness that did not go beyond, for most of those involved, supporting the election of a Labour government". In fact, the thousands of people actively involved in that fight shut down motorways, occupied decaying buildings in order to turn them into community centres and faced arrest and imprisonment – all the time attacking all politicians, Labour or Tory, for their support of repressive laws. The SWP were not involved in any of this activity. Instead, the SWP were forcibly arguing with those involved in this direct action to "support the election of a Labour government".

Monopolise Resistance was an attempt to challenge this sort of hypocrisy. The SWP can only pose as 'revolutionary' by rewriting history, denying the existence of a living, organic anti-capitalist culture in this country – one that sides with the majority of humanity in its fight against capitalism - and turning the anti-capitalist movement into sad little pressure group thanking 'left-wing' Labour MPs for speaking at their meetings. Well thanks, but no thanks - we want more than that. We want a movement that doesn't compromise with war, with racism, with exploitation with all the day-to-day shit that capitalism throws at us. And it's up to us to us to make it happen.

Read *'Monopolise Resistance – How Globalise Resistance Would Hijack Revolt'* in full at www.schnews.org.uk/monopresist/index.htm

OUR PAPER IS FOR SALE

WAKE UP! WAKE UP! IT'S YOUR NOT JUST A NUMBER

Weekly SchNEWS

Printed and Published in Brighton by Justice?

Friday 28th September 2001   **www.schnews.org.uk**   **Issue 324**   **Free/Donation**

CARDTRICK

"There is always an issue of the moment which government seize to introduce an ID card. Governments seek control, they seek power."
– *Simon Davies, Privacy International.*

With the threat of war hanging in the air, Bush, Blair and their cronies have wasted no time in threatening to undermine the very democracies they claim to be protecting. An opinion poll conducted in the glare of media scare stories found 70% of people would be willing to see some reduction in civil liberties and increased security in Britain. So, coming your way soon: ID cards, increased DNA profiling, even more CCTV cameras and a general crack down on anyone who dares question the glorious war effort. And while they are proclaiming to be on the side of 'freedom and democracy' the new Human Rights Act looks likely to be 'modernised' pretty soon to get rid of some of our, er, human rights!

Home Secretary, David Blunkett, has made a firm commitment to the idea of introducing compulsory ID cards as part of the fight against terrorism. But SchNEWS doesn't see how one card could stop someone strapping Semtex to themselves, walking into a shopping centre and blowing themselves up. As Liberty says: "There is no evidence to suggest that introducing national ID cards will help the fight against terrorism... Those who carry out terrorist attacks are often chosen because they are unknown to the police. ID cards only help you track people if you know who you are looking for, if you are certain they cannot possibly be carrying plausible fake papers, and if you stop them".

ID cards will inevitably lead to greater discrimination against minorities and a massive intrusion into our privacy for the rest of us. Not only that, but the government favours 'citizens cards' with health, tax, criminal and social security records. If you lose your card or have a problem/dispute with one agency, it would affect your dealings with all the others. And, what if the information on your card is wrong? The police have admitted that their national computer has errors of between 20% and 30%. As Simon Davies from Privacy International points out "A person cannot function without the ID card... In time the card will be required for gaining access to a building, getting swimming club membership, buying goods, renting a house, buying a travelcard. We can expect the card in Britain to become an internal passport."

But ID cards are just the tip of the repression iceberg. Politicians across the USA and Europe are rushing through new "Anti-Terrorist" laws. Last week European Union ministers drew up proposals to remove data protection and privacy directives and introduce knee-jerk oppressive laws: Every phone-call made, email sent and website you visit will be known to the police. They may introduce Europe-wide arrest warrants along with a list of presumed terrorists and expand the concept of terrorism to include the right to protest and civil disobedience.

Not to be outdone the UK is going even further. As if last year's brand spanking new Terrorism Act wasn't enough (SchNEWS 268) New Labour want another one including giving the police powers to arrest people not for any crime they've committed but solely for interrogation purposes! "Look Sarge, Asian man with a long beard." "Yes Constable, lets bring him in."

The Real Terrorists?

While the FBI have named amongst others Reclaim The Streets, Carnival Against Capital and the Animal Liberation Front as a terrorist threat, the US "intelligence" agencies including the notorious CIA are preparing to return to their Cold War tactics of bomb, bug and corrupt. So let's get this straight: people blocking traffic, dancing in the street or rescuing animals are terrorists while the US secret services are...well, here's some of their recent highlights:
*1951: CIA helps overthrow the democratic government in Guatemala, then backs new regimes who murder more than 100,000 Guatemalans over the next 40 years.
*1965: CIA provokes a coup in Indonesia leading to General Suharto taking power. In following weeks a half to one million people are murdered by death squads using lists provided by US State Department.
*1973: US sponsor a coup in Chile against the democratic government of Salvador Allende and help murder another 30,000 people, including US citizens.
*1984: World Court declares the US government a war criminal for placing mines in harbours in Nicaragua in the 1980s, a war which resulted in the deaths of over 30,000 innocent people.
*1989: US invades Panama, over 4,000 people are killed and they arrest President Manuel Noriega, one time CIA agent turned enemy (sound familiar?).
*1998: US bombs a pharmaceutical plant in Sudan claiming it was linked to bin Laden.

The attack deprived Sudan of desperately needed medical drugs. The CIA later admits that information linking the plant to Osama bin Laden was probably incorrect.

Introducing measures like ID cards won't stop the kind of terrorism seen on September 11th. It will, however, give governments a good excuse to clamp down even further on the world-wide anti-capitalist movements. All of course in the name of protecting our liberty and freedom.

* Burn yer ID card! Check out www.optional-identity-uk.cjb.net
* The US National Security Agency Echelon system can intercept all email, telephone and fax communications in Europe. Jam Echelon Day, October 21st, see cypherwar.com/echelon
* An independent tribunal has accepted that a blanket ban on releasing information held by MI5 introduced by Jack Straw, the former home secretary, is unlawful under the Data Protection Act. In future, the 300,000 people whom MI5 have files on, will be able to apply to see their files, but 'sensitive information' will still be held back, how much use is that?
* More info on these and other related stories, issues etc see: www.statewatch.org , www.privacyinternational.org.
* Check out other acts of US terrorism at www.thirdworldtraveler.com/

WHILE YOU WEREN'T LOOKING

While the corporate media are telling us to unite behind "our boys" the Government is quietly slipping through some dodgy stuff:

The mixed oxide nuclear reprocessing plant at Sellafield has been given the green light, this highly controversial scheme would normally be front-page news, but in the current situation is barely noted. The irony is that opening this plant will lead to a proliferation in the amount of plutonium available which terrorists would love to get their hands on.

Asylum seekers arriving in the UK will have even less rights of appeal against deportation.

In the USA right-wingers want to rush through more free trade agreements and are proposing cutting Capital Gains Tax, which will only benefit the rich, as anti-terrorism initiatives (we kid you not!).

And, of course, with the terrorist attacks there were calls to push ahead with the "Star Wars" missile defence system, which would have been useless on September 11th

ANOTHER BRICK IN THE WALL

As New Labour marches full steam ahead, privatising the parts even the Tories didn't dare to reach, a relatively new corporate beast has emerged: the public-sector outsourcing* firm. It lies in wait ready to snap up contracts anywhere it can, from education to hospitals, prisons to defence. And you can see why - the outsourced education market alone is already worth £2.5 billion with Neo Labours recent white paper on education indicating that up to 300 failing schools could be handed over to the private sector.

In January 2000, Cambridge Education Associates (CEA) became the first company in the country to get a piece of the outsourcing action taking over all seventy of Islingtons' schools, in a seven-year deal worth a potential £130 million. When SchNEWS asked them at the time why they were getting involved in education they told us it was because "we care."

Within a few months they announced that one of those schools they "cared" so much about - Angel Primary - would have to close because of poor results and surplus places. Despite the fact that 'surplus' places would vanish if the Council cut class sizes from 30 to 25. Despite the fact that results were improving, despite a campaign by teachers, pupils and parents and an independent panel refusing to endorse the closure plans, the school adjudicator said tough – the school must close.

CEA's parent company are civil engineers Mott Macdonald (involved in such prestigious projects like the Newbury Bypass and the road destruction at Twyford Down). Of course closing down Angel has nothing to do with the value of its site, right next to the Business Design Centre and a proposed shopping and entertainment development in the borough's fashionable commercial centre. In fact just three days after closure was finally announced, the Business Design Centre was given permission to nearly double its number of visitors.

One local resident told SchNEWS "CEA's parent company Mott MacDonald are responsible for the design of channel tunnel terminal at nearby Kings Cross St. Pancras - a small diversion under Copenhagen St to Angel school would provide a direct rail link to the Business Centre. The playground could also be converted to a lorry park which the Centre needs when it hosts major events - this is a guess but am I right?" As Esther Gonzalez, whose son goes to Angel points out "The plan has nothing to do with the education at the school and everything to do with the value of the site."

At the beginning of the month CEA were fined £300,000 by Islington Council for failing to reach performance targets.

Corporations are slowly taking over Britain's schools so they can make them into profit making businesses instead. In their pursuit of strategic moneymaking, it's not just our schools they're interested in… SchNEWS can't think of a company better suited to educating our children than SERCO plc. which also invests in and manages atomic weapons establishments (such as Aldermaston) and radar facilities at Fylingdales (Fylingdales base on the North York Moors is essential for the Star Wars programme). SERCO will manage the biotechnology programme for the UK's Department of Trade and Industry. They part own the Premier Custodial Group which built and now runs prisons and young offenders institutions such as Kilmarnock, Nottingham and Medomsley secure training centre. On top of this they manage prisoner tagging and monitoring systems, police number plate identifying technology, speed cams, the new national traffic control centre (which collates info from coils embedded under roads) and one hospital... so they would be in a good position to monitor us all rather effectively should we be made to use ID cards. To tell them what you think, call: 01932 755900.

* **Gatecrash Labours Party** this Sunday. Labour's annual conference starts in Brighton. Surrounded by a security cordon and hundreds of cops, against a background of imminent war, the government will make decisions behind closed doors. Those who oppose their agenda of creeping privatisation, the criminalisation of asylum seekers, the UK subsidised arms trade, and the outlawing of protest are invited to crash their party. Meet 1pm at the Level in Brighton. For more information contact: gatecrashing@yahoo.com or call 01273 298192 Website: www.new-labour.com

SCHNEWS VOCAB WATCH
* Neo-Labour calls it 'outsourcing', SchNEWS will stick with privatisation.

Unhappy Anniversary

"America's name is literally stamped on to the missiles fired by Israel into Palestinian buildings in Gaza and the West Bank. Only four weeks ago, I identified one of them as an AGM 114-D air-to-ground rocket made by Boeing and Lockheed-Martin at their factory in Florida, the state where some of the suiciders trained to fly."
- Robert Fisk, Middle East Commentator

On the 28th September of last year, Ariel Sharon, the then Israeli opposition leader, along with 1000 fully armed troops from the Israeli Defence Force (IDF) went to 'guard' Jerusalem's Haram-al-Sharif Mosque by the golden Dome of the Rock. The 28th September is a significant date for Palestinians because it marks the anniversary of the Sabra and Shatila refugee camp massacres, which took place in Lebanon in 1982 (see SchNEWS 279). Ariel Sharon was the one who ordered that massacre of hundreds of people so its not surprising that turning up to Islam's third holiest shrine with his henchmen in tow on this anniversary was the flash point that started the present Intifada. Since then 673 Palestinians have been killed by the IDF with up to 28,000 injured and this figure rises everyday. Some, like Mohammed al-Durrah a 12 year old boy who was shot dead while trying to hide behind his dad on the second day of the uprising, have remained a potent reminder of the terror experienced by Palestinians on a daily basis. Others, however, are only statistics now that people around the world have become used to the regular killings.

So how is this ethnic cleansing allowed to go on? Well America funds Israel to the tune of £3 billion a year to keep its well-armed friend in the hostile Middle East, so they look the other way when the Israeli State is accused of acts of terrorism. On September 13th, while the world had its attention on the USA, the IDF invaded the Gaza Strip and the West Bank with tanks and bulldozers, shelling apartment blocks, offices and shops. And a government spokesman said at the time, "This is the strong beating the weak" At the moment there is an American imposed cease fire in Israel/Palestine, but without any visible concessions to the Palestinians it is unlikely to last. Fisk is outraged, "we are supposed to hold our tongues, even when Ariel Sharon - a man whose name will always be associated with the massacre at Sabra and Shatila - announces that Israel also wishes to join the battle against 'world terror.'" More info: www.gush-shalom.org or www.indymedia.il.org

...and finally...

The annual Blaggers Guide to the Labour Party Conference is out, and for those of you who want a good drink/debate and some free food here's some of the highlights.'Politics and progress: democracy, civil society and political renewal. Sound boring? - not at all! Home Secretary David Blunkett will be at this Sunday Telegraph/Demos event agonising over taking away more of our rights. Come and put your point of view (if having a point of view is still legal by then).' 'The globalisation debate - car capitalism be regulated? A right old ding-dong between Clare Short, George Monbiot and some geezer from BP/Rio Tinto. Our favourite tho' is 'Building a sustainable aviation policy.by The Airport Operators Association.' Er, might we suggest not flying. To find out when and where these and other talks are taking place get your copies from the Brighton Peace Centre.

INN JOKE

Sick of the McPub and the closure of many traditional locals in order to sell of the land for development, regular boozers, sorry readers of Schnews will be celebrating after a groundbreaking decision in the European Court of Appeal. Courage was forcing publicians to buy barrels of beer from them which were costing up to £100 more than they could get the barrels on the open market. 800 publicians took the company to court, some went on rent strike, and all suffered evictions and bankruptcies for their trouble. The European ruling overturns a previous decision by the English Court of Appeal which had said that if publicians signed a contract – even if it was illegal – it was binding! Each individual case will now have to be reconsidered and although many landlords have lost their pubs, it does demonstrate that sometimes if you stand up to the corporate bastards, you can get a result! Mines a pint Micky!!!

Inside SchNEWS

Stuart Durkin is 5 years into a 13 years sentence - for streaking through the Vatican! He's looking for communication with the outside world, so get scribbling:2A,Casa Circondariale, Mamma Gialla, Via S Salvatore 14/B, KM 1800 Cap, 01100 Viterbo, Italy.

FRIENDLY FIRE?

the Israeli army are trying to get the M16 A3 assualt rifle declared a non-lethal weapon to allow its use on the civilian population for 'riot control'. Thousands of Palestinians have become permanently crippled from bullet wounds suffered during stone-throwing protests, mostly due to the fragmenting bullets fired by M16s. The ammunition often breaks into tiny pieces after initial penetration, ripping up muscles and nerves and causing multiple internal injuries.

SchNEWS in brief

Anti-War Demos in your area: see Party & Protest section on the SchNEWS website **'**Monopolise Resistance** - how Globalise Resistance would hijack revolt' is a new SchNEWS booklet. See it on our website or send two first class stamps + sae for a copy ** If you'd like to get involved in writing SchNEWS, help with the website or the mail-out come to a **SchNEWS training day**-call to book your place ** **SchNUSIC:** 18 tracks, 70 minutes. 'Music and culture to unite the underground'. £7 inc.postage from the SchNEWS address. www.dirtysquatters.com ** **Stop Star Wars Demo**, 13 October at Menwith Hill 10am-4pm Contact Campaign for the Accountability of American Bases (CAAB) www.caab.org.uk.

disclaimer

SchNEWS warns all readers going thru an identity crisis, there's now a card for every occasion. Honest.

Opportunism in the face of tragedy

by Gillian Murdoch

Repression in the name of anti - terrorism

In the atmosphere of global xenophobia and paranoia which followed the September 11 attacks, many countries used the opportunity to justify crackdowns on ongoing domestic dissent, tighten surveillance and push through new 'anti-terrorist' legislation. For some countries [like UK] September 11 legitimated draconian anti-terrorist laws which had been introduced during the past few years anyway, while others just carried on with the same human rights abuses they'd always done, whether they wrote new legislation to legalise it or not. Here's a round up of some post 9-11 anti-terrorist rubber stamping worldwide...

The European Union

Under the post September 11 "Anti-terrorism roadmap" the EU has added two new databases to the planned Second Generation SIS (Schengen Information System – see SchNEWS 312).

The first database would cover public order and protests and lead to: "Barring potentially dangerous persons from participating in certain events [where the person is] notoriously known by the police forces for having committed recognised facts of public order disturbance."

The second database would be a register of all third country nationals in the EU who will be tagged with an "alert" if they overstay their visa or residence permit - this follows a call by the German government for the creation of a "centralised register".

Spain

Spain used its presidency of the EU to push through new proposals to target anti-capitalist protesters across Europe, with more cooperation between police forces and the introduction of an EU wide arrest warrant. Their own anti-terrorist zeal goes back well before September 11 and they continue to attack Basque political group or publications – accusing them of ETA (Basque militant separatist army) affiliations and terrorism. On October 1st police raided and imprisoned 13 people who were involved in the Basque prisoners support organization Gestoras Pro-amnistía. (For more see SchNEWS 343) The Spanish government admitted to 'tracking' a number of activists websites for intelligence gathering including Barcelona Indymedia (move over Maxwell Smart). www.euskalinfo.org.uk

France

On November 15, France rushed through 'The Law on Daily Security' (LSQ): a package of anti-terrorist laws which are scheduled to remain in force until December 31 2003, giving the police expanded powers to search, monitor communications and heighten security in public places – all in the name of cracking down on "terrorism" and "delinquency." www.lsijolie.net

United Kingdom

The UK's latest anti-global terrorism effort, the Anti-Terrorism, Crime and Security Act became law on December 14 2001. The new Terrorism Act defines terrorism as "the use or threat of action" designed to "influence the government or to intimidate the public ... for the purpose of advancing a political, religious, or ideological cause". Actions cited include those involving "serious violence against a person" in Britain or abroad. The act covers fundraising.

Expanding the Terrorism Act 2000 (for a rundown see SchNEWS 251, 268, 300), it allows for the freezing of terrorist funding and legalises the indefinite detention of foreign nationals without charge or trial. Detainees can be held with no evidence that they are even thinking of committing a crime, and may be 'certified' as a terrorist

Graphic: Martin

suspect if there an 'unspecified link' either to a so-called terrorist organisation, or to someone else who is a member of one.

The opting out of Article 5 of the European Convention on Human Rights (which outlaws detention without trial) was justified with the soundbite: 'The presence of extremists in the United Kingdom at this time and for the foreseeable future creates a situation of public emergency threatening the life of the nation.'

As a result Asian and north African communities were openly targeted for surveillance and repression in exactly the same way the Irish community was in the 1970s and 1980s. Between 11 September 2001 and 18 January 2002 there were 124 'terrorism-related' arrests. A significant number of those arrested in the post-11 September hysteria have already had any suggestion of terrorist involvement dismissed but remain imprisoned on pretexts connected to their immigration status. With the government putting the pressure on to speed up deportations and effect more 'removals', this is an excuse to trawl minority communities, conflating anti-terrorist and immigration powers.

In March MI6 announced it was seeking to double its recruitment of front-line officers for the "war against terrorism," justifying the need for more spies by claiming that recent events 'pose the greatest threat to Britain's security in 60 years'.

In the same month twenty one [mainly Islamic] groups were banned under new terror law, adding to the list of groups targeted in the Terrorist Act 2000 such as the PKK, the Kurdish Workers' Party; ETA, the Basque separatist group; LTTE, the Tamil separatist group, a number of Sikh organisations, Al Qa'ida of course and more. The Home Office concedes the large majority of the groups on the list have not attacked British targets.

www.statewatch.org/news/2002/apr/01sis.htm

Germany

Rushed through are a package of anti-terrorist laws, amending existing laws, strengthening immigration control and secret services to an extent unknown since Nazi times. New supervisory powers give virtually unlimited access to data from telephones, emails, bank accounts to government intelligence and police. Surprise surprise a lot of the laws are pointed at outsiders living in Germany - with the 'alien central register' law being upped, and records of fingerprints and other documents of asylum seekers being kept for ten years.

India

On October 24th the Prevention of Terrorism Ordinance (POTO) became law. This gives the police wide powers of arrest, it allows up to six months detention without charge or trial for political suspects. It also made government, army officials, and other paramilitary forces immune from prosecution for any action taken "in good faith" when combating "terrorism". POTO modified 1985's lapsed Terrorists and Disruptive Activities (Prevention) Act (TADA.) Under TADA, tens of thousands of politically motivated detentions, torture, and other human rights violations were committed against Muslims, Sikhs, Dalits, trade union activists, and political opponents in the late 1980s and early 1990s. In the face of mounting opposition to the act, India's government acknowledged these abuses and phased TADA out in 1995.

In May this year **Thailand** agreed to join **Indonesia, Malaysia** and the **Phillipines** in an anti-terrorism pact to "defeat a militant network they say is bent on creating a single regional Islamic state." The four-way pact would allow anti-terrorism exercises as well as combined operations to hunt suspected terrorists, the setting up of hotlines and sharing of airline passenger lists. www.helpkashmir.org/poto/poto1.htm

Russia

International concern for human rights abuses in Chechnya appeared to wane after the September 11 attacks, although Russian forces in Chechnya have continued with extrajudicial executions, arrests, and extortion of civilians. Since September 11 alone, at least one person per week has "disappeared" after being taken into custody by Russian forces.

The Kremlin has laboured to link the Russian operation in Chechnya with the global fight against terrorism. On September 12, Russian President Vladimir Putin declared that America and Russia had a "common foe" because "Bin Laden's people are connected with the events currently taking place in our Chechnya."

Jordan

In October Jordan amended its Penal Code and press law "to cover all the needs that we are confronting now," said Prime Minister Ali Abul Ragheb. The amendments expanded the definition of "terrorism", and introduced loosely defined offences restricting freedom of expression and expanding the scope of offences punishable by death. It allowed the government to close down any publication deemed to have published "false or libellous information that can undermine national unity or the country's reputation," and prescribed prison terms for publicising in the media or on the internet pictures "that undermine the king's dignity" or information tarnishing the reputation of the royal family.

In January Fahd al-Rimawi, the editor-in-chief of the weekly political paper al Majd, became the first known victim of the amended penal code. He was questioned for four hours by the General Intelligence Department (GID) and then detained for three days at Jweideh Prison in January 2002. He was charged with "writing and publishing false information and rumours that may harm the prestige and reputation of the state and slander the integrity and reputation of its members".

Somalia

Since **Somalia's** Islamist group al-Ittihad was linked with al-Qai'da and the bombing of the US embassies in Kenya and Tanzania in 1998, the threat to people's freedom since September 11 is not a case of the Somalian government rushing through anti-terrorist laws. Rather the threat comes from the US, who are poised to inflict terror themselves in the name of preventing terror. US and German warships are patrolling the waters around Yemen, Sudan and Somalia, and to prepare the country for being hit, earlier this year the US closed down international banking to it, as well as cutting off the internet and restricting phone communication.

Nigeria

In October Nigerian Police were reported to be making efforts to "revive" their anti-terrorism squad in the aftermath of the terrorist attacks. The squad, was set up by the late dictator General Sanni Abacha, and disbanded after Nigeria returned to democracy in 1999.

The idea had critics worried. In all its years of existence, not a single terrorist was arrested or prosecuted. Instead, it was used to terrorise the media, human rights community, the pro-democracy movement and other real and imagined enemies.

Canada

The Government, proposed four repressive anti-terrorist laws modelled on the US Patriot Act. Bill C-36, the Canada Police State Act, was enacted on December 24th 2001. It allows new powers of "preventative arrests of people suspected of terrorism" for up to 72 hours based on police suspicion and removes the right to remain silent. It defines protests that interrupt public facilities as acts of terrorism, and allows suspects' property to be confiscated.

Under the Bill anyone who associates with listed person or organisation can be by association defined as a terrorist. Property and bank accounts can be frozen. www.canadianliberty.bc.ca

Chile

The Mapuches, the most active radical group in Chile fighting repression and land rights, have felt the brunt of the crackdown after September 11. After one newspaper spread the rumour that a Mapuche web-page was done by a so-called 'Bin Laden Corporation'. Government officials asked an Appeals Court to apply the Anti-terrorist Law to any Mapuches who attack Endesa Chile, a subsidiary of Endesa Espana, the company building a controversial dam on the Biobio River.

Colombia

A Bush administration "policy review" about Plan Colombia is moving the goalposts further to allow Colombia's military to use future US aid - guns, helicopters, intelligence and training - to attack domestic 'terrorists' - in other words any group who are defending the country and it's people against the neo-liberal onslaught. Likely targets are leftist Revolutionary Armed Forces of Colombia (FARC), National Liberation Army (ELN) guerrillas, the United Self-Defence Forces of Colombia (AUC) and anyone else who steps out of line. (see Plan Colombia article in this book)

United States

In early October Bush announced he was creating the Office of Home and Security, to co-ordinate the government's 46 "anti-terrorist" agencies. Modelled on the CIA's Vietnam War Phoenix Programme, the office came into effect in March 2002, with Tom Ridge, former Republican Governor of Pennsylvania, as director. The proposed 2003 budget gave homeland security $38 billion - roughly double the budget allocation for the previous year.

State lawmakers in the US responded to the September 11 terrorist attacks by drafting more than 1,200 bills – an average of 24 per state! They ranged from making terrorism a capital crime to requiring teachers to lead students each day to sing the national anthem. Iowa lawmakers made terrorist crimes punishable by life imprisonment or death. In Pennsylvania, a bill would require students to start each day with the pledge of allegiance or the national anthem. In October the USA Patriot Act was approved by Congress without debate and signed into law. It put into place the most sweeping expansion of state powers to spy, search, restrict speech, arrest, incarcerate, interrogate, punish, deport, and withhold information the United States has ever seen, all unchecked by judicial review.

Australia

On September 13, Defence Minister Peter Reith cited the US attacks and terrorism to justify his (1950's style conservative) government's effort to prevent asylum-seekers from entering Australia. These remarks came as the Australian government overturned a court decision that it had illegally detained hundreds of migrants from Afghanistan.

A bundle of post September 11 counter-terrorism legislation is currently pending which is mainly about giving the government covert access to electronic communications and banning organisations on the basis of secret intelligence information.

Aotearoa/New Zealand

The NZ version of the UK RIP Bill enabling covert access to communications is being delayed due to public resistance. The Security Intelligence Service has cashed in on the paranoia by launching a 'dob in a terrorist' hotline.

WAKE UP! WAKE UP! WAKE UP! IT'S YER CITY WIDE

Weekly SchNEWS

Printed and Published in Brighton by Justice?

FOR SALE

Friday 5th October 2001   **www.schnews.org.uk**   **Issue 325**   **Free/Donation**

NIGHTMAYORS

"When we tell them that a mayor would have total power for four years; would not be able to be controlled or voted out in that time, no matter how incompetent or corrupt; and would be able to act in total secrecy, they almost universally reject the notion as frightening". - Tom Davidson, Labour Campaign for Open Local Government.

With President Blair telling us to pull our bloody socks up and be more like America, it's good to see Councils up and down the country calling for referendums on directly elected mayors just like they've got in the States.

In Brighton ex-squatter and ex-Council leader Our Lord Steve Bassam has been spearheading the Yes-please-we'd-love-a-mayor campaign (oh and while we're at it, can I be the first one please?). In his 'strictly confidential discussion paper' Lord Bassam said the Yes campaigners "should talk the language of democracy, accountability, openness, anti-corruption and strong public services" by - er - electing a mayor. "What frustrates this sector is red tape, overlong decision-making and a lack of leadership" Bassam continued.

Mayoral Chains

'Democracy and openness'- hmmnn, a directly elected mayor would be all-powerful and help to get rid of all that silly debate stuff and nonsense about 'public consultation' - that democracy is supposed to be about. SchNEWS ain't saying the present way of doing things is much copeither , but as local Green councillor Pete West argues "An executive Mayor would wield enormous influence without any formal duty to consult or the immediate control of backbench councillors."

'Anti-corruption'? Over in the U.S. the most popular hang out for Mayors when they leave office is in prison, where over 50 of them currently reside. Lets' hope Lord Bassam doesn't end up there.

'Red tape and overlong decision-making?' We think he means cutting the time given to all those pesky members of the public who complain about unwanted planning applications.

And as for *'strong public services'.* Come again? Is this why the New Local Government Network (NLGN) are so involved countrywide in pushing for directly elected mayors and harp on about

wanting to 'modernise' local democracy

This Network, which just happens to have been co-founded by (none other than) Lord Bassam, has generously given a £2000 interest free 'loan' to Brighton's pro-Mayor campaign.

Crapita

But just who are these Networkers? Well, you won't believe the coincidence but some of NLGN's 'corporate partners' are the very same firms that are snapping up public services up and down the country as they're privatised. Companies like Capita (Lord Bassam was a paid consultant to them. He even tried to flog them Brighton's Housing Benefit and Council Tax Service when he was leader.); KPMG - one of the world's largest accountancy firms, who've made rich pickings from 'advising' clients on the massive profits to be had in the public sector. (Busy bee Bassam was a paid consultant to them as well); Serviceteam - who are taking over Brighton's refuse collection; Amey, Jarvis and Serco, moving into a classroom near you; and of course Deutsche Bank - although SchNEWS aren't too to sure why a German bank wants to 'reform British local government?'

So, why do these corporations want directly elected mayors? Capita gave it away when they told a House of Lords Committee that a strong leader who can 'personally commit the council' made it easier for firms like theirs to 'develop partnerships' - meaning making it easier for firms like theirs to take over public services and run them for profit without any fuss. And with the privatisation of public services worth £5 billion a year and rising it's no wonder firms like Capita are after an even bigger slice of the council cake.

* The Brighton Allies for Democracy Vote No campaign have produced a newspaper. Send an SAE to 192 Ditchling Rd., Brighton, BN1 6JE www.ourpower.org.uk/

"**SchNUSIC**" New compilation CD featuring 70 minutes of music, 18 bands (including Digidub, Inner City Unit and 2000 DS) from 8 different countries. Covering a range of music to unite and excite the underground: hip-hop, electro-mental, dub-drum & bass and more. £7 inc. p&p (cheques payable to Justice?) from SchNEWS. www.dirtysquatters.com

---

INSIDE SchNEWS

There's one place in the world where slavery is still regarded as entirely acceptable; inside prisons. Some prisoners are having to work for pence rather than pounds per hour – if they refuse they can be put in isolation and denied 'privileges'. Last year prison labour made the tidy sum of £52.9 million for private companies and the state. New Labour has decided that all prisons to be built from now on will be financed by private companies, no doubt earning them a few new corporate friends. In the UK, for example, Group 4's Altcourse Prison has paid for itself in only 3 years, with the next 22 years of its contract making pure profit for the company. This exploitation is only viable if prisoners go along with it. Work strikes, go-slows and sabotage are some of the best weapons prisoners have, and solidarity action by supporters outside can make a massive difference, as with the recent occupation of Hepworth Plumbing (see SchNEWS 317). For more info get yer hands on the book "In the Hands of the Enemy" by prisoner Mark Barnsley and his supporters. It costs £6, cheques payable to Justice for Mark Barnsley, PO Box 381, Huddesfield, HD1 3XX Tel 07944 522001 www.freemarkbarnsley.com.

* **David Blenkinsop** has been sentenced to 3 years for assaulting Brian Cass, the despicable managing director of Huntingdon Life Sciences.Write to him David Blenkinsop, EM 7899, HMP Bedford, St Loyes Street, Bedford MK40 1HG

* **Free and Critter**, two American environmental activists who were sentenced to 22 years 8 months and 5 ½ years respectively (see SchNEWS 308/309) are being moved between prisons by the US authorities to stop them receiving constant mail. Send Letters to them: c/o Free & Critter Legal Defense Committee, PO Box 50263, Eugene, OR 97405, USA.

* **Witness appeal** did anybody see a Womble get arrested at DSEI while he was assisting a woman who had been assaulted by police as the police were forcing people away from the Excel centre by the roundabout? Contact Mark on 07811 654721

BEACH PARTY

By the time you read this SchNEWS hacks'll be breathing a sigh of relief as the 'New' Labour Party go home and the massive £2 million security operation winds down. Along with all the usual over-the-top policing we expect when Neo-Labour come to town - police on every corner, shoot-and-quick armed response units, random vehicle searches, evidence-gathering teams waving video cameras in people's faces - they even concreted motorway crash barriers into the seafront road in case terrorists ram-raided the delegates' hotels!

For some, harassment started even before the 'conference' began, with cops using laws designed for terrorists and criminals on - you've guessed it - protestors, and those who didn't look straight enough. Hunt saboteurs doing the usual Saturday afternoon stall were told they couldn't set up by police - who then filmed the 'highly illegal' act of handing out leaflets. Over the course of the conference one sab was stopped a record-breaking 19 times - three times under Section 44 of the Terrorism Act, where it is an arrestable offence not to give your details (unlike all other stop and searches). The same sab has two civil cases against the police - Coincidence?

On Sunday the traditional lobby-the-Labour-Party demo was changed at the last minute to a pro-peace march along the seafront, flanked on one side by driving rain and on the other- by riot cops. While a samba band drummed out some kicking rhythms, assorted anarchists and others, having proclaimed their intention to gatecrash Labour's Party, decided to join the peace march. Although they didn't totally get into the spirit as they parodied the perennial lefty chants ("They say Big Mac! We say Prozac!").

During the march the level of police paranoia was higher than ever: most of the officers on the front line were wearing balaclavas under their helmets and they didn't have their numbers on. One protester was arrested for wearing a Palestinian flag as a scarf and four 'Wombles' were arrested for 'conspiracy to commit violent disorder.' They were surrounded and nicked by riot cops before the march had even started. It would seem they were nicked for standing out from the dark-coloured rain-drenched crowd because of their bright white overalls, helmets and padding. When questioned Chief Inspector Robin Smith said "They were singled out as the result of intelligence." Yeah right.

* The solicitors dealing with those arrested on Sunday mysteriously had their phone lines blocked all day.

* ID cards have been scrapped, for the time being at least, thanks no doubt to our front page last week.

* The US is bringing in the Patriot Act, because - remember kids as President Bush says – 'if you're not with us, then you're against us.' A new sinister Office of Homeland Security in the USA has also been created, headed by Pennsylvania Governor Tom Ridge who has praised the Third Reich's efficiency and how Mussolini did well to keep the Italian trains running on time! A new state political police is being formed, this new police force will operate "with extralegal authority" and operate outside the American constitution, and will be above the CIA and FBI.

(www.almartinraw.com/)

*To keep up to date with what's happening check out www.alternet.org

* SchWHOOPS! Last weeks web address for Jam Echelon Day on Oct 21st was wrong. It should read http://cipherwar.com/echelon

SchNEWS in Brief

The **Anarchist Bookfair** celebrates its 20th Birthday by moving to a larger venue, the Camden Centre, Euston Road, nr. King's Cross, London, 20th October 10am-7pm. www.anarchistbookfair.org ** Agency staff working on **construction sites** at government buildings such as the cabinet office are being kicked out of their jobs unless they provide security details that include where they've lived in the last 5 years, due to increased security measures after the USA terrorist attacks. ** Its getting exciting in **North Staffs**: there's a new local website for activists (www.actionnet-northstaffs.co.uk) and they had their first critical mass on Car Free day which will now be a regular event first Saturday of every month, 11.30am Queens Gardens Newcastle, contact topsyturvy@disinfo.net or 07880-841809 ** **Shortcuts to Manchester** is an ace new radical guide to taking direct action and interesting stuff to do in and around Manchester (centre of the universe - apparently) for a copy send SAE to Shortcuts, Dept 29, c/o MERCI, Bridge Mill, 22a Beswick Street, Manchester, M4 7HR. ** All you **gardeners** out there, get saving your vegetable and flower seed for a community seed swap event happening in Brighton next February. To find out more contact: 5 Wellsbourne, Findon Rd., Brighton, or call 01273 852457 ** An **anti McDonalds** protester has been awarded £1,500 damages by North Wales police for illegal imprisonment and malicious prosecution. The man was nicked for dropping a banner which read "McDonalds Makes You Sick" at Llandudno McDonalds on last years' World Day of Action ** ...and don't forget to target your local **McDogshit** during this years anti-McDonalds Day on October 16th . Get your Adopt Your Store leaflets from Veggies 0845 4589595 or contact the McLibel Support Campaign, 5 Caledonian Rd., London, N1 9DX www.mcspotlight.org ** In **Brighton** there will be a demo on the 16th outside SchNEWS favourite burger bar – meet 1pm onwards at the Western Road branch Tel 0870 7379000 or email barc@vegans.free-online.co.uk ** **Seeing Through the Spin** is an education pack produced in response to the corporate takeover of schools. It gives a fresh insight into the subtle processes of 'greedwashing'. £15 + £3 postage from Baby Milk Action, 23 St.Andrew's St., Cambridge, CB2 3AX. Tel 01223 464420, www.babymilkaction.org ** **The Pecan Centre** in Peckham offer free computer facilities for refugees and asylum seekers. 1-3 Atwell Road, London SE15. Tel: 020 7740 9200 www.pecan.org.uk ** On the 13th October there will be a **British Sign Language March** in Newcastle Upon Tyne, part of the campaign to get sign language recognised as an official language meet at 11am newcastlebslmarch@hotmail.com ** For more dates and things going on in your area check out the party and protest section on our website ** New to town and want to get involved in SchNEWS? Then why not get involved in the **SchNEWS Student Training Day**. Ring up and book your place now for the opportunity of a lifetime.

Return of the REBEL ALLIANCE. The irregular get together of Brighton's direct action rabble. Hear reports of what different groups have been doing/will do and take part in the discussion about the war on terrorism. 17th October, upstairs at the Albert Pub 7.30pm *sharp.*

WASTE OF TIME

Would you believe it but composting your own kitchen waste could be illegal! The Department for Environment Food and Rural Affairs has in its wisdom decided that to help stop the spread of foot and mouth disease kitchen waste cannot be composted as it will be spread on land. This has already affected Chesterfield Council's collection of kitchen waste and may damage community and farm site composters. So instead of being composted this kitchen waste has to be incinerated (environmentally damaging) or put into landfill, where rats, seagulls, etc. will have access to it and spread disease. If you think this idea is crazy contact Philip Walker of DEFRA, 020-7944-6404. Philip.Walker@defra.gsi.gov.uk

*For info about composting contact Community Composting Network, 0114-2580483 www.othas.org.uk/ccn

Positive SchNEWS

21st October is the 11th national Apple Day organised by Common Ground. Apples growers and fanatics all over Britain will be throwing apple day celebrations. Events in Sussex include apple archery, pin the maggot on the apple, apple bobbing and Morris dancing. Lots of apple varieties and cider tastings to those wishing for the ultimate apple experience. Sussex Apple Days: **20th** 12-4pm - **Stanmer Orchard**, **Brighton** Volunteers are needed for providing transport, setting up and clearing away. Contact Anne 01273 689532, email annedaisybellis@hotmail.com. **20th-21st** - **English Farm Cider Centre, Lewes** - Apple competitions and games including the Apple Stalk, Pin the Maggot on the Apple and Apple Archery, apple pressing, tasting, trade stalls, live music all day, licensed bar, Old Time Victorian Fair, apple produce and baking, hot food marquee, morris dancing. £1.50 entry, free parking. Contact: 01323 711411 For details on Apple Day events around the country call Common Ground 020 7267 2144 www.commonground.org.uk

...and finally...

From our Free Food correspondent.

As always, the Labour Party conference provided a kaleidoscope of opportunities to sample the traditional mix of food, chat, fine wines, and violent stomach cramp for those who indulged in too much canape and grape-fuelled political debate. At events such as the Leave Country Sports Alone reception, with venison and duck on offer, meat-eaters cleaned up; though everyone contributed to draining their wine supply. Better veggie and vegan buffet options were available at the Police Federation and (along with free beer) the Liquor Licensing Reform shindigs. Some of the more right-on discussions were lacking in refreshments, (though, like the Red Pepper debate on the 'War on Terrorism' were interesting in their own right) but with events like the Fabian Society 'globalisation' debate, you could feed your mind and your stomach at the same time. Few events, though, surpassed the 'New Labour - New World Wines' wine-tasting hosted by export credit company NCM. After the bash was listed in the anonymously-produced 'Bloggers' Guide' to the conference, one of the organisers from NCM noted; 'We have had quite a few homeless people come in. I didn't mind, we gave them all glasses of wine.' No cake, then.

disclaimer

SchNEWS warns all culture vultures if ya wanna help in the war against terrorism and stop the economy taking a nosedive then why not rush out and buy our new CD... P.S. don't forget our bargain basement books too. Honest!

Reshaping The World

Fisch

'New World Order' is the name given to this current phase of history where the world is governed in the interests of the corporations. It's also know as 'neo-liberalism' and is the consequence of the development of the same suppression rules used in colonialism, as well as the now institutionalisd economic empirialism of the World Bank/IMF/WTO. Stripping a country of its assets by privatisation or squeezing a country financially is one ways of keeping control, bombing it or having a war is another way of 'reshaping' the new world order.

100 days after the US and UK began its military campaign against Al-Qa'ida and Taliban targets in Afghanistan, the media adopted the attitude that the war is over. No matter that at least 4,000 had been murdered or that some 400,000 were displaced - either made refugees or their towns too dangerous to return to because of looters etc - the media found it unworthy of being top of their news agenda. However the US air force still continued a heavy, daily bombardment in the area around Zawar. As happened in Iraq and Colombia, the attack continues but the media attention has waned.

Demonstrating that the "war on terrorism" is a global action, 650 US troops have recently been sent to the Philippines to combat guerrillas, as well as intentions being aired of spreading the 'war' to Somalia. Iraq, still suffering the embargo, appears not to be so much of a military target, though there are movements of troops there.

It's true: this is another world war, but one that has been waging for long time. A war for capitalism, for hegemony. A multinationals' war for control of markets and resources.

President Bush, whose family is well connected to oil and energy companies, has called for an international crusade against terrorists who, he says, hate Americans simply because they are "the brightest beacon of freedom". Bush's rhetoric about fighting for justice and democracy is masking a less noble struggle for control of an estimated $5 trillion of oil and gas resources from the Caspian Basin.

One of the material results of the elder Bush's Desert Storm campaign in 1991, as well as guaranteeing the control of Kuwait's oil, was to secure access to the huge Rumaila oil field of southern Iraq. This area came under U$ control by expanding the boundaries of Kuwait after the war. American and British oil companies are heavily invested in Kuwait since being a British protectorate. Kuwait doubled its pre-war oil output as a result.

The Trepca mine complex in Kosovo, one of the richest mines in Europe, was seized last year by front companies for George Soros and Bernard Kouchner, two members of the New World Order gang who devastated Serbia. A similar geopolitical strategy to control the valuable mineral resources of the Caspian Basin underlies the planned aggression against Afghanistan, a Central Asian nation that occupies a strategic position sandwiched between the Middle East, Central Asia and the Indian subcontinent.

Central Asia has enormous quantities of undeveloped oil resources including vast amounts of natural gas, waiting to be exploited. The former Soviet republics Uzbekistan and Turkmenistan are the two major gas producers in Central Asia. A memorandum of understanding has been signed to build a 900-mile natural gas pipeline from Turkmenistan to Pakistan via Afghanistan, but the ongoing civil war and absence of a stable government in Afghanistan have delayed the project. India, Iran, Russia and Israel also have interests in the project. Afghanistan remains fundamental in the control of the area, as it was in the past when Russia and England competed for control of it.

Amoco, British Petroleum, Chevron, Exxon, Mobil, UNOCAL and Enrol before its collapse, are all engaged in a multi-billion dollar frenzy to extract the reserves of Azerbaijan, Kazakhstan, and Turkmenistan. All these companies are based in the countries leading the 'war for peace'. And an array of former cabinet members from the elder Bush administration have been actively involved in negotiations on behalf of the oil companies with these republics: James Baker, Brent Scowcroft, John Sununu and... Dick Cheney, now vice president of America. **BRISTLE**

War: What Is It Good For? Business.

War may well be a waste of resources but it's a brilliant profit maker for those who manufacture weapons and military equipment. Taking in consideration that the US, the UK (See SchNEWS 357) and all the other European governments that support wars are the main arms dealers, and a war such as Afghanistan is the best way to display their products. It's also a great way of getting rid of surplus stock - better to use than dump eh.

The U$ is spending $589,000 every minute on military - during the war and since (yes visit http://www.cdi.org/msc/clock.html). This is $850 million a day. Most of those expenses will be covered in a supplemental request that the Pentagon will forward to Congress later this year.

Meanwhile, spending on systems that have actually proved useful in Afghanistan is lagging far behind expenditures for costly pet projects favoured by the White House, key members of Congress, military bureaucrats and major weapons contractors.

Just when everybody thought that the militarist madness that had been developed in the Cold War was over, Bush - with backing by Blair - has come up with the idea that there were still enemies out there that we needed protection from. September 11 is now being used to justify this paranoia and so in December the Son of the Star Wars ballistic missile program received a $2.5 billion increase from the US Congress. **BRISTLE**

the world is watching...
FUCK THE WAR

BRISTOL 2001

From: Bristle

SPOT THE DIFFERENCE

CAN YOU TELL THE BADDY FROM THE GOODY?

ANSWER BELLOW ↓

WE CAN'T! THE NORTHERN ALLIANCE BIGOTS ARE AS BAD AS THE TALIBAN... JUST SERVING THE ALLIES' INTEREST THIS TIME!!

Black Berets

French intellectuals are to be deployed in Afghanistan to convince Taliban of the non-existence of god.

The ground war in Afghanistan hotted up yesterday when the Allies revealed plans to airdrop a platoon of crack French existentialist philosophers into the country to destroy the morale of Taliban zealots by proving the non-existence of God.

Elements from the feared Jean-Paul Sartre Brigade, or 'Black Berets', will be parachuted into the combat zones to spread doubt, despondency and existential anomie among the enemy. Hardened by numerous intellectual battles fought during their long occupation of Paris's Left Bank, their first action will be to establish a number of pavement cafes at strategic points near the front lines.

There they will drink coffee and talk animatedly about the absurd nature of life and man's lonely isolation in the universe. They will be accompanied by a number of heartbreakingly beautiful girlfriends who will further spread dismay by sticking their tongues in the philosophers' ears every five minutes and looking remote and unattainable to everyone else.

Their leader, Colonel Marc-Ange Belmondo, spoke yesterday of his confidence in the success of their mission. Sorbonne graduate Belmondo, a very intense and unshaven young man in a black pullover, gesticulated wildly and said, "The Taliban are caught in a logical fallacy of the most ridiculous. There is no God and I can prove it. Take your tongue out of my ear, Juliet, I am talking." Marc-Ange plans to deliver an impassioned thesis on man's nauseating freedom of action with special reference to the work of Foucault and the films of Alfred Hitchcock.

However, humanitarian agencies have been quick to condemn the operation as inhumane, pointing out that the effects of passive smoking from the Frenchmens' endless Gitanes could wreak a terrible toll on civilians in the area.

Speculation was mounting last night that Britain may also contribute to the effort by dropping Professor Stephen Hawking into Afghanistan to propagate his non-deistic theory of the creation of the universe.

When the dust settles on Afghanistan, will it be full of depleted uranium?

By Joanne Baker

There are serious and unanswered questions as to the current military use of depleted uranium (DU) in Afghanistan; questions which none of the mainstream media are addressing. Dai Williams, an independent researcher has concluded that, despite MoD denial, it is highly likely that the new generation of hard target guided weapons contain DU. These weapons, part of the Hard or Deeply Buried Defeat Capability Program, achieve their effectiveness by increasing the area/density ratio of the new Advanced Unitary Penetrator warheads. The only metals capable of this are DU or tungsten or a combination of the two. DU has the advantage over tungsten of being considerably cheaper and burning spontaneously on impact at an intense heat of 2,000 degrees which carbonises anyone in its range. The heat transforms much of the uranium into minute, insoluble, radioactive particles which can then be inhaled.

The controversy over the dangers of internal low level radiation is now on the political agenda. The UK Departments of Health and of the Environment have set up a new Working Group to investigate the health effects. According to many independent experts, low level alpha emitting particles which damage but do not directly kill the cell, would seem to be a major cause of the cancers, birth defects and immune deficiency syndromes that are besetting both military personnel and civilians in DU affected areas. Tests done in Berlin, show that some Gulf War veterans, with high levels of DU in the body, have three times the chromosome damage as people living in the vicinity of Chernobyl.

If DU is in the guided missile systems, then a vast tonnage may have been used in Afghanistan and the dry and dusty climate will enable the particles to be spread by wind as well as water. The contamination may extend to many parts of Pakistan. One particular concern is the bombing of the Karez, the underground tunnels in the mountains of southern Afghanistan which hold much of the regions fragile water supply. If these become contaminated with radioactive particles, the health consequences are unthinkable. DU has a half life of 4.5 billion years.

In the absence of any explicit information from the US/UK governments, the awful truth may only be known if or when the hospitals begin to fill with unprecedented numbers of cases of childhood leukaemia, congenital multiple malformations, or thyroid malfunction.

* A recent vote at the UN General Assembly resulted in a narrowly defeated effort by Iraq to have the question of DU contamination in its country properly investigated by the World Health Organisation (WHO). After extreme pressure by the US, 54 nations voted against it with 45 yes votes and 44 abstentions from countries not yet strong enough to directly oppose the US. Iraq suffers the legacy of DU from bombing during the Gulf War.

Direct Action Against Militarism and Depleted Uranium

THEY'RE THE ENEMY. THEY HIDE IN CAVES. WE'RE BOMBING THEM. WHO THEY ARE AND WHAT THEY THINK ISN'T SOMETHING YOU REALLY NEED TO WORRY ABOUT...

FA-BOOM!

Polyp

LIVE

Out Of The Frying Pan

Arif Ali (4) standing in front of the tents of the Jalozai refugee camp. He came with his parents from Kabul, arriving 4 days before the US air strikes.

Deaths caused by Al Qa'ida on September 11: nearly 3,000. Civilian deaths in Afghanistan because of the US led attacks they call 'Enduring Freedom': up to 28,000. What war on terrorism?

Before September 11 there were already over a million Afghanistani refugees fleeing a country ravaged by decades of war, political instability and drought. Immediately after September 11, when it looked like US attacks were imminent, nearly 250,000 Afghanis escaped across closed borders – the UN claiming that about 160,000 went to Pakistan, 60,000 went to Iran, and 10,000 remained in refugee camps within Afghanistan. Much trauma resulted from the upheaval, with only the

Zarmeena and her son Ali came from Kabul, crossing the border illegally into Pakistan.

These sisters, Mansoor (12), Naheed (10) and Shanaza (10 months) are from Kabul. They arrived in Pakistan 10 days before the US air strikes.

wealthier ones able to bribe border guards and maintain provisions during the journey. The toll of Afghani civilian deaths is far higher than just those known to have been killed by bombs.

The US air strikes since October 7th turned a dire situation into a total catastrophe for the average Afghani. While it is figured that up to 8,000 civilians have been killed by the US bombing – now it is estimated that another 20,000 could have died indirectly because of the war*. The droughts have compounded the hazards of displacement from home with people forced to travel long distances cut off from food and other supplies. They have spent the last winter in tents, at the mercy of aid. With the firm arm (and gun) of the Taliban rule gone, many have been murdered during incidents of looting and local ethnic conflict. And then there's the matter of depleted uranium bombs being used, the long term consequences of which may not yet be known.

When the US started bombing Afghanistan they mouthed empty promises that aid would accompany the attack to make up for the inconvenience of being bombed back to the stone age for the second time in twenty five years. What eventuated was that the international aid already being given to the country pre-September 11 was disrupted - and existing aid deliveries were lowered by 40% during the three month period after the bombing began.

* These figures are given by Jonathan Steele in The Guardian, May 20, 2002.

The media made out that the 'war on terrorism' had done the people of Afghanistan a big favour by removing the Taliban – who had ruled since 1996. The Taliban's strict Islam fundamentalism – which involved public hangings for those opposing them and other public atrocities (see www.rawa.org for the gory details) make them hardly ideal, but the removal of their heavy control and the ascendency to power of the Northern Alliance introduced rampant lawlessness, reminding people of the last time this alliance were in power before 1996.

Treena (15) arrived in the Jalozai refugee camp 10 days before the US air strikes. She said that she misses home, but that she's glad the Taliban have gone.

The US agenda to take out the Taliban involved arming and assisting an 'emerging coalition of oppositional forces' – a well-thought-out strategy which saw the Northern Alliance re-taking control. This alliance featured many of the same war criminals (such as Abdul Rashid Dostum, head of the Junbish militia), who as the Mujehadeen had ruled from 1992-1996. Their legacy was four years of massacres, rape and pillage leaving 50,000 dead in Kabul. Northern Alliance drug lords grow 70-90% of the world's opium, which mostly goes to the Triads in China - a huge racket involving banks and money laundering which the Taliban tried to crack down on.

Since October the people most subject to violence and oppression are the majority Pashtuns – who happen to be the same ethnic group as the Taliban. Despite all the maniacal fundamentalism, it is understandable that for many the Taliban would be preferable.

A lot of the homeless are in refugee camps because their houses were bombed – but many more are in the camps because their towns are subject to looting and ethnic persecution and they don't want to return.

With the US showing no regard whatsoever for the human consequences as they help a load of war criminals back into power, their agenda is obvious: putting Afghanistan on the path towards political stability? – you can eliminate that red herring immediately. Gaining military control of the region at any human cost because of its proximity to large petroleum reserves? You can read Bush like a book.

Aziz and Muhammad come from Kabul. Since arriving in Pakistan as refugees they have only had bread and water given to them as a daily meal.

Nida (10) and Meena (12) are sisters who came with their parents and their three brothers from Kabul into Pakistan.

RAWA's work continues in the midst of war

Sally Beaumont talks exclusively with Mehmooda, a member of the Revolutionary Association of the Women of Afghanistan.

Since the beginning of America's "Operation Enduring Freedom" the Revolutionary Association of the Women of Afghanistan (RAWA) have continued to provide support, education, and medical attention for the innocent victims of their devastated country.

With underground schools still running, RAWA have begun educating the young about their current positions and most importantly about truth. Speaking to Mehmooda, a RAWA member, she explained to me the changes which have ensued in their underground classes. "We have shifted some of our home based classes to the relatively safer places in all providences subjected to the air strikes. We have painstakingly tried not to stop the classes so that the students feel not much depression and fear."

Such classes involve covering the questions many Afghans are asking, as Mehmooda states, "The same holds true for the women's literacy courses, but the teachers are mainly trying to educate the women about the situation: What did the Taliban and their Arab accomplices do on September 11th in America? Who is Osama and his Al-Qaeda? What was the role of the U.S. and Pakistan in creating and assisting these criminals especially during the anti-Soviet war? Why the Northern Alliance should not seize power? We are raising awareness in the women, that there are millions of anti-terrorist people in the US and the West, who are peace loving and have sincere sympathy with the Afghan people. That they want to fight the germ of terrorism in a way without any negative effect on the already wounded people of Afghanistan and many other related points. We do our utmost to prove to them that notwithstanding our reservations, the current anti-terrorist war is not at all a religions war or a war against Islam and Muslims."

The refugee crisis in Afghanistan has escalated severely with an estimated two thousand Afghans fleeing daily. Many are met with the Taliban blocking routes and neighbouring countries closing off their borders. These innocent people are often fired upon and have no escape. The Islamic Republic of Iran deported over 2300 Afghan escapees, forcing them back into the war zone, as too did the Pakistani government, ordering its border guards to open fire on refugees attempting to enter the country - killing a 23-year old man and injuring a 13-year old child. Yet RAWA's work continues, supplying these refugees with much needed medical attention and supplies. "We have helped hundreds of women with their children to immigrate to Pakistan and accommodated almost all of them in the camps or elsewhere. Some of our mobile medical teams are going to stockpile as many supplies needed in a war situation as possible. We want to be helpful to our helpless people. That is why even none of the personnel of our mobile teams have taken refuge in Pakistan."

RAWA have also continued their extremely courageous work of covering events in their countries using hidden cameras and eyewitness accounts. And now the world is listening albeit not as much as it should to the undeniably courageous work of these women and the extreme problems that have plagued Afghanistan for decades. "We've received reports of civilian casualties. Few of them have been posted on our website and the rest are to be translated and posted on the site. Also we've filmed about 10-hour video footages from recent destruction due to the strikes, and interviews with victims. They all have already been given to world media and TV channels in Germany and other European countries."

"In the past few weeks we've been interviewed by over 500 journalists and publications the world over have published articles about RAWA. Among them are The Washington Post, The Guardian, The Los Angeles Times, The Chicago Tribune, ABC news, BBC, CNN, NBC and many more. However the changing situation has not affected our underground status in Afghanistan or even in Pakistan, because the Taliban are still at the helm and their Pakistani brethren are very much active in Pakistan. However, we are still mainly underground organisation."

With their current focus and illumination, RAWA's security is being hindered, even in Pakistan, as Mehmooda states, "Yes, we are being persecuted in Pakistan more than before and the Taliban are keeping an eye to hunt any RAWA activist wherever possible. However, it could be also said that the focus on RAWA has been positive because the world would know that the women of Afghanistan also resist the Taliban or other criminal fundamentalist bands like the Northern Alliance. RAWA is determined to continue the hard struggle against these enemies of mankind till the end. Anyway for the sake of our cause and to get the voice of our voiceless women heard around the world, we have to cope with danger."

From *The Paper* issue 24 www.thepaper.org.au

www.rawa.org

All We Are Saying...

In the aftermath of 11 September - and particularly once the attack on Afghanistan started - the 'anti-war movement' took flight. In the first week after the bombing started, there were around 400 known protests in 40 countries. 100,000 gathered in Rome, 30,000 in Naples, and despite all the blind ignorant patriotism and media rubbish, there were mass demonstrations in the US including 25,000 marching in Washington. All sorts of anti-war coalitions and networks sprang up all over Britain:

Muscling in immediately in London were the Socialist Worker Party/Socialist Alliance/Globalise Resistance grouping who convened what it hoped would be a Britain-wide coalition to Stop the War (STW) on the usual 'committee' basis (SchNEWS are gutted we weren't part of that - ed). As it turns out many groups around the country preferred to work with their own networks, staying out of the London STW framework.

A grassroots anti-war movement mobilised all over the country, in all sorts of amazing ways. Of course there were the headline events, such as the massive CND and Stop The War coalition demonstrations in London including the 100,000 strong 'Not In Our Name' march on November 18th, and 40,000 marching in solidarity with Palestine in May.

Anti-war demo outside Downing St, London, 21st October Pic: Alec Smart

More at the grass roots level: a vigil was held every day in Bristol outside the Hippodrme, and continued all through the winter.

Three coalitions emerged in Wales, one of them being the North Wales 'Coalition for a Just Peace', initiated by peace activists also involved in Welsh language activism and Plaid Cymru. As in Wales, the Scottish activist scene saw amicable relations between different elements: Women in Black, religious groups, trade unions, nationalists, greens, CND and other peace groups, and the Scottish Socialist Party all came together to form and support the 'Scottish Coalition for Justice not War'.

The Quakers played a role in the anti-war movement by opening up their meeting houses for action planning. Amongst others the Newcastle Stop The War group came through this – and went on to function as a loose network rather than a formal 'committee' system as preferred by the Stop The War bods.

Trafalgar Square, November 18th Pic: Guy Smallman

Trafalgar Square, November 18th. Pic: Lawrence Renee

Up and down the country groups – such as the 'Justice Not Vengeance' affinity group in London, and the ongoing 'Direct Action Against War Now' network (DAAWN) - held vigils and weekly meetings for months. Groups also campaigned against anti-Muslim and racist prejudice.

In February 2002 ARROW and Voices in the Wilderness UK hosted a visit by two relatives of Craig Amundson, who died in the Pentagon on 11 September. Craig's brother Ryan and his sister-in-law Kelly Campbell spoke out against military retaliation, and announced the formation of 'Peaceful Tomorrows', an anti-war network of US September 11 relatives www.peacefultomorrows.org.

There have been all kinds of civil disobedience, including the ARROW-initiated sit-down in Whitehall on 13 October 2001, when 600 people blocked off one side of Whitehall for an hour and a half; several blockades at Northwood, the headquarters of Britain's expeditionary forces (organised by the 'D10' group); lock-ons at Downing Street; lamp-post climbing in Parliament Square; sit-downs during some of the big marches (organised by 'DAAWN'); and 'die-ins' in Manchester.

In 2002 much of the focus of the anti-war movement moved to the threat of war on Iraq, and Israel's brutal occupation of Palestine. The media manipulated public attention by treating the war as having finished when the Taliban were taken from power – but the bombing and military presence continues (as it does in Iraq a decade after the Gulf War).

Thanks to Milan Rai

ARROW (Active Resistance to the Roots of War)
www.justicenotvengeance.org

Anti-war demo Bristol 11th October Pic: Simon Chapman

To sell a war you need professionals

When the Government of **Kuwait** needed to get its message across, we were there to help.

In 1991, PR consultants The Rendon Group and Hill and Knowlton Inc. represented 'Citizens for a Free Kuwait', a Kuwaiti government front group. In one of the largest and most sophisticated propaganda campaigns in history they successfully persuaded a sceptical American public to support war against Iraq.

When the **CIA** needed propaganda expertise they turned to us.

After the Gulf War, The Rendon Group was hired by the CIA to conduct a covert propaganda campaign against Saddam Hussein, which included blocking criticism of the sanctions. Their fees totalled almost $100m. A Rendon spokesperson said "Every two months or so there would be a report about starving Iraqi babies. We'd be on hand to counter that."

Today we are the **Pentagon**'s first choice in managing their communications needs.

In October The Rendon Group was hired by the Pentagon to help shape their communications strategy for the War on Terror.

John Rendon, who describes himself as "an information warrior and a manager of perceptions," is charged with spinning the war to the peoples of the world.

Because

sometimes democracy is not enough

For more information:

WWW.PRWATCH.ORG
Lots of info on the PR industry.

Voices in the Wilderness
www.viwuk.freeserve.co.uk
Campaign to break the immoral sanctions against the people of Iraq.

Corporate Watch
www.corporatewatch.org.uk
Information on corporations.

The **RENDON** Group Inc.
Information as an element of power

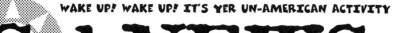
SchNEWS

Weekly

Printed and Published in Brighton by Justice?

Friday 12th October 2001   www.schnews.org.uk   **Issue 326**   **Free/Donation**

COURTIN' TROUBLE

"This legislation is, in effect, a protection of war criminals" - William Pace, Convenor of the Coalition for the International Criminal Court.

While America tells the world to get behind its 'global war against terrorism' and support the bombing of Afghanistan, a law is being rushed through that will scupper attempts to set up an international criminal court - a court which would be the very body to bring to justice those responsible for the attacks on September 11th. The proposed law has the backing of Bush and has already been passed in the House of Representatives.

The Coalition for the International Criminal Court was formed in 1995 and is a network of over a thousand non-governmental organizations and international law experts from every corner of the world. It's pushing for the creation of a permanent and independent International Criminal Court (ICC) that "will investigate and bring to justice individuals who commit war crimes, crimes against humanity and genocide." 42 countries, including the UK, have signed the treaty which ICC Convenor William Pace, reckons "will be a powerful international legal tool in the fight against global terrorism." The US however doesn't want anything to do with it, complaining that "its power could be easily misused to make capricious arrests of American officials or military personnel abroad." Because as everybody knows, the rest of the world commits war crimes but not the good ol' USA.

So using the current climate of patriotic hysteria Republican lunatic Senator Jesse Helms is pushing a bill of extreme anti-ICC legislation - The American Servicemembers' Protection Act. The Act aims to stop the convention getting the magic number of 60 countries signing up to it - which is how many signatures are needed to make the ICC international law.

Amongst the highlights the Act threatens to cut off military aid to countries that ratify the ICC treaty - apart from NATO, Israel and Egypt - hoping this economic blackmail will stop weaker countries signing up. These are often the countries which are backed by the US, have bad human rights records, and in some cases are the places where war crimes are being committed. The Act would mean that the US military would not take on any UN peacekeeping roles unless they were made exempt from ICC prosecution. It would prohibit US cooperation with ICC inspectors even in a case of international terrorism and give the American President "all means necessary and appropriate to bring about the release from captivity of US or allied personnel detained or imprisoned against their will by or on behalf of the Court, including military force." This in theory could lead to the invasion and bombing of Holland, since the ICC will be based in The Hague! As Richard Dicker of Human Rights Watch points out " the State Department has just endorsed a bill that authorizes an invasion of the Netherlands." No wonder critics are calling it the Invade the Hague Act.

All this hasn't gone to well with America's allies. A European delegate at the United Nations said that legislation "imposing military and legal reprisals is unprecedented and unacceptable." While Richard Dicker,added "This makes no sense. It hardly seems like a good moment for the U.S. to be threatening sanctions against dozens of countries simply because they want to bring to justice the perpetrators of crimes against humanity."

Forget the talk about a war on terrorism, America wants to be the worlds judge, jury and executioner. As comedian and activist Mark Thomas points out "In a sickening display of hypocrisy America is acting in its own narrow interests with typical double standards. Supporting terrorism is bad except when we do it, the rule of law is good except when it might be used against us, war crimes must be punished except if we commit them. Standing shoulder to shoulder? No chance! America's natural position is standing behind another country pointing a gun at its head."

* More info on the court: www.iccnow.org

TV WAR

While the western world watches the gigantic fireworks display on our TV 'screens' its easy to forget that real people are being bombarded each day. No matter what we are told about smart and precision bombing, many rockets will miss their targets and many targets will include civilians anyway – on the second night of bombing 4 UN workers whose job was clearing one of the most landmined countries in the world lost their lives while they slept.

Still, Bush and Blair say they haven't got an argument with the ordinary Afghani people which must be reassuring for those being bombed every night, or forced to flee, or whose UN food supplies have stopped. But don't panic, there's an American once-in-a-lifetime 37,500 one-day ration packs which will go far in a country with millions of starving people. Still, as President Bush

explained on Sunday "the oppressed people of Afghanistan will know the generosity of America and our allies." So, here have some of our free missiles as well. Still, the bombing has achieved one thing, managing to turn an existing humanitarian crisis into a disaster, which will cause the deaths of many more than were slaughtered in the World Trade Centre.

* SchNEWS is no apologist for the Taliban regime - check out some of the sickening stories posted on the website of the Revolutionary Association of the Women of Afghanistan (RAWA). RAWA is a human rights feminist organisation, and the site gives first-hand reports of atrocities, and inspiring stories about the ways in which Afghan women have been risking their lives fighting the regime. Check it out at www.rawa.org

* This Saturday (13) March for Peace 12 noon in Hyde Park (Marble Arch end) for march at 1pm to Trafalgar Square for rally. CND 020-7700-2350 www.cnduk.org./cnd. www.wombleaction.mrnice.net.Transport from Brighton 01273-620125

* Give Peace A Dance – happening in 45 countries and 100 cities across the world including synchronised dancefloor linkup when every DJ in every city plays the same track www.earthdance.org

* Anti-war demos and vigils are happening around the world. www.uk.indymedia.org/

* A dozen people occupied Brighton's army recruiting centre yesterday. Police closed off the road for an hour and arrested two people who scaled scaffolding and unfurled a banner saying 'sabotage the war effort.'

* Bypass corporate media war machine: www.alternet.org www.indymedia.org

REBEL ALLIANCE

The irregular get together of Brighton's direct action rabble. Hear reports of what different groups have been doing/will do and take part in the discussion about the war on terrorism. 17th October, upstairs at the Albert Pub, 7.30pm sharp.

* Pick up a booklet of groups involved in the Alliance at Brighton Peace Centre.

FRIEND OR FOE?

The USA's new buddies in Pakistan are now the good guys since they started siding with the US, but little attention has been paid to abuses of democracy and human rights in a country with a long history of military rule. Also forgotten is the fact that much of the anti-American feeling in Pakistan has been caused by the intervention of our old friends the IMF.

The Pakistan military regime, headed by General Musharraf, overthrew the last democratically elected government in 1999. In August 2001, Musharraf announced a schedule for elections and restoration of democracy but this has now been conveniently forgotten. The USA seems happy with this. Colin Powel, on NBC Television, said that the US has no concern over their nuclear programme and 'guarantees' that the Musharraf government will remain stable. Given their past history, however, this seems unlikely. Whilst they are currently sucking up to the US, not so long ago Musharref was declaring his support for the Taliban.

So why the sudden change of heart? Pakistan's alliance with the US during the Cold War earned it huge sums of IMF money, (as usual, this money didn't help the ordinary people but ended up in the hands of military generals, bureaucrats and corrupt politicians). Once the Cold War was over, Pakistan wasn't needed as a US base-camp. This meant 'pay-back' time. Pakistan is crippled by two drains on its annual budget: 40% goes on military spending, and another 40% goes on debt repayment. Any attempts at Democratic government in the past have been scuppered as they are forced to conform to IMF capitalist dictats in order to receive any support. As always, this means privatisation, taxation – in short, anything which makes money for corporations and makes life hell for ordinary people. So what does it take for the IMF to help this time? you've guessed it, siding with the USA. Since September 24th, sanctions imposed by the US for Pakistan's nuclear weapons use in 1998 have been lifted, and look to be followed by other countries including Japan and Australia. Other perks include $90 million in grants from the US and Japan, and drastic debt rescheduling by the IMF and countries including US and Britain - something that was never done for democratically elected governments.

Also forgotten or ignored have been the many human rights abuses committed by the current regime in Pakistan. The regime has been Islamizing key institutions since the early 1980's - sound a bit familiar? Human Rights Watch have released a report documenting horrific conditions for women, with domestic violence at levels of up to 90%. Honour-killings are common, and up to 60% of women prisoners are being detained under the Hudood Ordinance - penal laws prohibiting sex outside of marriage, which have had a devastating impact on women's rights (see www.hrw.org). So the message is, commit as many abuses of human rights as you want, test as many nuclear weapons as you can, and as long as you side with the US, you'll be OK. And meanwhile the people of Pakistan suffer on both sides.

*More info: www.labour.00server.com/LabourPartyPakistan

Inside SchNEWS

There will be a benefit night at Easton Community Centre in Bristol on 19th October to raise funds for legal fees and prisoner support for those arrested during the demos in Gothenburg and Genoa. Punk bands – Conflict, Icons of Filth, Bug Central, Disruptive Element and DJs playing Techno, Drum'n'Bass and Beats. Doors 10pm - 4am. £5.

SchNEWS in brief

Brighton's premier pirate station **Radio4A** is on the airwaves this weekend: (12-14) with music, party sound system and speech on 106.6 FM. e: Radio4A-subscribe@yahoogroups.com to receive latest schedules etc. ** **Sainsbury's** have put in another planning application for the **Brighton station site,** BUDD have organised a public meeting to continue resistance. Brighthelm Centre, Church St, 24th Oct. 7.30pm. ** Support your local radical info shop - The **Peace and Environment** Centre in Gardner Street has just stocked up with loads of AK Press literature, why not visit them instead of corporate bookshops. ** Call the office to book your place for the next **SchNEWS Training Day,** 24th Oct. 12 noon onwards. ** **Faslane Peace Camp** stepped up actions recently: occupying a 124ft crane for 12 hours and banner drops at Glasgow MoD buildings. Big blockade 22nd Oct., 01436-820901 www.faslanepeacecamp.com ** Speak Out Against Racism - **Defend Asylum Rights** - Hands Around the Home Office Vigil. Bring candles 5.30-7pm, Home Office, 50 Queen Anne's Gate, SW1. EU governments are meeting 16-17th October to discuss changing the 1951 Geneva Convention's definition of a refugee to tighten asylum laws. Contact: 020 7247 9907/07879 612 234 ** In a blow for companies trying to make a mint out of public services, **Brighton's bin service** is once again being run by the city council for a trial period of 18 months. The last private contractor, SITA, was forced out after the bin-men went on strike (see SchNEWS 308/309) and the council has been unable to find a 'suitable replacement. Which is a shame. ***Cannabis campaigner* Kevin Lippiatt has been repeatedly arrested while testing the laws surrounding cannabis for three years. Support him in Truro Crown Court at 10am, 24th Oct. Contact him: 31 Chapel Road, Tucking Mill, Cambourne, Cornwall. ** The next lot of **Hackney** community property sell offs takes place at Nelson Bakewell Auction, 1.30pm 15th Oct., Langham Hilton Hotel, Portland Place, W1. Community groups and residents will protest outside the auction, as well as a samba band and the Nelson Bakewell 'spoof estate agent' photographic display showing the vast extent of planned sell offs and closures. hackney4sale@yahoo.co.uk

WATERFIGHT

"The community set up burning barricades all day to try and prevent the police force from coming in to help the Council cut off the water of 1800 households…they shot 15 people, some with rubber bullets and some with live ammunition. A 5-year-old was shot in the back and one woman was shot three times. Some of the people who were shot seem to be missing." - Faizel, from the anti-eviction campaign.

In December last year the Capetown Unicity council demanded outstanding debts on council owned houses and businesses be paid within a month. Afterwards they began evicting families that could not pay and an anti-eviction campaign began. They have been successful in resisting the evictions and now the council have started to cut off the communities water and electricity. Eyewitness Ashraf Cassiem said at the time, "There seem to be a million police in the area. People are standing outside everywhere in the street weeping openly. The private workers and protection services have succeeded in carrying out most of the 1800 water cut-offs. People are desperately trying to reconnect their water with pieces of old hosepipe, and string - it doesn't seem to be working. Nobody knows where they can go now to get water."

More info: http://southafrica.indymedia.org or email - faiz@union.org.za

BACKTRACK

SchNEWS asks its readers to spare a thought for those poor shareholders of Railtrack who are suffering from the company collapsing this week after the government refused to give it any more cash. All those poor investors are losing money and threatening to sue the government for not bailing out Railtrack once again. Now, some of our more cynical readers might be thinking that these gold diggers deserve to lose the profits they made from the sell-off of our national assets, but maybe they should ask the relatives of the people who lost their lives at Paddington and Hatfield whether they should be reimbursed, seeing as the profits went to shareholders instead of rail safety.

Anarchist Bookfair

The Anarchist Bookfair celebrates its 20th Birthday by moving to a new larger venue at the Camden Centre, Euston Road, London (near King's Cross) on 20th October. There's gonna be loads of information, books, CDs and Videos. Here's a selection of stuff on offer:

"ON FIRE: The battle of Genoa and the anti-capitalist movement" This has sixteen different accounts of what happened in Genoa and has plenty of constructive criticisms of what tactics the movement should adopt. Essential reading and at only £3 it's a bargain. AK Distribution 0131-5555165 www.akuk.com

"The allotment handbook – a guide to promoting and protecting your site" by Sophie Andrews is a handy little book full of bite size pieces of info on everything from making allotments more sexy to inspiring community garden success stories around the country. Eco-logic books 0117-9420165. www.eco-logicbooks.com

"Monopolise Resistance? How Globalise Resistance would hijack revolt." A SchNEWS pamphlet that investigates the SWP front group. Get it from SchNEWS for 2x1st Class stamps + SAE – or come to our workshop at the bookfair.

And after being book worms all day why not come along to the after party at the Lord Cecil Pub, Lower Clapton Road. Bands include Riot Clone, Harum Scarum, Bug Central and Kismetic HC. Door tax £4 going to SHAC, Emmaz (soon to be opened @ social centre) and Anarchist Bookfair.

...and finally...

The World's Worst Job Revealed: Think you've got a crap job and living on hand outs? Well, spare a thought for Mohd Binatang who won the 'worst job in Singapore' award. He works in the local zoo collecting sperm samples from the animals, by giving them a spot of hand relief each morning. He starts collecting at 4am as the animals are usually standing to attention then. Apparently the orangutan likes to be kissed first, and the chimpanzees like a cuddle afterwards. However, the most difficult client is the elephant because of its size. Poor old Mohd has to use both hands, which makes him feel like a bell-ringer in a cathedral, and when the elephant finally comes, it's like "being sprayed with hot glue"(and they say size doesn't matter). The job is also affecting his sex-life, as he can't stop thinking about ejaculating rhinos and their horns. The animals' breeding habits are also sufferring because they can't be bothered to have sex anymore. So next time you moan about getting up for work, be thankful you don't work at Singapore zoo!

Subscribe!
Keep SchNEWS FREE! Send 1st Class stamps (e.g. 10 for next 9 issues) or donations (payable to Justice?) Ask for "Originals" if you can make copies. Post *free* to all prisoners. SchNEWS, c/o on-the-fiddle, P.O. Box 2600, Brighton, East Sussex, BN2 0EF.
Tel/Autofax +44 (0)1273 685913 Email **schnews@brighton.co.uk** *Download a **PDF** of this issue or subscribe at* **www.schnews.org.uk**

WAKE UP! IT'S YER SHOPPING AS THE BOMBS ARE DROPPING

Weekly SchNEWS

I shop therefore I am

Printed and Published in Brighton by Justice?

Friday 19th October 2001   **www.schnews.org.uk**   **Issue 327**   **Free/Donation**

DESERT STORM

Next month's World Trade Organisation (WTO) meeting takes place in the protest friendly desert of Qatar – with America and its allies using the 'war on terrorism' to try and push forward a new world trade round.

The WTO is the world's most powerful trade organisation, backed by its big business mates to eliminate 'barriers to trade' (annoying little things like environmental laws, workers rights…) and push for the privatisation of everything they can get their grubby mits on. But since the Seattle protests two years ago (SchNEWS 240) the WTO and 'free' trade in general has been facing a bit of a P.R. crisis. Since the attacks on America however, free trade has become, like shopping, a patriotic duty. According to US Trade Representative Robert Zoellick, trade "promotes the values at the heart of this protracted struggle." Meanwhile one New York Times commentator equated freedom fighting with free trade, explaining that the traders who died were targeted as "not merely symbols but also practitioners of liberty.... They work hard, if unintentionally, to free others from constraints. This makes them, almost by default, the spiritual antithesis of the religious fundamentalist, whose business depends on a denial of personal liberty in the name of some putatively higher power." We've heard of merchant bankers being called *other* things but freedom fighters is a new one to SchNEWS!

As for the protestors that have dogged international conferences ever since Seattle…well in the eyes of some the protestors' 'war' against capital and globalisation is no better than Bin Laden .

While dismissing the protestors, the majority of Western media has kept conspicuously silent about the stance taken by the poorest countries of the world. Tanzanian President, Benjamin Mkapa, speaking on behalf of the 41 Least Developed Countries said the group opposes a new trade round and that the "rules of the global economy and trade that end up making poor countries poorer, instead of narrowing the gap between the rich and poor, are rules that Tanzania has opposed and will continue to oppose with all its strength as co-ordinator of least developed countries." Still, what do the poor countries matter? At the end of last month, the WTO's General Council put up a draft declaration in which everything the rich countries wanted out of a new trade round was trumpeted while all demands of developing countries were ignored.

Trading Blockheads

Every day 37,000 people die from diseases such as AIDS, malaria, and tuberculosis. Most of these deaths are in poor countries where many life-saving drugs are unaffordable as they are patented under rules set by the WTO. At a meeting last month, over fifty developing countries proposed to reinterpret these rules to guarantee the right of governments to have access to affordable medicines. This was blocked by the US and Switzerland who issued a statement which, surprise surprise, mimicked the well-rehearsed views of corporate pharmaceutical companies.

The rich nations are going all gung-ho about expanding the General Agreement on the Trades in Services (GATS - SchNEWS 286) where water, education, hospitals,etc. are sold off to the lowest bidder. In the last two years there's been massive global resistance to privatisation of these services. But as one WTO official says GATS help "overcome domestic resistance to change" meaning once a country signs up to GATS and opens a service to WTO rules, it is practically impossible to go back on any agreement whatever the protests.

Meanwhile Sri Lanka has dropped its plans to ban the import of genetically modified food after a 'request' from the WTO, telling them the ban was against free trade rules. This came after pressure from the US, worried about its 4% of agricultural goods it exports to Sri Lanka. They argued that the ban had no 'scientific basis', despite concerns about GMOs being raised by scientific bodies from the World Health Organisation, to America's own Environmental Protection Agency. Many nations also have a moral basis for setting limits on GMOs. For instance, the insertion of a human gene into the fish tilapia makes it unacceptable to practitioners of some religions in Sri Lanka. Pete Riley of Friends of the Earth said "Bush's administration have once again been shown to dance to the tune of the biotech companies in lobbying for WTO action against Sri Lanka. It is time the US government and the WTO understood that individual countries have laws which reflect their culture and environment and are not merely satellites of the USA".

The protests that shut down the last WTO meeting in Seattle helped inspire a growing worldwide anti-capitalist movement. Now governments across the globe are using knee-jerk terrorism laws that will also come in handy to target protestors. Capitalist commentators are saying that the time has passed for the protesters with the Financial Times suggesting (*hoping*) that the anti-globalisation bandwagon has

been derailed "With America (and Britain) on the offensive, the counter capitalist movement is in retreat."

With the WTO meeting in the protest-free country of Qatar it's time to leave the world's elite to bake in the desert and take the struggle back to our communities.

* The west and WTO officials, worried about their safety since the bombing of Afghanistan, are trying to push Qatar into agreeing to move the meeting to Singapore.

* 'Free trade: trick or treat for the world's poor?' Westminster Central Hall, Storey's Gate, London. 3rd Nov. Speakers include Trevor Ngwane (Soweto Electricity Crisis Committee & Anti-Privatisation Forum, South Africa) and Kathy-Ann Brown (Trade negotiator for the Caribbean at the WTO) 6-8pm. free but to book a place contact World Development Movement 020-7737-6215 www.wdm.org.uk

* Trade Justice Parade 3rd Nov. Start at 12.30pm from Geraldine Mary Harmsworth Park, (Imperial War Museum), Lambeth Road, London for a march to Trafalgar Sq. 07870-823485 www.tradejusticemovement.org.uk

* Global Day of Action against the WTO, 9th Nov. "Work stoppages? Street parties? Public meetings? Squatted info-centres? What will you do?" Action ideas: Peoples Global Action www.agp.org. Manchester Earth First! 0161-2266814 mancef@nematode.freeserve.co.uk. London Reclaim the Streets, PO Box 9656, London N4 4JY; 020-7281-4261 www.reclaimthestreets.net

* Keep up to date with WTO goings on, check out Third World Network www.twnside.org.sg

EARLY CLOSING

Processions of drumming, dancing, bank-window-breaking, American-flag-burning and chanting protestors in Toronto successfully disrupted a day's trading on October 16th in the city's financial district. Despite a dozen arrests prior to the protest, and a heavy police presence, several thousand protesters from over 80 different groups gathered at five in the morning (which puts all us lazy British activists to shame) and blockaded streets in the city centre to protest against the policies of the Conservative government. Protesters went off into several different 'snake marches' after they had all met up, making it much harder for the cops to keep everyone penned in. Offices were empty at 9am, as financial workers went up on their way to work by large slow vehicles on main routes, with many being advised by their employers not to go to work. More info: http://ontario.indymedia.org and www.ocap.ca

WAR AGAINST WHAT?

While the world is busy watching Afghanistan getting bombed back in to the Stone Age, another American-sponsored war has reached its 1st anniversary. In autumn 2000 Bill Clinton authorised the start of Plan Colombia, (SchNEWS 273) a war supposedly against drugs, but which has had far reaching effects on the campesinos (peasant farmers) way of life, not to mention the bio-diversity of the Amazon Basin. Plan Colombia is the US Government's term for: (a) spraying rebel held areas with an extremely poisonous pesticide called Roundup Ultra to wipe out the coca plant. (Coca is a large part of campesino culture - the equivalent to drinking tea in England. Traditionally eaten raw, it's a valuable source of vitamins A, D and E and a cure for altitude sickness), and (b) to fund the Colombian military and right wing paramilitary to the tune of $1.3bn to fight against the rebel guerrilla army FARC who control 40% of the country. Trade unionists, human rights activists and campesinos living in the rebel held area have become victims of this dirty war, killed by death squads - decapitation by chainsaw is a common form of 'punishment' used. Because of these atrocities and the poisoning of their land, 315,000 people have been displaced in the last year.

Roundup Ultra, made by our old friends Monsanto, is a stronger version of Roundup, a cocktail of pesticides including glyphosate, cosmoflux and POEA. Normal Roundup has been shown to be hazardous to humans, the environment and animals, Roundup Ultra has even more dire effects with campesinos complaining of skin infections, hair loss, headaches, nausea, vomiting, and who knows what in the future, because this stronger version contains untested additives. Roundup was designed to be sprayed in small doses at ground level, not hundreds of gallons from the air.

'War against drugs' is a smoke screen to hide the real intentions. The U.S. imports more oil from Colombia, Venezuela and Ecuador than from the entire Persian Gulf and 80% of Colombia's oil reserves remain unexplored. As Stan Goff, a former U.S. special forces intelligence sergeant put it "The purpose of Plan Colombia is defending the operations of Occidental, BP and Texas Petrol and securing control of future oil fields…the main interest of the U.S. is oil." So it's no surprise that oil companies were pushing hard for the U.S. to provide military 'aid' to protect their interests in this country. Colombia has always had a history of strong grassroots resistance to neo-liberalism and that's what Plan Colombia is out to stop. For more info: www.narconews.com

Pull The Other One Up

Sometimes the law works on our side, especially for cases of people who trash GM crops. Since Greenpeace GM crop-pullers were found 'not guilty' of theft and criminal damage by a jury, the police and Crown Prosecution Service have been pursuing charges of Aggravated Trespass instead. This can only be tried by a Magistrate, and they tend to ignore "public interest defences", (e.g. GM crops cause pollution - so it's in the public interest to pull them up). But a High Court judge has ruled that there can't be any aggravation if no-one is working in the field. There are about 20 other crop-pullers awaiting charges, SchNEWS wonders what the Crown Prosecution Service will pick to do next. To find out where your nearest GM test site is - www.geneticsaction.org.uk/testsites or contact Genetic Engineering Network 020-7272-1586.

CARBON COPY

Pssst! Wanna buy some pollution? At the upcoming climate talks in Marrakech, Morocco (Oct. 29th - Nov. 9th), world leaders, big business and NGOS will create a new market of 'carbon credits' in global warming pollution. The smokescreen behind this is that it will enable more cost-effective market driven measures to be developed to combat global warming. But with the trade in credits worth US$13 trillion a year, its just another piece in the global capitalist babylon jigsaw. Countries with the greatest economic power will protect their own gas-guzzling ways, while cash-strapped poor countries will sell their credits. In future these countries may not be able to develop their industries without buying up pollution credits from the rich guys - reinforcing economic inequalities. It's not just all the work of the oil companies - international accountancy firms are rubbing their greasy palms in anticipation at facilitating the trade in emissions.

What about the environment? This seems to have been forgotten. A cut of 60-90% in greenhouse gas emissions is needed to stave off climate change, the pathetic 5.2% cut agreed at the last meeting will not be changed.

It is important to show resistance to this privatisation of our atmosphere. Rising Tide are calling for local actions to highlight climate change: street theatre, car-free-zones, paint cycle lanes, target your local gas guzzler firm, airline or branch of international accountancy firms like PricewaterhouseCoopers and Arthur Andersons, and demonstrate the effects of flooding. Info and ideas see www.risingtide.nl, UK contacts: www.risingtide.org.uk, 0113-262-9365.

* Changes to the way electricity is bought and sold in the UK have led to the withdrawal of a number of Combined Heat and Power plants (where excess heat from power plants is used to heat industrial areas, leading to a reduction in pollution). Also wind-farms have had their income cut by up to 60%, this is affecting the government's own target of producing 10% of electricity from renewable sources, it is currently a pathetic 2%.

* Reclaim the Streets have produced an excellent spoof leaflet about BP, called Beyond Petroleum? For a copy send an SAE to Reclaim the Streets.

Positive SchNEWS

Did you know that £6.5 billion worth of energy is wasted annually in the UK - £110 for every person in the country. To try and sort this out next week is Energy Awareness Week (27th-31st). For some hot energy saving tips and a free home energy action pack, call the Energy Efficiency hotline 0845 727 7200 or check out www.saveenergy.co.uk

Brighton Briefs

Anarcho Feminist Brighton Health Collective's first ever Herbal Co-op stall, at the Unemployed Centre, Tilbury Place, Fri 26th Oct 10.30-1.00, then every Friday after.www.geocitiies.com/anarchofeministhealth** SchWhoops! BUDD's meeting about the Sainsbury's development at the Brighton Station site will be in the Brighthelm Centre, North Road (not Church Street), 24th Oct. 7.30pm. ** Education for the 21st Century - Democratic approaches in education, with Yaacov Hecht (founder of democratic school in Hadera, Israel, & now runs the Institute for Democratic Education. Linked to proposals for a democratic school in Brighton. 7-9pm, 22nd Oct., Academy for Creative Training, 8-10 Rock Place, Kemp Town, Brighton, Tickets: Ian Cunningham 01273-703691, cunning@pavilion.co.uk

SchNEWS in brief

London RTS want contributions for a free newspaper about the 'war on terrorism' the West's lust for oil, racism, the repression of our movement and how people are trying to come up with a radical response. Send ideas, comments, material, cash etc. to them (details on front page) shells@gn.apc.org ** Sunday (21) Mass Sit-down for Afghan aid/against U.S. bombing. Meet Temple Place, London, 1p.m. 07947839992 ** Check out and distribute the excellent 'Against War and Terrorism' at www.struggle.ws/issues/war/pamOCT01.html ** COPEX have their annual British arms fair selling Internal Security, Riot Control and 'Less Than Lethal Munitions', Sandown Racecourse, Oct. 30th – Nov 1st, Campaign Against the Arms Trade will protest against this, meet 30th Oct. 10am, Esher Train Station. Contact 020-7281-0297, www.caat.org.uk ** An old London Greenpeace leaflet 'Why the Media Sucks' has been updated and is hot off the press at this Saturday's Anarchist Bookfair (10am-7pm Camden Centre, Euston Road, London). Donations wanted to help print 'Verbal Abuse' about government and media abuse of the words 'terrorism' and 'democracy'. Offers of help to hamsters@talk.to *** March: Saturday 27th, Gloucester "to demand a full enquiry before we are all wiped out by large faceless conglomerates who are rapidly claiming our land and heritage." Meet 12:30 pm. at The Park.

...and finally...

After Seattle, Prague and Genoa, watch out for the 'Walk for Capitalism,' apparently happening in cities all around the world on December 2nd, or D2, as they've it called. The pin-stripe brigade will take to the streets to proclaim their love for the free market economy. Probably. Fat cats will carry coloured ribbons to symbolise different strands of the 'get rich quick' theory: Navy blue - the rule of law, justice and the ideas of the American founding fathers; sky blue (get this) - creativity, benevolence and happiness!!! Since when did capitalism promote this stuff? We reckon somebody's pulling our plonkers but check it out for yourselves at http://walkforcapitalism.org

Meanwhile, U.S. corporations are telling people to march out to the stores and buy to take their minds off the war. An advert for gym equipment has a woman dressed in a leotard solemnly saying that America should be strong in this time of crisis… and what better way to keep strong than to buy one of our wonderful work out machines at only $399.95.

General Motors have brought out an advert showing an endless open road. "C'mon America, buy some wheels and burn some gas… .Forget about free speech and the freedom of religion. The greatest freedom is the freedom to drive…the freedom to escape…the freedom to just get up and go." But it's not all going their way. On the 23rd November there's going to be another 'Buy Nothing Day.' As Adbusters say "This year celebrants in more than 50 countries will opt not to spend any money for 24 hours, but instead to enjoy pranks, parades, street parties, credit card cut-ups –and some quality time with friends and family. Why not join us?" SchNEWS asks how long before this unpatriotic bunch are locked up for good. http://adbusters.org/campaigns/bnd/

Subscribe!

Keep SchNEWS FREE! Send 1st Class stamps (e.g. 10 for next 9 issues) or donations (payable to Justice?) Ask for "Originals" if you can make copies. Post free to all prisoners. SchNEWS, c/o on-the-fiddle, P.O. Box 2600, Brighton, East Sussex, BN2 0EF. Tel/Autofax +44 (0)1273 685913 Email schnews@brighton.co.uk Download a PDF of this issue or subscribe at www.schnews.org.uk

CONGO: THE WESTERN HEART OF DARKNESS

by Asad Ismi, October 2001

'I'm interested in land not [black people]'. *Cecil Rhodes*

RARELY has Western savagery been more destructive than in the Congo. After 115 years of Belgian colonialism and U.S. neo-colonialism, the Democratic Republic of Congo (DRC) today is a war-ravaged, balkanized country where an incredible 2.5 million people have died during the last 2 ½ years and 2.3 million have been displaced. OXFAM called this "the world's biggest humanitarian disaster." The catastrophic war which began in August 1998 has been imposed on the long-suffering Congolese by U.S. proxies Rwanda and Uganda which have occupied the eastern half of the Congo and are plundering and looting it with most of the proceeds going to the West.

KING LEOPOLD AND THE CIA

Genocide and plunder have been Western policy towards the mineral-rich Congo since the Berlin Conference of 1885 when European nations divided Africa between them, and King Leopold II of Belgium got the Congo as his personal property. Ten million Congolese were killed under Belgian rule which lasted until 1960. The Congo's population was cut in half. Belgian domination was marked by slavery, forced labour and torture aimed at extracting the maximum amount of ivory and rubber from the Central African country. The people of the Congo "probably suffered more than any other colonized group." Their hands were cut off for not working hard enough and on one day 1,000 severed hands were delivered in baskets to an official. Women were kidnapped to force their husbands to collect rubber sap and Congolese were shot for sport. Such atrocities were documented by George Washington Williams, an African-American visiting the Congo, who invented the term "crimes against humanity" to describe them.

The U.S. took over the Congo from Belgium in 1960-61 in a bloody coup after the CIA arranged the murder of Patrice Lumumba, the country's first elected leader. In his place the Agency installed its paid agent Colonel Mobutu Sese Seko who continued the looting and killing started by Leopold, for another 37 years. The U.S. considered the socialist Lumumba to be pro-Soviet and President Eisenhower himself approved his assassination. The CIA sent Sidney Gottlieb, its top scientist (under the code name "Jo from Paris"), to the Congo with deadly biological toxins to use on Lumumba. This particular assassination plot was unsuccessful but Lumumba was killed by Mobutu's troops on January 17, 1961.

Until his ousting in 1997, Mobutu was Africa's most brutal and corrupt ruler who massacred and tortured thousands of people, and plundered his country with U.S. backing. From 1965 to 1991, Zaire (as Mobutu named the Congo) - got more than $1.5 billion in U.S. economic and military aid. In return, U.S. multinational corporations increased their share of Zaire's abundant minerals. Washington justified its hold on the Congo with the pretext of anti-Communism but its real interests were strategic and economic.

The Congo borders nine African states. In terms of mineral wealth it is the richest country in Africa, holding the world's biggest copper, cobalt and cadmium deposits. The Congo contains 80% of the world's cobalt (essential for jet aviation, defence and other high-tech production), 10% of its copper, and one-third of its diamonds in addition to possessing considerable reserves of gold, uranium and manganese. Other resources include coltan (used in cell phones, jet engines and fibre optics), timber, oil, coffee, tin, zinc and palm oil. George Bush Senior was Mobutu's friend for 20 years, and has interests in mining companies in the Congo. In addition to getting a share of Congolese wealth, the U.S. used the country as a base to attack the left-wing MPLA government in Angola after it took power in 1975.

According to the World Bank, (a long-time supporter of Mobutu), 64.7% of Zaire's budget was reserved for Mobutu's "discretionary spending" in 1992. Official Zairian figures put the number at 95%. Such astounding pillage made Mobutu (according to himself) one of the three richest men in the world while impoverishing Zairians and destroying the country's infrastructure. One-third of Zaire's citizens died from malnutrition under Mobutu with "countless others" suffering permanent brain damage in youth.

A BALKANIZED CONGO

Mobutu's unlimited greed was his undoing. As long as he shared the looting with U.S., Belgian, French, British, Dutch and other Western corporations which dominated the Zairian economy, the U.S. supported him. But, as one observer put it, "when he kept too much for himself-and became an embarrassment - the U.S. was ready to see him overthrown." In October1996, the Rwandan army along with Ugandan troops invaded Zaire and by May 1997 had taken over the country and forced Mobutu to flee. To give the invasion the cover of a local rebellion, the Tutsi Rwandan forces called themselves the Alliance of Democratic Forces for the Liberation of Congo-Zaire (ADFL) and recruited Laurent Kabila, an exiled Congolese Marxist opponent of Mobutu's, as a figurehead leader. As the Wall Street Journal put it, "Many Africans [concluded that] the Zairian rebellion was the brainchild of Washington from the very start." Rwanda and Uganda are the U.S.' "staunchest allies in the region". Paul Kagame, the Rwandan leader, was trained at the U.S. Army Command and General Staff College at Fort Leavenworth, Kansas. U.S. Special Forces had been training the Rwandan army since 1994 in counterinsurgency, combat and psychological operations. This included instructions about fighting in Zaire. Rwandan soldiers were also trained at Fort Bragg, North Carolina (U.S.), in July-August 1996 (just before the invasion), in land navigation, rifle marksmanship, patrolling and small-unit leadership.

Also in August 1996, Kagame visited Washington to discuss his concerns about Hutu refugee camps in eastern Zaire with U.S. officials. The Hutus are the majority ethnic group in Rwanda (85%) while Tutsis made up the minority (15%). In April 1994, the Hutu government had unleashed a genocide that killed 800,000 Tutsis and 50,000 Hutus in 89 days. Kagame's Tutsi rebel force, the Rwanda Patriotic Army (RPA) then invaded Rwanda from Uganda and took power. A million Hutus fled to eastern Zaire. Kagame considered the Hutu refugee camps a "dangerous threat to his regime" because Hutu militia who had carried out the genocide were amongst the civilians. As one observer put it, "it was clear to the U.S....that Kagame was prepared to act and that this was certainly in the U.S. government's interest."

Once the Rwandans had installed Kabila in power in Congo, his relations with them quickly deteriorated. In July 1998, Kabila expelled Rwandan and Ugandan forces from the Congo. He cited as his reasons a failed assassination attempt against him and the Rwandan army's killings of Hutu refugees. On August 2nd, Rwanda and Uganda invaded the Congo and occupied its eastern half where they remain today having set up surrogate "rebel" armies called Congolese Rally for Democracy (RCD-Goma-created by Rwanda) and Movement for the Liberation of the Congo (MLC-created by Uganda). Angola, Zimbabwe and Namibia sent their armies to support Kabila and Burundi joined the Rwandans and Ugandans. Thus began "Africa's First World War" involving seven armies, which has killed 2.5 million people and further devastated a country crushed by more than a century of Western domination.

This domination is being continued through Washington's use of Rwanda and Uganda to partition the Congo and loot its resources. The U.S. backed the Rwandan/Ugandan invasion of the Congo and according to Human Rights Watch apparently justified it. The Washington Post has reported that U.S. soldiers were sighted in the company of Rwandan troops in the Congo on

149

July 23 and 24, 1998. At the start of hostilities, the U.S. reacted with "a remarkable silence." When a statement was issued it explained that the invasion was intended to counter genocide and blamed the Congolese government for failing to deal with border security. Susan Rice, U.S. Assistant Secretary of State for African Affairs, told Congress that the U.S. "fully understands their [Rwanda and Uganda's] legitimate security interests in countering insurgent attacks from Congolese soil." Rice added that foreign intervention in the Congo was "unacceptable" but Washington declined to call for the immediate withdrawal of its close allies, the Rwandan and Ugandan forces, which it has trained, armed and financed. If foreign intervention really was unacceptable, the U.S. could have ended it by cutting off its considerable military and economic support for Rwanda and Uganda and sanctioning the countries. Instead, Rice pressed for a ceasefire in place and pressured Kabila into signing the Lusaka Accord which treated the conflict as a civil war and called for a step-by-step withdrawal of foreign troops (in 180 days) rather than an immediate one.

The result is a partitioned Congo with Rwanda and Uganda still occupying the eastern half having ignored all deadlines for leaving. The ceasefire is regularly violated. Kabila accepted the Lusaka Accord only because of the implicit U.S. threat that "refusal would be met by even greater assistance to the rebels and the potential dismantling of the entire country." This message was dramatically reinforced on January 17, 2001, when Laurent Kabila himself was assassinated on the same day that Lumumba had been, forty years ago. Joseph Kabila, Laurent's son, took over as President. Thus the U.S. has ensured continued Western dominance of the Congo by destroying the country itself as it existed when Mobutu was overthrown. Just as in the Berlin Conference of 1885, the West is again redrawing the Congo's boundaries and this process is once more accompanied by plunder and large-scale killing.

ARMIES OF BUSINESS

According to a U.N. report released in April 2001, Rwanda and Uganda are looting and plundering the resources of the eastern Congo and illegally exporting them to the West. The eastern Congo contains most of the country's minerals. The report titled "Report of the Panel of Experts on the Illegal Exploitation of Natural Resources and Other Forms of Wealth of the Democratic Republic of the Congo" details "mass-scale looting" and extraction carried out by Rwanda, Uganda and Burundi in the occupied zones between September 1998 and August 1999. During this time, the eastern Congo was "drained of existing stockpiles, including minerals, agricultural and forest products and livestock." Rwandan, Ugandan and Burundian soldiers visited banks, factories, farms and storage facilities to remove their contents and load them into vehicles. In November 1998, the Rwandan army transported seven years worth of coltan stock (about 1,500 tons) to Kigali (Rwanda's capital). Following the looting of stockpiles, Rwanda and Uganda have been extracting diamonds, gold, coltan, timber and coffee from the eastern Congo and illegally exporting these to the West. Rwanda has made U.S.$250 million in 18 months from coltan exports alone. According to the "Christian Science Monitor," every day cargo flights full of diamonds, gold and palm oil leave the Congo for Kigali and Kampala (Uganda's capital). Seven to ten such daily flights come into Kigali. Most of their cargo is loaded on to planes bound for Europe. Diamond exports from Rwanda and Uganda to the West have surged since 1998 yet neither country has any diamond mines. During 1999-2000, Uganda exported U.S.$3 million worth of diamonds. Diamond dealers in the Congo provide U.S.$2 million a year to the Rwandan army.

The looting and extraction of resources has been accompanied by the "constitution of criminal cartels" in occupied areas, created or protected by top military commanders. The U.N. report blames Presidents Kagame and Museveni (of Uganda) for "indirectly" giving "criminal cartels a unique opportunity to organize and operate in this fragile and sensitive area.;" the document warns that these cartels which have "ramifications and connections worldwide... represent the next serious security problem in the region." Significantly, the U.N. report points out that the illegal exploitation of the eastern Congo has been abetted by Western companies, governments, multilateral institutions and diplomats. Rwanda's coltan exports are transported by Sabena, the Belgian national airline, while Citibank carries out the required financial transactions. Ramnik Kotecha, the U.S. Honorary Consul in the eastern Congo, promotes deals between Rwandan coltan sellers and U.S. companies. Kotecha himself also deals in coltan.

Uncertified timber from occupied Congo has been imported by companies in Belgium, Denmark, Japan, Switzerland and the U.S. Western governments rewarded Rwanda for invading the Congo by doubling aid to the country from $26.1 million in 1997 to $51.5 million in 1999. The U.S., Britain, Denmark and Germany were the bilateral donors. Rwanda could thus spend more money on the war.

Rewards have been promoted for Rwanda and Uganda by the the World Bank too, which has praised the latter's economic performance following its Congolese diamond and gold exports. The Bank has pushed the case of both countries for the Highly Indebted Poor Countries initiative (a new debt relief programme) and dismissed the fact that Uganda's improved economic statistics stem from its illegal exploitation of the Congo.

The U.N. report also lists 35 companies illegally importing minerals from the eastern Congo through Rwanda but does not give the national origin of these companies. Instead, the report specifies the destination of the material. Twenty-six of the companies' destinations are in the West. The firms include Cogem, Transintra, Issa, Finconcorde,Cogecom, Tradement, MDW, Sogem, Soger, Cogea, Finiming, Cicle, Eagleswing, Union-Transport and Banro Resources, a Canadian company (see section below). Ten of the 35 companies are importing coltan to Belgium; three are importing the same resource to the Netherlands, three to Germany, two to Britain and one to Switzerland.

Along with plundering the eastern Congo, Rwanda and Uganda have committed "devastating human rights abuses" according to Human Rights Watch (HRW). The Rwandan army and RCD Goma "have regularly slaughtered civilians in massacres and extrajudicial executions" as well as tortured and raped villagers. As Alison Des Forges of HRW put it in April 2001, "While Ugandan commanders were plundering gold, looting timber, exporting coffee and controlling illicit trade monopolies in the Ituri district, their troops were killing and otherwise abusing the local population." Uganda's encouragement of (and participation in) fighting between the Hema and Lendu ethnic groups has resulted in 7,400 deaths. Human rights violations are widespread on the Congolese government side as well including "indiscriminate attacks on civilians, extrajudicial executions [and] rape." Kabila's allies Zimbabwe, Angola and Namibia are also profiting from the war. However, the Kabila regime cannot be accused of being a foreign military occupier; nor did it initiate the current war.

HEART OF DARKNESS

The destruction of the Congo says much more about the West than it does about the Central African country. It reveals most clearly that the West is largely a criminal enterprise, the prosperity of which is based on the genocide of Third World people and the theft of their resources. The Congo is perhaps the worst example of this but the West has followed the same policy in Asia, Africa and Latin America for centuries. In this sense, Western countries can be seen as a murderous mafia led by their godfather the United States government for which no amount of blood and wealth is enough. Today, the perpetrators of the Rwandan genocide are being tried in Tanzania. It is time to try those responsible in the U.S. and Belgium as well for more than a century of genocide and plunder in the Congo. And that will just be the beginning of dealing with the West's horrendous crimes.

This article is dedicated to Patrice Lumumba.

WAKE UP! WAKE UP! IT'S YER TRIP'D OUT

Weekly SchNEWS

Printed and Published in Brighton by Justice?

Friday 26th October 2001　　　www.schnews.org.uk　　　Issue 328　Free/Donation

DRUG-CRAZED

The anthrax crisis in the United States has thrown into sharp contrast the double standard world of the 'haves' and 'have-nots'.

In the wealthy corner we have America and Canada who this week threatened drugs manufacturer Bayer that unless it reduced the price of its anthrax antibiotic drug Cipro, it would change its laws, override Bayer's patent and get other companies to make cheap copies of the drug. Tommy Thompson, US Secretary of Health and Human Services, said "They are going to either meet our price…or else we're going to go to Congress and ask for some support to go in and do some other business." Not surprisingly Bayer caved in and will now sell America and Canada cheaper Cipro at the knock down wholesale price of 95c a pill– rather than the original $4.50.

Bayer, who had initially threatened to sue the Canadian government for breach of patent, were one of the 39 corporations that took South Africa to court when the country said it would use emergency legislation to make cheap generic drugs to treat people with AIDS. The corporate court action collapsed after worldwide condemnation (see SchNEWS 290).

The hypocrisy of America and Canada must be *sickening* for the developing world. For many years, the US has been acting as the pharmaceutical industry's policeman, threatening trade sanctions against any country that wanted to make cheap drugs for its population.

FANCY SOME TRIPS?

Following intense lobbying by US corporations, the World Trade Organisation introduced TRIPs. Sorry readers, this isn't some mind expansion drug but stands for Trade Related Intellectual Property Rights. TRIPs set enforceable global rules on patents, copyrights and trademarks, for the first time this included living things. This means that genes, cells, seeds, plants and animals can be patented and 'owned'. By 2006 even the poorest member states in Africa will have had to pass their own national legislation to become TRIPs-compliant and fully signed up respecters of patents on new drugs – or face the trade sanction consequences.

Only last month nearly sixty developing countries asked for a declaration to be agreed at next months World Trade Organisation (WTO) meeting in Qatar to re-interpret WTO rules to give governments the right to have access to affordable medicines. For example, AIDS medicine, which costs $20,000 with patents costs just $200 without. However, this declaration was blocked by Switzerland, Japan - Canada and the United States. Mimicking the line of the pharmaceutical corporations, they argued that the protection of pharmaceutical patents is necessary to encourage research into new drugs. Unless of course these cheap drugs are needed urgently for those countries with the financial clout to cower corporations and break world trade rules.

> Number of people in Africa infected with AIDS: 25 million
> Number of people in Africa who have died of AIDS: 17 million
> Number of people who have died of anthrax in America: 3

TRICK OR TREATY?

President Bush recently refused to sign an agreement strengthening the 1972 Convention on Biological Weapons, despite it being ratified by 140 other countries. Last month it was revealed that the Pentagon had secretly built a germ factory in the Nevada desert capable of producing enough deadly bacteria to kill millions of people. One proposal awaiting approval is the manufacture of a more potent version of anthrax using genetically engineered biological agents. So while the American public is worrying about anthrax attacks, their own government is developing biological weapons, but rest assured readers the development of lethal germs to wipe out millions of people is for 'defensive' measures only.

The threat of severe biological weapons attacks probably doesn't come from terrorists but countries. As Prof. Barbara Rosenberg, from the Federation of American Scientists' Working Group on Biological Weapons says: "… these attacks now are nothing compared to what is waiting for us

in the future when it becomes possible to genetically engineer new kinds of agents. These things are not easy to do it's much more likely that these attacks would come from a country, not a terrorist group."

Another threat to the world comes from chemical weapons; Russia has 40,000 tonnes of the stuff is supposed to destroy in the next few years. The USA is committed to destroy its stockpiles as well, but how will we know it has destroyed them? Go and inspect their stockpiles? Er, well you can't, you'll just have to take their word for it. The 1997 Chemical Weapons Treaty allows "challenge inspections", where any country can demand to inspect another countries stockpiles, but the USA has a unilateral exemption from this. There is an Organisation for the Prohibition of Chemical Weapons (OPCW), whose job it is to inspect military/industrial premises, but the OPCWs work has been severely hampered by the USA not paying its dues and blocking OPCW inspectors.

The US have become experts at opting out of and blocking weapons treaties, justifying this with excuses of self-defence and national security. But while they say they do not use chemical or biological weapons directly against populations, they have been poisoning people through its "war on drugs" in Colombia where over 300,000 people have been displaced because of the US funded spraying of poisonous pesticides in their country. Now that's what SchNEWS calls paying a high price for 'freedom'.

* For information on biological weapons check out www.sunshine-project.org

* For more information about America's secret biological warfare programme read "Germs: Biological Weapons and America's Secret War." By J. Miller, S. Engelberg and W. Broad (published by Simon and Schuster).

@ANTI-COPYRIGHT - INFORMATION FOR ACTION

Terror Attack

On 17th October, Rehavam Zeevi, an ultra-nationalist member of the Israeli cabinet, was assassinated by the Popular Front for the Liberation of Palestine (PFLP). Zeevi, ironically, was about to resign from Sharon's cabinet the next day because they weren't right-wing enough for him as his views made Atilla the Hun look like a woolly liberal. He thinks Palestinians should be expelled from Gaza, the West Bank and Jerusalem, are 'lice', 'vermin' and 'a cancer', Jordan should be "annexed" and no one should be allowed to enter Israel unless they can speak Hebrew. Western governments, predictably, condemned this killing in strong terms - Blair said it was a "contemptible act of violence", Bush called it "a heinous crime", and Koffi Anan, the UN Secretary General, said it was an "appalling murder." So let's get this straight when Palestinian civilians are massacred by Israeli tanks, F1-16 fighter jets and Apache helicopter gun ships the most that is said by Bush, Blair and their cohorts is that the killings are "not helpful" and would "jeopardise" the peace efforts - *whatever they are*. But when a racist bigot is assassinated the shit hits the fan. Double standards we think.

Since September 11th 110 Palestinians including women and children have been killed by the Israeli Defence Force (IDF) as tanks blast their way into Gaza and The West Bank supported by jet fighters and helicopters. As SchNEWS went to press Beit Rima, a West Bank village was attacked by large numbers of the IDF and, sinisterly, was closed off to ambulances and the media. "What is amazing about this situation is that medical teams were not allowed inside the village and we know that there are people in there who need our help" said Yunnis al-Khatib, the president of the Palestinian Red Crescent Society, "What happened there was a massacre." With the number of casualties rising each day it's a scary time for the Palestinian population. Ata Manasra, who lives in Bethlehem, says in a plea to the world "We are not safe at all. We might be targets of their bullets of hatred at any time. What can you do for us? Please don't leave us alone...We are targets of terrorism. We are a target of a state terror."

For more info check www.indymedia.il.org or www.gush-shalom.org

* Samar Alami and Jawad Botmeh wrongly fitted up and jailed for 1994 bombing of the Isreali Embassy in London (see SchNEWS 278, 286) have just had their appeal heard and the judges will be giving their verdict sometime in the next two weeks. The campaign is asking people to go to Appeal Courts, The Strand when they reconvene for the verdict. More info 07958680449 or check www.freesaj.org.uk

Pipe Dreams

Actions are planned around the world in support of resistance in Ecuador to a new oil pipeline through the Amazon rainforest. It will allow Ecuador to double its oil production, and create a boom in new oil exploration in the Amazon. The pipeline runs through 11 protected forest areas including the Mindo Nambillo Cloudforest Reserve, home to some 450 species of birds. The government squashed the public review process three weeks after the release of a 1,500-page Environmental Impact Assessment and by fast tracking licensing for the project. The oil is destined for consumption in the United States, which gets oil from Ecuador, Colombia and Bolivia.

See Amazon Watch's Report "The New Heavy Crude Pipeline in Ecuador: Fueling a Second Oil Boom in the Amazon" at www.amazonwatch.org

SchNEWS in brief

Benefit for Afghan Refugees this Sunday (28) with The Brighton Agitators, Tragic Roundabout and DJ Bin Liner and the Funky Jihad plus video propaganda by Guerrillavision and comedians from Voodoo Vaudeville, 7-10.30pm, at Gloucester Club, Brighton, free food before 8pm, £3.50/£4. ** **Hallowe'en Fun-Raiser for 9 Ladies Anti Quarry Protest Site**, 9pm-late, 31st Oct. Technocauldron and Raggadubdungeon DJs and SchMovies at Volks Tavern, Madeira Drive, Brighton. http://pages.zoom.co.uk/-nineladies ** **Another SchNEWS victory** – last Friday Brighton and Hove voted an emphatic no to plans for a directly elected city mayor (see SchNEWs 325) ** Budding activists should get along to the **West Country Activist Gathering**, to discuss everything from genetics, anti-globalisation, Afghanistan etc. Nov. 10th, St Werburghs Community Centre, Horley Rd, Bristol 10am-6pm. Full disabled access. £3 donation on the door, No dogs, alcohol or hierarchies, www.geocities.com/westcountryactivist ** **Hackney** now has its very own site on http://uk.indymedia.org letting community groups, workers and residents to post their own info about how the cuts in the bankrupt borough are affecting them and link up with similar struggles around the country. There's also a newsletter now out Hackney NOT 4 Sale. Details 07950-539254 hackneynot4sale@yahoo.com ** No war but the class war (Now **Brighton Against the War**) meet every Monday 7.30pm upstairs at the Hobgoblin Pub, Brighton. ** There's a new group being set up to start a **small school/learning centre** in Brighton and there's a meeting all about it on 2nd Nov 7pm at the Pheonix Community Centre Brighton Tel 245042 for more details ** This Sunday (28th) at 6pm there's a meeting upstairs at the Albert, Trafalgar St, Brighton, to discuss **council funding cuts** to essential voluntary and community groups and the fact that homeless people being disallowed benefits if they can't prove a connection to Brighton ** **Arjuna whole food co-op**, in Cambridge who have been running for 31 years are desperately looking for new members to get involved – otherwise the shop could close. Contact: 12 Mill Rd, Cambridge, CB1 2AD, 01223-364845 ** The **Colombia Solidarity** delegation has returned from Colombia and want to give talks for next 6 weeks. They want events on International Human Rights Day (10th Dec.), to focus on Colombia. colombia_sc@hotmail.com ** The big blockade of **Faslane Naval base** saw cops arrest 170 people. Info www.tridentploughshares.org/0845-4588366. ** **Schwoops!** The Reclaim The Streets number printed in last weeks SchNEWS was wrong: it should be 020-7281-4621

Positive SchNEWS

LEAF (Linking Environment And Farming) is a charity that aims to help farmers adopt sustainable and viable agricultural practices. They aim to create a better public understanding of farming through a nationwide network of demonstration farms. They are holding a series of open meetings exploring the current state of UK agriculture and how farmers are moving forward in positive ways. Issues covered include sustainability, local food production, conservation, countryside management and a visit to the LEAF Virtual Farm. There are meetings in Chester, Sussex, Harrogate and Peterborough. Details from LEAF 02476-413911 www.leaf.uk.org

NATSy Boys

Only three months since it was controversially part privatised (so called public-private partnership), it looks like the National Air Traffic Services (NATS) is set to become the 'Railtrack of the skies'. Faced with massive debts the company may soon have to beg the government for emergency cash, as well as cutting a fifth of their management and support workforce. NATS bosses are blaming their problems on the recent collapse of the aviation industry after Sept 11, but even before this the safety of our airspace was sliding off the rails. Faced with a predicted 50% increase in the number of flights in next ten years NATS cunning solution was to make cuts of £60million over two years with massive redundancies. Yet they still weren't able to make the investment in the service that they were required under the terms of the privatisation. It now looks likely that NATS maybe re-nationalised in a Railtrack-type deal. Coming next in the successful public-private partnership trilogy is the privatisation of the London Underground, which is already running into problems before it's even left the station.

Rent Boys

Newham Council, the poorest borough in the country, has ditched the privatisation of its Housing Benefit after the wholesale cock-up of the service by the CSL group. New claims were taking three months to process, while three UNISON shop stewards were dismissed by CSL for the "gross misconduct" of exposing the working conditions and procedures within the company. The three had brought attention to the fact that thousands of documents were being closed without processing to 'massage' the backlog figures. The contract is expected to return to the council before Xmas, by 'mutual' agreement. Email: housingbenefit@hotmail.com

...and finally...

It's alright sisters, the battle is over! According to the adverts in shop windows of Thornton's "1975 - women get equality" *(did we miss this happening?),* "2001 - women finally got what they wanted - 5 new Belgian chocolates." Forget freedom from oppression, sexual harassment, discrimination and violence, what we need is corporations selling us sugary junk at the expense of exploited workers across the world. Four women from Manchester were so outraged by this offensive propaganda, they visited two of the shops in central Manchester to show them what they thought, graffiti-ing window displays with "2001 - women get what they want - freedom, justice and equality" and "Smash Patriarchy!", and plastering them with posters about exploitation of women. When intrepid SchNEWS reporters tried to get Thornton's opinion on the advert, first response was a terrified 'no comment'. A cagey Press Liason told us that complaints had been 'minimal' and denied the extent of attacks on the shops. Let Thornton know what you want via their website www.thorntons.co.uk, which also has details of local branches. (The Manchester women note that spray glue is very quick drying and strong.........)

disclaimer

SchNEWS warns all readers we reserve the right under guarantee to limit without prejudice the taking of our TRIPs. Honest.™ This does not affect yer statutory rights.

WAKE UP! WAKE UP! IT'S YER THAI'D AND TESTED

Weekly SchNEWS

Printed and Published in Brighton by Justice?

Friday 2nd November 2001 www.schnews.org.uk **Issue 329** **Free/Donation**

LUNCH OUTS

"Genetically diverse food resources underpin world food security. It is farmers who have developed these resources and their rights are being destroyed." – Patrick Mulvany, Intermediate Technology Development Group.

Next week was meant to be the beginning of the UN World Food Summit in Rome, where world leaders were due to meet to make major decisions to help reduce world hunger. But after the hijack attacks in the US the full conference was postponed probably until June next year, instead a small scale annual meeting is still taking place although no decisions will be finalised. The World Trade Organisation (WTO) meeting in Qatar, however, is still going ahead, which goes to show that free trade liberalisation (giving free reign to multinational companies to steamroller over human rights and the environment) is more important to our world leaders than fighting starvation and securing global food security.

Five years ago at the first world food conference agreements were made to try and reduce world hunger. One of the most important moves was the agreement to introduce a new legally binding convention to ensure that living things couldn't be patented - called the *International Treaty on Plant Genetic Resources for Food and Agriculture* (PGRFA), that would directly oppose the WTO's TRIPs (Trade Related Intellectual Property Rights, where companies can 'own' plant varieties they have 'developed').

The PGRFA aims to ensure the conservation, sustainable use and 'free flow' of the genetic resources of food crops, and also tries to ensure that if corporations use a food crop, farmers who've helped to develop it receive a fair share of the benefits. It could also ensure that genetic information from crops were public property stored in public gene banks, and could limit the increasing use of intellectual property rights where organisations can claim ownership over seeds and genes. The agreement is well overdue, over the past century over 90 percent of world crop varieties have been lost from farmers' fields.

Thai'd Up

"...its [Jasmine rice] acquisition by the US is an example of Biopiracy and this is why the Treaty is needed" – Pinit Korsieporn, Thai Director of Foreign Agricultural Relations.

Thailand is one of the biggest rice producers in the world, producing Jasmine rice, which is made up of several of the most desired varieties in the world. This unique group of rice varieties has been grown and developed by Thai farmers for thousands of years with seeds being handed down over generations and shared. To the Thai people the concept of anyone 'owning' this rice is simply absurd. However this is about to happen as a University of Florida professor, with full backing of the US Government, is working on genetically manipulating the rice to enable it to grow in the US climate. Then he plans taking out a patent on it and selling it to the US public as "Jasmine" rice, thus undermining the export of Thai Jasmine rice and the livelihood of thousands of Thai farmers. About one third of Thai Jasmine rice produced every year is exported to the US.

Such biopiracy shows the urgent need for protection for the world's small farmers. But over the 5 years since they were first discussed the PGRFA regulations have been watered down to the point that if they're ever agreed they'll be pretty much irrelevant. And there's no prizes for guessing whose been putting up the most opposition, er, yes, the US and the European Union with a hefty bit of shoving from the biotech companies. As the treaty now stands, although there will be no right to patent seeds, genes from seeds will be allowed to be patented. Because of this most countries are refusing to sign up seeds into the treaty, which increases its ineffectiveness further. But even if the treaty does live up to its original aims the one big question is whether the WTO bully boys will allow it to override their unfair-trade rules or even have an equal footing. Either way the chances are looking slim for the world's farmers who may soon be forced to wave goodbye to the free exchange of

* 815 million people in the world regularly go hungry.
* 62 million people face food emergencies caused by natural and man-made disasters.
* One fifth of the world's children do not eat enough calories or protein.
* 18 million people in East Africa still rely on food assistance.
* Britain chucks out £500 million of safe and edible food each year.
* 1.4 billion people around the world are believed to depend on saving their own seeds for their food security.

CRAP ARREST OF THE WEEK
For circulating a bit of paper!

Neil Sorensen, a delegate at this week's Food and Agriculture Organisation (FAO) meeting in Italy, was booted out and locked in jail for the night. His crime ? While the Americans are using the Conference to try and get on as many FAO sub-committees as possible, Neil circulated a memo pointing out the destructive corporate led nature of the US and asked people to stop them getting on *any* committees. FAO have now apologised for being a bit over the top!

CRAP SACKING OF THE WEEK.

Following from last week's *And Finally...* A girl lost her Saturday job at Thornton's, for the heinous crimes of eating one of their chocolates!

---

seeds and their rights to profit from seeds they've developed over thousands of years of innovation.

So after years of negotiations, those in power look like they will be offering the world an empty bowl. As Pat Mooney from RAFI/ETC Group remarked recently, "By participating, both NGO's and grassroots groups, lend legitimacy to these international meetings, but if they continue to refuse to listen to them, and translate that into action for good, then it's time to stop taking part."

For the latest information check out www.ukabc.org and www.itdg.org

* March for Trade Justice. Saturday 3rd November, starting from Geraldine Mary Harmsworth Park, outside the Imperial War Museum, Lambeth Road, London SE1 at 12.30pm, the Parade will go to Trafalgar Square (speakers at 3.30pm). www.tradejusticemovement.org.uk

BOMBED OUT

At the same time as randomly dropping food parcels from their planes, America have also been dropping cluster bombs. Cluster bombs are extremely nasty weapons that are used instead of landmines to hit moving targets, when released the bombs separate into smaller bomblets, up to 5 percent of these remain unexploded. Just like landmines they pose a great threat to innocent civilians. By some bizarre coincidence both the food parcels and the cluster bombs are yellow. When this was discovered the US was forced to broadcast a radio message warning the people of Afghanistan not to touch any yellow coloured objects they find particularly in areas where bombs have been dropped. Well they can say goodbye to their monthly meal then!

HOME AND AWAY

On Monday, in a blaze of publicity, Neo-Labour announced that they're getting rid of the much hated voucher system for refugees (see SchNEWS 254 & 267). The 'humilliating and demeaning' voucher system is going to be replaced with I.D. cards and 'holding centres'. From next Autumn all asylum seekers will be made to live in ex-army camps, old holiday camps or purpose built centres which are gonna be built 'away from the general populace' i.e. in the middle of nowhere. Seeing as they'll be cut off from society the government has decided that there will be no need to even give them vouchers to buy food and clothes as all this will be provided at the detention centres. Sounds like prison to us. Mohammed Asif, a spokesman for refugees living on the Sighthill estate in Glasgow, agrees "These reception centres will create a lot of problems. It is like prisons. It is against our basic human rights. They have done this to satisfy the opposition and some sections of the media".

I.D. cards are gonna be a double whammy to hit refugees. From January it'll be compulsory for them to carry the cards at all times - which will be a green light for the cops to stop and search anybody who looks foreign. Sheyda, who fled persecution in Iran, is worried about this: "People came here because they were afraid in their country, they had no freedom to speak, no freedom to think. They were in prison. And they do not want this."

* Public meeting about new detention centres Nov. 6th at the Bowen West Theatre, De Montford University, 37 Lansdowne Road, Bedford 7pm. More info 07786 517379. www.barbedwirebritain.org.uk

* Earlier this month police raided the offices and homes of people involved in 'Libertad!' confiscating computers, hard discs, and documents, because of the online demonstrations they organised against Lufthansa. The airline company, targeted because their planes are used to deport refugees, are claiming the 1.2 million hits caused economic damage. Er, that's the point.

OK KO'd

The Manchester OKasional cafe was illegally evicted this week by builders and police who kicked in the shop front window to gain access before nicking all the occupants.

The OKasional Cafe collective have been squatting empty buildings for the past four years and the current eviction is the most violent and heavy handed since the retaking of the Hacienda in 2000.

All those arrested were charged with nicking electricity – despite the collective contacting the electricity company. This Saturday is expected to see Manchester's biggest peace demo against the war in Afghanistan, and the squat, handily sited opposite the peace gardens and cenotaph, had been acting as an info shop for anti-war views.

* 'Shortcuts to Manchester' is an excellent little booklet telling you everything you need to know what's going on in the City. For copies send an SAE to Shortcuts, Dept 29, c/o MERCI@Bridge 5 Mill, 22a Beswick St., Manchester, M4 7HR.

* The rules for (legal) **eviction of squatters** have changed, but it doesn't really make much difference to what will happen, it's just that the forms are different. Get your update for your **Squatter's Handbook** by sending an SAE to Advisory Service for Squatters, 2 St Paul's Road, London, N1 2QN, 020-7359-8814. Squatter's handbook's available from them for £1.57 (in stamps, cheque or postal order).

Inside SchNEWS

There have been 17 more arrests in Sweden following June's demos against the European Union Summit in Gothenburg, Sweden (SchNEWS 310). Most charges are for rioting and property damage, the arrests came from police footage taken during the protests – with more arrests in Scandinavia and Germany expected during the winter. Fifty people have already faced charges, resulting in sentences of between 9 months and five years. "The quality of the prosecutor's case has sunk to low levels and gullibility has been a huge factor in the local court and court of appeal in Gothenburg, after the riots in June. Some of the sentences pushed by the prosecutors have been as long as those for murder. The sentences have, to the highest degree, been political." writes Sweden's Motkraft bulletin.

Prisoners may receive books and letters, but as time goes on they are receiving less. Paul Robinson is the only UK citizen in prison in Gothenburg. Letters of support and for a full list of prisoners write to Solidarity Group GBG, c/o Syndikalistiskt forum, Box 7267, SE-402 35 Gothenburg, Sweden solidaritetsgruppen@hotmail.com

* Bonfire night benefit for Mark Cullinane banged up in a Moroccon prison for the past five years. The campaign needs to raise £1,500 otherwise he'll do another year inside. Bands include d.s.g., Digi Dub, Flatpig, Dead Plants, X-it (all of which feature on the SchNUSIC CD – available from us for £7) as well as DJ's and performers. 5th Nov 8pm – late, Concorde 2, Brighton, £6. www.dirtysquatters.com

* Spanish anarchist prisoner Eduardo Garcia has been freed on parole. Eduardo, a prominent political activist was fitted up with a 20 year jail sentence after being accused of sending letter bombs (SchNEWS 294). A demonstration organised outside the Spanish consulate (20 Draicot place London - Sloane Sq.tube.) at noon, 9th Nov is still taking place.

TREE CARE TREAT

"We can work with nature, harvesting in ways that cause minimum disturbance and sustain beautiful and productive woodlands for ourselves and other species." – Ben Law.

At this time of year, when the autumn leaves are falling, you might want to consider what's being done to preserve what's left of our forests. 'The Woodland Way: A Permaculture Approach to Sustainable Woodland Management' by Ben Law is a wonderful book that goes to the heart of such matters. Ben's been working the land in the UK and elsewhere for 20 years. In '92 he settled in Prickly Nut Wood, Sussex, where he uses the principles of permaculture (a way for us daft human beings to work with nature rather than destroying it) to look after himself and the abundance of life in the place where he lives.

Prickly Nut Wood is incredible. SchNEWS scribes walked round in a daze when they visited last year, grinning from ear to ear at what Ben is achieving largely on his own. The local ecosystem is used to provide food and shelter, and a variety of incomes help enable self-sufficiency. Power from wind generators and solar panels provides lighting and electricity for a shower and email/phone communication with the outside world. 'The Woodland Way' is full of practical tips on forest management and useful for anyone interested in permaculture. Well inspiring. Available from Permanent Publications, 01730 823311 www.permaculture.co.uk. They also produce Permaculture magazine and a catalogue of books and details of permaculture/ sustainable living courses around the country.

SchNEWS in brief

The **Corporate Watch website** now contains new in-depth profiles of many companies including Unilever, Nestle, BP and ASDA. www.corporatewatch.org.uk ** Celebrate **Word Power's 7th birthday**. Readings and music, 7.30pm 9th Nov. Assembly Rooms, George St., Edinburgh. Tickets: £5/£3.50 from Word Power, 43 West Nicolson St, 0131-6629112 www.word-power.co.uk ** **Anti-privatisation Conference**, 11.30am-5pm, 3rd Nov., St Mary's Neighbourhood Centre, Upper Street, Islington, London. Speakers and workshops on opposing privatisation of public services, fighting anti-union laws and defending union rights. www.unionsfightback.org.uk ** '**We Are Everywhere**' are looking for contributions for a book/CD-ROM and website that promises to be information for inspiration. Contributions via their website www.weareeverywhere.org or post to Everywhere, c/o 55 Rectory Road, Oxford OX4 1BW UK. ** **Project Censored** publicise stories the mainstream media ignores and are now broadcasting censored stories on the web every Monday 7-8pm www.sonoma.edu/ksun. Also see www.projectcensored.org. ** The first **Voice of the People Celebration** aims "to bring people together from all walks of life and all areas of North Staffs to create a positive and fun space in which ideas and information can be shared." 12.30pm, 3rd Nov, Tontine Square, Hanley, Stoke-on-Trent. ** A **super summit in Ottawa** (16-18th Nov), has been arranged to replace the cancelled Washington IMF/World Bank. meeting. Would you believe it, a demo is planned on the 17th! Housing, legal, medical, food and other logistic aspects are being organised by Global Democracy Ottawa. www.flora.org/gdo/ ** There are anti **World Trade Organisation** (see SchNEWS 327) demonstrations planned across the globe. www.agp.org. 11.30am, 9th Nov: No to WTO picket outside the Qatar Embassy, 1 South Audley Street, London (New Bond St tube).

WAR Briefs

Anti-war actions are happening continually countrywide. See www.indymedia.org.uk for what's happening in your area or call CND 020-7700-2393 ** This Saturday (4th) public meeting - Stop the WAR - Help build an anti-racist, anti-imperialist, anti-war coalition. 4pm Millman Street Community Centre, Millman Street, (Russell Square tube) ** Tues 6th: 'Hidden agendas behind the war in Afghanistan', public meeting hosted by Worthing Eco-action at the Downsview pub (West Worthing Station), 7.45pm. ** Saturday 10th: Stop the War march and rally in **Brighton.** 12 noon at the Level. ** The following weekend, Sunday 18th there's a Stop the War march in London. Assemble 12 noon, Hyde Park. Coaches from Brighton – tickets from the Peace Centre in Gardner St.

...and finally...

Pumpkin Up The Volume.

Members of the Belgian Pumpkin Liberation Army have stolen 53 Halloween pumpkins to turn into soup for poor people. The pumpkins were taken from gardens in Leuven and given to Food not Bombs, who will make soup from them to feed the poor. It's the first time the Pumpkin Liberation Army has struck and hopefully the last but the ghoulish raiders have said they want to start a worldwide web of organisations "fighting against the improper use of pumpkins."

disclaimer

SchNEWS warns all readers hungry for info for action not to bite off more than they can chew. Honest.

Norwegian Hood Squatting in Norway

Long Live Blitz!!

This May sees BLITZ, Norway's best known squat, celebrating a double decade of activism - "20 years out of control"

BLITZ was born during the heyday of Oslo squatting in the eighties, when hundreds of folks got pissed off with having nowhere to go. Picking up their crowbars and defending their right to free space against police brutality and harsh penalties, over 100 people took over the four storied central Oslo house in 1982.

Since then several generations of activists have passed through Blitz, helping defeat the local Conservative Government's repeated attempts to shut it down. For years much of the political activism was directed against the City's building and housing policies, but lately the focus has switched to anti-fascism. Blitz based activists gather intelligence on what the Nazis are up to, and spread that information via a magazine, as well as militantly stopping Nazi gigs and concerts. The closest the building came to closure was in 1994, when it was bombed as a result of it's anti fascist actions and campaigns, luckily no one was hurt.

Those who like the music say Blitz has been the city's best underground concert scene for years - Bands like 'Life... But How To Live it?' 'So Much Hate' and 'Stengte Dører' (all influential on the continental Hard Core scene in the late 80's early 90's,) have all rocked the space. On top of which RadiOrakel, the first women's radio station broadcasts from the loft, and there's also a bookshop, vegetarian café, meeting space, banner painting room, and band practice space.

Visit BLITZ at Pilestredet 30c, 0164 Oslo, Norway call 0047 22.11.23.49. www.blitz.no

(Right) The writing on the wall: A slogan known among Oslo`s squatters and homeless since 1970, demanding the castle for social squatting (The king out, we need the castle)

Cheers Camilla

Brakkebygrenda (BBG) 'With Homes On Wheels'

After a second trip to Berlin with a friend we both bought caravans in which to live, and we settled in Oldtown, Oslo in May 99. During the two first weeks of squatting land a couple more people joined us with their caravans, then another. A month later we got evicted and moved 15 metres away, got evicted again and moved 20 metres further. After four evictions in three months we had moved 150 metres from the first place and the local authorities were pissed at us. Ha-Ha!

They towed us away and gave us a fine. We paid the fine and got our homes back and moved to an unused and deserted area in the same part of town. We got evicted and moved around in the same neighbourhood two more times. After finding a deserted, seemingly ownerless and preservable house from 1840 severely damaged by fire and neglected since 1987, with a spacious back yard with plenty of room for homes on wheels, our numbers grew fast. We've now got nine people, a dog, cat and a rat living on the 600-700 m2 of land all year round. We cleared the space, which seemingly had been used as a local dumping ground, built a toilet, composts, a common livingroom/kitchen and a storeroom, and are constantly trying to develop environmental and ecological solutions for our waste. Living in BBG in the city feels like living in a secret garden - with all its trees and singing birds of the summer.

With nine single homes now in BBG there's no space for any more. Now it's up to other people to create more "wagenburgs" in Oslo whilst we hope to develop out squat, and to fight for our right to stay, and to be a resource to our local community."

brakkebygrenda@yahoo.co.uk

Hausmannsgate 40

In September 1999 Boligaksjonen, a local housing action group, squatted Hausmannsgate 40, an old three storied nineteenth century building. Initially providing a home for 20 people, the squat is one of three still going strong in Oslo today. Boligaksjonen are growing stronger and gaining a broader network of activists. Now established in several cities in Norway, they are working for more social housing, establishing housing co-ops and the right for a place to live, as well as ploughing through the bureaucracy, squatting and pie throwing of course.

Get in touch: ba@lbf.no web: http://squat.net/boligaksjonen/

MARRAKESH RECESS

COP 7 Climate Talks November 2001

Amsterdam, Nov 6th: 50 local activists in The Netherlands protested against the use of emissions trading in the Kyoto Protocol, by selling air to passersby on the streets of Amsterdam. While the Samba band whipped up the crowd into a hip-swinging frenzy, "carbon traders" attempted to sell people their own air, which they could then take home in jars to pollute as they please. Luckily, there were climate heroes on hand to let people know the real costs of carbon trading. Highlight of the day was a young American women asking one of the activists, "Where do you get the air from?"

Moroccan Activists Turn Out Against COP 7, Nov 7th: When a group of Moroccan activists in Marrakech for the COP 7 were refused entry into the conference (why ever not? – ed) they took their message to the street. The group Attac Rabat began distributing information about climate change and neo-liberal economics in French, Arabic and Tamazight (one of Morocco's Berber languages) and had info-stalls at Marrakesh University. (At the same time the campus was enjoying a visit from three truckloads of soldiers because of an exhibition by students from Western Sahara about their struggle against Moroccan occupation.)

Attac Rabat were in no mood to join in discussions about plans such as emissions trading which they fundamentally disagreed with, and were very critical of NGO's from the 'north' who wasted their time discussing 'least bad' ideas and were heavily biased towards issues relevant in the north. The activists job was made harder by police harassment.

Korean Activists Protest During COP 7

As the world's bureaucrats gathered for the COP7 Climate Change Convention in Marrakesh, Korean climate change activists, Risingtide Korea, began a week of protest actions.

Since coming together three months before the conference, Risingtide have organised their own internet newsletter and campaign, done info tours, and run public debates on climate change issues.

On the 3rd of November, Korean Ecological Youth accosted a group of Korean industrialists as they set off for Morocco from Inchon international airport. Bringing banners, pickets, and the local media with them, they ran a mock interview with one of the industrialists, and generally tried to piss the corporate types off.

Four days later a series of rallies took place in front of the Ministries of Commerce, Industry and Energy, The American embassy, Shell, KCC and the Congress Building, to draw attention to how industrial circles and government collaborate with the global carbon business.

On the 9th of November, the last day of COP7, the Korean Risingtide crew marched through Seoul with other activists in an anti-WTO demo, ending the week of protests with a well-earned street party.

'Was it a fair cop in Marrakesh?'

Perhaps it was a signal of approval from on high. The night before a deal was done at the climate negotiations in Marrakech, the heavens opened and drought-stricken Morocco got some much needed rain. But then perhaps it wasn't. The rain stopped after half an hour, and the weather system moved on to neighbouring Algeria, where over a thousand people were killed in flashfloods and mudslides.

Of course very little of these outside realities filtered through to delegates meeting in the cloistered confines of the Marrakech Palais de Congres, despite an expedition to a mountain valley nearby where 250 people were killed in a similar flash flood event in 1995. Instead, delegates were busily occupied with finalising the small print needed for implementing the Kyoto protocol, resuming the good work from the COP6 in Bonn in July.

But if the climate negotiations were complicated before, now they were almost completely unintelligible to anyone without a degree in law. Several delegates from poor countries and small island states confided that the linguistic gymnastics had made it nearly impossible for them to contribute. Their only option was to take refuge in the regional positions taken by the Alliance of Small Island States (AOSIS) and the G77 and China group of developing countries.

Making resolutions for a sustainable future? Forget that - the main objective of this conference was to keep the Kyoto protocol alive and make sure Russia and Japan were still in the fold. In order for Kyoto to come into force, parties representing 55% of industrialised country greenhouse gas emissions need to have ratified – which would only happen if the EU, Japan and Russia signed up. Canada was wavering, and Australia, which had just re-elected its dark-ages Howard government, still looked certain to stay out. Of course the US is out. Russia was in a strop because it was demanding double its 'sinks' allocation – that bit of the carbon trading scam that says the amount of carbon dioxide (CO_2) your forests suck in counts as tradeable carbon credits and threatened to back out unless the other countries agreed – which to keep Kyoto going they did. Russia stands to be a big winner with carbon trading because since its economic decline its fossil fuel consumption is down, and vast forests give it a lot of carbon credits (or so called 'hot air') to sell. (Don't ya love the way at these conferences it's always 'Germany says...' 'Canada agreed...' when representing whole countries are small groups of unelected delegates sitting at card tables with a namebadge saying 'Canada' on it - ed).

The phrase 'fiddling while Rome burns' comes to mind.

WAKE UP! WAKE UP! IT'S YER FOR US OR AGAINST US

Weekly SchNEWS

Printed and Published in Brighton by Justice?

Who yer lookin' at buddy?

Friday 9th November 2001   **www.schnews.org.uk**   **Issue 330**   **Free/Donation**

BUSH BEATERS

"It's going to be important for nations to know they will be held accountable for inactivity. You're either with us or you're against us in the fight against terror." - President Bush.

"We refuse the choice that is offered by both sides in this conflict - you are either for us or against us. As anarchists we obviously see little attraction in the sort of religious state fantasized about by Bin Laden and enacted by the Taliban. But we also oppose the fake democracy of the western states where politicians are bought by oil companies, refugees are criminalised and where corporations rule." - Anarchist Platform statement.

Last Sunday, Nicaragua went to the polls knowing that a vote for one of the candidates, Daniel Ortega of the Sandinastas, would be a vote that could see vital American humanitarian aid to the worlds poorest speaking Spanish country cut off. Worse the election of Ortega would in the eyes of the United States make them 'against us' in the fight against terrorism.

You see the Sandinastas and America go back a long way. In '79 a revolution by the Sandinastas ended the brutal Somoza family dictatorship - a few years later and the Sandinastas won elections convincingly. America however refused to recognise the left-wing government, which started to seize and redistribute land and businesses. Instead the CIA funded the Contras, a right-wing paramilitary group, who waged a campaign of terror that destabilized the country and led to 50,000 deaths.

To keep the Contras war chest healthy the CIA allowed the import of tonnes of Contra cocaine to sell mainly as crack in the inner city ghettos across America. The US Drug Enforcement Agency (DEA) was obstructed from investigating Contra groups and their agents. Former DEA agent Michael Levine said "I watched the CIA protect drug traffickers ... I have put thousands of Americans away for tens of thousands of years for conspiracy with less evidence than is available against Ollie North and CIA people." The CIA have even admitted this in an internal report, with retired CIA inspector-general Frederick Hitz saying "There was a great deal of sloppiness and poor guidance". Which is basically bureaucrat speak for "We knew about it and we didn't care."

Bush-shit

In 1990 the electorate finally voted for a US favored candidate and the CIA spooks got what they wanted. But eleven years on America are still sticking their oar into Nicaragua's business. Over the past few weeks they've used money, free food and propaganda to get their Liberal Party candidate into power. Pressure was successfully put on the Conservative candidate to drop out of the election to prevent splitting the anti-Ortega vote. A US ambassador wearing a Liberal Party baseball cap went on an emergency food-aid distribution trip. Jeb Bush, the President's brother and governor of the state of Florida, home of one of the dodgiest US election results in history, attacked Ortega in an apparent lack of irony because he "neither understands nor embraces the basic concepts of freedom, democracy and free enterprise."! He then went on to accuse Ortega as someone who has condoned international terrorism - and his whole rant was duly reprinted in a Nicaraguan paper as an advert by the Liberal party.

In the end the Sandinastas lost the election but the actions of America speak volumes about its foreign policy. On the day it began bombing Afghanistan George Bush announced "If any government sponsors the outlaws and killers of innocents...they have become outlaws and murderers themselves." But it seems that this doesn't count if it is US sponsored death squads that are carrying out the killing. As the journalist John Pilger points out "The Bush family's violence, from Nicaragua to Panama, the Gulf to the death rows of Texas, is a matter of record. Their war on terrorism is no more than the continuing war of the powerful against the powerless, with new excuses, new hidden imperatives, new lies."

Terror Camp

Where did all those Latin American dictators and their terrorist henchmen go to fine tune their 'skills'? - the School of Americas in Georgia, USA. In 1996, the US government was forced to release some of the school's training manuals where, among other top tips for terrorists, they recommended blackmail, torture, execution and the arrest of witnesses' relatives. Last year the school was closed down, then re-opened immediately under the snappily named Western Hemisphere Institute for Security Co-operation. But as one senator commented, apart from the name, nothing at the 'school' has really changed. www.soaw.org/

* Bypass the corporate media war machine www.alternet.org/ or www.zmag.org

* Read about the CIA in 'Washington's War on Nicaragua' by Holly Sklar (South End Press, 1988), ISBN 0896082954. Or, 'Killing Hope: US military & CIA Interventions Since World War II' by William Blum (Common Courage Press, 1991) ISBN 1567510523.

Biscuits not Bombs

Army and navy recruiting offices occupied in Brighton, banners hung on the BBC building in Manchester denouncing the 'Blair Broadcasting Corporation'. The Department for International Development squatted by people demanding food not bombs for the Afghani people. These are examples of people taking direct action to show their opposition to the war.

* There's also loads of protests going on, to see what's in your area check out www.indymedia.org.uk or www.stopwar.org.uk or call CND 020-7700-2350.

* There's a demo against the war in **Brighton this Saturday** (10th) Meet noon at the Level. And don't forget the **Stop the War demo** Sunday 18th. Meet at 12pm Speakers Corner, Hyde Park, London - there will be an anti-capitalist block. info@rhythmsofresistance.co.uk

* Info on researching companies send £1 + SAE to 16b Cherwell St., Oxford, OX4 1BG www.corporatewatch.org.uk

* Campaign Against Arms Trade, 11 Goodwin St., London N4 3HQ. 020-7281-0297. www.caat.org.uk

* Daily Express journalist Yvonne Ridley, who spent ten days as a prisoner of the Taliban, is speaking out against the war. At the Brighthelm Centre, North Road, Brighton, Tuesday 13th 7.30pm 01273 692880

* Brighton Against the War meet every Monday 7.30pm upstairs at the Hobgoblin Pub, London Road (nwbtcw@yahoo.co.uk)

Looking for something a little different for the folks this Yuletide?
Here's some Christmas prezzies for the collaterally damaged. Real life action man accessories, armoured tank tops, special vests to keep out the winter chill (and the odd bullet). Find all these toys at www.bdec-online.com for the "ultimate reference to British defence, equipment, technology and services". Thousands of products used by the Ministry of Defence and the firms that make them.

They aren't of course the sort of things you can buy in your local shop, so why not log on, find what you want, then get a bunch of mates to go and pay some of those nice companies that are investing in war a visit. We're sure they'll welcome you with open arms.

SHAFTED

"We have had an unfair trial that was followed, after a long wait, by an unfair appeal. This was a political trial from day one and we are totally innocent. We were only convenient scapegoats. A huge amount of evidence is still hidden, all of which points away from us. We will carry on the struggle for our freedom and justice as part of the larger struggle for our people's freedom and justice" Samar Alami and Jawad Botmeh 1st November.

Last week, in an extremely dodgy political verdict, high court judges dismissed the appeal by Samar Alami and Jawad Botmeh against their 20 year jail sentences for the bombing of the Israeli Embassy and Balfour House in '94 (see SchNews 278, 286). A large amount of evidence was covered up by various secret services including MI5 and Special Branch and a leaked senior MI5 manager's report pointed towards the involvement of Mossad (Israeli intelligence service) in the bombings. Police, the prosecution and the secret services also withheld evidence to the court under Public Interest Immunity certificates, which MI5 and other secret police outfits use to cover up their dodgy dealings if they end up in court. David Shayler, the ex-MI5 officer, also made a statement that the security services knew that the Israeli Embassy was about to be bombed but his superiors did not act on this information. Why not? Well, at about the same time the Palestinians and the Israelis were involved in peace talks held in Oslo and Israel had the most to lose from the peace talks. So what better way to derail the peace talks than to plant a bomb and then claim 'terrorists' have broken the ceasefire. Incidentally no one was killed or even injured in the explosion. Like the MI5 man said, Mossad were involved in the bombing and they needed to blame someone else.

For more info check www.freesaj.org.uk

TRUNK CALL

What would it be like if the world had no Esso? (Exxon-Mobil to the rest of the world) Would the globe really be warming if there were no Oil giants? What if there was no Bush in the Whitehouse? That's what people will be thinking during National Tree Week (26th Nov – 2nd Dec) supported wholeheartedly by ..er, Esso. So through Tree Council events up and down the country school children, community groups and individuals can learn how driving everywhere in Esso fueled cars helps to care for trees across the UK.

www.stopesso.com

* Instead why not take part in Treesponsibility's Tree Week (at the same time), who think that "taking care of your local and global environment is something not to be left to multinational corporations." Contact 10 Broughton St, Hebdon Bridge. HX7 8JY. 01422-843222 www.konsk.co.uk

* Stop Esso campaign benefit, 13th Nov., including Hexstatic (Ninja Tune), Pressure Drop & Tru Thoughts. 9:30pm-3am, Concorde 2, Brighton. Tickets £5 from Brighton Peace and Environment Centre.

* Exxon Mobil are to have their $5 bn fine for the worst US oil spill reduced after a federal court ruled the sum was too high. They must also be pleased with neo-Labour endorsing new guidelines allowing more branding of teaching materials and activities, in schools, by corporate sponsors. **Seeing Through the Spin** is an education pack produced in response to the corporate takeover of schools. £15 + £3p&p from Baby Milk Action, 23 St Andrew's Street, Cambridge. CB2 3AX 01223 464420 www.babymilkaction.org

SchNEWS in brief

It's **Landmine Action Week** – but maybe America's got the wrong end of the stick by dropping cluster bombs and now daisy cutter bombs on Afghanistan ** This Saturday there's an **Anti-War Benefit** with Earth Tribe, DJ's and speakers, proceeds go to refugees and anti-war protests. 8.30pm till 2am £4 /3 at the Arsenal Tavern, 175 Blackstock Road, London N4 (Finsbury Pk Tube) ** Tune **into Radio 4A** in Brighton this weekend (Fri-Sun) on 106.6 FM. Saturday nite is an all women DJ's techno party. Also live on the web at www.piratetv.net ** Another Brighton Pirate Radio **Rage FM,** broadcasts every weekend on 92.1 FM. ** If you want to hear about the real costs of Britain's **food** policies get along to a meeting on Monday (12) at the Pitshanger Manor Museum, London 7-9pm Call 020 8231 2076 to reserve a place. ** When a tearful kid noticed that a statue of Ronald was missing from outside **Ronald McDonald House** in America a nationwide search was started. The 5ft solid PVC statue was found later in the day hung by the neck from a tree. Maybe Ronald doesn't like his job anymore! ** There's another **Eclectic City Community Centre** up and running in Newcastle at Bewick House, near the train station and Forth pub. It's been open to support the global days of action against this weekend's World Trade Organisation meeting. Get involved 07810 496941 www.tapp.cjb.net ** To get hold of the new Corner House Briefing on global warming **'Democracy or Car-bocracy'** see www.cornerhouse.icaap.org or cornerhouse@gn.apc.org ** **War Cry** is a new radical newsletter for those living or working in West London. For a free copy, send a SAE to West London Anarchists & Radicals, BM Makhno, London WC1N 3XX.**The Highways Agency have an exhibition about the controversial **Lamberhurst bypass** in Kent at Lamberhurst Primary School this weekend. The bypass will be built through National Trust Land at Scotney Castle and through an Area of Outstanding Natural Beauty. www.lamberhurstbypass.com

Barry Horne R.I.P.

Animal rights prisoner Barry Horne has sadly died in prison from liver failure during a hunger strike. He was sentenced to a massive 18 years for arson. He was convicted following a series of arson attacks in the early '90's on Boots the Chemist stores, who had been exposed by the Animal Liberation Front as still testing on animals after it managed to persuade everyone it was an animal friendly company. In prison he went on three hunger strikes to try and get the newly elected Neo-Labour government to honor its pre-election promise of a Royal Commission on vivisection, but they still haven't honored their promise. After the third hunger strike lasting six weeks his eyes and kidneys were damaged. He has since been on a number of hunger strikes and his last was believed to be over the government's handling of foot and mouth disease.

* The trial of three people from Shac (Stop Huntingdon Animal Cruelty) on conspiracy charges is getting underway, there will be weekly Monday demos at Huntingdon Life Sciences Labs, Cambridgeshire, details 0845-458-0630. www.shac.net

Positive SchNEWS

The growing anti-war movement is one of the most diverse movements this country's ever seen. A new organisation Muslims for Justice and Peace was formed in opposition. Many of the people involved in setting it up have never been involved in protesting before, Shaheed Saleem, one of the organisers, says "Our main point is trying to get the majority of Muslim people involved; people who look at CND and SWP banners and say 'this has nothing to do with us'. We're saying we do have a place in the movement". Other Islamic groups such as Islamic Relief, a UK based charity have decided to help by bypassing aid agencies and sending out aid directly to Afghanistan using their own convoys. * Muslims for Justice and Peace: justpeace_uk@yahoo.co.uk/ * Islamic Relief www.islamic-relief.org.uk.

*Asian Women Unite! have a meet up point for Asian women to march together on the 18th November London anti-war demo. Meet at exit 9 of Marble Arch underground station 12pm. More info: 020-7424-9535.

SMUT

Spitalfields Market Under Threat (SMUT, nice acronym) is in it's 14th year of campaigning to preserve Spitalfields Market as a public space. The indoor market in between Brick Lane and Petticoat Lane is now seriously under threat from Spitalfields Development Group who want to demolish the market and create a 'soulless' office space. The developers are seeking planning permission at Tower Hamlets Town Hall, Mulberry Close, Docklands, Nov 21st at 7pm. Last time the developers bused a load of Yuppies down to the council meeting and 'sloshed them with champers'. To preserve the market rather than privatise it, contact www.smut.org.uk or 020-7503-1965.

...and finally...

Clare Short our lovable International Development Secretary has been mouthing off in the lead up to this weekend's World Trade Organisation meeting in Qatar. According to her, anti-capitalist protesters and the al-Qaida network are virtually indistinguishable claiming that "since 11th September we haven't heard from the protesters. I'm sure they're reflecting on what their demands were because their demands turned out to be very similar to those of Bin Laden's network". Um yeah, well as SchNEWS can exclusively reveal secret anti-capitalist and al Qaida discussions in the Afghan desert recently broke down due to severe ideological division and the fact that most of us refused to grow beards (especially the women).

Forget anti-capitalists, SchNEWS spotted scary similarities between Bin Liner and Bush.
Terrorists: Leader is the spoiled son of a powerful politician, from extremely wealthy oil family.
US Govt: Leader is the spoiled son of a powerful politician, from extremely wealthy oil family.
Terrorists: Leader has declared a holy war (Jihad) against his enemies; believes any nation not with him is against him and God is on his side.
US Govt: Leader has declared a holy war (Crusade) against his enemies; believes any nation not with him is against him and God is on his side.
Terrorists: Operate through clandestine organisation (al Qaida) with agents in many countries, uses bombing, assassination and other terrorist tactics.
US Govt: Operates through clandestine organisation (CIA) with agents in many countries, uses bombing...
Terrorists: Leadership was not elected by a majority of the people in a free and fair democratic election.
You get the picture.

disclaimer

SchNEWS warns all readers the Bushes are scrubbing out enemies so need pruning back. Honest.

491 Gallery

"The Temporary Autonomous Zone is like an uprising and doesn't engage directly with the state, a guerrilla operation that liberates an area [of land or time or imagination] and then dissolves itself to reform elsewhere/elsewhen before the state can crush it." Hakim Bey

491 gallery has seeded within a building which has been abandoned for 8 years since the completion of the M11 road link. In place of racist graffiti once found covering the walls are artworks and sculptures by local and visiting artists. Where human faeces was once festering over the floor, people play, dance and relax. In the outside yard, 8 years of fly tipping, rat pits and rotting matter have been cleared to make way for an evolving garden, pond, sauna, and stage. Broken windows are fixed and act as projection screens for passing people and traffic, lighting up what has for nearly a decade been an eyesore, an empty skull.

491 is one of a number of temporary autonomous zones that have sprung up from the Warp Experience. The infamous multimedia extravaganza centred around a 24 hour play, that used to take place regularly at the Drome in South London.

The previous tennants of the building were more into high art and needle work

491 is a place where structure isn't too rigid, allowing everyone here to challenge themselves to doing something quite extraordinary. As neighbour Bright from Malawi wrote in the comments book "This place bears no resemblance to what it was 4 months ago, even movie directors wouldn't dare do this. It is a great thing when an idea has found its time to come, and time has come for Leytonstone to support The Art Organisation."

491 is an evolving play-space, currently offering workshops every week-day, regular events including Iggy Shark & co. theatrical productions and Michelle's Meta Conceptual Cabaret. People are invited to join us for Working Weekends; all in all a place for people to come and find out what they might like to offer, what dreams they might like to realise.

491 is getting closer to the community, soon to take part in the Leytonstone Arts Festival in July, providing street theatre and a somewhat subversive Leytonstone Fringe Festival. We will also join the Swaines Green Festival helping save green land in Epping from private development.

491 When faced with the possibility of a recent eviction of 491, the local council was moved enough to suggest two possible properties to move to, not wanting to lose the 'art activists' of Leytonstone. (STOP PRESS – the owners have now agreed to a peppercorn rent agreement for the next three years, giving the place medium term stability).

491 As of June 2002 the community has grown to eighteen people, living in and around the gallery. Those sleeping in the building are part of the breathing exhibition which is this living arts piece – while others come in to support particular projects and events.

491 acts as the base for several other projects including Festival of Flight, Masala Theatre Productions, and is home to teachers, playwrights, craftspeople and more.

491 will soon open the 'workshop' a place for artists to create and sell their work.

491, Grove Green Rd, Leytonstone, London E11 Tel: 07932 762 5871

Computer Game Review: State of Emegency

It's good to know the kidz are being edukated by games such as **State of Emergency** which follows the plot of the 'Corporation' who have taken over the country and established a shopping paradise. In **State of Emergency** you are part of the resistance taking the battle to big business. You can either run rampage through the shopping malls Black Block style creating economic damage or join with the resistance in toppling 'The Corporation' though acts of sabotage, social unrest and subterfuge.

The game itself is a third-person perspective game where you undertake missions on behalf of the resistance. You can grab any object and use it as a weapon; from bins to discarded police billy-clubs. In toppling The Man, you have to deal with rampaging street gangs, cops and the army. The game settings range from shopping malls to prisons to office blocks and overall the action is fast paced.

Is it really subversive though? Salon.com (the mainstream web-mag) called it "a little less prole, a little more Proudhon." The official game site features fly postings that are subvertised with a distinctly anarchist message, "Uprising is the only chance for personal freedom and liberty".

It may be a shameless cash-in of the anti-capitalist movement but at least offering some alternative ideas to gamers whose choice is dominated by pro-military and/or pointless violence based games. It has placed politics in front of people who previously considered serious issues to be whether Quake or Unreal was the best first-person-shooter.

Reclaim the screen - but are they donating the profits to Indian farmers?

A Taste Of Freedom

"FREE DOM" in Wroclaw, Poland, is an autonomous cultural centre, set up in the heart of the Polish community. "Free Dom" ("dom" means "house" in Polish) began life in the middle of the 1990s, when a group of friends squatted a small house (called "REJON 69") near the centre of Wroclaw. During the next three and a half years the group formed a small community and organised a range of cultural and political events, like punk concerts, festivals, and regular 'food not bombs' events. In 1999, they were forced out by bailiffs, police and the local authority.

The next building they squatted only lasted two weeks, but important ties were being created and an 'eviction party' elicited considerable support from the local (Jewish) community and brought the squatting issue into the media spotlight for the first time. After a big campaign, demonstrations, leafleting and expressions of support from residents, the local authority handed the building over to the squatters in September 2000.

Despite its dilapidated condition the house was opened, after a year of repairs, in the spring of 2001. In place of the ruins were an alternative library, an info cafe, a dark room, silk screen printing and spaces for art gallery exhibitions, cinema and concert rooms.

Acts like Citizen Fish, Catharsis, Sin Dios, Tragedy, and many local bands have played there. Every Sunday there is 'Food not Bombs' event which gives squatters a chance to skillshare, provide food and eat together with local homeless people and socialise.

This also creates scope to engage with local people who have been made aware of a resistance to the new demands of capitalism on a country that had no motorways before 1996 and some of Europe's last great forests. Now, however, there is a new 126km road between Wroclaw and Nogawczyce - part of the Trans European Network and built by a consortium of British firms headed by WS Atkins.

'Free Dom' plan to start a local newspaper to give out independent information, promote alternatives to capitalism and provide more opportunities for community involvement.

They have started activities with the city kids, who have made the building their own. Together with their parents they hold parties and feasts, games and painting for children.

Also part of the plan is to begin an after school programme where kids can get help with homework and spend their time creatively with juggling, theatre, and photography workshops.

One resident explained the purpose of the centre: "The idea and function of the cultural centre is to be a place where people can come, without money, and realise non profit projects/ ideas, or just have a place to meet. This house is the only legal place like this in the city." Co-operation with other squatter groups is essential for the survival of all. With the World Bank eyeing up the silverware and describing Poland as 'one of the most advanced transition countries in the region' (ie: it's flogging everything), it is time for the local groups to radicalise and work together to ensure their mutual futures.

In November they hosted a congress for Polish autonomous groups and are trying to build a support network across Poland, particularly for those affected by Polish law which does not recognise squatters' rights. Police are often aggressive and bribes are accepted currency to delay eviction. 'Free Dom' is a legal centre and doesn't have the same problems as other groups attempting to reclaim old buildings as community spaces. However, because they are 'legal they have to fulfil bureaucratic rules as laid down by fire police, building and government inspectors.

Many of these rules are absurd and unachievable because the activists don't have enough money to pay the bribes (and don't want to). This curtails the organisation of events and work with children. It could also lead to the eventual closure of the building.

Support is needed, especially from abroad. Said a resident "When the local government see that some international group and individuals supports us, it will help us in negotiations." You can send letters of support to: Free Dom, ul.Jagiellonczyka 10c 50-240 Wroclaw, Poland.
E-mail: freedom69@go2.pl
A direct letter expressing support to the City Government (Wroclaw Fax: +48 71 344 78 29 would also help.
For more information go to: www.ainfos.ca

WAKE UP! WAKE UP! IT'S YER SEVEN YEARS OLD TODAY!

Weekly SchNEWS

Printed and Published in Brighton by Justice?

"Play it backwards for a birthday message from Bin Laden."

Friday 16th November 2001   www.schnews.org.uk   **Issue 331   Free/Donation**

BLUNKETT BAN

"The government is using this bill firstly to introduce the indefinite detention of suspects on the say-so of the security services, and secondly to introduce a whole series of new powers which have nothing to do with terrorism." - Statewatch

With the UK now under a 'State of Emergency' Home Secretary David Blunkett this week announced another brand spanking new terrorism bill, this time with added internment - that's trial without jury - for any foreigners suspected of being terrorists. Those lucky enough to be locked up would be able to appeal to a special immigration tribunal but not have access to the security information that led to their arrest in the first place! Even better, the suspected terrorist could remain in prison indefinitely, subject only to six monthly reviews.

The emergency order which says the events of 11th September are 'threatening the life of the nation', is a technical twist to allow Britain to opt out of Article 5 of the European Convention on Human Rights, which rather inconveniently bans detention without trial.

Still, we've seen internment before during the Gulf war. Writer Abbas Shiblak was one of more than 100 Iraqis and Palestinians who were said to be linked to terrorism and detained without trial in the UK. Shiblak had in fact been a critic of Saddam when the UK was still busy selling weapons to Baghdad (Saddam was still considered a good guy then). After months of imprisonment the suspects were released without a single one of them being charged or deported.

Internment was also re-introduced in Northern Ireland in August 1971 as an attempt to crush the IRA. During one night the Army sealed off whole areas raiding homes and taking away hundreds of Catholic men for detention without trial. All were subjected to brutal treatment, 12 in particular were selected for 'special' treatment. These twelve were secretly moved from the internment clearing centres to an unknown destination and held for seven days. They had hoods on their heads throughout, had no idea where they were and were kept completely isolated. They were severely beaten, forced to stand spreadeagled against walls until they collapsed, given hardly any food and subjected to 'white noise', which prevented them from sleeping. All the while being constantly interrogated. It was a new technique of sensory deprivation designed to disorient the mind and help the authorities to find the 'truth'. By March 1972, when London took over direct rule of Northern Ireland, some 924 people were interned. The vast majority were Catholic who were eventually released without being charged. The mass arrests led to widespread rioting, twenty-three deaths and increased support for the republican movement. As Amnesty International pointed out, "Internment measures have resulted in human rights violations and failed to deter political violence in several parts of the world."

WET BLUNKETTS

It's only been 16 months since the last Terrorism Act was passed (see SchNEWS 268) and it's already been used on peaceful protestors. The existing Act defines terrorism as "The use or threat of action, designed to influence the government or to intimidate the public or a section of the public, made for the purpose of advancing a political, religious or ideological cause." Which is why at a recent EU Terrorism Summit after September 11th one of the Prime Minister's spokesmen boasted "we have some of the toughest laws anywhere in the world." But obviously not tough enough for Blunkett who's got even more (Santa) clauses on his Christmas wish-list.

So shut up CND – time to forget about letting people know that nuclear trains might be running through their towns. Beat it peace campaigners, no more protesting outside nuclear bases. Stop whinging Amnesty, who cares about foreigners being locked up without trial? Put a sock in it Privacy International, what's wrong with telecommunications companies storing every email, phone call, or fax we've ever made.

So don't you airy-fairy lot forget that in order to safeguard our civil liberties against the terrorist threat we must…er, take liberties away.

* See the Anti-Terrorism, Crime and Security Act in full www.statewatch.org

---

CRAP ARREST OF THE WEEK

For kissing a cop… A 77 year old was recently nicked for kissing a female cop on the cheek. The amorous OAP grabbed the WPC, planted a smacker on the shocked rozzer's face and was promptly arrested for his misdeed. He was bound over to keep the peace for six months by magistrates. Mind you, kissing a pig has got to be one step from bestiality.

ANTI-CLIMAX

After 4 years of negotiations a final agreement was reached last week on the Kyoto Protocol aimed at reducing climate change. It sets targets to reduce emissions of greenhouse gases by a measly 5.2% by 2012, which is pathetic when you consider that it's estimated that what is really needed to stabilise the climate is a cut of 60-90%. It's unlikely though that even this small target will be met, with the agreement including massive loopholes which will allow richer polluting countries to buy carbon credits off of those who have credits to spare (see SchNEWS 314/315). The fact that the US aren't having anything to do with the protocol also makes it totally irrelevant before it's even signed since they produce a quarter of the world's greenhouse gases. George W's reasoning for pulling out of the talks in July was that it was "unfair because it exempts developing nations", but er George, isn't that fact that the US uses 20 times more energy than India and 300 times more than Mozambique slightly more unfair?.

*Vigils outside American Embassy every Monday 5-7pm

* December 1st Stop Esso protests outside petrol stations throughout the country. To adopt your local store go phone 0870 010 9510 or www.stopesso.com

*December 8th March from Embassy of drought stricken Afghanistan to the US Embassy in solidarity with the victims of climate change- passing the Ethiopian and Bangladeshi Embassies on the way. Meet 11am Prince Consort Road, South Kensington tube, London www.campaignagainstclimatechange.net

* To get yourself informed about climate change get hold of a copy of this months Ecologist. £3.50 plus p&p from The Ecologist Unit 18, Chelsea Wharf, 15 Lots Road, London SW10 0JQ tel: 020-7351-3578 www.theecologist.org

*For more info on climate change check out www.risingtide.org.uk

*Next week in London (19th) there's a conference called 'Transport in a Renewable Era' For more info contact Matt on 0207 752277 m-mckay@imeche.org.uk

---

BALFOUR BEATEN

"We are delighted. We were not expecting this, because Balfour Beatty was fighting hard for the dam. This Ilisu campaign is a great example of environment and human rights groups fighting together to be effective." - Kerim Yildiz, spokesman for the Kurdish Human Rights Project.

After shedloads of direct action this week Balfour Beatty announced they were pulling out of the Ilisu Dam project in Turkey. This incredible victory is an inspiration to us all. Comedian and activist Mark Thomas, on tour in Brighton this week, had SchNEWS hacks cracking-up with his quips about shutting down Balfour's Annual General Meeting: "The Kurdish Human Rights activists were raging about the atrocities being committed by Turkish government in the Ilisu area, and Friends of the Earth, they were really angry too. I mean they were tutting - loudly - and looking very cross…and the Quakers normally pacifists to the end shoulder-barged their way onto the platform. At this point a couple of big, mean looking Group 4 security thugs started pacing towards us with intent and in the blink of an eye two very skinny, attractive environmental activist women had rugby tackled them to the ground…"

As the chief executive of Balfour Beatty, Mike Welton, explained "Balfour Beatty believes the project could only proceed with substantial extra work and expense and with considerable further delay. Accordingly, in concert with Impregilo of Italy, it has decided to withdraw from the project."

The Dam planned for the Kurdish region of Turkey and would have made more than 30,000 homeless and affected up to 78,000 people. It would have drowned dozens of towns and villages including the world historic site of Hasankeyf, submerging a total area the size of Greater Manchester. This massive dam would also have made it possible for the Turkish government to control the flow of the Tigris river into Syria and Iraq - no prizes for guessing that this would've been seen as fightin' talk. As part of an international Swiss-led consortium including 7 multinationals and 8 governments, Balfour Beatty were seeking $200 million in export credit guarantees from the British Government to build the dam – that's British taxpayers money that would have been used to pay for the ethnic cleansing of Kurds in Turkey.

The World Commission on Dams (WCD) published a report of large-scale hydroelectric dams in November last year saying, "in many cases dams have led to the irreversible loss of species populations and ecosystems." It went on to explain that "Impacts of dam building on people and livelihoods have been…devastating." In other words, Dams are NOT environmentally friendly and they are NOT a viable answer to increasing energy demands if you care about anything other than profit.

The Ilisu Dam is now not likely to go ahead. But, there are 22 other dams planned in the Tigris and Euphrates basins in Turkey that must be stopped. Amec, another British construction company, want to build a dam in Uyseffely in the Jordanian minority region of Turkey. If their plans go ahead they will displace 12-15,000 people and its predicted environmental impact goes off the scale. They are trying to secure a £68 million export credit guarantee from the taxpayer - that means if Turkey defaulted on the payment, taxpayers will foot the bill. See www.foe.co.uk and www.ilisu.org.uk, or call 01865-200550.

WAR ISN'T TOPPS

Children in the States are being brainwashed by Topps swap cards who claim "Our cards deliver the details in a medium with which they are familiar and comfortable." about their series called "Enduring Freedom". The deceptive cards depict George W. Bush and the US military in a nice clean sanitised image as they save the world from the "evil doers". Check out the slickening details at www.topps.com/enduringfreedom.html. But free thinking kids are being urged to bunk off school on 5th December and get involved in the international strike of pupils against the war. Contact: nonalaguerrelille@altern.org

* Check out the new anti-World Trade Organisation/anti-war spoof of the SUN "newspaper" at the big anti-war demo in London (Sunday 18th, noon, Hyde Park, www.stopwar.org.uk), or see www.the-spun.co.uk. And why not join the SchNEWS block at the demo and help us give out some of these bloody newsletters (if we're not at the demo check out the nearest pub where we will be trying to become the drunk block). After the demo why not get down to the blatantly squatted café on Drummond Street, (nr. Euston station). Hosted by the Goblins with food & drink, DJs, films and anarchy. Followed by an eviction party on evening of 21st.

* A medical student, Carlos Geovanny Blanco Leguzamo, has been shot dead at an anti-war demo by police at the Colombia National University, Bogota. The police had invaded the University campus, undeterred the students stayed on campus overnight for further protests. www.midiaindependente.org/

* There's a call to take non-violent anti-militarist direct action on International Human Rights Day (10th December). There's a blockade of the British Military Joint Forces Hq, Northwood, meet 7.30am, Northwood Tube, or get in your own affinity group and go to Northwood or your own target. www.northwood.cjb.net. 07950-567099. Preparation day, 1st December, phone for details.

They Shot the Sheriff

The Trident Ploughshares campaign has made a formal complaint about comments made by a Sheriff during a court case at Faslane trident nuclear base. "I look upon you so-called peace protesters as parasites, causing untold damage to fences, disrupting the base and wasting this country's money which could be spent elsewhere." Er, wasting money? Trident costs Britain £1.5 billion a year. And a bit more than a few fences would be damaged if one of those friendly missiles ever went off.

SchNEWS in brief

Fox Hunting is likely to start again soon in most of the country, so why not get involved with the Hunt Saboteurs contact 0845-4500727 www.huntsabs.org.uk ** 24th November is the 8th Anniversary Demo against **Campsfield Immigration Detention Centre**, Campsfield House, Kidlington, near Oxford 12 - 2pm. www.closecampsfield.org.uk. Followed by a meeting of the anti-detention network at 2.30pm in Oxford. Further info/transport details phone 01865-558145 or email bmackeith@aol.com ** **Sweatshop Labour Just End It!** On the 24th Nov there's a conference against child and sweatshop labour at University of London, Mallet St, WC1. 11am till 5pm. Speakers include Dita Sari, a prominent Indonesian trade unionist who spent time in prison because of her political activity. She will also doing a speaking tour around the country call 07904 431959 to find out where. www.nosweat.org.uk ** A man has been sentenced to a year in prison after climbing through an open window at **Keynsham Police Station** in Bristol. The cheeky robber stole two mobile phones and the keys to a police van, which he then used as a getaway vehicle!

The Rebel Alliance

Brighton's direct action get-together is happening next Wednesday (21st) 7.30pm Upstairs at the Albert pub on Trafalgar St. Followed by a discussion about the war.

Inside SchNEWS

Today Satpal Ram starts his 16th year of imprisonment for murder. He was viciously attacked by racists in a restaurant and in self defence stabbed one of the attackers who later died after refusing medical treatment. The Criminal Cases Review Commission (CCRC) has admitted he was the victim of a prolonged attack, but believe he was wrong to defend himself. They have provisionally rejected Satpal's legal team's submission after sitting on the case for four years. Please **URGENTLY** send protest to the CCRC, Alpha Tower, Suffolk Street, Queensway, Birmingham, B1 1TT. Tel: 0121-633-1800. Fax 0121-633-1823. Email: chairman@ccrc.gov.uk Letters of support to: Satpal Ram, HMP Blakenhurst, Hewell Lane, Redditch, Worcestershire B97 6QS. More info and sample letter at www.appleonline.net/satpal

…and finally…

Let's face it there's loadsa consumer crap out there, especially mobile phone accessories. *"We all like to relax in the sun and we're sure your mobile or cordless phone feels the same. Here's its very own deck chair, so while it sun itself by your side, you'll never miss a call.* Except that you'll never get a call if yer that sad! If you are stupid enough to fall for that why not have a $500 bikini. This useless bit of cloth says on the label "Should not be worn in the sun or water". Er, what's the point of that then?

Alternatively you could save your hard won cash and give consumerism a rest on Buy Nothing Day, 23rd November. www.adbusters.org

Or why not take a leaf out the fanclubber book where 30 fake shoppers bought and returned goods throughout the day every 1 minutes for six hours! This caused the store massive inconvenience and they were obliged to honor all the returns causing the tills to run out of money at one point! www.fanclubbers.org

disclaimer
SchNEWS warns all shopaholics that Justice can be seen to be blind so pull yer finger out! Honest.

STORMING THE WORLD INC SUMMIT

THE WORLD INC ARE HAVING THEIR ANNUAL SUMMIT AT THE HEAD QUARTERS IN BABYLONDON.
ARE YOU INVITED?

Buyouts, mega mergers and colossal trade deals put the whole world into the hands of two enormous multinational conglomerates - who ruled the world as partners, dealing with countries and companies alike, with the media monopolies doing their propaganda for them.

They came to be known as 'Coke' and 'Pepsi' - not because they were led by these two, but by the fact that one owned Coke, the other Pepsi. Both sold essentially the same products which were made in the same factories in China, South America and South East Asia.

Every year executives and leaders from the two powers came together to pretend to listen to regional voices, rubber stamp a few resolutions and enjoy the wine and mini-golf in their high security HQ in Babylondon. The real agenda of the World Inc was in fact to maintain the front that there were two players, when really it was mostly all run by the same people.

This year at the summit the only remotely thorny subject under discussion was the deal for Volkswagen to do a direct swap of Congo for Peru - currently owned by Motorola - which would mean that Coke then controlled all of South America.

The World Inc Headquarters in Babylondon featuring the two towers which represent the two conglomerates. Locals call it the 'two cans'.

PREDICTABLY THERE WAS A BUILD-UP OF OPPOSITION

As usual there was the rash of counter-conferences against the summit around the world; ranging from corporate PR greenwash frenzies featuring paid-off keynote speakers and delegate junkets through to red flag waving march and megaphone affairs down to heavily policed events of political activists in regions fighting the havoc the 'two cans' had caused to their environments and livelihoods.

In the days leading up to the summit, protesters began to head towards the centre of Babylondon. In response to this the media began parroting the overblown police claims of a 'Terrorist influx descending on Babylondon'...

Again there was a 'call for action' to converge on the summit centre and ruck at the fence with the sponsored para-military force geared up for the occasion.

This inner city squat protecting the last scrap of green in the centre of Babylondon became the convergence centre for the 'Summit Else' alternative event against the World Inc Summit. The centre stood in the shadows of the 'two cans'...

PEOPLE BEGAN ARRIVING IN THEIR DROVES...

The 'Summit Else' event was a counter-conference of the 'official' counter-conference: Government sponsored publicity pointed most of the protesters who didn't know otherwise to the Babylondon Liberal Forum (BLF), a convergence centre and accommodation point the city council had put on. The propaganda was so good that most protesters didn't know that BLF was in fact a front group working for the Home Office in an attempt to control the protests. On the surface it was a friendly place to be to meet people, there was free food being handed out and nobody stopped you doing anything. This made covert surveillance much easier.

(above) The Babylondon Liberal Forum - spot the spook!!

Convoys of dodgy vehicles banked up on the edge of the city as they were searched, and many were refused entry.

(right) The day before the planned mass demonstration thousands were building up at the BLF centre.

Fleets of chartered coaches brought in hundreds of members of 'Hijack Resistance' to Babylondon. Following these were truckloads of red banners and newspapers. Immediately they made their presence felt with megaphones barking out orders to party members who enthusiastically waved and cheered at seemingly everything the speakers said. The spokesperson for Hijack Resistance denied that they were mostly all Redskyists.

REMEMBER - WE'RE THE ONLY ONES HERE WHO UNDERSTAND THE ISSUES SO SELL THEM OUR PAPER...

YES WE WILL

The Campaign Against Camping Mats performed an action where they cut a load of camping mats to pieces in a protest against the production of useless plastic products by slave labour in debt-ridden non-alliance countries. They were to wear the cut up mats during the demonstrations the next day so they could sweat while wearing them in the sun in solidarity with sweat shop labourers.

The Summit Hoppers Movement jetted in during the days before from all around the globe.

'...HELLO MAKE IT QUICK PHONE CREDITS ARE REALLY EXPENSIVE IN BABYLONDON ... ER I THINK I'LL BE GOING WITH THE POSH BLOCK - THOUGH MY ANARCHIST THEORY IS A BIT RUSTY ... SEE YOU DOWN THE FRONT ... BYE.'

Last but not least the Brew Block finally showed up

I CAN'T BELIEVE HOW CHEAP THE BEER IS HERE...

A lot of protesters couldn't get into the centre of the city of Babylondon because their ID card numbers appeared blacklisted on the International Terrorist Register. As a matter of course anybody entering the city centre who the police suspected of being a protester was searched.

THEN... THE BIG DAY OF ACTION CAME...

The protesters divided into different 'blocks' according to their mode of tactic to protest against the World Inc Summit

The party block lead the charge in the morning. They immediately took off in a direction away from the World Inc Summit centre, with the international samba band generating a street carnival atmosphere.

The camera block's tactic was to photograph or video everything which moves, and then immediately upload all the images onto the internet. The tactic works well when they can get evidence of police violence, but many of the other protesters equally didn't want to be caught commiting criminal acts on film, and often attacked the camera block. This block was possibly the least likely to breach the summit centre security.

By 11AM the heavies were out on the street: the International Avin' It Block. A coming together of many nationalities with the simple principle - going out and fucking avin' it on the street. Safety in numbers and anonymity. This is the block always most threatening to the summit security - but it's got other fish to fry: like banks, franchise shops, car dealerships and anything else that's a symbol of Babylondon. Every Avin' It Block is rumoured to be infiltrated by police, and we will never know what leads some to the 'dark side' of smashing up working class peoples' cars and corner shops.

The Posh Block moved off in the afternoon tagging itself at one point behind the Avin' It Block, revelling in the fact of being united - however briefly - with a genuine working class struggle. They would text-message their friends at home to tell them so.

The Brew Block burst out of the blocks at about 4PM, and those who were sober enough caught the last bit of the Avin' It Bloc, while others stayed on to mind the kettle at the 'Summit Else' centre. Later on smaller affinity groups roamed the town in search of open off-licences.

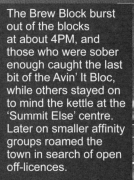

ANYONE GOT A LIGHT?

None of the blocks realistically came near to actually threatening the summit security zone - except the party block which danced their way right to the last line of the police defence before the gates. But by this stage the samba band had done their three tunes about ten times each and lost momentum.

Meanwhile, during all this, in a quiet back room in the conference centre the Chairman of Volkswagen Group and the CEO of Motorola shook hands on the deal that would give Motorola control of Congo - and therefore most of the world's supply of coltan used in mobile phones. This would also mean that Peru could now be fully absorbed into the South American Combined Economic Zone. In fact this was a publicity stunt as the deal was done out six months previously.

Summit officials duly issued a press statement in the late afternoon announcing that the leaders had all agreed to cut poverty, foreign debt and carbon emissions, when actually they had spent the day playing mini-golf.

THEN THE UNBELIEVABLE HAPPENED...

MOMENTS LATER THE TWO WORLD INC CANS COLLAPSE

Within seconds the building disappears in a dust cloud. It is not immediately visible how much of the building is still standing because of the smoke, but the two cans are definitely gone. Inside this building, presumed dead are the leaders of the handful of corporations which own the planet, their leading PR-spin overlords, and the presidents of the fifteen alliance countries. Tragically hundreds of support staff - cooks, lift technicians, waiters, waitresses, receptionists etc are killed in this incredible attack. The protest stops and everybody stares at the inferno in stunned silence.

The whole city centre is overcome with thick smoke. Luckily for the protesters - because their attempts to get near the summit centre during the day were such dismal failures, they are all at a safe distance to run away from the clouds of rubble which are crashing to the ground. At this moment everybody is united in their struggle to get clear of the danger area, with the divisions that separated the protesters gone: Hijack Resistance, Avin It Block, Brew Block, Party Block and Posh Block all help one another escape.

NNRRRNNNNRRROOOWWWWW SSSHHNNNWWWWWAAAAANNNNNN

After what seems an eternity - but is probably more like about half an hour, the dust clouds start to settle and the moment of it has passed. People gazing up from the Summit Else centre can barely believe their eyes as the shadows of the cans are no longer cast on its roof.

Then - just when it seemed like nothing else outrageous could possibly happen, those standing outside the 'Summit Else' squatted centre hear something which sounds a bit like somebody twiddling with a 1970's synthesiser...

SSSSSSHHHHHHHHHHHHHHH

Materialising before them as if by magic is what appears to be five human beings and a mechanical dog. They introduce themselves...

"Hello Earthlings. We saw your website and call-out for action and thought we'd race across the galaxy to lend our support for the demo. Call us the 'hologram block' because what you're seeing is holograms of ourselves - so it's pointless to shoot at us. Incase you're wondering who bombed the summit - it was us. I suppose you could say we are intergalactic anarcho-confrontationalists. We used old ex-cold war missiles bought in an auction on our planet, and we think they've done a good job of getting rid of the fucking parasites your planet has suffered for far too long. Thirty men controlled 99% of your planet - that's taking the piss as far as we're concerned. Those thirty are now dead. We realise that things are going to get a bit wobbly and changeable on Earth because of this, so be brave. Remember it's for the best."

WAKE UP! IT'S YER DODGY DESERT DEALINGS

I'd trade it all for a little bit more...

Weekly SchNEWS

Printed and Published in Brighton by Justice?

Friday 23rd November 2001   **www.schnews.org.uk**   **Issue 332   Free/Donation**

D'oha!

"The rich nations are still negotiating primarily in the interests of their major multinationals. And they are still shutting the poor nations out of the negotiating process. The more cynical trade watchers say that this is the way trade negotiations have always been conducted." - Barry Coates, World Development Movement

It ended in victory for protestors in Seattle two years ago (see SchNEWS 240) but in the Qatar desert last week U.S. Trade Representative Robert Zoellick was celebrating, "Today the members of the World Trade Organisation (WTO) have sent a powerful signal...we have removed the stain of Seattle." After six days of 'talks' in Doha, Qatar, a last minute declaration was produced, with the wealthy nations describing the new trade round as the 'Doha development round' - supposedly good for the world's poor and good for the world's economy. This outrageous declaration was practically written by the US and European Union alone and delegates from poorer countries were forced to sign.

The Declaration came after complaints of bully-boy tactics from the powerful nations who used arm twisting and threats of loss of aid and debt relief. This and fear of being branded 'deal breakers' responsible for global recession if they didn't comply, forced poorer countries to sign on the dotted line. Richard Bernal one of Jamaica's official delegates, explained the pressure, "We are made to feel that we are holding up the rescue of the global economy if we don't agree to a new trade round here."

This 'new' development round will only further the goals of the rich and powerful and line the pockets of corporate shareholders. As Barry Coates from the World Development Movement points out "For the world's poorest countries...little has changed - their exports are blocked, their businesses are wiped out by foreign multinationals and their farmers are driven off their land by subsidised exports from the rich countries... The EU and US have exploited the vulnerability of poor countries in order to force their agenda on them. Even where it appears that developing countries may benefit, the Declaration is so riddled with holes and get-out clauses that the gains are likely to be illusory."

Mark Curtis from Christian Aid added, "Poor countries have come away from Qatar with a fistful of crumbs but they're yet to have any significant slice of the WTO's cake."

* What does this trade round mean? You tell us! There's gonna be more talks to clarify things the WTO have talked about before, and a commitment for all WTO member states to start talks on four new issues at the next ministerial meeting in two years time. Got that?

"Eat my shorts"

Forty two countries and hundreds of cities around the world saw protests during the WTO meetings.

In **Aoteroa**, New Zealand, the hometown of Mike Moore, director of the WTO 200 people went on a 'tour of capitalist greed' around the city. In **Bangkok**, Thailand 1,500 farmers, jasmine rice producers, trade unionists and HIV/AIDS activists marched from Bangkok's World Trade Centre to the US Embassy. In **New Delhi** India 500,000 peasants, landless labourers, youth, women and trade union activists took part in civil disobedience. **Seoul**, South Korea 20,000 marched for labour rights in the midst of neoliberal restructuring and to show solidarity with international protests against the war on Afghanistan. **Ljubliana**, Slovenia Despite heavy snow 2,000 had a street party that shut downtown, and in **Teheran**, Iran, 500 workers rallied peacefully at the Tehran University campus. For a full list www.nadir.org/nadir/initiativ/agp/free/qatar/index1

* Read the daily reports from Doha www.foodfirst.org/

* Check out www.gatt.org/ for the truth about the WTO

* 'The WTO's Hidden Agenda,' confidential documents between business and UK government officials pushing for a pro-business WTO.www.corpwatch.org

More than 80 countries now have per capita incomes lower than a decade ago and, as the United Nations development programme points out, it is often those countries which are highly 'integrated' into the global economy that are becoming more marginal. For example in spite of the fact that exports from sub-Saharan Africa, have reached nearly 30% of GDP the number of people living in poverty there continues to grow. Even the International Monetary Fund admits, "in recent decades, nearly one-fifth of the world population has regressed."

CRAP ARREST OF THE WEEK

For looking after an injured friend.

While demonstrating outside the home of the owner of Newchurch guinea pig farm (supliers to the vivisection industry), 2 protesters were hospitalised after a vicious attack by security. One man suffered three large head wounds and was beaten so severely he was left unrecognisable while the other needed his head stapled back together after being bludgeoned with a club. When the cops turned up they ordered all the activists to leave immediately under Section 42 of the Criminal Justice Act but one man refused wanting to stay with his severely injured mate until the ambulances had arrived. For this act of kindness he was nicked while the thugs were left alone. www.guineapigs.org.uk

POISONED CHALICE

The Mexican government lost its appeal against a decision made under the North American Free Trade Agreement (NAFTA), the free trade area covering Canada, USA and Mexico. Like the WTO, NAFTA removes "barriers to trade", such obstructive unnecessary things like labour laws, environmental and health regulations.

All poor old Metalclad Corp wanted to do was build a toxic waste dump in San Luis Potosi, Mexico. Local people took direct action to stop it being built because it would poison the local water supply and forced the local government to refuse planning permission and declare the site part of an ecological reserve. This was however - thanks to NAFTA - a barrier to trade, an infringement of the corporations rights (yes, corporations feel pain as well you know) and illegal. So the company sued for $90 million in damages, including compensation for lost profits and future business! They got $16.9 million in the end, but we're sure for the Californian based company that will do nicely thank-you-very-much.

NO-MAN'S ISLAND

The small island of Tuvalu in the Pacific Ocean has become the first victim of climate change. The island's 11,000 inhabitants are being forced to abandon their homes as sea level rise has caused coastal erosion, increased storms and salinization of their drinking water. New Zealand has agreed to accept all of the island's residents. Tuvaluans are laying the blame on the U.S: "...they've effectively denied future generations of Tuvaluans their fundamental freedom to live where our ancestors have lived for thousands of years." Current estimates reckon that sea level could rise up to 1 metre during this century this could this would inundate not only islands but large parts of countries such as Bangladesh which could cause millions of climate refugees. www.earth-policy.org

HEATHGROW

Residents of west London were stocking up on earplugs this week after the government announced the go ahead for a fifth terminal at Heathrow. British Airways insist that the new terminal is needed to boost the economy. After a 4 year planning enquiry, the planning inspector agreed but did go on to say that this should be the last new development at Heathrow. Oh yeah? Well that's what they said when they allowed Terminal 4 to be built. As the Middlesex Gazzette so rightly predicted in 1947 *"An atomic bomb dropped at Heathrow could not spread devastation more widely than the disruption caused by the construction of an airport on this spot."*

If you think you've got noisy neighbours then imagine living under the Heathrow flight path, about 1 million people do, and have to put up with a plane flying over their house about every 90 seconds from 4.30am to 10pm. For them, Terminal 5 will mean more and probably bigger planes, such as the new European airbus. It is also going to mean more road traffic; with an estimated 49,000 extra car journeys in what is already the most congested area of the south east. For them the continued creation of a mega-airport on their doorstep is totally unacceptable just so the government can boast 'our airports bigger than yours'. As one local resident says "They call it progress, but it seems like sheer greed to me."

If the aviation industry continues to grow then it's likely that there's going to be many more airport expansions. To make sure this and other controversial schemes aren't slowed down by whinging do-gooders Neo-Labour are 'modernising' planning laws. Which in effect mean that if ministers decide a scheme should go ahead in 'the national interest' then there is next to bugger-all anyone can do to legally oppose this. Planning inquiries are to become discussions on how roads are landscaped or what colour that new nuclear power station should be, but the public will just have to trust the government that the scheme is needed and the proposal of alternatives or questioning the need will be ignored. The Campaign for Planning Sanity is opposing these changes and have organised a training weekend 8-9th Dec in Birmingham www.onlincam.freeserve.co.uk

* This Saturday (24th) November, HACAN ClearSkies who've been campaigning against Terminal 5 are marching in London. Meet Whitehall Place (just off Whitehall) at 11am. 020 7737 6641 www.hacan.org.uk

* Flying may be a cheap way to get across the globe, but not only is it concreting the countryside, it also plays a massive part in the cooking of the planet. For example a return flight from London to India emits as much carbon as the average person in the world generates in a year. Flying is the least energy efficient form of transport and the fastest increasing source of greenhouse gases. Look at this website before you book a flight: www.chooseclimate.org

* A protest camp on the route of the proposed A6 bypass near Alvaston, Derbyshire want more people to live on site. Directions 07812434217, dot@theadora.screaming.net

* Doormice, protected under EU and UK law, have been found on the route of the proposed Lamberhurst Bypass. Doormice are according to English Nature a 'key indicator of ancient woodland'. www.lamberhurstbypass.com

*There's a growing campaign against the proposed Tyne road tunnel under the river between North Tyneside and Jarrow, which will greatly increase traffic and pollution in the area. More info from 0113 2428150 www.tyne-crossings.org

Positive SchNEWS

The Planning for Real process has been used in many areas to get local people together to talk about what they'd like to see happen to improve their communities. Using a scale model of their area people can identify problems and then discuss what they'd like to see happen and how that can be made to happen. Help and advice on how to run a Planning for Real advent are available from. The Neighbourhood Initiatives Foundation at, The Poplars, Lightmoor, Telford TF4 3QN 0870 7700339 www.nifonline.org.uk

SchNEWS in brief

Demo Saturday 24th, 2pm at the Glen, **St.Leonards on Sea** , East Sussex. Developers have moved in despite the local residents association trying to raise money to buy the land and preserve it as an open space for community use. The Glen is a small natural oasis of woodland, wetland and scrub, much of it is ancient woodland, and home to badgers, newts and owls. 0845 458 9572 e: save_the_glen@hotmail.com ** A group of **intercontinental anti-capitalist artists** have an exhibition in East London (9th –16th December) and want more contributions from artists (any medium). E-mail: alturnertiveart@yahoo.com ** A US Government funded $2.5 million bio-prospecting project of Mayan medicinal plants and traditional knowledge in the **Chiapas** region of Mexico has been 'definitively cancelled'. This is a victory for the indigenous people as they can now propose their own alternative approaches to using the resources. ** **Mayday 2002 Planning Meeting** Sunday 25th 2pm, London Activist Resource Centre, Fieldgate St (Whitechapel tube) Located behind big Mosque email: londonmayday@yahoo.co.uk

INSIDE SchNEWS

Three organisers of the Stop Huntingdon Animal Cruelty (SHAC) have received one-year prison sentences for "Conspiracy to Cause a Public Nuisance". The charges related to the publication of the SHAC newsletter, which allegedly encouraged readers to call more than once, send black faxes and unsolicited mail to Huntingdon Life Sciences (HLS) employees and investors. The reason for targeting SHAC campaigners was that they have been successful in bringing a multi-million pound company to its knees in a few years. Originally there were a lot of conspiracy charges, including incitement to cause mental grievous bodily harm (which never reached court), and incitement to cause criminal damage (a plea bargain was entered and only a year sentence was given instead of up to four years).

But when it comes to prosecuting animal abusers the authorities seem less keen. One HLS employee received only 50 hours community service for punching a dog in the face and HLS only received slap on the wrist for breaches of the Good Laboratory Practice regulations for their fraudulent science and horrendous record of animal abuse. Recently HLS were found guilty for failing to hold an AGM, but received an unconditional discharge. Another prosecution against the Managing Director and board members is expected soon.

Despite the jailings the SHAC campaign continues contact www.shac.net 0845-4580630.

Send letters of support to those jailed: Heather Avery (TE1951) and Natasha Dellamaigne (TE1952), both at HMP and YOI Highpoint, Stradis Hall, New Market, Suffolk, CB8 9YG. And Greg Avery (SS9142), HMP Belmarsh, Weston Way, Thamesmead, London, SE28 0EB.

SUMMING UP

"According to a Police spokesman, only 25 people attended Sunday's Peace Rally in Trafalgar Square - the other 50 odd thousand 'were just tourists who'd picked up banners by mistake.'" - www.spin-on-this.com

SchNEWS reckons about 55,423 ½ turned up (neither the ridiculously low 15,000 reckoned by the mathematically challenged boys in blue nor the exaggerated 100,000 claimed by the stop-the-war coalition). The usual suspects (peaceniks, anarchos and socialist paper sellers) were joined by all sorts of 'ordinary' people, home counties mums alongside inner-city Asian youth, students and masked up muslim women in a show of solidarity with the oppressed and bombed of Afghanistan.

* Earlier this week Laura Bush and Cherie Booth both made patronising speeches to the western press denouncing the burka (full veil) worn by Afghani women as an example of women's oppression under Islam. Obviously Afghani women are suffering and they deserve our support, they are being bombed by military servicemen (and women!) and made homeless and starved by the existence of war. The Taliban have undoubtedly oppressed women but this bit of media spin is a cynical ploy to prop up the so-called War-on-Terror. Before this the UK and US cared little about Afghani women, and they'll undoubtedly forget about them soon.

* Politicians and businessmen alike are having wet dreams about the moneymaking potential of the newly acquired Afghanistan. The World Bank is helping to make these dreams a reality by hosting an international conference in Pakistan next week to talk about rebuilding the country. In reality it's about rebuilding in the western image and exploiting for profit. Their first priority will be oil, but then they'll probably turn their attention to making sure the people are 'free' to work in sweatshops or as prostitutes. Um' we wonder if Cherie will still be speaking up for women then.

* Last Saturday, fifty Trident Ploughshares campaigners padlocked themselves to the gates of Downing Street for an hour before being cut free, no-one was arrested. On Monday, they occupied the offices of Rolls-Royce in London who construct nuclear reactors for submarines launching cruise missile attacks on Afghanistan. Trident Ploughshares: 07876-593016/07752-378993 www.tridentploughshares.org

* 1st December is Prisoners for Peace Day organised by War Resisters International. 0207 72784040 www.wri-irg.org

...and finally...

Shaggy Dog Story. A drunk who claimed he had been raped by a dog was jailed for 12 months by a judge. Martin Hoyle, was arrested by police after a passing motorist and his girlfriend found a Staffordshire bull terrier, called Badger, having sex with him at the side of a road. The couple had stopped to help because they thought Hoyle was being attacked by the animal. But when they got closer they saw that he had his trousers round his ankles, was down on all fours and the dog was straddling him from behind. Another passing motorist contacted the police and Hoyle was arrested as he walked with the dog down the road. Hoyle told police "I can't help it if the dog took a liking to me. The dog pulled my trousers down." Hoyle's barrister said the accused had no memory of the incident because of his drunken state, but was now very remorseful and incredibly embarrassed.

disclaimer
SchNEWS warns all readers that we are an oasis of truth in a desert of bullshit. Honest.

SHAC - A year in review

It has been a pretty eventful year for the campaign against Huntingdon Life Sciences as Stop Huntingdon Animal Cruelty (SHAC) continues to have more influence over the shares than the company does. The highlight of the year however was getting the biggest backer, Stephens Inc to pull out of HLS, with them passing on both their shares and their loans. Stephens are a huge private bank well known for their dodgy dealings, but even they were unable to handle the pressure put on them in the UK and in the US. Stephens, the largest shareholder, had bailed the company out in January when the NatWest loan was called in, and gave them more money. Thus they were directly responsible for HLS continued survival. Stephens went all out to defend their investment, and swore they would never give in to the animal rights activists. But in January this year they caved.

This was the biggest of a good number of companies falling by the wayside after SHAC turned their attention on them. HLS were turned into pariahs in financial circles as more large shareholders sold up and they lost all their stockbrokers and market makers which enabled the shares to trade.

It got so bad for them they attempted to move the shares to the US, but as the accompanying article tells, that too is being successfully blocked. Never has a company had its public presence so completely seized by a pressure group.

However, the campaign did not stop there. Customers and workers continued to be targeted with numerous home visits. One unexpected home visit was when 300 protestors switched county and turned up on the door step of managing director Brian Cass's house! Mobile demos, both in the City of London and around the country continue to be highly successful, and the main focus of anger has now been redirected towards HLS's insurers Marsh UK. There have been large numbers of run-ins, lock-ons and just general picketing of offices. And SHAC has truly gone global, with demos in numerous European countries and as far away as South America and New Zealand.

Unfortunately, all this success has attracted some rather insane policing as democracy gets mangled by the powers that be.

There was a big show trial of three SHAC people in November. The police and company were very hopeful that all three would be sent down for a very long time, and that would be the end of the campaign. How very wrong they were. They were found guilty of incitement over a Scooby Doo cartoon, but by the time you read this they will all be free. To the police and HLS's dismay, the campaign simply continued from strength to strength.

SHAC has declared that 2002 is the year to finish HLS, and they believe the end is in sight. The company is on the run, and the animal rights people keep winning the victories as persistence pays off.

IF ORDINARY PEOPLE BEHAVED LIKE- RAILTRACK

HEY, CAN I PLAY TRAINS AS WELL?!

YETH

SORRY IS NOT ENOUGH. SO YOU GIVE ME ALL YOUR POCKET MONEY AND I'LL FIX IT FOR YOU...

Kicking Corporations

How Stop Huntingdon Animal Cruelty took on the finance world and won

FOLLOWING AN UNPRECEDENTED campaign during 2001 and 2002, animal testing company Huntingdon Life Sciences (HLS) has been forced to withdraw from the London Stock Exchange and failed in its attempt to re-list on a US stock market, due largely to the campaigning of Stop Huntingdon Animal Cruelty (SHAC). SHAC have stepped into the world of the stock market, taken the business people on at their own game, and are now finding that a great way to attack a company is from the angle of the shareholders and making life impossible for a firm in the fickle world of the stock market. No you're not reading a page from the Financial Times - put your executive toys away and read about how to bring your favourite company to its knees…

We have seen the share price of HLS crash totally. The company has not been able to prevent SHAC influencing shareholders and driving away most of their financial backers. For a publicly quoted company to maintain support from investors and management wages it is dependent on the share price rising, and to tackle this involves using the system against itself: The strength of a company is measured by its share prices, and this is a significant way it raises cash, especially if it is in serious debt or needs to expand. There is a close connection between debt and share price, as banks and other institutions will offer loans and bonds based on it. If the share price subsequently falls the creditors get worried, and a significant fall could see creditors demand their money back.

So with HLS already in turmoil, with their main creditors NatWest Bank under an all out attack, and with the share price having fallen from 350p to under 200p, it was time to attack: First tactic was to go after shareholders - lists of which can be obtained for any public company from Companies House. There are two types of shareholders: the small, private investor and the "institutionals" like investment and pension funds and banks.

The city institutionals were targeted first. Using the negative publicity surrounding HLS, activists staged public demonstrations outside offices, and stormed PR events to disrupt and embarrass. Taken back by the storm of negative publicity many of them sold up, stating the bad performance of the share price as their reason for getting out. This served to make the shares even more unattractive and fall lower.

Next the small shareholders: Names and addresses were posted on a website so everyone could see their association with the animal torture company. Local groups took to dealing with the shareholders in their area, with all sorts of amusing, inventive and effective tactics. The result was electrifying and the media went nuts. Shareholders freaked as it dawned on them that the animal rights movement now knew exactly where they were. They started getting protests outside their homes, inundated with mail and calls, even visits from the ALF. They sold in droves and the share price continued crashing.

It hit the desired vicious circle; the more the share price fell, the more it encouraged people to sell, bringing it down further.

Naturally, those selling the shares had to find buyers, which was happening because the shares were being sold at a pittance of their previous value. Hence the second phase of the operation, going for those promoting the buying and selling: stock brokers and market makers.

A stock broker is the company that provides a small shareholder access to stock markets. A market maker is a company that takes on a stock to provide a market in it, facilitating the stock brokers and encouraging liquidity. The key buzzword here is 'liquidity', roughly how easy it is to buy and sell shares in a company, and associated with the volume being traded. Generally large volume of trades pushes up the share price, creating a market for them. An illiquid stock is one that generally falls in value because it hard to trade and there is thus little volume of shares.

HLS were about to lose liquidity: From the London Stock Market, it was simple to find the brokers and market makers. Shareholders were suddenly told by their brokers that they would no longer deal in HLS shares, and those that held their shares in 'nominee accounts' by the brokers were told to sell up or take them elsewhere. The market makers likewise rapidly disassociated themselves, with the desired effect.

The name HLS has become a joke in the City of London, their share price was stuck between 2 and 4p (less than their nominal value), valuing the company at around 9 million (much less than the value of its actual assets), and there was no chance of the shares ever recovering. The City works pretty much on rumour and gossip, so plant a story and it can rapidly spread, even causing panic. The City got dose after dose of this until everyone knew that HLS was bad news.

Meanwhile, SHAC USA deftly removed all eight of HLS's American market makers using similar tactics. The share price for the 'ADR' system which allowed limited trading in the shares in the US also collapsed, and they fell off all US stock markets until they reached the 'pink sheets' - where shares go to die. Many of the big institutional investors will not invest in shares that have ended up on the pink sheets. More investors were frightened away.

Desperate to recover, HLS planned to move their shares to the US. They took their shares off the London Stock Exchange, arranged a dummy company, Life Sciences Research Inc (LSR), and moved all the shares to the new company. But there was a hitch: just as a deal with a market maker was formalised with LSR, an article appeared in the New York Times profiling the aggressive campaigning tactics of guess who. The market maker promptly pulled, before a single action against them had occurred. HLS managing director Brian Cass is quoted as being "confounded and frustrated"!

Eventually HLS scraped the bottom of the barrel and found a small Colorado market maker with fraud convictions called Spencer Edwards to take them on. But just when it looked as though the transition to the new name was going well, several shareholders homes were invaded, and offices occupied and soon after Spencer Edwards faxed through that they were getting out. LSR shares never saw light of day. It was a brilliant victory for SHAC, and an outright disaster for HLS.

Meanwhile the majority of their shareholders, the small UK investors, have been left stranded; their names are up on the website, and they are facing greater costs to get their brokers to deal in US shares. Under pressure from SHAC, HLS has managed magnificently to shaft its backers and shareholders.

What now for HLS? The LSR deal to move to the US is in tatters. They are still essentially a private company with no share price, a lot of angry shareholders and duped creditors, upset that the shares they swapped their debt for are pretty much worthless. SHAC met them on their financial territory and is winning this crucial battle in the drive to close them down.

For SHAC see http://www.shac.net or ring 0845 458 0630

Locked Up For Being Too Successful

Letter to SchNEWS from SHAC campaigner Heather Avery written while serving a 12 month sentence at Highpoint Prison on the charge of 'Conspiracy To Cause A Public Nuisance'

Dear SchNEWS,

Well here I am at High Point. Imprisoned for daring to get off my backside and say "enough is enough, I am going to take action to stop this horrendous suffering." Locked up for speaking out, locked up for exposing Huntington Life Sciences, locked up for motivating others into action, locked up for being far too successful, locked up for caring.

I was part of the campaigns that closed Consort Kennels and Hillgrove Farm. Consort Kennels caved in just 10 months into the campaign. Over 200 Beagles were legally re-homed. Many were snatched to safety in the middle of the night. Others were grabbed in broad daylight and carried across country to a new life. Feelings were so strong at Consort that activists were openly tearing the walls down brick by brick.

People said we would never close Consort. We knew we would. They said we'd never close Hillgrove Farm. We knew we would. Hillgrove Farm gave in just two years into a relentless campaign. Success came from that important word-relentless. These places were hammered from every direction day in and day out (not to mention the nights). In short they didn't know what hit them and certainly didn't know which direction the next blow was coming from. Over 800 cats were re-homed when Hillgrove closed. More importantly the business was forced to close and they were unable to breed and sell any more cats for vivisection.

Huntingdon Life Sciences was our next target. We needed new tactics but the principles were still the same. Relentless pressure, actions, imagination and innovative tactics. Whatever the target we always try to stay focused and positive. We always have an unwavering certainty that we will win. We have to because it's not our necks on the line. Our motivation is always the animals who are suffering. A sense of real urgency runs through all of us with the knowledge 500 animals are needlessly killed at HLS everyday.... one at a time, each one an individual whose life is precious to him/her as ours is to us.

It was 5 o'clock in the morning when Laddie warned me that the police (about 30 of them) were creeping down my front path. He was up at the window growling and snarling. It was August 2000. The next thing I knew the police were up to their usual amateur dramatics shouting and trying to smash the front door in. I had my house ransacked and was arrested and charged with 7 outrageous offences (they do try it on!). By the time it all came to court a year later it was reduced to "conspiracy to incite a public nuisance" and we got 12 months. The whole operation took 42 police officers full time (we had been under extensive surveillance for many months) and cost in the region of £1.2 million. One Cambridgeshire cop was overheard saying in court when we were sentenced "we won't be trying that again!". Obviously the aim was to stitch us up for 3-5 years in prison and for SHAC to fall apart without us.

I have been fortunate enough to share a cell with Natasha (my co-defendant) and our stay in prison has been treated as a holiday. The rest has done us a lot of good. I have made the most of every single day here. I feel mentally and physically stronger than ever before. Of course it's easy to feel like that with such a short sentence. I have missed my dogs, family and friends but unless you can escape I've found it's best to be positive and do something productive every day.

I have read about other political prisoners around the world and realise that I have it easy here. The other prisoners here at High Point have expressed nothing but support for us in our fight to close HLS. Some of them have even turned vegan!. Even some of the prison officers have made comments such as 'I think it's brilliant what you're doing', 'you shouldn't be in here', 'I hope you close them down'.

It struck me when I first arrived at High Point how much it looked like HLS with the huge fences topped with razor wire. The big difference being that I would be released alive and well. Being in prison hasn't helped me to empathise with the animals at HLS because there is no comparison. I don't want to empathise with them I am going to save them.

With determination, belief and hard work I believe almost anything can be achieved. Whether you're fighting for people, animals or the environment don't be distracted or pushed off course. Keep at it. I know there will be many more victories along the way. Unlike most people, when activists and campaigners like you or I die we'll be able to say we did everything we could to end cruelty and fight injustice.

All I want to do now is get back out there and smash HLS.

Stay free and good luck with all your efforts.
Love and respect
Heather

"I've never eaten anything organic. Wouldn't want to compromise my impartiality!"

SchNEWS Of The World EXCLUSIVE

OSAMA SPEAKS OUT

Al Qa'ida Agents In Florida Rigged US Presidential Elections.

US Intelligence has revealed that secret Al Qa'ida agents operating in Florida twelve months before the September 11 attacks interfered with voting cards to give George W Bush the election

Osama Bin Laden has admitted "The Florida recount - it took many men, and was a very tedious business. Although we all mostly still voted Democrats we owed George and Jeb a favour and

The Tenth OKasional Cafe

In a world of disintergrating culture and increasing psychic disease, decay, and disorientation, it's always good to watch people get positive stuff together rather than seeing it fall apart. Taking control of a space when you have a clear focus can be a really amazing experience. This Easter a totally new group of people took on the shape shifting banner of the Okasional Café to do just that – and Manchester's most lively and creative alternative venue had its 10th incarnation!

The Okasional Café is put together by a loose non-hierarchical collective of people who have taken empty buildings in Manchester and transformed them into wicked spaces. Squatting allows us to take back some space for inspiring stuff that could not happen otherwise in today's over-commercialised society. It also makes the point that land and space should not only be available to rich developers to turn into yuppie flats or posh bars. In previous cafes there have been vegan meals, free parties, live music, inspiring films. Drumming workshops, other workshops, direct action and political meetings, benefit nights,

poetry evenings, free shops, art exhibitions, banner making, kids space and always stacks of information about alternative radical stuff going on in Manchester and further afield. The OK Café is run by people working voluntarily and any money made is ploughed back into supporting radical action to make the world a better place. Decisions are made collectively at meetings before and during the café, and everyone is welcome to get involved.

The space itself is free and open to anyone who wants to put it to good use. When you find out about the next one, just come on down and help us make your ideas happen.

The 10th Okasional cafe was a squatted pub the Pack Horse , a beautiful old Manchester pub on the end of Deansgate – don'tcha just love squatted pubs! This building was taken on the 14th of March and since then there has been vegan food, chilled music, free parties, live bands [shout to Solinky who were excellent!!], two Beyond TV interactive screening nights, a poetry evening, a benefit for Peat Alert, a subvertising workshops and more.... Our collective was most impressed however, with that lovely loo. With the toilets all having been knocked down, we had to be creative, and our wonderful plumbing friend (you know who you are!) managed to plumb us in a pukka loo. Anyway, on a more serious note, we weren't able to keep the space for long as yet again, the owners kicked us out to turn this lovely pub into yet more yuppie flats. There was a final benefit party on Easter Saturday to raise money for a new Earth First! Minibus. But not to worry, we hope to reappear another day another place, to shed another ray of light into Manchester life.

To stay in touch with the Okasional Café between squats, and to get involved with helping make the next one happen call 0161 226 6814, come to a Beyond TV show or look on the Loombreaker website. We always need more hands and everyone can help in some way - even if it's just a bit of cleaning.

Loombreaker http://www.loombreaker.org.uk
BeyondTV http://www.beyondtv.org/pages/ok_cafe.php
Advisory Service for Squatters www.squat.freeserve.co.uk

Dita Sari's tour of the UK

Dita Sari is a trade union leader. She doesn't look much like your average British trade union leader - she isn't old, male, fat, drunk, lazy or white. She doesn't behave much like one either.

She is a leader of the FNPBI, the largest, independent trade union federation in Indonesia. Aged just 29, she has spent three years in jail under the Suharto dictatorship, during which time she nearly died of typhoid. She was arrested for her part in a strike of textile workers in a suburb of Jakarta. Arrests, violence and intimidation, from the Police, the Army, the bosses and armed gangs of muslim fundamentalists are a regular feature of the class struggle in Indonesia. But still they fight.

Dita was recently awarded a $50,000 dollar human rights award from the Reebok Foundation. Unlike Tony Blair who'll take money from any one who's offering and allow their cash to colour his policies, Dita screwed up Reebok's plans to greenwash their record on human rights and threw a spanner in the works of the corporate openings of the Winter Olympics, where she was due to collect her award. Pointing out that Reebok had sweated that money from the backs of workers in Indonesia, she refused the money.

Dita came to the UK at the end of 2001, at No Sweat's invitation and spoke at our conference about Sweatshop Labour on November 24th and to meetings of students, campaigners and trade unionists across the country. She told us what was going on in her country and was keen to hear what was happening here.

She appealed to us not just to boycott companies like Reebok, but to make real solidarity with the workers in the garment industry abroad and also at home. She urged a linking up of the anti-capitalist movement, the anti-war movement and the workers' movement in the fight to radically transform the world. You couldn't imagine John Monks of the TUC or, much worse, Sir Ken Jackson of Amicus making the sort of speeches she made!

No Sweat: www.nosweat.org.uk

WAKE UP! IT'S YER GETTING AWAY WITH MURDER

Weekly SchNEWS

Printed and Published in Brighton by Justice?

Friday 30th November 2001 www.schnews.org.uk **Issue 333**

Simon Jones
1973 - 1998

LICENCE TO KILL

"The judge has decided Simon's life is only worth fifty thousand pounds." - Tim Jones, Simon's brother.

"The law's refusal to punish these serious crimes is just one more indication of how little importance our law makers give to casual workers' health, safety and right to life." - Simon Jones Memorial Campaign.

Bosses up and down the country were yesterday celebrating the fact that killing your workers won't get you locked up behind bars after a jury trial at the Old Bailey. Richard James Martell, general manager of Dutch-owned Euromin, based at Shoreham, was found not guilty of manslaughter and his company found not guilty of corporate manslaughter, over the death of Simon Jones in 1998. Instead they were given a £50,000 fine with £20,000 costs for breaking health and safety regulations.

Simon Jones was killed on his first day of work when he was sent as a casual worker to Euromin. After just a few minutes 'training" he was unloading cargo inside the hull of a ship. Within a few hours he was dead after having his head almost severed by the grab of a crane thanks to a cost cutting exercise by the boss.

But yesterday at the Old Bailey that mattered for nothing – Simon was just another statistic, one of the hundreds of people who die at work every year, while he companies that employ them get off scot free or have to pay pathetic fines.

As the Simon Jones campaign said, "We are painfully aware that in 21st century Britain the fight for the most basic of workers' rights - the right not to be killed or injured at work - is still being fought. The Crown Prosecution Service has put obstacles and obstructions in the path of this prosecution at every turn. The Health and Safety Executive have consistently shown themselves to be either unwilling or unable to take the necessary action against employers to ensure he safety of workers."

It took over three and a half years from the day Simon was killed for the trial to get to court. The Crown Prosecution service (CPS) had to be dragged kicking and screaming every step of the way until in an historic U-turn they were told by two High Court judges that they were adopting an approach that was "baffling" and "beggared belief" over their refusal to prosecute. That it even got this far was because of a relentless campaign by family and friends.

In the dock

The death of Simon was tragic, but no accident. In fact it was a direct result of the low paid 'flexible' economy (let's call it 'flexploitation') which is now endemic throughout the country. The growth of casualisation, where people are forced into low paid jobs with little or no training, no job security, no sick pay and no holiday pay means bigger profits for companies – but more deaths and injuries for the people working for them.

For Simon this meant he was sent to Euromin to work as a stevedore by temp agency Personnel Selection. As Emma Aynsley, Simon's girlfriend at the time pointed out "He was doing one of the most dangerous jobs in the country for about £5 an hour with no training whatsoever. It was like asking someone without a driving licence to drive an articulated lorry."

Since the abolition of the National Dock Scheme in 1989 casualisation has returned to all British docks. Within four years of the end of the scheme, the accident rate on the docks had leapt by a third. But profits for the companies involved had also leapt with a 41% saving in wages caused by five thousand redundancies and a cheaper labour force with much fewer rights.

One of the sacked Liverpool dockers (see SchNEWS 165/6) who went on strike to stop the casualisation of their jobs, joined Simon's friends when they shut down Euromin a few years back. He told SchNEWS at the time "We went on strike for over two years to prevent deaths like this, which are inevitable with an untrained, casual workforce. Before casualisation, this sort of thing would never have happened. If these companies are allowed to get away with employing casual staff to do skilled jobs the death toll will just keep rising."

D.I.Y.

Simon wrote for SchNEWS and was involved like all of us in supporting the Liverpool dockers' strike. This also meant that from the beginning, the memorial campaign set up in his name was committed to taking direct action to ensure that his death wouldn't be brushed under the carpet like so many others. The list of actions to make the authorities take notice has been impressive. The campaign occupied and shut down Euromin for the day; occupied and shut down the temp agency Personnel Selection that sent Simon to his death. Occupied the Department of Trade and Industry on the day that Simon's case was being debated in Parliament; shut down Southwark Bridge outside the Health and Safety Executive's HQ until they got to speak to the director, and picketed the CPS for their failure to prosecute.

If it wasn't for Britain's casual labour economy Simon would still be alive. And if it wasn't for the direct action campaign that has been fought for the past few years Simon's death would have been brushed under the carpet.

So what does this now mean? That scumbags like James Martell can carry on cutting safety corners to squeeze an extra pound of flesh, and temp agencies like Personnel Selection will carry on sending anyone anywhere as long as they can keep half their wages?

SchNEWS knows that under the present law it is almost impossible to find anyone guilty of corporate manslaughter charges and no doubt there will be calls for the laws of the land to be changed. But we also know that it isn't just laws that need to be changed, but a whole new world built, one where people are more important than profit, where people like Simon Jones aren't killed just to make some boss or shareholder a little richer.

* Simon Jones Memorial Campaign, PO Box 2600, Brighton, E.Sussex, BN2 OEF www.simonjones.org.uk

* Watch 'The Navigators' on Channel 4 this Sunday (2nd December) at 10pm. Directed by Ken Loach the film shows how, since the privatisation of the rail industry, experienced workers who used to be in charge of rail safety have been replaced with casual inexperienced labour – with frightening consequences. The film was written by Rob Dawber, a railwayman who died earlier this year from mesothelioma, a cancer caused while working with asbestos on the railways. http://rob.dawber.net/

* 'Fighting to Win' is a pamphlet about various strikes with a section on deaths in the building industry. Copies from Revolutions Per Minute, BCM Box 3328, London WC1N 3XX www.red-star-research.org.uk/fightframe

GENE-TRICKS

Reports in the scientific journals Nature and New Scientist show that genetically modified (GM) crops have contaminated all of North America. In Canada where GM oil seed rape has been grown commercially for six years, GM pollen and seed is now so widespread it is difficult to grow conventional or organic strains without them being contaminated. Not only that but also some GM plants are developing into superweeds, as they have acquired resistance to more than one weedkiller by crossing with other GM strains.

In Mexico wild maize growing over 60 miles away from GM varieties have been genetically contaminated. Of course the long-term effects of wild plants being contaminated by GM crops is totally unknown and may have knock-on effects on the animals that feed on them, we just don't know. So in the light of these findings will the government halt GM crops? Will capitalist pigs fly?.

 * The snappily titled Treaty on Plant Genetic Resources for Food and Agriculture (PGRFA) (see SchNEWS 329) was adopted at the United Nations Food and Agriculture conference at the beginning of the month. In theory the agreement should have totally undermined the biotech companies control over genetic resources in food crops, unfortunately it's unlikely to happen. Under international law the terms of new treaties should overrule older ones, this meant this treaty would have trumped the World Trade Organisations (WTO) TRIPs Agreement (see SchNEWS 328). But carefully placed wording in PGFRA appears to suggest that the WTO will still be able to continue to be genetic bullies on behalf of the biotech giants www.ukabc.org/

* Pharmacia the American Pharmaceuticals group will next October sell its share of the biotech firm Monsanto. An industry analyst said, "If management does not have to give presentations every year on Frankenfoods that can only be a good thing." Check the cybersquatted www.monsanto.org - telling you exactly what to expect from this nasty biotech company.

ANARCHRISTMAS

This year we've saved the expense of producing a glossy Christmas catalogue, but we thought we'd better slobb out some enlightened Christmas presssie advice:

If granny put her ecstasy testing kit to good use last year then she'll love the latest **Class War Anti-Jubilee Calendar**, and for days that she feels too tired to take part in the class struggle, she might find the **Housmans Peace Diary** more relaxing. Calendar £6 from "London Class War" Box 467, London E8 3QX. Diary £6.95 from "Housmans" 5 Caledonian Road, London N1 9DX.

To guarantee a seriously rocking Christmas why not get yer hands on a copy of the **SchNU-SIC CD** with something for everyone; punk, dub , folk, techno. To get your copy send £7 to SchNEWS . Alternatively if feel like 2002 might be the year to start cleaning up your act then get hold of **'Go M.A.D!'** It includes 365 easy ways to help change the planet, from taking a natural love drug then counting little creatures and putting a spider plant on your desk. Only £3.99 + £1 p&p from The Ecologist 01626-832225.

And if you want to miss boring Bond re-runs this Christmas and are stuck for alternatives why not curl up with a nice SchNEWS annual? (details on our website)

SchNEWS in brief

Ourpower in Brighton & Hove want to form an alliance of residents and community groups to discuss and take action for the type of city we'd like. Meeting: Sat. 1st 11am-1:30pm, Friends Meeting House, Ship Street, Brighton info@ourpower.org.uk. **Actions at all Brighton Esso** garages, Sat. 1st as part of the national day of action. Meet noon outside Esso in either Hove, Lewes Road, Hollingdean Road, Dyke Road or London Road (Patcham) www.stopesso.com ** **The Black Cat Collective** in Bristol wants more people to get involved in "the destruction of Capitalism and the overthrow of the State". 07905-720575, Black_Cat_Collective@yahoo.co.uk ** Over 2000 people protested last week against three major dams in **Lesotho**, South Africa. The police responded violently injuring three elderly women. The protesters were demanding fair compensation for the property that will be submerged www.irn.org/programs/lesotho/ ** **Manchester Radical bookfair** Sat. 8th at Bridge 5 Mill, 22a Beswick Street. Info 0161 273 1736 merci@gn.apc.org ** Sat 8th is also **Kebele** community centre's sixth anniversary free party at Easton Community Centre, Bristol. 0117-9399469 kebele@marsbard.co.uk ** **March against US obstruction of the fight against climate change** (catchy). The US government refused to sign the Kyoto treaty despite being the world's largest polluters. March in London from Prince Consort Rd, 11am, 8th Dec. to the US Embassy, Grosvenor Sq. Also weekly climate vigils, 5-7pm Mondays at the US Embassy. Tel 07903-316331 www.campaignagainstclimatechange.net.

Inside SchNEWS

December 9th marks 20 years since the arrest of **Mumia Abu-Jamal**, the American radical black journalist, in Philadephia for allegedly killing the police officer Daniel Falkner. At the latest court hearing new evidence was denied consideration by the prosecution. The new evidence was a video taped confession by someone who claims to be guilty of Falkners murder. Mumia remains on death row. Saturday 8th December is a global day of protest to demand Mumia's immediate release from prison. www.freemumia.org

* American eco-activist **Rob 'Ruckus' Middaugh** has been sentenced to three years for his involvement in the Mayday 2001 Reclaim The Streets celebrations in Long Beach, California. He accepted a plea bargain rather than risk a 16-year sentence if found guilty of all charges. Rob now has two "strikes" in America's "three strikes and your out" rule, which means if he's nicked again he could face 25 years in prison. Send letters to: Rob Middaugh #6859467, PO Box 86164, Los Angeles 90086-0164, USA.

* **Robert Moaby** is on remand for allegedly sending threatening e-mails to the Director of the Bank of New York (who fund the vivisectors Huntingdon Life Sciences), would like to receive letters: Robert Moaby GF7721, Hospital Wing, HMP Jebb Avenue, Brixton, London SW2.

* A Trident Ploughshares activist has just received a vindictive three months in prison for Breach of the Peace for her part in the Big Blockade of the Faslane Nuclear Base. The harsh sentence might be something to do with her comments about the Scottish legal system. Write letters of support to **Jenny Gaiawyn**, HMP Cornton Vale, Cornton Road, Stirling, FK9 5LY.

* Independent footage is urgently needed of the police operations outside Euston station, on **Mayday** this year, to help in a trial starting on 3 December. If you can help contact Moss & Co. solicitors on 020-8986-8336 andrew@mosslaw.co.uk

Anti-War Actions

There's a mass action in opposition to militarism and violence next weekend (Sunday 9th and Monday 10th December) at **Northwood Military Joint Forces Headquarters**, London. December 10th is also International Human rights day. The 9th will be a mass rally/blockade of the military HQ and the 10th will be organised on an 'affinity group' basis – basically, get together with some mates, go along to a training day beforehand and hey presto, you have an affinity group! There will be legal support at the event. Meet 10th Dec. 7.30am Outside Northwood tube station. More info: 07950 567099 www.northwood.cjb.net

'Stop Star Wars: Stop War Spying: Stop Afghanistan War' is a women's only gathering at Menwith Hill military base to protest against the star wars military programme. Meet 12th December, 10 am onwards in the lay-by opposite the Black Bull pub on the A59, 7 miles west of Harrogate, just before you get to the golf-balls. Women should go for the day & be self-sufficient because there are no facilities. Tel: 01943-468593 flossiemintballs@aol.com

SNATCHED

On 25th November an 'immigration snatch squad', raided a flat in Streatham, south west London, one person fell to his death from the balcony, trying to escape. He is the fourth person to die this way since 1994. With the government planning a ten-fold increase in arrests of failed asylum seekers. How many more deaths will there be? Jenny Jones, Green Party member on the Greater London Assembly, is furious "there should be an immediate halt to the operation of the asylum snatch squads and the Government should review the targets it is imposing on the Immigration Services"(and maybe the methods they are using). More info National Coalition of Anti-Deportation Campaigns 0121-554-6947. www.ncadc.org.uk

* Protest outside the Yarl's Wood refugee detention centre in Bedfordshire. At 2pm, Sunday 2nd December. More information from www.stoparbitrarydetentionsatyarlswood.co.u

* Hands Off Asylum Seekers - Candleli Vigil 6th December at St Martin-in-the-Fields, Trafalgar Square, London, 6pm - 7.30pm Info 0121-554-6947.

...and finally...

Hunts around the country are preparing to resume their murderous 'sport' in foot and mouth free areas from 17th December. A permit system means their followers will only be allowed on roads 'cos of the risk of spreading the disease. Unfortunately for the hunts there's a certain faction who follow hunts (the one with the black hoodies) who aren't easily controlled, and who will still be legally entitled to use footpaths near the hunt. This has angered the fanatical Australian hunter Janet George, who claims to 'speak for the countryside'. She is openly advocating violence towards Hunt Sabs encouraging farmers and 'stewards' to hold down and spray sabs with disinfectant 'from head to toe'. But we don't think the sab will take kindly to being sprayed with animal tested toxic chemicals…

If Hunts can't control their 'followers' they could loose their licences, now wouldn't that be a shame! Contact the Hunt Saboteur 0845-4500727 www.huntsabs.org.uk

disclaimer

Subscribe!

Keep SchNEWS FREE! Send 1st Class stamps (e.g. 10 for next 9 issues) or donations (payable to Justice?) Ask for "Originals" if you can make copies. Post *free* to all prisoners. SchNEWS, c/o on-the-fiddle, P.O. Box 2600, Brighton, East Sussex, BN2 2DX.
Tel/Autofax +44 (0)1273 685913 *Email* schnews@brighton.co.uk *Download a PDF of this issue or subscribe at* www.schnews.org.uk

WAKE UP! WAKE UP! IT'S YER STIRRED NOT SHAKEN

Weekly SchNEWS

Printed and Published in Brighton by Justice?

"With friends like these who needs enemies."

Friday 7th December 2001 www.schnews.org.uk **Issue 334 Free/Donation**

FROM RUSSIA WITH LOVE

"We have certainly come to see the scourge of terrorism in Chechnya with different eyes." **- Lord Robertson, NATO secretary general.**

"Why are we terrorists? What would you do if Russia came and destroyed your villages and killed your children?" **- Chechen rebel.**

With Russian part of the international "war against terrorism", the plight of ordinary Chechens caught up in Russia's very own "war against terrorism" is still falling on deaf ears. Now the West merely 'disagrees' with Russia's bombing of the country back into the dark ages and has better things to do than worry about the endless accounts of torture, killings, rape and disappearances of the civilian population.

The recent conflict started after a number of bomb attacks in Moscow, which were blamed on Chechen rebels. Russia used this excuse to re-invade Chechnya in September 1999 to destroy the 'terrorists'. Russian troops captured the capital Grozny - already a pile of rubble after the last war with Russia five years earlier - and in the process killed up to 40,000 civilians. Although the main conventional war between Russian and Chechen forces has largely ceased, human rights organisations have reported a rise in the disappearance, torture and summary executions of detainees. Chechnya has been called the Wild West' of Russia and Human Rights Watch says it is in transition from an internal armed conflict to a classic dirty war. The United Nations have condemned Russia for "excessive and indiscriminate" use of force by its troops, but because Russia is still a military superpower - and one of the five permanent members of the UN Security Council - it knows it can get away with it.

TORTURE

In Grozny most of the population is female, all with tales of mass round-ups of males between the ages of 16 and 50. Isa is one of these men. He was taken to the Khotuni camp and was kept in a pit measuring 1m by 3m half filled with water with five other men. While being 'interrogated' he had cigarettes stubbed out on his body, his fingernails pulled out, his feet beaten with clubs and was then gang raped. Isa was only released after a ransom was paid, but the five others, along with thousands more, were tortured and then killed. Round ups of all men from villages take place under the guise of looking for terrorists and rebel leaders, but in reality the reasons for detention are arbitrary. In one case, following a bomb explosion

that killed five Russian soldiers, tanks and troops invaded the village of Sernovodsk. Most males were rounded up and taken into a field outside the village. Among them was Khamaz Yusupov, who described to Human Rights Watch beatings and electroshock torture to his ears, teeth, and arms. Another woman was detained when soldiers found a picture in her house of her in traditional dress standing next to a man with a beard. For that 'crime' she was taken to a military base where she was tied to a pole, beaten for several days then dumped half unconscious at the side of a road. Men have now shaved off beards and destroyed all photos of themselves with beards or in military uniform for fear of being branded a Chechen rebel. In February this year 51 bodies were found in the abandoned village of Dachny, less than a kilometre from the main Russian military base in Chechnya, sixteen of those found were last seen in the custody of Russian troops. Many of the bodies showed evidence of torture with broken limbs, flayed body parts, severed fingertips, and knife and gunshot wounds. Rozita, a grandmother, was detained in January and held in a death camp outside the village of Khottuni. She was thrown into a 4-foot deep pit with heavy logs as a roof so she couldn't stand up and kept there for 12 days. She was then taken out to be interrogated and tortured with electrodes attached to her body and the current turned on. "Yes I screamed something terrible. It hurt a lot when they turned on the current. The FSB (Russian secret police) people said, 'You aren't dancing well enough. Let's add some more voltage.'" Rozita was only released when her relatives and fellow villagers paid a ransom.

In the 19th Century Russia conquered Chechnya after a war that lasted over half a century. After World War II, Stalin deported the whole population to Serbia for "re-education" but the Chechens eventually returned to their homeland. With the break up of the Soviet Union Chechens unsurprisingly wanted independence. In 1991 pro-independence Jokhar Dudayev won 90% of the vote, so Russia sent in troops, Dudayev imposed martial law and Russia pulled out. In 1994 civil war broke out between Chechen government forces and the Russian sponsored Chechen Council, providing Russia with the perfect excuse to again invade sending in 40,000 troops and destroying the capital Grozny. By the time a peace deal was negotiated, giving Chechnya autonomy within Russia, 60,000-100,000 people had been killed.
* To find out more on Chechnya see http://tchetchenieparis.free.fr

Anna Politkovstaya, a respected Moscow journalist, also fell foul of the secret police when she visited to Chechnya to find out about the human rights abuses. After she had seen the pits for herself she was arrested and tortured, all the while her captors reminding her that FSB take their orders direct from President Putin himself.

As one human rights observer commented "The war is not a response to Chechen terrorism. It is an attempt to divert attention away from the social and economic crisis in Russia. Its goals are to restore the standing of the military in Russian society, and to secure Russian control of the oil and gas pipelines running through Chechnya. But unlike Kosova or Kuwait, the world has just sat back and watched Russia's scorched earth policy." With Russia now part of the united front against terrorism SchNEWS has to ask yet again - who are the real terrorists?

CONVOY

In January this year a food aid convoy went from France to Chechnya. Taking over a month their journey was littered with problems. For 11days they were held up by customs and harassed into paying over 17,000 Roubles in various fines. But the food reached its destination and given to refugees who had received no food aid for three months. Xavier Rousselin, one of the organizers of the Trade Union Convoy for Chechnya told SchNEWS, "The state of health of the refugees - physical as well as mental - was terrible. There was an epidemic of hepatitis and another of tuberculosis... The approach of a new winter without adequate heating and without correct food could be catastrophic. Without care, some people will soon die." Another convoy is on its way this week to help rebuild a school in Gronzy and one in the refugee camp of Bart. More information: cst@ras.eu.org

Anti-Anti-Terrorism

With the Anti-Terrorism, Civil Liberties are for Wet Liberals, We Need More State Security Bill (see SchNEWS 331) rushing its way through parliament here's a few details of events against the Bill.

* On International Human Rights Day (Monday 10th) there's a candle lit vigil 'last chance to say no to detention without trial'. Parliament Sq., London (Westminster tube) 6pm - 8pm. More info from: 020-7417-6375 or Asad.Rehman@amnesty.org.uk

* Charter for Basic Democratic Rights. Discussion on why Labour's anti-terror laws threaten us all. 6.30pm, Dec. 11th, Friends House, Euston Road, London. More info: 07753-658875 charter@socialistfuture.org.uk

* For the latest Terror bill news see: www.blagged.freeserve.co.uk/ta2000/

* The electrohippie collective have an online lobbying/direct-action in December, against the Anti-terrorism bill. Important days for participation 6th, 10th 11th, 12th, and the days following the passing of the new law. www.fraw.org.uk/ehippies/

* For the latest info about next weeks Brussels protests including your rights at the Belgium border check out www.uk.indymedia.org/

POSITIVE SchNEWS

It's official - the residents of Garstang, a small town in Lancashire, are some of the most ethical consumers around. It's the first town in the world to be recognised as a fair trade town by the Fair Trade Foundation. Their produce is marked with a guarantee that people receive a better price for their work. In 1992 there were only 5 places in Garstang that sold fairtrade stuff, but after years of campaigning another 8 have also started selling it too. Now seven out of ten local people say they choose to buy it over the usual more exploitative stuff and many only buy local produce (they also have a local produce directory).

To become a fair trade town or city you've got to get the local council to pass a resolution which supports and promotes it, put a sign up declaring it and promise to serve tea and coffee that hasn't ripped people off at yer meetings. Fairtrade products have to be readily available in at least 10 shops (more if you're a city). Find out more at www.garstangoxfamgroup.fsnet.co.uk.

Gene Camp

Believe it or not - a protest camp has been granted PLANNING PERMISSION! Highland Council in Scotland gave the Munlochy Vigil permission for two caravans, a yurt and a toilet to remain next to the site of a GM crop they're protesting against until the trial ends next summer. Contact: The Munlochy Vigil, The Layby, By Roskill Farm, Munlochy, Ross-shire IV8 8PA.

* The biotech industry have out of the goodness of their wallets produced a magazine entitled "Your World" to distribute in Scottish schools, and would you believe it the magazine presents a totally distorted view of the issues surrounding GM. A campaign has started to try and stop the booklet being distributed and a guide has been produced entitled "Your World or their World" www.scottishgenetixaction.org

* Flowering GM oilseed rape plants have been discovered in a field in Linconshire. The site was used earlier in the year for farmscale trials and the plants should have been destroyed to prevent them flowering and cross pollinating with other plants. Friends of the Earth are now trying to get Aventis, who were responsible for the trial, prosecuted.

SchNEWS in brief

Tonight (Friday) 7.30pm talk about **Plan Colombia** and it's effects at the Phoenix Community Centre (next to Freebutt Pub) Brighton. ** Keep your wrists busy this weekend at the **24hr letter writing vigil**, organised by Amnesty at the Friends Meeting House, Ship Street, Brighton, 9am Sat 8th - 9am Sun 9th. ** The **Spitalfields Market Under Threat** campaign lost the first part of their battle to save the market. Planning permission has been given to an office block despite there being no environmental impact assessment. This is being challenged in a bid to stall the work www.smut.org.uk ** The **Sheffield Digger** a radical publication dealing with environmental, social and political stories in the Sheffield area has been re-born. Help with printing costs, distribution and volunteers wanted: The Sheffield Digger, c/o Brambles Resource Centre, 82 Andover St, Sheffield, S3 9EH. email: jimthackery@yahoo.co.uk ** Benefit Gig for the **Campaign Against Depleted Uranium**. 11th Dec. 8pm-late. Night and Day Café, Oldham Street, Manchester. £3.50/£4.50, with Scapa Flow, Polythene, Desolation Angels and more. ** "**Stanleys exploits, or Civilising Africa**" a new pamphlet by anarchist writer David Nicoll, from the Kate Sharpley library. Their Winter 2001 catalogue is out for Christmas http://flag.blackend.net/ksl/sharpely.htm ** Three **Trident Ploughshares** activists are today to be awarded the "Alternative Nobel Peace Prize" by the Swiss Parliament for "a model of principled, transparent and non-violent direct action dedicated to rid the world of nuclear weapons." Info: 08454-588366 www.tridentploughshares.org ** This Sat (8th) **SLAG** (South London Action Group) have their first shindig at 31 Morecombe Street, SE17 www.slagfest.org.uk/ ** Over 15,000 workers took part in a march demanding more pay in Bucharest, **Romania**, at the end of the march striking workers urinated on the Ministry of Labour building to show their anger! ** 30 people occupied the offices of the **Scotts Company** last week as part of an ongoing campaign against peat extraction at Hatfield Moor, Doncaster, one of the last remaining raised peat bogs left in England. Leeds EF! 0113-2629365 leedsef@leedsef.org.uk ** 6 activists calling themselves **Sodexho Screws Refugees For Money** (catchy eh?) occupied the Sodexho European Management centre and disrupted their work for the day before being nicked, taken to Croydon copshop and charged under section 4 of the Public Order Act 1986 – threatening words/behaviour (!) for their trouble.

STUNNED

The owner of the Dutch Experience Café in Stockport, Colin Davies, is still on remand after police raided the café and his home and found large quantities of cannabis. The Café opened in September to try and provide low cost marijuana to medical users. Despite newspaper claims to the contrary, the cafe is still open. On the 24th there was a mass smoke-up at Stockport police station and twelve people were arrested. Around 70 people turned up to a further protest on December 1st. Contact The Dutch Experience, Stockport Village, Hooper St, Stockport, GTR Manchester, 0161-480-5902 www.dutchexperience.org/

Limited Edition Mark Thomas Bootleg Video, Live in Brighton.

See 2 hours of Mark in fine form the day after Balfour Beatty pulled out of the Ilisu Dam. Get it from SchNEWS for £8 + 80p SAE. Buy this and help fund the next SchNEWS book.

Inside SchNEWS

Prisoners always appreciate a bit of mail at this time of year, so why not send some Christmas cards. Here's a few prisoners who'd appreciate a line or two from you – for others check out the Anarchist Black Cross website www.brightonabc.org.uk

* **Mark Barnsley**, WA2897, HMP Whitemoor, Longhill Road, March, Cambs PE15 0PR. Serving 12 years after being attacked by a dozen drunken students.

* **Inaki Garcia Koch**, Carcel de Pamplona, C/san Rogue, Apdo 250, 31080 Irunez, Pamplona, Navarra, Spain. Serving 5 years for cutting cables on the construction site of the Itoiz dam.

* **Harold Thompson**, #93992, NWCC, Site 1, Route 1, Box 660, Tiptonville, Tennessee 38079, USA. Long-term anarchist prisoner

* **Paul Robinson**, KVA Karlskoga, Box 7, 69121 Karlskoga, Sweden. In prison for his part in the Gothernburg anti-EU demonstrations

* **Neil Bartlett** FW7083 HMP Lewes Brighton Rd. East Sussex BN7 1EA England. On remand on suspicion of making hoax telephone calls to animal abusers.

* **The SHAC 3** each serving a year for 'Conspiracy to cause a public nuisance' for encouraging readers in their newletter to phone and fax Huntingdon Life Sciences –**Heather Avery** (TE1951) and **Natasha Dellamaigne** (TE1952) both at HMP and YOI Highpoint, Stradis Hall, Newmarket, Suffolk CB8 9YG and **Greg Avery** (SS9142) HMP Belmarsh, Weston Way, Thamesmead, London SE28 0EB.

* **Jeffrey Luers (aka Free)** sentenced to 22 years 8 months in prison for setting fire to several sports utility vehicles because of the environmental damage these gas-guzzling vehicles cause. Letters c/o the legal defence committee FCDLC PO box 50263, Eugene OR 97404 USA

* **Jeffrey Archer**... Unfortunately SchNEWS couldn't track down his address.

...and finally...

SchNEWS just couldn't make it up, last Sunday was the first annual walk for capitalism. Three dozen capitalists, (or two as the police saw it) walked through Westlake Park in Seattle waving signs such as "Help a starving child in Africa. Give him capitalism." "Make Money Not Class War." and "Capitalism is more important that democracy." - OK, these were held by *anti*-capitalist protestors, who infiltrated the march.

Tym Parsons, the Seattle coordinator of WalkForCapitalism complained "We knew they had something in the works. Their aim was to infiltrate our organization and discredit it by way of parody."

Er, SchNEWS reckons you did a good enough job of that yourself, with one passer by commenting "I find it all very amusing. I don't think I've ever seen a protest for capitalism before. Don't these people already have what they're fighting for?"

The question is why did they choose to celebrate D2 (they've even nicked the name) with something as inefficient, ecologically sustainable and downright un-capitalistic a walking? SchNEWS reckons they would have also got more people onboard if someone had promised to bung each person who turned up £25 and a packed lunch (well that's the only reason us rent-a-mob lot ever bother turning up to demonstrations.)

Have a laugh, look at their website www.walkforcapitalism.org

disclaimer

Subscribe!

Keep SchNEWS FREE! Send 1st Class stamps (e.g. 10 for next 9 issues) or donations (payable to Justice?) Ask for "Originals" if you can make copies. Post *free* to all prisoners. SchNEWS, c/o on-the-fiddle, P.O. Box 2600, Brighton, East Sussex, BN2 2DX.

Tel/Autofax +44 (0)1273 685913 *Email* schnews@brighton.co.uk *Download a* **PDF** *of this issue or subscribe at* **www.schnews.org.uk**

HACKNEY NOT 4 SALE

Hackney NOT 4 Sale is a local action group that was set up to resist the crippling budget cuts that are being imposed by Hackney Council. Hackney NOT 4 sale is fighting for proper public funding of services to be run in the interests of the community.

The group first met spontaneously early in 2001 when a nursery was squatted and used as a community centre after closure by the Council (Atherden Community Centre – see SchNEWS/Squall Yearbook 2001). The next action, a spoof estate agent, got such a great response that Hackney NOT 4 Sale decided to form to support new and existing campaigns. The group feels a massive concern about what is happening in the provision of public services as well as in the processes of local democracy and accountability. There are cutbacks in leisure and education. Community halls and playgrounds on estates are being sold. Library services and parks are under threat. Council workers have had huge cuts to their pay and conditions. Social services have lost millions of pounds of funding and the Council are mis-using resources by prioritising their own schemes rather than properly supporting services and essential voluntary groups.

In 2001 Hackney NOT 4 Sale squatted a shop on the high street and installed a spoof estate agent. On display were details of all the community buildings and other properties owned by Hackney Council that have been put up for auction or otherwise threatened. School buildings, nurseries, buildings used by voluntary groups, green spaces, garages, public toilets, houses and shops have all been under the hammer. The West End hotels which hold the auctions have been picketed and the bidding has been disrupted by members of the group and many others from the community. People were forcibly removed after vocally challenging the sales or singing protest songs while others were involved in fake bidding and even 'purchasing' buildings before quietly leaving.

The publicisation of the Council's programme of property sales and questioning the legality of some of the Council's actions has led to a number of properties being withdrawn and, for the meantime at least, saved. Other buildings have been removed from the auctions at the last minute and sold in backroom deals.

Why is Hackney up for sale?

Why is Hackney in this crisis? The current situation is not new – its history is long and complicated – but the solutions being proposed are part of the problem and will not benefit local people.

The recent cuts are being imposed after an unprecedented directive from central government was given to the Council in 2001 to balance the books. The New Labour Council obliged by slashing budgets and their uptake of privatisation has been similarly eager. The government has given top accountancy firms £3.5 million to balance the budget and restructure management in preparation, it seems, for greater privatisation. But the use of private companies only adds to Hackney's problems as the private companies perform even worse than the Council and residents are left to foot the bill. In one disastrous episode, the Council lost £38 million to the company ITNet who were contracted to collect Council Tax and pay housing benefit (which they failed to do). Individuals have been made homeless, Housing Associations have faced bankruptcy and the Council itself lost out on government grants for failing to collect enough Council Tax.

The ways in which services are being taken out of public hands are numerous. The government is handing over control of the education of Hackney's kids to a trust, and Labour councillors recently told campaigners that they should expect all council nurseries to be closed or privatised within five years. PFI (Private Finance Initiative) schemes to build and run local leisure and community services are the norm. One PFI leisure centre scheme was way overdue and over budget when it finally opened, draining funds from facilities elsewhere in the borough (some have closed as a result). Libraries and voluntary groups are having to apply for special funds for parts of their core requirements. Even the deer reserve in a local park is threatened with closure unless private sponsorship can be found.

Fraud, corruption and plain bad management have long been part of the culture of Hackney's local government. During the last couple of years alone, two councillors have been sent to jail for election fraud and the Chief Executive resigned hurriedly, receiving a hefty pay-out of £100,000. Increasingly executive-style decision-making structures are being introduced while basic democratic processes are withdrawn. The availability of government money targeted at 'regeneration' has seen the establishment of unelected quangos and partnerships and the kind of gentrification that the Council wants is often in conflict with the improvements the local community needs.

Deprivation and debt... a familiar story

Hackney is the fourth poorest borough in the UK and yet, instead of being given extra funds, its history of borrowing and losses has left it with a massive debt. Capital from the sale of community properties is going straight into debt repayments. Hackney NOT 4 Sale says 'Drop the Debt!' and stop making the people of Hackney pay for the mess that local and central governments have created. It's not much of a leap to see how Hackney and a country in crisis such as Argentina are experiencing the same forces- the power of international capital, politics that focus on the individual rather than community (and yet is quite happy to sacrifice both), and a lack of the kind of democracy that listens to and gives control to ordinary people. The man with four kids working in a meat canning factory in Buenos Aries has found his

meagre income diminish to nothing during devaluations enforced by 'structural re-adjustments'. And the single mother in Hackney Wick has to work but has two children in need of Council nurseries which no longer exist. The Council is even selling off the playground on the estate where she lives. The playground will then be turned into new housing priced way out of her reach. What are the prospects for her children?

Act locally

Hackney NOT 4 Sale wants to bring the issues of globalisation right into the local arena and make links with similar struggles in other boroughs around the country. In many ways, Hackney is a test bed for the forces that will soon be evident everywhere. From the government's unprecedented removal of education from local authority control to the borough's being the first to experience an untested postal ballot system, Hackney becomes the pilot study for more universal application. The threats of cuts and privatisation are long term but so are our goals.

It is difficult to get information from the Council about what they are up to, so pooling our knowledge is vital. Our regular newsletter helps people find out about what is happening locally and spreads the word on various campaigns. None of us has much faith in the system; some of us believe voting will not change anything, but we all believe that alternatives are possible. We start from the idea that while diverse struggles are being waged and sometimes won, working together can achieve much more.

Hackney is a diverse, culturally rich community with many opportunities for social change. It is an exciting and exhilarating place in which to live and work. We believe in organising and taking action for ourselves, empowering others to do the same and supporting others who are attempting to improve things for themselves and their communities. People are coming together to build co-operative, creative, informed, empowered and non-commercial alternatives for the future.

There are many campaigns in Hackney, some of which are aided and abetted by Hackney NOT 4 Sale such as a weekly picket by Hackney library workers engaged in a long running pay dispute with the Council who refuse to implement nationally agreed pay rates. They are setting up a library users group to successfully stop the closure of a library and fight for long-term improvement in the service. Other campaigns include ones against cuts and closures in nursery, education and youth services; and a coalition to stop huge cuts to the Freedom Pass for those who have difficulty getting around.

Contact

hackneyNOT4sale@yahoo.com, 07950 539 254, Box 7, 136-8 Kingsland High Street, London E8 2NS

'Down with consumer society'

WAKE UP! WAKE UP! IT'S YER WELL CONNECTED

Weekly SchNEWS

Printed and Published in Brighton by Justice?

Friday 14th December 2001   www.schnews.org.uk   **Issue 335**

Privatisation of education its going like clockwork!

CASH FOR CONNEXIONS

"Connexions is just one corner of a well-designed jigsaw puzzle which, when complete, will reveal a picture of education from which all freedom, all notions of public service and accountability to an electorate have vanished. The family silver is long gone, and now our children are being sold off." Action on Rights for Children in education (ARCH)

Connexions - coming soon to a high street near you, a re-mix of careers, benefits, housing and welfare advice for all you teenagers out there. Connexions, yet another scheme from Neo-Labour, the idea behind this one is to provide teens with a personal mentor and a 'one-stop shop' to help them get on the career ladder. Introduced in pilot areas by the Department for Education and Skills (DfES) in Spring this year it is now to be extended throughout England. On the face of it is just an upgrading of the old careers offices, but behind the glitz, big business is muscling in.

The Learning and Skills Act 2000 gave the DfES unprecedented powers to gather information about students from all schools, Local Education Authorities, social services, Young Offender Teams, probation services, police and benefits agencies. This gives government the chance to build up comprehensive records on every aspect of the lives of the population between the ages of 13-19.

As ARCH points out "The 'Connexions' database has already introduced what is effectively a national identity scheme for teenagers. The implications for all citizens if it is maintained into adulthood are extremely worrying."

So who will have access to all this confidential information? Will it be deleted? And can individuals check its accuracy? The DfES haven't even bothered to reply to letters from ARCH. Terri Dowty from the group said "They say the idea is to give youngsters a 'joined-up service' but it's all about tracking. They are saying things like 'no young person should be invisible to us'."

But were sure some of the 'business partners' involved in Connexions are rubbing their hands at all that handy market research. Take 'Young Enterprise', a so called charity set up by business whose board consists entirely of representatives from Nestle, Marconi, Bull UK, KPMG and more of the usual suspects. Or what about the 'Careers Enterprise Group' whose parent company is Vosper Thornycroft, who do a good line in warships.

EDUCATING CAPITA

In May this year the government awarded a £100 million contract to Capita to develop a Connexions smart card scheme for over-16s. In return for attendance and achievement, students earn points, which are recorded on their Connexions card. They can then hot-foot it to a website to obtain consumer goods and discounts on such essential items as a Big Mac'n'fries. While they watch the screen, the screen watches them and draws up consumer profiles based on the pages they choose. Capita insist that young people can opt out of this monitoring - but run the risk of losing discounts if they do. As ARCH point out "The incentives to join the scheme are almost irresistible to teenagers; the opportunities to collect vouchers or discounts on goods and services is a blatant marketing ploy directed at young people and one which encourages a shallow association of education with consumerism, rather than building an ethos which fosters the right to education."

Big business has been gagging to break into education for decades. EU Trade Commissioner, Pascal Lamy, has said that education is 'ripe for privatisation' while Gerhard Cromme, the Chair of the European Round Table of Industrialists – the most influential pressure group in Europe - said last year that all schools should be privatised and subjected to market forces like any other business! Cromme also took a pot shot at "lazy" students who study subjects which have no relevance to industry. As ARCH said " In view of the increasing control which the business sector is gaining over education, and the size of the profits enjoyed by 'edubusiness', it is not unreasonable to ask whether our children are regarded as individuals, or merely as raw materials in the development of the economy. The direction and content of education needs to be in the hands of democratically elected representatives and not multinational corporations."

Action on Rights for Children in education (ARCH) PO Box 19, Lydbrook, Glos GL17 9WA www.arch-ed.org

---

BOOTLEG MARK THOMAS VIDEOS UP FOR GRABS

For just 8 quid plus 80p of stamps on a SAE you can get yer mits on a 2 hour special filmed in Brighton. All proceeds go to the next SchNEWS book. Send us an SAE to 55 Canning Street, Brighton BN2 0EF

CRISP NOTES

Walkers crisps and The Sun newspaper are blatantly breaking the law by encouraging kids to "engage in an unhealthy eating activity." Both companies who are jointly running the "books for schools" campaign are forcing kids to munch their way through £15 worth of crisps for a £4 book. Tesco has a similar scam going with its 'free' computer promo - the snag is that mum and dad have to spend a whopping £250,000 pounds on groceries before little 'Jim' gets a £1,000 computer for his school. The Consumers' Association has slammed both promotions for being nothing more than a "high level" branding campaign aimed at kids. Psst! Want some free stationary for little 'Jims' school? Why not contact jazzymedia who are offering free exercise books, files and diaries emblazoned with 'ethical advertisers' logos, companies include-Pepsi, Adidas, BT and Sunny Delight!!!

In a throw back to the days of the fascist Ministry of Popular Culture a snitch line has opened in Italy to collect info about teachers carrying out 'propaganda work in the classroom'. After one month 300 reports of teachers speaking 'badly' about Berlusconi and the goverment had been collected. Propaganda work includes showing videos of the G8 meeting or criticising the involvement of big business in schools.

COPWATCH

* Cops are stalking commuters in London who look like easy victims in mugging black spots Scotland Yard has revealed. The scheme called 'guardian angel' involves plain-clothes cops secretly following people to their home car or taxi ready to jump if the 'victim' is attacked. Meanwhile other plain clothed cops have been wandering around carrying laptop computers and mobiles to attract muggers. Despite this massive operation street crime has continued to soar while the scheme has yet to nick a single mugger!

* London cops are planning a register of kids who exhibit 'criminal potential' Anyone caught tagging, skipping school or even talking back to teachers runs the risk of being put on a database so cops can monitor their behaviour as they grow up! The plan was unveiled by Ian Blair, London's deputy police commissioner last month. Director of Privacy International, Simon Davies, said the registry was tantamount to police "profiling gone mad."

TRUCKIN' CRAZY

Did you know the distance that food is transported by road increased by 50 % in just over twenty years? Or that between a third and 40 % of all UK road freight is thanks to food travelling around the country?

'Eating Oil: Food supply in a changing climate' is a major new report launched this week by Sustain and Elm Farm Research Centre (EFRC) which takes a look at how far our food travels to get to our plates. The report also exposes our dependency on imports and on fossil fuels to produce, process, package and distribute the food we eat.

In the Report, Sustain said that the UK's food system had become "almost completely dependent" on oil, and that internationally, food distribution was a major cause of pollution and climate change. The organisation also criticised this food system because, for the sake of international trade agreements and political commitments, many countries essentially just swap food. For example, in 1997, the U.K. imported 33 million gallons of milk and exported 71 million gallons, instead of just exporting 38 million. Likewise we exported 195,000 tones of pork while importing 240,000 tonnes and exported 102,000 tonnes of lamb while importing 125,000 tonnes. Call us thick but this sounds like a waste of fuel, time and money. Ah but we forgot, governments and big agribusiness make huge profits through international trade. By supporting local food suppliers, we can all help to reverse this damaging set of priorities.

Other problems highlighted include loss of nutrients in food, increased incidence and spread of diseases like Foot and Mouth, and major animal welfare problems.

Poor countries producing food for distant markets are not necessarily seeing benefits through increased and often intensive production for export. The report reveals how such trends could be reversed through industry, government and public action.

The report's author, Andy Jones says, "The food system has become almost completely dependent on crude oil. This means that food supplies are vulnerable to increases in petroleum prices or any shortfall in oil supplies, as demonstrated during the fuel protests in the UK in 2000. Food distribution is also a major contributor to climate change and other forms of pollution. The environment and society cannot continue to bear the costs. We need to invest, now, in regional and local food systems combined with fair trade initiatives that will bring about a more secure, sustainable and fair food system."

Sustain, 94 White Lion Street, London, N1 9PF Tel 020 7837 1228 www.sustainweb.org

*One way to reduce organic food miles is to increase UK production. The Organic Targets Campaign rally and lobby will take place on 23 January 2002 to encourage government to adopt an organic action plan with a target of 30% agricultural land to be organic by 2010. For more information from sustain 0207 837 1228, email: otbrally@sustainweb.org.

* Wanna find out who grows what in your area? Log onto the interactive www.bigbarn.co.uk site type in yer postcode and a map will appear displaying local producers in your area.

CHINESE CRACKERS

It's official – after fifteen years of asking, this week China finally got to join the World Trade Organisation (WTO). Right wingers in the US had used China's dodgy human rights record to stop them joining, when in reality it was a cover for their determination to keep Washington's grip on international trade. Last year China was the seventh biggest exporting nation in the world, and the eighth biggest importer (together worth more than £327bn) and so, surprise, surprise, this won the right wingers over. For the average Chinese person on the street, details of this trade marriage have remained obscure. As soon as the English version of the agreement went on the web, the site crashed after hundreds of thousands logged on. The 900 page Chinese version is still not available - nothing to do with government worries over the likely massive protests once people find out what's going on.

The International Forum on Globalisation doesn't hold out much hope for China's people, "Any obstacles in the path of operations and expansion of global business enterprise must be subordinated. In practice these 'obstacles' are usually policies or democratic processes that act on behalf of working people, labour rights, environmental protection, human rights, consumer rights, social justice, local culture, and national sovereignty."

With a lowering of Chinese barriers to trade, small Chinese farmers will be swamped by cheap imports from US agribusiness.

While China's leaders now expect a bigger share of world trade with their club membership card, it's unlikely that the US and the EU will reduce import quotas for textiles and clothing, two of the country's main exports. In effect this will mean that while China must lower its barriers to trade, it can forget drastically improving its trading chances cos richer nations won't follow suit. At US insistence it is possible for countries to deploy special measures against China and curb its textiles and clothing exports for 8 years and any other products for 12. This would otherwise be illegal under WTO rules. The WTO say 'If you wanna be in our gang, first you have to survive the initiation ceremony'. Anyone still think free-trade means a level playing field?

FIGHTING MAD

On International Human Rights Day (Dec 10th) dozens of people went to Northwood in London to protest against the military action in Afghanistan, and against militarism in general. Northwood, has been described as the British "nerve centre" in the war on Afghanistan. It's the British military joint forces headquarters, which means it's connected by secure links to the Ministry of Defence in London and the hidden Downing Street bunker known as Cobra. Australian Ploughshares activist Ciaron O'Reilly commented, "We have come here today in a spirit of non-violent resistance and in solidarity with the past, present and future victims of the state terror that flows from this base." Activists daubed red paint around the place, scattered photos of Afghan children, stopped traffic and generally made their presence felt. Three protestors were arrested, held for 12 hours and charged with criminal damage. They have a date with the wigged ones at Watford Magistrates Court on December 13th. For pics of the action on the day, or for more info Tel 07904 450307 email: d10northwood@gmx.net or check out their website www.northwood.cjb.net.

Inside SchNEWS

"Books are a little lifeline for prisoners, offering knowledge, inspiration and a little bit of sanity in a totally insane environment." Mark Barnsley, Full Sutton Prison.

After a threatened legal challenge by prisoner John Shelley and the Prisoners Advice Service, HMP Full Sutton have been forced to end its blanket ban on prisoners receiving publications from Haven Distribution. They were forced to admit that the ban infringed on prisoners rights to freedom of expression, protected by article 10 of the European Convention of Human Rights. Haven has been sending out free books and publications to prisoners since 1996. To get a copy of their catalogue of fiction and non-fiction books, send a second class stamp to - 27 Old Gloucester Street, London, WC1N 3XX

* Another person who'd like some christmas cards and books to cheer him up. Stuart Durkin has served 5 years of a 13 year sentence in a Italian prison for streaking through the Vatican naked! He is in his cell 20 hours a day with nothing to do - write to him at II A-9 Casa Circondariale Mamma Gialla, Via S Salvatore 141B, KM 1800 Cap, 01100 Viterbo, Italy

* There's a conference on the abolition of prison on the 26th January 2002. There will be a few speakers but emphasis is on discussion. For more info Email: prisonabolition@hotmail.com.

SchNEWS in brief

Stop ESSO protest this Saturday (15) at Lewes Rd and Dyke rd stations 12 noon more info www.stopesso.com** **Winter Moot 2002** The Earth First! motley crew are having another knees up in Manchester on the weekend of the 26th and 27th of January. Accommodation available from Friday night and so it'll cost around £10 each including food. Manchester EF! 0161 226 6814 mancef@nematode.freeserve.co.uk ** **The Nicaragua Solidarity Campaign** is organising a trade study tour to Nicaragua and meetings with local and national organisations working on debt structural adjustment and trade, 16-25 February. 020-7272-9619, nsc@nicaraguasc.org.uk ** **Justice for Mark Barnsley** Campaign picket of the Home Office, Queen Annes Gate, London. Sat 20th 12.30-2.30pm. 07944 522001 www.freemarkbarnsley.com **Alveston protest site** against the by-pass want people to go and live on site in trees or tents. Info at bypass.18.com Tel: 01332 733540 ** **Radio 4A** will be transmitting this weekend (14th-16th Dec) on 106.0 FM tune in for underground music, party music and speech based piracy. www.radio4a.org.uk ** **Surrey Activist Group (SAG)** is holding a demo against capitalism and war this Saturday (15) in Guildford town centre. Assemble outside main train station at 1pm. Please bring flyers, flags, banners, & friends. This is a demonstration not a paper sale! saggymail@hushmail.com ** Four Swedish teenagers have been found guilty of **high treason** for throwing a cream cake at King Carl Gustaf's face. The boys shouted, "For King and country" as they lobbed the tart to protest against the Swedish monarchy. The pie-thrower was fined 100 days wages and his mates were each fined 80.

...and finally...

A Robin Hood wannabe in Canada, known as the "briefcase bomb bandit" has been holding up banks and giving all his loot to charity. Robert Henry Arthur robbed banks in Calgary, Edmonton and London, Ontario by pretending he had a bomb in his suitcase. "He was not a selfish man for a guy who threatened to blow himself up and kill people, he did good things with his money" said a Canadian police Sherrif.

disclaimer
Schnews warns all readers that we refuse to learn our lesson. Honest.

Pic: Guy Smallman

BUSTING THE EU IN BRUSSELS

By Jasper

The first person you will hear talking about the EU summit in Belgium last December, may well be the country's prime minister Guy Verhofstadt. He'll soon announce it was so great, we contained all the protesters and from now on all EU summits will be there. As to prevent this, here's a read up on what actually happened.

For the general public, the first sign of mayhem became apparent when the Mayor of Brussels, Freddy Thielemans, assured the viewers of the state television news that the first coach of violent Dutch and Belgian ecoterrorists had been intercepted. He had ordered confiscation of illegal radio and cellphone bugging devices, as well as the usual ski masks and knives.

The broadcast rather forgot to mention that this illustrious group had just occupied the European chemical industry lobby headquarters (CEFIC). A day before the start of the summit, it was a successful attempt to disrupt that stressful final effort a lobbyist needs to make, in order to get that "Yes, Prime Minister" sounding just right.

CEFIC is one of the largest and most powerful lobby organisations but has managed to stay out of the public eye until now. It has a record of opposing the most meagre attempt at environmental regulations for the chemical sector. Some files accidentally misplaced by the chaos also revealed efforts to undermine EU restrictions on animal testing.

Eco-radical disorganisations from Holland and Belgian co-operating in the action stated they had discovered that direct action is a much more enjoyable way to spend your summit hopping holidays than a dull march. And hey, if you hide a camping knife and short wave radio in your coach you will surely make the papers as well!

Something very astute in the Belgian activist scene, where action strategies of big NGO's and four fiercely competing flavours of authoritarian socialism make a meal of potato pie, potato soup, mashed potatoes and potato custard. French fries were also originally a Belgian invention.

After chains and lock-ons were cut and all activists arrested, deportation was imminent for the foreigners participating. Dutch deportees stopped their coach from leaving the city by climbing

out of the roof windows. After a good row with their riot police broke out, they were brought back to the police station hall to negotiate, which they then occupied. They refused to be deported until their comrades from Spain and Italy were sent to Holland as well. In the end the Belgian foreign department requested it's Dutch counterpart that these would be allowed on Dutch ground. The Dutch government refused and the deportations took place.

At the union members march the day after, the chemical workers union confided to Radio Bruxxel it very much supported the occupation. The union had recently been to Toulouse, France, where bad safety had caused the death of several in an explosion in a chemical plant. Investments in work conditions are dropping and companies are lobbying to downgrade safety and health regulations.

The unions had their demonstration on the Friday the 13th, but there was neither bad luck for the weather or the number of people in the march - with 80.000 people it was the largest demonstration in Belgium for years.

The next day saw the main parade of the "anti-globalisering" movements, in Brussels renamed "anders-globalisering" ("anders" meaning different), around 25.000 people, neatly divided in thirteen different blocks with subcategories as well.

When the demo came together in a manifestation, police sealed off the area. After body searches and ID checks, police violently attacked people sitting around a campfire on the street. Officials refused to tell what happened to them and a demonstration was staged around the jail, where the solicitor of the earlier arrested people was arrested himself and charged with conspiracy to form a violent organisation.

On Sunday the anarchist demonstration converged with a wild Reclaim the Streets set up by libertarians and artists, who had earlier squatted an old train station and set up independent radio all under the name Bruxxel. Instead of choosing the obvious target of the conference centre, the street party situated it's autonomy throughout the poor district of St. Giles. Police then sealed off the entire block for several hours. This standoff ended when protesters confronted the black block clad undercover police who were trying to provoke them. Their identities were revealed by activists and then broadcast on television.

In the run up to the climax of the Belgian EU presidency different organising groups could not get along at all. Unions split off from the main d14 platform, as well as Bruxxel and the anarchists. Of course, reformists asked the anarchists to help them with the socialists again. At EU ministerial council meetings in Leuven and Gent, well sorted street parties were staged. While the previously very fragmented anti-authoritarian groups, took over the streets and connected with each other, the ministers - politically and literally on the defensive - had to lock themselves up in fortresses, shielded off with nasty barbed-wire.

In Belgium protests were not taken up much in mainstream media, let alone internationally. While a few banks and a police station were seriously trashed, there were few other confrontations. One interesting sight was some Brits in black with those lovely Socialist Workers Party bandanas having a go at a few Mercedes. Well, they aren't all bad.

The Belgian and Brussels governments and police went to an enormous effort to look like they are the mister cools of handling big summits, so they can be in charge of hosting all the EU summits in a year or two. This is now likely to happen, and it was the message the media followed. While the brutal images of Göteborg and Genoa did lead to some representations of the ideas behind the protests in the media, without violence, content isn't very interesting for most editors.

However, effectively penetrating a summit's 'red zone' is becoming nearly impossible unless you manage to airdrop in unseen (or mysteriously all have security passes, like the 60 people who disturbed the climate conference in The Hague in 2000). Not being represented by the media makes stopping the work of corporate lobby groups an attractive strategy. After lobbyists were stalked in The Hague in October last year Paris also saw lobby buster action at the inauguration of Business Action for Sustainable Development (BASD)*. In Belgium, the year before the summit the European Round Table of Industrialists (ERT) was occupied. The Barcelona EU summit in April 2002 saw a whole day of proper lobby busting activity as affinity groups roamed the city having a go at various headquarters.

While you can equally doubt the legitimacy of national governments and the EU, corporates do not (yet) have a crate of tear gas grenades behind the reception desk.

So if you have a conference haunting your town, who are ya gonna call...

Some interesting links:
www.anarchy.be - portal for libertarian Belgium
www.bruxxel.org - Bruxxel coalition
www.groenfront.nl/english - eco-activism across the Channel
www.aseed.net/cefic-action - backgrounds on CEFIC

* The BASD is a joint effort by the International Chamber of Commerce (ICC) and the World Business Council for Sustainable Development (WBCSD) to undermine any binding regulations at the Earth Summit taking part in Johannesburg, August/September 2002. Their slogan is, take a deep breath here it comes: people, planet, profit! Web: www.basd-action.net. It is not yet clear when they will be naming their events with letters and numbers.

All Brussels pics: Guy Smallman

BECKHAM SHOCK:
Al Qa'ida Link

Osama Bin Laden claims from his Kabul dug-out:

"We wanted David Beckham out of the World Cup at all costs. His foot injury was part of our plan. I fancied Senegal. We strongly advised Ronaldinho to aim for the corner of the net before the England game. We achieved the desired result even

WAKE UP! WAKE UP! IT'S THE *MAS PREZZIE YOU'VE ALWAYS WANTED

Weekly SchNEWS

Printed and Published in Brighton by Justice?

WINTER SOLSTICE 2001 www.schnews.org.uk **Issue 336** **Free/Donation**

TRIAL AND TERROR

"The world does not need a war against 'terrorism', it needs a culture of peace based on human rights and justice for all."

Irene Khan, Amnesty International Secretary General

The events of September 11 and the campaign against terrorism are being used across the world as an excuse for governments to bring in more repressive laws, along with redefining and widening who the terrorists could be. And if that means taking away the very freedoms that governments claim to be defending, well, that's surely a price worth paying.

In Britain we can feel proud that we are leading the way in the race to the bottom of the civil liberties barrel. On Monday the Anti-Terrorism, Crime and Security Act became law – two days later eight people became the lucky winners in the 'we've decided you're a terrorist so were locking you up without trial' Christmas draw.

This hotch-potch of a bill includes not just internment (see SchNEWS 331), but a whole host of civil liberty busting BLAH. As Raif Smyth from the Coalition Against the Terror Act said "The truth is, the mandarins at the Home Office have used the Bill as a Trojan horse to get into law all the dodgy proposals at the bottom of their filing cabinets." In Europe, heads of state are pushing ahead with an "anti-terrorism roadmap" with plans to add two new databases on the Schengen Information System (SIS - see SchNEWS 312). SIS already holds files on nearly one and a half million people. One of the new databases would cover public order and protests and lead to, "Barring potentially dangerous persons from participating in certain events." Such as ant capitalist protests outside international summits by any chance? 'Targetted' suspects would be tagged with an "alert" on the SIS computer, barring them from entering the country where a protest or event was taking place.

In the Czech Republic, a new law permits the prosecution of people expressing sympathy for the attacks on New York, or even of those sympathising with the sympathisers! Already one Czech journalist, Tomas Pecina, a reporter for the Prague-based investigative journal Britske Listy, has been arrested and charged for criticising

the use of the law, on the grounds that this makes him, too, a supporter of terrorism. Meanwhile in Turkey, that well known human rights haven, just publishing a book by Noam Chomsky could land Fatih Tas with a fine or spell in prison, under the country's anti-terrorism laws. Chomsky apparently overstepped the mark when he wrote in 'US Interventions': "the Kurds have been oppressed throughout history... but that changed (in 1984) tens of thousands of people were killed, two or three million had to migrate, 3,500 villages were destroyed... an intense ethnic clean-up." So while it's ok for the Turkish state to carry out attacking the Kurds, it's terrorism and "separatist propaganda" to talk about it.

COURT-KNAPPING

In America, more than 1,200 people have so far been held in connection with the attacks on September 11th - most because of the colour of their skin. The majority of those arrested have nothing to do with terrorism, but have been jailed for minor visa violations that normally would be ignored.

Take Ali Al-Maqtari, a Yemeni immigrant who spent eight weeks in jail. Al-Maqtari told the Senate Judiciary Committee about being interrogated for 12 hours, lied to by the FBI, accused of beating his wife, then locked up unable to contact his wife or solicitors. All because his wife wore a head scarf to a recruiting centre when she enlisted in the Army, spoke in a foreign language (French), and because soldiers found box cutters and New York City postcards in their car.

Or what about Samir Khalaf, a Palestinian who worked at a petrol station in Connecticut.

Number of civilians killed in World Trade Centre	**3,234**
Number of civilians killed in Afghanistan by U.S. Bombs http://pubpages.unh.edu/~mwherold/	**3,767**
Money raised by UK and American citizens for victims of September 11th	**£900m**
Money raised by UK and American citizens for Afghanistan refugees	**£14 m**

He went to the hospital with chest pains on Sept. 12. People thought he was acting suspicious. They called the police, who called the FBI. After his emergency operation, the Feds took him - against doctors' advice - to jail. There he remained, charged with failure to get a work permit. However, he was in the country legally and was quickly cleared of terrorism suspicion and an immigration judge ruled at the beginning of October that he could go home. But then the Immigration and Naturalization Service wouldn't let him go until November.

Michael Boyle, solicitor for Al-Maqtari, told the US Senate meeting discussing the Department of Justice actions that these aren't isolated incidents, but are "part of a pattern of excessive detention and disrespect for the rights of non-citizens."

The war on terrorism has become a war on people – if you're the wrong colour, have the wrong views, or are merely in the wrong place at the wrong time, then you better watch out because you could potentially be the next terrorist.

*Coalition Against the Terrorism Act c/o Haldane Society, Conway Hall, 25 Red Lion Square, London WC1R 4RL Tel: 0845 458 2966 http://go.to/ta2000 * Read full story of America's detainees on www.alternet.org

Brussel Sprouts

As the Belgium government held the final EU meeting of their six-month Presidency, cops were out on the streets of having a good old ruck with protesters at the summit of Laeken.

Undercover cops, dressed in black, were seen directing protesters to smash up the Palace and attack shops, only this time the international black bloc were having none of it. Instead of following their instructions protesters surrounded the 15 cops and herded them into a corner and held them there until riot cops had to rescue their mates. For info on the meeting http://belgium.indymedia.org/

DON'T RIOT FOR ME ARGENTINA

As SchNEWS goes to press food riots and strikes in Argentina have led to a state of emergency as President De La Rue's economy finally hit rock bottom this week after just two years in government and nine economic plans.

South America's second largest economy has been in recession for the last four years as government attempts to tie the Peso to the dollar lead to the sell off of state owned utilities and the countries gold reserves. This has left the country with a £90bn debt and unemployment running at nearly 20% as the government caves in to pressures of the free market. Nearly half the population are below the poverty line - with a further 2000 people joining them every day.

Behind it all lies those global loan sharks the International Monetary Fund (IMF). Continual reliance on IMF policies has stripped the country of its assets and left them with few alternatives and huge debts. When the loans looked perilous more was given. The bigger the debt the bigger the interest repayments: the more for the bankers, the less for the people. The west has looted Argentina of its finances and left them the bill to boot.

On the brink of financial and social collapse with debts they cannot repay and people anxious of food shortages in a country formerly self-reliant the IMF may give another billion. This will mean further cuts of £2.7bn. But cuts from where? The government last week even sold off private pensions from already strapped public sector workers in order to repay international creditors. Money is now worth nothing and people have resorted to their own methods in order to eat (see SchNEWS 319).

Protesters armed only with pots and pans met police armed with tear gas, water cannons, CS gas and rubber bullets. The state of emergency has led to 16 deaths including a 15 year old boy shot by a shopkeeper; hundreds of arrests and 108 injured as young and old take to the streets.

20,000 people marched on to the presidential palace. Police issued warnings of arrests for an illegal gathering, after 15 minutes they opened up with plastic bullets. "The incredible thing is that not a soul is on the side of the police, so everyone who drives by honks, people walking by try to help, clap, boo the cops, throw things".

The food riots began in the provinces but spread into Buenos Aires, banks have been destroyed and the Israeli embassy attacked. In Cordoba Argentina's second biggest city civil servants set fire to the city hall in protest of the governments economic plans. One protester said 'I have never seen anything this intense in Argentina in all my life'. According to press reports this isn't just about getting rid of the government, most Argentinians do not trust any of their politicians and are revolting against the whole political class. Find out more http://argentina.indymedia.org

BYKER GRAVE

You might think that an organisation called the Environment Agency (EA), with over 10,000 full-time employees and an annual budget of £655m could be expected to look after our environment. Well think again, this government Quango*, just like the Health and Safety Executive, seems more concerned with protecting the interests of business than safeguarding the environment. Alan Dalton one of the board members of the EA has been saying what SchNEWS thinks, he spoke up and criticised the Agency, but for his honesty the Board Chairman sacked him.

Alan Dalton was appointed to the Board of the EA to look at the workings of the Agency. His report is scathing of top-level management, he says "…the real role of the board is essentially negative. In that, should the EA step out of line with government policy, too much, then the board will come into action to reign-in the EA." He was even told this by a senior civil servant that the Labour government didn't want any "surprises"!

One of the biggest failings of the Environment Agency has to be with regard to the Byker Incinerator in Newcastle (SchNEWS 260). For a period of six years 2,000 tonnes of highly toxic ash from the incinerator was spread on allotments and paths. This was against the incinerator's licence; the ash should have gone to landfill. The ash should have also been analysed and the results sent to the EA, but this never happened either. According to the EA "the Duty of Care is intended to be self regulatory …there is no legislation requiring the Agency to productively ensure that all waste stream from all waste producers are properly and legally dealt with. This would require a huge resource commitment which is simply not available." So they just trust polluters to tell them they aren't polluting? Brilliant!

When the practice of spreading the ash was revealed, studies by Ergo Laboratories of Germany found that dioxin concentrations were up to 800 times above the 'safe' level. However when the EA studied the allotments 18 out of 20 tested, contained only half of what Ergo found. The reason? Ergo took their own samples, the EA and the Food Standards Agency (another dodgy Quango) used the highly scientific approach of asking the polluters to collect the samples! The EA was going to press 19 charges, but quietly dropped 17 of them including the most serious one of causing harm to health, the company received small fines for the other two offences.

On the Byker fiasco and incineration in general Alan Dalton says: "I have no faith in the EAs ability to regulate the current domestic and toxic waste incinerators in England and Wales.

For the full report read the Winter 2001 edition of Toxcat from Communities Against Toxics, PO Box 29, Ellesmere Port, CH66 3TX,0151-339-5473, ralph.ryder@communities-against-toxics.org.uk, for £2.50

* SchNEWS Vocab Watch: Quango - Quasi-autonomous non-governmental organisation, which is a government body supposedly independent from the government.

Inside SchNEWS

"He did not receive a fair trial. The justice system is stacked against poor people, against people of colour, and against political radicals. And Mumia Abu-Jamal fits all three criteria...I think the entire justice system in our country needs to be re-examined." Howard Zinn, Historian.

You've probably heard about Mumia Abu-Jamal the former Black Panther and journalist – the most famous death row prisoner in the US – well, his death sentence was overturned on Tuesday by a District judge in Philidelphia. This ain't as good as it sounds. The Judge responsible, has refused Abu-Jamal's request for a new trial, upholding his 1982 conviction on first-degree murder charges. So while Jamal knows he isn't going to be killed by lethal injection, its pretty likely he'll stay in prison, period. The judge gave state prosecutors 180 days to conduct a new sentencing hearing, and ordered that Abu-Jamal be given a life sentence if authorities do not meet his six-month deadline. Philadelphia District Attorney Lynne Abraham said her office would lodge an appeal, while Jeff Mackler, from the Mobilization to Free Mumia Abu-Jamal group said "If they give him to a life sentence without bail, that's totally unacceptable to us."Mumia was convicted of having shot a police officer in 1981, who had pulled over a man over the road from Abu-Jamal who had been in his taxi. Celebrities, death-penalty opponents and foreign politicians have since rallied to Abu-Jamal's cause, calling him a political prisoner and saying he was railroaded by a racist justice system.

* Two weeks ago, hundreds gathered in his hometown of Philadelphia to demand his release on the 20th anniversary of the Faulkner shooting. The peaceful demonstration was marred by police violence. At least seven protesters were arrested and beaten. For more info check out www.nyc.indymedia.org

...and finally...

Last Sunday the Countryside Alliance went to Edinburgh to march against the anti-hunting bill going through Scottish Parliament. As they stomped through the Edinburgh streets they were joined by members of a 'splinter' group the Real Countryside Alliance. Waving banners like 'Aristocracy Against Democracy', 'I Love Torturing Animals' and 'Put the Blood Back into Sport' the group joined the front of the march for several minutes. For some reason the hunters didn't seem to pleased with their new found friends, with one woman brandishing a knife and another hitting one of the gatecrashers across the head with her own placard. The cops then confiscated the banners and threatened to charge the protestors with 'Breach of the Peace'!·

* Tally ho for another season of killing as the ten-month ban on hunting ends this week. First bunch of hunts out were the Duke of Beaufort lot from Gloucestershire, with another thirty recommencing animal terrorism again this weekend.

*Feeling bloated after yer crimbo dinner? Fancy a day out in the country? Call the Hunt Saboteurs Association 0845 4500727 www.huntsabs.org.uk

Schristmas Message

SchNEWS warns all readers that in this time of peace and goodwill expect to see Osama escape disguised as Santa, George 'WW3' Bush sing 'White Christmas' (with Bill Clinton on sax) and Tory Blair stuff a turkey while us bunch of terrorists have a few weeks off…see you 'orrible lot next year (or the 11th January to be precise). Ho..ho..ho..nest.

SchNEWS in brief

Looking for a New Year Resolution? Why not get involved in **SchNEWS** – we need writers, researchers, envelope stuffers, web designers, town distributers. Come along to our next training day on Wednesday 16th January. Ring the office to book your place ** This week protestors dressed as **pigs occupied** BOCM Pauls **animal feed mill** in Exeter. The porkers shut down the mill for 5 hours to protest against the continued sneaking of genetically modified organisms into the food chain via animal feed. Tel: 020 7272 1586 www.geneticsaction.org.uk

** A study by a **Cornell University** researcher suggests that living in a house surrounded by woods, meadows or other natural habitats is good for a child's mental health - for which Schnews gives them the 'Bleedin Obvious' study findings of the year award ** 'Local Voices' in **Newbury** will be commerating the 6th anniversary of the beginning of the 'Battle of the Trees' to prevent construction of the Newbury Bypass. Meet 13th Jan 11am in Northcroft Lane, by the leisure centre. Info: 01635 47437 ** **Take-Over-The-Streets** in-line skating event in London every Friday (subject to weather). Meet Duke of Wellington Arch, Hyde Park Corner 7:30pm. Info at www.citiskate.com

THE RALAHINE LEGACY
BIOREGIONAL FOOD PRODUCTION IN THE MODERN WORLD

The State is not something which can be destroyed by a revolution, but is a condition, a certain relationship between human beings, a mode of human behaviour; we destroy it by contracting other relationships, by behaving differently.
- Gustav Landauer

I am a traveller by trade
I only have what I have made
A fortuneteller too, they say
And I can take you all away
- Sandy Denny

Bismark, the German Chancellor, once remarked unkindly or perhaps ironically that if the Irish ruled the Netherlands it would be under water, but if the Dutch controlled Ireland they could feed Europe.

There may be some truth in this anecdote. The Dutch are model farmers, even in remote unforgiving places like Connemara where the topsoil is found in the crevices between the granite rock. The Irish, by comparison, have struggled with the concept and practice of agriculture as a means of growing food to feed their populace. Farming is an industrial activity. Land is turned over for the use of monocultures like wheat, oaks, barley, potatoes and sugar beet or for the raising of cattle, and, where bogs and rocks predominate, sheep are grazed which denude hill and mountain side. The country's daily food needs, including vegetables and meat, is met by imports. Ireland's own production of food, especially dairy produce and meat, is mostly for export – as it has been since the land clearances of the 18th century.

The idea that people should grow their own food and keep animals for their own needs is given no credibility. Organic farming is not taken seriously, except by non-natives. Gardens are for lawns skirted by roses. Self-sufficiency is a hippy phrase. Bioregionalism is a word few understand and such a thing as a worker-led agricultural co-op is a nasty communist scheme. "Do we want to be organic farmers or waitresses or do we want to get on with it?" was the prevailing theme as Irish society opted for post-modern urban prosperity in the early 1990's.

A researcher taking the time to find out why this attitude prevails might see a government policy which only encourages industrial agriculture because the state abandoned the concept of community-oriented agriculture in the 1950's when it decided to make modern Ireland a haven for the chemical corporates. This was to boost its gross national product at the time when the World Bank, the International Monetary Fund, the General Agreement on Tariffs and Trade and US-led corporate capital was mapping out the first territories for the establishment of globalisation. Our researcher might also conclude that the majority of Irish land is unfit and the climate too variable for small-scale farming and gardening, that the amount of effort would not produce sufficient foodstuffs, that the Irish do not have what it takes to be farmers, unlike the Dutch!

GAMBLED AWAY

The real reasons have both historical and contemporary precedents. Bismark might have had a different opinion of food production in Ireland if a utopian ideal in the early decades of the 19th century had been allowed to flourish and gain popularity. Modern agriculture might have included industrial, community, and family farming. Instead the agricultural co-op founded in Ralahine, near the Limerick-Ennis road in County Clare, in 1831 is a fragment of Irish history hardly known. Where it is known, it is dismissed as a failure. Ralahine failed because the proprietor of the land, John scott Vandeleur, retained legal ownership of the estate. It did not fail because labour-intensive, worker-led, agricultural co-ops do not work.

This was the lesson of Ralahine, James Connolly wrote in Labour and Irish History. "Had all the land and buildings belonged to the people, had all other estates in Ireland been conducted on the same principles, and the industries of the country also organised, had each of them appointed delegates to confer on the business of the country at some common centre such as Dublin, the framework and basis of a free Ireland would have been realised."

In a moment of madness not unusual among the Anglo-Irish landlord class, Vandeleur's utopian scheme crashed when he lost at the gaming tables, fled the country, and allowed a Limerick relative to file for bankruptcy against him. There has been a suggestion that he was set up, because the British establishment did not want to see anarchist-style co-ops springing up all over the west of Ireland – particularly at a time when it was desperate to remove pesky peasants from the land, to turn it over to grazing for livestock, and increase the size of each farm.

The tragedy here is that a proliferation of food producing co-ops might have prevented the famines, which raged from the 1820's until the 1840's, because the peasant Irish would have had access to a variable food supply which they controlled. This is crucial. Famines are not caused by lack of food. They are caused by the lack of access to food and the inability, for various reasons, of people to grow or pay for it. In Ireland in the mid-19th century a species of potato known to suffer blight was the staple crop for the peasantry, as it was for most of the poor of northern and western Europe. They became dependent on it. When the crop failed successively the people starved, died of disease, or fled the country. They did not do this without a fight because they knew who the architects of their misery were.

A select committee of the House of Commons on 'The Employment of the Poor in Ireland' noted at the time that "those districts in the south and west presented the remarkable example of possessing a surplus of food while the inhabitants were suffering from actual want. The calamity may, therefore, be said to have proceeded less from the want of food itself than from the adequate means of purchasing it, or, in other words, from the want of employment".

Vandeleur's personal motives for setting up the co-op are not known. They were not as altruistic as some have argued. Vandeleur did not make it easy for the co-op workers. The rent he required the society to pay him was higher than the national average at the time, and while the workers did begin to amass savings from their earnings it would have taken them many years to accumulate sufficient funds to pay for "the stock, implements of husbandry, and other property" belonging to Vandeleur.

Yet the Ralahine co-op had a positive effect on the well-being and health of the workers. Edward Thomas Craig, the manager of the co-op, wrote that rural Ireland presented "a melancholy picture of a rich soil only partially cultivated, and a willing people unemployed". Irish peasants, Craig believed, did not know what to do with the land! What he should have added is that they were kept ignorant by a social system that was driven by a combination of absentee landlords, their Irish agents, the catholic middle-classes, catholic priests, and a belief system founded on religious autocracy. Their other problem was access to land and seed.

So it was natural that the established order would object to Vandeleur's Folly – the epithet given to the enterprise by Margaretta D'Arcy and John Arden when they told the story as a stage drama in 1978 – because they did not believe the peasants could look after their own interests. "Others objected to the system," Craig observed, "because it was not in accordance with the established rules of political economy."

Despite the opposition, Vandeleur's utopian dream was made a reality by the shrewd management of Craig and the industriousness of the workers. "The peasantry began to hope and indulge in the expectation that other landlords would adopt similar arrangements on their estates," wrote Craig. It wasn't to be. The conditions for the genocide of a people had been put in place. One million people are believed to have died as a result of the 'Great Hunger' of the 1840's and as many more immigrated.

MEAT IS MONOCULTURE

What happened at Ralahine resonates through to the modern era. Large monocultural farming, with its emphasis on industrial and technological fixes, damages land and poisons eco-systems. It also produces high profits for land-owners, speculators, corporates, governments, and shipping agents. Roughly one 12th of the global population do not own the land they farm, "including a near majority of agricultural populations in south and south east Asia, central and south America, and southern and eastern Africa". With seed production now under the control of the corporates, and governments introducing legislation to outlaw seed saving, the means to self-sufficiency are being challenged. No land, no seed, no food.

The western world's obsession with meat has seen global consumption of beef, mutton, pork, and poultry climb to 217 million tons in 1999 - a five-fold increase since 1950. Most of this protein finds its way onto the plates of the rich (relative to their geographical location). The countries where land is used to produce meat have high levels of poverty and malnutrition. Export cash crops like coffee, cocoa, tea, sugar, and soybeans have the same effect. Rich, fertile land is owned, controlled, and used for raising meat, feed, or cash crops – all destined for the western consumer. Rice, wheat, maize (corn), and potato are the staple carbohydrate-rich foodstuffs for the majority of the 6.2 billion people who inhabit the planet – rice feeding almost two thirds of the human population – yet more cultivated land is being used for animal fodder (soybeans) and cash crops (coffee). Production of soybeans, used as a protein supplement in animal feed in the US, requires more land than wheat and corn. Despite a fivefold increase in land use for soybeans since 1950, the yield has increased by only a half. The consequence has been to clear more land for the cultivation of soybeans. In 2000, coffee production shot up ten percent to 7.1 million tons. Most of the world's coffee, which is harvested in central and south America, is consumed in the stress-filled, industrialised world.

The result of this is malnutrition and starvation among the poor, and obesity and immune dysfunction among the rich. One billion people are under-nourished while one billion are over-nourished. Obesity is the cause of 300,00 deaths annually in the USA. Diabetes now affects 154 million people globally.

RALAHINE REVOLUTION

The alternative is a quiet non-violent revolution, which is gaining more credibility in central and south America, Asia and in fringe communities (such as islands) than in the western world. Yet wherever you look around the world, people are coming together to create co-operatives and movements which combine worker participation with fiscal realities and ecological solutions. Food centred eco-villages are lighting up like tiny beacons everywhere. Barter schemes, local currencies, and mutual aid clubs are working alongside capitalist economic methods of exchange in many communities. Movements set up to preserve and reclaim soil, trees and, water can be found in diverse locations such Australia, Germany, America, India, Ireland, and China.

What all these activities have in common is a gradual drift towards a bioregional paradigm, which – in a post-oil, post-consumer world – will be necessary if we are to feed ourselves no matter where we live. Without oil, food production and distribution will grind to a halt. But before that happens industrial agriculture will play a part. Ecologist David Pimental sees a grim future for a world dependent on the present system of food production. "When global, biological, and physical limits to domestic food production are reached, food importation will no longer be a viable option for any country." Despite an increase in global food production, world hunger is also increasing leaving only one solution - indigenous land ownership and bioregional production.

It would be easy to be cynical about these seemingly insignificant gestures on behalf of an eco-centred future. Many of the eco-co-ops and eco-villages in the western world lack significant social dimensions because they do not involve the indigenous communities. They tend to be elitist and isolationist in their orientation so from the start they have been seen from the outside as something that can be dismissed because, particularly in English language speaking countries, they have been characterised by the Beatrix Potter - JRR Tolkein - Edward Abbey - loving set. People who have never had to work in factories or live in dysfunctional families or suffer racial abuse or breath toxic pollution or experience gaol, alienation, discrimination, sectarianism, migration, or any of the everyday aspects of the lives of people in murderous urban ghettos and factory towns and crowded cities.

If any bioregional model of society is to take hold, it will have to embrace social as well as ecological issues. Despite five decades of warnings about the disintegrating ecology of the planet and analyses that our social problems have their roots in our domination of nature and labour, not one single leader of any country anywhere on the planet has taken notice. A report Walter Goldschmidt prepared for the US government in the 1980's found that small farm communities had better economies than agribusiness communities, were more stable and contributed to a higher standard of living. The US Department of Agriculture refused to release the report.

Just to make sure that the masses do not give it a thought, the media in all its forms has dismissed all ecological-centred activity as a threat to business, jobs, profits, and our benign material societies. If people cannot be persuaded to think ecologically, asking them to accept bioregional solutions to a problem they cannot see is a blind step into a scary world. Kirkpatrick Sale, in his impelling book on bioregionalism, does not underestimate the personal and social obstacles. "It will take some broad and persuasive education to get people to realise that it is not the bioregional task that is irrelevant but precisely the business-as-usual politics of all the major parties of all the major industrial nations, not one of which has made ecological salvation a significant priority, not one of which is prepared to abandon or even curtail the industrial economy that is imperilling us. And it will take patience to lead people past their fear and lingering hatred of the natural world, which grows as their ignorance of it grows."

His words are echoed by Chellis Glendinning: "We need to integrate into our lives a new philosophy that reflects the wisdom of what we are learning in our recovery and the wisdom of the kind of cultures that all humans once enjoyed – earth-based, ecological, and indigenous."

The Ralahine Co-op is not our past, it is our future and it is beginning to happen. The island of Cuba is a model organic farm. Arainn, off the west coast of Ireland, is becoming one. Regions of India have flourishing eco-villages that are self-sufficient in food. Projects to turn lawns into small-scale gardens in North America are modelled on European examples, particularly in Austria, Germany and Switzerland. It has been estimated that the USA could be self-sufficient in its food needs if it turned over all its lawns.

John Holloway argues that the struggle for radical change is now part of our everyday lives and that revolution must be understood as a question, not as an answer. It was a question posed by the peasant workers of Ralahine. The reclaiming of food production is the answer.

*An Talamh Glas (bluegreenearth) is a globally oriented collective working on two specific projects

– the publication BLUE (www.bluegreenearth.com) and;

– the Ripple Project (an educational programme designed to help individuals and communities plan and set up bioregional food and craft producing centres, rural, and urban woodland forests and gardens. Info from: atgblue@yahoo.com).

WAKE UP! IT'S YER MODERATE VOICE OF ANARCHIC REASON

Weekly SchNEWS

Printed and Published in Brighton by Justice?

Friday 11th January 2002   www.schnews.org.uk   Issue 337   Free/Donation

FULL OF MELCHETT

"The majority of NGOs and activists do not understand how public relations firms are helping corporations manipulate them. This is a fundamental strategic mistake." - Andy Rowell author of Green Backlash.

This week Peter Melchett the former head of Greenpeace UK made famous for helping to trash genetic crops in Norfolk has turned coats and become a consultant for Burson-Marsteller - the biggest public relations (PR) company in the world.

Ironically Burson-Marsteller (B-M) are the PR Company for the genetic engineering company Monsanto. They specialise in 'greenwashing' - making corporations look like they're being nice to the environment when in fact they're doing the complete opposite. B-M have done PR makeovers for such nice companies as Union Carbide after the Bhopal gas leak killed up to 15,000 people in India, and Exxon after the Exxon-Valdez oil tanker ran aground in Alaska causing the worst oil spill in history. They even defended the 1980's military dictatorship in Argentina that saw 35,000 civilians 'disappear'.

Melchett says he isn't compromising his principles as he will choose which companies to work with (but with the likes of Monsanto, BP, Nestle, Shell, Unilever, Sainsbury's and British Nuclear Fuels on their books that's some choice!).

But talking to environmentalists is standard a tactic used by PR companies to green a company's image. *Managing Activism*, published by the UK Institute of Public Relations, describes this process, in typical PR speak, as "two-way symmetrical communications" which "offer a way forward where the company does not have to give in to activists or persuade them to give in." And the hiring of activists is described by PR Watch as "a crude but effective way to derail potentially meddlesome activists". It seems that Melchett is being led up the genetically modified garden path.

CON MERCHANTS

"It is easier and less costly to change the way people think about reality than it is to change reality." - PR adviser Morris Wolfe.

The modern PR industry dates back to the 1930s when companies realised they could use World War I style propaganda to deal with social movements and unions. PR companies are not interested in facts only images. B-M advise clients to concentrate on 'stories - not issues' and 'symbols - not logic', because "...symbols are central to politics because they connect to emotions, not logic". And these 'symbols' end up being reported in the media as crap lifestyle stories with the real issues not discussed. This is especially unsurprising since B-M is in partnership with ITN (Independent Television News) running the Corporate Television Networks (CTN) - which use ITN staff and facilities to make promotional videos for business clients - CTN videos have ended up in ITN broadcasts.

When the likes of Melchett give endorsements it makes the stories and symbols gain credibility with a cynical public. When cash strapped environmental charities take a few quid from companies, they do little to further their causes, yet greatly benefit the image of the companies involved. The WorldWide Fund for Nature accepted $1 million from oil firms Chevron and BP for a conservation project in Papua New Guinea (between them BP and Chevron make over $20,000 million profit per year). In return, leaked documents from Chevron revealed, "WWF will act as a buffer for the joint venture against ... international environmental criticism". In 2000 WWF held back publication of a damning report on tropical forest destruction, for fear of upsetting the companies it named.

It is not just charities and activists that are used by the PR companies. There are a whole load of front groups set up to present a different picture to what environmentalists are saying. In 1989 B-M set up the Global Climate Coalition to discredit warnings about climate change; people involved in the Coalition include most of the big oil companies, motor manufacturers and chemical companies.

PR companies also specialise in creating their own grass roots groups. In North America and Australia this has led to the rise of the Wise Use Movement.

WORLD POWER PROPAGANDA

Burson-Marsteller is the biggest PR company in the world, with offices in 32 countries and 1,700 employees.

B-M is owned by the WPP group, who own 17 other PR companies.

Believe it or not but WPP began life as Wire & Plastic Products a small British company making shopping baskets! In 1985 it was bought up by Martin Sorrell, financial director of Saatchi & Saatchi, he then acquired lots of marketing and PR companies and is now the world's largest communications group with a massive ability to influence the way people think.

REBEL ALLIANCE

Get together of Brighton's direct action groups (7-8pm), followed by Life Before Profit – a rally to stop the corporate killers (8-9.30pm), then DJ's (till 12.30 am). Monday 21st January at the Komedia, Gardner Street, Brighton.

Using campaigning tactics similar to environmental groups they scare farmers, forestry workers, miners, etc. into thinking that the environmental movement is out to destroy jobs and ways of life. Thousands of timber jobs in North America have been lost to automation, economic rationalisation and export of raw logs, but environmental protection is used as an easy scapegoat. Behind these groups which present a front of concerned citizens and workers, are big businesses. For example People For the West! who claim a membership of 18,000 is funded by 200 companies and 12 of its 13 directors are mining company executives!

So how do PR companies deal with yer uncompromising activists? Well it is that age-old tactic, divide and rule - exploit differences in the movement by co-opting the more conservative elements and ridiculing the radicals. PR companies divide activists up into categories such as radicals, opportunists, idealists and realists. 'Idealists' are educated and altruistic and should be changed into 'realists' who are willing to work within the system for change and 'opportunists' are simply careerists who want jobs and power. So Melchett seems to have migrated from an idealist to an opportunist. The most problematic group are the 'radicals' who want to change the system or have underlying political motives, the tactic of the PR gurus is to isolate the radicals from the support of the realists and idealists. Labels like extremists and terrorists are attached to anyone who refuses to compromise or takes effective action. But since PR companies are not interested in issues, only stories then this sort of doublespeak is unsurprising.

SchNEWS thinks maybe a leaf should be taken out of the PR experts' book and we should start describing radical capitalists as uncompromising extremists using terror tactics to destroy the environment and wreck people's lives in the pursuit of profit.

* Further Info: PR Watch produces a regular bulletins: www.prwatch.org, read "*Global Spin*" by Sharon Beder (Green Books) or "*Green Backlash*" by Andy Rowell (Routledge).

POSITIVE SchNEWS

We know that reading SchNEWS can sometimes be a bit of a wrist slashing experience, so we thought we'd dedicate a page of the first issue of 2002 to positive news stories. - Stories of people getting together in their communities to come up with grass-roots solutions to some of the world's problems...enjoy it while you can because it'll be back to the depressing stuff next week.

TRANSPORT

Critical Mass – is held in cities all over the world where people sick of the dominance of cars take to the bike as a sustainable solution, ride en-masse through the streets. These events are often regular, check the SchNEWS party and protest section on our website to find out ones in your area. Other means of bringing bikes into cities have included cyclists painting their own bike lanes on roads, and the now famous Reclaim the Streets events held across the world. * York has a critical mass bike ride on Sat. 2nd Feb, starting at Clifford's Tower at noon. "It will also be emphasising climate chaos, so people are encouraged to dress up in snorkels, wet suits, rubber rings, armbands etc. We would also like people on foot as well on bikes to talk to and hand out stuff to motorists and passers-by." socs203@york.ac.uk

* If yer fed up of cycling on dangerous main roads why not design your own back-street routes. Maps designed for cyclists for both urban and rural routes are available. Visit www.sustrans.org.uk

* Vivaldi – a four year sustainable transport plan is being introduced for Bristol. This includes 'home-zones' – taking traffic out of residential zones, revamped cycle lanes, schemes to power buses with alternative fuels, a new tram system, a 'clear zone' in the city centre, park and ride schemes and more to rescue Bristol from its traffic problems. www.sustrans.org.uk

HOUSING

For many people finding secure, affordable housing is one of their main worries. At this time of year when people are sleeping rough in freezing temperatures it is shocking to find out that there are seven empty homes for every homeless household in England. In the Burnley Wood area of Burnley, Lancashire, 1 in 10 houses are empty. The local Council's solution to the problem has been to let the properties rot and then bulldoze them. A number of local residents though were fed up and managed to secure a grant to set up a new social housing company. The company makes no profit and uses an idea called "Homesteading". The company buys empty properties, improves them if necessary, then charges a low rent, some of which is kept back in a special fund for a mortgage deposit for the residents if they choose to buy their own house later. Any profit made by the company goes into a special recycling fund to buy other properties. A similar scheme is now also reviving empty properties in areas of Sheffield. More info Empty Homes Agency www.emptyhomes.com 020-78286288

Another way to solve your housing problems is to get involved in a co-op. Housing co-ops are essentially housing associations run by the members (who are also the tenants), so as well as getting secure and often cheap housing you are also your own landlord. There are loads of existing co-ops around the country who are often looking for new members, alternatively why not set up your own? To find out more contact Radical Routes, 16 Sholebroke Av, Leeds LS7 2HB 0113 262 9365 www.radicalroutes.org.uk

RECYCLED HOUSING

Alternatively why not put your waste to good use and collect it all to build your own house. The Bishops Wood environment centre in Worcester is built from recycled waste such as old telephone directories and used car tyres, but even better they've got guinea pigs grazing on their turf roof. Take a virtual tour of the centre at www.4seasons.org.uk/centres

* There's a Green Architecture Day on Saturday 26th January at the Phoenix Centre, Brighton The day includes talks on sustainable buildings, including the Brighton Earthship. For more info phone 01273-503613 or see www.brightonpermaculture.co.uk

FARMING

There are loads of schemes popping up around the country aimed at cutting out the supermarkets and making it easier for people to buy direct from local farmers. One such scheme is Community Supported Agriculture (CSA) which is not only great for customers but also helps farmers so they don't have to sell their souls to supermarkets. The Soil Association defines CSA as "a partnership between farmers and consumers where the responsibilities and rewards of farming are shared." Fundamental to CSA is the mutual support between the farmer and the consumer with some degree of commitment. For example a vegetable grower may draw up a budget reflecting the production costs for the year and community members sign up and purchase their shares either in a lump sum or instalments. In return for their investment members receive a box of fresh, locally grown food once a week. As the Soil Association points out "CSA gives farmers and growers the fairest return on their products. They receive a guaranteed market for their produce – and can invest their time on the growing rather than looking for customers. As with all types of local food initiatives – box schemes, farmers' markets, food co-ops etc the local economy is stimulated by consumers supporting local business, the grower is also part of a community and is no longer isolated. Community members benefit enormously by receiving fresh, locally grown produce on a regular basis. Education about where food comes from and how it is produced is also a strong feature of these schemes. Most CSA schemes welcome members to come along to open days and even help with the harvest. As CSA farms are directly accountable to their consumer members, they strive to provide fresh, high-quality food, typically using organic and bio-dynamic methods."

There are currently about 100 CSA's in the UK and the Soil Association are currently working on ways to expand the idea. Lets all join up and watch the supermarkets crumble.
Soil Association 0117 929 0661 www.soilassociation.org/

ENERGY

Residents of Ollerton a former coal mining village in the East Midlands are shedding the area's destructive past and are building a new sustainable village on the former colliery site. After the closure of the colliery and the collapse of the coal industry in the 1990's the villagers were left with nowhere else to go. Looking to the future the community got together and formed the Sherwood Energy Village. The new village will be at the cutting edge of sustainability with a bio-mass power generator, educational facilities, energy efficient housing, cycle trails, sustainable construction design and materials, clean industrial developments and water recycling instead of the traditional polluting drainage systems. Conference and education centres on the site will also provide local employment. Info: www.sherwoodenergyvillage.co.uk

To find out about other energy saving and sustainable developments contact Centre for Alternative Technology 01654 705950 www.cat.org.uk

SEEDY SATURDAY

Brighton gardeners should get along to St George's Hall, St George's Road, Kemptown for a community seed swap. There will be speakers and films on biodiversity, the importance of seed saving, bio-piracy, genetics and related gardening topics, displays and stalls by community allotment groups and organic seed companies – as well as the seed swap itself.

With five corporations fighting for control of the world's food production, millions of acres of farmland being planted with genetically modified crops and 97% of our vegetable varieties lost in UK in the last 100 years Seedy Saturday is a response to these problems. Seed saving is a way all of us can do our bit to protect bio-diversity keeping rare and outlawed varieties safeguarded for future generations. It is taking place on February 9th 11am till 4pm and entrance is just £1. 01273 882552 or email baggage@primalseeds.org

SchNEWS in brief

6th Pedal Power Convention is at RISC, 35-39 London St., Reading. Sun 10th Feb, noon -6pm 013444-482266 www.c-realevents.demon.co.uk ** Fieldgate, also known as the London Action Resource Centre is set to open shortly in Whitechapel, and will be a resource for people interested in the growing movement for a co-operative, non-hierarchical and ecological society. The overall idea is to have a permanent building with meeting room/exhibition space, office, library, roof garden and prop and banner-making basement. One of those involved told SchNEWS "This is an exciting development on the London and UK direct action scene. It's also one of many similar projects coming together both in and outside the capital, other examples being the Sumac Centre in Nottingham, Bridge 5 in Manchester and Emmaz in London." Help needed with building and admin work, contact 020-7281-4621 or fieldgate@gn.apc.org ** Bypass corporate media – tune into pirate Radio. This weekend Radio 4A is back 106.6 FM www.radio4a.org.uk

...and finally...

Want to be an activist from beyond the grave? Want to avoid your death being part of the ruthless funeral industry? Have a DIY funeral personalising your special day, use a low-impact cardboard or home-made coffin, or get buried in a woodland and plant a tree instead of using a gravestone. Having bodies buried on land provides a legal battle for a would-be developer taking tunnelling tactics to new extremes! To find out where the woodland burial sites are in UK and advice about alternative funerals, contact the Natural Death Centre. 020-8452-643 www.naturaldeath.org.uk

Disclaimer
SchNEWS warns all readers we're up to our neck in Melchett every day. Honest!

FASLANE FOCUS

JANUARY 2002

The USA has bombed the following countries since 1945:

China (1945-46 & 1950-53)
Korea (1950-53)
Guatemala (1954 & 1960)

Indonesia (1958)
Cuba (1959-60)
Congo (1964)

Peru (1965)
Laos (1964-73)

Vietnam (1961-73)
Cambodia (1969-70)
Guatemala (1967-69)

Grenada (1983)
Libya (1986)

El Salvador & Nicaragua (all of the 1980s)

Panama (1989)
Iraq (1991-99)
Sudan (1998)

Afghanistan (1998)
Yugoslavia (1999)

THERE IS NO CRISIS - WAR IS BU$INE$$ A$ U$UAL

RETURN ADDRESS:
FASLANE PEACE CAMP, A814, SHANDON,
NR. HELENSBURGH, DUMBARTONSHIRE, G84 8NT,
SCOTLAND

WE KNOW WHERE YOU LIVE:

Schnews
c/o On the Fiddle
PO Box 2600
Brighton

The following is excerpts from the wonderful Faslane Peace Camp zine, re-laid out for this book.

FASLANE PEACE CAMP
a beginner's guide

WHO, WHAT, WHY, WHEN, and WHERE???

WHAT:

F.P.C. is a collection of 11 caravans, a bus, a tipi, a bender, a tree house, and various sheds and self-built structures.

WHY:

The camp's purpose is to oppose nuclear weapons and live in an alternative way to the society that produced them.

Britain's nuclear weapons system is four 'Trident' submarines, with nuclear warhead missiles, which are based at Faslane Naval Base.

WHEN:

NOW!!!! The camp has been here permanently since 12th of June 1982. Protests and a temporary peace camp existed before that but there has been a solid presence since '82.

Hopefully we will be here 'til the nukes are got rid of.

WHERE:

F.P.C. is on the east verge of the A814 road, which leads to HMNB Clyde and beyond. The Camp is therefore visible to all traffic coming towards the base from the direction of Helensburgh.

We are about 30 miles west of Glasgow, by the Gareloch, a river Clyde estuary sea loch. Faslane Naval Base is on the Gareloch.

BAe Blockade

The 20th November was Universal Children's Day and a group of Peace Campers joined other activists to protest outside British Aerospace's main offices in Edinburgh. We started early at 7:30am in the morning and eight people blockaded the two main entrances. People used lock-on tubes to join themselves together and threw red paint at the gates. Also the gates of the back entrance to the offices were mysteriously D-locked together.

The action was to highlight the thousands of children who are injured or killed each year through wars. The U.K. is the second largest arms exporter in the world and British Aerospace are Britain's main arms company. They are well known for exporting arms to repressive regimes such as Indonesia, Turkey and Colombia. The Indonesian military have been responsible for the deaths of more than a third of the population of East Timor and military equipment supplied by British Aerospace such as Hawk jets have been used against the East Timorese. Many of the people on the action believed that the workers at the Edinburgh offices should take responsibility for the people that are killed through the weapons that are sold by their company.

The action was successful as a significant amount of disruption was caused to the morning shift and lots of leaflets explaining what we were doing were given out to workers. The police were called but when they came they seemed quite happy about us blockading and after two hours and no arrests we went home and had a cup of tea.

Kirsty

PS - A few days later it was on the news that BAe Systems was losing profits significantly. So there.

Fran

The action went swimmingly. Pics: www.motherearth.org

Kitty and myself managed to cut a nice hole through the fence and into the razor wire. We crawled into the rolls of wire and stayed there for over six hours which is a record as far as I know. We kept each other warm, hugged each other while we were slowly surrounded by guard dogs and matching MOD-plods and a quad-bike and while alien-like infra-red cameras were filming us. All the arms we need.

Strangely enough being arrested was a liberation for me. Locked inside four walls, but for doing something which is against the law, but not against my conscience is a liberation. Nukes???

Not in my name!!

You can restrain my mind, but not my soul!

After the Summer Camp I visited the Peace Camp in Faslane and discovered it such a nice place that I had to come up here and live.

So be warned, don't visit this Camp ever, you might end up living here. Just like me and all these other nice people. (Kidding of course, pop in for a cuppa any time!)

Ludd

Coulport Summer Disarmament Camp

About 100 people, non-violent, direct action, vigils, fence cutting, camp fire, swimming actions, painting a Trident submarine, blockades, decoys, dancing, annoying the police (non-violently and fluffy, of course). Crawling on your hands and knees at night for five hours soaking wet up the wrong hill, nice people, Trident Ploughshares, 68 arrests, and lots of new friends from all over the world!

All these things could be found at this camp. This little space is not nearly enough to tell you how fantastic this camp was. From my own actions, I did one blockade at the gate of Coulport and two attempts at cutting into the Base.

On my second attempt I was joined by Kitty from London. We also had two other teams cutting into the Base at the same time and numerous groups of decoys to distract the M.O.D.'s attention.

Kind policeman lends a hand with the lock-on.

Partick Crane Action

After having had our eye on this particular building site for weeks, initially for "only building for the rich", we'd decided to occupy the crane for anti war reasons, taking up banners ("welfare not warfare" and "Blockade Faslane Oct 22"), food, water, extra clothes, and extra tarps for cover. Alex, Mary and I started climbing at about half 6 on the morning of Sunday the 7th October.

After a bit of a struggle with our backpacks up the narrow ladders we made it to the top of the 129 ft high crane then dropped and tied the banners. Well that was the exciting bit really. Now came the making of a shelter and looking out over Glasgow and down at the fab support gathering at the base of the crane.

Amanda and Rachel were busy sending out press releases and informing journalists from the warmth of Bab's and Brian's house (Thanks to B and B) while Ian, Sue and Anna were handing out leaflets and dealing with the coppers on the ground.

The support was fantastic. People were driving by just to see as they'd heard about our action on the radio. A local preacher took a bunch of leaflets and handed them out to his congregation. The local shop-owner gave us his support and talked of his disgust with the money going into military action and luxury housing while people are sleeping on the streets. We were definitely speaking for the majority!

In the afternoon the cold wind and periods of rain really got to us but we'd decided to occupy the crane for 12 hours. We were brightened up by the people in their cars and on the streets that just kept on waving, tooting, etc. Some of the Crusty Mansion crew came to relieve Amanda, Rachel, Sue and Ian.

We waited and watched the most beautiful sunset. At 6:00 pm we slowly climbed down, waiting 10 minutes on each platform and singing "you can't kill the spirit". Then once on the ground we were arrested but the police let us walk to the end of the site together, still holding hands and singing. We were met by Steve and Paddy and, as we hugged, we heard someone say; "They've started bombing Afghanistan………"

Marjan.

---

this card was found by the roadside.....

Upgrading the Camp

Slowly but surely…. we have ideas for new traditional long house, comprising two wheelchair accessible living spaces, visitors centre, library and an office. This will obviously take a long time to complete, especially as it involves taking down our oldest caravan "Bagend" (previously know as "doves", many moons ago), and the winter is not the best time to start building.

In the meantime we are continuing to widen the existing footpath to make it more accessible for wheelchairs and the new plumbed hot bath is also accessible - we still need sturdy handles to make the flushing loo good for folks getting in and out of wheelchairs.

We have a new lovely caravan "Unity" (it was donated by a member of the Unitarian Church in Glasgow- THANK YOU!!), a new bender and a new tree house!! WHOOPEE!!! The tree house is my lovely new home.

We have many new residents- we are now up to 23 and frankly not enough space for all - it is almost a hotbed system!

We also (shhh!! Don't tell the MOD) now have better access to the beautiful woods at the back of the camp.

Anna.

Heather planting potatoes.

Okblock - Big Blockade in Faslane

On Monday, 19th October 2001, around 1000 people came to Faslane to join the Big Blockade of the nuclear base. Aiming to keep the base closed for one day, the blockade started at 7 a.m. before the first shift of workers would start. At the Northgate, the main entrance to the base, around 900 people blockaded by either sitting on the ground and linking with armtubes or dancing and singing in the street to the sounds of the sambaband and successfully closed the base until 1pm when 178 people were already arrested and people started to form a big circle symbolising a hug for peace, standing in a moment of silence.

Among those arrested were veteran campaigners Pat Arrowsmith (71), Judith Pritchard (79), and Dumbarton couple Bobby (86) and Margaret (83) Harrison. David Mackenzie, of Trident Ploughshares and Scottish CND said: "To have these numbers shutting down the Trident base on a wet Monday morning shows the determination of protesters to keep going until this obscene weapon is banned."

Aaarghgh!! The submarine's on fire!!!

A source in the base revealed to us that at 10:30 on 17th June 2001 there was a fire on Number 5 berth, where I knew one of the Swiftsure (nuclear powered submarines) was berthed.

About 15 minutes later, it was said the Strathclyde Fire department was called off, but it was seen (and heard!) coming by the camp a bit later.

I assumed the message had reached them too late, so that, already on their way, they came to check out the fire anyway.

So I started calling the press, telling them about the above and asking them to let us know what the M.O.D.'s story was as well (Nothing appeared in the papers but it was reported on the radio).

Well, the M.o.D. had said there was almost a fire due to "hydraulic fluids" spilling, but that it didn't actually start (aye, right).

F.P.C. says there must have been a fire. Or otherwise the fire dept. of Strathclyde wouldn't have been called in, as there's a firefighting unit inside Faslane.

Your listening ear,
Marjan

DAILY LIFE AT FASLANE PEACE CAMP

I meant to write this article two years ago, under the title "What it's like for a newcomer at Faslane Peace Camp" but I never got round to it. I still thought it would be interesting to write it because people always ask "what do you do all day?" as if we are stuck for things to do (My arse! It is quite the opposite my friends...).

The camp is under surveillance 24 hours a day by the MoD (Ministry of Defence) police. They drive past the camp to the bus stop at the south end of the camp where they turn around and go back towards the base again. Often they wait in the bus stop for a bit if they've got nothing better to do or if we go to talk to them. They are usually quite friendly, you get to know some of their faces after a while and I think they know that we are keeping them in their jobs somewhat by being occasionally mischievous. One day I had a really good chat with one of them, quite a young chap although he'd been in the job for ten years, and he asked why I was at the camp. "Because I think nuclear weapons are bloody silly," I replied. He agreed with me and admitted that if he had known what he knew now before he had taken his job he wouldn't have taken it - but now he's got it, it's good pay, stable, and he has wife, kid and mortgage to pay. I think this is the case for a lot of workers at the base - they don't morally agree with nuclear weapons, but they need jobs to pay mortgages and support families, and what else is there in the area?

So the Mod Plod, as we affectionately call them, drive by every 15 - 20 minutes and usually radio through "No change at the peace camp." Sometimes they radio "Vehicle number six at the peace camp" - all cars that park at the camp get given a number, depending on how often they visit - but to be boastful, my van was vehicle number one because it lived here. When it was alive, boo hoo. Or they might radio through "Six people at the fire pit" (the fire pit is very visible from the road) or anything else untoward they might notice...

The MoD police can only arrest you for things to do with the base. The 'real' police we have here are the Strathclyde Constabulary, who the MoD might call for non-MoD related offences, but this is rare and it takes a long time for them to come. The Gareloch is also patrolled by the Mod Plod, but different chaps in boats - they have Ribs (Rubber Inflatable Boats) which go dead fast and look really fun, and Police Launches which are bigger, have cosy looking cabins (I always imagine them playing cards and drinking whisky in there), and chug along very slowly. A very bright flashlight from either of these boats often greets one when taking an evening stroll on the beach, which can be most unpleasant but is good for puppet shows, but also a friendly wave will be reciprocated.

Enough about them - what about us? Well the peace campers rise at different times. Frankly I always get up quite late, or later than I'd like to on these short winter days - there is really only full light from about 8am to 4pm. Sometimes we have 'jobs meetings' where we discuss what needs to be done that day and who's going to do it...

Every day lots of wood needs to be chopped. Wood is our only fuel for cooking and heating - we have a Rayburn stove which has a hotplate for cooking on the top, the fire compartment on the left, and an oven on the right. It also has a back boiler that heats water. The back boiler is plumbed into a normal boiler the same as you might have in a house, which supplies scalding water (if you're lucky) to the kitchen hot tap and the hot tap in the bath. Sometimes the boiler actually boils and then you can make cups of tea straight from the hot tap! The Rayburn is quite a temperamental creature, sometimes you start cooking at noon to make lunch and it's just about done by suppertime... So we have an outside fire too sometimes. It's quicker for boiling the kettle and on a nice day it's good to sit around enjoying the view of the busy A814. Then one can also wave at all the passers-by that stare from cars, take photos out of the window, shout "get a JOB", and other such pleasantries, or lob half finished bottles or Irn Bru from the window. We have a sign that says, "Toot to Trash Trident", so we get the odd friendly honk. The funniest is the tour coaches full of grannies and granddads that drive slowly past the camp one way, as we wave enthusiastically (well, I do), then turn in the bus stop at the end of camp and drive slowly back the other way so everyone on the coach gets a good look. Once one of these coaches stopped, the driver shouted, "can we stop for a cuppa?". I hollered "Yes, of course," and motioned them over but they weren't really up for it. At the time we had a sign that said "Faslane Peace Camp, intrigued? Pop in for a cuppa", but it was stolen one night by some drunken sailors and is being held as evidence...

Anyway. Wood. Fires. All the caravans and other dwellings are heated with wood too so everyday we have to get some more wood from the forests up the back, the log fields (a field where trees had been felled, chopped, left in the rain for a few years, just nicely seasoned for burning - unfortunately a limited resource), the beach, or if we're lucky enough to have a van to fill, we can go further afield and get a van full of wood which will last a few days. My first winter at the camp was spent continuously trudging trough wet forests, getting wet firewood for the outside fire and wet feet that never dried. This was the year the communal caravan burnt down and there was no indoor kitchen (plaintive violin music...). So. We get wood. Then burn it, thereby staying warm and being able to cook. Then we get more wood. Then burn it.

There is always cooking, tidying, washing up, sweeping, cleaning etc. to be done. There is also always mud everywhere, it being Scotland and winter and all that rain. Shopping, for 20 people, usually needs doing every day. We get bulk whole foods from 'GreenCity' in Glasgow, they deliver our order to the camp, but fruit, veg, bread, and hardware etc. we buy locally in Helensburgh. The Camp bank account is held in Helensburgh too, so any cheques lovely people send us have to be taken in, and if we need to withdraw cash we have to get two signaturees to sign and one to take it in. Then the account book has to be written up, a tedious job that always takes longer then you think, and only sometimes adds up first time!

I'm quite into hitching in and out of town. The A814 road is usually very busy - good for hitchhiking, (usually with a supportive local, or even supportive submariner), not so good for hearing each other talk in the camp. Hitching is a really good way of getting to know the locals and telling them about the camp. If I hitch out of Helensburgh (not to be done with all 60 tonnes of shopping- it's worth paying the extortionate £1.20 bus fare for the 6 mile journey back) it's a good opportunity to invite my driver in for tea and show him/her the camp - something I wish more people would pop in for but I think they are usually too intimidated by preconception and local myth...

On a "normal" day, people just get on with what needs doing; fixing roofs, gardening, making shelves for the kitchen, painting caravans inside and out, making burners to fend off the encroaching winter, plumbing, making livings spaces (treehouses, benders), raking leaves for the compost loo, changing the barrel in the compost loo (a most fragrant affair), making banners, planning actions, canoeing the Gareloch to see which subs are in the base and keeping the sublog up to date, canoeing the Loch to pester in/outgoing subs, babysitting one of two nine-month old babies currently living on site, fixing the fence around the camp, writing letters to the local newspaper, reading people's right wing Tory replies in that same newspaper, sorting out stalls, keeping the mailing list up to date, replying to letters people send us, keeping the food kitty (we all pay £2 a day and some poor sod has to keep track of it all), and much much more....

Then every once in a while we get wind that a nuclear warhead carrying convoy is coming our way, usually the next day. We rush around phoning people on our convoystop list, arrange a time and place to meet to drive off, hide in some bushes, and ambush the poor unsuspecting convoy. Crawl under it, climb on to it, and tell the big tale back of civvie cars what the hold-up is about: nuclear weapons on our roads. Often someone tracks the convoy to see which route and how long its taking and can then also let the ambushers know when to expect it. In fact, that is exactly what happened today and why I've actually got into writing this whole piece, except I was actually in the tracking car intending just to take photo's and not to get nicked. Due to another convoystop (the legendary Summer Solstice one) where all 11 of us got arrested near Stirling, held over for court the next day and given bail conditions not to come back to Stirling I have ended up in the police cells for breaking bail. The car was pulled over for a routine check (aye, right), just as we were in front of the convoy and the Central Scotland (that's Stirling area) police said to Marjan: "You've got bail conditions, haven't you?", just as she tried to tell them her name was Emma. They continued to me, "and you've definitely got bail conditions". Oh bollocks! We were about 50 yards inside Stirling council boundaries (not that there are any signs to tell you this). If I'd known I would end up in a police cell for hours on end, I would have jumped on the convoy further up the road with everyone else!

Another part of peace camp life is endless time-consuming court appearances and supporting other people on theirs. Most cases for offences at Faslane or Coulport are at Helensburgh District or Dumbarton Sheriff Court. The latter is usually for more severe acts. Often cases are postponed and postponed and postponed, but when you finally come to trial, there's not much persuading the JP or Sheriff that what you did was actually for the greater good because nukes are actually really evil. They still insist that YOU breached the peace of someone (usually that someone isn't even there) then give you a hefty fine. If you refuse to pay it you end up in jail. Then at least you get clean top and a trophy (an SPS Corn ton Vale t-shirt).

I've not been to jail yet, but I guess I will soon cause I do not intend to give the state more money to pour into army's, war, nukes, etc. and shall tell the judge character so immediately. Unless I defend myself so well that they find me NOT GUILTY, and start campaigning against nukes themselves.

Anna.

Radical Routes

It's a tough job but someone's got to do it - Keveral Farm, Cornwall.

We live in what is essentially a one party state, most differences between the major political groupings being no more significant than factional arguments within a single party, with each political brand in thrall to unelected business interests so wealthy and powerful that resistance would mean removal from the political arena. Every five years we are permitted to endorse this dismal situation by placing the traditional mark of the illiterate against the name of a politician not bound to keep the promises they have made to get elected and over whom we have no further control.

Those two strokes of a pencil conveniently excuse us from direct responsibility over our political lives and the political life of our neighbourhoods and towns. We abdicate our social and political responsibility into the hands of a small political elite kowtowing to a plutocracy and are told that this is what democracy is about.

On one level or another increasing numbers of people are recognising the futility of supporting mainstream politics, faith in the existing system is lapsing. What are we to do instead? What practical steps can be taken take to evade control by the established order and how do you go about building a different society?

For around twelve years Radical Routes has been developing a network of independent co-operatives holding collective ownership of urban housing and rural land and buildings for groups and individuals working for social change. Radical Routes also aids small worker controlled businesses involved in socially useful work, supports and promotes de-schooling and home education and helps facilitate the development of radical clubs and social centres.

All these projects are bases from which we can begin to build a society of people who see the value of co-operation over wasteful and destructive competition, who can work without the results of their labour being diverted to share holders, managers and directors and play without these same people filling their pockets. Who actively oppose the environmental and ecological destruction which goes hand in hand with relentless production of absolutely anything at any cost provided that it makes money

for someone who already has more money than they know what to do with. Who will not tolerate exploitation, oppression and injustice and who have the imagination, confidence and practical enthusiasm to develop alternatives through grass roots participatory democracy, egalitarianism and, from time to time, hard work.

Radical Routes currently has around 37 member groups within an area from Central Scotland down to Cornwall and Sussex and from Norwich across to West Wales. A further 25 or so groups are associated, being like minded and generally speaking 'on board' but not formally members. Radical Routes can be contacted at:

16, Sholebrook Avenue,
Chapeltown, Leeds, LS7 3HB.
Telephone: 0113 262 9365.
E-mail: radicalroutes@cornerstone.ukf.net.
Web: www.radicalroutes.org.uk

The network is financed through supporters investing in Rootstock, the financial arm of Radical Routes. So why keep your cash in a bank where it's liable to be used to fund all manner of exploitation, environmental destruction and otherwise ethically dodgy projects when it could help to support the development of grass roots control and social change? Rootstock can be contacted at:

50, Whateley Road, Handsworth, Birmingham B21 9JD.
Telephone: 0870 458 1132.
E-mail rootstockltd@yahoo.com
Web site: www.rootstock.org.uk/

SchNEWS Of The World

EXCLUSIVE

Bin Laden: "POTTERS BAR - IT WAS US."

"Potters Bar and Hatfield - only we could have master-minded such operations."

The truth about rail chaos in England is revealed in this candid interview with Osama Bin Laden.

"Tony Blair is a staunch ally of our bid to destroy British railways. I am advising him strongly to privatise the London Underground - and he is taking the bait" admitted Bin Laden. "We have had Al Qa'ida infiltrators in Jarvis and Balfour Beatty for many years, waiting for the right moment to strike - but until now these companies have done a brilliant job themselves to send

IT'S YER WE CAN'T KEEP MEETING LIKE THIS.

AT LEAST IT GETS ME OUT OF THE OFFICE.

Weekly SchNEWS

Printed and Published in Brighton by Justice?

Friday 18th January 2002   www.schnews.org.uk   **Issue 338**   **Free/Donation**

TALE OF TWO CITIES

NEW YORK

"The World Economic Forum is, in a way, a big cocktail party for the global corporate elite. As an organisation, it has no power to actually set policy, but it creates a space in which international "leaders" can hash out their vision for the rest of us. In their own words, "they are fully engaged in the process of defining and advancing the global agenda." More specifically, it's our globe, but it's their agenda."

- NYC Indymedia website.

Anti-capitalists will be descending on New York at the end of the month to protest against the world's largest gathering of government and business leaders, the World Economic Forum. (WEF). According to protest groups it will be the biggest thing to hit New York since Sept 11th. It has switched to New York from its traditional Swiss home of Davos for the first time in 31 years as a token of support for the City. The invitation-only meeting last year attracted over 3,000 delegates, including Britain's Chancellor Gordon Brown and Microsoft's Bill Gates. In fact you'll find a whole host of SchNEWS' favourite corporations from BP to Boeing and Nestlé rubbing shoulders with media moguls and politicians.

The decision to host the meeting in NYC was announced the day after the election of Mayor Bloomberg, whose company, Bloomberg L.P., is a member of the WEF. Politicians and business leaders are hoping that the event will stimulate NY's lagging economy post Sept 11th - and the plan to divert badly needed public funds into such an event and its security bill are sure to benefit NY locals. The police, famous for their zero tolerance attitude, have been given the green light for military-style tactics, traffic will be halted around the hotel and a 'frozen zone' created, with the cops announcing that since Sept 11th they're ready for anything.

The WEF – the club who helped create the notorious World Trade Organisation and the General Agreement on Tariffs and Trade - say that their meeting this year will focus on finding ways to "reverse the global economic downturn, eradicate poverty, promote security and enhance cultural understanding." Another World is Possible, one of the groups organising the protests against the meeting, see it rather differently. "They'll be looking to rescue failing

corporate giants, exploit working people, clamp down on dissent, and puree the diverse communities of our world into a single, American-style consumer culture."

After Sept 11th the world's media have been saying that the anti-capitalist movement is dead – but with 100,000 at Brussels for the EU summit in December, 50,000 in India during the WTO meeting in Doha - protests, big and small, have continued around the globe. New York will show that it's certainly business as usual for global resistance. Another World is Possible say "The WEF is in for a surprise…the movement for global justice is alive and well and growing, and ready to stand in the way of their five-day corporate cocktail party!"

* February 2nd will be the universal day of action against the WEF. To find out more information see at www.accnyc.org or www.anotherworldispossible.com

* WEF Counter-Summit and National Student Mobilization, January 31st to February 3rd at Columbia University in New York City, for more information see www.studentsforglobaljustice.org/

MUNICH

Every February the NATO Munich Security Conference takes place. This year the official organiser of the conference is BMW's own Herbert Quandt foundation. It's a meeting of administration officials of the NATO-member states and about 200 military strategists, generals and experts on military equipment - the alliance between capital and the military could hardly be better demonstrated. For the participants of the Conference on Security Policy the central themes are the planning of current and future wars, the establishment of powerful, mobile armies, the development of new billion-dollar weapons systems and this year (surprise, surprise!) 'Terrorism' and 'global security' which could mean anything really (just ask David Blunkett). It's obvious that it is only the security of the US and the EU and its capital that is

being discussed at the conference. What security does this system offer a Bolivian small farmer or Philippine woman working 16-hour days in a branded-label textile sweatshop? How secure is the future for the unemployed youth in the suburbs of Paris, or for a refugee in a deportation prison at Frankfurt Airport?

The conference has a pretty good track record. In 1998 US military operations in Iraq were on the agenda and the question of using German air force bases. Last year they talked about how the EU could join in with the US Missile Defence System madness. A conflict of interests between the USA and their European NATO allies call for their own EU-military block was resolved in November last year, when the foreign and defence ministers of NATO members took over the West-European Defence Union - this is being replaced by the EU 'rapid deployment force'. By 2003 this new intervention strike force of 60,000 soldiers is due to be available for 'assignment' anywhere around the globe, which means the EU will have its own private mobile army.

Just to show some appreciation for all the effort over the years and all the good work NATO are doing in Afghanistan a well known travelling circus will be in Munich for a 'Carnival against NATO'. From 1st –3rd February, the Pink n Silver brigade will be causing a commotion in Munich while others stuff custard pies in the faces of WEF (World Economic Forum) in New York. email:muenchen@rote-hilfe.de www.anti-nato.de.vu/

201

BLOCKS AWAY!

Faslane in Scotland is home to all of Britain's Trident (nuclear) submarines. Last year there were two massive sit down blockades where over 500 people were arrested. The courts still haven't dealt with all those arrested at the first one in February and haven't even began to deal with those nicked at the blockade last October. And those cheeky tridenting protesters are coming back for more. The 'Block n Roll' is taking place between 11-13th February and the aim is to have three days of rolling blockades and actions. There's accommodation available, so why not go up and join the court queue, or maybe try and provide us with a crap arrest. Call the action line for more info 0845-458-8361 or email: big_blockade@hotmail.com. www.gn.apc.org/tp2000/

* It's on late, so it must be good! The documentary '**Nuke UK**' will be on Channel 4 tonight at 2:10am, it follows four members of Trident Ploughshares at the blockade last February.

* **Three days of protest at Devonport, Plymouth** at the beginning of February. The focus of the demonstrations is the arrival of the first Trident submarines to Plymouth scheduled to berth on Monday 4th February. One of the organisers told SchNEWS "The protest is against Trident and against the storage of large quantities of nuclear waste at the Dockyard, representing a significant threat to the 270,000 people of Plymouth." Protests include a protest march and sit down blockades across all 5 gates of the Dockyard on the Monday. There will be accomodation on Saturday for people who want to go to workshops and discussion forums. Tel 07803620390 or e-mail tstaunton@aol.com

* '**Challenging the arms trade**' public meeting with Chris Cole who has recently published "A Matter of Life and Death", about the arms trade. 7:30pm, Tuesday 22nd, in the Meeting House, 7 Victoria Terrace, London. Tel: 0131-669 5591, www.araucaria.org.uk

SCHOOL REPORT

"Lately, our public servants appear to have gone surveillance-crazy, particularly where our children are concerned. It seems that hardly a week goes by without the announcement of yet another database to monitor selected groups of children in some way - small wonder that the Data Protection Commissioner has just announced her resignation" - ARCH.

A government's wet dream of complete surveillance of their citizens is making massive progress under Neo-Labour. At the end of last year we had Connexions cards for teenagers (See SchNEWS 335), and at the beginning of this year the government has sneaked into the Annual School Census the personal details of pupils which is usually anonymous.

The School Census is always carried out for statistical purposes but in this year's forms schools need to supply names and addresses with all the information which will then be stored on a central database. From starting school each child will now issued with their own personal student ID number which will follow them through their childhood (and possibly further). ARCH (Action for Rights on Children) reckon this is a 'National Identity Scheme' and want the DfES to halt the census until there is open honest debate. But don't hold yer breath. www.arch-ed.org/ or 01594-861107.

SchNEWS in brief

'One law for them.... Another one for us!' - the **Mark Barnsley** benefit CD is available from: PO Box 381, Huddersfield. HD1 3XX, £7 UK, £8 Europe, & £9 Rest of World, cheques payable to Justice For Mark Barnsley. ** Irregular Records have a benefit CD for **Medical Foundation For The Care Of Victims Of Torture** in support of Asylum Seekers. It's called ARTICLE 14 and includes Chumbawumba, FunDaMental and others - www.irregularrecords.co.uk ** Denied access to your personal history by social services? Check out **www.careleaversreunited.com** for legal advice and support ** After Ilisu - Lessons For Export Credit Reform, Corporate Governance And Regional Stability - 7.30pm, 22 January 2002, Grand Committee Room, House of Commons, Westminster, London SW1. Organised by the Ilisu Dam Campaign. Speakers include Tony Juniper and Mark Thomas. 01865-200550 or ilisu@gn.apc.org ** **12 hour Benefit Gig for Red Cross Afghanistan Appeal** this Saturday (19) at the Cardiff Coal Exchange 2pm to 2am. Confirmed acts include Blue Horses, Zion Train Sound System, Alabama 3's. www.afghanplightnight.com ** **The Underdog** is "Walthamstow's monthly shit-stirring rag" put together by the Walthamstow Anarchist Group. Email wag@fuckmicrosoft.com or check out www.tao.ca/~lemming/wag ** The **GM crop trashing craze** has spread all over the globe, recently in New Zealand 1300 GM potato plants were destroyed at a research lab. ** **BUDD Open Meeting**. To discuss the latest dodgy proposal by Sainsbury's at the derelict Brighton Station Site . 23rd, 7.45pm at Church of the Annunciation in Washington Street, Hanover, Brighton. ** And don't forget next weekends (26-27) **Earth First! Winter Moot**, in Manchester. A get together to discuss thought provoking issues and tactics and hopefully inspire each other, as well as entertainment in the evenings. Accommodation and food available for £10. Manchester EF! 0161 226 6814 or mancef@nematode.freeserve.co.uk ** And don't forget the four day **Wakefield Festival of Rhubarb** at the end of this month. Call 01924 305841 for details.

Inside SchNEWS

A **Chiapas prison** in Mexico felt the full force of inmates' unrest earlier this month as 1,000 rioted against appalling conditions, beatings and corruption. All credit goes to the Prison Warden Fidel Velazquez, a retired military officer who oversees a brutal regime, he has denied all reporters, families and human rights groups access to inside the prison. Family members blockaded an access road in protest, facing around 200 anti-riot cops armed with shields, clubs and assault rifles. Members of a civil rights group joined the relatives in blocking access to the prison, demanding the release of at least 100 inmates who they say are political prisoners. www.eco.utexas.edu/faculty/Cleaver/chiapas95.html

* **Dave Blenkinsop** has been given 18 months for liberating 600 guinea pigs from animal abusers. Write to Dave Blenkinsop EM7899, HMP Birmingham, Winson Green Rd, Birmingham, B18 4AS.

* **Prison Abolition or More Prisons?** A conference on the abolition of prison. Saturday 26th January 10.30am – 5pm at Conway Hall, 25 Red Lion Square, London (nearest tube Holborn) email prisonabolition@hotmail.com or SAE to Prison Abolition Conference c/o BM Hurricane, London, WC1N3 XX

CHOC BLOC

A red and black anarchist flag flew briefly from the top of the Argentinean embassy in London last week. A group of anarchists calling themselves "Those Pesky Kids" occupied the Embassy in solidarity with the people of Argentina, who are protesting against the government and IMF imposed reforms (SchNEWS 336). They gave the Argentinian Ambassador his very own personal reception, giving him a box of Ferrero Rocher chocolates in a parody of the classic advert.... "oooh, with these chocolates you are really spoiling us."

So what logical punishment did the pesky kids receive? Six protesters received bail on condition they don't go within 100 metres of any embassy. Still, at least the magistrate had the sense to drop another condition imposed by police and allowed the defendants to talk to each other!

Argentina was once heralded as the golden child of economic liberalisation but has now plummeted into a state of poverty and chaos, saddled with $155 billion debt and unemployment levels of 18%. The economic collapse is due to the expansion of free-market liberalisation and the imposition of IMF enforced Structural Adjustment Programs including the relentless privatisation of public services. These very same policies have caused ruin elsewhere, from the privatisation of water in Bolivia to the chaos of Railtrack in Britain.

With the economy going down the pan, Argentineans are taking matters into their own hands not only be taking to the streets but by creating a bartering system, handling the equivalent of over $400 million a year, with well over a million people involved (SchNEWS 319). The system is kept highly regulated, avoiding the influence of existing power bases in Argentina. It seems like the people of Argentina don't agree with Tony Blair's belief that global capitalism is helping the world's poor. http://argentina.indymedia.org/

TRADE BLOC N ROLL

A major trade war between the USA and EU looks on the cards after the World Trade Organisation (WTO) once again ruled against US corporate tax breaks. Companies like Boeing and Microsoft have been cashing in on "illegal subsidies" to the tune of $4 billion. So what's going on here is the US preaching free trade to the rest of the world, whilst stuffing the pockets of its own companies. This is the third time that the WTO have ruled against US subsidies. One influential US businessman said if this isn't sorted out "things could easily get out of hand". While Robert Zoellick, the US trade representative said this could unleash "a nuclear weapon on the trading system".

...and finally...

Lard of the Rings.

The British Lard Marketing Board aim to change lard's bad image and promote the benefits of lard. Sneaky tricksters have set up a spoof website complete with a history of lard, lard merchandising and some exciting new recipe ideas, such as "Roulard: Take a block of lard from the fridge and roll it out to about half an inch thick. Sprinkle it with herbs, or parsley or grass cuttings. Roll it up. Looks and tastes delicious on the cheese tray at a posh dinner party." Alternatively lard has some non-culinary uses such as: "Lard is excellent for adding a danger element to Scalextric tracks - particularly those shiny-surfaced chicanes with the lumps either side."

www.blmb.freeserve.co.uk/frameset.html.

disclaimer

SchNEWS warns all blubberers to sort out the greasy leaders living off the fat of the land. Fat chance.

Subscribe!

Keep SchNEWS FREE! Send 1st Class stamps (e.g. 10 for next 9 issues) or donations (payable to Justice?) Ask for "Originals" if you can make copies. Post *free* to all prisoners. SchNEWS, c/o on-the-fiddle, P.O. Box 2600, Brighton, East Sussex, BN2 2DX.

Tel/Autofax +44 (0)1273 685913 *Email* schnews@brighton.co.uk *Download a PDF of this issue or subscribe at* www.schnews.org.uk

Bayer Hazard

On 23rd January 2002, around forty people blockaded the UK headquarters of the German multinational chemicals company Bayer to highlight Bayer's acquisition of Aventis Cropscience. The acquisition makes Bayer the biggest GM company in Europe, and the majority of crop trials in the UK in 2002 will be run by them.

Arriving at Bayer House in Newbury shortly after dawn, protesters used scaffold tripods and a human chain with metal arm tubes to block access to Bayer's car parks. A few of the protesters managed to enter the building but did not remain inside for long. Others managed to block both the main front and rear doorways into the offices by sitting in pairs within the revolving doors bicycle D-locked together by their necks. Bayer's staff found themselves unable to reach their offices. After completing the planned three-hour blockade, the activists left peacefully of their own accord with no arrests. www.bayerhazard.com

The late 1990s saw the formation of several huge life-science/genetics companies including Aventis, Monsanto, Astra-Zeneca and Novartis, committed to the idea of combining human healthcare and crop protection interests in one company. But despite free-trade barriers being pushed aside the whole way by the WTO, allowing these companies privileged access to all international markets, they haven't had it easy because of bad publicity, and all those pesky direct action campaigners all around the world causing trouble for them.

So these companies have gone through sell offs, mergers, name changes, and anything else their PR consultants suggest, just to survive. In October 2001 Aventis sold its CropScience division to German chemical giant Bayer for 7.25bn euros (£5bn), making Bayer the second biggest pesticide producer in the world after Syngenta. They now own over half of the GM crop varieties currently seeking approval for commercial growing in the EU, including nine varieties of oilseed rape and one of maize, all of which are modified to be tolerant of the herbicide glufosinate ammonium, or Liberty (which they also own). Should the de facto EU moratorium on the commercial growing of GM crops be lifted, Bayer will be best placed to flood European fields with GM crops. They will also be responsible for the majority of GM field trials, including the controversial farm-scale trials, over the coming year.

Bayer has a history of corporate crimes that makes even old-school bio-tech baddies Monsanto seem like angels. In 1925 they were one of the companies that merged to form IG Farben, and during the second world war were involved in forced labour in their factories and produced Zyklon B, the gas used in gas chambers. More recently, Bayer was one of a group of pharmaceutical companies who took the South African government to court for allowing the production of cheap generic versions of HIV drugs. Earlier this year they were forced to withdraw one of their leading pharmaceutical products, the anticholesterol drug Baycol or Lipobay, which was linked to over 50 deaths. And then there's the poisoned Peruvian kids and the nerve gas...

For more skeletons and background information check out **www.cbgnetwork.org**

Bayer Hazard

Bringing genetically modified crops to a field near you

BAYERHAZARD

WWW.BAYERHAZARD.COM

With its takeover of Aventis Cropscience, Bayer has become GM Public Enemy No 1 in the UK and Europe. Bayer is new to GM crops but has a long and sinister history. Find out more about Bayer and GM crops, as well as its involvement with heroin, the Holocaust, withdrawn pharmaceuticals and toxic chemicals at www.bayerhazard.com

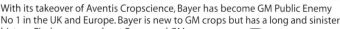

Bayer Hazard

This subvert was brought to you by Bayerhazard.com Anti-copyright 2002. Contact bayerhazard@lycos.com

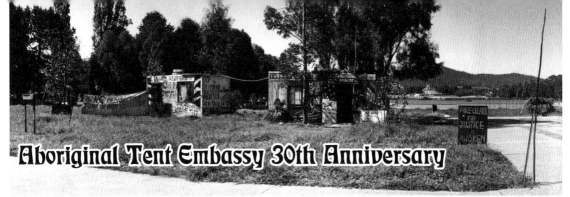

Aboriginal Tent Embassy 30th Anniversary

On January 26th 2002 the Aboriginal tent embassy in Canberra (Australia's capital) celebrated its thirtieth anniversary - making it the longest running protest camp in the world (that SchNEWS knows of).

A ten day 'Festival of Living Lore' was held in celebration of earth culture with workshops, storytelling, dancing, yummy grub, music, indigenous culture, earth-lore, singing, poetry, earth, magic, action, sacred fire and dreaming. People from all over Australia, both indigenous and non-indigenous, converged on the embassy to join the celebrations.

A Black History

"It is thirty years today since the embassy was put up in 1972 when four people come down from Redfern (Sydney), Billie Craigie, Tony Kurrim, Michael Anderson and Bert Williams, and they put up an umbrella on the lawns, and the umbrella grew into tents. We maintained the site there for about 6 months. [Then] in the early hours of the morning the police moved in and that was the start of the first protest on this site. And it was the first time ever in the history of Australia, that there was a violent confrontation on the lawns of Parliament House. It was the first time ever that Aboriginal peoples, stories about Aboriginal sovereignty went out to the rest of the world. Now we've been fighting here for 30 years." Isabel Coe.

At the time the embassy was first established it was opposite the front steps of Australia's parliament house where it couldn't be ignored (parliament moved to a new building further up the road in 1988). Since then many hard fought rights have been achieved, despite the camp infrastructure having been destroyed several times over the years by police, but a constant vigil has been maintained throughout. The tent embassy is an enduring symbol of the struggle of the Aboriginal people.

During the commemoration elders announced:

"We, the Aboriginal people and nations of this land, now known as Australia, hereby declare our original and continuing sovereignty over our lands and waters. Aboriginal sovereignty has never been extinguished. It has merely been impeded, by the use of violence, by the first fleet of British boat people in 1788 and those who followed. We hereby reclaim our sovereignty, our inherent right to be governed by our own laws, in harmony with the land to which we belong. We are taking our rightful place in our ancestral lands, which are our birthright, our sacred inheritance, handed down from generation to generation since time immemorial from the beginning.

We invite representatives of the colonising government… to come to the fire for peace and justice at the Aboriginal tent embassy and listen to the elders about continuing violation of the laws of this land."

But the tent embassy now faces the its biggest threat yet: the federal government are hoping to replace the thirty year old autonomous zone outside their old seat of power with a bit of polished marble across the park they're calling 'Reconciliation Place'. Already the national heritage listing bestowed on the tent embassy in 1983 for unique cultural and political value has been transferred from the tent embassy to the new shrine, a "white mans monument to a black mans tombstone".

After thirty years of struggle, the tent embassy is still serves as a major platform for the voices of Aboriginal Australia. There is still a long way to go until the rights of the first nation peoples of Australia are recognised and this 214 year long war is ended. Like the rising of the Moon and the Sun, so shall the Aboriginal nations of Australia rise up!

thanks to Bilbo & Belle

The beginning of the tent embassy in 1972.

WAKE UP! WAKE UP! IT'S YER SENT TO THE TOWER

I'm paying peanuts for this company

EMCALI

Weekly SchNEWS

Printed and Published in Brighton by Justice?

Friday 25th January 2002   www.schnews.org.uk   **Issue 339**

TOWER STRUGGLE

Colombia's second city Cali is today on a city wide stoppage in support of 800 workers from the Sintraemcali Union. For the past 31 days they have been occupying a 17-storey communications tower, the home of the state owned Emcali, who supply water, electricity and telephones to the city.

With the support of the Cali community, the workers - who have been there since Christmas Day - are demanding that the company isn't privatised, that there are no price increases and the corrupt company officials who have siphoned off money for years are prosecuted.

Apart from the riot police around the tower, the square surrounding it is in the hands of the people and has been "transformed into a beehive of collective action."

A huge makeshift kitchen is feeding the hundreds of occupying workers with breakfast, lunch and dinner. Across the road is a stage where people make speeches, play music and try to keep people's spirits up. On some days there have been 20,000 supporters outside, and every few days there is a big meeting of several thousands. All around the square, the walls are adorned with banners with slogans such as "Better to die for something than live for nothing". Squatting such a sophisticated communications tower also has its advantages – with workers beaming video link-ups around the world.

Colombia is not a place for the fainthearted. It has been in a civil war for the past 40 years, and in the past ten alone over one and a half thousand trade union activists have been assassinated. Since 1994 workers from the Sintraemcali Union have successfully fought off *sixteen* attempts to privatise Emcali - and the heavy price they have paid has been murders, assassination attempts and the forced exile of many workers. The leader of Sintraemcali is just 33 but has already survived three assassination attempts, and workers occupying what has now been dubbed Robin Hood Towers, cover their faces knowing that even if they are victorious right wing paramilitaries could exact revenge at any time.

Over recent years the paramilitaries have managed to grow in parallel with the US initiated Plan Colombia, a two billion dollar largely military aid package supposedly aimed at the eradication of cocaine production (see SchNEWS 273). However the paramilitaries have been untouched by this military war on drugs, despite admitting that they fund themselves largely from drug production in the areas under their control.

As Mario Novelli from the Colombian Solidarity Campaign, who is currently in Cali as a Human Rights Observer points out "Could it be that the US is fighting not against drugs, but against resistance to the imposition of an economic model based on privatisation, budget cuts, and rising inequality? If it is, then the stakes at this negotiation table here are high, for if the Cali community and Sintraemcali stop the privatisation of public services, and prevent price increases for the poor, then they are not just preventing government plans, but the plans of the IMF and the World Bank, and their US masters. Plans that seek to ensure that Colombia fits in to the neo-liberal block being developed across the region." With the occupation now entering a fifth week and messages of solidarity pouring in from around the world, negotiations are now taking place at the highest level. As Mario Novelli says "We are beginning to get the feeling that the world is starting to take note of what those inside the tower already know: this is an historic battle."

* There will be a mass picket of the Colombian Embassy today (25th) 4-6 pm at 3 Hans Crescent, Knightsbridge, London (back of Harrods). The Union is facing bankruptcy so if you want to make a financial contribution to the strikers send cheques payable to "Colombia Solidarity Campaign" with SINTRAEMCALI on the back and send to Colombia Solidarity Campaign, PO Box 8446, London N17 6NZ . 07950-923448, colombia_sc@hotmail.com

* The campaign have also organised a conference: 'Plan Colombia - Clearing the Way For the Multinationals', 23rd-24th February at Conway Hall, Red Lion Square, London WC1 (Holborn tube).

* Mario Novelli, who has been sending daily bulletins back from the occupation, will be speaking immediately on his return from Colombia on Saturday 2nd February at the CORAS Centre, 161 Lambeth Walk, SE11. (Vauxhall tube) 4pm

For general news on Colombia see www.colombiareport.org/

PROFITS ON TAP

"Here in Bolivia $25 million is the annual cost to hire 3000 rural doctors, 12,000 public school teachers or hooking up 125,000 families who don't have access to the public water system. Which of these are you suggesting Bolivia should do without in order to pay you?" - Jim Schultz -director of the Democracy Center in an open letter to Riley Bechtel, Chief Executive of Bechtel Enterprises.

In February 2000, just months after it took over the water system of Bolivia's third largest city, Cochabamba, an American corporation Bechtel hit water users with enormous price increases. They forced some of the poorest families in South America to literally choose between food or water. A popular uprising against the company, repressed violently by government troops, left one 17-year old boy Victor Hugo Daza dead and more than a hundred people wounded. Due to the protests Bechtel was forced to leave and the water supply handed back to public ownership (see SchNEWS 286). Then in November last year Bechtel decided to add to the suffering it had already caused by demanding compensation of $25 million against the Bolivian people – compensation for its lost opportunity to make future profits.

The employees of the consortium didn't leave empty handed. They took the hard drives from the computers, the cash left in the company's accounts, and sensitive personnel files. They also left behind an unpaid electric bill for $90,000. Now it's saying it wants more.

In his letter to the company Jim Schultz continued "Your losses, however you may calculate them, are numbers on a ledger. Mrs. Daza's loss is buried in a cemetery. No one will be representing her in your arbitration. For Bechtel, with revenues of more than $14 billion annually, $25 million is what you take in before lunch on any given workday." www.democracyctr.org

* Tell Riley Bechtel - the 51st richest person in America - why does he need to take any more money from the one of the poorest countries in South America. email: rbechtel@bechtel.com

---

White label Mark Thomas Video. Live in Brighton at the Gardner Arts Centre. For £8 + 80p postage on an SAE from SchNEWS.
Apologies to all those who have ordered a copy, the first batch we got had a dodgy soundtrack (not our fault) but now we've had more copied. If we sent you one please send the old one back and we'll get another one to you. If yer still waiting you'll get one soon(ish).

Within Tent

The Australian Aboriginal Tent Embassy celebrates its 30th anniversary this Saturday (Australia's national day, otherwise known as 'Invasion Day'). The camp was started in 1972 by a group of Aboriginals who decided that unlike other nations, theirs wasn't represented by an embassy – so they set up camp outside the then national parliament house. After several violent evictions over the years, and the seat of power since having been moved up the road, this embassy remains right under the noses of the government. It is the longest running protest camp we know of in the world. There is a celebration the 'Festival of Living Lore' 18-28th Jan on the site, featuring music, but also elders from all around the land, activists and supporters will gather around the sacred fire to pray for Aboriginal Sovereignty, and world peace. living_lore@start.com.au

Cops cop Kop

These days some people are saying that the new rock'n'roll is… terrorism. Well the Dutch police thought so this week when they arrested Marc - lead singer of the band 'Kop' and Barcelona squatter - in an Amsterdam supermarket accusing him of ETA (Basque Militant Separatists) collusion. Then just to show how 'rock'n'roll' cooperation between police across Europe has become, the Dutch boot boys did their Spanish mates a favour and violently raided and searched the Amsterdam squat where Marc was staying.

Marc is accused of having given a list of names of Cedade members (a Spanish neo-nazi group) to ETA, he is now in an isolation cell waiting to be extradited back to Spain to face trial.

Following his arrest the legalised squat 'Vrankrijk', described by the local scum rag the 'Telegraaf' as a 'hotbed for terror', was raided by 200 cops who prevented people phoning lawyers. One woman needed stitches after being batoned. Terrorist items seized were some water pistols, a couple of books in Spanish and two mobile phones.

The Spanish government is using the frenzy against 'terror' to legitimize their ongoing campaign to terrorise anyone that goes against their agenda. People fighting for autonomy of Basque Country are lumped in with ETA – and labelled co-conspirators in their terrorist acts. Squatters, anarchists and anti-globalisation protesters are all feeling the force of 'terror' in Spain.

* March against the Anti-terrorism, Crime and Security Act. 12.30pm , 2nd February at Temple, London. Called by the Federation of Kurdish Community Associations to highlight the Kurdistan Workers Party becoming a proscribed (banned) organisation. Tel 078790 24737 e-mail: fedbir@yahoo.co.uk

Bollockswood

Hollywood is a propaganda machine – a new movie about the American 'aid' involvement in Somalia in the early nineties coincides with the fact that Somalia is likely to be targeted next in the 'war against terrorism'. This film represents the US as peacekeepers rather than the killers of 10,000 Somali civilians. Bush officials have met with Hollywood representatives, who have committed themselves to 'initiatives to support the war on terrorism', and "Black Hawk Down" had to be OK'd by the White House. Already the US has closed down international banking channels into Somalia, cut off the internet from the country and restricted its phone communications. New York group ANSWER say "The Pentagon has unfinished business, they have a "black eye" and must return with a vengeance. This is the goal of Black Hawk Down." www.internationalanswer.org.

SchNEWS in brief

People disrupted an **Air Defence Systems Conference** at the Hatton in London on Wednesday. Armed with stinkbopted mbs the protesters managed to ruin the nice suited men's £350 buffet. The chair of the meeting, Gordon "Come on lads let's get 'em!" Wilson joined army types and govt ministers in trying to assault some of the protestors. The boys in blue appeared, did their usual dithering and false arrest thing, charged no-one and the talks were disrupted! ** **Anti-GM protesters** this week blockaded chemical giant Bayer's UK headquarters on the day the company floated on the New York Stock Exchange. Bayer need to raise capital on Wall Street to take over Aventis Cropscience, who run most of the UK field trials. Bayer's share price has plummeted following revelations their anti-cholesterol drug Baycol had been linked to almost 100 deaths. www.bayerhazard.com ** Wanna get clued up on climate change? **Rising Tide** have a weekend course, Feb 22-24, Ruskin College, Oxford – everything is free, but only if you never went to college 01865 241097 soaringskywards@yahoo.co.uk ** There's a **Fun-Raiser** benefit gig with DJs and SchMovies for the Centre for Alternative Technology Weds 30th at the Volks, Brighton 9pm till late. Next day is **180 Degrees at the Volks** (Thur 31st), psychedelic techno/ trance DJs, 10pm-3am, £2. All money goes to the Indonesian rainforest project. ** **Esso-bashing** resumes this Saturday (25) at the Dyke Road Esso station (Brighton) from 12 noon. www.stopesso.com ** A Seminar **'Crisis in Nigeria's Niger Delta'** Organised by the Centre for Democracy and Development (CDD) and the Royal Commonwealth Society (RCS) in London, Sat 26th. Presentations by authors and activists on terrorism and corporate violence, with a focus on Shell. 1-3 pm at the RCS Club, 18 Northumberland Ave, London, WC2. morten@cdd.org.uk www.corporatewatch.org.uk/profiles/profiles.html ** An **underground explosion of art** in a squat in London, 13-15 Feb. Gallery plus extra events - film night on the 14th - Live music and performance on the 15th with refreshments, crafts, clothing and a book swapping stall throughout. Artists should contact in advance to ensure showcase space. Artist line: 07092 012299 or Email: randomartists@whoever.com ** Check out the excellent **Space Hijackers** website for anarchitects, London-based pranksters, bloggers' guide and general funny business. www.spacehijackers.co.uk

Positive SchNEWS

Refugees from Nicaragua and El Salvador fleeing war and persecution in their own countries set up a model village in Finca Sonador, Costa Rica in 1978. The community now has 350 members who've been living a sustainable lifestyle surrounded by swathes of beautiful rainforest. Now though they're facing the prospect of their surroundings being ruined by the Man from Del Monte who wants to cut the trees down and replace them with pineapple trees. They need to raise money urgently and are looking for people to buy their own bit of the forest. 100 euros will buy you 400sq metres. www.dieschwalbe.de

Inside SchNEWS

Dave Blenkinsop, recently jailed for 18 months for the 'crime' of liberating 600 guinea pigs has been moved to HMP Bullingdon, Patrick Haugh Rd, Arncott, Nr Bicester, Oxon, OX6 0PZ – prison number EM 7899

Sab Hunt

Hunting has resumed countrywide now that the foot and mouth fiasco has been declared over. Hunts are up to their usual tricks again, hunting not just foxes, deer and hares, but anti-hunt protestors as well.

In Cornwall a hunt sab was hit by a horsebox trailer which was driven straight at him. At the Chiddingfold Hunt in Sussex huntsman Jonathan Broise shouted "Let's sort this out once and for all", grabbed a hunt sab, dragged him in front of the horse of the 'whipper-in' who then rode over him. Simon was lucky to escape with bruises.

In Sussex cops are conspiring with hunts to prevent effective action by sabs, but despite 40 cops on Saturday a few sabs managed to slip through the net and disrupt the Southdowns hunt, who made no kills. This extra effort in Sussex is probably due to the new Sussex Chief Constable who has previously said that he doesn't like sabs.

In Northants the police arrested a hunt steward (hired thug) for kicking and punching a sab. Later the sabs managed to stop a fox being dug out of an earth and the hunt packed up two hours early.

So don't let all the bad stories get you down, most sabs don't get beaten up and they do save the lives of foxes, deer and hares, more than the Neo-Labour government have done despite all their election pledges. Hunt Saboteurs Association: 0845-4500727 www.huntsabs.org.uk

Refugee Roundup

About midnight on Monday five Romanian refugees escaped unjust imprisonment at Campsfield Immigration Detention Centre. Unfortunately that leaves nearly 180 wrongfully imprisoned refugees and other migrants still imprisoned in the Centre.

*130 refugees detained at Yarlswood detention centre went on a 24 hour hunger strike last week in protest at their conditions. Their grievances were inflamed when a Daily Mail report described their conditions at Yarlswood as luxurious.

*Theres a demonstration outside Campsfield this Saturday (26) 12pm – 2pm to give support to the detainees imprisoned inside. Bring kites/ ballooons/music! Campsfield House Immigration Detention Centre, Langford Lane, Kiddlington, Oxford www.closecampsfield.org.uk

* Last Saturday more than 150,000 people took to the streets of Rome to protest against proposed new immigration laws in a massive grassroots demonstration organised by SenzaConfine (No Borders). Find out more at www.noborder.org

...and finally...

SchNEWS would like to give the Most Undeserving of Charity Award Ever to... US Defense Secretary Donald Rumsfeld, who has just accepted over $10,000 towards the rebuilding of the Pentagon, from the children of Moorefield Middle School, West Virginia! All part of the unbelievable-but-true, brand spanking new 'Show Pride in Your Military Act' created by a lunatic West Virginian congresswoman Shelley Capito. Congress attached Capito's legislation to the 2002 Defense Authorization Bill, which became law when President Bush signed late last year. "We decided on donating to the Pentagon because a lot of us have been to Washington, not too many of us have been to New York." said a student. Apparently the students felt the attack on the Pentagon was "sort of in their backyard" and wanted to help.

Subscribe!

Keep SchNEWS FREE! Send 1st Class stamps (e.g. 10 for next 9 issues) or donations (payable to Justice?) Ask for "Originals" if you can make copies. Post *free* to all prisoners. SchNEWS, c/o on-the-fiddle, P.O. Box 2600, Brighton, East Sussex, BN2 2DX.
Tel/Autofax +44 (0)1273 685913 *Email* schnews@brighton.co.uk *Download a* **PDF** *of this issue or subscribe at* **www.schnews.org.uk**

Colombia has Plan Colombia, Bolivia has Plan Dignity, now Brazil has Advance Brazil and Mexico has Plan Puebla Panama. Put 'em all together and you get...

PLAN COCA COLA

THE USA IS AN ADDICT. The country is addicted to petrol and cocaine - and will do anything to get its next fix. But like many addicts it's in denial, and now the people of Colombia and Bolivia are part of a plan to ensure that the US never goes without again.

PLAN COLOMBIA: COULDN'T GIVE A FARK

Colombia's President Andres Pastrana originally proposed Plan Colombia as a $7.5 billion development plan to address the country's related problems of drug trafficking, civil war, and economic underdevelopment. $4 billion for the Plan was to come from Colombia itself, mainly through the privatisation of publicly owned utilities. Pastrana asked other countries and international lending organisations for the rest, and the US used this chance to create their very own 'plan Colombia'. So far only Spain has committed $100 million to the Plan, whilst other European countries have held back because of the $1.3 billion grant the U.S. is giving to the Colombian military. This money significantly changes Plan Colombia from a regional development initiative to an aggressive military engagement with what the U.S. calls "narco-guerrillas".

Only 20% of the overall money allocated by the U.S. will be spent on socio-economic aid. The rest will be spent on advanced military hardware supplied by major U.S. defence contractors. The original proposal called for a 55% military aid and a 45% developmental aid split within the $1.3 billion plan. The final U.S. proposal leant heavily on the military side. It supplied the newly created counter-narcotic divisions 30 Black Hawk helicopters, 33 UH-1N helicopters and a $341 million upgrade to radar facilities. This was the single largest arms sale to any Latin American country since the Cold war.

Aside from the huge amounts of money being made by its arms companies, the U.S. has substantial economic interests within Latin America. By 2010 overall U.S. trade with Latin America is set to surpass trade with Europe and Japan. Colombia is the U.S.'s seventh largest oil supplier and has discovered vast oil reserves within its territory. Venezuela has the largest petroleum reserves outside the Middle East and is the U.S.'s largest oil supplier. The U.S. has wanted to decrease its oil reliance on the Middle East and shift its purchasing to Latin America. Venezuela and Colombia increasingly figure in this equation. With so much at stake, what was supposed to be a development project has turned into an excuse for the US to build up its military presence in the region, and to make money from it.

Plan Colombia is not just a US government initiative. Its being spurred along by corporations who stand to gain if US influence in the region increases. Occidental Petroleum, a major oil producer in Colombia has lobbied Congress intensively for the safe passage of Plan Colombia (along with major defence contractors). Washington's interest merges with U.S. corporate interests not only through the aim to increase access to Colombia's markets, but also in eliminating the rebels who have consistently bombed oil pipelines and whose presence destabilises this crucial oil region. The FARC are part of a complex and newly emerging radical opposition to U.S. interests within South America. It is Latin America's largest guerrilla movement with approximately 20,000 combatants who are principally concentrated in the south of Colombia. A lot of the funding for the group comes from taxes it imposes on businesses in the territories that they control. They acknowledge that along with all businesses within their zones of control, they also tax coca cultivation. Also in existence, and concentrated in Colombia's north, are well armed right wing paramilitary groups, the largest of which is the umbrella organisation, the AUC (United Self-Defence

Forces of Colombia) which has 5-7,000 combatants. They are responsible for 80% of the 4000 politically motivated murders that happen every year in Colombia.

In northern Colombia coca cultivation is largely industrialised on large well-organised "coca-estates" run by powerful landowners and paramilitary gangs. In the South there is a pattern of small-scale coca cultivation by peasants displaced through the decades of civil war and unequal landholding. The trafficking networks are concentrated in the north of Colombia and connected to the paramilitaries and the countries ruling elite. These networks are responsible for the international traffic in cocaine and the laundering of the money this trade produces, and yet the U.S. has completely ignored these in Plan Colombia.

Current U.S. policy on Colombia will not fund any development programs in areas not completely under Colombian government control. This effectively rules out funding for areas in the southern regions which will be most affected by Plan Colombia, because they are controlled by the FARC. Most of the 300,000 peasants in the Colombia's southern region of Putumayo are either directly or indirectly dependent on the coca trade. If poverty is the root cause of drug cultivation then it would make sense to put most of the money from Plan Colombia into developmental programs, crop substitution schemes, and land reform but the US obviously have other ideas.

Plan Colombia seeks to eliminate the most immediate threat to U.S. interests - the FARC - but at the same time this gives the US an excuse to build bases in Colombia as well as countries like Ecudor and Panama - which under the plan will remain. A permanent military foothold in the region - they don't give a FARC.

The US has a plan for the whole of Latin America and Plan Colombia as it turns out is only a part of it. The intervention and influence of the US in the region has been increasing continually...

PLAN DIGNITY: BOLIVIANS DON'T DIG IT

In Bolivia it has taken the catchy name Plan Dignidad (Plan Dignity). Its based on a law passed in 1988 that makes the traditional cultivation of coca illegal. This is like saying corn in its natural state is chicha or wheat is whiskey. The law proved to be a total failure after 10 years: There was no substitute for coca as a crop, millions of dollars went to corrupt government officials and, nothing to the farmers. The text of the plan says that the "stigma of narco-traffic inhibits the free flow of capital and goods to Bolivia" which means its objective is to create Bolivia as a safe haven for neo-liberal global investors. 5000 families will be relocated, from the Chapare region to impose this plan and it will be supported by the build up of troops to speed the process along.

At the moment there are 8,000 police and troops stationed there. The plan is a fight against the peasant population, not against drugs. Between 1995 and 2000 there have been over 4000 arrests of men and women and young people, over 2,500 injured, 49 killed. The people of Chapare and the Yungas are defending the coca leaf and their land. The government said they could provide three alternative crops in 1988 but have so far failed to deliver.

Plan Dignidad says "2002:"zero coca en Bolivia". The peasant families in Bolivia have decided "2002: with our coca, land and territories." The plant has been traditionally grown and used in the area for centuries. The plan has not fought against the drug trade, this has been just used as an excuse to get money from donor countries. Instead the government has pursued a plan of forced land reform, militarisation and harassment of the peasant farmers, in the tropical regions of Bolivia. Growing coca has become a symbol of protest, a way of trying to hold on to traditional ways of life and a way of resisting the US led land grab being pursued under the name of 'dignity'.

Like in Colombia people are organising to resist the plan. Resistance is mostly organised by peasant federations, by the people most directly affected by the plan. "We do mobilisations like national blockades. If they do blockades in the six Federations of the Tropics, nobody gets past. To get them through the government has to use the armed forces, police. And in this way, with gas and bullets, they manage to disperse us." (Silvia Lasarte Flores, the leader of the Peasant women's federation)

The peoples whose lives and homes are being taken away are offered no alternatives. Despite the laws being in existence since 1988 nothing has happened in the region to encourage farmers to move away from growing coca. Plan Dignidad is another way in which the US is increasing its influence in Latin America, under the pretext of a 'war on drugs'. Like in Colombia it affects only the poor, and like in Colombia also people are fighting to preserve their way of life.

ROAD RAGE: PLAN PUEBLA PANAMA

By Penny

Plan Pueblo Panama was proposed by President Vincente Fox of Mexico in 2001. It was promoted as a way of bringing the neoliberal "fruits of globalisation" to the region South and south East of Mexico city, and extending them to Guatemala, Belize, Honduras, El Salvador, Nicaragua, Costa Rica and Panama.

Little known outside the region, the mega-project will create an elaborate infrastructure of railways, ports, highways, roads and airports. They will connect together the development of the agricultural, fishing, timber and energy industries. Dams, gold and uranium mines, platforms for petroleum extraction, and chemical intensive palm plantations, will be built. Multinational corporations will be licensed to engage in bio-prospecting and tree felling in an area that holds 10% of the world's bio-diversity.

Central to the plan are tax and legal incentives designed to expand the maquiladora (assembly plant) concept. This is where manufactured U.S. goods are assembled in low wage factories and then returned to the U.S. via new transit corridors. Supported by the World Bank and the Inter-American Development Fund, PPP would represent a massive cost saving to U.S and European multinational companies. Both shipping and freight times to the

U.S and Asia will be drastically reduced. PPP would also create the foundation for the implementation of the Free Trade Area of the Americas by 2005. However the project seems to have been designed for the benefit of the international economic powers - especially the U.S. It is based on the exploitation of the Central America's impoverished populations.

There are plans to build 70 hydroelectric dams to power the meta-project. These will have the devastating effect of diverting the drinking water of the local populations. In the state of Chiapas in Mexico alone, 32 dams are planned. They will flood jungles, canyons, rivers, and archaeological ruins, in an area of outstanding natural beauty. If these projects are realised up to a third of the Peten in Guatemala could be flooded, along with up to eight hundred archaeological sites in Peten and Chiapas.

The hydroelectric dams would also help dislocate and disrupt the indigenous populations of the region; who have a long history of resistance against government and business exploitation. These displaced populations would then provide a convenient workforce for the maquiladoras proposed by the PPP.

In Mexico the plan seems to represent a counter-insurgency strategy to eliminate and undermine the largely Mayan resistance in the area. In the Lacondon and Monte Azules areas in Chiapas several zapatista autonomous municipalities and communities are being immediately threatened with expulsion. Military and paramilitary presence has been significantly increased in the area.

Thousands of small projects are planned throughout Central America under the PPP. Taken as a whole, the plan will deny indigenous inhabitants the right to control and protect their lands and to decide the future of their own development. For the indigenous, the PPP represents a plan to homogenise their cultures and way of life, shifting the importance from agriculture to manufacturing.

Civil society organisations, and indigenous communities throughout Mexico and Central America, have repeatedly voiced their resistance to Plan Puebla Panama. The reasons for this are obvious - it has been formed for and by the interests of large multinational corporations and those in government with close ties to investors in the plan.

Representatives of N.G.O.'s, civil society, and indigenous groups, held regional conferences and demonstrations throughout the last year in Mexico and Guatemala to address the impacts of PPP. Through these meetings they hope to address the effects of the project on local communities, to create alternative plans for economic development, and plan strategies for a unified campaign that transcends borders. In the short term they aim to use legal instruments, create educational documents, and improve communication networks. The long-term goal is to develop and maintain strategies to defend land and resources; as well as educate local communities.

Resistance is a daily struggle for many indigenous communities in Mexico. They live with the threat of impending expulsion. Many have witnessed the growing military and paramilitary presence. A communiqué from Ricardo Flores Magon zapatista autonomous municipality in rebellion in Chiapas, Mexico on the 25th March 2002 testifies to this:

"Today we are saying it quite clearly, the project to exterminate our indigenous communities through dislocation and relocation is a strategic part of the Plan Puebla Panama and of its economic interests, which are attempting to extend neo-liberal policies and projects to the south and south- east of Mexico and all Central America... The PPP is also a counter-insurgency plan, because neo-liberal interests find themselves thwarted by our indigenous communities and our different cultures which understand land as mother, as a communal good that cannot be used for the benefit of just a few, because it cannot be destroyed or stolen in order to be made private and in order to take its wealth....We are not going to permit the dislocation nor the relocation of our communities, we are going to defend them with everything we have in our hands, in our truth rights, and reason. We are going to defend our lands and communities as the territories and rights of our indigenous people."

Chiapas indymedia - http//chiapas.indymedia.org
Global exchange - www.globalexchange.org

PLAN EXPLOITATION: ADVANCE BRAZIL

Heavily under the influence of both home grown and foreign fat-cats, the Brazilian government thinks it's a good idea to blow $45 billion on an Amazon development plan dubbed 'Advance Brazil'. After the dismal failure of the Trans-Amazonian Highway (TAH) in the 1970s many Brazilians don't have much faith in this new development drive. Soon after its construction the sediments of the Amazon Basin made the highway unstable and it often flooded during heavy rains, blocking traffic and leaving crops to rot. Harvest yields for peasants were dismal since the forest soils were quickly exhausted, and virgin forest had to be cleared annually. Logging was difficult because commercially valuable trees didn't grow together in the same place and erosion from wind and rain ruined the land after clearing. Many colonists, unfamiliar with banking and lured by easy credit, went deep into debt. Instead of boosting the economy the TAH got Brazil into financial strife. So why would Advance Brazil be any different? The simple answer is it won't.

With various financial commitments to the IMF, the World Bank and the Inter-American Development Bank as well as trade agreements with other countries and global corporations, the Brazilian government's hands are variously tied. They are also under pressure from Brazil's business elite and influential landowners that aspire to the heavily advertised capitalist dream of wealthier nations. In comparison to the heavily industrially and economically developed Western European countries, Brazil is poor. Over 6.5 million families are without accommodation and 10 million lack the necessities to meet basic living standards. For these reasons Brazil's Government says that Advance Brazil is the way forward and the Amazon must be exploited. Various Advance Brazil schemes are already on the go, including the building of new roads, dams, railroads, waterways, ranches, oil pipelines and mineral extraction works, but opposition is also building.

ECOLOGY

In 1950, tropical rainforests covered 14% of the earth's land surface - now they only cover 6%. Nearly 40 percent of what's left is in the Brazilian Amazon.

According to a US-Brazilian study Advance Brazil is set to destroy about 42% of the rainforest by the year 2020. This will mean the loss of countless animals, trees, plants, insects, birds, reptiles, amphibians and fish because over half the world's 10 million species live there. Deforestation will also affect both local and global water cycles because one-fifth of the world's fresh water circulates in the Amazon Basin. Advance Brazil projects will also impact upon medicinal research – already much of the active ingredients in today's cancer-fighting drugs come from organisms found only in the rainforest, and there's many more that western medicine is yet to use.

ROADS

"Illegal logging and land-clearing are rampant. New roads that cut into the frontier almost always initiate a process of spontaneous colonisation, logging, hunting and land speculation that is almost impossible to stop" - William Laurance, Smithsonian Tropical Research Institute, USA.

In order to 'colonise' land, large numbers of people from city slums have been given cash incentives to move – the word used is 'transmigrate' - to rainforest locations for a cash incentive, but often the settlers are unable to farm their land, and they are forced into wage slavery for big agricultural developments or mineral extraction works. "Slave labour in Brazil is directly linked to deforestation," says Cláudio Secchin, director of the Ministry of Labour's special antislavery Mobile Enforcement Team. The large companies exploit the surplus of labour, to the point that several workers who have fought for rights have been killed. "I can't read so maybe a half-dozen times I was ordered to burn the identity cards and work documents of workers who I had last seen walking down the road, supposedly on their way out. We also found heaps of bones out in the jungle, but none of us ever talked about it" said one worker on the Brazilian Indymedia website.

DAMS

"Dams have already displaced more than one million Brazilians from their lands, and if there is no resistance, another 800,000 people will be expelled with the construction of 494 new dams in the next 10 years." – Movement of Dam affected People (MAB).

The Brazilian government is still trying to rustle-up investment, ignoring the comments of the World Commission on Dams (WCD) that "in many cases dams have led to an irreversible loss of species populations and ecosystems." The WCD also highlighted the fact that, "Impacts of dam building on people and livelihoods – both above and below dams - have been … devastating." Often led by MAB, opposition to dam building has been growing. In March 9 anti-dam protestors were hospitalised in Sao Paulo after clashes with the police in Rio Grande do Sul State. The demonstrators were part of a national campaign of protests against Brazil's hydropower energy policy and marked the fifth International Day of Action Against Dams and for Rivers, Water and Life. 500 people marched to the site of the Inter-American Development Bank's annual meeting in Fortaleza in northeast Brazil because the bank plans to finance many new dams. A spokesperson for the International Rivers Network said, "These dams would flood over 10,000 sq km of the Amazon rainforest, affecting indigenous communities and endangered species." Brazils history of dam building has been about as successful as its Trans- Amazonian highway, with over 2,000 Dams left to crumble unused in the last ten years.(www.mabnacional.org.br)

LAND

The largest opposition to Advance Brazil is Moviemento dos Trabalhadores Rurais Sem Terra (MST). The MST is a landless workers movement that organises mass land squats and actions to oppose the unequal distribution of land in Brazil and fights for workers rights. On 17th April 1996, Brazilian military police killed 19 landless workers in Eldorado, Carajas in the state of Para. 600 families connected to MST had occupied the highway to protest about delays in land reforms. The military police sent in to 'open up' the highway blocked it with troops instead and then opened up their weapons on the crowd. 19 workers were shot dead, 13 at point-blank range, and hundreds were left wounded. Oziel, an 18 year old MST organiser was grabbed by military police and tortured in front of everyone before being beaten to death. Seven years passed and finally in May this year Colonel Mario Colares Pantoja and Major Jos Maria Olivera (the Commandant of the troops responsible for the massacre) were sentenced to 158 Years imprisonment. And on the 18th May, 600 landless people connected to MST squatted a farm belonging to President Cardoso's family in Buritis, Minas Gerais. They occupied the farm to pressure the federal government to settle 200 families and to support other settlements in Minas and Goiao. The government brokered a deal with MST, publicly called the activists 'terrorists' and had 16 organisers from MST arrested during a so-called inspection of the farm for damage. The government has shown that they are incapable of protecting the human rights of indigenous people. The MST on the other hand has become famous for its actions and has received several Human Rights awards. It has also created 60 food co-operatives as well as setting up a large-scale literacy program. (www.mstbrazil.org)

GREENWASH

The 6th March represented a small victory for environmentalists when Brazil's Agrarian Reform Institute cancelled thousands of false and undocumented land ownership claims following a parliamentary investigation of squatters on Amazon public lands last spring. Roughly half of the reclaimed lands have been proposed as areas of strict protection such as national parks and ecological reserves. The other reclaimed areas will be protected as 'extraction' reserves and national forests, which means that the government can authorise the 'use' of the land, wood and minerals to anyone they reckon is committed to 'sustainable development'. The problem is, there's nothing 'sustainable' about developments which destroy the Amazon, flood tribal land and exploit the people.

www.solcomhouse.com/advancebrasil.htm

Substandard Safety

Dockyard gets go ahead to turn south west city into nuclear dustbin

by Roy Norris

3rd February 2002 - Marchers at the Devonport Dockyards in Plymouth upon arrival of the first Trident submarine brought there for a refit. Pic: Simon Chapman

AFTER AN eight-month "investigation", on the 6th November 2001 the Environment Agency announced that the Plymouth Devonport dockyard's owners - DML - can increase the amount of radioactive tritium it discharges into the nearby River Tamar by nearly 700 per cent. All this in a city of 270,000 people.

On top of that the dockyard is about to begin a programme of refitting Vanguard-class nuclear submarines, a process which will see radiation leaking into the river and the atmosphere for at least the next ten years. Already four scrapped nuclear submarines are stored afloat there - three of which have already had their spent fuel removed leaving the highly contaminated reactors intact and radioactive waste remaining on board. The Navy has also confirmed that all subsequent submarines could be decommissioned there; which will see 20 scrapped nuclear submarines lolling about in the area. Each one carries - not counting the spent fuel - around 160 tonnes of radioactive waste. This will effectively make Plymouth the MoD's national radioactive waste dump.

Recently declassified reports from the Nuclear Powered Warships Safety Committee written in 1965 state: "...the Committee could not recommend Devonport as an acceptable site for a refitting yard for nuclear submarines" because of its proximity to peoples' homes. More recently independent nuclear consultant, John Large, has said he sees 'no substantive change' in safety arrangements at the dockyard since 1965. And in fact there's a new variable - sure to put people at ease: the dock facility was sold into private hands in March 1997 to the only bidder, DML (Devonport Management Limited) at a bargain price.

The largest shareholder in DML is a US company - Brown and Root - who achieved notoriety in the early 1990's when it became subject to the largest lawsuit in US history after it was discovered that the concrete reactor casing in a nuclear power plant in Texas it was involved in constructing was full of air-holes. Brown and Root is owned by American multi-national Halliburton whose Chief Executive is Dick Cheney, US vice President.

Plymouth Dump Information Group, tel. 01752 337 482. www.members.aol.com/pdig

---

Bin Tax Victory

Court orders Cork Corporation to collect non-payers' bins

After a marathon protest and despite the jailing of seven activists from our campaign, Cork Corporation's strategy of bullying the people of the city into paying twice to have their domestic rubbish collected, ended in disarray. The deathblow for the Corpo came with a decision made by the Supreme Court that it had a statuary obligation to collect domestic rubbish within the city.

Despite the fact that it is the Supreme Court that has dealt this blow to Cork Corporation, it has been the ongoing and sustained campaign led by Householders Against The Service Charges (HASC), that is responsible for the victory. By organising weekly protests, by preparing to take the Corpo on head-on and even go to jail, HASC ensured that the issue stayed alive during a difficult period. This has now paid off and everyone can feel proud of the achievement, not least because it will give heart to other campaigns throughout the country.

But where to now? Clearly, the aim should be to continue with the basic but important job of getting more workers in Cork to refuse to pay the Bin tax. With the Corpo losing it's main weapon of threat against people, as a result of the Supreme Court decision, this should be easier. A non-payment poster/ leafleting campaign is vital, particularly in the lead up to the new round of yearly bills.

Although building non-payment might seem obvious, there are clear problems ahead with the probability of a general election. Some activists in HASC will want to see HASC opting for the avenue of 'endorsing a candidate' in the lead up to the election. There is also the possibility that HASC will have some of its resources diverted in this direction. Anarchists oppose this. As we see it is vital to keep the focus in the campaign directed at building 'mass non-payment' and solidarity. This is the real threat to the Corpo's long term strategy and the only sure one that will guarantee us victory.

http://struggle.ws/wsm/bins.html   www.stopthebintax.com

WAKE UP! WAKE UP! IT'S YER HEAVILY SUBSIDISED.

Weekly SchNEWS

Printed and Published in Brighton by Justice?

Friday 1st February 2002   www.schnews.org.uk   Issue 340   Free/Donation

FOOD FIGHT

"Everywhere on these Isles, rich and beautiful habitats have been ploughed, bulldozed and sprayed out of existence, not as a result of need but in response to farm subsidies" – Graham Harvey, The Killing of the Countryside

This week the Policy Commission on the Future of Farming published its long awaited report on what they see as the future of agriculture in the UK. Commissioned by the government in the wake of the foot and mouth crisis, it recommends changes in the way we produce our food, namely that more money be spent on organic farming methods and subsidies towards the protection of the environment rather than for food production.

Foot and mouth was just the latest in a long line of disasters to illustrate the unhealthy state of UK farming. Since the introduction of subsidies in the last few decades, farming has largely become an industrialised process just like any other manufacturing industry. Many parts of Britain could be described as agricultural wastelands, devoid of wildlife and plants. Look out across the countryside in some parts of the UK and you will see endless fields of chemically contaminated monocrop, separated not by hedgerows but by roads and barbed wire. Over 10,000 miles of hedgerows disappear each year. 97% of meadowland has been lost since WW2, and many water courses have been heavily polluted through extensive f chemical use. Prof. Jules Pretty of the University of Essex has calculated that even before foot and mouth, the hidden costs of industrial agriculture to our health and environment added up to £2.3billion a year.

It's estimated that in the last 2 years at least 40,000 people have lost their jobs in agriculture. Many people have come to accept the failures of the modern farming system as the price we have to pay for cheap food. But with the taxpayer contributing to the £3billion in subsidies paid to farmers each year, each family is actually paying an extra £10 a week.

Supermarket Sweepstakes

On the face of it we'd have to agree with Tony Blur for once, who welcomed the new report saying that "the current situation benefits no-one: farmers, taxpayers, consumers or the environment". But er, sorry Tony but we think Tesco might disagree with you there. Supermarkets are raking it in, with Tesco's profits rising every year in the last decade, last year amassing over £1bn. The supermarkets' power on our food chain has become almost complete, and the result has been that our agricultural land now looks like the supermarkets they are servicing.

A fifth of farms, mostly the wealthy ones in this country received 80 percent of the annual production subsides. This misdistribution of subsidies has been compared to the government choosing to subside grocery shops, and giving all the money to Tescos and Sainsbury's. And farming just like the retail world has had its casualties - small farms are closing all the time while the large monoculture farms (yer Tesco equivalent) keep growing. But even these big farms are being screwed by the supermarkets they serve. For example a litre of milk in March last year costs 22p to produce, farmers were being paid 17.6p for each litre, the supermarket was selling it for 35p, that's 17.4p profit for supermarkets and a bill of 4.4p to tax payer for subsidies, which means that we are subsidising the supermarkets! Overall today in the UK only 9p of each pound you spend ends up in the farmer's pocket.

Food Chained

Marion Shoard the author of "This Land is Our Land" told SchNEWS that this idea of environmental subsidies assumes that farmers know what's best, yet considering that they're the ones who've been busy destroying the landscape in the first place, putting our faith in them helping to restore it is a bit laughable. Marion believes that the best way to shake up our agricultural system is to get rid of subsidies altogether. She believes that land prices would then plummet and farming would become more profitable, this would then allow land to be bought by environmental and social groups for the public good.

This sounded like a good idea so we tried to track down some farmers who've

---

* Only 8% of UK farmland is given over to crops that provide for people directly. The rest goes to feed livestock.
* We would need only a fifth of our current cultivated area to be self sufficient in this country if we grew food for only human consumption.
* In 1970 the average household spent 25% of its income on food, the equivalent figure today is little more than 10%.
* In 1950 there were 221,662 food shops in Britain, by 1997 this had gone down to just 36,931.

CRAP ARREST OF THE WEEK

For Canoeing without lights!!
Last Friday, Faslane peace protestor Jenny Gaiawyn was arrested and charged with 'breach of the peace' for canoeing without any lights around the Gareloch where those nice Trident submarines live. For that crime she spent 3 days in police custody and is due in court on the April 2nd (should be April 1st)

managed to survive without subsidies, but unfortunately we couldn't find any. Not surprising really when the price farmers get for their produce is often less than it costs them to produce it in the first place. But regardless of whether or not redirecting subsidies are the solution to our problems, nothing is likely to change until there is a serious shift in the balance of power in the food chain. The biggest villains of all are the supermarkets who've made us believe they're providing us with cheap food. The report does nothing to challenge the powers of supermarkets, which isn't surprising when you consider that Peter Davis from Sainsbury's was a member of the Committee. Professor Pretty points out "The quest for even cheaper food is at the root of all these problems. It has encouraged farmers to cut corners, compromising food safety, animal welfare and damaging the environment."

* Further reading "The Killing of the Countryside" by Graham Harvey. For a history of the landownership in Britain read "This Land is Our Land- The struggle for Britain's Country" By Marion Shoard. Loads of information on supermarkets at www.corporatewatch.org.uk

Positive SchNEWS

It isn't necessarily true that farming and environmental destruction need to go hand in hand. Ragman's Lane Farm in Gloustershire is one of many commercial farms now being run successfully using permaculture ecological principles. When Matt Dunwell and Jan Davies took over the farm in Gloucestershire, in 1990 the Valuer commented that its 50 acres of grassland could only provide half of one salary, which would be true were it only a conventional farm. But now the farm employs three full-time people. The farm sells most of it's food locally and they run regular courses to pass on their knowledge - the next one is 23-24 February is 'Growing and selling vegetables'.More info Mandy Pullen Ragman's Lane Farm, Lower Lydbrook, Glos, GL17 9PA. 01594 861173 www.permaculture.co.uk

* And don't forget Seedy Saturday next Saturday 9th February at St.Georges Hall, St.Georges Rd, Brighton 11am – 4pm. Find out how to bypass the corporate seed industry and pick up some outlawed vegetable seeds. Volunteers needed to help out call 01273 882552 email baggage@primalseeds.org

Andersen Fairy Tale

Would you get McDonalds to advise you about healthy eating? Or BP to sing the praises of free electricity from the sun? Well, Neo-Labour thought it would be a good idea to ask accountancy firm Andersen to write a report on the Private Finance Initiative (PFI) – the scheme where the nation's public services are flogged off to the private sector, who then lease them back to the taxpayer! Andersen said PFI was a great idea and would save money – but forgot to mention that it would also make them lots. They've already made millions thanks to 37 PFI schemes they've already got their sticky little accountants' fingers in. This company is so dodgy that even the Tories took them to court and banned them from any government contracts for 12 years. This didn't put off Neo-Labour though. Before Blair's government came to power, they were advised by Andersen about the windfall tax, capital gains tax and advanced corporation tax and in the summer of 1996 more than 90 Labour MPs attended an Andersen seminar on 'how to be a minister'. Patricia Hewitt, now Trade and Industry secretary, used to be head of research at Andersen Consulting.

Since coming to power, Neo-Labour continued to follow Andersen advice on how to flog off our remaining national assets like Air Traffic Control, the London Underground, defence research labs, schools and hospitals. Andersen has also given expert advice on Railtrack, the Jubilee Line Extension, British Nuclear Fuels, education action zones, the management of local education authorities as well as doing the accounts for the Millennium Dome....

Andersen are making the news at the moment for helping to cover up the collapse of energy giant Enron – which last year entered the record books by becoming the biggest company to go bankrupt in US corporate history. Not only did Andersen receive $25 million for its Enron audit work, where you would have expected to see that Enron's accounting was bullshit, but also $27 million for its Enron consultancy work, which probably explains why they turned a blind eye and also why one US Senator commented "If Enron robbed the bank, Arthur Andersen drove the getaway car."

Lately Andersen have been busy shredding as many Enron documents as possible – all in the interests of recycling and making more bedding for hamsters of course.

All Along the Watchtower

Last week the Glastonbury Festival got its music license – after announcing that there would now be a zero tolerance policy against gatecrashers. In an open letter, organiser Michael Eavis wrote "Most of you probably know that for years a lot of people have been getting in…without tickets. Over or under the fence, forgery, scams - whatever. This year things have to change for good, otherwise the Festival will be gone, forever." To stop the gatecrashers there will be a new 3.6 metres high floodlit fence, "that can't be taken apart, climbed over or tunnelled under", with watchtowers and CCTV.

Glastonbury has become a victim of its own success. Thanks to the free festival clampdown, financially crippling restrictions and police protection rackets on anyone who wants to put on a festival, focus has turned to one of the few that has survived. As Andy from Festival Eye magazine told SchNEWS "It's about time the Stonehenge Free Festival was brought back."

* Keep up to date with festivals, parties and protests on the schnews website.

Super-CALI-fragilistic-expealidocious!

On Tuesday, workers from the Colombian City of Cali, who have been occupying the communications tower of Emcali since Christmas Day won an historic victory (See last weeks SchNEWS). An agreement was signed by the Colombian government, the Mayor of Cali, and the union guaranteeing that the company will not be privatised, that there will be no price increases this year, and that a high level anti-corruption inquiry will investigate and bring to justice all of those people who have siphoned off public resources from the company in recent years. If you want to hear more, Mario Novelli whose been sending daily reports from the occupation, will be speaking this Saturday(2) at the CORAS Centre, 161 Lambeth Walk, SE11.(nearest tubes Vauxhall) 4pm. Tel 07950-923448

SchNEWS in brief

A detention centre for **Migrants 'Sans Papiers'** was occupied and wrecked last Saturday in Bologna, Italy. ** **Defend Council Housing** national conference next Saturday (9) in Birmingham. www.defendcouncilhousing.org.uk, 020-7987-9989 ** **Mr Gluck's Radical Dairy-** a squatted social centre/info shop/café has opened at 47 Kynaston Road, Stoke Newington, London. 020-7249-6996 ** **A day of film, workshops and musicology** 2 Feb from 11am, with an evening party at the newly opened 217 Resource Centre on Swansea High Street. www.geocites.com/swan_net/ ** Jeff Halper, of the Israeli Committee Against House Demolitions and Salim Shawamreh, twice the victim of house demolitions, will speak on the subject: **Palestine and Israel: A Just and Viable Peace?** 12th Feb,7.30 p.m Brighthelm Centre, Brighton ** '**Stop the War on Dissent:** - the threat to civil liberties posed by the Terrorism Acts'. 7pm, 12th Feb, Grand Committee Room, House of Commons, Westminster (er, that is the place where the terrorism acts were passed).020-7586-5892, knklondon@gn.apc.org ** **Worthing Eco-Action** meeting next Tuesday (5) about the planned direct action campaign to stop the destruction of the countryside around Titnore Lane in Durrington. 7.45pm, upstairs at the Downview pub, West Worthing Station ** Two new indymedia sites to check out - **Indymedia Ireland** www.indymedia.ie/ and **Bristol Indymedia** www.bristol/indymedia.org ** '**Last Orders for the Local'** is an ace little pamphlet looking at how your local boozer is being corporate themed out of existence. Send some stamps and an SAE to ACATAC c/o BM Combustion, London, WC1N 3XX ** Campaign meeting on '**Planning a green paper'** 9th Feb 10am-5pm International student house,229 Great Portland St. London 0161 9590999 planning@onlincam.freeserve.co.uk ****Jill Phipps Memorial Day**, An animal rights activist who was killed on a demo against live animal exports.2nd Feb 12 noon Darley Oaks Farm.

BCUK YOU

The Burma Campaign UK (BCUK) have managed to get lingerie giant Triumph International to close down its Burma-based manufacturing site. The company was targeted for its part in supporting the military regime. It was charged by the UN's International Labour Organisation with a 'crime against humanity' for the oppression and exploitation of Burma's people. A spokesperson from BCUK said, "This should serve as a warning to other companies operating in Burma - get out now or you could be next." Burma Campaign UK, 020-7281-7377, www.burmacampaign.org.uk

ROAD TO RUIN

"This road will also increase regional air pollution, increase congestion, increase air & noise pollution for people using the bridle paths, underpass and the children at the school, increase traffic into Derby, increase pollution in an Air Quality Management Area, destroy wildlife habitats, make all alternative journey modes longer, and all for 20 seconds off journey into city " Dorothy, a Derby resident

The protest camp at the site of the proposed Alvaston bypass is calling for more people to join the protest camp there. The site has a kitchen and tree houses, but bring your own accomodation tent space may be limited! www.alvaston-bypass.i8.com

Inside SchNEWS

Colin Davies is still on remand for opening an Amsterdam style coffee shop in Stockport last September. His friends and family have kept the café open since then so drop in for a (BYO) spliff. Colin's next court hearing is on Valentine's Day. 0161-4805902 www.dutchexperience.org

International Day of Solidarity for **Leonard Peltier**, Saturday 9th February. Next Wednesday will mark the 27th year since the American Indian Movement activist was framed and arrested for killing two FBI agents at the Pine Ridge Reservation. www.freepeltier.org.

DOLE FACED

This week saw a two-day nationwide strike by benefit agency staff. SchNEWS spoke briefly to one of the strikers to find out what's been going on "The government want to merge the benefits and employment service into one agency Job Centre Plus which isn't a bad idea, but they want it all done in open plan offices. What we are asking for is that in every office when we think things might get violent that there is an area where staff can be behind screens. No one thinks its bad when post office or bank staff work behind screens, its basic health and safety."

"The first pilot open plan office opened in Harlesden two weeks ago, and already someone smashed the place up with a bike chain. In Lewes someone set fire to the benefit agency and one worker was followed out of Balham dole office and was kicked to a pulp at the tube station. Before the strike we were bombarded with government propaganda films – one was about benefit changes in Australia and how since they've gone open plan its safer. We found out that violent assaults have actually gone up and two members of staff have been killed. More strikes are planned with the threat of overtime ban and work to rule, but the Government are telling managers not to negotiate with the union. It seems they want to undermine us and push through more privatisation."

...and finally...

Ever thought of becoming an anarchist? Pay: Crap; Chance of Arrest: High; Bosses: None; Fun: Loads. By the time you read this you'll have missed Brighton's first anarchist job fair. St James Street job centre 'kindly' allowed a dozen dirty anarchists and a dog, to run an info stall on the premises for over an hour! Those pesky kids thought they might as well give an alternative option to the MOD who had an open day there. The police, always keen to promote the anarchist cause, suggested that the stall be moved outside (so as to reach a wider audience of course). Don't worry though you needn' wait till the next open day. Start today! Jack in yer job, have a lie in, cause trouble and then save the world.

disclaimer You'd have to be a mad cow to thin that SchNEWS gets a government subsidy (don' mention the dole cheques). Honest.

DIGGING FOR VICTORY

by Tony Rebel Green

When the Brighton and Hove Economic Partnership announced that it would be a good idea to build on the Eastbrook allotments they dressed the idea up by calling it 'urban renaissance'. Now my dictionary says that renaissance means a 'new birth', which brings to mind something beautiful and not quite the ugly grey office blocks the Partnership want to erect on whatever greenery in

Urban renaissance? Which would you choose?

Brighton is left out of the South Downs National Park.

In fact my version of 'urban renaissance' is very different. In our city there has been a massive increase in the uptake of allotments over the past couple of years for a whole variety of reasons. Be it the constant food scares or people just wanting a little bit of the 'good life' it has meant there has been something of an allotment renaissance. But even when sites are half empty and derelict, this does not mean that they should be seen as 'waste ground'. They are still a valuable resource to the treasured, acting as important green lungs for our towns and cities, as green corridors and homes for wildlife, as tranquil places for people to chill from everyday life, as magical places for kids to play.

Many others like the idea of growing food but find the idea of taking on an allotment a bit daunting. Luckily in Brighton and Hove there are plenty of community groups where you can get involved for a few hours each week, learning and working with other likeminded people in exchange for some fresh produce. Not that all these groups are just about growing veg, some are also about trying to reconnect people with the land. Recently, one women told me that while she was digging her garden, her neighbour's six year old asked if she was going to grow chicken and would not believe it when she was told that chickens come from eggs! So on our site, it's not just producing food that's important, but also about showing kids that spuds and carrots come from the ground and not plastic bags. These community groups are a perfect way of 'thinking globally, acting locally', and with a bit more support could sell their surplus food to their local neighbourhoods. Surely it is better to get fresh produce on peoples plates picked that day with all the health benefits, as opposed to food that has been flown half way across the world, with all the environmental consequences. In fact most of the ecological cost of food is not growing it, but its transport, distribution and processing.

Just think for a minute what you had for dinner last night. Did those potatoes come from Egypt and beans from Kenya? Is that apple you are munching on from New Zealand? These sorts of food are usually flown by plane, and air travel is the fastest growing source of carbon dioxide emissions, which is warming up the planet and causing climate change.

· For every kilo of kiwi fruit transported from New Zealand 5kg of carbon dioxide is pumped into the atmosphere

· 1 kilo of asparagus flown from California produces 4kg of carbon dioxide. If they were grown in Europe 900 times less energy would be produced

· 1 tonne of food in the UK now travels an average of 123km before it reaches the shelves, compared with 82km in 1978

Most of Europe's orange juice comes from Brazil. Demand for orange juice has doubled in the last decade, yet in this country there is a richer source of Vitamin C that grows everywhere - rosehip. During the Second World War when it was impossible to get oranges, children were given days off school to go and pick rosehips - by 1943 450 tonnes were picked a year.

And how about this for madness. Vegetables being sold in two superstores on the outskirts of Evesham in Worcestershire were grown just one mile from the town. But before they reached the shelves they had been trucked to Hereford, then to Dyfed, then to a distribution depot in Manchester, from where they were sent back to Evesham. Not surprisingly a quarter of our road traffic is now transporting food.

The BSE and foot and mouth crisis makes a mockery of those that argue that our present way of farming gives us cheap food. On the contrary the current system ensures that we end up paying three times for our food - once over the counter, a second time in tax subsidies for farming and a third time in cleaning up pollution. As the Soil Association points out "The quest for ever cheaper food is at the root of all these problems. It has encouraged farmers to cut corners, compromising food safety and animal welfare and damaging the environment. We all end up paying a heavy price through our taxes to clear up the mess." Professor Jules Pretty of the University of Essex has calculated that even before foot and mouth, the hidden costs of industrial agriculture to our health and our environment added up to at least £2.3 billion a year!

So growing food on our allotments and sharing it with others is a positive, practical step to help reverse this trend. But is it possible for places like Brighton and Hove to become self sufficient in food?

In my book 'Seedy Business' I went round interviewing older Brightonians, who spoke of a fairly self-sufficient town not so very long ago, that was surrounded by pig farms, orchards, smallholdings and allotments. If we are to rid ourselves of our present unsustainable agricultural system then once again every village, town and city will have to grow some of it's own food. Can it be done? Well when Cuba faced economic crisis in the early 90's it turned to organic food production and by 1998 the Capital City Havana had gone from producing virtually no food to 115,000 tonnes with this figure rising all the time, with every available green space and patio being utilised.

The popularity of farmers markets shows that when people are given the choice they will buy fresh locally produced food. So couldn't the South Downs be covered in orchards and small scale farms?

* Couldn't our vegetable peelings, tea bags and green waste be collected and turned into compost?

* Couldn't we have more community groups with demonstration gardens to teach people who want to learn about gardening?

* Couldn't every school that has the space have its own urban farm?

This is the sort of urban renaissance I dream of, a place where our allotments and green spaces are seen as community treasures - not rich pickings for ugly office developments.

'Seedy Business - tales from an allotment shed' can be read at www.seedybusiness.org

Also read:

'The Allotment Handbook' by Sophie Andrews (eco-logic books)

'Wild Food' Roger Phillips (Pan 1983)

'The Food miles report: the dangers of long distance food transport'/ 'Food miles action pack: a guide to thinking globally and eating locally' both by SUSTAIN, 94 White Lion St., London, N1 9PF http://www.sustainweb.org

MARK BARNSLEY IS FREE

STOP PRESS: Mark Barnsley was released from Whitemoor Prison, 25th June 2002. (yay!!) We have included the statement from the 'Free Mark Barnsley' website as an update, and although this development may make the article below seem by-the-by in Mark's case, there are many others wrongly imprisoned, and this still stands as an example of the things campaigns to free them are up against...

Statement on 'Free Mark Barnsley' website:

Justice for Mark Barnsley Campaign, are overjoyed to announce that miscarriage of justice prisoner Mark Barnsley was finally released from Whitemoor prison on the morning of Monday 24th June 2002.

Mark walked out of maximum securty HMP Whitemoor to loud cheers and applause from waiting supporters. Friends, eager to welcome Mark out of prison had travelled from around the country and included an official delegation from the NUM, complete with their National Union banner.

After having his first decent breakfast in 8 years at a local cafe and thanking everyone for coming, Mark set off back to South Yorkshire where he will be living for the foreseeable future. He was later reunited with his children. Mark's youngest daughter who is now 8 years old, last saw him outside a prison when she was just 6 weeks old.

After spending over 8 years in just about every Maximum security hell- hole the prison system has to offer, Mark is in good spirits and obviously glad to be finally out. Mark and his campaign would like to take ths opportunity to thank everyone who has supported him over his 8 long years of wrongful imprisonment.

Whilst Mark tries to re-build his life and adjust to living in the outside world again the Justice for Mark Barnsley campaign will continue to help him get the justice which is long overdue. Mark has been released after serving two thirds of his 12 year prison sentence but he has yet to clear his name and have his wrongful conviction overturned. Prior to his release Mark refused to sign his licence on the principle that he is an innocent man and freedom is his right.

Another Year Inside

Mark has made solidarity an abiding principle of his political life- both in prison and during his life outside. Throughout 2001-2002 he and another dedicated prisoner-activist, John Bowden, held regular monthly hunger strikes in solidarity with the Turkish hunger strikers.

Mark has also always refused to work inside and has sought to highlight the injustice inherent in prison labour. In August 2001, supporters of the campaign took direct action against forced prison labour in Britain, invading and shutting down Hepworth Building Products in Edlington, South Yorkshire. Hepworths use prisoners at HMP Wakefield to package their products for 32p an hour. Mark commented "I really hope actions against companies like this carry on; they are an easy target on the outside and it is so inspiring to those on the inside. Prisons themselves can stand up to pressure but the companies that profit from them can't. This is what I call real solidarity." With New Labour proposing a Custody-to-Work scheme which will pave the way for a US style prison-industrial complex - such action will need to be repeated whenever and wherever companies seek to profit from prison labour.

At the beginning of 2001 The Justice for Mark Barnsley Campaign started regularly picketing the then Prisons Minister Paul Boateng's Harlesden surgeries to protest Mark's segregation and his subsequent transfer to HMP Wakefield. By May Boateng was gone and David Blunkett was Home Secretary, so we took the battle to his doorstep.

Militant as the Justice for Mark Barnsley Campaign has continued to be, there is an obvious downside to all this. It's now eight years since Mark entered the prison system - and while it is good news that the Criminal Cases Review Commission has begun to investigate his conviction it remains a disgrace that so few are involved in campaigning to free a working class anarchist militant so obviously fitted up. In the last year, Mark has continued to be shipped from jail to jail-Frankland, Wakefield, Leeds, Whitemoor - with long spells in segregation.

We've lost count of the number who've written to Mark to promise that "they won't sleep until he's free" and then must decide to keep their insomnia to themselves as neither we nor Mark hear from them again. Just as bad are those who let us down by failing to turn up on activities because "it was raining" or "I had an hangover" or "I caught the wrong bus". The bottom line is that if you call an activity in support of a prisoner and it's poorly attended, the message to the state is that the prisoner has sweet f.a in terms of support and so he or she is exposed to the danger of further repression on the basis that there's little in the way of active solidarity to prevent it. If you say you'll be there and aren't - you don't just let the prisoner down you put him or her at risk.

The media continues to operate a "blackout" policy in relation to the campaign. We've been told Mark's politics make him "not innocent enough", that the case is too old to be newsworthy etc etc. Whatever we do, however many press releases we send out, the mainstream media acts as if we don't exist. When we marched on Downing Street (and you'd think the first protest against the new government on their first day in office might be worth reporting) the press asked the police to shut us up as they thought our presence might deter new Cabinet Ministers from stepping out for a photo opportunity!! So much for a critical and independent media. It's not just in relation to Mark's case - the fitting-up of working class people and their abuse in the prison system rarely makes the news. Our prison population goes through the roof, the gap between rich and poor grows ever wider-but the papers are full of mobile phone thefts and carjackings and the crimes of Enron disappear. New Labour wants to believe that the working class doesn't exist (except as jail fodder) and the press are determined to report the news as if the wish were reality.

We'll continue fighting until Mark is free and his name cleared. We need more people to get involved. One of the strengths of the campaign has been the space it's offered for an older generation of working class anarchists to work alongside the new generation of anti-capitalist militants around groups like Earth First! Such collaboration has been a real gain and we hope it will continue.

Justice for Mark Barnsley Campaign
email: barnsleycampaign@hotmail.com
www.freemarkbarnsley.com

Prisoner Support

It is important to support those imprisoned for their beliefs - one day it could be you. Read about how you can help a prisoner - see 'Prisoner Support' in the DIY Guide section of the SchNEWS website, or read it in last year's SchNEWS/Squall Yearbook 2001 annual. Also: www.brightonabc.org.uk.

WAKE UP! WAKE UP! IT'S YER ROTTEN APPLE

Weekly SchNEWS

Printed and Published in Brighton by Justice?

NOMINEES

IGNOBLE PRIZE FOR WAR

Friday 8th February 2002   www.schnews.org.uk   **Issue 341**

BIG APPLE PIED

"This was perhaps the first action that was entirely put together by the 'bad' protesters. By standing up and taking action anyway, despite all the police and military force and manipulation of the press and public opinion we know are being marshalled against us, we are sending a message to the world that it is not necessary to be ruled by fear: we refuse to bow down to terror, just as we refuse to terrorise anyone else."
-David Graber, New York Anti-Capitalist Convergence.

It was the usual thing we've come to expect - media hysteria and police threats aimed at scaring the numbers down. There was a difference though - this was New York in the wake of September 11th, where everyone knows someone whose been touched by the horrors of that day. President Bush had just announced trillions more dollars for the military and declared that anyone not supporting his policies was an Enemy of America. This was people taking to the streets to tell Bush and his corporate string-pullers that he didn't voice their grief - and he didn't bomb in their name.

The wartime atmosphere that has been whipped up by Bush and his billionaire pals in the wake of September 11th is aimed at directing grief and anger so that anyone challenging unbridled exploitation and the rule of powerful elites can be identified as supporting mass murder. More than a bit ironic considering who payrolled Bin Laden in the first place (the US government), but if you control the media, why waste an opportunity to promote capitalism as the alternative to barbarism rather than its creator? And that's what the World Economic Forum's travelling circus in New York was all about.

For the first time in its 31-year old history, the WEF was meeting outside Switzerland. They were all there - 2,700 delegates from Bill Gates to Colin Powell to less likely world-leaders like Bono and Naomi Campbell chinwagging over cocktails. It's estimated that they spent $100 million between them on food and entertainment - so, just another boozy weekend for these folk, living the high life amongst the cleaners and cooks who make it all possible for them in the first place. As the New York Anti-Capitalist Convergence put it, "The WEF's choice to relocate to Manhattan is a cynical exploitation of grief, fear, and terror they hope to exploit those emotions to make it easier for them to crush us."

The main protest on Saturday started off with a Reclaim the Streets (RTS) that immediately turned into a walk in the park - Central Park that is. In the wake of the collapse of the Argentinian economy there was a definite Latin American vibe with samba, tango dancers and a whole lotta people banging on pots and pans, traditional symbols of resistance in Latin America. While the New York gutter press was trying to scare people off the streets, the people here were determined to have a party.

The RTS wound its way through Central Park to the start of the main march where about 12,000 protesters had gathered. It was a wide array of people, mainly from the US, marking the fact that in New York the rich and powerful don't speak for the people - and that grief over the horror of September 11th doesn't equate with support for the most right-wing government the US has ever seen (well, since the last one...) People vilified by the press as irresponsible troublemakers were demanding world-wide economic equality and an end to corporate power.

It was an entirely peaceful protest, but of course, this meant that the media who had talked up the violence pretty well failed to report the protests when they happened.

FAWLTY TOWERS

And the 7,000 cops who had been mobilised for the event didn't sit quietly by just because the march was peaceful - at the beginning they arrested a group of demonstrators carrying plexiglass shields painted with colorful images. Janik Lewis, one of those arrested, said "Without any warning at all, the cops came running, targetting specific people, I had my face thrown into a barricade, some were pepper sprayed and battoned." Along with others, he was detained for 30 hours at the Brooklyn Naval Yard and charged with 'illegal assembly' at what was supposedly a legally permitted demonstration.

Smaller protests and action continued after Saturday's big event. Dozens were arrested on Sunday afternoon in New York's East Village when a 'snake march' - where people link arms and dance along streets and sidewalks in an unpredictable route - was met with riot police. New York Police Chief Raymond W. Kelly called for a crackdown on "hard core protestors". He must have heard his own call as dancers and walkers were met with pepper spray, violence and mass arrests. No permit for this one guys - you're goin' down!

As L.A. Kauffman of Reclaim the Streets said, "Some people were frustrated by the constraints under which we operated here, but holding these actions at all was a bold step. Our movement is very much alive and seasoned enough to make solid and strategic choices based on circumstances." Or as one protestor from Brooklyn put it, "Seattle galvanized the movement. It said that we mean business. Today showed that there's a sizeable contingent of Americans who are fed up with corporate globalisation."

** 18 year old Sherman Austin became one of the first people nicked under the new USA Patriot Act, when 25 heavily armed FBI, Secret Service, and LPYD cops stormed his house and nicked him for masterminding anarchist website Raise the Fist. But not before asking him stupid questions. "Would you like to see George Bush Killed?" and "Why have you grown your hair, are you trying to disguise your identity?"

CRAP ARRESTS OF THE WEEK

Despite a ban on all demonstrations by Munich Council 10,000 people still protested against the NATO Conference on Security Policy last weekend, where government officials hobnobbed with 500 odd military experts. Central themes were the planning of current and future wars, the establishment of powerful mobile strike forces and the development of new billion-dollar weapons systems.

A few days before, the city council passed a law declaring all protests during the Conference illegal. The whole city was declared a "red zone", road blocks, were set up preventing people getting to Munich by train, coach or car, known activists were warned in letters and phone calls not to protest, organised info points and sleeping places were closed down and several people were arrested before it all began.

The police then desperately tried to prevent meetings and spontaneous demonstrations during the next three days, arresting people at random - 849 people in total – including a speaker at a press conference! Bans on demos are common in Germany, with one protestor telling SchNEWS "People usually still go ahead but it gives the cops more powers to nick people."

The main Trade Union building was surrounded by police for several hours, with people complaining that the last time the police threatened an official trade-union building was in 1933 when the Nazis seized power. Meanwhile Bayern Munich football club gave the police 1000 free tickets for their game against Bayer Leverkusen as a thank you to all the out of town coppers who'd been drafted in!

DON'T BOLIVIA THE HYPE

It's all kicking off again in Cochabamba, where two years ago massive protests halted the planned privatisation of the water system, (see Schnews 339). This time the battle is over Coca. For several months, the government has totally militarised the region in order to stop the traditional cultivation of the Coca plant, they have started a "war on drugs" – but the real objective of evicting peasants and indigenous people is that the land can then be sold to multinational companies. Over the last few weeks, dozens of demonstrators have been killed by the Army. Four soldiers were also shot during clashes which is a bit suspect considering the peasants don't carry guns on demos. Using this as a pretext the government had 60 community and union leaders arrested. The Bolivian human rights organisations have already denounced the abuse that they have suffered, such as beatings and wounds, electric shocks on the teeth, etc.

Parliament also voted the repeal of the parliamentary immunity of Evo Morales, one of the most popular deputies and foremost union leaders of the country. He now stands accused of being the "intellectual author" of the soldiers' deaths. Radio +, which belongs to the peasant confederation has been heavily damaged and closed down by the police, while organisations of other social sectors in solidarity with the peasants have also been brutally attacked. www.democracyctr.org/.

GUATEMALA'S GOING ON?

* Fancy a holiday that does more good than harm? Then we have just the thing – all you need to do is pack yer bags, pick up a passport and shift over to Guatemala to work as a human rights observer. The Guatemalan peasants union, (CUC) are urgently calling for volunteers to help defend their land rights and rights to protest without being killed. A British human rights observer told SchNEWS, "For the last three months the union has been in occupation of five large farms in the district of Izabal. They have also been blocking the main roads at strategic points and holding huge demonstrations in the capital…On the 23 and 24 of December three men were killed on the farms by the paramilitaries. As a consequence the union is desperate for foreign peace observers and human rights volunteers." If you're up for helping - waste no time – email them on: cuc@guate.net (in Spanish) and get yer flight booked.

POSITIVE SchNEWS

After going to a overcrowded and overpriced National Science week event sponsored and polluted by Glaxo Wellcome, a mum and her daughters were so unimpressed they decided that they'd run an alternative science event. They helped set up an informal network of people 'SEASoN' - South East Alternative Science Network, who've organised the Brickhurst Science Funday on the 16th March. The event will concentrate on ethical and environmental science and will run workshops principally for children on science, sustainability, nature and the environment. They'd like to get in contact with people who would like to help, or that can help with running a workshop or doing displays. Also if you'd like to attend the event then you need to book a place in advance. Tel: 01892 863 941 www.geocities.com/seasonscience/home

SchNEWS in brief

Brighton's Premier Pirate Radio Station February 8-10 on 106.6F. Local DJs and music Sunday pm Free Speech – including SchNEWS 4pm. Live web broadcast at: www.radio4a.org.uk **This weekend starting on Friday (8th) the 10 year anniversary since the start of the M11 road campaign. There will be an exhibition celebrating 10 years campaigning against Road building, being held at a house formerly used by security on the M11 Road Protest. 491 Grove Green Road, Leytonstone, London Images in Exile a photographic exhibit about refugees around the world by Howard Davies 25 Feb - 3 March (Closed Sat). The Meeting House, Sussex University 9.30am- 4.30pm. On Thursday 28 Howard Davies will speak about his work 6pm in The Meeting House** Seven people were arrested on Monday at Devonport naval dockyard during a protest against the refitting of nuclear weapon submarine HMS Vanguard there.** Next week 11-13th is the 'Bloc and Roll' at Faslane naval base, Scotland. Transport is going from around the country. Call the action line 0845 458 8361 www.gn.apc.org/tp2000 ** Want to keep up to date with the Enron scandel –"not just a business scandal, it's an indictment of our entire financial and political system" then check out www.alternet.org ** Next Friday (15) Lupercalia party is a benefit for the Queeruption DIY gathering in March, with cabaret, performers, kissing and whipping booth. It's in Shoreditch, East London for info/directions: 07947 489 617 or e-mail: info@queeruption.com.** Around 40 activists halted work on construction of a new logging road and bridge into the Weld Valley in Tasmania. The area has been nominated for inclusion as a world heritage site. A permanent camp has been set up to highlight the plight of these ancient wilderness and river systems www.tasforests.green.net.au

INSAINSBURY'S

For years Sainbury's and their accomplices have been trying to build a supermarket on a derelict site next to Brighton Station. In 1997 the original proposal was strongly opposed by local residents, and was refused planning permission by the Council, a decision upheld by a Public Inquiry. Since the start public consultations have been organised by BUDD, in the absence of a democratic council. These consultations have shown that when residents have their say, they are well capable of sussing out that more developments will only benefit the fat cats.

Undeterred, Insanesbury's are back again, clutching a new (nastier) development application. This 'exemplar of 21st century urban development' includes (unsurprisingly) a huge supermarket, two luxury hotels, a car park that will obliterate the Sunday market, and "housing for key workers" (read yuppie flats). Never mind sustainability or open spaces – bring on the pollution say Brighton Council. The Council rejected the last application, but are set to accept the current proposal cos they have a development quota they have to maintain, passed down from Westminster.

The decision is due to be made at the end of the month. As well as a massive letter writing campaign, following last year's May Bug Ball further direct action is in the offing: watch this space…

Fundraiser for community resistance next Monday (11th) from 9pm, the Hobgoblin Pub, London Road. Protest outside Sainsbury's, London Road. Sunday 16th Feb from Noon. Bring banners, noise. Background info: www.solarcity.co.uk/BUDD

Inside SchNEWS

Nicolas Sguiglia has been issued with a deportation order after police violently attacked a demo outside Malaga immigrant detention centre in Spain. Nico was one of those nicked, after people blocked roads and chained themselves to the gates of the centre to try to stop vans carrying detained Nigerians who were on there way to being deported, from getting through. Although Nico has full legal rights to live anywhere within the E.U the Spanish government is using a loophole which allows them to deport foreign nationals without them being convicted of any crime. The international campaign to prevent his deportation can be found on www.noborder.org and support is needed urgently before the appeals deadline on Feb 15th.

* Benefit party for Nico This Saturday (9) at the Radical Dairy, 47 Kynaston Road in Hackney, N16
* Two people who demonstrated against Britain's biggest arms fair are on trial next week (11-13) charged with "obstruction of the railway" an offence which carries a maximum penalty of two years imprisonment. The two were nicked after handcuffing themselves to the doors of a Docklands Light Railway carriage. They were trying to prevent delegates from Angola, Turkey and various other renowned supporters of human rights, arriving at the conference which in 1999 was found to be selling anti-personal mines in clear breach of the UK Anti-Landmines Act. The pair will be defending themselves on the grounds that they were acting in order to prevent a greater crime. Show your support outside Snaresbrook Crown Court,75 Hollybush Hill at 9:30am Monday. Campaign Against Arms Trade 02072810297 www.caat.org.uk,

MAN. DISUNITED

Last Saturday, 50 people hung banners and leafleted around Manchester's historic Free Trade Hall, demanding that the building be returned for use by the general public. The hall is built on the site of the Peterloo massacre when militia attacked a mass meeting being held in protest of the Corn Laws and as part of the campaign for universal suffrage. The Free Trade Hall is a key monument of the struggle for democracy. It was built in 1840 to house the great Corn Law debates and to provide space for Manchester people to hold political, religious and cultural public meetings. The Manchester Corporation bought the Free Trade Hall in May 1921, "so that the Hall should not be lost to citizens." But now Manchester Council is all modern and new and have sold it as part of the councils asset-stripping programme to fund the Commonwealth games being held there this July. It has been sold to a private developer for £4 million, and is currently scheduled for 95% demolition to make way for a £45 million luxury hotel. Demolition is due to begin on 11th February www.freetradehall.org

...and finally...

Australia's Tabloid TV stations lost face big time last Tuesday when they fell for a story about a gang of jobless sewer-dwellers plotting and getting militant in Melbourne. Gutter journalism sank to a new low when the country's biggest stations both paid for an expose on a fictional group of bin-raiding drain-dwellers called the Dole Army. The unemployment activists behind the hoax are happy with the attention – their www.dolearmy.org website received thousand of hits after the TV "exposes"… "They lapped up like dogs," said one Dole Army rep.

disclaimer
SchNEWS warns all fat cats you've made a dogs dinner of it. Honest guys.

THE DUST SETTLES

...and the organised left expose themselves as the fad-rebel wankers we always knew they were

By FLACO

New York, 2nd February, back on the streets against the WEF Forum. Pic: NYC Indymedia

Three weeks ago New York City got to host the World Economic Forum. As a 'tribute to the victims of September 11th', Manhattan taxpayers got to indulge a bunch of tobacco, oil and airline magnates, and a wannabe-planetary-cabinet of shady statesmen. Collectively, these people are responsible for an infinitely greater number of deaths and shattered lives than the combined kill-rate of every Arab who ever strapped on a C4 corset.

The WEF - think Bilderberg group with Bono in tow - is yet another (yawn) boys-club of capitalism's shot-callers. Cue Troy McClure: "You may remember us from such classics as Davos, and Melbourne's (later upstaged) own S11 (2000) street fight..." Anyway - it was their antics that sparked the alternative World Social Forum in Porto Alegre, Brazil (another nice idea quickly colonised by red flag hierarchies), and twice yearly mass protests from across the anti-capitalist spectrum. But not this time.

Patriot Act and Bush-whack rhetoric aside, it's fairly predictable that the lefty-millionaires Sierra Club should bottle out of confrontation with the power brokers in the post-S11 city of tears. No real surprise either that the AFL-CIO unions and the host of 'Global Justice' NGOs of every shade of red and green balked at the idea of ruffling the feathers of New York's finest. As the city's press, on both the left and the right, cranked up the spectre of an "al Qaida like black bloc" (Village Voice) massing like "barbarians at the castle gates" (Newsweek). A string of Direct Action Movement 'faces' lined up to distance themselves from anyone whose agenda aimed for anything greater than a moratorium on badger baiting. "Vandalism is inexcusable," lamented John Sellers, the caribina king of the ludicrously-bankrolled Ruckus Society. Needless to say, the reporting (in an almost blanket fashion) concentrated on the differences in tactics

between the anarchists and the liberals. No space was given to the gaping ideological chasm between the RaisetheFist militia on Fifth Avenue, and the 'raise the Tobin tax' lobbyists munching vol-au-vents with the delegates in the Waldorf Astoria foyer.

In the event, a few thousand anarchists and assorted revolutionary types took to the streets and, amidst an outpouring of sympathy, the 'poor darlings' of the NYPD dutifully kicked the shit out of them and threw a couple of hundred in jail.

The events in New York merely illustrate how the organised left (in the UK as elsewhere) has used September 11 to re-position itself in an, at best, more compliant, and at worst, more authoritarian stance.

Liberal Britain has been split between the trembling lips and disappearing tails of those who are content to wrap themselves in a tear-stained stars and stripes and vanish up Uncle Sam's arse, and those who have (at last) been freed to brandish their handcuffs and lay down their own blueprints for a capitalist super-state. Either way, Britain's left-wing have finally exposed themselves as the fad-rebel tosspots we always knew they were.

"Standing protesting outside Gap is a strange thing to do when civilians are being killed in Afghanistan," Globalise Resistance's Guy Taylor tells a fawning Andy Beckett (Guardian G2, Jan 17 'Has the Left Lost Its Way'). The implication being that before September 11 - before perceived public support for resistance to world dictatorship evaporated in an explosion of dust, glass and cello music - it was perfectly natural to be protesting outside Gap as civilians endured a blitzkrieg of Allied firepower in Palestine, Indonesia, Columbia and Iraq. Beckett goes on to quote a stream of liberal left-wing tossers who's politics were so well-founded that they'd managed to pull off complete ideological U-turns after a only couple of weeks of heart-tugging ('poor old America') Newsak.

'Formerly hardcore left-wingers' were apparently getting all gooey over Tony Blair's Montgomery makeover. The Ecologist ran a debate titled: 'Is the anti-corporate globalisation movement a finished force in the post-11 September world?' Guardian columnist Suzanne Moore was just one of those, converted by the smell of cordite, giving it the: "I was wrong to oppose the bombing," line as the Taliban fled Kabul - as if the women of that city had thrown their oppressors out themselves, and were not about to become the latest subjects of a US-manufactured puppet state.

As a rule, the anti war movement in Britain has been reluctant to confront the illegitimacy of the warring authority. Though opposed to the bombing, most silently-accept a 'first world'/US orchestrated 'solution' to Afghanistan: namely the Western annexation of Central Asia.

To be fair, this reactionary slide had begun well before the World Trade Centre attack. The SWP (perhaps after finally accepting the absence of 'workers' in its ranks) had already switched its preferred handle to 'Globalise Resistance'. Having left it a little late to fasten their name to the anti-capitalist upsurge of 1999 (as they had done with the Poll Tax, CJA etc), they wasted no time ramming branded

Who's been shining their helmet? NYC, 2nd February.   Pic: NYC Indymedia

anti-war placards into the hands of pacifist old ladies and fearful Muslims as Blair strapped on his flak jacket. No sooner had the first F-16s scrambled and Globalise Resistance was morphing again - this time into the Stop the War Coalition.

Anti-capitalism (a phrase that was itself adopted by liberal left-wingers trying to avoid any pro-revolutionary tags), has been dropped altogether by the left in favour of "movement for globalisation with justice". You may laugh, but the underlying thought processes behind this repositioning are a little more sinister.

One leading voice of the liberal left is the New Internationalist magazine. Their January/February issue was subtitled 'Another World is Possible'. The introduction promised "visions" of "many diverse pathways into a better, fairer world". The reality merely reinforced what Orwell pointed out over sixty years ago; that the organised left's version of 'democracy' is little different from the right's, and despite the tags, they have no intention of doing away with the constraints of capitalism - and would merely replace the domination of private capital with that of state capital. Or to bring that observation up to date 'a (neo)liberally-distributed amalgamation of the two'. Global PPPs anyone?

The 'visions' put forward by the NI's gathered worthies are 'diverse' in the same way the aims of the navy are 'diverse' from those of the air force. Every proposal in the magazine is legislative and authoritarian. According to the writers, elected bodies could be re-jigged, governing institutions formed, legislation passed and treaties re-written. The lack of aspiration is depressing... unless, of course, you're setting yourself up for a seat in 'the world parliament'.

The World Parliament is Lord Monbiot's offering. Another spin on electoral 'representative' democracy peddled with all the fervour of a Republican governor. Completely disregarding the lessons of history, where electoral democracy has failed to either represent or serve the people (other than those 'elected' and their chums), Monbiot taunts would-be detractors with: "Power exists whether we like it or not... so we might as well democratise it". You can't dis-invent the Bomb - eh!

As if a host of similar statist adventures (every election anytime/anywhere, the policy reversal of all elected bodies - e.g. the German Greens, the failure of Kyoto, the carbon trading style legislative loop-holing that followed, Nato - and it's complete disregard for law/anybody else, the failure of; the EU; every other power-invested institution to address anything other than its own pay checks ...and so on) hadn't all resulted in those in power completely fucking over everyone else, Monbiot goes on to outline his global hegemony leading the rest of us skipping to milk and honey-dom. He never mentions, however, if two wolves and a sheep were doing the catering...

Joining Monbiot in the NI is Jim Shultz ('executive director of The Democracy Centre'), who uses the genuinely inspiring example of the Cochabamba people's ejection of the Bechtel water company from Bolivia, to 'envision' - not for people everywhere to rise up against their usurpers, not for the global rejection of economic dictatorship, not even for the ditching of the Free Trade Area of the Americas (FTAA) agreement and all similarly oppressive

international trade treaties, but (wait for it) a 'bill of rights' to ensure the FTAA does not overrule regional laws. Go Jim. Go...!

Maybe we should be grateful that the left has come clean - shaken off their Seattle rain capes and returned to bickering about vote counts and electoral funding. For some time, the rhetoric of the leading left wing/environmentalist NGO's has been almost indistinguishable from that of the World Bank's... - though admittedly, this revealed precious little about either faction's agenda

But, the question remains - how wide is the influence of the organised left and their liberal overlord companions - and how substantially are they capable of stemming the rising revolutionary tide anyway?

There are those who hope they are well capable; the bods from the FBI who spent half of last month dismantling LA's RaisetheFist.org with the site's founder, Sherman, locked in the basement; the EU's Working Party on Terrorism who are right now in Spain, drafting a document on intelligence sharing about political activists in order to stamp out "violent urban youthful radicalism"; the President's Commission on Critical Infrastructure Protection (PCCIP) and the half dozen US state and private sector bodies it initiated under the National Security Council and Department of Defence (to name but two) to combat 'hacktivism' and 'cyberterror!'; the Swedish authorities who have just rejected the appeals of eight activists, each serving between 3-4 years, for using SMS messages to stop their mates getting hammered by police at the EU summit in Gothenburg last year; every boss, landlord and New Labour voter; every shareholder, whip-cracker and charity director, (insert your own 'come the revolution they'll be the first against the wall' list here), and everyone else who, overtly or covertly, revels in the deal capitalism has dealt them.

Back in Porto Alegre, undoubtedly the left's blueprint for a 'world parliament' (in his keynote address Chomsky called it a sketch of the beginnings of a 21st Century International), the predictable has happened. Two years in, and the 2002 Forum is already playing host to corporate lobbyists, media clowns and WEF delegates ("jumping ship from NYC"). Naomi Klein (one of the 10,000 invited 'delegates') describes the WSF as at risk from "turning from a clear alternative into a messy merger" with their New York antithesis.

In protest to what Znet's James Adams calls "left-wing corporatism", 600 attendees of the alternative Jornadas Anarquistas - Anarchist Journeys - (some of the 50,000 'excluded' internationals who had travelled to Porto Alegre to unite and discuss outside the 'conference centres') "broke off from the opening march and occupied a three story house, building barricades in the streets, in order to emphasize that, as one IMC (Independent Media Centre) poster put it, 'Porto Alegre isn't the social democratic paradise that the PT (Brazilian Workers Party) makes it out to be.'" (The PT control the municipal government and view the WSF as a party conference - draping the town in their flags, propaganda and party faithful.) Needless to say: " Local police, under the command of the PT, and dressed in full riot gear, surrounded the house immediately, nearly running over one squatter at a particularly high point of tension." Familiar?

However - despite the fifth International looking set to follow the first into a dog-pit of flying fur and shattered dreams, perhaps things are not so bleak. The 50,000 who gathered outside the auspices of the WSF in Porto Alegre, and the two thousand that took on the WEF in New York - plus the tens of millions who have already learnt the hard way that genuine, direct, democracy will never follow a recount, a rebrand or any amount of reform - do not look like they are about to jack-in the revolution because Washington's 'busted' the safety catch off its Winchester.

Undoubtedly the atmosphere of resistance has changed. But just because the warmongers were quicker to colonise the airwaves it doesn't follow that they win the (global) war. By shirking off tha protest-chic, the reformist-statist-liberal-left has finally brough some clarity to the message they have been concealing from disgruntled 'democrats' for years - namely, that they do not seek the overthrow of illegitimate power, merely its replacement. Now that's clear, we can get on with the fucking revolution!

WAKE UP! IT'S YER HAD A SCHNOG YESTERDAY?

Weekly SchNEWS

Printed and Published in Brighton by Justice?

Friday 15th February 2002   www.schnews.org.uk   **Issue 342   Free/Donation**

WAILING WALLS

"British headlines are full of suicide bombs, raids on Jewish settlements, inter-Palestinian violence. My experience of the past few weeks has included listening to Israeli F16 bombers flying low over Gaza City for two consecutive nights. That is the real drama being played out in the grim day to day existence of Palestinians." - Rev. Lucy Winkett (Human Rights Observer).

One day in 1998 Salim Shawamreh and his family were eating dinner at their home in Anata, a Palestinian suburb of Jerusalem, when the house was surrounded by two hundred Israeli soldiers. They were given just 15 minutes to pack their bags before their house was destroyed.

Salim tried to stop the soldiers and was attacked then arrested; his wife locked the doors, trying to keep their six children safe. The army responded by breaking windows and throwing in tear gas. Salim's 'crime' was that he didn't have a permit for his house. He owned the land that he had bought to house his family, who were living in cramped conditions in a refugee camp. But every time he applied for a building permit to build his house legally, according to rigged Israeli law, he was refused.

What happened to Salim and his family is what Jeff Halper from the Israeli Committee Against House Demolitions describes as the "Kafka-esque administration system designed to wear the Palestinians down...laws, zoning, planning, permits, settlements, roadblocks – all designed to control and confine the Palestinians." In the past few years 250 by-pass roads costing $3 billion dollars and all funded by the US have been built to bypass Palestinian settlements - cutting the Palestinian state up into small isolated islands. In the Jewish settlements there are bungalows and swimming pools, and well-watered land, whereas in Palestinian Khan Younis a population of 200,000 people doesn't even have a sewage system. For the Israeli government this war of attrition is much more preferable than using the army, because images of soldiers shooting at stone throwing youths does not go down well internationally. Much better, and much less newsworthy to drown the Palestinians in bureaucratic despair.

Currently over 180 Palestinian children are being held as political prisoners in Israeli jails where they are subject to violence and denied basic rights such as family and lawyer visits and the right to continue their education.

Peace House

During the demolition of Salim's house local villagers and people from the Committee Against House Demolitions tried to stop it being destroyed - seven were injured including a 16 year old who lost a kidney. The Red Cross gave the family a tent where they lived by the ruins of their house, until a new one was built with the help of hundreds of people. Just 24 hours later however and the army were back with the bulldozers - this time even taking the tent because it didn't have a permit! Yet again hundreds of people helped to rebuild it, and again it was demolished, the army even digging up the foundations.

The destruction is just one of the many hundreds in a fresh wave of house demolitions that are taking place in Palestine. But Salim's house, dubbed the Peace House, is also a symbol of the resistance that has taken place, with Arabs and Jews working together to take direct action to stop the demolitions and to rebuild those houses that have been destroyed. Support from the Israeli people is important – they can get in front of bulldozers and will only be arrested. If a Palestinians did the same they may be shot.

In other countries not quite so powerful as Israel, you would be hearing words like ethnic cleansing and Apartheid (there are now Jewish-only beaches) but then this is the fourth biggest military power in the world receiving goodwill and good cash (£3 billion a year) from the most powerful nation in the world – USA. As the Palestinian Authour, Edward Said commented, "Israel's cruel confinement of 1.3 million people in the Gaza Strip, jammed like so many sardines into a tiny place surrounded by a barbed-wire fence, and of nearly two million in the West Bank - all of whose entrances and exits are controlled by the Israeli Defence Force - has few parallels in the annals of colonialism. Even under Apartheid, F16 jets were never used to bomb African homelands, as they are now sent against Palestinian towns and villages."

Last Orders

In the past few weeks nearly 230 Israeli army reservists, many of them officers, have signed a petition saying they will refuse to serve in the occupied West Bank and Gaza Strip because Israel is "dominating, expelling, starving and humiliating" the Palestinian p   opulation. The army revolt

is the biggest since the start of the 16-month Palestinian uprising. One of them, Lieutenant Ishai Sagi, has described how, during one two-week stint in the West Bank, he was ordered to open fire at Palestinians who picked up stones for throwing at the troops. "Everything that we do in there - all the horrors, all the tearing down of houses and trees, all the roadblocks, everything - is just for one purpose, the settlers, who I believe are illegally there. So I believe that the [orders] that I got were illegal and I won't follow them again."

Last Saturday 10,000 people in Tel-Aviv, demonstrated their support for those sentiments under the banner "The Occupation Is Killing Us All", demanding an immediate end to the occupation of Palestinian land and solidarity with the growing number of young Israelis who are refusing to serve in the occupied territories. See: www.seruv.org/

* The Palestine Solidarity Campaign are calling for a boycott of Israeli goods and tourism. Box BM, PSA, London, WC1N 3XX. Tel. 020-7700-6192. www.palestinecampaign.org
* 26th Feb The Case Against Sharon - Michael Verhaeghe, part of the legal team in Belgium who are trying to prosecute the Israeli Prime Minister for war crimes, is speaking at Goodenough College, Mecklenburgh Square, London WC1 8pm. www.indictsharon.net
* See New Palestinian Indymedia site: http//virtualpalestine.org/update
* Also see www.btselem.org

Recommended reading:
- Pity the Nation by Robert Fisk (Simon & Schuster 1991).
- Drinking the Sea at Gaza by Amira Hass (Owl Books 2000).
- Fateful Triangle: the US, Israeli and the Palestinians by Noam Chomsky and Edward Said (Southend Press 1999).

BLUNKETT CHECK

Last week saw the publication of "Secure Borders, Safe Haven: Integration with diversity in modern Britain" the government white paper on asylum seekers. David Blunkett described the paper as 'tough but tender'. But the Refugee Council don't see anything tender in it, describing it as a kick in the teeth for refugees, increasing the numbers of detained asylum seekers, and doing nothing to improve the application process.

With the paper came the announcement that Campsfield Detention centre near Oxford will soon be closed. Although this is great news for those campaigning for Campsfield's closure, the next few years will see the places in secure centres increasing by 40%. The white paper includes plans for 'asylum villages' to house refugees' families while their applications are processed. Although refugees won't be locked into 'villages', proposed locations are so remote that refugees will unlikely be able to leave because of travel costs, and those refugees who turn down the governments kind hospitality won't be entitled to any financial support whatsoever.

On top of detention, refugees will also enjoy a 'streamlined' application process with no improvements in fairness or access to legal advice. And should their applications be refused they're on the first plane home before they've even packed their bags. www.refugeecouncil.org.uk

*Demonstrations are taking place at Campsfield on the last Saturday of every month while it remains open. www.closecampsfield.org.uk

DEATH ROW

In March 2000 Zahid Mubarek was murdered by his racist cellmate. His family, despite demanding a public inquiry into Zahid's death, have been ignored by the Home secretary David Blunkett. In September 2001 in a judicial review Judge Justice Hooper asked the Home Secretary to reconsider and order an independent investigation into Zahid's murder. Despite the ruling, Mr Blunkett still refuses to meet the Mubarek family, preferring instead to appeal against the judge's decision. Blunkett's appeal starts next Monday (18th). The verdict will have a profound impact on how suspicious deaths are dealt with by public bodies. Suresh Grover, of the National Civil Rights Movement stated that "The Home Secretary is petrified of losing because he believes that other victim families with similar deserving cases will also successfully demand public investigations and inquiries."

* Picket the High Court, Strand, London 18th February 9.30 am.
* 'Justice for Zahid meeting, Committee Room 8, House Of Commons London 7.00 pm, 25th February. Info: call Suresh Grover 020 8843 2333 sgrover@monitoring-group.co.uk
·For information on miscarriages of Justice in the UK www.mojuk.org.uk/

FISHY CHIPS

The future of 'Great British cuisine' could take a battering if ActionAid are successful in patenting salted chips. Under bizarre new patent rules ActionAid have found that by re-inventing the ready salted chip, they can demand chip shops pay a licence fee to add salt to their chips. Luckily ActionAid won't be robbing us of beloved fried product – just showing us how things are for farmers in developing countries, who have to live with this sort of theft, which is becoming common practice, thanks to greedy corporations patenting traditional crop varieties and local skills. Tel 020 7561 7636 www.actionaid.org.uk

SchNEWS in brief

Want to see a model of the shiny, **new Brighton Sainsbury's** supermarket development? Check out the plans at Brighton Library next week (18-23), or view at www.buddbrighton.org. Next BUDD meeting: 7.45pm, 20th Feb, Church of the Annunciation. **Protest against the Sainsbury's development** at London Road Sainsbury's, Brighton at Noon, this Sunday (17th). Info: occupy_resist@hotmail.com 01273-298192 ** A new website www.worthinga27.freeserve.co.uk highlights the campaign against the proposed **development at Titnore Lane** in Worthing which will trash ancient woodland. ** On Monday Julio Galeano became the first person killed as a reprisal for a successful strike against **privitisation in Cali**, Colombia (see SchNEWS 339). Julio, a community leader and strike committee member was assassinated by paramilitiaries as he left his home. Striking workers and members of the Colombian food workers union - who are taking Coca Cola to court for complicity in the assassination of trade union leaders - shall be at the **'Plan Colombia: Clearing the way for the Multinationals'** Conference on Saturday 23 February Conway Hall, Red Lion Square, London WC1 (Holborn tube). Colombia Solidarity Campaign, contact us at PO Box 8446, London N17 6NZ. Tel 07950 923448, email colombia_sc@hotmail.com ** **National Demo to End Student Poverty**, Reinstate the Grant, Weds 20th Feb, Coaches from University of Brighton, tickets £1 from UBSU offices, 07812 148919 ** **London Underground** is back on the 1st Sunday of each month from 2pm at London Activist Resource Centre (LARC), corner of Fieldgate & Parfett Street, London E1. ** The next meeting of the **London social Centres network** is on Feb. 20th 7.30pm Sebbon Street Community Centre, Sebbon Street, Islington London N1 Email: Londonscn@yahoo.co.uk ** **Justice Not Vengeance** – Relatives of 11th September attacks speak out against war and for an end to sanctions on Iraq. 7pm, 21st Feb, Friends House, Euston, London. www.justicenotvengeance.org ** **National Anti-War Anti-Sanction Conference**, 23rd-24th Feb, Kingsley Hall, Powis Road, London E2. £10/£5. Details from glenn@viwuk.freeserve.co.uk or 0845-458-9571. ** **The Block 'n' Roll** protest the beginning of this week saw three days demonstrations against the trident nuclear submarines in Faslane, Scotland. About 600 protestors turned up and 188 people were arrested including a mother and her 8 month old baby! A vanload of senior Navy officials was stopped and locked on to and protestors succeeded in keeping the gates of the military base closed for the three-day period. Tel: 0141 4231222www.faslanepeacecamp.com. ** The cheeky all new **Faslane Focus** is out – to read all about the exploits of the crap arrest specialists from the peace camp send a couple of quid to Faslane Peace Camp, A814, Shandon, nr.Helensburgh, Dumbartonshire, G84 8NT, Scotland ** **Earlier this week** York university managers attempted to flush 400 protesting students out of University buildings by deliberately setting off fire alarms. The attempt backfired when students chose to stay put, unlike the local fire services, who where not amused. ** **Sam Karoba**, spokesman for the Alliance of Papuan students and the Highland Tribal Council, has had a bounty put on his head by the Indonesian army. Sam is investigating the murder of the one of the leaders of the Papuan independant movement. Fax letters of protest 006296731642 and 006221356404 www.eco-action.org/opm

Chomsky at the bit

Fatih Tas was acquitted yesterday in Istanbul of charges of producing propaganda against the unity of the Turkish state. Fatih might well have spent over a year rotting in a Turkish jail, however, if it were not for the intervention of star witness Professor Noam Chomsky.

A relieved Mr Tas stated after the acquittal that "If Chomsky hadn't been here we wouldn't have expected such a verdict". Tas faced imprisonment under anti-terrorism laws simply for translating and publishing Chomskys work, which was highly critical of the US for supplying the Turkish Government with weapons that would ultimately be used for "intensive ethnic cleansing" against the Kurds. Chomsky supporters said he would petition the court to add his name to the charge sheet. "He will say 'I am here, I wrote this book and if there is a crime I should be tried too',"

The Turkish authorities have a history of 'information management' that extends beyond labelling free thinking publishers as terrorists. Little over a year ago the Turkish Government threatening 'action' against Microsoft for content relating to the Armenian genocide included within Encarta on-line encyclopaedia.

Quite how the Turkish authorities expected Encarta to 'gloss over' the genocide of approximately 1,500,000 Armenians between 1892 and 1921 is another matter.

POSITIVE SchNEWS

The Glaneirw Housing project in North Wales is combining the skills of the New Futures Association, Endless Knot and Travellers' School Charity. The group is creating a community housing co-operative for 20 families to live as a sustainable community when they're not travelling. The project hopes to create an environmentally sustainable resource centre where produce and crafts can be produced to sell locally. Over the summer fortnightly camps for travellers children aged between 9-15 are being organised with loads of classes on offer including bender building, food foraging, self-defence, cookery and computing skills. Tel 01239811929/ 0845 2818571 www.tsct.co.uk

...and finally...

Reebok, that well known champion of human right's has attempted to award Dita Sari, an Indonesian labour activist with a 'Reebok Human Rights Award'. The multinational reckons it honours, "champions and torchbearers in the fight for a better world" with its annual £35,400 Award. Shameless Jill Tucker, from Reeboks Hong Kong office said, "We feel like we are fighting for the same thing" and somehow managing to keep a straight face. Reebok are but one of many shoe and clothing companies to have their 'sports goods' manufactured on the cheap in Indonesia by sub-contractor companies. In their plants, the workers are lucky to get paid $1.50 a day. "They then have to live in a slum area, surrounded by poor and unhealthy conditions, especially for their children," said Dita Sari. "At the same time, Reebok collect millions of dollars of profit every year, directly contributed by these workers. The low pay and exploitation of the workers of Indonesia, Mexico and Vietnam are the main reasons why we will not accept this award."

For info contact: No Sweat 07904-431-9 www.nosweat.org.uk

disclaimer
SchNEWS warns all Zionists not to have a GodA mighty chip on their shoulder as it's already been patented Honest.

Subscribe!
Keep SchNEWS FREE! Send 1st Class stamps (e.g. 10 for next 9 issues) or donations (payable to Justice?) Ask for "Originals" if you can make copies. Post *free* to all prisoners. SchNEWS, c/o on-the-fiddle, P.O. Box 2600, Brighton, East Sussex, BN2 2DX.
Tel/Autofax +44 (0)1273 685913 *Email* schnews@brighton.co.uk *Download a PDF* of this issue or subscribe at www.schnews.org.uk

INDEPENDENT SOURCES IN PALESTINE

The following is a snapshot of how independent/activist news sources relayed events of the latest Intifada from Palestine. The timeline is taken from Palestine and Israeli Indymedia. The eyewitness reports are from a variety of independent information, alternative media sources and email lists.

Until the 1940s, the Jewish underground in Palestine was described as "terrorist". Around 1942, as news of the Holocaust spread... the terrorists of Palestine, suddenly began being described as "freedom fighters".
EQBAL AHMAD, TERRORISM: THEIRS & OURS, SEVEN STORIES PRESS, 2001

In order to prepare properly for the next campaign... it's essential to learn from every possible source. If the mission will be to seize a densely populated refugee camp, or take over the casbah in Nablus, then [we] must first analyze and internalise the lessons of earlier battles - even how the German army fought in the Warsaw ghetto.
AMIR OREN, EDITORIAL IN HA'ARETZ - ISRAELI DAILY NEWSPAPER - JAN 25 2002

March 30, 2002, 12:15: Bethlehem: IMC-Palestine is experiencing intermittent mortar shelling from the vicinity of Beit Jala. Israeli Occupation Forces (IOF)* have invaded Beit Jala. Palestine prepares for all-out war with Israel.

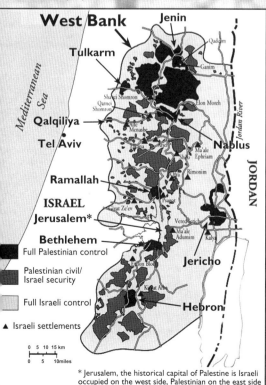

West Bank

Jenin
Tulkarm
Qadom
Ganim
Shake Shomron
Qarnei Shomron
Elon Moreh
Qalqiliya
Alfe Menashe
Tel Aviv
Nablus
Ma'ale Ephraim
Shilo
Rimonim
Ramallah
Psagot
ISREAL
Givat Ze'ev
Jerusalem*
Vered Jericho
Ma'ale Adumim
Kalya
Bethlehem

Jericho

Etzion Block

Kiryat Arba

Hebron

Mediterranean Sea — **Jordan River** — **JORDAN**

■ Full Palestinian control
▨ Palestinian civil/ Israel security
□ Full Israeli control
▲ Israeli settlements

0 5 10 15 km
0 5 10 miles

Jerusalem, the historical capital of Palestine is Israeli occupied on the west side, Palestinian on the east side

20:00: Ramallah: Electricity and water are cut off. International observers confirm Red Crescent ambulances are being targeted by the IOF. Tanks surround Bethlehem. Israeli aggression at checkpoints has been growing the last few days. This afternoon, an 18-year-old woman suicide bomber from Deheishe camp struck in Jerusalem. Arafat says he is ready to be a martyr and is calling all Palestinians to take up arms.

I'm sitting in the hot sun on the roof of the Bethlehem TV building. It's near the centre of Bethlehem, next to a major crossroads called Bab al-Zqaq and the main dual carriageway between Deheishe refugee camp and the largely Christian municipality of Beit Sahour. The flat crackle of automatic rifle fire echoes down from the old city, along with the occasional thud of tank shells. From the road below, separated from me by a low parapet, comes the occasional ear-buzzing bang of gunfire from the bored Israeli soldiers. They know we're in this building, and they don't like us, so it's just a form of sporadic harassment.

I'm here, at the moment, as a volunteer with Palestine Indymedia Centre (http://jerusalem.indymedia.org). The site went live a couple of days before the biggest re-invasion of Palestinian towns and cities in years – the return of the tanks to Ramallah, Bethlehem, Nablus, Jenin, Qalqiliya, Tulkarm and Hebron.
SARAH IRVING, BETHLEHEM IMC

Bloody hell. Just got out of Ramallah. I had been staying at the hospital - it was safer and I was useful there...

Sometimes there was not enough food. Everybody not anaemic donated blood. The patients that were able to make it to the hospital in time had gun shot wounds. I saw many corpses with close range wounds - execution style. The morgue is over-full.

The Israelis are lying about what is happening - they did enter Ramallah hospital on Sunday, I was there. The press is censured, unable to report what is occurring as they are also prevented, detained, threatened, injured, or escorted out. I hear that news in the States is very pro-Israeli. Americans need to be aware that their news is

What is INTIFADA?
An Arab word meaning 'abrupt waking up from sleep' or to 'shake off' something. It is the word used to describe the Palestinian uprising against Israeli occupation, breaking free from the compromised position they are in. The second Intifada began in October 2000

a Palestinian term, the Israelis use IDF (Israeli Defence Force).

very biased. They need to re-evaluate their definition of terrorism and who the terrorists are.

AN UNNAMED US NURSE VIA E-MAIL FROM JERUSALEM APRIL 2

April 01, 2002 Three international activists are shot at in **Bethlehem**, with Australian activist Kate Edwards (AKA Sharron) injured critically needing emergency surgery in a Beit Jala hospital to remove bullet fragments from her stomach.

April 03, 2002 Tanks enter **Nablus**. Estimates suggest 200-300 tanks deployed around the city are meeting resistance from Palestinian defenders.

The refugee camp is nothing like I expected - no tents or shacks, but small stone buildings - 3m x 3m units per family. Eleven thousand people live in 1km square. Everywhere you go there is art work, murals and graffiti on the walls. Art lives on. Every street is covered with posters of martyrs - those killed while fighting, or just victims of the IOF. A lot of the posters are of young boys.

MARTHA -SCOTTISH CND ACTIVIST - from BETHLEHEM via e-mail April 1

April 03: Jenin: Israeli attempts to invade the camp with tanks are prevented by fierce resistance. Four more dead, including a nurse and a four year old boy.

April 04, 1530: Nablus: Israeli forces take over the An-Najah University. They are also in Balata and Askar refugee camps. Five confirmed dead.

There is no water or electricity at the hospital. The nurses in the neonatal unit must be taking turns ventilating the babies by hand. Some of the babies will die without oxygen - of all the indisputable innocents.

AN UNNAMED US NURSE via e-mail FROM JERUSALEM APRIL 4

April 04, 17.00: Nablus: Eyewitnesses say Palestinians civilians are being forced to walk in front of tanks as the IOF sweeps the area.

April 05, 0917: Nablus: The old city has been under helicopter attack since the early hours. Eleven casualties reported since last night.

The general theme is the tribal theme. The only voice (allowed in Israel) shouts that we are in a war between two tribes: a tribe of human beings, of pure good - the Israelis – and a tribe of sub-human beings, of pure evil - the Palestinians. The same voice says this is a war of life and death. Only one tribe will survive, so, even if we are not purely good, we must lay morality to sleep and fight to kill — or else the Palestinians will throw us into the sea...

This is not a 'war against terror'. This is a war OF terror, a war in which, in return for Palestinian guerrilla terror, we employ the [IOF] in two types of terror; the visible one - the killing and destruction which some try to explain away as 'defence'; and, the silent terror of occupation, of humiliation , of deprivation and robbery, of alternating exploitation and starvation. This is the mass of the iceberg, the terror that is a greenhouse for counter-terror.

Does Israel have a monopoly on labelling its rivals as Nazis? Supporters of the essentially Nazi idea of deporting all Palestinians, have been part of our Knesset and "legitimate" political map since 1984. Recent opinion polls show 35per cent of the Jewish public supports this 'solution'.

ASSAF ORON, A JEWISH ISRAELI ARMY "REFUSENIK", JERUSALEM.INDYMEDIA.ORG, PASSOVER EVE MARCH 29, 2002

April 05, 0340: Nablus: A woman dies when the IOF shelled her home. She is Zaha Sartech (30). Resistance is strong and, having disabled eight tanks, is keeping the Israeli military at bay around the perimeter of the old city.

April 06 1630: Clashes begin in **Rafah**. IOF amassing around Rafah, Khan Younis, Karni and Erez. The Gaza Strip is under complete closure and has been internally divided into four sections.

Got woken up by machine gun fire and tank shells. Things have quietened down now. Curfew has apparently been lifted until 5pm, although we don't know if that's Israeli 5pm or Palestinian. A group of internationals in the street breaking curfew yesterday encountered a group of Palestinian lads who'd just been released [from Israeli cells] and accompanied them to comparative safety - as the IOF often release people during curfew so they can arrest them again for breaking it.

SARAH IRVING, from BETHLEHEM via e-mail 11:51am APRIL 8

Curfew was reinforced an hour and twenty minutes earlier than announced on television, with no obvious warning to civilians other than the sudden resumption of gunfire. The sporadic fire at the IMC office where we are living, has increased considerably since Israeli Indymedia [in the hope of preventing the IMC being bombed] told the IOF our exact location, and the IOF put it out on their radio station..."

SARAH IRVING, from BETHLEHEM via e-mail 09:12 APRIL 9

Broke curfew yesterday to get [name snipped] clean clothes, and ended up trapped in the hotel whilst the IOF shot at journalists to keep them out of the street whilst they looted shops. We snuck round a back way, with about fifteen pitiful journos following us from about twenty yards, cameras trained, hoping they'd get some pictures of international chicks with no flak jacket getting blasted. There are a couple of really cool press out here, like Bob Fisk and Khaled from Bethlehem TV and the crew from Al-Jazeera, who are very brave and capable. But the rest seem to spend most of the time cowering round corners

At the entrance to Jerusalem's al-Aqsa mosque, a Muslem kneels on his prayer mat as an Israeli police officer maintains an armed vigil.

Pic: Alec Smart

Jenin

April 06, 2030: Nablus: Medical Relief sets up six field hospitals. One, a mosque in the old city, reports 50 people injured, three of those critically. There are five corpses in the room in which they operate. Israeli snipers shoot at any one trying to enter or leave the mosque. In the Askar refugee camp, Israeli helicopters shoot missiles leaving seven people injured. An ambulance given permission by the Israeli military to collect them has its tyres shot out.

We could not get through the checkpoint so travelled over the mountains by foot to get here. There were helicopters and drone planes flying overhead and I had my first encounter with the dreaded settlers. They are armed and very angry. We got to a village and an Arab family took us in. The grandfather had been arrested. He told us of the brutal treatment he received from the IOF, stripped naked, kept on his knees, no food or water for 2 days. His son is still being held. Next day, we walked for two hours into a deserted Nablus (city of 180,000) bullet holes in everything, this is the Holey Land we joked.
MARY KELLY - IRISH NURSE AND ISM (International Solidarity Movement) ACTIVIST via e-mail APRIL 11

April 06 18:00: Jenin: Al Razi hospital: Medics watch helplessly as 28-year-old Nidal Al Haj bleeds to death inside the hospital yard. Israeli snipers prevent anyone attending him. Fifteen dead bodies are reported in different locations. The Israeli army is systematically bulldozing houses in the camp, home to 15,000 Palestinians. They drop tear gas from helicopters. In the afternoon, occupation soldiers announce they will ceasefire to allow the women and elderly to get water. As those fetching water reach the camp's entrance, all are detained. Shortly after, residents say the Israelis call out to the resistance fighters to surrender to save the lives of the detained civilians. Detainees are seen strapped to the tanks and personnel carriers, which then resume their bombardment. The Israeli officer heading the Jenin reoccupation offensive is removed from duty having failed to take over the camp.

First Day April 3: I hear tanks and helicopters. The Israeli troops have entered Jenin City. All day the muezzin from the mosque is calling out for resistance: "Calling all Palestinians, Hamas, Fatah, Jihad. Resist the Army. We are on alert!" By Saturday, they have entered the camp. There are so many tanks. Snipers are everywhere.

The resistance tried to stop the Army from taking the camp and six Palestinians were killed and two Israeli soldiers. That's what the Israeli reports say. The resistance said Israelis will only take the camp over our dead bodies. The resistance used rocket-propelled grenades for the first time and three Israeli

Boy with fake suicide bomber's kit

tanks were destroyed. The resistance leaders say "there are a lot of surprises in store for the Israelis".

SATURDAY, APRIL 6 9.30am: Israeli troops broke into our house and took over the rooms. They broke furniture and seem very angry. They are rubbing dark camouflage cream on their faces. Some were nervous and I could see the hatred in their eyes. One of the soldiers spat at us. Then some soldiers took my father into a room using him as a shield while they were shooting out from holes they made in the walls. They moved all 24 — neighbours, cousins and relatives — into my uncle Sophi's room.

SUNDAY, APRIL 7: An Israeli soldier was shot in our house. He was seriously injured. There is blood all over his face and he is screaming. The other soldiers put bandages on his face and his arms and later, they put a drip with glucose in his arm. Later, he screams for his mother.

I am afraid they will take revenge. They scream at us in Hebrew. They tell us not to go near the window. One soldier is so angry he bangs his head against the wall. The Apache shells the camp all day and the soldier tells us: "We will not leave this place until all the armed men surrender." The Palestinian resistance keeps saying: "We will never surrender." The only muezzin left in the camp continues all day, telling the fighters to resist.

MONDAY, APRIL 8: The Apache keeps shelling. The houses are burnt. No one knows how many people have died inside their houses. Today there is fighting also in Nablus, where my uncle and aunt live. Today, Israeli reports say two Israeli soldiers are killed and five injured and 50 Palestinians are killed. Palestinian sources are different. They say there are hundreds of Palestinians killed. The radio also says there is a massacre here in the camp and the world knows nothing about it.
TRANSLATION FROM THE PERSONAL DIARY OF REEM SALEH (aged 15), JENIN REFUGEE CAMP, FROM JERUSALEM.INDYMEDIA.ORG

April 08, 20:02: Jenin runs out of water, food and medical supplies. People are drinking waste water.

The IOF are not allowing rotting bodies to be collected from the streets; they shoot at people who try to bring home the dead but do not shoot at the cats and dogs that have started to eat them.
MARY KELLY - IRISH NURSE AND ISM ACTIVIST via e-mail APRIL 11

April 09, 2002: Nablus: Israeli forces continue shelling. Twelve residents are killed. In Askar refugee camp, Israeli forces kill two residents. Hafed Sabra (60) and Amjad Abda (11). During the raid of the old city, the Israeli army take 1000 residents to Hawara military base. They close a field hospital at Al-Beik mosque. Loudspeaker announcements from jeeps say: "We are stronger than you - you are weak - there is no-one here to help you."

April 09, 2002: Jenin: More than one third of the camp has been destroyed.

April 10, 2002: Jenin: Israeli forces dig large holes in the Haret al-Hawarish area. Eyewitnesses see Israeli troops putting bodies in the holes.

TUESDAY, APRIL 9: A pregnant neighbour called Hyam comes knocking at our door. She is having pains and is frightened.

The soldiers scream at her to go away but she has nowhere to go, she says. She goes out on the street again with her little daughter who is waving a white cloth, like a flag. But they shoot at them anyway. When Hyam gets back to her house, her husband is gone, he has been arrested by the Israelis. Her other children were taken by her neighbour.

WEDNESDAY, APRIL 10: There is a radio report of a suicide bomber in Haifa on a bus. He came from Jenin. When the Apaches circle, the children put their hands over their ears and the Israelis tell them not to be afraid. "The Army knows we are here, you won't get rocketed," they say.

FRIDAY, APRIL 12: Another suicide bombing in Jerusalem. Every day is the same. On the news, I hear 13 Israeli soldiers are killed in Jenin camp. I don't know where it is, because there are explosions all the time. One of the soldiers says to my father: "Now we will not leave until every Arab is dead."

DIARY OF REEM SALEH (15) WHO LIVES IN THE JENIN REFUGEE CAMP. SHE TOLD AN INDYMEDIA TRANSLATOR THAT SHE ONCE WANTED TO BE A TEACHER OR A NURSE BUT NOW WANTS TO BE AN AMLIEH ESTESHHADIEH, A SUICIDE BOMBER.

Things in Bethlehem are bad, but things are bad elsewhere. Do we cancel food drops here to go to demonstrations against that bastard [Colin] Powell in Ramallah, leaving Bethlehem without internationals? God we need more people. We kind of thought that Powell's presence might at least inspire a brief pullback and give people a little respite. But not even that seems to be happening. The entire international community has sold out the Palestinian people.

SARAH IRVING, from BETHLEHEM via e-mail, April 12

April 13: Ramallah: After several attempts on his life, the IOF arrest one of the most popular figures of the Intifada, Marwan Baghouti - a senior Fateh leader and member of the Palestinian Legislative Council. Ariel Sharon says: "Like in every democratic country he will be tried and put in prison."

April 15: Khader Shkirat, General Director of Palestinian human rights group LAW, visits Barghouti, at the Russian Compound ('Moscowbiya') in Jerusalem. His hands and legs are shackled to a small chair, angled to slant forward so that he cannot sit in a stable position. Due to nails sticking out of the chair his back is bleeding. He is not allowed to sleep. Position abuse, known as 'shabeh', is a favourite of the Israeli General Security Service ('Shin Bet'). Barghouti's interrogators have told him they have his son in detention in Ashkelon and they are going to kill him.

The Intifada will not stop until there is an end to the occupation and the establishment of an independent Palestinian state. The shortest way to achieve this is to make the occupation have a high price. Our strategy is to fight. The [PA] leadership is not prepared for this, but the people are...

One month ago we called for the establishment of an Intifada government. This means to allow all the Palestinian factions who are united now (and this is the first time they are all working together on the ground) to have representatives in the Intifada government: to formally adopt the policy of the Intifada as the policy of the government. This is a good solution until we are somehow able to have general elections. The PA refused this, but the people have welcomed the idea.

FROM: A CONVERSATION WITH MARWAN BARGHOUTI BY TOUFIC HADDAD FEBRUARY 2001, BETWEENTHELINES.ORG

The thought of any activists cosying up with a corrupt dictator such as Arafat is a worrying one.

IAN F, BRISTOL PALESTINE SOLIDARITY GROUP

April 13, 2002: Jenin: Israeli army chief, Brigadier-General Ron Kitrey, tells Army Radio it has killed hundreds of Palestinians in Jenin. Fighting ceases when the Palestinian resistance ran out of ammunition. Unarmed men are being rounded up within the camp and taken for summary execution. Waddah Fathi ash-Shalabi, 35 and Abdul Karim Yusif Sa'adih, 38 are shot dead in front of a group of 150 men.

We entered Jenin camp on the morning of the 14th. It was a closed military zone, but the few soldiers that saw us did not intervene. The lower portion of the camp appears to be almost deserted, except for wandering goats. Every house has been damaged in some way.

Bulldozers have cut a 10 metre wide path from the north to the south of the camp so the tanks could get in. Many people have families buried inside, under the rubble.

The destruction in the centre of the camp is total... an area of 5000sq ft that is nothing but rubble in what was once the most populous, and poorest area of the camp. It was also the area of the strongest resistance.

Estimates vary between 250 – 350 homes demolished and 450 to 600 families, perhaps 2000 people, homeless. We saw bodies of six people killed inside their homes. They'd been there for about six days and it's been hot, decomposition is rapid. You know exactly where a body is because you can smell it.

Today, there is no food, water or electricity in the camp. We met two UN trucks that have been prevented access by the Israeli military for eight hours. They were happy to let us take whatever we could carry. To my knowledge the only international organisation in Jenin is Amnesty International who brought lawyers, took statements from some of the refugees, and filed cases against the Israeli government.

BRIAN WOOD COLORADO CAMPAIGN FOR MIDDLE EAST PEACE - via e-mail

On Thursday 12th April, in Bethlehem, I was filming tanks attacking ambulances. One of the soldiers shot at me, hitting my car about 10cm from my head. When he realised I wasn't shot, he told me to approach him slowly, to put my camera down, and take off my flak jacket and hardhat. They blindfolded me, put me in a tank, and took me to Etzion.

Etzion is not just a settlement. It is a new prison. When you enter blindfolded they ask you: "Are you a man? You will be a woman soon!" as they kick you in the groin. They shot

Pic: Alec Smart

Palestinian boys catapult stones against the brick walls of an Israeli Army bunker, Bethlehem, on the first anniversary of the intifada, September 2001

abuse at you, about your mother, your sister and your God.

They put me in one of the tents, with 41 other people. The youngest was 16, from Ayda camp. The oldest was 65, from Beit Jala. Rami, the Druze soldier, is in charge. He shouts in Arabic. He is about 20. He especially dislikes Palestinians. Once he pointed his gun at us and said that he would shoot us. He said he could just claim it was a mistake and no one could do anything.

The food was tinned military rations. They would open the can and put it in front of you, still blindfolded and handcuffed. You had to ask to go to the toilet. When you call, you're told to shut up. When you call many times, you are kicked in the head and body. One of the prisoners wet himself and started to cry. They make you stand if they think you are going to sleep. Sleep is just a few stolen moments. It was too cold to sleep at night.

KHALED'S STATEMENT ON RELEASE FROM PRISON 14 APRIL 12:52

April 16, 15:15: Nablus: The Israeli military cut the phone lines and destroy the water supply. Of the four camps in Nablus, at least two, Balata and Askar, have been without food, water, and electricity for 13 days. The camps are sealed off by soldiers and tanks. As of last night, they are shelling the camps.

There are few patients in the hospital, not because there are few injuries or deaths, but because ambulances are not allowed to reach the dead and dying. A Red Crescent ambulance driver told me he has been arrested four times in a week. They are forced to take off their clothes, handcuffed, blindfolded and made to stand in the sun for two or three hours while the soldiers shoot their guns. He showed me the bullet holes and broken windows in the ambulance.

Yesterday a boy found an unused tank shell. It exploded and left his eyes burned shut, his body blackened and blood pouring from his stomach. His cries revealed a voice in the process of changing. He could not have been more than 12 years old.
MARY KELLY – IRISH NURSE AND ISM ACTIVIST – via e-mail APRIL 15

April 16, 2002 16.30: Nablus: A group of internationals, attempting to deliver humanitarian aid to the Askar camp are intercepted by the IOF.

Today we planned to take food and medicines to Belata and Askar refugee camps which have been under attack and curfew for weeks. We were six Palestinians - a Doctor and 5 paramedics - and 25 activists - 15 from France, 5 from the UK, 3 from US, 2 Danes and myself from Ireland. We met an army checkpoint with IOF soldiers and one tank. We declared our mission, showed our passports and got through to Belata.

Our efforts to visit Askar were stopped by two tanks which blocked our way. The soldiers fired warning shots from machine guns. We turned back and were stopped at the same checkpoint but this time they did not let us through and wanted to punish us for taking food to Belata. They made us wait for two hours. Suddenly, we were surrounded by four tanks and two police vans. Machine guns were fired into the air. Things escalated quickly. We were told that they wanted to arrest the Palestinian doctor and the five paramedics, but that we [the internationals] could leave. We refused to leave without the Palestinians. They warned us that things would get ugly if we did not obey. We quickly formed a protective ring around our Palestinian friends. A concussion grenade exploded into our group, then the soldiers started beating us kicking, punching and rifle butts were used. They managed to drag the four Palestinian men away from us, beat them, forced them to kneel and handcuffed them. We were very shocked to put it mildly! Many of our group were injured, especially the men, but we still had the two Palestinian women in our midst. They threatened us with more violence but we refused to move and linked our arms tightly around the women. They destroyed the film in our cameras.

We refused to leave until they returned the four men. A stand off situation went on where we expected another attack from them. We let them know we would not move until they returned the four men. After what seemed like a lifetime, they returned the prisoners to us and allowed us to go home. They beat us but did not win.
MARY KELLY - IRISH NURSE AND ISM ACTIVIST via e-mail

April 19: Nablus: IOF raids in Naseiriah neighbourhood kill one. In Nablus, seventy Palestinians, including many children and women, are killed during the attack. They are buried in a mass grave during a 5-hour lift of the curfew imposed on the city.

April 19: Gaza Strip: Fifteen Israeli tanks attack the town of Rafah in the southern Gaza Strip early Friday, killing at least three Palestinians in the Brazil neighbourhood. A 15-year-old boy is shot dead in the Sweidiah neighbourhood.

April 22: Gaza Strip: Four Palestinian children are wounded, including a three-year-old shot in the head, when Israeli troops fire on them as they threw stones at Israeli bulldozers.

April 24: Ramallah: A delegation from the EU, holds talks with Arafat today. This is the ninth day that the moqata'a (presidential compound) has received no food or water. The Israeli authorities refuse to allow the injured out. One activist has a broken back, another went out to speak with some of the soldiers and was told: "Tell them to come out, then we will shoot them."

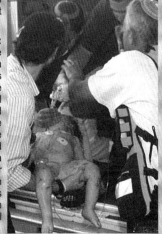

International law forbids the building of the settlements, but 34 new settlements have been constructed in this year alone. Collective punishment is illegal. But Israel has now escalated from interrupting food shipments to completely shutting off water to the city of Ramallah, endangering the lives of 120,000 people. The shelling of innocuous Palestinian civilian structures such as power plants, schools, and sewage facilities, is occurring at an alarming rate. Unarmed civilians are being killed on a daily basis. Israel is making a mockery of international human rights law, and by its tacit acceptance, the UN is severely eroding its credibility in the region and beyond.

NETA GOLAN AND IAN URBINA, MOQATA'A COMPOUND

April 25, 14.00: A group of over 50 internationals join a 1000-strong Palestinian civil society march to protest against the continued siege of their town, and to demand an immediate withdrawal from Palestinian territory.

16:00: Seven people are injured at the protest in **Ramallah,** one of them with a bullet to the head, who dies hours later. Although clearly unarmed, tear gas, sound bombs and live ammunition are used.

Bethlehem: A Palestinian ambulance, shot-up by IOF machine guns while transporting a patient - the driver was killed.   Pic: Alec Smart

The Director of the Red Crescent in Jenin was killed with a doctor when their ambulance was bombed by an IOF tank in March. Two medics were killed in Gaza and two in Turkharem. Over the past 19 months, 225 medical workers have been wounded. Many [people] have died due to ambulances being stopped and shot at, and many women have given birth in horrifying circumstances while being held up at checkpoints.

MARY KELLY - IRISH NURSE AND ISM ACTIVIST April 25

April 25, 2002: Jenin: A truck bringing aid from the USA is turned back by residents of the camp. The boxes, including baby clothes and toys, are marked 'a gift from the United States'. Some of the goods were clearly manufactured in Israel. One man points to the destruction caused by two US made Apache helicopter missiles and says: "This is the biggest gift we got from America."

April 27 12:00: Nablus: A woman in the Kalandiya camp, holds close the body of her dead child, torn apart by an explosive "dum-dum" bullet. Pointing at her other sons she cries: "I did not hate Israelis, nor did my sons. I don't want to hate them. I don't want my sons to kill their sons. Help us."

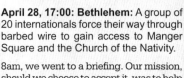

April 28, 17:00: Bethlehem: A group of 20 internationals force their way through barbed wire to gain access to Manger Square and the Church of the Nativity.

8am, we went to a briefing. Our mission, should we choose to accept it, was to help break the month-long siege at the Church of the Nativity and get food and a team of international observers inside. The Israeli army had been shooting indiscriminately at the church ever since 26 people had been allowed to leave safely a few days earlier. Two parts had been set on fire by the army the night before, and a man had been killed there that morning. The hope was that the killing would stop once there were internationals inside.

We travelled to Bethlehem via back roads to avoid checkpoints, switching vehicles from time to time, decamped and walked in small groups to be less obvious…

Someone brought card and a marker pen and drew a map. "There's the church, there's the square, these are the alleyways we'll approach through. This is the barbed wire we'll have to go over. There's a tank here and another one here. There are snipers here, here, here, here and here." Oh. Not just security cameras then?

We stuffed toilet paper in our ears in case of stun grenades. We soaked scarves and hankies in case of gas. We were told, if we were shot at, they'd almost certainly be shooting over our heads, in front of us or at the ground, so under no circumstances should we run or get on the ground…

I've never been so scared in my whole life. Perched on a step with Kate and Marcia, Trevor and the two Nathans. Feeling my pulse thundering through my temples. Trousers falling down… why didn't I sew a top button on them? Out of the alleyway, into the wide square, tanks in front, the church ahead, a shout, no shots, a roll of barbed wire approaching, how am I going to get over it without getting caught up? My hands are full. Walking though it, pulling my trousers along with me, walking as fast as my legs will go, ignoring the shouts, the backs of the people in front my only focus, dimly aware of a khaki man running, glancing across at him grabbing someone, can't see who, wrestling them down, walking faster, wanting to run, people ahead running, still no shots, running too.

Shield the door and the doors open and hands are reaching out, taking the food we're passing in, a woman pushes through into the church. That's meant to happen, all the food bags are in. The door closes. We've done it. A quick hug of pure joy. "Faster. Come on." Israeli troops in front of us, blocking the way, linking arms, trying to push against the line. Pulled apart from each other, still clinging to Trevor's arm. Jeff bleeding. Sitting down, legs round Marcia, physically lifted from the ground and carried into the Peace Centre, dumped on the floor. Skulking in a corner hiding the dictaphone tape recording of the action in my pants.

Bizarrely, a khaki man says to Huwaida: "We're not at the University of Michigan now you know." At some point in some other life, they were both at the same college in the US, this Israeli soldier and this Palestinian-American activist.

The soldiers were unimpressed: "We were really close to a Final Solution and now you've ruined it." Final solution frighten me. There had been signs of an intent to storm the church and end the siege with an intense burst of violence, potentially the deaths of many of the refugees inside. Yeah, we ruined it, and amidst all the uncertainty of being detained by them, there was a defiant high, which their fury only fed.

We were separated and asked to call the people in the church and tell them they had to come out. Apparently the Palestinians inside the church wanted the internationals to leave, but rather than simply ask them to go, they had asked the negotiators to ask the soldiers to ask us to ask them to leave. Yeah right.

After a while I climbed out of the window of the office I was locked in, reached up to the rafters above and swung myself onto the roof of the Peace Centre. I knew the trapeze training would come in handy one day. The stars looked amazing up there, the moon just past full, so much more real than the tanks surrounding it. There was nowhere to escape to and eventually they got me down.

Hands bound, we were put in a lorry and taken to the Bethlehem checkpoint. The women were taken out, tied hands and feet and put on the floor of a van. We were driven to the middle of nowhere and they opened the back doors. Bastards… they were going to dump us in the arse end of beyond at two in the morning, having taken all our ID and phones…

JO WILDING - UK ACTIVIST AFTER DEPORTATION

Church of Nativity - IOF tank approaches in a cloud of tear gas

My first glimpse into the darkness was of two armed Palestinians, dressed in flak-suits, crouched aiming rifles at us as we passed through the gate. As the gate was closed, torches were lit, our faces checked, then the door to the main church opened. We walked through to a rousing reception from the 150 or so Palestinians waiting on the other side.

Spokesmen of the various factions formally welcomed us, thanked us and made it clear we were free to leave at any time. We explained that we intended to stay until the siege was concluded.

It was explained that there were IOF snipers on or in most of the surrounding buildings. We were shown the sniper crane. This crane 100-200m in height, which looked down into church complex, was fitted with a camera and rifle remotely controlled by an IOF soldier on the ground.

The church itself is a complex of courtyards, offices, gardens, halls, priest's quarters, towers and tunnels. We were shown an office burnt out by IOF incendiary devices. One man had been killed by a sniper, while fighting the fire. All the windows in the upper reaches of the church were smashed and the walls pockmarked with bullet holes.

We were shown a bell tower where a few weeks earlier the bell ringer had been shot and killed, and a rooftop area where we were told an IOF assault team had been repulsed with fatalities on both sides.

There were thirty priests from the Armenian, Franciscan and Greek Orthodox traditions who share the church in an uneasy alliance of faiths. Of the approximately 150 Palestinians, about two thirds were civilians the remaining third armed. All those present were adult males excepting a handful of nuns and the three female international activists. It was clear that all those present were there of their own accord and that reports of a hostage situation were totally unfounded.

The Palestinians had not eaten properly for weeks. Many were gaunt, all looked thin. A few people were obviously ill. One man was falling in and out of consciousness and occasionally having fits.

ALISTAIR HILLMAN - UK ACTIVIST - report posted on www.squall.co.uk after deportation

Pic: Alec Smart

A peacekeeper from TIPH (Temporary International Presence in Hebron) in 'Prayer Walk' - a neighbourhood evicted and destroyed by the IOF after a Jew suffered a bullet wound from an unknown assailant in the vicinity.

April 29: Bethlehem: Nidal Hueida, 28, is shot dead in the compound of the besieged Church of the Nativity.

The sniper crane afforded the IOF a view into the otherwise invisible courtyards of the church. This crane was routinely raised, lowered, and moved. People would get used to a habitual safe route around the complex, which would suddenly be rendered dangerous. It was in this way that many of the deaths and injuries occurred. While we were there, one man was shot. We had been speaking with him the day before. He was friendly, the father of eleven children. The IOF claim he had been pointing a gun out of the church. The Palestinians claim he was hanging out his washing out to dry.

Food was distributed by a committee, which arranged the cooking of one meal a day. A typical meal for one person would consist of between half and one cup of a weak spiced soup containing maybe five pieces of pasta or a sprinkling of rice, a few leaves and perhaps 10-20 lentils. On sparse days, some people would cook up a weak salty soup of mustard leaves found in the gardens, and others would fry lemon leaves until edible. While we were there, three deliveries were made: our delivery; the only token effort by the Israelis that included pot noodles (a press stunt - enough for 10 people); and a delivery by Bethlehem women. It was an exceptional week in terms of deliveries.

ALISTAIR HILLMAN - UK ACTIVIST - report posted on www.squall.co.uk after deportation

April 29, 04.00: Hebron: Israeli forces enter the Palestinian port of Hebron. Nine Palestinians are killed and 25 wounded. Several buildings are destroyed, including a television station. Throughout the day Israeli tanks patrol the city while sporadic shooting is heard. A curfew is in place. Ninety Palestinians are arrested 'suspected' of being connected to Saturday's attack against the Israeli settlement of Adura.

May 01: Hebron: Overnight more than 300 people are detained following what witnesses describe as the 'targeting of students'. Student houses are attacked and one is firebombed. The IOF is preventing fire crews from attending.

May 02: Gaza: Sabha Abu Ghanem, 48, is hit in the chest as Israeli tanks and bulldozers are used for incursions in the centre and south of the Gaza Strip.

May 05: Bethlehem: The siege at Nativity Church continues. There are conflicting reports in the media concerning the situation and treatment of some of those inside.

The last days were exhausting. Time and again, the negotiations appeared to be hours from closing and then would break down. One event of note occurred a few days before the end when we were asked to leave by a Palestinian "go-between" negotiator. He claimed the negotiations had finished, that we were to leave immediately, and that the Palestinians would leave one hour after us.

We were in contact with a representative in the compound in Ramallah who was in direct contact with Arafat. We were told that we should not leave as the negotiations were in no way closed. Italy was not accepting the exiles and no agreement had been reached as to how the weapons in the church would be decommissioned. The "go-between" spread rumours and caused a situation where it appeared we were deliberately holding up the proceedings. Tensions between us, and some of the Palestinians, were high.

Later that day, our consulates applied similar pressure. I explained that they were misinforming me, and they should not bother to contact me anymore. By nightfall, Italy's refusal to accept the exiles was in the press, and tensions dropped.

Next day, many Palestinians thanked us for not leaving and seemed aware of the trickery that had been attempted. We were lucky to have contacts we could trust both inside and outside the church which enabled us to make the right decision for the people in the church and to avoid the political wrangling.

ALISTAIR HILLMAN - UK ACTIVIST - report posted on www.squall.co.uk after deportation

May 06: Internationals held: Nathan Musselman, Nathan Mauger, Tom Kaoutsoukos begin a hunger strike in solidarity with Trevor Baumgartner, Huwaida Arraf and Jo Wilding who are themselves in the fifth day of a hunger strike in protest at their detention. Today, two of them are hospitalised and, despite tests showing their blood sugar levels to be dangerously low, they are returned to detention. At least two have been deported without due process. The rest are denied information or access to lawyers. The men are being held at Kiryat Arba, an illegal settlement in Al-Khalil (Hebron). 152 foreigners have been refused entry to Israel since April 3, including a Greek team of doctors, Italian members of Parliament, and British, Belgium and French peace campaigners.

May 06: Hebron: Dozens of tanks, which had been gradually pulled out in the past weeks, come back in force. Soldiers brake into houses and offices, destroying equipment indiscriminately. Hundreds of inhabitants are arrested and ordered to strip almost naked, to show they are not wearing explosives.

May 07: Nativity Church, Bethlehem: Under arrangements brokered by the US and EU, 13 Palestinian militants will be sent into exile in Cyprus while 26 others will go to jail in the Gaza Strip. The other Palestinians inside the church are interrogated then set free in an effort to end the 36-day standoff.

May 07: Israeli forces move back in to Deheishah camp.

May 09: Apaches and F16's sporadically shell the Balata refugee camp. Tanks are again moving on the Jerusalem road…

TO CONTINUE THIS COVERAGE GO TO THE FOLLOWING WEBSITES:

Palestine Indymedia
http://jerusalem.indymedia.org

Israel Indymedia
http://indymedia.org.il

Women in Black
http://www.womeninblack.net/

Hebron Christian Peacemaker Team
http://www.prairienet.org/cpt/hebron.php.

LAW Society (Palestinian human rights group)
http://www.lawsociety.org/

Palestine Solidarity Campaign -
http://www.palestinecampaign.org/

Electronic Intifada
http://www.electronicintifada.net

International Solidarity Movement
http:// www.rapprochement.org

WAKE UP! WAKE UP! IT'S YER INQUISITIVE

Weekly SchNEWS

www.schnews.org.uk

Friday 22nd February 2002   Free/Donation   Issue 343

SPAIN IN THE ARSE

"Terrorism is not only a group of commandos who act, but is a project that tries to root itself in society, and to combat it, it is also necessary to struggle against the social, economical, political and also communication structures which support and nourish it" - *Jaime Mayor Oreha, Spanish Minister of Internal Affairs.*

When Oreha spoke at the European Conference on Terrorism in Madrid in January last year his government was already cracking down on Spanish citizens' civil liberties; long before September 11th and the beginning of an international 'war on terrorism'. In the past year alone, belonging to the wrong political party, supporting prisoners, teaching the Basque language, publishing books and records, editing a magazine, being in a band, running a radio station, or simply being a journalist has become a crime in Spain. There have been mass arrests with people taken to isolation wards where they are often tortured then released a few days later without charge. This targeting of Basque political activists has now spread to anarchist and other radical movements, with raids and arrests being part of a general clampdown.

Euro nicked!

No surprises then to find that Spain is using its presidency of the European Union to push forward radical proposals that would label demonstrators at European summits 'terrorists'. The document, issued last month to the European Working Party on Terrorism, states that they have "noticed a gradual increase…in violence and criminal damage (at anti-capitalist protests) orchestrated by radical extremist groups, clearly terrorising society." The proposals go on to state that this 'new breed' of terrorist menace are "organisations taking advantage of their lawful status to aid and abet the achievement of terrorist groups' aims."

Post September 11th, the European Union agreed new legislation for combating global terrorism, along with a European arrest warrant. The Spanish proposals go further, asking for a more proactive EU wide database to keep an eye on protestors. They reckon that this extension "would provide a very helpful tool in preventing and, where appropriate, prosecuting violent urban youthful radicalism, which is increasingly being used as a cat's-paw by terrorist groups in order to achieve their criminal aims."

But it's not just Spain that is widening the definition of terrorism; we in the UK are 'fortunate' enough to be protected by some of the world's toughest anti-terrorist legislation. Barrister Stephanie Harrison, from the Campaign Against Criminalising Communities reckons that the Terrorist Act 2000 (SchNEWS 268), alongside its even tougher little sister, the Anti Terrorism, Crime and Security Act 2001 (see SchNews 331), are not only criminalising dissent amongst the locals, but are a direct attack on the rights of vulnerable groups - mainly immigrant communities.

Dr Ghayasuddin Siddiqui, Leader of the Muslim Parliament of Great Britain told SchNEWS that the situation within the British Muslim and Arabic community is becoming unbearable. "We are the target of this legislation - there is a witch hunt going on - a fishing expedition… Innocent people are being harassed, families are being disturbed, children traumatised… there is a climate of fear in our community". And it doesn't stop there, as new legislation allows instant internment, providing the police with powers to detain people indefinitely without trial. Often based on the most circumstantial of evidence, Asians and Muslims the length and breath of this fair and pleasant land are finding themselves being detained under this new legislation. Dr Siddiqui's message is clear "The whole Muslim community is frightened, intimidated and traumatised; as a result the people are not getting involved in community activities, and people are asking 'is it worth it?'"

In January Yasadigimiz Vatan, a Turkish language socialist weekly magazine had its last two issues confiscated by police who said it was "property for the use of terrorism." Vatan has been distributed in the UK for the past two years so what has changed? According to one of its workers "The Terrorism Act 2000, which is not being used to fight terrorism but to fight democrats and prevent press freedom in this country."

Estella Schmidt from the Kurdish

National Congress (KNK) told us that as far as UK based Kurds are concerned it is more a case of harassment than actual detention. Demonstrators are constantly being filmed, and follow up calls from police to homes of Kurds is commonplace often late at night and unannounced."These people are not from this country, and despite protesting innocently, and making it quite clear that they are not supporting terrorists, they are still harassed by police - it is similar to the way the Irish have been treated in the past."

As the Spanish example shows, it's not long before the authoritarian finger starts pointing at anyone who dares to disagree. Raif, a lawyer from Coalition Against the Terror Acts, told SchNEWS "With so much police activity against refugees and Muslims, many people are becoming complacent. This new document confirms exactly what we've been warning of for ages. All effective dissent will be treated the same: you are either with them or you are a terrorist and outlaw."

* Coalition Against the Terror Acts c/o Haldane Society, Conway Hall, 25 Red Lion Square, London WC1R 4RL www.cacc.org.uk http://go.to/ta2000

* To find out more about crack down in Spain http://barcelona.indymedia.org/

* The Kurdistan Workers Party (PKK) is today mounting a legal challenge to its banning under the Terrorism Act 2000. The PKK are one of 21 political groups whose activities were outlawed under a Proscribed Organisations Order which came into effect in March last year. Peace in Kurdistan Campaign 020 7586 5892

* On Wednesday people across America wore blue triangles to show support for the thousand plus people - mainly Arabs and Muslims - who have "disappeared" since September 11th. Many of those detained are being held on the basis of secret evidence - or no evidence at all. Prisoners are held without being allowed any contact with a lawyer, and the US government is refusing to reveal their identities, nationalities and whereabouts.

To find out more go to: www.laresistencia.org

* For a list of anti terrorism events check out the party and protest section on our website.

BASKET CASE

Pepe Rei, editor of radical Basque paper 'Ardibeltza' was imprisoned last year without charge (See SchNEWS 303)– on the allegation that ETA (militant Basque separatists) were using his paper for information, and so therefore *he* was supporting terrorism.

After being released 5 months ago because of lack of evidence, the same judge has shoved him back in prison again without any evidence and upped his charge to 'membership of an armed organisation'! 'Ardibeltza' has been banned, but a similar paper has since started on the French side of the Basque Country called Kalegorria. www.kalegorria.net (in Euskal/Spanish)

THE ITALIAN JOB

"In my opinion these raids were meant to intimidate some of the only independent media in the country. Now that Berlusconi has given more money to RAI, the Italian equivalent of the BBC, he has direct control or influence over 90% of Italian print and radio media, state owned or otherwise."
– Indymedia spokesperson.

On Wednesday morning, the Carabinieri (Italian paramilitary police) raided three social centres that were partly being used as offices for Indymedia. Two attorneys from Genoa gave the order for the nation-wide operation in which police seized computers, archives, and equipment as part of an ongoing enquiry investigating the events of last summers anti G8 protest in Genoa. The raid was meant to confiscate footage and info on the brutal police raid of two buildings during the protests (see SchNEWS 314/315). These were being used for accommodation, medical, media and legal services by protestors and the raids received international condemnation. Amnesty and the United Nations have each ordered independent enquiries into police conduct.

One of the social centres raided was the Cobas Trade Union centre, which with over 10,000 members is the biggest of its kind in Italy. During the raids police confiscated over 160 hours of original video footage of the protests including film of the murder of Carlo Gulliani by police and the school raid. Two days ago Italian Defence minister Skajola admitted that he did in fact give the order of 'shoot to kill' if any sizeable number of people moved into the red zone during the protests. A spokesperson from Indymedia told SchNEWS, "It's not likely that they will use the stuff they've nicked from Indymedia to properly investigate and try the police for murder and excessive violence. We reckon they'll just use it to identify and arrest more protestors…they already have loads of cctv footage of the protests, why else would they need ours too?"

Indymedia was established in Seattle to cover the protests against the World Trade Organisation, and the idea has now spread across the world. In the Berlusconi controlled media world of Italy, Indymedia is one of the few independants – during the G8 demonstrations they were getting over one million hits a day.

A demonstration will take place at the Italian embassy in London on Saturday. There will also be a demo in Rome on March, 16th. http://italy.indymedia.org Check out www.indymedia.org.uk for updates.

POSITIVE SchNEWS

Question: How do you turn a vegetable into a dangerous pollutant?
Answer: Simple, just put it in the bin!
As much as 40 per cent of what households throw away in their bins is compostable, and yet the UK currently composts just 3 per cent of its total waste. So instead of being put in a compost bin and being turned into an amazing organic pick-me-up for the garden, it gets thrown into landfill sites where it produces methane, a potent 'greenhouse' gas and 'leachate', a liquid pollutant which can contaminate ground water supplies. Composted household waste - ideally home made - is an excellent alternative to using peat. Alternatively you can buy peat free compost, or hold of some animal dung. For a guide to home composting check out www.hdra.org.uk/

SchNEWS in brief

This years **Big Brother Awards** are being held on 4th March at the London School of Economics. To check out the nominations for Worst Public Servant and Most Henious Government Organisation go to www.privacyinternational.org/bigbrother/uk2002/ ** **Street Medic** training weekend, essential first aid training for activists. 9-10 March at the film Akademie, overtoom 301, Amsterdam. Details cia_infocafe@disinfo.net ** The next **Mayday 2002** meeting is taking place on Sunday 24th Feb at The Calthorpe Arms pub on Grays Inn Road, London 2pm** **Central America** Conference with speakers from the continent, food and creche 9 March at Liverpool Institute for Performing Arts, Mount Street, Liverpool, and Sunday 10 March at The Casa, 29 Hope Street £12/5. Info and tickets from ruth@esnet.co.uk ** A strike at a Paris McDonalds that has been going on since October has ended in victory, with the workers winning their right to go **back to work**- lucky them!. This was the longest strike in McDonalds history www.ainfos.ca ** A planning meeting for possible actions during the next **NATO conference** in Prague at the end of the year is being held from 9-10th March For more info email: intersec@csaf.cz ** A community conference on the proposed changes to the council system in Brighton and Hove organised by '**Our Power**' 23rd Feb 2-5pm at Brighthelm Centre www.ourpower.org.uk

AVIN' A PEASANT TIME

During the 1970's a number of peasant struggles started in Pakistan, with the most successful and militant land-grab taking place in Hashtnangar, an area close to the Pakistan-Afghan border. Organised by the Mazdoor Kissan Party (MKP), the peasants were able to liberate the area from feudal land-owners, who had always brutally oppressed the poor with the full backing of the state. Since those days, Hashtnagar remains a liberated area despite several attempts by the state to evict the peasants, with nearly 300 people losing their lives in 30 years of conflict.

Taking advantage of the "War-Against-Terrorism" hysteria, the Pakistani government is once again trying to take-over the lands of Hashtnagar. They also aim to retake Okkara, Khanewal, Sargodha and Pak-pattan in other parts of the country in order to reverse gains made by the peasant movement in Pakistan over the past 10 years.. On 22nd January, 3,500 police armed with guns, tear-gas shells, armoured vehicles and jeeps attacked the village. Tractors were used to destroy peasant crops. MKP party activists and students surrounded the armoured vehicles to stop them firing into the crowd. Police attacked another village several kilometers away in the hope that they would have an easier time of it since the men of the village weren't around. The peasant women attacked the convoy and again the police had to retreat. The same night police arrested a peasant leader called Gulab Gul.

In retaliation peasants attacked a police convoy, capturing some police officers, before going on to raid the police station where Gul was being held. Peasants then threatened to burn down the police station if their leader was not released! The entire area was surrounded by police arresting people who hadn't even participate in the fighting. 16 arrests were made in total, 8 of which were of people so old they couldn't even walk properly without support. The situations is very tense and may erupt into full scale armed conflict at any time. www.ptb.be/international/

Inside SchNEWS

Ulla Roder, an anti-trident nuclear protestor was arrested at the Faslane anti-Trident Blockade last Wednesday, is being held on remand until the 25th March. Ulla has refused to accept restrictive bail conditions and so police have said they will hold her for five weeks, even though this amount of time is far in excess of any sentence she would receive for the actual 'offence.' Write to Ulla at Cornton Vale Women's Prison, Stirling, Scotland SK9 5NU.

FIRED UP

Last Friday part of Yarl's Wood detention centre in Bedfordshire, which only opened in November, was burnt down. The fire followed disturbances after an elderly detainee was being moved to hospital in handcuffs after a three-day delay.

At Yarl's Wood, as with other detention centres, asylum seekers are locked up prison-style. According to Emma Ginn from the Campaign to Stop Arbitrary Detention only 4 % of asylum seekers in centres are awaiting removal deportation, most haven't even had a hearing. There have been almost constant hunger strikes in protest at conditions since November. 07786 517379 www.stoparbitrarydetentionsatyarlswood.co.uk/

FOR PEAT'S SAKE

On Monday activists stormed six UK offices, plants and peat extraction sites in protest against the destruction of rare peat bog habitats. The actions were part of the campaign against Scotts, the worlds biggest horticultural multinational.

Peat Alert is a recently formed national campaign network, which aims to stop peat extraction in the UK and Europe. Danielle Locke, a spokesperson for the network explains, "Some of the most diverse and exciting habitats on this island are being systematically destroyed by the peat industry. Thorne and Hatfield Moors, Britain's two largest Peat bogs which support over 5,500 species, are being turned into grow bags by US Multinational Scotts. Once again, the call for resistance must go out to defend what little nature we have left."

The Moors are home to 25 endangered species and are an essential haven for fast disappearing peat bog bio-diversity. English Nature, Peat Alert and Thorne and Hatfield Conservation Forum say that despite decades of extraction having severely degraded Hatfield Moor, regeneration is possible if peat extraction is stopped. In a few years they reckon there won't be enough peat left to allow this diverse bog ecosystem to re-establish itself. Scotts disagree, claiming that the hydrology of the peat bogs is so badly damaged by years of peat working, it can no longer be restored and is not worth protecting. So, they're gonna keep digging rather than handing the sites back to English Nature to conserve.
* Easter blockade 2002! 25–28 March. 4 days of direct action at the Scotts Peat works, Hatfield Moor, near Doncaster. Bring tents and equipment, food provided. 0113 2629365 www.peatalert.org.uk

...and finally...

Fourteen activists were banged up in Guildford nick for ten hours on Monday after police arrested them for the burglary - of three pieces of paper! After a seemingly smooth Peat Alert office occupation against horticulture multinational Scotts, the activists who were driving home, were considering writing a book on 'how to plan and execute the perfect action' when they were pulled over by police and nicked. They have now been dubbed the Guildford 14 (plus one).

Subscribe!
Keep SchNEWS FREE! Send 1st Class stamps (e.g. 10 for next 9 issues) or donations (payable to Justice?) Ask for "Originals" if you can make copies. Post *free* to all prisoners. SchNEWS, c/o on-the-fiddle, P.O. Box 2600, Brighton, East Sussex, BN2 0EF.
Tel/Autofax +44 (0)1273 685913 *Email* schnews@brighton.co.uk *Download a* **PDF** *of this issue or subscribe at* www.schnews.org.uk

Orthodox Jews burn Israeli flag

March 30: This week, orthodox Jews around the world - including Jews in Manchester and London - burnt the Israeli flag to show their opposition to the Zionist state.

Rabbi Yisroel Dovid Weiss, spokesman for Neturei Karta International announced:

"The Zionist experiment has reached its inevitable conclusion. Death tolls mount and no viable solution is in sight. Slowly the Jewish people are awakening to the reality of Zionism... By burning the Israeli flag we are symbolically declaring that the Israeli state, contrary to its absurd claims, is not representative of the Jewish people. In fact, its denial of our faith and its brutalization of the Palestinian people, renders it antithetical to Judaism.

Zionism refuses to accept our status as people in exile. It is the task of world Jewry to remain patriotic citizens of the lands of their dispersion and pursue peace with all men. In the Holy Land, this means welcoming Palestinian sovereignty over the land. Accordingly, we will carry the Palestinian flag at the flag burnings."

Italian Indymedia Raid

By Samantha Savage

When media activist Andrea 'Blutaz' Masu awoke in the early hours of 20 February he found himself face to face with a member of the infamous Carabineiri paramilitary police force. 'Who are you?' shouted the uniformed officer who had one of Blutaz's video cameras in his arms. 'No, who are you?' Blutaz replied from his makeshift bed.

It has since emerged that the police raid on Italy Indymedia's Bologna base (http://italy.indymedia.org) had been ordered as part of an on-going government intimidation campaign. Since the now infamous anti-G8 protests which unfolded in July last year, several independent news operators across Italy have been targeted by the government including Indymedia and Rome-based Radio Onda Rossa, which had its broadcast licence withdrawn earlier this year.

'It wasn't just Bologna', explained 27 year-old Blutaz, who has been trying to find ways to continue his film-making and journalism since his equipment was seized. 'The police raided social centres throughout Italy ... Florence, Turin and the COBAS trade union offices in Taranto [a city in southern Italy] all on the same day.'

The official search warrant - carried out to seize materials on behalf of the Genoa Public Prosecutor - stated that the raid was aimed at gathering information on the violence "committed both by the protesters and against the protesters". It identified Italy Indymedia as being a crucial web-based point of information-gathering throughout the protests and stated that the raid was aimed at building up a "complete reconstruction of the events". Until now the Italian government has undertaken three limited enquiries into the summit-based violence and has yet to bring any official to justice. Several protesters - both from Italy and further afield - face long jail sentences on conspiracy charges connected largely to property destruction.

Many groups - including Amnesty International, the United Nations and representatives at the European Parliament - have continued to call for a genuinely independent enquiry into the bloody events which unfolded in Genoa last year and there is a growing sense of disquiet about the official explanation for the raids. "We want justice, of course we do ... Genoa was an outrage", explained Matteo, an Italian media activist who has been monitoring events in his homeland. "These raids were completely political - the police have got all the footage they could need ... they had helicopters and CCTV cameras everywhere ... also, they didn't raid any of the mainstream media ... The government has failed to give us a genuine enquiry and these raids are everything to do with intimidation and have nothing to do with justice".

Indymedia Italy are now challenging the state's decision to carry out the raid and there have been several mass actions across Italy, including Reclaim the Media Day in Rome on 16 March which saw a reported 20,000 on the capital's streets. There were also solidarity protests in several countries including an action in London in late February which saw people gather at the Italian embassy to tie video tape to the columns of the swanky Belgravia-based consulate.

Within Italy the mood of repression is growing. The March raids on Indymedia Italy were carried out by over 200 policeman backed up by dozens of armoured personnel carriers. Blutaz recounted the situation with disbelief and compared it to his first-hand experience during the notorious school raids which took place in Genoa last year. "I think my lucky angel must be having a holiday - I was in the school opposite Diaz on the night that it was raided and when I woke up to see a Carabineire officer staring at me that morning in Bologna I thought I was dreaming".

Pertini School - the building opposite the Diaz school where dozens of sleeping protesters were beaten and hospitalised by police officers in July last year - had hosted the international Indymedia network for the duration of the G8 summit. Police destroyed computers, media equipment and communications facilities during the raid and a legal battle for compensation is on-going. Pertini

Some Important Dates For Indymedia

January 1994: Indigenous people and supporters take control of Chiapas region in southern Mexico as part of the Zapatista uprising which rejects Mexican government controls and US interference. A new movement is born which utilises the Internet in an unprecedented manner as part of an attempt to internationalise their struggle

May 1998: Thousands of protesters from around the world converge on Geneva, Switzerland having organised one of the first and most effective global days of action;

The web is highlighted as the principle tool of international communcation

June 1999: Across the world people occupy financial centres in an effort to draw attention to the role played by banks in creating world poverty. London's financial heart - The City - is besieged with protesters who organise a flow of information direct from the streets to a web-uploading facility in the south of the capital. It is little known that J18 Sydney sewed the seeds for IndyMedia. Sydney based Catalyst created 'active' websites [www.active.org.au] based on a open publishing system. Their code is now used by the majority of Indymedia sites.

November 1999: People from across the world converge on Seattle, USA to shut down the World Trade Organisation (WTO). Indymedia makes its world debut with a full database-driven web presence

and for the first time people can upload their reports from anywhere in the world; Indymedia website gets more hits than the CNN website for the duration of the WTO summit

May Day 2000: International demonstrations see mass protests from Sydney to London; Mexico City to Milan; Bombay to Buenos Aries. UK Indymedia is launched under the shadow of a mohicaned Winston Churchill amidst the chaos of the Guerrilla Gardening action in Parliament Square

September 2000: Thousands descend on Prague, Czech Republic to shut down the 55th annual general meeting of the World Bank and the International Monentary Fund (IMF). The international Indymedia network is bolstered as DIY media activists from across the globe meet face-to-face, often for the first time

also played host to the umbrella group Genoa Social Forum (GSF) along with a range of other groups including legal teams, medical teams and radio project Radio G.A.P (www.radiogap.net) who also had equipment destroyed or seized.

The announcement in March by Italian Prime Minister - Silvio Berlusconi - to appoint several of his political allies to key executive posts within the Italian state-owned broadcasting corporation RAI has sent ripples across the Italian political system. Italian commentators have dubbed their own state a 'Banana Republic' and have called into question whether freedoms of expression can be guaranteed given that Berlusconi now personally owns - or has direct financial control over - 80% of the country's entire TV network.

"In Italy the state has a strong control over the press" explained Blutaz. "Indymedia Italy turned that on its head in Genoa - we issued hundreds of press passes to an army of dedicated DIY journalists ... now the state wants its revenge".

A film detailing the events around Genoa and the situation following the protests in light of the clamp down on civil liberties titled 'Genoa Red Zone' is due for release from late May. Check http: //uk.indymedia.org for further information.

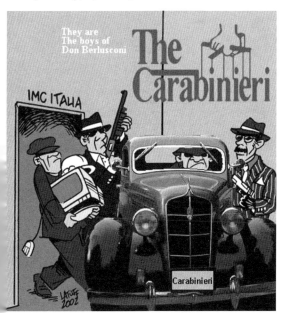

Carabinieri Style Attack In UK
by IMC-UK 12:09pm Sat Feb 23 '02

London police think they are Carabinieri as they attack peaceful demo outside the Italian embassy

At 2PM 35 people congrated outside the Italian embassy in Grosvenor Square in London in a peaceful protest with banners saying TELL THE TRUTH and SIAMO TUTTI INDYMEDIA (WE ARE ALL INDYMEDIA), holding video cassettes to symbolise the seizing of film in Italy. Video tape was also strung across the embassy front, and leaflets explaining the demo, the Italian IMC press release and the statement from the Italian legal team (who were also raided) were handed out.

Everything was calm and peaceful for 10 to 15 minutes with a small samba band playing until one police car turned up and the officers started to attack the crowd, pushing people off the pavement into the road. When people voiced objections and the legal right to protest, they were punched in their faces and batons were drawn.

One officer with number 320 repeatedly attacked peaceful demonstrators even after they had moved off the pavement. Several people have been injured, and 2 arrested.

One police officer was heard to say "I DONT GIVE A FUCK ABOUT THE LAW".

The protestors moved to the square/park and were being trailed by police when this report was coming in. Eventually seven police cars and six vans turned up. More reports later, including stills and video.

Two people have been arrested and later released with the charges of public disorder and threatening behaviour. They are due to appear in Court next Wednesday.

April 2001: Indymedia networks in Canada follow protesters as they successfully breach security at the Summit of Americas conference in Quebec, Canada.

June 2001: Indymedia Sweden break the story when police in Gothenburg shoot and injure a demonstrator as thousands force their way into a business-dominated European Council meeting

July 2001: 300,000 people arrive in the Italian city of Genoa to protest against the G8 and the decisions it takes. World leaders from eight of the world's most powerful economies meet to a chorus of discontent; Protester Carlo Giuliani is shot dead. Indymedia Italy has its offices raided as police beat sleeping protesters

September 2001: New York Indymedia launches 911 - a humanist video exploring

the contradictions in state and fundamentalist terrorism

November 2001: Indymedia Argentina reports live from the Latin American state as the economy and political system collapses after IMF-imposed austerity packages drive poverty stricken Argentinians to the point of starvation

March 2002: Indymedia Jerusalem is launched days before the brutal invasion of the Palestinian territory by the Israeli armed forces; Indymedia remains online throughout and provides a crucial line of information from the besieged state.

April 2002: Desert IndyMedia sets up in the back of a truck at the Woomera protest camp, Australia and provides incredible footage and photos of the break out of detained refugees.

There are now Indymedia groups in the following countries:

Congo	Czech Republic
Nigeria	Finland
South Africa	France
Zimbabwe	Germany
Argentina	Greece
Brazil	Ireland
Canada	Italy
Chiapas	Netherland
Colombia	Norway
Mexico	Portugal
United States	Russia
Uruguay	Spain
Israel	Sweden
India	Switzerland
Palestine	UK
Australia	Wales
New Zealand	**New IMC sites**
Indonesia	Bolivia
Austria	Basque Country
Belgium	Tijuana

High Priority: Priory Park, Southend

"The ancient Priory of Prittlewell must be perpetually used as a public park." With these words in 1917, local businessman Robert Jones donated the area now known as Priory Park in Southend on Sea, Essex, to the local council to stop planners building on it.

However, in yet another example of local councils overruling public interests with commercial ones, the residents of Southend have been fighting council's proposal to widen an existing road through the centre of town at the cost of a significant strip of land and several hundred mature trees in the town's most popular park. Not only does the park contain Prittlewell Priory, founded in 1110 with gardens and fountains, and function as the lungs of the town, it is also an area of wildlife diversity with squirrels, tawny owls, kestrels, two species of woodpeckers, bats, rooks and more.

However in 2001 the local council unveiled plans for the dual carriageway relief road around the northern side of the town centre, despite a previous failed attempt in 1974. But they were unprepared for the local backlash and almost immediately the Priory Park Preservation Society was born, and the campaign was taken up by free local newspaper *The Yellow Advertiser*. Since then all sections of the community have joined in demonstrations in the park and outside the civic centre. Twelve petitions with over 18,000 signatures were sent to the council, as well as one to Southend's MP Teddy Taylor as *The Yellow Advertiser* publicised the campaigns. It did a cut-out-and-send coupon campaign, of which the council received 26,000, and initiated the yellow ribbon campaign - with yellow ribbons appearing everywhere from car aerials to bicycles, in peoples' windows as well as around the condemned trees.

In response, the council decided to hold a public consultation (as if they hadn't got the message by now) by sending out calls for public responses in another local rage more likely to tow the party line - *Civic News*. The response to this, though much smaller was still blatantly opposed. Yet despite the tremendous amount of community action to 'Save Priory Park', all the alternative plans proposed by the council involves some of the park going. They see it as part of the 'regeneration of the town'. There's also the small matter of the Thames Gateway - a plan to create a new freight and commercial port at Shell Haven, the old Shell Oil plant, situated on the Thames estuary between Southend and London, and housing developments to accompany it. It's the usual circus of behind the scenes business deals and backhanders. The campaign continues. Visit www.ppps.org.uk

Women Speak Out
Radical Dairy, London, 8-10 March

Women Speak Out is a gathering for women interested or involved in DIY political, social and environmental activities. The weekends have provided squatted autonomous space for workshops, discussions, food and music. There have now been five events, last year's was held in Brighton in June 2001, and this year's in London on 8-10th March 2002 at the Radical Dairy coinciding with International Womens Day.

Women Speak Out is an exclusively women only space, an idea that has become quite controversial. Numerous activist men *and women* have said that they do not understand why there is a need for women only spaces, and while admittedly there are many women who do not need spaces like these for their support, there are many that do. For many these spaces offer a gateway into alternative politics and ideas.

The direct action movement values outspoken, assertive, confident and self-assured people, which is understandable given its DIY, "take-control-of-your-life" goals. The problem is, however, that while direct action validates all of these often positive traits, there is seldom room for anything else. Meetings or events filled with assertive, type-A activists - be they male or female - often leave people who don't interact in this way feeling marginalised and ignored. This is just one of the problems that women-only spaces seek to address.

During the weekend at the Radical Dairy there were some very different workshops, such as a talk from the group FORWARD – who oppose female genital mutilation; WEN, who came to show us radical composting; Hackney Cycling Campaign, who did a 'cycling for the terrified' session; and then workshops on rape survivors, body image, creative writing, cartooning and lots more. Saturday night was given over to a performance of the Vagina Monologues by all the women in the room (we're v. experimental y'know); bands The Sisters of No Mercy and The Drag King Ska band, with Little Lou on the decks.

Women only space is not anti-male, nor is it a condemnation of male activists. To the writers of this article, it is simply a way of creating an alternative - offering women an opportunity to interact, connect, and network in ways that may be overlooked or overshadowed by the larger activist community. We need women-only spaces to give us the confidence to behave and speak as we like so we can take that confidence out into our daily lives. No place should be dismissed if it is a source of strength and solidarity between people - if it allows people to become more fierce and defiant in challenging all aspects of the oppressive capitalist system that we all live in.

For details of the next gathering, which would be fantastic if held somewhere up North, email: womenspeakout@yahoogroups.com.

* Also, to mark International Womens Day there was an action at Holloway Prison. On 8 March, 20 or so women held a roving noise demo at the London women's prison to highlight the growing numbers of working class women being imprisoned for crimes of poverty. Women inside the prison were really responsive and waved and shouted back to those on the outside, and one group on the outside managed to stop a van containing women prisoners from entering the gates for 45 minutes.

WAKE UP! WAKE UP! IT'S YER SON OF A BITCH

THIS WILL TAKE HUNDREDS OF YEARS

weekly SchNEWS

www.schnews.org.uk

Friday 1st March 2002   **Free/Donation**   **Issue 344**

LADIES OF THE FIGHT

On March 2nd hundreds of women kicked off in the streets of London's West End. Armed with stones and hammers they smashed windows in Regent Street, Piccadilly, the Strand and Oxford Street, causing thousands of pounds worth of damage. Three women leapt out of a car in Downing Street and threw stones at the Prime Minister's house and the home office. Altogether about 120 women were arrested, 80 years ago, in 1912.

March 2nd marks 80 years since this mass suffragette demo. Protests took over the streets for nine months before women realised they would have to step up their militancy to get their voices heard. Women started burning the turf of golf courses with acid spelling "VOTES FOR WOMEN", breaking street lamps, torching letterboxes, chaining themselves to Buckingham Palace gates and attacking politicians on their way to work. Women planted bombs in empty houses and unused railway stations. They started massive fires. In February 1913 women blew up part of David Lloyd George's house - probably Britain's most famous politician at that time. Their first suffragette martyr was Emily Davison, killed when she threw herself under the Kings horse in June of 1913.

A year later over 1,000 suffragettes had been sent to prison for destroying public property. The jailbirds went on hunger strikes, and after the policy of force-feeding started looking too hard-line, the government watered down their response with the Cat and Mouse Act. This stopped the force-feeding, allowing the women to go on hunger strikes, and to get weaker and weaker. When they were very weak they were kicked out of prison so any deaths would not embarrass the government.

Forty years of peaceful protesting failed to win any changes for women. Women's suffrage only became a national issue when the suffragettes turned to violence. The first windows were smashed in 1908 and direct action continued until World War I. Once British women had gained the vote a token gesture in any democracy - the struggle continued.

The First International Women's Day took place in 1908. Nine years later, after months of struggles and strikes, thousands of Russian women took to the streets to protest food shortages, high prices, the world war, and general impoverishment. Their defiance led to the last push of the revolution, and within a week Czar Nicholas II had gone. This day, the March the 8th, 1917, was then adopted as the official date for International Women's Day. In the early days International Women's Day was celebrated as a socialist holiday honouring working women. The third annual International Global Women's Strike has upped the profile of protests across the world on the same day.

Next Friday thousands of women will take to the streets and continue the centuries old traditions of disobedience twenty-first century style.

LASS IS MORE

This year's protests are being called as a reaction against the US government's militarist response to September 11. Women's groups are pointing out that amongst the hysteria nothing was said of the 35,000 children who died of hunger that same day, and every day, as a consequence of the policies of the World Bank and the International Monetary Fund. More than $800 billion is squandered globally in military budgets that destroy life and guarantee the submission of Third World countries to globalization. The US government has already invested $40 billion in this new war.

Demonstrations are planned in over 60 countries to highlight these global injustices as well as calling for recognition of women's unpaid, underpaid and undervalued work in and out of the home. In previous years' demonstrations, men have been forced to stay indoors for the night in the Colombian capital of Bogota and those that snuck out were pelted with eggs and flour. Meanwhile women in Uganda held a co-ordinated sit-down across the country, which led to the awarding of free hospital services.

Masked-up sex workers marched through Soho to protest against the council's attempts to evict them from their homes, and against trafficking being used as an excuse for deportations.

This year's planned demos range from one woman in Bolivia who has announced that she's planning to go on the game to support her family to huge high profile marches expected to attract thousands of protestors.

In India groups are organizing a meet-

ing in Pithora where village women will put their demands to officials. They are calling for equal pay for equal work, land rights, safe drinking water, health and medical facilities, removing "untouchability" against Dalit people, and a bonus for Tendu leaf (smoke stick business that Tribal women particularly work in). "We are also raising our voice against globalisation, the World Trade Organisation, and the IMF which is affecting our people adversely."

In Argentina The Sindicato de Amas de Casa (Housewives Union) in Santa Fe which has co-ordinated the Strike since 2000, is holding daily women's assemblies in the poorest neighbourhoods as part of the popular uprising.

Women in London will be bringing pots, pans, and brooms into the town centre for an Argentinian-styled "cacerolazos" – pots and pans protest - in solidarity with their South American sisters. These noisy protests have become a feature of Argentinian life since last year's economic collapse. The first massive cacerolazos protest against IMF/World Bank policies brought down the government last December. Banging on pots and pans – the "tools of the trade" of those who do the vital but unrecognised work of feeding and caring, has become the symbol of the Argentinian uprising. The pots are now empty in most Argentinian households, but they are loud.

The London Strike Committee have organised a Whistle Stop Tour to Sweep Out the Global Killers: taking in Shell, Ministry of Defence, Institute of Directors and finishing at the World Bank. Lesbian/bisexual women are invited to march with the Dykes on Strike contingent. Rhythms of Resistance will be round for drum & dance Samba! Women mental health system survivors will protest outside a psychiatric hospital based near Shell.

Contact: International Wages for Housework Campaign, Crossroads Women's Centre, 230a Kentish Town Rd. NW5 2AB 020 7482 2496 http://womenstrike8m.server101.com

* *The Transfiguring Sword: The Just War of the Women's Social and Political Union.* Cheryl R. Jorgensen-Earp, University of Alabama, 1997.

* *The Disinherited Family.* Eleanor Rathbone, Falling Wall Press 1986

BUSHED AROUND

13 Bushmen from the Gana and Gwi tribes have been arrested on their ancestral land in the Central Kalahari Game reserve in Botswana, for hunting without a license. Despite having lived by hunting and gathering in the same area for 20,000 years, the government is now forcing the Bushmen to apply for hunting licenses! The accused were severely beaten and now face 5 years imprisonment. Two Bushmen bringing food and water to the communities whose supplies had been cut off by the government were told that entry to their ancestral lands was forbidden. The two were later allowed in but were told that in future they would have to have a special permit or pay to enter the reserve.

The Central Kalahari Game Reserve was set up in the 1960's as a home for the Gana and Gwi Bushmen, whose ancestral lands include the reserve area. Yet since the mid-1980's, the Botswana government has waged a campaign of harassment to force them off land that is theirs under international law. Last week they terminated supplies of water and food to those who were still resisting. They also seized solar powered radio transceivers, provided by Survival International, their only source of communication with the outside world. Hundreds of Bushmen have been trucked into government resettlement camps where they can't continue their traditional way of life. The families who remain on their land are now totally isolated and at risk from thirst and starvation.

The government claims it can't afford to continue to provide water and other services to Bushmen communities in the reserve, even though it costs only $3 per person per week. Behind the government's attitude is a deep-seated racism - the president himself has called the Bushmen 'stone-age creatures.' His government wants to open the reserve to tourism, and believes the Bushmen would be in the way. SchNEWS wonders if the areas rich diamond reserves may also have something to do with it. Info: 020-7687-8731 www.survival-international.org

POSITIVE SchNEWS

The Slough Environmental Education Development Service (SEEDS) have been busy in that most sexy of towns since 1997 "linking environmental and social justice through the principals of earth care, people care and fair shares." Projects include teaching kids in 17 schools about the environment and getting them to grow trees themselves, from seeds, that are then planted out in tree nurseries and eventually in the school grounds. The Herschel Park Extension project is a 10-acre local nature reserve on an old landfill site where over 2000 native trees have been planted and a one-acre wildflower meadow created. A Woodland Crafts Skills Pilot Project is providing training to disadvantaged and excluded groups, with a derelict coppice in the Chilterns being managed and the materials used for making craft products.

For the future SEEDS is hoping to establish a permanent crafts workshop at the old Council Nurseries, and tapping into the diversity of the towns population – with Asian, Afro-Caribbean gardens etc. – to supply organic vegetables to local people.

As Janine, one of the workers of the project explains "I find myself apologising for living here sometimes – but I shouldn't. This is so exactly the sort of area where the principles behind our work can make such a huge impact on peoples lives and for future generations."

SEEDS, 1st Floor 29 Church Street, Slough, SL1 1PL Tel 01753 693819 Email: theseedstrust@netscapeonline.co.uk

SchNEWS in brief

Benefit for the **no to Sainsbury's campaign**, Albert Pub, Trafalgar St, 7pm Monday 4th with bands and the MayBug Ball Video. ** The **2002/3 Animal Contacts Directory** is out now. An impressively comprehensive directory of everybody involved in animal welfare: from hunt sabs, to riot grannies and sancturies for donkies from the Holy Land. Get your copy from Veggies, 245 Gladstone Street, Nottingham NG7 6HX Tel 0845 4589595 £4.95 + 85p p&p www.veggies.org.uk ** Joint **Worthing Eco-Action** and **Protect Our Woodland** meeting to decide on what to do about council plans to cover Titnore Woods with concrete. Tuesday 5th 7.45pm @ the Downview pub, West Worthing station. www.worthinga27.freeserve.co.uk ** **Aspire**, Leeds' occasional squat venue opening today. Free gigs, parties, radical films, good food and other things www.a-spire.org.uk 07796 343085 ** **Last chance rally opposing GM trials** in Long Marston 9th March Startford Upon Avon Town Hall 12pm start, coaches to the field trial at 2pm. Transport from around the country 020-72721586 ** **Injustice**, the film about deaths in police custody has been screened at the Crown Prosecution Service and the Attorney General has agreed to meet with families of those that have died. It's also being shown at the Duke of York's in Brighton on 10th March, 4pm. www.injusticefilm.co.uk ** Last year Argentinas economy went into freefall, leading to massive riots and strikes (SchNEWS 336). **Argentina Arde** (Argentina burns) a documentary on the uprising and its brutal suppression by the police. See it at a special SchNEWS screening 11th March 8pm upstairs at the Albert pub, Brighton.

Fartin' Around

Last week Dutch activists caused a stink at a carbon trading conference in Amsterdam. Armed with water pistols, blue wigs and "farting-gas" they held up the conference for 2 hours. But their demands for an immediate 60% reduction in greenhouse gases was not met, instead 13 of them were arrested. Carbon trading is a dubious capitalist scheme, which claims to deal with global warming by giving emission reductions a monetary value which can be traded. Unfortunately it probably won't make much difference for the climate, but it will undoubtedly make a lot of fat cats even fatter. .www.risingtide.nl

Police Lose Face

A man who was arrested outside the Labour Party Conference last September for wearing a Palestinian flag as a face mask, has won his appeal against the conviction. He was charged under Section 60 of the Public Order Act for failure to remove his facial covering.

A solicitor told SchNEWS: "...the judge said that police had overstepped the mark: that it was wrong for the police to ask everyone to remove facial masks – and then arrest anyone who didn't comply – unless they had reason to believe that a person was deliberately concealing their face."

Police will get the message that they can't assume things like cycle masks at critical masses are an offence. The good thing about doing demos in Britain is that it always rains - the perfect legal reason for needing that toasty balaclava.

Inside SchNEWS

On the 19th February, Dr Margaret Jones was sent down for 40 days by the Bristol Magistrats court for painting stuff like, "What have Iraqi's ever done to deserve this?" "UK Iraq policy equals atrocities and failure" on the Foreign Office building. Her other 'crimes' were cutting a hole in the fence at Aldermaston where nuclear weapons are kept and 'breach of the peace' for sitting down at Faslane. Write to Margaret at: Eastwood park prison, Eastwood Park, Falfield, Wotton Under Edge, Gloucestershire.

GREAT SCOTT!!

On Wednesday the UK government announced that US multinational Scotts will be paid £17.4 million to immediately hand over Thorne Moor, in Yorkshire and Wedholme Flow in Cumbria to English Nature, the government wildlife watchdog. The Government has decided to buy the company's peat extraction rights in order to turn the moors into nature reserves.

However, another site, Hatfield Moor, which is a Site of Special Scientific Iinterest, will continue to be degraded for a further two years even though Scotts is being paid shedloads to sling its hook.

The campaign to stop peat mining on these moors has been going on for over 10 years, but according to Craig Bennet from Friends of the Earth, "little was achieved until campaigners started targeting specific companies and retailers... Now we have to really focus on pressuring retailers and companies so that we don't just export the problem. Environmental groups in other countries haven't woken up to the peat issue yet and it is our duty to export the campaign to the rest of the world."

Last week, environmental activists occupied seven of Scotts office buildings, factories and peat extraction sites as the latest in a series of direct-action protests against the company – and the planned Easter blockade of Hatfield Moor is still going ahead with Peat Alert declaring "We should also target other companies such as Sinclairs and Westlands who will continue to extract peat after Scotts pull out."

* Easter blockade 25-29 March 0113-2629365 www.peatalert.org.uk

Hanging Around

Nine Greenpeace activists occupied a rubbish incinerator in Lewisham this week closing it down for nearly four days. The nine attached themselves to industrial rubbish grabbers and suspended themselves above a stinking mound of waste ! They were protesting at the discharge of dioxins which are known to cause cancer. Early on Thursday morning 'special' bailiffs were brought in and spent all day to get the protestors down off the grabbers. At the same time other protestors were sneakily working or sealing the flues. Speaking from the top of the chimney Greenpeace volunteer Mark Strutt said "We are 300 feet up and we intend to make it as difficult as we can for the bailiffs to get to us. We are sealing the chimney flues to keep this toxic plant closed for as long as possible. Every hour this incinerator remains shut we are protecting people from cancer causing chemicals and other poisonous gases."

The government has already admitted that one in three Britons are taking in the maximum amount of dioxins that is considered 'safe' and more than half of Britain's babies and toddlers exceed this limit. Info: 0207 8658255 www.greenpeace.org.uk

...and finally...

The Spanish government recently decided to stamp down on yob culture by banning drinking on the streets. In Madrid the local troublemakers were outraged and so took to the streets, national police in riot gear were called in to give 'em a good twatting. Unfortunately for them they weren't facing a load of pissheads, but the local municipal cops (protesting about the extra work this law would give them) who'd also been trained in unprovoked violence, and so gave a good as they got. Just proves that coppers don't care who they beat the shit out of. Pictures at www.stlimc.org front.php3?article_id=1775&group=webcast

Subscribe!

FORT BLOCKADE BUSTED AFTER 5 YEARS

Fort Gook

On March 5, 2002, the five year camp in the Goolengook Forest, in East Gippsland in South-East Australia, was busted. At the time the camp consisted of a fortress across the road complete with moat and drawbridge; tunnels, tree sits, bridge and culvert lock-ons, and five or six ferocious defenders. The raid took place at 4:30 in the morning, with a force of forty policeman and Department of Natural Resources and Environment (DNRE) officers, and as the defenders locked on, the officers burned the fort and all their belongings in a bonfire. The latest round of the battle for Goolengook had begun…

Logging On

Goolengook forest is in the remote far-east of Victoria. It contains 273 rare and endangered plant species and 43 endangered animal species – and the government's own scientists recommend that its delicate mosaic of warm and cool temperate rainforests be left entirely intact. In 1997, Goolengook was logged for the first time – with round one of the battle to save it leading to more than 300 arrests, including Tasmanian Greens Senator Bob Brown. Less than 100 hectares was clearfelled at this stage and the logging stopped but the camp remained. Tenaciously reinstalling a new system of defenses between the existing roads and the remaining old growth, a watch was kept. A de facto drop in centre for eastern Australian activists, Goolengook became a home, a training ground, and an icon of the precarious fate of one of Australia's last undisturbed forests.

Late in 1998, the coupes at Goolengook were burned with aerial napalm bombs as part of routine "management" of previously wet forests - five protestors were caught in the shower but luckily survived. Again in early 1999, Goolengook was invaded as bulldozers and chainsaws flattened hectares of forest – which led to "Woodstop," a "this-is-not-a-festival" of direct action. Goolen-geeks from across Australia returned home to the primeval forests to tell them loggers where to go. And go they did. But the camp remained. In early 2000, as part of a series of attacks against forest camps throughout Australia, eleven brave defenders were violently assaulted at the camp by a lynch mob of 50 loggers trying to scare them away. The camp remained. This time, we built a fort.

March 5 – April 9, 2002

The part of Goolengook under attack this time was in one of the National Sites of Biological Significance listed by the original surveys. It's the chunk of old growth between the two previously logged sets of coupes, spanning the untouched catchment of the Little Goolengook River. The law enforcement went up a few notches with the use – for the first time in Victoria – of "exclusion zones": prohibiting members of the public from a given area of crown land – on the word of the regional forestry manager alone. Worse, the zones moved from day to day, sometimes from hour to hour – and because of this cars were towed and impounded, possessions confiscated, and more than 75 people were arrested for "trespassing". Enforcing the exclusion zones for five weeks were 24 hour shifts of DNRE officers, as well as police who guarded the access roads to Goolengook, as well as logging machines.

Under this guard – and under floodlight at night - four coupes were logged at once. In response protesters took to the tactic known as 'Black Wallabies' where people run through the areas where trees are being felled, suddenly making it too dangerous to work. Bulldozer tracks, the pneumatic arms of log loaders, dragons in the road, culverts, and bridges were locked on to, treesits went up next to overnight cop camps along the coupe borders, and groups ran missions through the bush carrying food and supplies to them. There were nearly as many rescue camps as cop camps – on the road, in front of the gates, in the coupes, along the river. Still the forest factory was working full-tilt: and in five short weeks, another 100 hectares of Goolengook had been cleared.

There are more than 20 coupes scheduled to be logged in these areas over the next three years and while rumours fly about when and where that will be – one thing's for sure: we'll be there.

www.geco.org
www.goolengook.forests.org.au

Weld Valley, Tasmania

Tasmania's forests played host to blockades, festivals, community actions and sabotage over the 2002 logging season…….

The Weld community blockade in the south east of Tasmania was the first blockade camp in the area for five years. The picket was established in early February to save more than 3000 hectares of unlogged, old-growth forest in the Weld Valley, an area immediately adjacent to a World Heritage listed area. Forestry Tasmania has proposed 800,000 tonnes of woodchips to be removed from this and adjacent forests for incineration in the proposed Southwood Wood fired power station and industrial woodchipping complex. The camp was established in early February and busted four weeks later.

A week prior to the police raid of the Weld blockade $3m (£1.2m) of damage was caused to logging equipment in another coupe. Four specialised log excavators and other equipment was destroyed – and activists were labelled as 'eco-terrorists' with activist group Future Rescue picked on in a media expose. The police asserted that the culprits must have had knowledge of operating such machinery, and the pattern of previous similar vandalism clearly suggests that it was part of a logging contractor war.

For its duration the Weld Valley campaign was home to between 30 and 40 people. It consisted of a tree platform mounted 30 metres off the ground which was constantly maintained. Lines ran from the platform to a double locked forestry gate, locked once by forestry to stop public access, and then re-locked by the community to stop forestry. Activists also spread the action to a nearby old growth coupe in the Picton Valley by halting work and talking to workers.

On March 6th after almost twenty-four hours of intensive police build up in the nearby town of Huonville, police moved in at dusk to break up the camp. Police cordoned off the forest in which the camp was situated, denied media and local residents access and declared the area an exclusion zone. The people who were in camp, now within the exclusion zone, were issued with the command to leave or face arrest for trespassing. An independent cameraperson was initially arrested, then the two police liaisons who were asking why this person was arrested were both also both nicked for trespassing.

During every logging season right across Australia similar blockade camps and civil disobedience actions are held. Although it's devastating when a blockade is busted, forest campaigners are a determined and resilient bunch and the struggle is always maintained regardless of the police, the intimidation, the smear campaigns and the logging trucks.

...ling the golden gook

OSAMA'S TERRIBLE SECRET

The Titanic - "our iceberg was magnificent"

OSAMA BIN LADEN now admits to sinking the famous ocean liner.

"We had to time it to perfection - the plan was a masterpiece" he told SchNEWS Of The WORLD. "I just wished I'd had a hand in the number of lifeboats. That was the time to...

the icing on the cake. The whole plan was the work of genius. We learned a lot from it and moved onto more ambituous plots

Pie In The Sky

March 6th A group calling itself 'Pie in the Sky', part of the Rising Tide UK network, disrupted a top-level conference on the new market in trading carbon dioxide emissions at the London's Kensington Palace Hotel. The conference, titled 'Emissions Trading Schemes Objectives, Implementation and Future Opportunities', featured representatives from Shell, the International Emissions Trading Association, the UN, CO2e.com, DEFRA, KPMG and the EU, and last but not least – Pie In The Sky.

Making their unscheduled presentation a little after elevenses - as the Shell rep was waxing lyrical on the new profit opportunities presented by this new market in emissions – in came a suited-up posse with a banner reading 'Emissions trading? Pie in the sky!' and leaflets. The delegates were reminded that emissions trading was little more than a profit-making opportunity for the companies that were responsible for current huge levels of CO2 emissions, an insult to the people of the global south, whose lives and livelihoods are under threat (if not already underwater). A UN representative told a friendly leafletter to 'Piss off!', though remained silent when asked if he could be quoted. The 'Pie in the Sky'ers left the hotel when requested by security staff, leaving an email address on their leaflets in case anyone had further questions. It is not known to what extent the rest of the day's proceedings were eclipsed by the morning's unexpected events.

The Return Of Pie In The Sky

March 18th: A second London high-profile emissions tradi conference this time at Holborn's Kingsway Hall Hotel w disrupted by 'Pie in the Sky' on the 18th of March. Called 'Profiti from Opportunities Presented by the Kyoto Mechanisms', featured the quote 'Position yourself to grasp the outstandi opportunities offered to business and finance by the Kyo Protocol'. You couldn't make it up. Giving presentations we Arthur Andersen, EU, Swiss Re, WWF, CO2e.com, Shell, Frien Ivory & Sime, KPMG, 'The Environment Business' (don't kno who they are, but they sound dodgy), and Ernst & Young. Pie The Sky walked in, gave out leaflets, 'discussed' the issues w the delegates before the security forcibly ejected one, and othe remained to talk.

FBI PRESS CONFERENCE

Uuh... I'm afraid I can't give you any information on that,... uuh...yes, we are investigating into that matter at the moment ...uuh...no, I cannot tell you anything about that right now No...I am not in a position to talk about that... but we are in fact presently looking into these issues... no, I can't answer that.. Sorry, I do not have the authority to speak on this ... yes we are aware of this problem but I'm afraid I cannot go into details Of course we are doing everything in our power to gather more specific information and we will go to all necessary means to be able to achieve all those goals which we have defined here. ...Thank you you're welcome

WAKE UP! WAKE UP! IT'S YER OILY RAG

Weekly SchNEWS

www.schnews.org.uk

'...the oil drilling is going ok but the locals are giving us some trouble.'

Friday 8th March 2002   **Free/Donation**   **Issue 345**

OIL-DERADO

"If they are moving toward a violent solution, encouraging the military toward violence, then they are playing with fire. The business sector continues to criticise us. So why don't they do something to help this country, like bringing back the $120 billion they keep in banks overseas?"
- Tarek William Saab, Head of Venezuela's Foreign Policy Committee.

Three years ago Chávez was elected president of the fourth largest oil producer in the world. On a tide of public support he won with the biggest majority in four decades. The population of Venezuela were eager for drastic change. They wanted a government that would rid them of corruption and redirect the country's oil wealth from the pockets of multinationals and towards the poor of Venezuela. In Venezuela 80 per cent of a population of 24 million live in poverty.

Chávez set about changing the Constitution. Out went the prescribed Washington model of elections and political parties, and in came a participatory democracy with an emphasis on popular assemblies, social movements and continuous referendums. As a result Venezuela's new constitution now includes guarantees for indigenous, and women's rights, free healthcare and education up to university level.

To reduce corruption Chávez restructured the courts and the legal system. In a country where the prisons are amongst the most dilapidated and dangerous in the world he met with prisoners and convinced them to hand over their weapons while promising to look at the prison conditions and the injustices of their sentences.

He also introduced two new laws that have brought him to the edge of his demise and the country to the brink of a right-wing coup. Firstly, he increased the tax paid on oil exports from 16 to 30 per cent and passed a new energy law that requires 51 per cent government participation in all oil ventures.

Secondly he introduced a land reform bill. The bill makes it possible for the government to take land that has remained unproductive for 2 years and re-distribute it to the poor. Within the law there is provision that extends credit to any private farmer who wants to make his land productive rather than lose it. The bill is broad and does not differentiate between farm, private and church land.

These two laws have prompted powerful sections from the unions, middle class, rich, media, high ranking military officers and the Catholic Church inside Venezuela to call for Chávez's resignation. In the words of investigative journalist Greg Palast "the Church says the meek will inherit the earth, but not while they are alive."

The right-wing opposition are using tactics similar to those used to oust Salvador Allende in Chile during the early 1970s. The rich are being used to create a feeling of chaos and paint a picture of Chávez as the 'dictator'. The military will then be encouraged to mount a coup seemingly for the sake of the country.

No More Mr Nice Guy

Criticisms of Chávez's reforms outside of Venezuela have come from financial institutions, governments, and the CIA. The IMF is even willing to bankroll an interim government according to James Petras, professor at the State University of New York. He believes the IMF and other financial institutions are creating an economic crisis to oust Chávez. He says, "There is no economic crisis. The economic problems facing Chávez have always been there; they are problems that Chávez inherited. Venezuela is an oil rich country that pays its debts and follows IMF guidelines etc."

George Tenent, head of the CIA and Colin Powell, US Secretary of State have both been critical of Chávez. They claim that he is undercutting American foreign policy by opposing US counter-narcotics aid to Colombia, providing oil to Cuba and giving political support to guerrillas and anti-government forces in neighbouring Colombia.

While Chávez has a long history of 'irritating' the US by attacking its foreign policy he has been careful not to allow himself to become involved in the civil war in

Thorn in the Bush

Never one to miss an opportunity at winding up the US Chávez has:
*Sold oil to Cuba despite a ban imposed by the yanks.
*Wanted to start an OPEC Bank to lend money the worlds poorest countries.
*Turned down US offers of 'military' aid after the floods of Dec 99, fearing this would lead to a permanent US presence in the country
*Criticised Plan Colombia's massive military programme for threatening to "Vietnamize" the conflict.

Colombia. Chávez declared Venezuela neutral and has helped in the release of hostages from the FARC (Revolutionary Armed Forces of Colombia) and helped the Colombian government during the peace talks.

Chávez has a vision for a new world order "Rather than accepting the imposition of models and economic policies, what we should do is march in the direction of a system of international relations based on equality and mutual respect" he says.

Sounds like for a change there's a leader who's not prepared to sell his people up the river and go along with what neo-liberalism forces on his country. When four high ranking army officers called for him to be overthrown, each one was interviewed by a joint civilian and military team and released the next day. Imagine if that had happen here or in the US - the officers would have been charged with treason and thrown in prison.

James Petras, believes that "Chávez is an extremely moderate politician who is being hammered for not allowing drug-surveillance flights over Venezuela, being opposed to Plan Colombia (SchNEWS 273) and working with OPEC."

Perhaps the most important figure in the foreign-sponsored destabilisation campaign is Alfredo Peña, the Mayor of Caracas and critic of Chávez. Peña has been visiting Washington recently meeting with the World Bank and the state department and is being groomed to replace Chávez.

The irony of all this is that the backer of the coming coup, the US, is under the administration of a president who stole the presidency in a coup d'etat.

According to Greg Palast "No one wants to stand next to President Hugo Chávez of Venezuela these days, much less be in the same room as him. He is a dead man walking. It's not so much a case of if he gets assassinated it's just a matter of when".

For more info on dodgy dealings in Latin and North America visit: www.rebelion.org , www.el-nacional.com

SchNEWS recommended read: *'The Best Democracy Money Can Buy'* by Greg Palast published by Pluto Press. 'Exposing the Truth about Globalization, Corporate Cons and High Finance Fraudsters.'

Dam It All

Arundhati Roy was found guilty on Wednesday of 'criminal contempt' and given a symbolic one day prison sentence in Tihar prison, New Delhi and a fine. The judges said they were going easy on her because she was a woman! Nothing to do with the fact that she's an internationally renowned author and winner of the Booker Prize (one of her opponents once called her the 'hooker with the booker'). The charges were brought by a group of lawyers who said that she had shouted abuse at them at a demo in front of a court where approval was being given for construction of the Narmada Dam (see SchNEWS 280) which will displace more than half a million people if it's completed. But raising your voice in protest against this is obviously a bigger crime.

The campaigners did have some good news recently. The Rehabilitation & Resettlement sub-group refused permission for further construction because they aren't happy about the resettlement of people who have become homeless because of the dam. Following this announcement, people from the Narmada valley ended a two-day sit-in in Delhi.

* After the recent great news that direct action had forced Balfour Beatty to pull out of the Illisu dam - which promises to drown dozens of towns and villages including the world historic site of Hasankeyf, and making 78,000 people homeless (SchNEWS 331) - now the Export Credit Guarantee Department which was backing Illisu is thinking of backing another dodgy construction project in Turkey to the tune of £68 million. This times it's construction company AMEC which is building the Yusufeli dam on the River Coruh in north east Turkey. The dam will make 30,000 people (mostly ethnic minority Georgians) homeless, impact on the surrounding environment, drown important cultural and archeological heritage, affect the supply of water to Georgia, and cause serious erosion on the Black Sea coast. At Hasankeyf, the Turkish government made the mistake of leaving the city standing, and therefore worth defending. It will not repeat this error. It intends to bulldoze Yusufeli in July, whether or not the dam is ready to be built, in the hope that its people and their supporters will give up once there is nothing to be saved but rubble. The people of Yusufeli and the surrounding villages will simply be dumped elsewhere. If they were to be given new homes the costs of resettlement would be greater than the value of the electricity the dam will produce.

The people who fought the Ilisu scheme are turning their attention to the Yusufeli dam and are targeting AMEC at their AGM on the 8th of May in Manchester. If you'd like a free share so you could go along then phone 020 7490 1555 or email kathb@foe.co.uk asap.

* For more info on the Namada www.irn.org Limited Edition Mark Thomas Bootleg Video, Live in Brighton. See 2 hours of Mark in fine form the day after Balfour Beatty pulled out of the Ilisu Dam. £8 + 80p SAE from SchNEWS.

On An Emission

Activists from a group calling itself 'Pie in the Sky' - part of Rising Tide UK - this week disrupted a top-level £300 a head conference on the new market in trading carbon dioxide emissions. The soiree brought Shell, the International Emissions Trading Association, the UN, KPMG and the EU together to hear about the profit opportunities presented by this new market in emissions. Carbon Emissions Trading is pie in the sky: it pretends to be a solution to climate change, but is in fact the privatisation of the atmosphere. (See SchNEWS 311)

Rising Tide 07762 252932
www.risingtide.org.uk

SchNEWS in brief

Brighton's premier pirate station Radio 4A hits the airwaves again this weekend (8-10) – if the home office don't pinch their equipment first. Catch 'em on 106.6 FM over Brighton and www.piratetv.net worldwide. More details www.radio4a.org.uk ** **International Solidarity Movement in Palestine** are organising a fortnight for direct action 29 March- 12 April. They're keen to hear from anyone interested in doing solidarity action in the UK. email saritasinpelo@hotmail.com details from www.rapprochement.org ** Next Wednesday (13th) sees the launch of a weekly **vigil** outside the **Botswana High Commission** to protest against their treatment of the **Gana and Gwi Bushmen** (See last weeks SchNEWS). Noon- 2pm, 6 Stratford Place, London W1 (nearest tube is Bond Street). Tel: 020 7687 8700 www.survival-international.org ** **Free Trade or Fair Trade?** Public meeting to celebrate Fairtrade Fortnight (4-17 March) with speakers and a video next Thursday (14), 7.30 pm Brighthelm Centre, North Road, Brighton www.tradejusticemovement.org.uk ** **Picket of New Scotland Yard**, Monday 11th, 12:30-2pm to demand full investigation into the death of Shaun Rodney. Contact Newham Monitoring Project 020 8555 8151 ** Check out the new McDonalds Workers Resistance website at http://www.mwr.org.uk ** Glasgow's **Govanhill Pool: Southside Against Closure** is organising a community conference called "Making Waves" about the impact community action can have, locally and globally. It's being held at Langside Hall, Shawlands, on 23/4 March www.saveourpool@aol.com ** Next Thursday (14) two **Cubans** will be in Brighton town to answer questions about everything from Guantanamo base, green Cuba and the anti-capitalist movement. Cuba is a 'rogue state' to some and a 'spanner in the works of capitalism' to others. The Debating Chamber, Falmer House University of Sussex 2pm. Race Hill Pub 1 Lewis Road 7pm 020 7837 1688 www.boycottbacardi.com ** **Index on Censorship** are showing the **Injustice** film about deaths in police custody next Wednesday (13) 6pm at Prince Charles Cinema, 7 Leicester Place off Leicester Square, London. Panel discussion after with the film director, Nick Cohen from the Observer and Brenda Weinberg, sister of Brian Douglas who died in police custody ** Three seperate strikes against **logging sites in Southern Tasmania** have left the companies with a $3,000,000 damage bill. The logging contractors are still too much in shock to speak to the media and they have labelled the actions 'environmental terrorism', unlike massive deforestation for profit which is, er.....

Positive SchNEWS

Did you know that there are over 20,000 species of edible plants in the world and yet fewer than 20 species now provide 90% of the world's food? Plants For A Future, with their two demonstration sites in Cornwall and Devon, have for the past 13 years been growing and collecting information on thousands of these.

Anyone interested in getting involved and helping with the organisations 'woodland gardening, vegan-organic horticulture, the use of perennial plants and a sustainable way of life' should get along to a weekend 'Shaping the Future of Plants For A Future' 6-7th April at their Blagdon Cross Site in North Devon

Plants for a Future 1 Lerryn View, Lerryn, Lostwithiel Cornwall, PL22 0QJ Tel 01208 872 963 www.pfaf.org/
* Read Ken Fern's book 'Plants For A Future - edible and useful plants for a healthier world' (Permanent Publications 1997), or get in touch for a copy of their plant catalogue.

Inside SchNEWS

Emily Apple, a die-hard anti-capitalist non-stop direct action activist is being sentenced at Snaresbrook Crown Court next Wednesday (13). Emily and a friend handcuffed themselves to a docklands light railway train during protests against the Defence Systems Exhibition International last September (scc SchNEWS 322) The 'exhibition' was Europes' biggest arms fair, catering for dictators and oppressive regimes throughout the world, selling landmines hawkjets, cluster bombs, rocket launchers, anti-ballistic missiles, you name it. The action stopped delegates on the train - literally in their tracks - from reaching the place. Her friend has been acquitted but Emily was convicted and now faces up to two years in prison, with the judge during the trail declaring that 'Society needs a break' from Emily.

People are meeting for a breakfast with her in the park in the grounds of the court on: Wednesday March 13th Snaresbrook Crown Court, 75 Hollybush Hill, E11 (nearest tube Snaresbrook) at 9am. Tel 07789 528 043
* Also at the infamous arms fair a WOMBLE (those with the white overalls, padding and helmets) who was acting as a medic, was found not guilty of "using threatening words and behaviour" after he was nicked for the crime of trying to help someone who had been assaulted by the cops. The case provides an important precedent as the judge didn't accept the cops' claims that people wearing padding and white suits were there to be violent (unlike the non-violent people down the road busy selling weapons to each other) He also clearly sided with the defence after asking if he'd been wearing anything to identify him as a medic. Will a hat with a massive red-cross on it do?

Shit Happens

Last Thursday about 500 people gathered on the steps of the Argentinan Congress building in Buenos Aires and began throwing carrier bags of their own shit, which they had painstakingly saved for days against the steps of Congress shouting such inspiring slogans as, "Put the shit where it belongs." and "Senators and members of congress - today we shit on you for a change" As a comment on Indymedia Argentina said "Shit isn't just any object - it's related to whether we eat or starve. What really disgusts us is the government, members of congress and all those who think we will continue to eat shit."
* Want to find out more about what's happenin in Argentina? Then get along to a SchNEWS public meeting next Monday (11) 8pm Prince Albert, Trafalgar St where will be videos and a eyewitness account and a chance for discussion

...and finally..

Fancy getting your own back on the cops for all those cameras in your face, Section 60 and all the general harassement? Well, next Wednesday (13th) the cops will be having their own demo/rally to protest against cuts in overtime and uniform allowance at the QE Conference Centre near Parliament Square and afterwards they'll be having a photo call outside the building. To see if they like a taste of their own medicine, bring cameras (to pick out the ringleaders), banners suggesting things like "Move along please, you've made your point" and "We understand, my daughter's a copper. If it starts to get ugly we might have to use citizens section 60 to keep them under control. Meet outside Politicos bookshop at 11am - make sure the "hardcore, violent elements" don't ruin it for everyone! For more info e-mail insurrectionist73@yahoo.co.uk

Disclaimer

Subscribe!

EU SUMMIT BARCELONA 9-16 MARCH

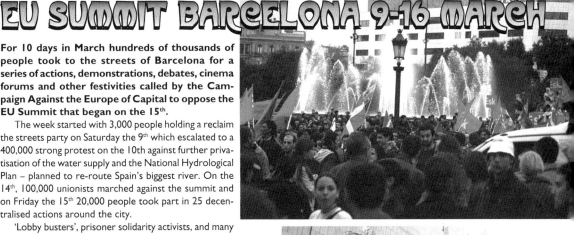

For 10 days in March hundreds of thousands of people took to the streets of Barcelona for a series of actions, demonstrations, debates, cinema forums and other festivities called by the Campaign Against the Europe of Capital to oppose the EU Summit that began on the 15th.

The week started with 3,000 people holding a reclaim the streets party on Saturday the 9th which escalated to a 400,000 strong protest on the 10th against further privatisation of the water supply and the National Hydrological Plan – planned to re-route Spain's biggest river. On the 14th, 100,000 unionists marched against the summit and on Friday the 15th 20,000 people took part in 25 decentralised actions around the city.

'Lobby busters', prisoner solidarity activists, and many other groups highlighted important issues around the summit, banners were hung at the Sagrada Familia church and other locations, critical mass bike rides clogged city streets. In the early afternoon, tensions increased as police surrounded the convergence centre and stopped and searched people all over the city. Police charged a large crowd of protesters on Las Ramblas (main avenue) and violently 'cleared' the area. In the evening they attacked another demonstration in Gracia and arrested several people. Prisoner solidarity protests went on all night, many were attacked by riot police.

On Saturday the 16th up to 500,000 people marched through the city. Protesters faced widespread police violence, including rubber bullets and tear gas, despite the majority of protesters being peaceful. Participants described premeditated, brutal and indiscriminate police attacks, that resulted in 80 people being arrested, bringing the total to 109 arrests in two days. In spite of the repression, spirits remained high and most considered the day a success. While much of the planning for the week of events had sought to minimise confrontation, the denial of basic rights that is now becoming commonplace in Europe was widespread - although not wholly unexpected - in Spain.

Campaign Against the Europe of Capital

www.pangea.org

Pics: Guy Smallman

Reclaim your media!
Rome 16 March 2002

-- From Italy IMC --

by breakthenews 11:59am Sat Mar 16 '02

A Street Media Party is taking place in Rome to support Radio Onda Rossa and IMC Italy for a free and independent information.

18.30 GMT: Under the control of a police helicopter the demo has reached the Colosseum and is turning into a massive party. Sound systems keep pumping music and news while videos are beamed on the walls of the buildings.

Along the route of the demo walls are covered with graffiti and Indymedia posters.

More than 20.000 people have converged to Piazza Esedra for the Reclaim your media! demo in Rome.

The demo has now moved in carnival atmosphere from Piazza Esedra and will reach the Colosseum for a final event that will include a live radio link with Barcelona and Buenos Aires. Several sound systems are alternating music and Radio Gap programs with breaking news from Barcelona.

A big truck hosts an Indymedia center with many computers and public access points where people are able to upload news from the streets.

The action has been called after 4 Italian social centres, allegedly housing indymedia centres, were raided by the police on Feb 20th. In the operation the police have seized audio and video material referring to the anti-G8 actions in Genova last summer and confiscated computers, archives, and equipment needed by hundreds of Italian activists for daily cultural and political activities.

In Italy the attack on independent information has also involved Radio Onda Rossa - an independent radio station in Rome, a node of Radio Gap network. On January 22nd, the ministry of communications has officially notified that its broadcasting license will be revoked.

Solidarity actions with indymedia are being held in Washington DC, Switzerland, Brasil, Barcelona, San Francisco, and many other places.

ZIMBABWE: THE ELECTION ASIDE

24 hour coffins in the Mbare townshop in Harare

Pic: Monty Strikes

by Mark Olden

In the run-up to the most crucial election in Zimbabwe's post-independence history on March 9 - 11 2002, more British journalists posing as tourists seemed to be in the country than real ones. Some of the vivid accounts of the dangers they were facing - for example Ann Leslie's in the Daily Mail - were slightly undermined by them being able to traipse unimpeded around Harare's luxury hotels.

President Mugabe and his ruling Zanu-PF party duly stole the election, the foreign press pack upped and left, and Zimbabwe went straight from front-page news to the news in brief columns. With the Middle East in flames, it wasn't surprising. That so much attention had been heaped on an African tragedy in the first place was - and can largely be put down to the potent symbolism of the land invasions, and the kith and kin factor in the murders of white farmers.

But while only the deluded - or Zanu-PF apologists - can deny the endemic violence, corruption and repression of the Mugabe regime, much of the British reporting on Zimbabwe has been afflicted by historical amnesia. Mugabe may be the architect of his country's present tragedy, but he's not a man without context.

Therefore, when he cranks up his anti-imperialist tirades against Britain and America, much of Africa is able to nod in agreement. They also know what he's talking about when he rails

against the IMF and the World Bank, (the fact that he orchestrated the crushing of the mass opposition that arose after his government accepted an IMF and World Bank economic structural adjustment programme with dire consequences in the early 1990s, is, of course, omitted). Mugabe's words also resonate in other former colonies when he harangues Britain for evading its obligation to fund Zimbabwe's land redistribution programme. Until the invasions of commercial farms started two years ago, 6,000 white farmers occupied half of Zimbabwe's mostly arable land.

Britain promised Zimbabwe hundreds of millions of pounds for land reform at the 1979 Lancaster House agreement that ended white minority rule - but it's never been delivered. Although the Blair government later promised £36 million for land reform if it was carried out legally and transparently, in November 1997 International Development Secretary Clare Short said in a letter to Zimbabwe's then Minister of Agriculture and Land, Kumbirai Kangai: "I should make it clear that we do not accept that Britain has a special responsibility to meet the costs of land purchase in Zimbabwe. We are a new government from diverse backgrounds without links to former colonial interests. My own origins are Irish and as you know we were colonised not colonisers." Short's arrogance was echoed not long after by Tony Lloyd, then a Foreign Office minister, who said Britain didn't owe Zimbabwe money for land reform because, "Colonisation is not something that people of my generation in Britain benefited from."

Travelling through Zimbabwe a month before the presidential election we saw the issue being played out on the ground. While Zanu-PF's re-distribution programme has seen vast tracts of land handed over to government cronies such as army chief General Vitalis Zvinavashe (who threatened a coup if the opposition Movement for Democratic Change were declared winners of the election), and Perence Shiri (in charge of the notorious Fifth Brigade which murdered up to 20,000 people in the 1980s), as well as Zimbabwe's Libyan sponsors - the land hunger that exist among the peasant population was starkly obvious. On one farm deserted by its white former occupants after another, they had flooded in and had carved out their plots.

At independence millions of peasants were living in infertile so-called Tribal Trust Lands - having been pushed out of their traditional homes over the last 90 years of white settler rule. So today, as Munyaradzi Gwisai, the socialist MDC MP for the Harare township of Highfield, points out - to the chagrin of his party's hierarchy - many of the war vets and peasants leading the land invasions are not merely puppets of Mugabe, but part of a genuine grassroots movement. Gwisai called for the MDC to adopt a more radical land position than Zanu-PF, but the party which has moved steadily to the right since it was founded out of Zimbabwe's civil society and trade unions in September 199* (adopting neo-liberal economic policies that have attracted western backers) rejected his advice.

But however great the need for land re-distribution in Zimbabwe is, the way Mugabe's regime has executed it over the last two years has led to agriculture in the country all but collapsing. The United Nations Development Programme (UNDP) recently said that 600,000 people in the country are facing starvation.

The massive queues that lined up to cast their votes a few months ago in an election whose outcome had already been determined, still line Harare's streets - only now they're queuing for hours to purchase mealie-meal, Zimbabwe's staple food. How much more the country's long-suffering - though incredibly resilient - people must endure, no one seems to know right now.

NAISSANCE, VIE ET MORT DES NATIONS

'Birth, life and death of nations'

WAKE UP! WAKE UP! IT'S YER SMALL GENE POOL

Weekly **SchNEWS** GM

IT'S HARVEST TIME!

www.schnews.org.uk

REAPER

Friday 15th March 2002 · Free/Donation · Issue 346

MONSTER MUNCH INC.

"Since genetic engineering manipulates the basis of life, the risks involved are more frightening than any other developed so far... We feel it is unjust of the richest of the world to expect us to bear the risks of their experimentation." - Tewolde Egziabher, Ethiopian Delegate (CBD).

In April UN delegates will be yapping about the state of the world's biodiversity resources over two-headed salmon and champagne at the sixth meeting of the Convention on Biological Diversity (CBD) in Holland. Set up during the UN Rio Earth Summit in 1992, the CBD have only just agreed on the useless Biosafety Protocol and The Law of the Seed. Neither will have the power to stop the legal or illegal spread of GMOs, protect farmers rights or stop finite resources being plundered for profit. This is because these UN organisations didn't have the power or force of will to fight powerful biotech corporations and the World Trade Organisation.

But the global commercialisation of genetically engineered crops and the complete control of our food chain by large multinationals, is still far from a foregone conclusion. In fields, boardrooms and courtrooms around the world the GM giants aren't getting an easy ride. Here's a short round up of just a few of the memorable events that ruffled the feathers of the biotech giants in the last 12 months.

Global Alliance
International Day Of Farmers' Struggle Against GMO

April 17th 2001 was declared 'International Day of Farmers Struggle Against GMOs' by Via Campesina (www.vicampesina.org), an international movement for small farmers, rural people, and indigenous communities. This day marked the launch of their International Alliance Against Agrochemical Transnatioanl Corporations, GMOs and Patents on Life, and the start of protests against the Free Trade Area of the Americas (FTAA) in Quebec City, Canada (see SchNEWS 302).

In February 2002 twelve nations including China, Brazil and India, agreed to join the alliance against bio-piracy and vowed to press for rules protecting their peoples' rights to genetic resources found on their land. The declaration - also signed by representatives of Indonesia, Costa Rica, Colombia, Ecuador, Kenya, Peru, Venezuela, and South Africa - echoed complaints long voiced by Indians and environmentalists: that wealthy nations are "prospecting" for species in order to patent or sell them. There are absolutely no concessions or benefits offered for the local people. Together the 12 nations in the alliance contain 70 percent of the world's biodiversity.

FTAA - Green Light For GM

The International Day of Farmers Struggle Against GMOs coincided with the Summit Of The Americas in Quebec where the finishing touches were put to the FTAA – a free trade agreement which believe it or not favours GM corporations and mass-scale agro-industry rather than small farmers. In the weeks leading up to the creation of FTAA the US government and its corporations attempted to reverse GM regulations introduced in several Latin American nations.
* In **MEXICO** the Senate had unanimously agreed to introduce labelling of GM foods but food corporations in the USA threatened sanctions and legal action through the North American Free Trade Area (NAFTA) unless they revoked the law.

* **ARGENTINA,** the country in South America most up-to-its-eyeballs in GM, where 90% of soya crops are GM, was threatened with sanctions by Monsanto unless it removed all its remaining regulations covering GM crops.
* **BRAZIL,** where agricultural exports are booming because consumers groups and foreign importers demanded a ban on GM crops, Monsanto threatened legal action using WTO rules to force the nation to open its doors to GM. In Florianopolis, 800 miles south of Brasilia, 2000 Brazilian women blockaded a supermarket that was selling GM food.

The **FTAA** is now the world's largest trade bloc and promises to operate like the World Trade Organisation, with tough sanctions for any nation whose environmental or health & safety regulations threaten the profits of multinational corporations. Like the WTO, the FTAA is almost completely controlled by the USA (where about 30 years worth of environmental regulations have just been scrapped) and it is feared that the USA will try to use the FTAA to ban the labelling of GM food throughout North and South America because such labels are an 'obstacle to free trade'. The WTO has taken away precautionary principles that GMOs have to be proven safe, leaving pro-GM lobbyists suggesting consumers spend their own money on the testing of GMOs.

French farmer Jose Bove appeared in Quebec City at the FTAA protest meeting, despite 'wanted' posters of him being displayed at every airport and customs post in the nation. There, on behalf of farmers' unions around the world he urged Canadians to destroy genetically modified 'seeds of death' and attack laboratories where GM crops were being developed. He said "people here must also join the resistance movement and not just make speeches. This means that GM crops must be destroyed, this means that the laboratories that continue to make these seeds of death must be attacked, this means that Monsanto and Novartis facilities must be attacked, they must not be given five minutes of peace. We have to fight against this because if it goes ahead, it means farmers won't be able to decide any more what they are going to grow. This is a fight which must be fought every day and in doing so you should not be afraid to break the law... all forms of combat are possible."

Mexico

"What's frightening is how fast it has spread" said Yolanda Lara, spokesperson for Oaxaca's non-governmental Rural Development Agency about the spread of GM corn in Capulalpan, a village in the hills of Mexico's Oaxaca State. Normally locals might be thankful for this new source of corn, the staple food of villages in the area. But they now know this corn is GM, which is surprising because GM crops have been banned in Mexico since 1998. Berkeley scientists have confirmed that this new corn is the spawn of Monsanto: it has the same DNA as the biotech giant's commercial GM maize. David Quist, responsible for the study suggests that "It's more likely that the contamination came from food aid brought into these regions. A lot of it comes from the United States and a lot of it is transgenic."

So under the guise of offering support to poverty stricken villagers in remote parts of Mexico, the US has managed to off-load tonnes of subsidised GM maize on unsuspecting shopkeepers and subsistence farmers. Locals are worried that the GM corn, which they say has been around in their shops for several years, will out-compete native varieties. The Berkeley study confirms their fears, suggesting that GM corn is likely to dominate local corn and may also threaten the research of the International Maize and Wheat Improvement Centre, home to the largest variety of endangered maize in the world. Quist believes a well-enforced ban on imported GM corn and a programme to encourage traditional habits of swapping and testing wild seeds is the way forward.

Phillipines

On the 29th August 2001, 800 people including many local farmers stormed one of Monsanto's experimental fields in South Cotabato, Mindanao. The operation took about ten minutes leaving police helpless. *"Faster! Faster!"* were the shouts as the protesters hurriedly uprooted the GM corn in the 1,700-sq/m experimental field of Bt-corn ('Bt' - Bacillus thuringiensis – genetically modified for pest resistance).

In October 2001, 300 people rallied in Isabela to protest against Monsanto's continued field testing of the genetically modified Bt-corn in the province. The protesters massed in front of the marketing office of Monsanto in Cauayan City and staged a noise barrage. Also that month, Swiss corporation Novartis AG confirmed allegations from Greenpeace that some samples of baby food it sold in the Phillipines did contain genetically modified soybean. Beau Baconguis of Greenpeace Asia said, "We should not be forced to feed our children with food the rest of the world is increasingly rejecting."

On 3rd January 2002 activists in the Philippines occupied unloading equipment to prevent over 17,000 tonnes of genetically engineered soya from entering the South East Asian food supply. In an early morning raid four people chained themselves to the largest soya factory in the Philippines where recent tests show widespread GM contamination. Protesters on inflatables then attached a large banner to the hull of the cargo ship, which was waiting to unload its contaminated cargo from America. The banner read *"USA - Stop Dumping GMOs in Asia"*. A year ago President Gloria Macapagal Arroyo's government promised to give consumers GM food labelling. Unsurprisingly nothing has happened yet.

India

India is the biggest cotton producer in the world so it was big news when, in 1998, 500 farmers committed suicide in Andhra Pradesh, a state in southern India, because of the failure of their cotton crops. Dr. Pushpa Bhargava, an Indian biologist, told the Indian Science Congress that the failure of the cotton seed in Andhra Pradesh in 1997 and 1998 should be investigated since Monsanto could have been using local seed companies to market bad seed in order to destroy the supply system. "The destruction of the seed supply and Monsanto's purchase of Indian seed companies would have ensured that Indian farmers had no option but to buy Monsanto's Bt cotton and in future Monsanto's terminator crops." The Indian farmers ain't taking this lying down and in 1998 the Karnatka farmers union occupied and burned down the three fields of GM cotton and 500 farmers occupied Cargill, the biotech multinational offices, throwing loads of their processing kit out of windows. They did loads of other actions too as part of 'Operation Cremate Monsanto' and hundreds of farmers and activists took part in the Intercontinental Caravan, which toured through Europe.

Vision 20/20: Short sighted

Vision 20/20 is a scheme to give large chunks of semi-arid Andhra Pradesh over to mass scale GM agro-industry. The area – with a population of 75 million – will see a reduction in farming labour as the area goes to mass scale farms, which could see 20 million rural people kicked off land. Farmers are to be encouraged to plant GM crops, including Bt cotton and vitamin A rice and a 600 sq km site in the so-called 'Genome Valley' is being set aside where biotechnology companies such as Monsanto will be invited to carry out trials.

The scheme is a hi-tech, export-orientated project funded by the World Bank and British aid money, and is being carried out by the International Food Policy Research Institute. Read their website (www.ifpri.org) and find out what their agenda is…"The potential role of genetic engineering to assure food security in developing countries while maintaining acceptable biosafety is an important aspect of this work.". In September 2001 they had an international conference in Bonn promoting Vision 20/20 and the sponsors were – guess who - Aventis CropScience, Cargill, Syngenta and Novartis (Wot no Monsanto? - ed).

The long sighted scheme shifts production in the semi-arid area from traditional, sustainable staples such as millet and sorghum onto the more lucrative crop of rice – which would require three million more wells to be sunk in an area that suffers from crippling droughts. This 'vision' also includes soy bean crops with Monsanto poised to introduce a progression of GM strains.

On Monday 18th March Indian women farmers were in London to challenge British Government aid to the Vision 20/20 programme. This action opposed the Memorandum of Understanding signed by Chief Minister of AP and Monsanto, which will give the company free rein to plant GM crops throughout Andhra Pradesh. The findings of an AP Citizen's Jury were presented in the House of Commons which unsurprisingly describes another resource grab by TNCs, opened up by free trade arrangements, and a displacement of people, and a privatisation and commandeering of traditional food crops (read the findings in full at www.iied.org).

To find out what you can do contact GAFF (Grassroots Action on Food and Farming) 01865 793 910 chapter7@tlio.demon.co.uk

Brazil

Despite pressure from the Brazilian government and Monsanto, the moratorium on commercial growing of GM crops still remains in place. This is thanks to a strong independent judiciary that was set up to prevent another dictatorship, and has resulted in the country having some strong biodiversity laws.

Canada

At the beginning of the year two Canadian organic farmers from Saskatchewan launched a class-action suit to get an injunction which would stop Monsanto and Aventis from proceeding with tests of GM wheat. They are also seeking losses from the company for the contamination of their crops. The two farmers allege that contamination in the region has become so widespread it is almost impossible for growers to certify their products GM free. Thanks to genetic engineering, rapeseed has now become a noxious weed in Canada. The local organic farmers group said "…losing wheat to genetic contamination would devastate organic farming…our very future is at stake." Info: www.saskorganic.com.

In April 2001a judge ruled that a Canadian farmer, Percy Schmeiser, violated Monsanto's patent by "unknowingly and unwillingly growing genetically modified (GM) oil seed rape." He now faces a bill for $105,000 and after 40 years of saving seeds and developing his own strain has had to purchase new seed wasting a lifetime's work. (see SchNEWS 300) Under Canadian patent law, as in the US and many other industrialised countries, it is illegal for farmers to re-use patented seed, or to grow Monsanto's GM seed without signing a licensing agreement. If biotech bastards such as Monsanto get their way, every nation in the world will be forced to adopt patent laws that make seed saving illegal. Schmeiser is in the process of an appeal of this decision – find out the latest on the case at www.percyschmeiser.com

France

On 29th August 2001, police in anti-riot gear prevented activists from taking down three fields of experimental maize. After a series of daylight actions, which were watched but not disrupted by small numbers of cops, the Prime Minister publicly criticised the destruction of GM tests and urged activists to stop. Undeterred some 100 radical farmers from the union Confederation Paysanne and other groups arrived at a test site in Sigalens and were met by between 100 and 150 officers carrying riot shields and truncheons. The protesters placed their tools on the ground in front of the police, but said they would be back. *"There is no question of having a confrontation. If we can't act today, we'll come back another day"*, one of the protest organisers said. A similar reception awaited the 100 or so activists who had planned to cut down two fields of maize near the village of Saint-Martin-la-Riviere, in west central France.

South Korea

In January a rally was held outside the Korean Food and Drug Association (KFDA) to demand that visiting U.S. trade officials stop pressuring South Korea into easing regulations on genetically modified organisms (GMOs). While visiting the KFDA U.S., trade officials were said to have requested that South Korean government

ease labelling restrictions on imported GMO products by raising the adventitious threshold level to 5 percent from the current 3 percent. In the EU the GMO free level is 1 percent.

Sri Lanka

On April 10, 2001 the Sri Lankan government bravely but in place the world's toughest ban on the imports of all GE foods. Unfortunately under pressure from the World Trade Organisation the ban had been indefinitely postponed.

Bangladesh

Farmers are rallying to oppose GM rice - their group UBINIG (Policy Research for Development Alternatives) stating that "Bangladesh farmers will resist it by any means, we want the farmers of Asia to take a united position against genetically engineered rice". Grassroots campaigns are fighting the misinformation which is helping spread the myth across Asia about Golden Rice being a 'wonder crop'.

USA

Monsanto the evil biotech giants were found guilty in February this year of decades of pollution in the small town of Anniston, Alabama. The verdict proved that the river in the town had been being pumped with nasty chemicals PCB's, which have been linked to cancer. The decision will now open the door for massive claims for compensation against the company.

May 13-20th 2001 was National Biotechnology Week in the US, and in California over fifty activists were tear-gassed by riot police while planting their own beans and corn at Syngenta's HQ. Meanwhile trials of GM strawberries, tomatoes and onions by DNA Plant Technology Holdings were destroyed by Night-time Gardeners.

New Zealand

The government has betrayed the majority of New Zealanders… They sold out to the GE lobby. That leaves the public no option but civil disobedience to protect our country from GE accidents and contamination." - Logan Petley Green Gloves anti-GM campaign group.

In March 1999 twelve people broke into a laboratory in an early morning raid and destroyed an experimental crop of rot-resistant toad-silkworm-potatoes and ruined Lincoln's Crop and Food Research Centre's NZ$200,000 project. This was the country's first major act of environmental sabotage in years.

The stakes are high because around 42 percent of New Zealand's exports involve food, and the pro-GM lobby have peddled a line about getting "left behind" in the global marketplace. Last year the Fonterra Co-operative Group - the dairy company which is also the country's largest transnational - said it would move its operations overseas if GM research didn't go ahead.

The pace of protest snowballed as the Government continued to ignore anti-GM campaigns. Last April a Research Centre was fire-bombed by a molotov cocktail. Just in case anyone misinterpreted the attack, a shed was graffitied with "No GE. Stop the tests," by a group called the Shadow Ministry for the Environment.

In October 2001 over a hundred Maori GMO protesters and their families set out from the far north of the North Island for a month-long march to parliament in Wellington. The day they arrived Labour Prime Minister Helen Clark announced that there would be GM field trials, and activists unveiled plans to stop it including 3000 who signed up to undertake non-violent direct action against genetically engineered crops. A month later forestry giant Carter Holt Harvey abandoned a field test for genetically modified pine trees and sheep.

In the latest big action this January, over 1000 genetically engineered potatoes were destroyed at the same Crop and Food Research complex that was first targeted by activists.

For the full stories and to keep up-to-date with the latest GM news around the world check out www.connectotel.com/gmfood

PUMP IT UP!

Last month in the Ecuadorian Amazon provinces of Sucumbios and Orellana thousands of striking construction workers and local residents protesting against the new oil pipeline were attacked by the country's armed forces. Three children were killed by asphyxiation from tear gas, close to forty people were arrested and over three hundred people were wounded after the military crackdown ordered by President Gustavo Noboa. Demonstrators occupied over 60 oil wells and 5 refineries-halting all construction on the pipeline bringing oil production to a near standstill and erected roadblocks. Nearby in the highland cloud forests of the Mindo, people continue to put their lives on the line by tree-sitting to block the pipeline's passage. The government declared a state of emergency for the provinces in defence of the oil multinationals, immediately suspending civil rights, and invoking the military to break up the demonstrations while the local radio stations were kept off the air.

Meanwhile on Monday Indian tribal leaders from Ecuador began the lengthy and expensive process of taking Chevron-Texaco to the US courts. This groundbreaking environmental class-action lawsuit, the first filed by foreigners in a U.S. court, is being watched closely to see if federal courts find American corporations accountable to crimes abroad.

"We simply want Chevron-Texaco to pay to clean up the damage it caused." The lawsuit asserts that Texaco installed detective drilling technology that led to the spillage of millions of gallons of toxic wastewater over a 20-year period. Rather than pump the poisonous water back into the ground - as is the industry standard, and as Chevron-Texaco does in the United States - they dumped it into hundreds of unlined pits. From the pits, the wastewater contaminated with oil and heavy metals slowly poisoning the rivers and wetlands of Ecuador.

"To Chevron-Texaco, the clean-up costs represent a small fraction of its annual profits," said prosecuting lawyer Joseph Kohn, "To our clients in the Amazon, this is a matter of life or death."

Texaco and Occidental Petroleum have extracted more that $60 billion dollars worth of oil from these provinces in the last 30 years, yet 90% of the region's population lives in poverty. Despite the huge profits from oil the locals surprise, surprise have seen none of the loot and all of the pillaging has left them impoverished and sick with cancer. www.amazonwatch.org

* At the end of last month a court gave the go ahead for the families of Ken Saro-Wiwa to take Shell/Dutch Petroleum to court for participation in crimes against humanity, torture, summary execution, arbitrary detention, cruel, inhuman, and degrading treatment. Environmentalist activist and writer Ken Saro-Wiwa, and eight other Ogoni activists were hanged by the Nigerian military government in 1995. The "Ogoni Nine" had opposed Shell's pollution and oil development in the Niger Delta. Saro-Wiwa told the military tribunal that sentenced him to death, "Shell is here on trial. The Company has, indeed, ducked this particular trial, but its day will surely come..."

Judith Chomsky, Attorney for the prosecution commented, "Shell had direct involvement in human rights violations against the Ogoni people. Any company that profits from crimes against humanity should be brought to justice wherever they are."

Lawsuits have also been filed against Exxon-Mobil by people from Indonesia's embattled Aceh province, Members of ethnic minorities in Myanmar (formerly Burma) against Unocal And Chevron-Texaco (again) by other Nigerian groups: www.earthrights.org/shell/appeal.html

---

SchNEWS in brief

A **Peat Alert** activist will talk about the campaign to save Britain's peat bogs and 4 days of direct action coming up at Hatfield Moors this Easter. 7pm Sunday 17th upstairs at the Hobgoblin, London Rd, Brighton www.peatalert.org.uk
** This Saturday there's a meeting to create a crew that the authorities can deal with to run a 4 day celebration of the summer **Solstice at Stonehenge**. It's at the Art Space, 491 Grove Green Road, Leytonstone London E11 (by Leytonstone tube station) 2pm 0798-402-6853 www.greenleaf.demon.co.uk/trcwp1.htm ** The South East Alternative Science Network are holding their first **Brickhurst Science FunDay** on Saturday at Brickhurst Farm in Pembury, Tunbridge Wells. The kids science and environment activity day has been set up as an alternative to the usual overcrowded and overpriced corporate sponsored science events. Tel 01892 863 941 www.geocities.com/seasonscience ** Manchesters **Okasional Café** will be back in business this weekend (Saturday 6pm) with a vegan supper and a gig with local bands. See www26.brinkster.com/okcafe/home.html for details of the location. ** Zimbabwe now has it's own Indy Media Centre http://zimbabwe.indymedia.org ** Two presidents resigned on the island of Mauritius in the Indian Ocean rather than give the green light to a new Prevention of **Terrorism Act**. Mass protests complained that the law was an infringement of human rights and an attack on the country's sovereignty, because it allows the CIA to interfere in national affairs. The law was eventually passed when the Chief Justice became president. ** The **Anti-capitalist Action group** will be hosting a number of workshops, discussions and film-showings on direct action at their newly occupied social centre this coming weekend. The social centre is in Cambridge: on "O" Covent Garden, on the corner of Mill Road just past the Kelsey Kerridge sports centre ** There will be a **Healing UK Medical Training** next weekend (22nd-24th) to teach people about first aid at demonstrations. It's at the London Activist Resource Centre, corner of Fieldgate and Parfett, St's, London, E1 (Whitechapel tubes) 020 7249 6996 healinguk@hotmail.com

Inside SchNEWS

Ever wondered why anti capitalist protesters always get over the top sentences for minor offences? Well, the Legal Defence and Monitoring Group (LDMG) have uncovered secret documents that tell judges to come down hard on activists. These documents were being passed to Crown and Youth Court judges after both May Day 2000 and May Day Monopoly 2001 festivities. The document titled "Mayhem" came to the attention of LDMG in June 2001 at Middlesex Guildhall Crown Court. The defence barrister Ed Rees QC asked to look at the document, but the court refused this on the grounds that it was secret! Sentencing in England and Wales is supposedly based on individual circumstances and the seriousness of the offence, but clearly in the case of anti-capitalists this is not the case. Glaring examples of over the top prison terms are Roger Davis who got 3 months for threatening words and behaviour, which results in a fine at worst, Karl Hodgkinson got 15 months for affray, and another person received a £1000 fine for common assault (the lowest form of assault). Paul Jones, spokesperson for LDMG told SchNEWS "The police have spent millions of pounds preventing the May Day actions from proceeding peacefully and in prosecuting people for minor offences. Now we discover that the judiciary is instructed to send those convicted to prison. Even the pretence of justice has been abandoned. We demand an amnesty for all May Day protestors." LDMG 07949 061 333 e: ldmgmail@yahoo.co.uk
*All sorts of pranks and actions are being planned for this year's **May Day**. For more info check out www.ourmayday.org.uk
* Brighton Anarchist Black Cross are hosting a **Mark Barnsley** info/debate night upstairs at the Albert, Trafalgar St. Monday 18th at 7.30pm. Mark has spent seven years inside after being attacked by 15 drunken students whilst out with his baby and a friend. Mark has spent all his time in maximum and high security prisons and has been denied parole as punishment for protesting his innocence. www.freemarkbarnsley.com
* **Emily Apple** the activist that "society needs a break from" didn't go to prison as feared (SchNEWS 345) but got a fine instead for locking onto a train carrying arms dealers to last year's arms fair in East London.

The Un-Dammed

Just 24 hours before a campaign was due to be launched against AMEC, for their participation in the controversial Yusufeli Dam in Turkey, the company announced its withdrawal from the project. The dam would displace 30,000 people, destroy many old churches, fortresses and a citadel aswell as displacing endangered red vultures and brown bears. The withdrawal of AMEC now casts doubt over the future of the whole project. Kerim Yildiz, Executive Director, Kurdish Human Rights Project said "We are delighted that AMEC has withdrawn from this project. For minorities on the ground whose homes, livelihood and ways of life are threatened by this project this a huge victory." www.khrp.org

POSITIVE SchNEWS

At Taurus Crafts in Lydney, Gloucestershire, peddlers will be connecting their own pedal generator to the national grid via a plug socket from 2nd-30th April.

Tom from 'Power of the People' told SchNEWS "The paperwork I have generated dealing with the natural grid, power supply companies, and planning department is enormous... In the Netherlands these same panels can be stuck on the roof, plugged in at a wall socket, and your meter will run backwards corresponding to the number of units produced No paperwork required". Info: 01594-836546 thomas.cousins@talk21.com

...and finally...

"The Corporation took over your country and proceeded to impose its strict rules or an unsuspecting public. Questioning this new authority led to unrest. Unrest led to full scale rioting." – So goes the blurb for a new Sony Playstation 2 game where armed with molotovs grenades and AK47s you fight the corporation The company backing it, Take-Two, will profit greatly from this anti capitalist bestseller at a time when it is in financial woes. Yet another example of a capitalist company selling th anti-capitalist idea. SchNEWS reckons its more fun (and risky) to get out on the streets and demonstrate than sit and smash things up o a TV screen.

Disclaimer
SchNEWS warns all readers if there's any seed o doubt go for the best of the crop. Honest

---

FROM BEHIND THE BARRICADE

Closed to corporate corruption - open to ideas

The building on the corner of the site: a hive of activity on a Saturday afternoon as the samba band and carnival dragon prepare to visit the nearby Sainsbury's store

It's early ... 6.30am. I wake up and try to stretch - but find myself tightly cocooned in a sleeping bag. My eyes slowly open - above me a double barn door, big enough to drive a truck through, stands barricaded shut. Scaffold bars brace rigid horizontals across the entrance. Buttresses of timber bite down hard on either side of me, immovable right angles dug into the concrete floor. I have camped up so close that I may as well be built into the barricade - as an early warning system - just in case it kicks off at dawn.

But it is not the heavy pounding of police sledge hammers or the splintering crack of crow bars that has woken me - not today. Today it is the silent shafts of sunlight that have pierced our fortifications, squeezing in between and under our defences with a cool morning breeze.

Taking a deep breath I sit up, rub the dust out of my eyes and think about breakfast. I struggle from the snug confines of my sleeping bag and wander over to the kitchen.

The room I'm in is a large windowless single space, rectangular, with a high pitched corrugated roof. The sunshine pours into the building through wide sky lights that run the entire length of the ridge. The rough brick work has recently been painted white, giving the confines of the four walls an extra sense of air and light. I guess the building is at least a hundred years old and despite its bright atmosphere it has some telling scars. One corner has a crack as big as your fist that runs like lightening from the ceiling to the floor. The rafters, though still solid enough to keep the roof up, have at some point in the past been charred black by fire. The building has survived much - but how much longer can it hold out against the world's most virulent and aggressive foe the corporate bulldozers?

I fumble with the dodgy connection on the kettle. My companions on the night shift are all still sound asleep after a long night of 'setting the world to rights'. They lie on makeshift beds, decoratively draped in the vivid patterns of charity-shop blankets. The lack of sleep does not bother me, in fact I have an irrepressible excitement in the base of my stomach - we are, after all, under siege. The water boils and I swill it round an empty coffee jar and drink the reassuringly bitter liquid in small appreciative sips.

The building that we are barricaded into is on the southeastern corner of a vast 13 acre site that is earmarked for development. It is adjacent to the Brighton mainline train station, right slap bang in the centre of our busy little city. Along its southern edge is a mix of second hand car dealers and garages. The western edge adjoins the high plateau of the station car park and the lower eastern side borders the ironically named "New England Street". It is a bleak and characterless road, itself the repeated victim of previous 'developments' - prefab high-rises, multi-story car parks, and cramped brick blocks of housing.

There is no northern edge, as the land continues along the route of an abandoned railway track that disappears up a thickly wooded path. This is a hidden world, where the secret people go to do their secret deeds. A landscape of disturbed earth, burnt out vehicles, broken glass and tangled undergrowth. Inhabited, as the wreckage would suggest, by arsonists, bag snatchers, joyriders, and junkies. But there is a wild beauty about the place, as with an overgrown cemetery, a place of return, where nature, red clawed, takes back her own.

Vipers and foxes haunt the shadows and hawks can sometimes be seen hunting from the surrounding tower blocks. Rare plants grow in the shade of the Ivy and Elder making it an officially designated conservation area.

Back behind the barricade, I make myself comfortable and begin to sketch out this article. Outside the rush hour traffic has begun to rumble by. The clean morning air thickens with exhaust and great tides of nine-to-fivers flow up hill to the station. Time for some background information...

The Poison

When the railways were privatised hundreds of miles of land – including this site - was given away to Railtrack to 'sweeten the deal'. Land that was by rights one of the country's greatest remaining public assets. Railtrack, (or the company that was formally called Railtrack), now wants to cut to the cash and run.

Our local council, in league with Railtrack, QED (the builders) and Sainsbury's, plan to develop the site into yet another large Sainsbury's superstore complex, (we already have three!) with car park, hotels and associated new roads. There has been no legitimate community consultation process and two proposals for a supermarket have already been officially scrapped.

There are many reasons given by residents for opposing the plan: It would damage the local economy by prioritising outside corporate interests over local traders and producers. There would be a severe detrimental impact to the environment and to health and safety caused by bringing more traffic into the already congested city centre. It is irrelevant to local issues such as the need for affordable housing - Brighton is currently suffering a housing crisis with "...house prices rising faster than nearly everywhere else in the country...the city has one of the highest levels of rough sleeping, higher than average unemployment and lower than average incomes." [1] (yet business interests call this a property "boom"). Brighton is in dire need of free community space and there is an urgent need for facilities for young people to get them off the streets without it costing them money - especially given that "levels of substance misuse and crime are all well above the national average" [2]. It disregards Brighton's unique architectural and artistic character. It will destroy a wildlife corridor. It threatens the thriving Sunday second-hand market. And the whole scheme depends upon the "development option", a highly controversial 'arrangement' which gives exclusive rights to the land to Sainsbury's, making a mockery of the democratic process as it excludes all other alternatives.

When the developers inevitably justify their actions with the cry "but we create new jobs!", they fail to mention that these will be at the lowest end of the pay spectrum, in one of the lowest paid parts of Britain [3]. Corporate Watch has this to add: "On average, the British Retail Planning Forum discovered in 1998 that every time a large supermarket opens, 276 jobs are lost. The New Economics Foundation has estimated that £50,000 spent by shoppers in an independent local store creates one job, whereas it takes £250,000 to do the same in a supermarket. This figure is also due to small local businesses employing other local small businesses as suppliers and for repair work, which supermarkets, for all their claims to support local communities, barely do at all.

Finding locally produced food in supermarkets is unusual, and even if it is labelled 'local', is still likely to have

May Bug Ball: the police briefly join the party but can't stop the samba band and leave.

travelled the length and breadth of the country before reaching the nearest supermarket to the place where it was produced (See SchNEWS 283). Almost all food sold in supermarkets is transported to distribution depots around the country before being distributed back to supermarkets. Sainsbury's, for example, has only 12 depots that distribute chilled goods. Besides, the 'Just in Time' delivery system, by which products are rushed to superstores as and when they are needed, means that trucks often travel only half full with only a couple of items. Besides the pollution implications of air and road freight, there are animal welfare and disease control implications". [4]

Why should our local environment and economy be forced to struggle or to go under, while outside corporations bleed it dry? And why has our "democratically elected" council put the interests of global monoculture before those of its local community? - Time for some direct action!

Dancing round the maypole - May Bug Ball.

The Antidote

As an antidote to this pernicious plan to corporatise our city further, a group of local residents has got together to do something about the situation. Already a group called BUDD (Brighton Urban Design and Development) and the Green Party have campaigned hard against the superstore proposals, but there has been little direct action. So last year in May, the ball was set rolling by a day long occupation of the site. The event was aptly called "The May Bug Ball" and was initiated by the collaboration of CRU (Community Response Unit) and SPOR. It included such unlicensed delights as a costumed carnival procession with samba bands and

a snarling carnival Dragon. A Maypole (complete with pixies), a wind and solar powered sound system, a kid's disco, a live music stage and the deeply satisfying sight of 50 police officers - who had repeatedly tried to shut us down with threats of violence - being drummed off site by 800 protesters full of the Beltane magic.

Exactly a year later the second wave of resistance is in full swing. This building (at the time of writing) has been occupied now for 3 months. In that time we have transformed it from an empty shell to a buzzing community centre and social space. Until Sainsbury's took us to court, (more of this later), we were open daily with a comprehensive exhibition about the proposed development, as well as displays about community-sensitive and sustainable alternatives. We ran creative workshops, including blacksmithing - using the building's built in forge, screen printing, a gallery, a cafe and coffee shop, a cinema, kid's activities - including discos for the local kids run by the kids themselves, a bookshop and info station, and local performance groups were able to build props and stage rehearsals.

We have also regularly picketed the nearby branch of Sainsbury's, given out information about the proposals and had a couple of "in-store" skirmishes with the twelve metre carnival dragon. On the first demo we had hand-painted a banner that turned the company's 'catch phrase' back upon itself, it read "Sainsbury's - making life taste bitter". A security guard took it upon himself to defend the company's honour - punched a demonstrator and tried to knock another from a ladder, he then snatched the banner and refused to give it back.

Understandably irritated that the local community was not only saying no to the superstore proposal but actively countering it Sainsbury's then took us to court to seek repossession. We turned up to defend ourselves and won an adjournment on a point of high cunning (many thanks to our legal friends and the Advisory Service for Squatters for advice). This gave us more time and the satisfaction of arguing through a legal defence that worked. At the next hearing Sainsbury's and their team of lawyers were not going to be caught out again and managed to prepare a case that won them the right to immediate repossession. We had a week or so before it came into force, a week in which we drew up action plans and ideas for tactical antics. Tat gathering runs went out all over town, skips were emptied of timber and scrapyards plundered for steel. We went on fund raising missions, organised benefit nights and hunted out the talents that could advise us on all things from using welding equipment to legal advice on resisting arrest.*

Day and night the building became a hive of activity. The blacksmith's forge was fired up and the hammer and anvil were put to work - from glowing red iron bars, bolts and fittings were wrought. A team worked 'till dawn welding a reinforced superstructure into and around the door. Across the night burst of fierce acrid light cut and fused the steel into solid immovable shapes. Cascades of molten sparks sprayed from the angle grinder and the pungent smell of burnt metal and ozone hung heavily in the air. Outside walls were daubed with messages of defiance and a banner was slung across the door that simply read "RESIST!"

Locked On

Then at midnight on Thursday 9th May 2002 the court order took effect - any that chose to disobey were now open to criminal charges. The barricade was locked into position and simultaneously our first press release went out.

The effect was instant, with the radio and TV calling us up at 5AM the following morning to arrange interviews and footage of the lock-ons. Some of us were barricaded inside, some formed a human chain across the outside, others unfurled banners from the roof. The bailiffs decided to play it cool and sent an undercover officer down to survey the situation. He kept his distance from the activity around the barricade - the sight of people being D-locked round the neck must have made him nervous - an eagle-eyed camera man spotted him and managed to gently squeeze him for information. He said that the bailiffs were undermanned for the job and would have to come back next week with reinforcements and the police.

Sure enough come Monday morning the eviction gang arrived with a crew of builders tooled up with crowbars.

They wandered around searching for a way over the high, barbed wired, perimeter wall. One finally managed to climb up and have a quick peek - but he soon jumped back down defeated. They huffed and they puffed through the cracks in the door but they couldn't blow it down. A police helicopter then arrived and began low sweeps of the area, presumably taking reconnaissance photos of the roof top and surrounding land. Finding no chink in our armour it flew back to its empty nest. After hissing through the door "We shall return..." the rest of the boys in blue (and fluorescent-acid-yellow) left, leaving the "law" unenforced and Sainsbury's still locked out.

So far they haven't come back, but there have been some intriguing developments...

All that next week we were getting prime time news coverage on TV, radio and in the local paper. It was then that the developers approached us and asked if we'd consider "going away" if they paid us - as they wanted to "avoid a scrap in public". Of course

Straight into the mouth of the beast: Demo at London Rd Sainsbury's, April, 2002

Banner drop on a busy Saturday shopping afternoon on London Rd.

we declined and sent a clear message back - it's not money that makes the world go round but a force of nature!

Unable to shift us, Sainsbury's PR department got to work trying to soften up the opposition elsewhere. The very next weekend, at a local workers co-operative open day, they managed to pay £1000 to the event organisers to hang a large banner across the public park. By associating themselves with well respected environmental groups they perhaps thought that they could influence public opinion. Sainsbury's are no strangers to the mass manipulation of consensus, after all they are not, as the event organiser who excepted their cheque, put it - "our local shop" but one of Britain's most powerful corporations. Last year Lord Sainsbury (Sainsbury's largest share holder while being the Parliamentary Under-Secretary of State for Science and Innovation and big time funder of GMO research - no conflict of interest there!) gave the Labour Party its single biggest "donation", (a total of £6 million in the last two years) [5]. The company runs controversial "cash for schools" campaigns (£28 million in the past 6 years) [6], and high profile media advertising daily. This particular PR stunt however, backfired and the banner was immediately "subvertised" to replace the banner we had lost to the violent security guard at that recent supermarket action.

There is a coded knock on the door - the day shift has arrived with fresh supplies. My sleeping companions stir, and breakfast is prepared. We continue our impassioned conversations from the night before and it's decided that now's the time to come out from behind the barricade and strike while the iron's still hot...

Watch this space - or liberate your own.

Amanita Muscaria

Supermarkets are part of the problem - not the solution!

• For more info check: www.solarcity.co.uk/BUDD
• If you live in the Brighton area and object to the proposed development write to the Planning officer, Paul Vidler, and your MP and tell 'em what you think
• Boycott Sainsbury's and all other supermarkets and large food manufacturers. Spend your money in locally owned shops where the profit stays in the area.
• Support small, independent suppliers, processors and retailers.
• Support local farmers by using their farm shops, Organic box schemes, going to farmers markets.
• Encourage small retailers to stock locally produced food.
• Help set up new methods of distribution locally, eg. co-operatives for marketing local produce locally, delivery schemes.
• Buy imported goods only when they cannot be grown in this country
• Lobby for more help for farmers to convert to organic production.
• Grow your own vegetables.
• Take an interest in where your food comes from and what is in it.
* If you would like to help the campaign you can get a "BARRICADE" t-shirt from: info@spor.org.uk or from the Peace Centre, Brighton.

Foot Notes: [1] Brighton and Hove Council Housing Strategy Report 2001/2002; [2] ibid; [3] The average gross weekly income in Great Britain is £400.00 , the average for the South East is £423.00, in Brighton it is only £352.40. Source, NES table E15 1999; [4]>www.corporatewatch.org.uk< Company profiles-Food & Supermarkets-Sector Overview.htm; [5]http://globalarchive.ft.com/globalarchive/article.html?id=011214001692&query=Sainsbury=Labour+donation; [6] www.sainsburys.com

TraShCO

£ A litre of our milk costs the shopper 72p. We pay the farmer 19p per litre, when it costs on average, 21p to produce it. Similarly, we sell white potatoes for 35p per kilo and pay the farmer 9p. So where does the rest go?

TOSHCO

£ Our chief executive earned £1,608,000 in 2001. In the last five years the net income of a 500 acre family farm plunged from £80,000 to just £2,500 forcing them into more intensive farming.

FIASCO

£ Meanwhile the taxpayer picks up the cost of industrial farming. We fool shoppers again with extravagant claims of 'price cuts' whilst raising the price of other goods instead. We even have a deal with a major rival not to undercut them on popular products.

Figures are accurate as of the 27th Feb 2002.

Selling farmers short

At Tescon, we pride ourselves with discreetly squeezing the maximum possible money out of our customers and suppliers. With our pre-tax profits for 2001 likely to be around £1.22billion, we're certainly succeeding!

Whats wrong with SUPERMARKETS

February 2002
Corporate Watch

Support the work of the **Small and Family Farms Alliance** (Tel: 01726 843647) and **Farmers for Action** (www.farmersforaction.org) who have been battling with supermarkets for a fair farmgate price. To find out why supermarkets are at the heart of many of the social and environmental ills that plague society, see the Corporate Watch booklet **'What's Wrong with Supermarkets'**. www.corporatewatch.org.uk

TESCON

Making you pay more

Every little hurts

WAKE UP! WAKE UP! IT'S YER PLAN SPEAKING

We lost the battle and they turned the site into a nature reserve - what a complete waste.

SchNEWS
weekly
www.schnews.org.uk

Friday 22nd March 2002   Free/Donation   Issue 347

PLAN GREEDY

"The proposed reforms represent the most significant erosion of civil rights in planning by any Government since the system was introduced in 1947. The measures are an ill-considered recipe for administrative chaos. They would favour big business to the exclusion of individuals and communities fighting to make their voice heard" - www.planningdisaster.co.uk

If you've ever been involved in fighting a planning proposal then you'll appreciate how bureaucratic and unfriendly the process is. When Neo-Labour came to power they made vague promises that this would change, which it has. Spurred on by their big business buddies and led by the Confederation of British Industry (CBI), they're busy pressing ahead with 'streamlining' the planning system to ensure that in the future planning considerations don't get in the way of making money. The government says these changes are necessary because the pesky public has made the whole process too time consuming. So in a recent Green Paper they laid down plans to scrap public consultation altogether for big projects such as major roads, rail links, airports, power stations and incinerators. Instead decisions will be made in Westminster with only the minimum amount of parliamentary debate. For smaller proposals the process is going to be speeded up in response to 'business need', this may include things like limiting the number of objectors at a public enquiries. There's also going to be a relaxation of development controls and the introduction of 'Business Planning Zones'- areas where businesses will be have free reign to carry on building without the need or permission.

Just Plan Lies

Local councils, who according to central government make poor and bureaucratic decisions, are also being cut out of the new streamlined process. Councils won't need to produce Local Plans anymore, instead powers are now being handed over to Regional Development Agencies. These have no democratic accountability, and are stuffed full of business representatives that are more interested in new trunk roads than sustainable development.

All these changes will add to an already heavily biased system that only allows developers but not objectors to appeal against decisions they don't like.

In Brighton the current pace of development is staggering. One of the most controversial schemes in the pipeline is the redevelopment of the Brighton Station

site. The story of people's attempts to stop business getting their hands on this land just shows what communities are up against.

Sainsburied

The site, one of the largest derelict brownfield areas in the south, was formerly public land owned by British Rail. It was handed over free to Railtrack, when the railways were privatised, who in the interest of their wallets flogged it to the highest bidder, the New England Consortium (NEC) a development group including supermarket giants J. Sainsbury's. In 1997 the consortium put in a planning application which included a Sainbury's superstore. The local council didn't think that the community would be interested in the application and so didn't arrange a public consultation. Locals disagreed and formed their own group, BUDD (Brighton Urban Design and Development), who organised their own public meetings and started to draw up plans of what Brighton people wanted the site to be used for. Nobody wanted the supermarket. The Council rejected the NEC application, a decision upheld by a public enquiry, and even went as far as saying they would always reject a supermarket on the site. Unfortunately this didn't put off Sainsbury's and their chums who last year submitted a new 'radical' application, allegedly an 'exemplar of 21st-century urban development'. It is so 'radical' and far out that it includes 2 hotels, a 200 space car park, offices, posh flats, crap bedsits for 'key workers' (nurses, teachers, etc), a language school, and oh yeah a supermarket! Unsurprisingly BUDD are equally opposed to this latest offering, which will do nothing to help the 15,000 odd households in the Brighton area considered in 'housing need', and which will also lead to increased pollution and congestion in the area. Town planning models have predicted that this heavily car dependant development will lead to a 35% rise in pollution in an area of town where nearly half of the people don't have a car, not to mention rises in noise pollution levels.

As supermarkets appear local businesses go down the pan; it's estimated that in the next 5 years 600 chemist shops will close as supermarkets open up their own in store chemists. Far from providing local employment as they often claim - one supermarket accounts for the loss of 276 full time jobs. A typical out-of-town superstore causes £25,000-worth of congestion, pollution and associated damage every week.

Brighton doesn't need any new supermarkets but the Council who've now changed their tune reckon this is the only way they are going to get a quality development for this site. The continued involvement of Sainsbury's in this scheme has little to do with what's good for Brighton but more to do with 'planning gain' - bribery to the rest of us - Sainsbury's are promising to build a road into the site and provide a building for community groups. This 'planning gain' has become a regular feature of planning laws, and result in supermarkets, office blocks and car parks in places that are well suited to low cost housing, or even being left as they are.

Right now urban development in this country is on the increase. In Brighton you can hardly pick up the local rag without reading a story about allotments or nature reserves being threatened with concrete. These new planning laws are going to ensure that communities will become increasingly passive onlookers as PLC's take over, with direct action still being the only way left to take a stand.

* Make some noise oustide London Road Sainsbury's, Saturday 23rd 10am.

* A decision about the application for the Brighton Station Site is due to be made by Brighton Council on 16th April, Demonstrate 3:30pm outside Hove Town Hall.

* Brighton Urban Design and Development 01273-681166 www.BUDDbrighton.org

* 'Check Out Chuck Out: A directory for campaigners against supermarket developments' Tel: 01865-791391 www.corporatewatch.org.uk

* Campaign for Planning Sanity 0161 959 0999 www.onlincam.freeserve.co.uk

EU'll Be Sorry

Last Saturday saw the end of the European Summit, held in Barcelona, descend into the usual rioting- plastic bullets, tear gas and baton charges from the cops and petrol bombs, cobble stones and burning banks from the protesters. The march, which organisers estimated at 500,000 strong (even though thousands of people were turned away at the border) was a noisy protest. And after over zealous cops attacked a few cheeky protestors all hell broke loose. The demo became noisier to the sound of breaking glass - banks, posh shops and fast food outlets becoming the instruments in place of drums and whistles. The match between Barcelona and Real Madrid was also disrupted for 7 minutes after activists d-locked themselves to the goalposts at the Nou Camp stadium! But what happened in the summit itself? Well, Tony Bleugh's new best mate is Silvio Berlusconi, who has members of the M.S.I.- the modern day Italian fascist party, in his cabinet - and, more importantly, also owns 90% of the Italian media. Berlusconi, Blair and the Spanish PM, Aznar have formed their own 'axis of evil' in Europe to promote their ideas of privatisation of state owned utilities, eradicating workers rights and not giving a toss about the environment. A lot of this was eventually agreed on with railways, electricity and gas companies destined to be privatised by 2004 (er, too late already done that in England). Even the moderate General Secretary of the TUC John Monks denounced Blair as 'bloody stupid' for siding with the most right wing governments in the EU. It seems to SchNEWS that all future EU summits are going to end up the same as Barcelona and Gothenburg and with more and more workers losing their jobs maybe the black block will increase in size. For more info including photos and personal accounts check out http://barcelona.indymedia.org/ (mostly in Spanish)

*Social movements in Spain are being increasingly criminalised as their government rushes to privatise everything. Students who've been involved in protests against the LOU (Ley Organica de Universidades) which will privatise the higher education system, are being listed as terrorists and are being tracked down and arrested. A protest camp in Sevilla, which lasted for 50 days, was violently evicted by police last month. www.antilou.org/

*This week in Monterrey, Mexico demonstrators held a peaceful protests at the UN aid summit where 50 heads of state were due to meet with IMF and World Bank bureaucrats to talk about how to plunge the poor countries even further into debt. http://mexico.indymedia.org/

* To find out about up and coming summits around the world www.protest.org.

Positive SchNEWS

Despite government targets to 'remove' 600 asylum seekers per week, and negative influences from the mainstream media, there are groups established and developing all over the country who want to show solidarity and support to people here seeking asylum and build links to benefit us all. In Gorton in January a 'Welcome to Manchester' event was held to bring people together with music, food, information and children's activities. As well as showing friendship, the idea was to provide a space for people to meet each other and develop joint responses to common difficulties. www.beyondtv.org.uk/gorton

* National Conference to Defend Asylum Seekers this Saturday (23rd) in Manchester 07941-566183 www.ncadc.org.uk

SchNEWS in brief

This Saturday (23rd) join the 'Long March for the Climate' - one year after Bush dumped the Kyoto Agreement. The 20 mile walk starts 7am at the ESSO HQ, Ermyn Way, near Leatherhead and ends at the US embassy in Grosvenor Square 5.30 pm. You can also join in at the final leg 3.30 pm, Imperial War Museum, Lambeth Road. Info 020 88553327 www.campaignagainstclimatechange.net ** There's another Fun-raiser next Wednesday (27th) at the Volks Tavern, Brighton 9pm onwards with all the usual DJ suspects – with all money raised going to a good local cause ** CND have organised a 'Don't Start Wars' demo next Saturday (30th) 020-7700-2350 www.cnduk.org/campigns/30march.htm ** On Monday protesters stopped a Trident nuclear weapon truck convoy for 30 minutes in the village of Balloch by Loch Lomond by getting in front of, underneath, and on top of the vehicles carrying the warheads. 13 people were arrested including one person who tried to super-glue himself to the convoy. Ouch! Nukewatch commented: "It is absolutely vital that we draw public attention to this criminally dangerous road traffic" www.nukewatch.com Tel: 07715 538652 or 0775 1477628 ** Help is needed in Essex to save over 100 trees that would be chopped to make way for a new road. Two Houses need to be squatted by Good Friday, they really need people to come and live-in (there's room for 10 people). For more info call: 0776 1975701 email: noroad2002uk@yahoo.co.uk ** Wales is finally GM-free now that a Flintshire farm has not been selected to run a third year of crop trials. ** There's a public inquiry into the pro's and con's of the building of a Lamberhurst bypass on 23rd April at Bewl Water Visitors Centre, Lamberhurst. www.lamberhurstbypass.com. ** From 29th March to 3rd April there will be a Women's Peace Camp outside Sellafield Nuclear Site. Info: 07751-450482, mia_kat@yahoo.com - This will be followed by a mixed peace camp (4th - 8th) Info: 20-8546-7795, info@youthstudentcnd.org.uk

R.I.P.

Jo, a protestor at the Nine Ladies Anti-Quarry Campaign in Derbyshire was tragically killed eight days ago by a fire, which ripped through part of the camp below where she was sleeping. The remains of the tower have since been removed, a memorial garden built on its site and a plum tree planted in her memory. www.nineladies.uklinux.net.

End of the Road

With the new roads programme around the corner the direct action crew are getting their act together. A gathering is being organised in Nottingham from 19-21st April to plan tactics. Friday 19th- from 7pm food, and preliminary meeting. Sat 20th- Update briefing on new road schemes and corporate links. Planning tactics and response. Sun 21st- meeting space for those wishing to build further on the day before. At Sumac Centre, 245 Gladstone street, Nottingham, NG7 6HX contact: 07813 505480 endoftheroad@hushmail.com. Bring: ideas, information, propaganda, bedding, roll mats (crash space will be provided), money for food and a contribution towards venue hire.

Inside SchNEWS

Donnie MacLeod, an organic farmer from Ardesier, near Inverness, has been jailed for 21 days for contempt of court. He admitted that he'd been present at the trashing of a GM farm scale trial at Rives Farm, Munlochy in June last year, but refused to point out anyone else who took part in the action. There will be a march this Saturday in support of Donnie from Inverness centre to the prison where he's held. Meet 11am outside Marks & Spencer, Inverness. Send letters and cards of support to Donnie MacLeod, 73125, B Hall, HM Prison Porterfield, Inverness, IV2 3HH.

The Munlochy Vigil have been watching over a GM field in Scotland since last year. The camp now has planning permission. Contact them GM Protest Caravan The lay-by near Roskill Farm, Munlochy, Ross-shire, Scotland IV8 8PA www.gmfreescotland.net

* Last week Spanish prisoners went on hunger strike to protest against invasive FIES units and to demand better prison conditions. FIES are isolation units in which prisoners are subjected to constant surveillance. Mail and phone calls are monitored, belongings are always being inspected, and torture is commonplace. The hunger strikers want: an end to FIES and all the isolation units; the end of dispersal where prisoners are sent far away from their hometowns, families and friends; the release of all prisoners with incurable illness like AIDS and Cancer and the release of all prisoners who have spent more than 20 years inside. The ultimate goal of this solidarity action is to completely shut down the prison system as part of radical social change.

ABC Spain: Cruz Negra Anarquista Secc Iberica, Paseo Alberto Palacio #2, CP 2802 Villaverde Alto, Madrid, Spain

* Paul Robinson, who was recently released from a Swedish prison where he has been in jail since the EU Summit protests in Gothernberg last June (SchNEWS 310) has been sacked from his job. Paul worked as a library attendant at UCL college for over 3 years and his union are appealing against the decision.

* Last Friday Dogan Tokmak became the 88th person to die in Turkey in a hunger strike against the new prison isolation cells.

Free For All Market

Police in Mexico, obviously intent on a bit of confrontation decided, in their wisdom, to raid a market at the heart of Chiapas to protect the interests of multi-nationals. Chiapas is a state in Mexico which the Zapatistas are fighting to make autonomous. This bunch of state-sponsored heavily armed lunatics marched in with riot gear to combat poor people selling counterfeit tapes and CDs in San Cristobal de las Casas, one of the towns taken during the Zapatista uprising of 1994. The indigenous people of Chiapas didn't take too kindly to this and retaliated by breaking into various shops for a bit of wealth redistribution and torching two police vehicles. The chaos did not last long, as the kill-joys came back with reinforcements, riot shields, helmets and tear gas and set about beating and arresting people.

...and finally..

SchNEWS loves it when governments get their priorities right. So hats off to the French for removing protestors' banners from above the Chamonix tunnel – because they are apparently unsafe. Unlike the 6,000 trucks a day that will soon tear down the valley when the road re-opens. ugatza@gmx.net

Disclaimer
SchNEWS warns anyone whose lost the plot would be a crazy plan not to take us away in a Paddic wagon. Honest.

For Peat's Sake

HATFIELD MOOR is an ecologically vital system for over 5,500 species and the subject of a campaign to save it from peat mining since the 70's. A recent deal by English Nature, meant that while the government paid Scotts £17.3 million to stop mining at three sites throughout the country, Scotts have been given two more years to dig at Hatfield Moor, which will irreversibly damage the peat bog. Peat Alert had already called a four day blockade of the peat works in the week leading up to the Easter Bank Holiday, the peat industry's busiest time.

An action camp for the four day blockade was planned for nearby. Before the site was taken, both night-time and daytime actions to Hatfield Moor had been taking place. Filling in ditches and blocking pipes to stop the peat being drained, plus other sabotage actions on the moors and at the works had caused at least £30,000 worth of damage. (Scott's estimate)

When people turned up to crack the prison training/RAF base site on the Saturday morning, they found it had passed from the Ministry of Defence's hands into a private landowner. The landowner turned up and gave us permission to stay and keys to his hefty lock! The police put pressure on both the landowner to evict us and the Green Tree Pub where we were meeting for the street party, but all involved supported us. The campsite was a fortress, complete with barbed wire rimmed fences and barricades, our own four flags flew from the old radar tower. An evidence gathering team was permanently stationed across from the site. The Anarchist Teapot provided field kitchen and Generator X supplied us with wind and solar power. Before the blockade begun, Scotts were ringing various other campaign groups asking what could they do to stop the blockade - all responded that they asked for it!

DAY ONE - 25th March: On the Monday morning the police were out in force with a helicopter, horses, dogs, landrovers and vans at the crossroads leading up to the peat works, and found some of our essential equipment while searching ditches. They tried to get a Section 60 (stop, search, demask) - at first denied but later granted - and a section 14 (designated protest area only) was put in place; between a post saying assembly start and point. About 100 people left the 'Green Tree' pub at one o'clock. The Section 14 was read out, but a bicycle sound system played music and various instruments and drums were played. Police formed lines to stop the march. People continued on holding reinforced banners, padding, hard hats and masks. We decided take the path of least resistance, running cross country and managed to seize the only exit road from the works.

The road was blocked for two and a half hours, with lorries unable to leave the works. 18 vans of cops in riot gear moved in, arresting everyone who stayed in the road (and some who didn't), so targeting specific individuals. An hour later there were thirty eight arrests, and two that got away. All were released by 5AM (except one for refusing bail conditions) The bail conditions were not to go within two miles of the works. A police map-reading error meant that everyone COULD go back to the site, and onto the south moors where most of the peat extraction takes place. No lorries left the peat works that night.

DAY TWO: On Tuesday some people went to a FoE demo. Others went out in small groups to try and find a lorry to blockade or went out on the moors ditch filling. The demo was meant to go to the works, but stayed in the designated protest area. Lorries were moved in convoy, with a heavy police escort.

A large police presence near the works meant a cross country ambush was not possible. Three people on the south moors were arrested for breaking bail conditions, although they weren't and were eventually released without charge once we had shown the police how to map read.

DAY THREE: On Wednesday we planned to blockade and lock on to the lorry convoy as they stopped at a roundabout on the A18 - the new exit route for the lorries. The normal exit route was not being used as it passed too near to our campsite! Continued police surveillance stopped play, but they once again held up the lorries at the peat works, so that no convoys left while we were at the roundabout.

DAY FOUR: On Thursday we tatted down due to diminished numbers. Vehicles leaving site were pulled over and followed by motorcycle cops. We left the camp in a convoy of five vehicles with a six police car escort into Sheffield. Despite only being able to block the road for three and half hours on the Monday, we seriously disrupted Scotts operation throughout the week. A lorry normally leaves the peat works every four minutes during that week. We slowed it to about twenty every six hours. We received a lot of local support for defending the peat moors and gave more people a chance to see the ecological destruction that is peat mining.

Many more people will now be back for both advertised and impromptu actions. Our next action will be a Mass Trespass on the moors on Saturday 11th May. It will be a chance to disrupt work and protest against the enclosure of common land that allows this ecological destruction to happen, and is also in remembrance of Benny Rothman from the 1932 Kinder Scout Mass Trespass who died recently. People will be going out and filling ditches, disrupting work between now and then and stickering and/or slashing the peat bags at Garden Centres. Why not join in!

Ring: 0778 7782259 or email: info@peatalert.org.uk and look at www.peatalert.org.uk,

Plus donations are very welcome! Please make cheques/P.O.s out to "Peat Alert" and send to: Peat Alert, c/o CRC, 16 Sholebroke Avenue, LEEDS LS7 3HB

Gabriel Nkwelle is a human rights activist from Cameroon who fled his country following his exposure of electoral fraud, after having been imprisoned five times for his political activity in that country. He came to England seeking asylum, and was put into detention. While in Rochester prison he publicised the treatment of his fellow asylum detainees and was transferred to Belmarsh Prison, Britain's most notorious top-security jail. With the support of BID (Bail for Immigration Detainees) he won bail after eight months imprisonment, and upon release worked as a volunteer at BID helping other detainees.

But days after receiving accolades at the Liberty/Justice human rights awards in December 2001 his bail was denied, he was back in detention, and set to be deported on Christmas eve, 2001. Only hours before he was due to board a plane his lawyers obtained an injunction giving him time to apply for a judicial review, so he remained back in detention in the UK. He was then prevented from being interviewed by the BBC by the Home Office – being told that 'this is not your country'. During his time back in detention he assisted other detainees in Tinsley House, Harmondsworth and Yarlswood with their bail applications.

After eleven months in detention he was eventually released on temporary admission from Yarlswood on the 2nd February 2002, and since then has continued to work defending human rights in detention centres including writing and public speaking.

While in detention he wrote several letters describing his experiences for distribution to the public – this is one…

Welcome To The Free World
letter from asylum seeker while in detention

09-10-00
Nkwelle Gabriel, TDOB41
HMP Rochester
Kent
MBl 3QS

Appeal For Urgent Intervention

Fellow human beings, fellow mankind, it is with great sincerity that I make this desperate appeal for your timely intervention in the horrifying and pathetic plight of asylum seekers in UK detained at HMP Rochester, Kent under Immigration Act 1971.

A subjected people have by right under universal standards and human principles the obligation to seek redress by any means internationally acceptable. I hold the view that all men were created equal and by virtue of their existence are vested with certain inalienable rights to be the sole masters of their destiny.

This has not been the case with asylum seekers in UK detained at HMP Rochester who from the beginning, because of their accommodating attitudes, have been slowly stripped of their human rights. With the oppressors' mechanism of 02/10/00 (HMP Rochester), now working full time to completely dehumanise and emasculate our people no matter what means including genocide. It is therefore time for asylum seekers in Rochester, Kent, and humanity as a whole to fight back.

Many people may not readily understand or agree with the reasons why asylum seekers should be clamouring to restore their rights equally as any other human being.

Asylum seekers detained at the notorious HMP Rochester, are treated worse than convicted criminals detained at the same HMP. Asylum seekers are held indefinitely without trial or initial decision on a claim made. This decision is taken by the immigration Service which does not explain the decision in detail to the persons concerned.

Asylum seekers held at HMP Rochester, Kent, have fewer rights than suspected criminals and often do not understand why they are being held indefinitely.

Not surprisingly, this causes mental anguish among detainees, many of whom have already survived horrendous ordeals in their own countries. The whole process of asylum seeking and being detained for a lengthy period of time in UK is extremely humiliating and distressing.

The way to refugee status is a long road. At HMP Rochester, Kent, asylum seekers are detained for long periods in the Echo and Delta wings. Cells are four by four metres - toilet included - two inmates per cell. The sixty by six metre area in the middle i[s] for games. Per day you are allowed six hours only in this area, fo[r] eighteen hours you are locked up in your cell. Echo wing house[s] one hundred and fifteen whilst Delta about sixty five inmates.

Being locked up makes you appreciate your freedom. Out o[f] everything in life, losing your freedom is the hardest situatio[n] to deal with. After months/years of incarceration the followin[g] are mentally deranged. Shi (Chinese), Saglam TDO6SO (Turk[ish]) Nwange (Kenyan), Fal TD0498 (Gambian), Shayanghi TC317[?] (Iraqi), Hammidou Deraji (Algerian), etc.

Inmates had attempted serious self-harm and nobody care[s] Medication is a forgotten issue, if you happen to be sick, the grav[e] should be your next home. Both medical and wing staff abus[e] asylum seekers racially, call them Kunta Kinte and saying wor[ds] like "…you all will be deported poor people", and "black coloure[d] monkeys". It's awful. I can't tell how awful I feel. The secret se[t] ever more secret, unhappy misled; "unless you know where yo[u] are, you don't know who you are."

In a recent survey of 02/10/00, a Romanian (Kvec FG 6796) w[as] seriously brutalised by five Echo wing members of staff (Archiba[ld] RCO5G, Brads RC062, S 0 Gamble RCO2O, Henderson RC0[?] and Mather RCO112) in my presence and others inmates for doi[ng] absolutely nothing.

Inmates from Delta say that a Kenyan who has been detain[ed] for fifteen months by Immigration Service without trial roast[ed] himself in his cell on the night of October 5th. None of the inma[tes] knows his whereabouts as from that night to date. Life witho[ut] freedom is a high price to pay.

Asylum seekers are kept in prison without charge, the sound [of] doors slamming and the ever constant keys echoing around the wi[ng] become our early morning wake up. If we are on remand, when a[re] we going to be sentenced? It's a question without an answer.

Expired food stuffs are always given to asylum seekers [at] HMP Rochester. When questioned, you are threatened to be tak[en] to the segregation unit. On September 25th a verbal system w[as] implemented by the governor, whereby asylum seekers detain[ed] at HMP Rochester must work seven hours in a workshop job [at] 0.25 pence per hour. He who refuses, is locked up till those in [the] workshop are back in the wing.

Today October 10th inmates are served with the worksh[op] compulsory memo. For God's sake, where on earth is an ad[ult] human being forced to do a job not of his/her choice and to

Bin Laden Royal Shock

The Queen Mum - we got rid of her. It was time for her to go

ROYAL SCANDAL

Details have come to light linking the Al Qa'ida network to the death of the Queen Mother.

A communique intercepted by British intelligence from Al Qa'ida sources brags about their role in the death of the Queen Mother, claiming they had "...been targeting her for some time". Osama himself is quoted as saying "I was take it or leave it really when it came to the Queen Mum. But then one of the brothers suggested her and I said 'oh go on then' and from then we

---

paid 0.25 pence/hour? Is it modern slavery? Where are we? Third world or first world? Some inmates have been trying to draw the attention of media, but once you are noticed, you are transferred to the segregation unit.

On the day in October I was to publish my appeal for urgent intervention, a member of education department whose name was not made known to me, betrayed me in the governor. At about 1310 hours, five members of staff (Whooten, Grimes, Henderson RC 096, Breds RC 062 and Virdler RC 158) rushed into my cell, moved out my inmate Ndoma TD 0534 to the TV room and seized all the appeal papers printed ready to be dispatched. That governor Lewis ordered the seizure.

As a detainee have I not got the right to express my view to the media?

We leave at tiptoe stance never knowing what to expect next as thousands of asylum seekers live in internal exile being continuously hunted for out right elimination like dogs. To us as people, there can be neither peace nor progress where unrestrained repression, assimilation, exploitation and human inequality reign supreme.

To you comrades, also battling your own personal hell; I wish you courage and with God's blessings a happy ending to all your woes. It will also help all of us disadvantaged people, to get together and aid each other in any way possible.

To all of you, whom God has blessed with justice, humanity's most cherished gift, human dignity and freedom, help us, the not so fortunate so we can have a semblance of it someday.

The situation now brewing here at HMP Rochester, has the potential of making the asylum seekers the flash point of a dangerous regional conflict. I call on you people to render any help you can to asylum seekers held at HMP Rochester.

The gratitude of asylum seekers will know no bounds. God crown our efforts with success and may he bless us all.

If you have any queries concerning the contents of this appeal, please do not hesitate to contact the writer,

Yours sincerely,

(signed)

Nkwelle Gabriel

for more information contact

Bail For Immigration Detainees

7833 625 033

8 Commercial Street, London, E1 6LS

bailforimmigrationdetainees@yahoo.co.uk

THREE MILLION MARCH AGAINST BERLUSCONI

Rome, Tuesday March 26th. Italian press reports claim up to three million attended the CGIL rally against Silvio Berlusconi and his plans for Labour market reforms, which will make it easier for employers to sack people.

Pics: Jess Hurd

EV'RY BODY NEEDS GOOD NEIGHBOURS

If it works for Unilever... Easton residents give the dealers a step up the advertising ladder. (The council jetwashed it off within 24 hours - wouldn't want anyone thinking something's amiss in the inner city)

Pic: Simon Chapman

When the revolution comes, we'll get rid of the police cos there'll be no more crime... yeah right. Anarchist utopias are all very well, but anti social behaviour is carving up communities in the here and now, and 'blueprints for the future' don't take knives off throats. In Bristol, one community awash with crack dealing scumbags - which the police refuse to tackle - has chosen to ditch living in fear, and take on the problem themselves.

By FLACO

Having sustained years of systematic beatings, communities all over Britain are finally imploding under the jungle-law/free-market greed-fest of smack and crack dealing and the anti-social, anti-people, anti-life bullshit behaviour it generates.

Skipping the idea of underpants over trousers (hooray), in favour of a pair of matching Jean Marie Le Twat cravats (boo), top UK crime fighting duo, Blunkett and McBlair (enough! – ed) dusted off some ol'-skool reactionary slogans in the hope the resulting confusion will camouflage the absence of intelligent policy. (...er, more boo...)

In March, Home Secretary David Blunkett managed to exit London and venture down the M4 to Easton in Bristol with a circus-full of performing home office clowns and tongue-lolling media in tow. The stunt of the moment, was the unveiling of his 'crime hotspots' and New Labour/Old Tory sus laws.

Much was made about the crime levels on Easton's Stapleton Road and the size of the resident black population. But the race card played (cynically) by Blunkett, and picked up (enthusiastically) by the press, has sod all relevance to the situation confronting local people.

Basically like dozens of inner city neighbourhoods nationwide, the community in Easton is being torn apart by smack and crack dealing and the anti social behaviour it generates. Despite Blunkett and the rest of the 'good people' distancing themselves from the 'criminal hardcore', the crack dealers, muggers and scumbags pimping out fourteen year old girls, are merely subscribing to the same greed driven mentality as every corporate CEO and Downing Street resident has since they minted the first fucking groat. The single message peddled by schools, governments and television, is the same one (often unwittingly) picked up and driven home by parents and peers alike. Namely, the only thing little Johnny should be concerned about is: how much money he can accumulate in his life, how many 'things' that will enable him to 'buy', and how much 'power' it will afford him. Society tells him - do anything, and step on anyone, in order to further your individual position - fuck over everybody who dares stand in your way. There is no society. There is no obligation to the greater community.

In Easton, the dealers (black and white - but increasingly immigrant Jamaican self-styled 'gangsta yardies') and the punters

jacking up on our doorsteps (black and white, some local, some not) all fuel the fear in the streets, and, the ranks of muggers in the underpasses. Hatred is the currency of choice on the streets – and every youngster sports a big-bad-sneer and mouthful of menace 'coz that's the way to be'. The police (more or less exclusively white) are totally unwilling to deal with the situation - or more to the point, they are content to let the situation in Easton escalate - it keeps the 'scum' out of the 'nice' parts of town - and the hope is, a well-nurtured crime ghetto may result in a cash injection from above. (Avon and Somerset chief constable Steve Pilkington said that without any more money - and Blunkett came with empty pockets - Labour might as well be trying to crack crime on the moon).

The tightly orchestrated Blunkett-junkett in March made sure no unsightly views were aired before the invited press and New Labour faithful. High salaried 'community-workers' and businessmen (including a locally despised loan shark) were ushered in to grip grin and pat his master's dog. Every press agency was on the guest list, but both Stapleton Road (it's a long road) residents groups were prevented getting near the minister by heavily armoured, and armed, police - the number of which Stapleton Road has never seen before, or since. (It was only a last minute tip-off about the visit that enabled residents to give the Home Secretary a good old Easton billboard style welcome... much to the shock of the camped out GMTV camera crew). In the event, two smack deals went down in full view of the thirty odd assembled old bill and special branch officers as Blunkett was doing his Diana-about. The few disgruntled residents, who had got wind of the 9am stunt, openly mocked the

'Spend fewer pennies... trash more communities, Easton doesn't need a home office stunt ... Blunkett'. Locals and cops join forces to welcome Blunkett.

cops, who pretended not to notice, safe in the knowledge the journalists present would obediently do likewise.

Like Trinity Road's [Bristol police station] sick-list, activists have continually shied away from tackling crime. Anarchist scribes paint us pictures of self policing utopias where criminality will disappear along with private property. All very well, but fuck all use to anyone facing a four-inch blade at the corner of the Easton way. Similarly, liberal whites recoil at the prospect of being on the 'wrong' side of a scrap with someone flouting asylum laws, or any conflict with even a hint of ethnic involvement.

It's horseshit. No one's denying the responsibility of successive administrations who have consistently denigrated and ghettoised working class communities, and used drugs, bad housing and poverty to keep people down and out (of the loop). But that does not free everyone else from shouldering some blame. If you are fucking over my community, you are a scumbag. Whether you're a corporate developer, a white racist cop or a black crack-dealing pimp, it doesn't matter. It doesn't matter sod all if you've dodged a fucked-up asylum system. Being a law-breaker doesn't make you a social activist. If you want to make money out of misery and destroy the community in the process, you are as much the class enemy as any titled parasite, and you need to be stopped. This is not a race issue. It's greed versus community.

Also, it's not enough to say to people who live in the area: 'Look, we don't want more police on the streets', or, 'we don't want fucking CCTV.' People who have been mugged, or whose kids go out to play and come home with needles in their hands, say, 'I'm sorry, but I'm fucking scared.' You cannot tell them: 'Oh no you're not.'

But, and there is a big but, many people (black and white alike) - here in Easton at least - are well aware that the solutions to their predicament will not come in a panda car or via a ballot box (however long you wait). They are sick of struggling up 'proper channels' only to be blocked by bureaucrats. They've stopped calling the cops, because they know the cops don't come. [The local beat officer at a post Blunkett community meeting confirmed that there is only one dedicated officer at any one time for the entire Easton, Eastville and St Judes area (an area the size of Brixton facing similar problems). To residents who complained of waiting three hours for a police response he said: "You're lucky we came at all".] The result is that several community groups have sprung up in recent months, all with increasingly militant agendas. One crack house has been shut down, dealers' phones have been 'cut off' and proposals are being sorted to reclaim large chunks of land. This isn't about vigilantism, but about taking control back from all bogus authority (whether that authority is backed by parliament, or by a machine pistol in the boot of a BMW).

Consensus won't come easy (the anarchists and the CCTV brigade are all in there together), but the alternatives on offer 'neighbourhood wardens' [ie: Reliance security rent-a-cops] from central government or 'gentrification' from the local New Lab/corpo-friendly council) are backed by no-one. We're all on a learning curve and we're not sure where it'll end up. But bitching bout it and doing nothing is, hopefully, no longer an option.

~NEIGHBOURS~
♪ EV'RYBODY ♪
NEEDS GOOD...

From **Daily Hatemail** Mayday 2002

SHOCK HORROR
FIVE DAY FESTIVAL OF FILTH!

Hundreds of self-declared sexual deviants, social misfits and anarchists recently CONVERGED on a residential street in London's East End. They blatantly SQUATTED an entire block of flats for an event advertised through shadowy internet sites as 'Queeruption 2002'. In an effort to keep the sordid goings-on under wraps, they refused to talk to the 'Daily Hatemail'. However we bring you this UNDERCOVER EXCLUSIVE, thanks to our intrepid reporter. She INFILTRATED their makeshift brothel and OBSERVED what can only be described as a depraved orgy of perversion.

Attendees, many of them FOREIGN, mingled happily. They included all kinds of punks, soap-dodgers, hardened protestors, hippies, New Age Travellers, dole-scroungers, extremists and EVEN former lesbian separatists. Some sported nose-rings, others Swampy-style dreadlocks, many obviously took delight in their own body-smells. They talked openly about SEX, and everything else. Among them we found proponents of anti-capitalism, sado-masochism, even 'asexuality' (!). The entire building had been decked in what passed for 'Art' among these dead-beats: mostly gaudy fabric held up with tape, obscene images and piles of junk 'sculpture'.

A board in the entrance hall detailed a sinister list of the 'workshops & discussions' ranging from the oddball to the downright irresponsible (eg. 'Does HIV cause AIDS?' Well, duh! Publicity for the event even exhorted parents to bring their CHILDREN along and make use of the 'creche' - one can only imagine the sick ideas these people would preach to such innocent youngsters. Most frighteningly, participants boasted of their plans to REPEAT this sickening spectacle around the world. Other cities with an underground minority of such freaks were mentioned: Hamburg, Stockholm, Montreal, Sydney, Barcelona and even Weston-super-Mare!

LONDON
QUEERUPTION
2002
Mind the Gap

Queeruption, an alternative queer gathering took place in a squat in Whitechapel from the 13th of March 2002. It was a five day international gathering for queer folk of all sexualities. The event was the continuation of a similar but smaller gathering that took place in London in 1998 and which has had sister events in New York and San Francisco in the last couple of years. The event was put up by a London based collective of anarchists (queer anarchists) who sought to offer a radical alternative to the commercial gay scene. Anarchism it is about combining radical sexual politics, with DIY, anti state/capitalist politics.

Inclusivity is central to Queeruption. Let's face it sexuality is more ambiguous than we usually give it space for. To the people involved in Queeruption 'queer' includes anybody that is challenging the societal norms that our sexuality has been squashed into. If you like shagging boys, girls, both, only yourself or nobody or if it changes according to the day of the week everyone is welcome in a queer space.

If you're interested in finding an alternative to the 'straight' gay scene (with its rampant consumerism & apathy), get in touch. Create some radical Queer community wherever you are.
http://www.queeruption.com

Shut up AnD fuck ME

257

Save Titnore Woods

BATTLELINES are being drawn in Worthing as a major battle to save a precious piece of Sussex countryside gets underway.

On one side are landowners and property developers hoping to make millions of pounds out of tarmacking over one of the last greenfield areas in the ever-expanding South Coast conurbation, with the collaboration of the Government and local authorities. On the other side are local residents and campaigners outraged by the horrific plans to build 875 new homes and an industrial development, together with the widening and

straightening of Titnore Lane to cope with the increase in traffic between the A27, A259 and the new developments.

The proposed road works would plough through rare ancient semi-natural woodland which has been there since the last ice age and is currently a Site of Nature Conservation Importance (SNCI). Several hundred trees would have to be felled, many over 150 years old and comprising oak, ash birch and willow. The woods are home to many species of wildlife, including dormice. Titnore Lane itself is part of our cultural heritage, reaching back at least to the Anglo-Saxon period and most probably way beyond that. It was part of a longer track that reached northwards across the South Downs and is rich in archaeological remains.

Public outrage has been ignited over the threat to Worthing's rural heritage in a big way, according to local campaigning newsletter The Porkbolter. They said: "It's been amazing. The protest group POW! (Protect Our Woodland!) was set up to be as fluid as possible - the idea was to encourage and empower people to act for themselves rather than try to control or direct the way they voiced their opposition." And that is the way it's been happening - people have been taking the initiative. "There have been floods of letters to the local press, home-made posters going up all over the place and people with petitions cropping up everywhere - one local bus driver even told us how he had been flagged down by a couple of Durrington schoolgirls just to ask him if he would add his support."

The swelling tide of public outrage certainly set alarm bells ringing at the local Tory party HQ. Although POW! was not involved in the local elections on May 2, the Durrington Conservative candidate Alan Whiteley saw fit to devote much of his "election special" newsletter to attacking the Titnore campaign. The newsletter said the Tory council would not be opposing the Titnore development because it "would be overruled" by central Government and suggested that all that was left to be decided were "the standards of services and amenities to be included in the development". The Tory leaflet tried to convince locals that "our lives are facing serious disruption from the invasion of Titnore Lane by the eco-warriors". It fumed: "Some Worthing people seem to believe they can achieve something by joining the May protest walk bringing whistles and a picnic. Do they realise they will be escorting seasoned activists into Titnore Woods? Will their stay be a brief or a long one? On the face of it 'Save Titnore Woods' looks a very good cause. But do the likes of Swampy actually 'Protect Our Woodland'?" The POW coalition, including Worthing Anarchists, SCAR and the Worthing Green Party, is openly claiming on its website the support of protestors from all over Britain and in Europe. "What on earth will the policing cost?" Alan Whiteley says: "Think long and hard before supporting these people. They have an agenda. It may not be yours."

Sadly for Mr Whiteley, it was the Tory agenda that was clearly not shared by the people of Durrington and he was humiliated at the polls, receiving less than half the votes of the Lib Dem winner. Furthermore the Lib Dems won three seats from the Conservatives across Worthing and gained control of the borough council. The Tories admitted to the Evening Argus the next day, May 3, that the Titnore Woods issue was one of the main factors behind their defeat. However, POW! was not lulled into a false sense of secu-

rity by the Lib Dems' pre-election pledges to oppose the development. Said a spokesman: "The battle has only just begun. The people of Durrington and Worthing know they cannot rely on politicians from any party to save the countryside." He added that the pressure for the site to be developed should not be underestimated. He explained that in the review of the Worthing Local Plan the inspector had rejected the idea of industrial development on the site but had approved the housing element. The landowners, the wealthy Somerset family, were also very influential locally and the property developers would also be trying to pull some strings, he said.

The three firms involved in the West Durrington Consortium are Bryant Homes (part of Taylor Woodrow), Persimmon Homes and the Heron Group, which is headed by Gerald Ronson, the disgraced tycoon jailed in the Guinness scandal in 1990. Having temporarily withdrawn their application to fine-tune it in line with the local plan inspector's comments, they would probably be dressing up their new-look plans as some kind of compromise, warned the POW! spokesman. He added: "We must not be fooled by this kind of manoeuvre, designed to muddy the waters and take the urgency out of opposition to the plans. "Any development at Titnore will be the thin end of the wedge for the area. What will be next? The west side of Titnore Lane behind Highdown? Clapham Woods?" The threat of an A27 bypass across the South Downs is also still looming and the new road from the A27 at Titnore would link in with this.

"It is vital to keep on fighting the greed machine every inch of the way. Only continual pressure, protest and commitment to taking all measures necessary will keep the bulldozers at bay. It will be a long battle but one that must won."

CONTACTS: POW! c/o PO Box 4144, Worthing, West Sussex BN14 7NZ

pow@worthinga27.freeserve.co.uk
www.worthinga27.freeserve.co.uk
worthing@eco-action.org
porkbolter@eco-action.org
www.eco-action.org/porkbolter

WAKE UP! WAKE UP! IT'S YER

Weekly SchNEWS

www.schnews.org.uk

YARLS WOOD TOWERS

"I mentioned Group 4 once but I think I got away with it."

Thursday 28th March 2002   **Free/Donation**   **Issue 348**

YARL-BOO SUCKS!

When I asked what the officers were doing with all this situation, they said there is no officers, cos they all run away. I just couldn't believe it... I saw that all doors and the gates (we had them along the whole corridors) were locked. No officers, no police, no fire brigade or anybody else. Only scared people everywhere...The some male detainees (mostly black) were trying to get people outside the building. Cos if it hadn't been for them we would all be burned in that fire."

- From a woman detained at Yarl's Wood during the fire.

It's been over a month since the Yarl's Wood Detention Centre in Bedfordshire burned down, but the true story of what happened on that day is still no clearer. The government's response -a promise to toughen up their policies with more detention centres, increased security, faster removal times for failed asylum seekers, and reduced access to the judicial system.

Yarl's Wood only opened last November -built at an estimated cost of £100 million and run by Group 4 under licence from the Home Office. To make asylum seekers feel welcome they've installed security equivalent to a category B prison, surrounded by 16ft high fences topped by razor wire with moving cameras and microwave detection units to prevent escape. According to the government the centre is supposed to house 'failed' asylum seekers facing immediate deportation, yet their own statistics reveal that only 46 of the 385 detainees at Yarl's Wood on the night of the fire were waiting to be deported.

Ever since the first people were locked up there has been constant protests about conditions. In January nearly all the detainees, went on hunger strike for 24 hours, while on the afternoon of 14th February, the day the fire started, trouble flared after a woman was handcuffed so she could be taken to hospital. At some point later a fire started. It's not clear where, although many detainees believe it started in the reception area to which they have no access. Shocking stories from those who were inside on the day are only now emerging.

"The incident started when detainees saw a woman aged about 55 being restrained and they were concerned for her safety. Women were told to stay in their rooms by staff. Families were waiting in their rooms for Group 4 to tell them what to do. Three hours later, when they became aware of the fire, and the building started to fill with smoke and heat, they were still inside waiting.

Exits and doors were locked. There was no evacuation by Group 4. Detainees got one another out of the burning building. Once outside, they saw others trapped in their rooms calling for help, unable to breathe. One man opened his door and found flames outside. Detainees shouted to Group 4 or the police asking them to help those who were trapped. With exits being closed, the only way out of the burning building would have been to try to smash their way through high security toughened windows which are designed to open only a few inches.

Some detainees tried to put the fire out themselves, but when they saw they couldn't, they shouted to firemen to come in. Others said police or Group 4 tried to push them back in to the building, or blocked their exit when they tried to get out.

Detainees, including a 2 month old baby, were kept outside most of the night in freezing weather. Bedfordshire County Council had transport, social facilities including a school available to provide respite care but they were not used. People were herded around the site by police/ Group 4, who shouted at them and tried to make them gather near to the burning building on tennis courts. When people protested, they pushed them on to the unused part of the building."

Deportation Department

Whilst Group 4 were busy locking the detainees inside it appears that fire fighters were being locked out from the burning building. Had they got they could well have prevented much of the estimated £38 million of damage. Home Secretary David Blunkett was quick to blame the fire and the lack of access for the fire fighters, on the detainees, complaining "Having removed asylum seekers from prison, we now find that our reward is the burning down of a substantial part of the facility, this is deplorable".

The Fire Brigade Union (FBU) however are refusing to tow the official line and have

---

There are 22 million displaced people in the world.
The top five countries of origin for asylum seekers in the UK are Afghanistan, Iraq, Somalia, Sri Lanka and Turkey. The average time for an initial decision on asylum applications is currently 14 months. Last year 69% of asylum applications considered were refused. Currently 2,800 asylum seekers are locked up even though they've committed no crime this figure is set to rise to 4,000 a year. This includes the detention of whole families.

---

attacked the Home Office and Group 4 for refusing to install a sprinkler system. Andy Gilchrist from the FBU said "It is clear that [they] have put their private profit before the lives of asylum seekers thereby treating them as second class citizens. Group 4 flatly refused to put a sprinkler system into these premises to cut their costs." Fire fighters who were at Yarl's Wood have also contradicted claims that it was asylum seeker who stopped them getting in to put out the fire. A spokesman said "None of the fire fighters has a bad word to say against the asylum seekers, we are only demoralised because we were prevented from doing our job." In the light of what they saw at Yarl's Wood, the FBU are now calling for the immediate release of all asylum seekers from detention centres until they can be made safe.

Group 4 is the largest security firm in the world, and are also involved in Campsfield detention centre. In 1997 after mass protests at Campsfield, 10 detainees were charged with rioting, but the subsequent trial collapsed after it became evident that the Group 4 security guards were lying and had themselves caused criminal damage. No action was ever brought against the company.

For those who were locked up in Yarl's Wood on that night of the fire 70 have now been transferred to prisons, some of them are in solitary confinement, although none of them have been charged with any offence. 19 are still missing, the official line is that they've escaped, although it can't be ruled out that they may have died in the blaze, a detailed forensic investigation of the site only began late February and is expected to take 2 months. In what is looking like a massive cover up, access by friends and relatives to many of those that knew what went on during that day has been denied, and key witnesses to events have been deported. Shakir Hussain a solicitor representing some of the asylum seekers, has already had one client removed without any warning "It seems to me that any potential witnesses were put in segregation and shipped out as soon as possible.". There is real fear among campaigners that these moves could stop investigators getting to the truth.

*Stop the lies. Demonstrate at Yarl's Wood Detention Centre this Saturday 12 noon till 2.pm Saturday. For directions tel: 07786517379

www.stoparbitrarydetentionsatyarlswood.co.uk

*Open Borders The Case Against Immigration Controls by Teresa Hayter (Pluto Press) www.barbedwirebritain.org.uk

SIZE MATTERS

"We are creators of new technologies... driven - this time by great financial rewards and global competition - despite the clear dangers, hardly evaluating what it may be like to try to live in a world that is the realistic outcome of what we are creating and imagining." - Bill Joy, chief scientist and co-founder of Sun Microsystems.

It's being called the next industrial revolution – and with one research institute announcing that hundreds of three-legged robots the size of a thumb, complete with onboard computers, powerful microscopes, and biosensors will be ready to manufacture nano-scale materials by the middle of this year, it's a science coming our way soon.

Welcome to nanotechnology. Once the stuff of science fiction, nanotechnology now seems the scientists' equivalent of porn.

But what is a nano? A nanometre is a billionth of a metre. If you put fifty million nanos side by side they'd be the width of a human hair. Where biotechnology manipulates genes to alter their natural molecular composition, nanotechnology aims to build pretty much anything atom by atom or alter existing structures.

Not surprisingly, the bio-tech and pharma-ceutical corporations, not to mention NASA and the trigger-happy US military, are busily developing and funding nanotechnologies. (The U.S. Defense Department announced it would be spending $180 million on it this year alone.)

The scope and impact of nanotech was brought home last month by researchers in Spain working with Kraft Foods. They are developing nano-capsules containing the colour, fragrance, and taste of tens of thousands of different drinks. The consumer would buy a generic liquid containing multiple-choice capsules (ranging from fruit juices to colas to wines and spirits). By exposing these capsules to different ultrasound or radio frequencies, the desired concoction would be released. Households would likely need nothing more sophisticated than a microwave-type device.

This technology is delivering a series of almost magical inventions that are the most phenomenally lucrative ever seen. Mihail Roco, the National Science Foundation's senior advisor for nanotechnology warns that, "a nano elite could command unlimited wealth and power" while Paul Thompson, a professor of ethics at Purdue University says "There are some disturbing similarities between biotechnology and nanotechnology. This is a technology that, once it's out there, can't be called back." As Pat Mooney of ETC group in Canada points out "Nanotechnology must become a serious issue for the Rio+10 summit If governments don't address it there, we could find ourselves dealing with social and environmental issues that will make biotech look insignificant."

Maybe that's why one of the most influential figures in computing Bill Joy wrote in Wired magazine that self-replicating nanobots are more dangerous than nuclear weapons and urged scientists to abandon nanotech for the good of mankind.

* To keep up to date with these issues check out the excellent www.etcgroup.org.

* The Institute of Nanotechnology will be holding a two day conference bigging up their new microscopic mates at the Dynamic Earth Centre in Edinburgh 24-25 April. www.nano.org.uk/dynamicearth.htm

* GM test sites for the coming year have recently been announced check 'em out at www.geneticsaction.org.uk

SchNEWS in brief

There's a benefit night for **Indymedia UK** next Friday (6th) at the Medusa, Barrington Rd., Brixton with 2 rooms of drum n' bass and house, VJ'S and a chill out space. Tax is £5/3, 10pm – 6am. ** The **Simon Jones Memorial Campaign** are asking groups and individuals to organise events for a national day of action against temp agencies that put profit before people on 24th April. To get involved call 01273 685913 or email simonjonesaprilaction@hotmail.com ** The **Mayday Festival of Alternatives** meeting has been moved to Thursday 4th April at the Union Tavern. Camberwell New Rd and Vassal Rd, Camberwell SE5. ** **Corporate-watch** have opened a new website in India to expose the social and environmental impacts of corporate investment in the country www.corpwatchindia.org ** **Schwoops** - the website for the 'Welcome to Manchester' event in last weeks positive SchNEWS should have read www.beyondtv.org/gorton/ ** 200 protesters marched through **Swansea** at the weekend in a protest aimed at putting pressure on the Environment Agency to refuse a license for the Crymln Burrows incinerator www.stic.org.uk ** And on Monday 100 residents in **Easton, Bristol** brought commuter traffic to a standstill to demand action about ever-rising levels of street crime in their area. www.bristol.indymedia.org ** **POW (Protect Our Woodland)** who are campaign-ing to save Titnore Woods near Worthing are meeting next Tuesday (2nd), Downsview Pub opposite West Worthing Station, 7:45pm www.worthinga27.freeserve.co.uk ** The Energy Minister in **South Korea** is studying how Thatcher dealt with the miners strike to try and end a five week long strike by power workers resisting privatisation (that'll teach em'). Thousands of strikers are now facing dismissal for creating a nice climate of labour unrest a few months before the football World Cup. www.labournet.net

Inside SchNEWS

Neil Bartlett has been sentenced to 4 years in prison for a series of bomb hoaxes against organisations involved in animal abuse. Write to him: Neil Bartlett FW7083, HMP Lewes, East Sussex BN7 1EA

Jonas Enander has just been given two years and 6 months for his part in the anti EU protests in Sweden last year. Letters to Jonas Enander, KVA, Aby-Funbo 755 97 Uppsala, Sweden. To contact the Goth-ernburg prisoner solidarity group e-mail: solidaritetsgruppen@hotmail.com

Positive SchNEWS

While places like Brighton have to put up with bullshit from developers about sustainable hotels, sustainable supermarkets and hey while we're at it, why not sustainable motorways, a Zero Energy Development is nearing completion in Beddington, Sutton near London. The mixed development of houses and offices will only use energy from renewable sources generated on site, is cutting water consumption by a third, reducing transport costs etc. It "aims to be a beacon, to show how we can meet the demand for housing without destroying the countryside. It shows that an eco-friendly lifestyle can be easy, affordable and attractive - something that people will want to do." www.bedzed.org.uk

* The occupation of the Harvest Forestry site in New England Road, Brighton continues with a host of events for the coming Easter weekend. Including a demo at London Road Sainsbury's on Saturday at 2pm. Call the hotline on 01273 622727 to find out what's happening.

DYING FOR A DRINK

Just in case you missed it the 22nd of March was World Water Day. It was celebrated in South Africa by remembering 260 people who have died in the recent Cholera epidemic. It started after the city council in Capetown started cutting off the water supply of people in townships who couldn't afford to pay for the 'service'. People who resisted were shot with live ammunition (see SchNEWS 326) Now the council have come up with the brilliant idea of auctioning off the houses of 400 families who can't pay, leaving them homeless. Most of the community were dumped in the poor quality council homes in Mfuleni in 1974, after being forcibly removed from other parts of the Western Cape under the Group Areas Act of the Apartheid government. The council homes were later supposed to be transferred to the tenants. The community agreed in a mass meeting last week that they would fight the eviction and, as a last resort reclaim the land they lived on before 1974 rather than become homeless after this second eviction.

In Bolivia they celebrated World Water Day by acquitting the _that murdered 17 year old Victor Hugo Daza during the protests over the privatisa-tion of the water system in Cochabamba two years ago (see SchNEWS286 and 339). Video footage from an independent Bolivian television network clearly showed Captain Robinson Iriarte de la Fuente, firing into a crowd of unarmed civilians, fatally wounding Victor in the head. This footage, seen by people in Bolivia and around the world, was apparently not considered as evidence at the trial. As a final insult, after the acquittal he was promoted to the rank of Major.

In Colombia, another person fighting privatisa-tion has been murdered. On 20 March, a leader of the Union Sindical Obrera (Oil Workers' Union), Rafael Jaimes Torra, was assassinated by paramilitaries. He is the eighty-fifth oil workers leader to be assassinated since 1988. To date no one has been prosecuted for any of these crimes. Rafael was involved in negotiations with the Colombian oil company Ecopetrol over their plans to privatise the industry. On Monday, two Ecopetrol workers, Jose Antonio Perez and Hernando Silva Cely, were abducted in Casanare and it's very likely that they will be tortured and executed. The government is doing nothing to obtain their release or prevent their deaths. To make helpful suggestions write to Dr Victor G Ricardo, Embassy of Colombia, Flat 3a, 3 Hans Crescent, London SW1X OLN. Fax: 020 7581 1829. Email: mail@colombianembassy.co.

More info: Colombia Solidarity Campaign 07950 923448 colombia_sc@hotmail.com

...and finally...

Ever had the wool pulled over your eyes by some yarn? In that case this pearl will have you in stitches. "We call upon activists throughout the world to join together in a Global Knit-In to challenge the G8 and the global corporatism it stands for. Our primary day of action will be Wednesday, June 26th 2002. On that day, we ask you to organise a group of knitters to knit at one of the seats of corporate power in your communities. Transform those spaces through knitting. We will also be doing a mass knitting action at a location outside the G8 meeting We'll show the G8 what we want through our people- and community-driven production.' Time to get that new balaclava sorted then eh? To get some anti-capitalist patterns e-mail knitting@activist.ca To find out more about the G8 protests in Alberta, Canada check out http://g8.activist.ca

Disclaimer

ESCAPE FROM WOOMERA

WOOMERA 2002 - AUTONOMADIC CARAVAN AND FESTIVAL OF FREEDOMS

by Alex Kelly

Woomera 2002 - Autonomadic Caravan and Festival of Freedoms - was held from 29th March to the 2nd April in Woomera, South Australia. It was a convergence that called together a variety of people and movements to 'make the journey' and 'draw the connections'. Woomera is situated 500kms north of Adelaide and is an incredibly poignant site due to the variety of issues which intersect here. Under the jurisdiction of the federal government, the Woomera township is a strange military town, established as a service town for the rocket testing range (still operational) and the now closed US spy base Narrunga. In close proximity is the Roxby Downs Uranium mine and the proposed site for a nuclear waste dump. The Woomera Asylum Seekers Detention Centre is one of six in Australia - not including the new off-shore 'initiatives' in Nauru. They are managed by Australasian Correctional Management, a subsidiary of USA corporate prison giant Wakenhut Corrections.

Even before the September 11 2000 anti-WEF protests in Melbourne (the original S11 - ed), a 'journey to Woomera at easter' had been discussed, and prior to S11 an 'xborder' action at the Maribyrong Detention centre had made the links between globalisation, freedom of movement and borders. By mid 2001 a small group began the call out for a 'festival of freedoms' for the Easter weekend 2002 at Woomera. Like previous events in Australia - S11, forest blockades, Jabiluka blockade et al, the word about Woomera spread fast. The Melbourne Woomera network meetings set up the space for autonomous actions - reminiscent of the pre-S11 AWOL meetings - and a huge groundswell emerged. People talked about a possible 500 coming, but it was hard to imagine - right up until the Friday morning when the buses started to pull in to the camp site - that over a thousand people would make the journey....

Despite the assertion that the Woomera Festival be more than single issue, the detention centre became the major focus of the five day camp. Even so attempts were made to forge links with local indigenous groups - a task to which great importance was attached, but not achieved that smoothly. Many of the city based activists lacked direct experience with indigenous communities, particularly remote ones, which risked misunderstandings, misuse of language, differing notions of "authority" and "sovereignty", and people not knowing who the elders or authority within each community were or even how to contact them. The Melbourne>Woomera network made contact with a number of Kokatha people,

and to my knowledge, were the only network who had done so. Although Woomera was to be decentralised - and was in nearly every aspect - this contact served to represent the entire camp. A letter from Eileen Wingfield to the protesters asserted, "When you mob come up to Woomera please think about how we have been fighting for a long time against Roxby Downs (uranium mine on their land). We have been busy all these years, trying to get control over our country. We don't get anywhere with them". Woomera raised many issues with regards to 'indigenous liaison' which remain unresolved, but are part of the learning process and the journey which the event catalysed.

So after the benefit gigs and workshops held around the country during the build up - buses were booked, tents, trucks, a water tanker, a shit-pit digger and more hired, a convergence booklet put together and legal and medical information gathered. It was time to make the journey!

MEET AT SPUDS

Thursday 28th March: In the morning members of the campsite working group as well as people from HMS Woomera (health and medical services) and desert Indymedia gathered at Spud's Roadhouse at Pimba to discuss establishing a camp site. Initially the Area Administrator (direct envoy for the Dept. of Defence) pointed us to a disused sports ground kindly set aside for the protest site - equipped with portaloos and fresh water - but he neglected to mention that it was two kms from the detention centre, and behind a 2.5 metre wire topped fence with only one access gate! Er thanks but no thanks. Later we arrived at a preferred location - much closer to the detention centre - and formed a circle with the vehicles and bedded down on that spot. A late evening police raid failed to move the camp despite unsuccessful attempts at arrest, and the site was held by a small number of protesters all night until the buses arrived the following morning.

WHOOPS THE FENCE FELL DOWN

Friday 29th March: Hundreds of people arrived from around the country and with tents erected en masse at this stage it was clear that we had won the first battle - deciding where to camp. Throughout the day more infrastructure was set up, a number of sound systems, Food Not Bombs, puppet making, legal, medical, workshop tents were put up, the desert indymedia centre established in the back of a truck, and a vast array of banners and

Protesters breaking in

Detainees breaking out

...tes, flags and costumers emerged. Local indig folk set up the 'Kokatha Peoples Embassy' near the site. At midday we received word that the detainees were going to do a 'sound action' and they wanted to see if we could hear them. We headed straight down to the federal check point where 200 metres of temporary fencing blocked the road - around one km from the detention centre itself. We could see them on the roofs of the buildings in the centre, and when the megaphones were shut down (!) we could hear them.

Later in the day 'No-one Is Illegal' had a meeting to discuss the civil disobedience action called for the following day, as others painted props and banners, including a giant pair of bolt cutters!! At around 5.40pm it was announced that contact with the detainees - via a mobile phone which I assume was smuggled inside and subsequently confiscated - had again alerted us to an action planned at 6pm inside the centre.

At this point the crowd headed across the desert aiming straight for the detention centre - and the following hour is almost impossible to describe...

Forming a long parade of colour and music, with music from a sound system on a truck, at first we reached within almost 500 metres of the centre - but no sign of police. Then at a five metre fence topped with razor wire we could see detainees well enough to wave and shout to each other. Still we couldn't believe how close we'd come. Next, unbelievably the fence came down!!

I was uneasy, I wanted to know where the police were, whether we were going to be hemmed in, beaten, and arrested. But we continued towards the detainees and next thing we knew we were at the last two fences - topped by huge coils of razor wire - which separated us from the detainees. For a moment we stood on either side of the fence - straining our arms through the fence to touch, talking, crying... then - the unbelievable happened:

A bar was used to wedge open a gap in the fence and then people began to escape! One after another stage-dived into the arms of stunned protesters.

Despite the police finally moving in, detainees were still able to leap over them into the crowd - and as soon as they hit the ground they were surrounded and given clothes as a disguise and rushed back towards the campsite. After some fifty had escaped, police horses regained control of the fence. Police tried to pick detainees out of the throng, but ended up arresting a protester of Bangladeshi descent who they banged up for two hours.

This night back at the campsite protesters kept detainees huddled in their tents as escape plans were discussed. Some cursed that they hadn't developed escape plans, but how did they know that a number were actually going to get out! The police set up road blocks around the camp and 200kms south at Port Augusta, and they sent undercover and uniformed police through to sweep the camp for detainees. Without speculating about the whereabouts or even how those people got away - for fear of jeopardising their chances at freedom - to date the official figures are that eleven are still free.

HOW DO YOU FOLLOW THAT?

Saturday 30th March: The Saturday was surreal, but much calmer than Friday night. Lots of people had not slept, and people were dazed, trying to get their heads around the magnitude of the previous nights events. This time the action went straight up the road and knocked over the fence at the check point, some people heading all the way to the centre, other opting to block the road and dance on the "No Entry" signs that were now lying in the dust.

A number of people were arrested for "trespass" and taken away to Woomera lock-up where a number of protesters and detainees who had been captured the previous night, were being held. A number of people have been charged with harbouring a detainee and their court cases will start in May. Detainees were charged with escaping and in the mean time most of the 39 recaptured have been moved to Port Headland detention centre.

ROXBY ROLL

Sunday 31st March: Sunday saw the delivery of hundreds of new, sealed toys intended for the 39 children in detention - but these were deemed 'unhygienic' and a 'security risk' and it appears that the toys ended up going to local charities instead. Following this a final march around the detention centre was called. Woomera is divided in to four blocks, so our aim was to reach the far side of the centre to communicate with other people face to face. The police presence was much stronger than on the previous two days, but still we were able to approach the immediate perimeter fences. A note was thrown over the fence in a rubber glove saying "Australian people, we are hostage in our rooms we can't move any where and also the ACM give us sleeping tablets in the food, nobody can do anything, please help us."

On Sunday another small group of excellently dedicated crazies jumped on bikes and had a critical mass bike ride to Roxby Downs uranium mine. Their aim was to "draw the connection with our organic machines between Woomera and Roxby, human rights, indigenous rights and land rights."

At least two former detainees made the journey to Woomera. One of them spoke to fellow Afghani Hazara people in Woomera on the Sunday, and later translated what he had said to them: "We can not pull down all the fences today, it would be too dangerous for you and for us. There are people here from Germany, America, England, Spain, every state in Australia and we are going to go back and tell everyone, everywhere about this, and we are going to do everything we can to help you. We will never forget you." This man had only been freed from this centre two weeks before, and now had a temporary protection visa (which does not guarantee sanction into Australia).

We are all illegal until no-one is illegal.

http://www.woomera2002.com
Desert IMC http://melbourne.indymedia.org/woomera-archive.php3

HOLY SHIT! IT'S YER FAITHFUL

Weekly SchNEWS

Printed and Published in Brighton by Justice?

Friday 5th April 2002   www.schnews.org.uk   Issue 349

Don't worry 'W', I've got a final solution and you can still have your war with Iraq

STATE OF TERROR

History is repeating itself…This is fascism, how they [the Israeli soldiers] are dealing with people, detaining them in big schools and interrogating each one, writing numbers on them…people are terrified. The Israeli soldiers are shooting everything. Life here has totally stopped; it's dead. This is terrorism against civilians. It is organised terrorism by the state…this is an organised war against a whole people who have no weapons to resist tanks, and helicopters and F16s." - *Ashraf, a Palestinian imprisoned in his home in Ramallah.*

It's Monday in Beit Jala, a small town near Bethlehem and 150 people from the International Solidarity Movement and dozens of Palestinians are marching peacefully in the deserted streets. They are attempting to visit families besieged in their homes, before Israeli tanks block their path. Two of the marchers start to move towards the tanks with their hands up in order to negotiate, but soldiers open fire at both the crowd and the reporters that are there. Eight people are injured, one seriously.

Other activists are holed up with Yasser Arafat in his headquarters. Mario Lill from Brazil's Landless Workers' Movement (MST) is one of those who are acting as human shield and has become a sort of war correspondent broadcasting live to Brazil. Others such as anti-globalisation French farmer Jose Bove are arrested in the compound by Israeli troops.

Wednesday and two thousand people including internationals, Israeli and Arab civilians gather at a checkpoint near Ramallah trying to get humanitarian aid delivered to the besieged town. Soldiers fire tear gas and baton charge people. One of the protestors was Yehudith Harel "Two Israeli faces surfaced today. One is the decent and humane face of the Israeli Anti-war movement – an alliance of Israeli citizens Jews and Arabs, adamant to struggle together for Justice for the two peoples. The second is the ugly and brutal face of the Occupation mentality and practices threatening to crush us."

CASUALTIES

People from around the world have been volunteering in the occupied territories of the West Bank for over a year, taking non-violent direct action like clearing roadblocks and acting as willing human shields to protect the Palestinian people. Invited by Palestinian activists, these international supporters live and work in solidarity with them – a similar call out to the one made by the Zapatistas in Chiapas, Mexico. People from abroad can often get away with a lot more when protesting, partly because they have the eyes of the international press on them - until Monday that was, when live ammunition was fired at the international observers for the first time.

As for the Palestinians, even the doctors, nurses and paramedics are being used by the Israeli army as human shields or forced to strip and sit on their knees at gunpoint in the streets. Israeli forces have stopped ambulances delivering aid or picking up the wounded and are detaining the Palestinian Red Crescent society and aid workers. *120 Palestinian paramedics have been killed in the last 18 months.*

As Israeli tanks roll in to Palestinian settlements, they destroy telephone lines and cut electricity and water supplies. All men between the ages of 16 and 50 are rounded up. Some homes are destroyed, others have their windows blown out and walls dynamited as soldiers move from home to home. Soldiers occupy other homes forcing the residents to live together in a single room, with little or no access to telephone lines, news coverage or even food and water.

An entire civilian population is being openly terrorised after over 50 years of occupation by the Israeli State.

Michael Ben-Yair, former Israel attorney general said, "The Intifada is the Palestinian people's war of national liberation. We enthusiastically chose to become a colonist society, ignoring international treaties, expropriating lands, transferring settlers from Israel to the occupied territories, engaging in theft and finding justification for all these activities…we established an apartheid regime."

Lev Grinberg (Director of the Humphrey Institute for Social Research at Ben Gurion University) sums up the situation: "Suicide bombs killing innocent citizens must be unequivocally condemned; they are immoral acts, and their perpetrators should be sent to jail. But they cannot be compared to State terrorism carried out by the Israeli Government. The former are individual acts of despair of a people that sees no future, vastly ignored by an unfair and distorted international public opinion. The latter are cold and "rational" decisions of a State and a military apparatus of occupation, well equipped, financed and backed by the only superpower in the world."

While Palestinians are being shot dead by Israeli troops and Americans wage 'War on Terrorism' BAE Systems, the world biggest arms trading company, are laughing all the way to the bank as their share prices have increased by 13.8%. Why not congratulate them at their AGM on May 3rd? To get involved, contact: Campaign Against Arms Trade 0207 2810297 www.caat.org.uk

---

* Boycott Israeli goods protests happening around the country this Saturday (6th) including: Waitrose, Western Road, Brighton 11am; Sainsbury's, Queens St. Cardiff 10am; Marks and Spencers Oxford St, Swansea Midday. To order boycott leaflets and stickers and find out events happening in your area email: big@palestinecampaign.org or call the Palestine Solidarity Campaign 020 7700 6192

* Saturday 13th April National rally and demonstration for Palestine. Assemble 2pm, Hyde Park to Trafalgar Square. Tel 020 7272 2888.

* To find out about more about the International Solidarity Movement www.freepalestinecampaign.org/

Bypass the corporate media
www.jerusalem.indymedia.org,
www.zmag.org
www.palestinechronicle.com,
www.alternet.org.

* Nearly 400 Israeli Defence Forces reservists are refusing to serve in the occupied territories. Read their reasons why www.yesh-gvul.org

OUTBACK FIGHTBACK

"Before we knew it we were all inside the perimeter fence… face to face with the detainees, only a few metres of steel railing and razor wire separating us. This was an incredibly emotional moment, people were crying, reaching through to touch hands, I will never forget those peoples' faces. …Then quite suddenly some of the men managed to break some of the fencing, it seemed to actually be quite weak. One by one they clambered out, stage diving down onto the excited mob of protesters. Still the police seemed to be paralysed, maybe they couldn't believe what was happening. The escapees melted quickly into the throng of people, swapping t- shirts and hats and running with us in big groups back to camp." – *Miranda*.

Last weekend an asylum seekers' detention centre in the Australian desert was broken into by 1000 protesters, 50 'detainees' managed to escape – and a few are still unaccounted for. This was part of the Woomera 2002 Festival Of Freedom – a tour of actions held around the desert town of Woomera 500kms north of Adelaide which was to call in on the detention centre, then move onto nearby uranium mines. Working with the local Kokatha and Arabunna peoples, this 'festival' was to combine the issues of uranium, refugees and indigenous land rights: Rebecca Bear Wingfield of the Kokatha people said that aboriginal people did not want the refugees to be imprisoned on their land, and also pointed out the connections: 'the uranium mined ends up as bombs and depleted uranium weapons is used in wars which create more refugees'.

In the days leading up to the protest a camp had built up near the detention centre and on Friday protesters took cutting tools to the centre and passed them to the detainees to help free themselves. That night the campers were huddled in tents with asylum seekers and heard horror stories about both Woomera and the places the people had come from. The next day protesters tried to move detainees out, some succeeded, but others were caught and are up on charges of aiding and abetting escapees – and bizarrely found themselves sharing cells with asylum seekers. Detainees claim that tear gas is used in the centre, and after the breakout some who had contact with the protestors were tortured and beaten.

Since 1994 the Australian asylum policy has been to bang up all asylum seekers – kindly housing them mainly in remote desert centres such as Woomera where people can wait for years for a verdict, and many are now prepared to risk possible deportation and death rather than suffer the conditions. Already this year Woomera has seen riots, hunger strikes, suicide attempts and people sewing their lips together in protest about their treatment.
www.noborders.org.uk, www.woomera2002,com
www.melbourne.indymedia.org

MONEY TO BURN

Yarls Wood detention centre in Bedfordshire which was the scene of the fire in February (see SchNEWS 348) closed this week. Unfortunately this wasn't due to a change of asylum policy by the government, but a result of the insurers whacking up their premiums. Just to guarantee that they won't be out of pocket over February's incident though the insurers have put in a claim for £97million against Bedfordshire Police Authority. www.ncadc.org.uk

SchNEWS in brief

Organisers of this years Mayday Festivities are getting more than their fair share of police attention. Police have successfully manage to persuade web hosts not to host their site www.ourmayday.org.uk the site is currently up and running but Met Police are threatening to raid the current host. The **May Day Festival of Alternatives runs from 16th April-6th May**** Mayday Meeting Sunday April 7th to discuss actions, ideas, affinity. The London Action Resource Centre (LARC), Fieldgate and Parfett Street, E1, 2pm, Tel 07786 716 335 festivalofalternatives@yahoo.com ** **No Sweat Comedy Cabaret** fundraiser for Indonesian workers featuring Rob Newman and Atilla the Stokebroker, next Friday (10th), 7pm The Bread and Roses, 68A Clapham Manor Street SW4 Tel 07904 431 959 www.nosweat.org.uk £10/5 ** The 20th is an **alternative health/healing day at the Radical Dairy**, 12-6pm 47 Kynaston Road, Stoke Newington, London, N16 ** 'The history of foxhunting and land ownership in Britain', which digs all the dirt on the Countryside Alliance is a new pamphlet available for £2.50 inc postage RPM Publications, BCM Box 3328, London WC1N 3XX 07967 886257 www.red-star-research.org.uk ** The Council meeting to decide the future of the Brighton Station site has been postponed. There's still a **Dragon and Drums demo with samba band** this weekend against Sainsbury's meet 1:30pm Saturday x-Harvest Forestry building New England Road ** Plans to widen the A303 road near **Stonehenge** are currently in the pipeline. An alliance is now forming to try and make sure it's not built www.savestonehenge.org.uk ** Next Monday is **Roma Nation Day** it will be marked in this country with a celebration march starting at noon in Victoria Tower Gardens, next to the houses of Parliament. Bring refreshments for the picnic in the park and flowers for the ceremony ustiben.2@ntlworld.com ** **End Factory Farming - before it ends us** a rally and march against factory farming. Meet Noon at the level, Brighton. Sat 13th 01273 777688** **Women, Peace and Security** a meeting with speakers from International Alert and Widows for Peace at University of London Union building, Malet Street, 2-4.30pm, 14th April Tel:020 8467 5367 www.peacewomen.org ** **Close Down Harmondsworth Detention Centre** 11.30am - 1.30pm 15th April email: closedownharmondsworth@hotmail.com** The **End Of The Road Direct action gathering** to build resistance to the new roads program and the corporate dominance it fuels. Is happening from 19-20th April at the Sumac Centre, 245 Gladstone street, Nottingham, NG7 6HX. Info 07813 ** **Stop Huntington Animal Cruelty** week of action 20-28th April 0845 4580630** There's a **National Day of action against Profiteering Employment Agencies** on the 24th April – the 4 anniversary of Simon Jones death. The **Simon Jones Memorial Campaign** are asking supporters across the country to mark the anniversary of Simon's death by demonstrating, in whatever way they see fit, at an employment agency in their area that profits from casualisation. Phone (01273) 685913 simonjonesaprilcamp@hotmail.com, www.simonjones.org.uk ** **To keep up-to-date with what's going on check out the party and protest section on our website**

Inside SchNEWS

A day of Action for Mark Barnsley is planned for Saturday April 13th Meet at 11am at Meadowhall bus station near Sheffield. (M1 Junc:34) to picket the Home Office Minister David Blunkett at his surgery. Mark is currently serving 12 years in prison after being beaten up by 15 drunk students. Now in his eighth year of his sentence h'es not been eligible for early release because he continues to maintain his innocence. www.freemarkbarnsley.com

TANKS A LOT

The Kurdish New Year (Newroz) was celebrated with fires and dances in traditional Kurdish dress towns and cities in Turkey**.** Millions of people demanded the use of the Kurdish language, the abolition of the death penalty, the recognition of their cultural identity, and universal democratic rights and support was voiced for the national leadership of Abdullah Ocalan and for his immediate release.

Turkey responded in its usual manner. In Istanbul and Mersin, they outlawed Newroz, police armed with tanks, water-cannons and plastic bullets attacked and killed two people, with more than one thousand arrested and hundreds hurt. Threats and intimidation, house arrests, confiscation of the Kurdish colours and arrests for talking in the Kurdish dialect as well as obstruction of speakers were ordered in many of the towns. In one instance police threw a hand grenade into an apartment. Despite all this, there were a greater number of revellers than previous years.

FIGHTING DIRTY

36 people were nicked on the first day of the Peat Alert Protests at Hatfield Moor which started on Monday 25th March, with more during the next four days. The threat of the four day blockade to the Easter DIY sales of peat was so much that US-based Scotts contacted groups to see if there was anything they could do to stop it. Er, how about stop digging. Scotts is due to phase out work at Hatfield and neighbouring Thorne Moors over the next two years, but continuing extraction at Hatfield could mean it will be too late to save the moor. Once again a big police presence stepped in to protect corporate interests with helicopter, vans with cops in riot gear and this time a section 14, making it an arrestable offence to get on the road that needed to be occupied to stop the lorries. After some scrambling over the moors the road was secured for a few hours stopping all traffic to and from the works, this continued with some peat drainage filling done on the moors for extra fun. Peat Pixies also helped delay Scott's operations after sneaking in the end of last week and slashing and ruining thousands of prepared peat bags. www.peatalert.org.uk

...and finally...

Disciples of Cupid in Calcutta, India have won a victory for passion. The Lovers Organisation fo Voluntary Exhibition (LOVE) have been protesting for more space in the city for courting couple to give each other mutual admiration, without being disturbed by police and passers-by. After hugging and kissing at the Mayors office for th right to snogging space, the local mayor Subrat Mukherjee has now agreed to let lovers enjo each other's company in 'free love zones' along the river Ganges The Mayor warned howeve that these zones are for lovers not love makers LOVE says their campaign will not end here, wants a public library and a consultancy to b set up for lovers, and legal recognition of lov letters written during courtship.

Disclaimer
Mum's the word. Honest.

The Radical Dairy - the movement moves in

A subjective account of 5 months at the Radical Dairy by a one of the Dairy Collective

In the creation of the social centre there is direct action. Confronted with a landscape designed for alienation, division and subjugation, the reclamation of disused space is a political act in itself; to then make such space available to the community is to further this action.

We squatted a disused corner-shop in North London and built in it a library and infoshop with free internet access; a large social area with tables, furniture, noticeboards, bar, etc.; a fairy-lit magical basement complete with sound system; a healing room (doubling as crash space); a toolshed, a bikeshed and a handsomely stocked kitchen. More people got on board as the project got underway, and we soon had a full diary of events happening every week. Regular workshops such as yoga, massage, voice and drama workshops, discussion groups, english for non-speakers, as well as more

sporadic (and often spontaneous) socials and cafes to raise funds for various groups and causes. Wednesday night, which alternated weekly between a women's cafe and a queer cafe, became one of the most popular nights, along with our regular Friday night acoustic social and the fully plugged-in and turned-up Saturday night party. Sundays would find our friends from Indymedia cooking a vegan roast and screening films up in the library, whilst the Dairy collective recovered from the week's energy and the weekend's excess in the basement.

The police harassment that the Dairy was subjected to in April, beginning with intimidating surveillance and culminating in a full T.S.G. raid in which the computers were taken (sorry kids, no more internet...) and the connection to the National Grid was cut off (no more D.J. workshops either...). This was a deliberate attempt by the police to alienate the centre from the community around it, and was also part of their Mayday crackdown. This attempt backfired on them immediately as local residents came out to express their disgust at the police state being brought to their doorstep and to demonstrate real passion and solidarity with our project. The community came into its own that day; many people who we may not have otherwise met, but who had heard about the place or whose kids had been using it, came around in the days after to offer their support or even to get involved. Though the nights since the raid have been gas-lamp and candle-lit, the warmth of feeling about the Dairy has continued. We hosted a Health Day a week after the raid, which was a real success.

The five month running of the Dairy hasn't always been plain sailing. There are lots of lessons to be learnt on the way. How far can people be trusted with the building and equipment? How are things dealt with when friction between people becomes apparent? Easy when it's black and white, not so easy when it comes in the subtle shades of everyday practicality. People are no longer 'out there', they're in here with you, drinking tea. Your revolutionary duty happens now, over a hob-nob or two. There's a fine line between social centre and activist ghetto. The key to keeping the latter at bay is the open-door policy, but it must be accompanied by an open-heart, open-mind policy on the part of those who are looking after the place.

Another factor to bear in mind is stress. All the members of the Dairy collective have had other things going on in their lives. The stress caused by day-to-day living can unfortunately find expression in the social centre, especially if the division of tasks and time spent taking care of the place is unequal. A balance must be sought between the desires of all involved, otherwise a situation can develop in which one or two people feel that they are putting all the work in, while everyone else feels cajoled into applying themselves to someone else's work ethic. For similar reasons, the establishing of a time-limit on a social centre could be a good idea, as it may prevent the dismal drizzling-off of burnt-out people from what began as an explosion of energy and enthusiasm.

The Dairy collective is now changing, new places are opening up along the same lines which are much more conducive to hosting busy events, etc.. From the time of writing, it looks like the Dairy may continue, but perhaps with the emphasis on the library/infoshop side of things, or a more relaxed day-to-day diary as opposed to the hectic one we've had for the last five months.

Whatever happens from this point onwards, we have learnt more about ourselves and each other in five months than we could have possibly imagined. The Dairy has been an experiment; an example to ourselves and others that our mutual desires and combined energy can bring about something more lasting than a single day of action. The more that this occurs, even if places last a matter of weeks, the stronger, more permanent, more lasting and more broad-based the movement will be. Every time anarchy becomes a living reality - even if between a handful of people - the closer we get to changing the big picture. "Viva la Liberacion!"

Police raid
Radical Dairy Social Centre

Communique 12th April: This morning over 30 riot police stormed into the Radical Dairy Social Centre in Stoke Newington as part of the Mayday campaign of repression.

30 riot police in conjunction with London Electricity used a hydraulic ram to force entry to the Radical Dairy. The police said that they had a warrant to investigate the abstraction of electricity and the misuse of drugs. No drugs were found but a computer [which was used as part of a free internet service for local residents] was seized as "proof" of abstracting electricity!!

The police also read out a statement saying that because a Mayday leaflet was displayed in the window of the Social Centre that it proved that the building was used as "part of the infrastructure to Mayday" , which now seems to be an illegal act! No one was arrested but the centre is now without electricity. During the raid angry residents came out onto the streets and gave the cops hassle. This is the third visit the cops have made to the dairy. The first being on Friday April 5th. They used the guise that they had broken down outside the dairy and were waiting for a repair vehicle, that obviously explained why they were outside for three hours taking peoples photographs!! On this occasion they left after the local residents came out in support of the Radical Dairy, which has been offering free events like Yoga, Shiatsu massages, vegan cafe, DJ workshop for kids, Drama and singing lessons.

The second occasion was on Tuesday April 9th, three cops from different police stations inc. a video camera were filming the structure of the building. The police were there for only 10 minutes as again local residents including a women with her child complained at the continued harassment of the collective which runs the centre. A statement will be issued by the Radical Dairy within the next few hours. Meanwhile the centre needs all the help it can get.

Come down to 47 Kynaston Road, Stoke Newington, London N16. Phone 020 7249 6996 for more news.

International Indigenous Youth Conference (IIYC)

April 17-21, 2002 Baguio City, Philippines

" What is the most precious thing to man? Life! If Life is threatened, what ought a man to do? RESIST! This he must do, otherwise he is dishonoured, and that is worse than death. If we do not fight and the dam pushes through, we die anyway. If we fight, we die honourably, I exhort you all then - FIGHT!

So said Macliing Dulag, one of the many martyrs of the Cordillera struggle for ancestral land and self-determination in the Phillipines. He was leader of the Cordillera peoples who opposed the building of the Chico Dam project during the regime of the former dictator Pres. Ferdinand Marcos. He was assassinated by the military in 1982.

Eighty three participants of the International Indigenous Youth Conference came together at this historic gathering of indigenous youth from around the world to share our experiences and forge a common voice in responding to the challenges of globalisation.

We represent indigenous youth of the colonial borders of Australia, Fiji Islands, New Zealand, Solomon Islands, Bolivia, Ecuador, Panama, Canada, United States, Finland, Norway, Russia, Bangladesh, Burma, India, Indonesia, Thailand and Philippines. The conference was hosted by the Cordillera Peoples Alliance -Youth Commission under the theme "Building Solidarity Among Indigenous Youth in Asserting Indigenous Peoples' Rights Amidst Globalisation."

We learned a lot from our hosts, a country up to its eyeballs in debt to the World Bank and IMF, where development has not solved poverty. For indigenous peoples development means that we can expect our rivers to be poisoned, our traditional ways and economies ravished and our methods of survival destroyed leaving us dependant on the state, just how they want us. The strategies of destruction and assimilation of indigenous peoples are the same worldwide; divide the community, destroy the resources, assimilate the culture and then use what's left to boost tourism for the country. Culture becomes a commodity of the dominant or colonising society.

However to enforce these policies and objectives of assimilation and eradication governments are often engaged in military occupations and conflicts with indigenous people or territory is militarised as a by-product of capitalist aggression. US troops in response to the 'War Against Terrorism' have been reintroduced in the south of the Philippines in co-operation and in exchange for military spending with the president Gloria Macapagal Arroyo and her government. The people suspect that the US is using the Abu Sayef as a justification for US imperialism, to get their foot in the door in Asia and to strip the resources in this country. Accompanying the deployment of US troops is human rights abuses,

sexual exploitation of women, corruption and the persecution of activists and advocates of democracy. Recently a young woman on a fact-finding mission in the south with human rights group *Karapatan* was killed by government forces who accused her of being a part of the New Peoples Army (armed guerrilla movement).

Every day indigenous people and people who speak out for justice for all are being killed or silenced, and our land from Russia to Canada to the Philippines and everywhere is being expropriated for capitalist profit at the cost of our lives, traditional ways, and our subsistence economies. It is time to unite our struggle against corporate and government policies that put the rights of profit ahead of the rights of people.

Resolutions

• To firmly stand to assert our right to self-determination and to the full recognition of our inherent rights as indigenous peoples

• To fight mega-infrastructure projects that result in the economic, environmental, and physical displacement of our communities

• To continuously advocate existing laws that uphold our collective human rights and to mobilise against laws and institutions which do not serve our needs or justice, such as the World Bank, IMF and WTO

• To revive our culture, languages, spiritual values and traditional structures of governance

• To affirm and uphold the rightful status of women as equal in society, family, the workplace and the movement for social transformation

• To expose, oppose and condemn the Imperialist and US State led wars of Aggression, which target the world's poor

• To strengthen the solidarity of indigenous youth against all forms of colonisation, foreign, domestic hegemony and state repression

• To unite with all the oppressed classes and sectors of the world and actively participate in international actions

• To link with other socially progressive movements that work to fight globalisation

• To establish concrete forms of organisational formation by building region wide networks

• To join all forms of struggle to end all forms of oppression, racism and discrimination against Indigenous Peoples

• To call upon the United Nations and States of the world to recognise and adopt in full the Declaration of Indigenous Peoples Rights in it's original text.

• To assert the right of indigenous peoples to free, prior and informed consent over all issues concerning them

www.redwiremag.com

thanks Tania Willard

COPYLEFT HACKERS

The exploitation of our world's resources is one way that commercial interests are eroding our environment and common heritage, but also the wholesale copyrighting and patenting of concepts as well as objects is a another. The implications of **private ownership of knowledge** are deeply disturbing. Companies are staking their claims on living organisms and even annexing genetic material from humans, a trend supported and enforced by the unelected and undemocratic World Trade Organisation. In these cases the term "protection of intellectual property" is no more than a cover for an institutionalised regime of robbery, which allows and encourages corporations to take, with coercion and/or force, that which is not theirs - and then withhold it from those who cannot pay their prices.

There have been a few attempts at loosening the tightening strangle hold on the ownership of information, for example material (such as SchNEWS) which is published as "**anti-copyright**" – making information free to be reproduced and proliferate. But things have been taken to a further, interactive level…

There is a simple idea which has built into it a viral strategy that not only **proliferates and develops knowledge freely but also protects itself** against usurpers - so effectively that many corporations feel increasingly threatened by its dramatic advances into their fortified territory. It is an idea that has its roots in the computer hacking community, though it isn't intrinsically electronic, and has aspects that are profoundly philosophical and politically potent. It is the concept of "**Copyleft**".

Copyleft started life with the "open source" computer movement that was begun by Richard "Math-You" Stallman in 1984. Stallman, a hacker working at MIT (Massachusetts Institute of Technology) had become disillusioned with the way in which private companies had bought out the various projects he and his colleagues had been working on. He realised that to "protect" software ownership by keeping its "source code" secret was actually damaging to software evolution.

Commercially produced software is of low quality, bug-ridden, and the unknown source code prevents any possible improvements being made by the user. Stifling the free flow of ideas weakens the whole field and stagnates the craft. Stallman, angered by the profiteers, left MIT, started the Free Software Foundation (FSF) and resolved to create a superior software product that would be free for all to use. The name of this software is GNU.

To make this possible Stallman drew on his experiences of shared information in the hacking community. The first problem was the work load: a programming project of this scale is daunting, especially for Stallman alone. The other problem was that any "open source" code that he wrote could later be co-opted and sold on as a proprietary product. It was in solving these problems that Stallman went on to form the next part of his idea, a part that some would argue is as important as the actual software, if not more so. With the help of a lawyer he reinvented the parameters of his trade and drafted a radically new concept, the General Public Licence (GPL) or, as it's better known, **Copyleft**.

Instead of restricting the rights of the user the Copyleft licence protects them. It ensures the product is free for all to use and remains free. It stipulates that the source code must be open, allowing people to modify and improve upon the original. If such modifications are made then these modifications also must carry the Copyleft licence – and the resulting software is free (freeware). Not only does this have obvious benefits for the end user but also it means that any bugs can be ironed out and that many more people can contribute to the project strengthening and perfecting it.

GNU and the Copyleft concept swept around the world like wild fire. The Copyleft agreement became the written constitution of many hackers, a symbol of idealistic and technical achievement and unshakable integrity. It has paved the way for many free packages:

The brightest star in the open source galaxy is currently **LINUX**, an operating system originated by Linus Torvalds, a Finnish student, in the early 90's. Now, after years of combined work with other hackers, (including Stallman), Linux is so stable and strong that it is used on 18 million computers worldwide [1]. In fact Linux and its allied components, is so good that it is considered the imminent successor to all commercial operating systems and ultimately the nemesis of the corporations grand plan.

So, from software design, which is perhaps seen by some as a rather rigid and formulated craft, a high quality free and flexible system arises, that has organically evolved from a sharing community spirit - (and wipes the floor with the cut-throat commercial opposition). What other applications could Copyleft have… ?

For practical purposes Copyleft works better in some areas than in others. People have tried with books and music but have had problems, after all, few "Artistes" would approve of persons unknown tampering with their work. However, within the **electronic music** scene there is a thriving community of hacker-types who openly share sound sources and techniques.

www.wikipedia.org is an on line Copyleft encyclopedia which contains 19,000 entries and can be added to by anyone.

Another example of a successful application has been the Openlaw project at the Harvard Law School. Here lawyers work through cases in an open forum, unlike the usual method of working out challenges behind closed doors and only giving out the end result publicly. Wendy Selzer who runs Openlaw says, "We deliberately used free software as a model. The gains are much the same as for software. Hundreds of people scrutinise the 'code' for bugs, and make suggestions how to fix it. And people will take underdeveloped parts of the argument, work on them, then patch them in." In this way the case that the Openlaw project is currently working on, a case pronounced unwinnable in the beginning, has now gone through the entire legal system to the Supreme Court. Those involved strongly believe that the open strategy is a particularly effective way to help citizens rights and community groups [2].

As a graphic artist, I too would like to contribute what I can towards extending the applications of Copyleft - I feel that graphic communication is an area in which the concept could thrive. The manipulation of information by the mass media and the private ownership of almost everything creates the ideal climate for the contagious spread of information scrawled anonymously over the blank concrete walls that try to block us in or keep us out. And for just such a purpose I have thrown together three simple arcs to form a stencillable Copyleft sign, which is, naturally, copylefted and there for the use of anyone who may need it. **May your mark count.**

[1] New Scientist 2/2/02 Graham Lawton p35-36
[2] New Scientist 2/2/02 Graham Lawton p37
Books: Rebel Code. Glyn Moody. Allen Lane Penguin Press 2001

INFO WAR ILLEGAL COMBATANT

Four Steps To Heaven

Ex World Bank Economist Spills The Beans About IMF

This is a shortened transcript of an interview by Alex Jones with investigative journalist Greg Palast where Palast delivers his shocking findings about the systematic way the IMF and World Bank crushes countries, citing information from fired ex-chief World Bank economist Joe Stiglitz and leaked WB and IMF documents. This first appeared in March 2002 on American K Talk Radio (www.infowars.com)

Greg Palast (GP): ...I spoke to the former chief economist, Joe Stiglitz who was fired by the World Bank. It was like one of the scenes out of Mission Impossible, you know where the guy comes over from the other side and you spend hours debriefing him. So I got the insight of what was happening at the World Bank. In addition to this ...other people handed me a giant stash of secret documents from the World Bank and the International Monetary Fund...In fact, I was supposed to be on CNN with the head of the World Bank Jim Wolfensohn and he said he would not appear on CNN ever if they put me on. And so CNN did the craziest thing and pulled me off.

We found inside these documents that basically they required nations to sign secret agreements, in which they agreed to sell off their key assets, in which they agreed to take economic steps that are really devastating to the nations involved and if they didn't follow those steps they would be cut-off from all international borrowing. You can't borrow any money in the international marketplace. No one can survive without borrowing, whether you are people or corporations or countries...I've got inside documents recently from Argentina, the secret Argentine plan. This is signed by Jim Wolfensen. By the way, just so you know, they are really upset with me that I've got the documents, but they have not challenged the authenticity of the documents. First, they did. First they said those documents don't exist. I actually showed them on television. And cite some on the web...So then they backed off and said yea those documents are authentic but we are not going to discuss them with you and we are going to keep you off the air anyway. So, that's that. But what they were saying is look, you take a country like Argentina, which is, you know, in flames now. And it has had five presidents in five weeks because their economy is completely destroyed.

Alex Jones (AJ): Isn't it six now?

GP: Yeah, it's like the weekly president because they can't hold the nation together. And this happened because they started out in the end of the 80s with orders from the IMF and World Bank to sell-off all their assets, public assets. I mean, things we wouldn't think of doing in the US, like selling off their water system.

AJ: So they tax the people. They create big government and big government hands it off to the private IMF/World Bank...This is like one of the biggest stories ever...

GP: So what's happening is - this is just one of them. And by the way, it's not just anyone who gets a piece of the action. The water system of Buenos Aires was sold off for a song to a company called Enron. A pipeline was sold off, that runs between Argentina and Chile, was sold off to a company called Enron.

AJ: We are talking to Greg Palast. He is an award-winning journalist, an American who has worked for the BBC, London Guardian, you name it, who has dropped just a massive bomb-shell on the globalists and their criminal activity - there is no other word for it. He now has the secret documents. We have seen the activity of the IMF/World Bank for years. They come in, pay off politicians to transfer the water systems, the railways, the telephone companies, the nationalised oil companies, gas stations - they then hand it over to them for nothing. The globalists pay them off individually, billions a piece in Swiss bank accounts. And the plan is total slavery for the entire population. Of course, Enron, as we told you was a dummy corporation for money laundering, drug money, you name it, from the other reporters we have had on. It's just incredibly massive and hard to believe. But it is actually happening. Greg Palast has now broken the story world-wide. He has actually interviewed the former top World Bank economist.

Continuing with all these points... I mean for the average person out there, in a nutshell, what is the system you are exposing?

GP: We are exposing that they are systematically tearing nations apart, whether it's Ecuador or Argentina. The problem is some of these bad ideas are drifting back into the U.S. In other words, they have run out of places to bleed. And the problem is, this is the chief economist, this is not some minor guy. By the way, a couple of months ago, after he was fired, he was given the Nobel Prize in Economics. So he is no fool. He told me, he went into countries where they were talking about privatizing and selling off these assets. And basically, they knew, they literally knew and turned the other way when it was understood that leaders of these countries and the chief ministers would salt away hundreds of millions of dollars.

AJ: But it's not even privatization. They just steal it from the people and hand it over to the IMF/World Bank.

GP: They hand it over, generally to the cronies, like Citibank was very big and grabbed half the Argentine banks. You've got British Petroleum grabbing pipelines in Ecuador. I mentioned Enron grabbing water systems all over the place. And the problem is that they are destroying these systems as well. You can't even get drinking water in Buenos Aires. I mean it is not just a question of the theft. You can't turn on the tap. It is more than someone getting rich at the public expense.

AJ: And the IMF just got handed the Great Lakes. They have the sole control over the water supply now. That's been in the Chicago Tribune.

GP: Well the problem that we have is - look, the IMF and the World Bank is 51% owned by the United States Treasury. So the question becomes, what are we getting for the money that we put into there? And it looks like we are getting mayhem in several nations. Indonesia is in flames... The Chief Economist, Stiglitz was telling me that he started questioning what was happening. You know, everywhere we go, every country we end up meddling in, we destroy their economy and they end up in flames. And he was saying that he questioned this and he got fired for it. But he was saying that they even kind of plan for the riots. They know that when they squeeze a country and destroy its economy, you are going to get riots in the streets. And they say, well that's the IMF riot. In other words, because you have a riot, you lose. All the capital runs away from your country and that gives the opportunity for the IMF to then add more conditions.

AJ: And that makes them even more desperate. So it is really an imperial economy war to implode countries and now they are doing it here with Enron. They are getting so greedy - they are preparing it for this country.

GP: I've just been talking to, out in California just yesterday, from here in Paris, the chief investigators of Enron for the State of California. They are telling me some of the games these guys are playing. No one is watching that. It's not just the stockholders that got ripped off. They sucked millions, billions of dollars out of the public pocket in Texas and California in particular.

AJ: Where are the assets? See, everybody says there are no assets left since Enron was a dummy corporation - from the experts I've had on and they transferred all those assets to other corporations and banks.

GP: Yeah, the system has gotten completely out of control and these guys knew exactly what was happening. Well, you have to understand that some of the guys who designed the system in California for deregulation then went to work for Enron right after. In fact, the British have some responsibility here. The gu who was on the audit committee of Enron, Lord Wakeham. And this guy is a real piece of work, there isn't a conflict of interest that he hasn't been involved in.

AJ: And he is the head of NM Rothschild.

GP: There isn't anything that he doesn't have his fingers in. He's on something like fifty boards. And one of the problems, he was supposed to be head of the audit committee watching how Enron kept the books. And in fact, they were paying him consulting fees on the side. He was in Margaret Thatcher's government and he's the one who authorised Enron to come into Britain and take over power plants there. And they owned a water system in the middle of England. This is what this guy approved and then they gave him a job on the board. And on top of being on the board, they gave him a huge consulting contract. So you know, this guy was supposed to be in charge of the audit committee to see how they were handling their accounts.

AJ: Well, he is also the head of the board to regulate the media.

GP: Yes, he is, because I have run into real problems, because he regulates me.

AJ: Go through these four points. I mean you've got the documents. The IMF/World Bank implosion, four points, how they bring down a country and destroy the resources of the people.

GP: Right. First you open up the capital markets. That is, you sell off your local banks to foreign banks. Then you go to what's called market-based pricing. That's the stuff like in California where everything is free market and you end up with water bills - we can't even imagine selling off water companies in the United States of America. But imagine if a private company like Enron owned your water. So then the prices go through the roof. Then open up your borders to trade - complete free marketeering. And Stiglitz who was the chief economist, remember he was running this system, he was their numbers man and he was saying it was like the opium wars. He said this isn't free trade; this is coercion trade. This is war. They are taking apart economies through this.

AJ: Well look, China has a 40% tariff on us, we have a 2% on them. That's not free and fair trade. It's to force all industry to a country that the globalists fully control.

GP: Well, you know Walmart - I did a story, in fact, if you read my book. Let me just mention that I've got a book out, "The Best Democracy Money Can Buy" about how, unfortunately, America has been put up for sale. But I have a story in there about how Walmart has 700 plants in China. There is almost nothing in a Walmart store that comes from the United States of America, despite all the eagles on the wall.

AJ: Exactly, like 1984, then they have big flags saying "Buy American" and there's hardly anything --- it's Orwellian double-think.

GP: What's even worst is they will hire a factory and right next to it will be the sister factory which is inside a prison. You can imagine the conditions of these workers producing this lovely stuff for Walmart…I talked to a guy, Harry Wu, is his name and, in fact, he broke into, he's been in Chinese prison for 19 years. No one believed his horrible stories. He actually broke back into prison, took a camera with him and took pictures of the conditions and said this is the conditions of factories where Walmart is getting its stuff made…

AJ: I was threatened to be thrown off TV here in Austin when I aired video of little girls 4-years old chained down, skinnier than Jews in concentration camps, to die. And I was threatened, if you ever air that again, you will be arrested.

GP: Well you know, it is horrifying stuff that, unfortunately, I have been handed and Stiglitz, it was very courageous for him to come out and make these statements. The documents really sealed it because it said this is what really happened. They really

do say sign on the dotted line agreeing to 111 conditions for each nation. And the public has no say; they don't know what the hell is happening to them.

AJ: Go back into privatization. Go through these four points. That's the key. It sends billions to politicians to hand everything over.

GP: Yeah, he called it briberization, which is you sell off the water company and that's worth, over ten years, let's say that that's worth about 5 billion bucks, ten percent of that is 500 million, you can figure out how it works. I actually spoke to a Senator from Argentina two weeks ago. I got him on camera. He said that after he got a call from George W. Bush in 1988 saying give the gas pipeline in Argentina to Enron. That's our current president. He said that what he found really creepy was that Enron was going to pay one-fifth of the world's price for their gas and he said how can you make such an offer? And he was told, not by George W. but by a partner in the deal, "…well if we only pay one-fifth that leaves quite a little bit for you to go in your Swiss bank account". And that's how it's done…

This guy is very conservative. He knows the Bush family very well. And he was public works administrator in Argentina and he said, yea, I got this call. I asked him, I said, from George W. Bush? He said, yea, November 1988, the guy called him up and said give a pipeline to Enron. Now this is the same George W. Bush who said he didn't get to know Ken Lay (CEO of Enron) until 1994…A month before Bush took office, Bill Clinton, I think to get even with Bush's big donor, cut Enron out of the California power market. He put a cap on the prices they could charge…That upset Enron. So Ken Lay personally wrote a note to Dick Cheney saying get rid of Clinton's cap on prices. Within 48 hours of George W. Bush taking office, his energy department reversed the clamps on Enron. OK, how much is that worth for those guys. You know that has got to be worth, that paid off in a week all the donations.

AJ: Listen at the bombs you are dropping. You are interviewing these ministers, former head of IMF/World Bank economist - all of this, you've got the documents, paying people's Swiss Bank accounts, all this happening. Then you've got Part two, what do they do after they start imploding?

GP: Well, then they tell you to start cutting your budgets. A fifth of the population of Argentina is unemployed, and they said cut the unemployment benefits drastically, take away pension funds, cut the education budgets, I mean horrible things. Now if you cut the economy in the middle of a recession that was created by these guys, we are really going to absolutely demolish this nation. After we were attacked on September 11, Bush ran out and said we got to spend $50 to $100 billion dollars to save our economy. We don't start cutting the budget, you start trying to save this economy. But they tell these countries you've got to cut, and cut, and cut. And why, according to the inside documents, it's so you can make payments to foreign banks - the foreign banks are collecting 21% to 70% interest. This is loan-sharking. If fact, it was so bad that they required Argentina to get rid of the laws against loan-sharking because any bank would be a loan-shark under Argentine law.

AJ: Part 3 and Part 4. What do they do after they do that?

GP: Like I said, you open up the borders for trade, that's the new opium wars. And once you have destroyed an economy that can't produce anything, one of the terrible things is that they are forcing nations to pay horrendous amounts for things like drugs - legal drugs. And by the way, that's how you end up with an illegal drug trade, what's there left to survive on except sell us smack and crack and that's how…

AJ: And the same CIA national security dictatorship has been caught shipping that in.

GP: You know, we are just helping our allies.

AJ: This is just amazing. And so, drive the whole world down, blow out their economies and then buy the rest of it up for pennies on the dollar. What's Part 4 of the IMF/World Bank Plan?

GP: Well, in Part 4, you end up again with the taking apart of the government. And by the way, the real Part 4 is the coup d'etat. That's what they are not telling you. And I'm just finding that out in Venezuela. I just got a call from the President of Venezuela.

AJ: And they install their own corporate government.

GP: What they said was here you've got an elected president of the government and the IMF has announced, listen to this, that they would support a transition government if the president were removed. They are not saying that they are going to get involved in politics - they would just support a transition government. What that effectively is saying 'we will pay for the coup d'etat', if the military overthrows the current president, because the current president of Venezuela has said no to the IMF.

He told those guys to go packing. They brought their teams in and said you have to do this and that. And he said, I don't have to do nothing. He said what I'm going to do is, I'm going to double the taxes on oil corporations because we have a whole lot of oil in Venezuela. And I'm going to double the taxes on oil corporations and then I will have all the money I need for social programs and the government - and we will be a very rich nation. Well, as soon as he said that, they started fermenting trouble with the military and I'm telling you watch this space: the President of Venezuela will be out of office in three months or shot dead They are not going to allow him to raise taxes on the oil companies. (SchNEWS Note: weeks after this interview Chavez survived a weekend coup in late April 2002 see SchNEWS 351).

AJ: Greg Palast, here is the problem. You said it when you first came out of the gates. They are getting hungry, they are doing it to the United States now. Enron, from all the evidence that I've seen was a front, another shill, they would steal assets and then transfer it to other older global companies, then they blew that out and stole the pension funds. Now they are telling us that terrorism is coming any day. It's going to happen if you don't give your rights up. Bush did not involve Congress and the others who are supposed to be in the accession if there is a nuclear attack in the secret government, Washington Post -"Congress Not Advised of Shadow Government." We have the Speaker of the House not being told. This looks like coup d'etat here. I'm going to come right out with it. We had better spread the word on this now or these greedy creatures are going to go all the way.

GP: I'm very sad about one thing. I report this story in the main stream press of Britain. I'm on the BBC despite Lord Wakeham. I know he doesn't like me there. I'm in the BBC, I'm in the main daily paper, which is the equivalent of the New York Times or whatever, and we do get the information out. And I'm just very sorry that we have to have an alternative press, an alternative radio network and everything else to get out the information that makes any sense. I mean this information should be available to every American. I mean, after all, it's our government.

Recommended reading - Greg Palast 'The Best Democracy Money Can Buy' (Pluto 2002) – 'Exposing the truth about globalization, corporate cons and high finance fraudsters.'

www.gregpalast.com

270

Argentina Special

SchNEWS issue 350 featured a four page special about Argentina written mostly by our mate who had just returned from the country and had witnessed the recent dramatic events covered in the articles. For the annual we have turned this into an eight page spread with pictures and a font size a bit easier on the eyes...

TAKING THE PESO

Last December, the people of Argentina rose up in fury against the economic disaster wrought on them by their government, hand in hand with big business, banks and the International Monetary Fund (IMF).

The world watched on TV as pictures of supermarkets and food shops being looted showed a country at breaking point. On the evening of the 19th of December President De la Rúa appeared on Argentinian TV, refusing to resign and instead imposing a state of emergency. Within minutes of his broadcast, the people took to the streets. In Buenos Aires, an estimated million people left their homes and headed for the main Plaza de Mayo, banging pots and pans, chanting 'El estado de sitio, que se lo meten en el culo' (the state of emergency, they can stick it up their arse), and demanding the resignation of De la Rúa and the whole government. 'Que se vayan todos!' (out with them all!) quickly became the main slogan, and after two days of protest and repression which left some 35 people dead, President De la Rúa obliged and fled.

Since then, Argentina has been through an astonishing time. TV news has become a surreal portrait of a country turned upside down - a Congresswoman's house is set on fire by a mob outside after her son shoots a protestor from inside; a group of artists hold a 'mierdazo' - a shit-throwing demo - on the steps of Congress under the slogan 'Putting the shit where it belongs'; farmers bring hundreds of chicks they can't afford to feed to the steps of a provincial government house - when another march, of piqueteros, arrives, they scoop up the chicks and take them away to eat. Popular assemblies have sprung up in barrios (neighbourhoods) all over the country, and the unemployed workers' movement, the piqueteros (picketers), have stepped up their road-blocking activities. As these two currents of protest form tentative links, the loan sharks of the IMF, despised by the people, are in town again to impose their will on a government desperate for more 'assistance' and still willing to go to any lengths to get it.

The Mothers of the Plaza de Mayo - mothers of some of the 30,000 who disappeared during the military dictatorship, who wear distinctive white headscarves - were beaten out of the Plaza by police on the 20th December. TV pictures of this caused outrage, and sent thousands onto the streets.

Eye Witness Account Of The Uprising

An eye-witness account of the uprising of the 19th December, posted in English on indymedia

The presidential palace - the Casa Rosada - on the central Plaza de Mayo

" I was watching television, seeing the lootings and the uprisings in the country's interior. Suddenly the president appeared on the screen, he was talking about differentiating between criminals and the needy. He spoke quietly, almost elegantly, trying to sound in charge. He said he had announced today the state of emergency. I knew that it is unconstitutional in Argentina for the president to declare a state of emergency, only the congress can do that. I was disgusted and I turned off the TV.

I started hearing a sound…a very quiet sound, but growing. I went to the balcony of my apartment and looked out - people on every balcony banging pots and pans. The sound got louder and louder… it was a roar, and it wasn't going to stop. I saw some people on the corner of the street I live, no more than 10. I put on a shirt and went down. On every corner I could see people gathering in small groups. This is a comfortable middle class neighbourhood, but everybody's been fucked by what's going on, and it's been going on for far too long. On the corner of the next street people had started gathering on the middle of the streets. Banging spoons against pans, waving flags…in a few minutes we were something like 150 people.

We started walking. Nobody seemed to know where we were going or what was gonna happen…an hour had gone by since the banging started and the noise wasn't stopping, coming from every corner of the city. As we walked, people were joining us, it was exciting, almost manic. The feeling of regaining your own power. I looked back and suddenly this spontaneous demonstration was a couple of blocks long. I could see people in suits and people in working uniforms. I could see young girls in nice clothes and senior citizens in old clothes.

I could see the small businessman who is suffering from higher and higher taxes and it's about to lose his house from his bank loans and the young man who has been excluded by the system and couldn't get a job for 4 years. Everybody was represented. It was amazing. People cheered from the balconies, small pieces of shredded paper falling slowly to the streets…singing, banging, marching.

When I got to Congress, a couple of thousand people were already there and I could see more people coming in from every corner. It felt like a party. The flags waving, the chants, the clapping. A guy at the top of the steps lit some sort of smoke-flare - pink smoke all over the place. I looked around, I don't know why but I started feeling tense. People kept on coming and we started marching to the Casa Rosada. Things didn't feel exciting anymore, it felt tenser and tenser. I could see some fire on the street ahead - a small trashcan on fire. I kept on walking. Some people were quietly singing and clapping but I saw other small fires. I had entered a column that came from a tougher neighbourhood than mine. I don't blame them - they've been fucked way harder than anybody else and hunger breeds anger. A young guy was banging a stick against a street sign, and this thirtyish guy, skinny and dressed in really old jeans and shirt, holding a young girl in his arms, said something to him. The young man looked back, he saw

the columns of people. I could catch this phrase from the skinny guy "Look at how many we are". I looked back. I saw and felt what I felt at the beginning. Everybody was there, everybody was represented, we were so many.

When I got to Plaza de Mayo a couple of thousand were there and they kept on coming. People started coming in on cars as well as marching. Young people, old people, families - the people. I walked around. Amazed. I was thinking that not many days you go to the balcony to check the noises coming from the streets and you end up being a witness to a presidential deposal by social uprising. Suddenly I was pushed in the back by somebody. When I regained balance I saw people running away. Somebody was yelling "Sons of bitches" right next to me. Out of instinct I started running with them. I ran half a block, stopped and looked back. I saw thousands of people running.

Somebody passing me said something about the police. I couldn't quite understand…my nose started itching. I looked back - in the plaza, 500 metres back, I could see smoke. People's eyes, they were reddening. My throat hurt. I ran. People were going off in all directions away from the plaza. The smoke got higher and higher. I took off my shirt and covered my nose and mouth. My eyes itched. I got pretty far and looked around. This guy in a Miami Florida T-shirt, absolutely middle class said he now understood what the piqueteros felt. I suddenly realized I was crying. I didn't know if it was from the tear gases or from impotence and anger.

* Serious street fighting followed, that night and the next day. 35 people were killed during the two-day insurrection which ended in De la Rúa's resignation. 5 were shot dead by police in and near the Plaza de Mayo (one, Gustavo Ariel Benedetto, was killed by a bullet fired from within the HSBC bank), and many others were killed by police and shop-keepers during lootings.

Thirty five people were killed over the 19th and 20th December, some shot on the streets by police, others by shop-keepers and police during lootings

Silver Tongued

Argentina, a once-prosperous country, is now facing the same problems of poverty as the rest of the continent. Its journey from economic parity with France, at one time, into seemingly endless debt and economic crisis, has been called a process of 'LatinAmericanisation'. So who's made us cry for Argentina? International Monetary Fund, come on down.

Argentina has, for the past two and a half decades, been the IMF's star pupil. It sold off everything, right down to its "grandma's jewels," with foreign firms taking over key sectors of the economy and the utilities. Companies like French multinational Vivendi Universal, which in 1995 bought most of the water system before sacking staff and raising prices, up 400 % in some areas. Or the Spanish oil company Repsol, which snapped up the state-owned YPF, sacked thousands of workers and turned the only oil company in the world not making a profit, into a money-spinner estimated to have taken $60 billion out of the country. Or the Spanish Telefónica, which bought up most of the privatised telephone system for a bargain basement price, then whacked up the prices to way above those paid anywhere else in the world and made a tidy profit of $2 billion in its first year.

Argentina obediently deregulated its markets and tried to make its workforce more 'flexible' (meaning you work longer for less pay.) It has jumped through all the IMF hoops, with promises of prosperity at the end of them, yet now finds itself with a $150-billion-dollar foreign debt, with 30% of its GDP going every year on interest payments alone before December. It is still paying part of the debt, despite having supposedly defaulted.

Loan Sharks

The first IMF loans were to the military junta in 1976 and since then, this 'debt' has been paid off by the Argentinian people many times over - and not just in pesos. Argentinians used to call their country the bread-basket of the world, and say that in a country bursting with natural resources and a huge agricultural sector, nobody could ever go hungry. But now 40% of the people live below the poverty line and up to a hundred die every day from poverty-related illness, with food parcels and medicines now arriving from Spain and neighbouring Brazil.

In a ruling two years, ago a federal judge summed it up. "Since 1976, our country has been put under the rule of foreign creditors and under the supervision of the IMF by means of a vulgar and offensive economic policy that forced Argentina down on its knees in order to benefit national and foreign private firms."

Despite the economy being in free-fall, two documents leaked to investigative journalist Greg Palast show that, for the deluded economists at the IMF, what the country really needed to get it back on its feet was even more structural adjustment! So it's more cuts for state pensions, salaries, unemployment benefits, education and health, all of this ensuring that the burden of this so called 'adjustment' falls, as ever, on those who can least afford it.

Anoop Singh, leader of the IMF delegation currently in the country, admitted it was "the worst economic crisis any country has had." He then promptly listed a new set of demands Argentina must implement immediately before they even get to see how much 'aid' they'll receive. In a veiled threat he commented, "without an IMF agreement, it will be very difficult for Argentina to recover." Since 1983 there have been nine IMF stabilisation plans in Argentina, 'helping' the country out.

But it's not just the IMF that wants more adjustment. Other financial institutions are still licking their loan shark lips, saying Argentina's crisis should not be seen as an obstacle but as an opportunity because, the reasoning goes, the country is so desperate for cash it will do whatever the IMF wants. "During a crisis is when . . . Congress is most receptive," explained Winston Fritsch, chairman of Dresdner Bank AG's Brazil. Meanwhile, a couple of Massachusetts Institute of Technology economists writing in the Financial Times, go even further. "It's time to get radical… (Argentina) must temporarily surrender its sovereignty on all financial issues . . . and give up much of its monetary, fiscal, regulatory and asset-management sovereignty for an extended period, say five years."

When Greg Palast interviewed the former chief economist, Joe Stiglitz - fired by the World Bank for questioning its economic wisdom - Stiglitz told him about 'IMF riots' "Everywhere we go, every country we end up meddling in, we destroy their economy and they end up in flames." He went on to tell Palast that the IMF even plan for riots, because as the people revolt, capital drains out of the country (helped by IMF inspired abolition of currency controls) and whoever's left in charge has to go begging back to the IMF for more money. They don't mind handing some out, as long as the country agrees to even more demands, and they turn a blind eye as politicians fill their pockets in return for their compliance.

On Tuesday the IMF did just that, agreeing to give Argentina $5 billion of its promised, frozen $22 billion loan programme. And where will that money go? To where it's really needed - paying the interest on the debt. The debt gets bigger, the cuts get harsher - and the money doesn't even have to leave Washington. The people of Argentina know the IMF aren't there to help them. The only people the IMF dish out their dollars to are those who in their view really need it; the banks and big business, the rich and the powerful. For them, the Argentina experiment has been a stunning success - Shame about the people though, eh?

* Greg Palast's 'The Best Democracy Money Can Buy' (Pluto Press, 2002) www.gregpalast.com

* www.corpwatch.org

* www.50years.org

Payback Time

Last year, as the country slipped into total crisis and it looked likely it was going to default on its eternal debt, IMF conditions dictated that the government should make massive cuts in public spending. State workers' salaries were cut by 13%, as were state pensions, in yet another round of austerity measures which helped to push people's patience right to its limit. Argentina has paid and paid for its addiction to IMF 'assistance', and it looks as if it will be paying for years, in ways it never thought possible. The deployment of Argentinian troops to the Gulf War and to Bosnia are examples of favours called in by the USA, as is the training of Colombian airforce pilots in Argentina. US and Latin American troops, commanded and financed in Washington, have carried out exercises in Argentina without Congress's approval, and despite this being in violation of Argentina's constitution.

Argentina is about to vote, for the third time, against Cuba's human rights record at the UN, this time as a proposer of the motion. It has promised Washington to 'work for the liberty of the Cuban people,' to the disgust of the Argentinian people and Fidel Castro, who has yet again called the government 'yankee boot-lickers'. Another member of the Cuban government expressed sympathy for Argentina, locked in to 'carnal relations' with the USA, for the way the USA is 'humiliating and pressurizing' Argentina while denying it the funds to resolve the situation imposed by 'the dogmatic imposition of the neo-liberal model'. And there's more to come for Argentina. On January 12th, the New York Times reported US Secretary of Defense, Donald Rumsfeld, as saying the US might be willing to financially assist the Argentinian government, if they were permitted to install military bases in Tierra del Fuego, the southernmost tip of the Americas. The governor of the province has secretly authorised bases, where the US will be allowed to detonate underground atomic bombs - but only for 'peaceful ends'. So that's alright then.

Fear And Loathing In Buenos Aires

The following is a condensed version of eye-witness reports sent to Schnews from Buenos Aires in January.

Fri, 18 Jan 2002

The streets are emptier in Buenos Aires, at night, than I have ever seen them. In the centre of the city in the daytime it's as crowded as ever, and queues for exchange bureaux and banks stretch around blocks. There's a new feeling in the air, of anxiety and barely-surpressed anger; walking down the main pedestrian avenue, Florida, I heard a woman laugh too loud, and everyone jumped and shot her alarmed stares. 'Ladrones usureros' - usurers, thieves, is scratched onto the marble plaque outside the Bank of Boston. Lloyds and HSBC banks have put up enormous metal panels over their windows. In the provinces, banks are being ransacked every day. The TV news shows protest after protest; today in Santiago del Estero, in the North, there are barricades in the streets and brutal police repression of the mostly middle-aged working men who are demanding 'Dignidad para el obrero' - dignity for the workers. In La Quiaca, people are crucifying themselves every day, 5 hours each in the hot sun, while the children hold signs saying 'pan y trabajo' (bread and work) and 'luchamos contra el hambre' (our struggle is against hunger). Yesterday, after a cacerolazo outside the Supreme Court to demand the resignation of its 9 judges, the people went to the home of one of the judges and continued there. This form of protest is called an 'escrache', or 'outing', and was first used in Argentina by the HIJOS - sons and daughters of the disappeared - to expose repressors and members of the military government to their neighbours. Politicians and judges can't walk the streets for fear of being recognized - a friend was queuing at a bank the other day when a judge drew up in a car and tried to go in. Everyone started abusing him - 'ratta!' (rat), 'corrupto', 'hijo de mil putas' (son of a thousand whores), until he took refuge in his car and left.

Peoples' fury at their inability to access their savings, due to banking restrictions, is worsened by news of 386 trucks stuffed with cash, which ferried an estimated 26 billion dollars to the airport after banking restrictions had been imposed, for transfer to Uruguay and beyond. Given the numerous stories of massive 'capital flight' over the early days of this crisis, and of businesses and banks which mysteriously took out fortunes before and during the strict new measures, people think most of their money will never be seen again. But there are many for whom the corralito means nothing - they have nothing in the bank. Unemployment is at well over 20%, and there is hunger in many areas. Pensioners are badly affected - they have had no pensions since November, and millions of workers are also going unpaid. The state medical system, PAMI, has collapsed due to lack of funds. There is an extreme shortage of insulin and other common drugs, because they are imported and because many drugs were withdrawn from the shelves by pharmaceutical companies, in order to protect prices. In the outlying, poorest barrios people have arms and use them, but actual robberies are outstripped by paranoia and vigillanteeism, born of government disinformation about supposed widespread looting of homes. Many people are trying to leave the country, reluctantly but seeing no future in Argentina - when it was reported this week that Poland was to join the EU, a queue formed immediately at the Polish embassy. Thousands of the large Chilean population of Mendoza have gone home, as have many of the Bolivian, Peruvian and Paraguayan migrant workers. People talk bitterly of institutional corruption from top to bottom. Now, as well as blaming the IMF, the free market economy forced on them by Menem (the whole-sale selling off and privatisation), and the constant flight of capital abroad, people are beginning to blame themselves. It's bitter and humiliating.

Yesterday we went to the general assembly, the 'Interbarrial', of the almost 100 neighbourhood ('barrio') assemblies of Bs. As. in Parque Centenario, and attended by about 2,000 people. There were speeches from each barrio, telling of their experiences, listing actions they planned and putting forward proposals. There was a lot of talk about the Supreme Court and continuing the protests against it until all the judges resigned - or to go in and boot them out themselves. The media was denounced by many speakers for its lies and distortion; meanwhile, the news that there were TV crews from Japan, Spain, UK and Finland present at the assembly was greeted with cheers, while the mention of a US TV crew met with angry whistles and boos. There were no Argentinian TV crews present at all. Speakers suggested that anyone who had held a political post in the last 30 years should be disqualified from ever doing so again. They denounced the new budget and banking reforms due to be announced this week as measures that were bound to suit the 'yanquis' (USA) - the new economy minister is a veteran of 20 years' service to the IMF. It was agreed that the visitors from the IMF due here on Tuesday should be greeted with a 'cacerolazo'. A speaker proposed that 'we stay in the streets till they have all gone' and commented on the importance of showing that it's not just the corralito they are against; that they want to change it all. There was a minute's applause for those who died during the repression which followed the first cacerolazos of the 19th and 20th of December and chants of 'Policía Federál, la verguenza nacionál' - the Federal Police, a national disgrace. Barrio after barrio made its proposals, and when the voting through of the main proposals went ahead they were:

· Que se vayan todos (that all politicians should go)
· No to payment of the external debt
· Justice and punishment for the murderers and repressors
· Nationalisation of the bank and the privatised companies
· The Supreme Court - out!
· Return the money to depositors.

Tue, 29 Jan 2002

On Friday night, the 25th January, a national 'cacerolazo', agreed at the assembly, began at 8pm with the sound of pans clanging from balconies and in the streets and park of the capital. By 10pm, the enormous Plaza de Mayo was starting to fill and the noise was already deafening, a cacophony of metal on metal; spoon on saucepan, lid on lid, kettle on cheesegrater. Along the Avenida de Mayo a steady stream of people was pouring into the square; 'asambleas barriales' (neighbourhood assemblies) arriving from the barrios, hundreds of families and thousands of old people. The clang of metal on lamp-posts and traffic signs sounded over the massed pots and pans, while the clapping of those who had come empty handed was by now inaudible. The rain was coming on and off in the heat, but everyone acted like they hadn't noticed as the square filled with banging, chanting people. Over the rhythm of beaten pans, chants were constantly breaking out; the favourite, sung by nearly 20,000 football-style, was and almost always is: 'Que se vayan todos, que no quede ni uno solo' (that they all go, that not a single one remains). And, jumping and pointing at the President's Casa Rosada, cut off from the square by fencing and lines of stony-faced cops, 'A minute's silence for Duhalde, who is dead'. I look at the faces of the police behind the fence and I think I see fear and shame; later, I reconsider.

By 11:30pm, the rain is pouring down in buckets, creating rivers around the kerbs of the plaza and washing across the square, but the crowd only bangs the pots harder and jumps faster, chanting louder, 'Que llueve, que llueve, que el pueblo no se mueve' (let it rain, let it rain, the people are staying here). And suddenly, unexpectedly, almost on the stroke of midnight, the 'represión' begins. Motorcycle police appear and begin to fire teargas and rubber bullets, causing panicked running here and there; as people on their way home along the Avenida de Mayo approach the wide Avenida 9 de Julio, a line of cops appears and fires teargas and rubber bullets from the front and from side-streets. In the Plaza, people taking shelter from the rain in front of the cathedral are fired upon with gas and rubber bullets. The demonstration had been noisy but entirely peaceful - on TV reports, there is just a single image of a youth throwing a molotov cocktail at lines of police who have already emptied the square. It is an incomprehensible response in already volatile times. I hear a report on the radio of a woman of 70, on the ground badly wounded, her legs full of rubber bullets, and a young man with two in his head. Back home, we watch on TV as 20 people, under arrest, are forced to lie face down

in the rain with their hands above their heads - 'It's just like during the dictatorship', someone says. There are still 300 demonstrators at Congress, completely surrounded by police. They are chanting and jumping - 'El que no salta es policía' (whoever's not jumping is police). We see three young men with their arms over their heads being thrust towards a police bus. Their t-shirts are pulled over their heads from the back by police and at least one is bleeding heavily from the head. A policeman in soaked t-shirt and shorts is directing uniformed officers as they hustle

the lads onto the bus. In the bar someone says - 'These sons-of-bitches haven't even been paid' (thousands of people have gone unpaid, some for months). 'No importa', says someone else '- lo hacen de onda'. (They don't mind - they do it for fun).

PS. This morning, tho' some of the press made the point that the demo had been entirely peaceful and the police action unprovoked, most of the TV news, as always, reverted to type and lied. As graffiti here in the barrio where we are staying says, 'Nos mean y la prensa dice q' llueve' (they piss on us and the press says it's raining).

'They piss on us and the press says it's raining' - Graffiti in Buenos Aires

Money For Sale

The banking restrictions, known as the corralito (meaning the corralling or ring-encing of bank deposits), was imposed at the beginning of December, when nervous savers, feeling disaster approach, started to withdraw their money from the banks. Since then, its rules have changed almost daily, allowing a certain amount to be withdrawn each month, but also forcibly converting most savings, 80% of which had been deposited in dollars for security (!) into pesos at extremely unfavourable rates. Those who insisted on keeping their deposits - which exist on paper only now as the money is no longer in the country - in dollars, have been forced to accept bonds which may or may not be repaid in the next year or so, and almost certainly not in dollars. And those with pesos can only watch as the peso falls from one-to-one with the dollar, where it had been artificially pegged for eleven years, to a low of 4 a few weeks ago. The stated Supreme Court, in a manoeuvre calculated to save its own skin from moves

in Congress to impeach them and from the angry threats of the people to go in and kick them out, decreed the corralito unconstitutional on the 1st of February. Some savers laid down their pots and pans to queue at the court for individual court orders to their banks to return their deposits, but banks have generally ignored these. Those with a lot of money or influence routinely skip out of the corralito with their money, either on the nod from their banks or through clever dealings with shares in Argentinian companies on the New York stock exchange.

It's a different story for businesses, which have been generously compensated by the (bankrupt) state for the peso-fication of their debts in dollars. Plans for the peso-fication, at one-to-one despite the plummeting peso, of debts contracted in dollars was intended to help individuals with debts like mortgages, who could never dream of repaying them in the devalued peso, and was going to apply only to debts of less than $100,000. But an investigation by reporters on the TV news show 'Telenoche Investiga', who were all sacked and their programme never broadcast, uncovered the truth about

how the debts of big business came to be included in the rescue plan. On the 12th January, heads of large Argentinian corporations held a secret meeting with President Duhalde and three other members of the cabinet. They were told by the president that it might be possible for their massive debts to also benefit from conversion at one to one, if they were willing to make a 'contribution'. Even the millionaire CEOs were taken aback at the size of the bribe he was soliciting - it was to be $500 million dollars, in dollars and in cash. The reporter was told that the money was to be divided between members of Congress and the Senate ($200 million) who would have to approve it, $175 million for Mendiguren, Lenicov and Capitanich, the cabinet members present that day, and a tidy $125 million for Duhalde. One empresario refused and is now under investigation by the DGI (General Tax Directorate). The overall saving to businesses is estimated to be in the region of $20-30 billion dollars (YPF-Repsol oil, for example, has been able to halve its $310 million debt); the money will have to come from more cuts in public spending.

PIQUETE Y CACEROLA, LA LUCHA ES UNA SOLA

The two biggest types of organised resistance in Argentina are the popular assemblies and the piqueteros, the unemployed workers' movement which takes its name (picketers) from their trademark tactic of blocking roads.

The piqueteros set up camps on the asphalt of the highways

130 pesos a month. An email which arrived at Schnews last week from a British activist in Buenos Aires:

"There's loads of different piquetero organisations, and a lot of divisions, partly caused by old left parties. The CCC is the largest, and the most reformist [despite the name - Classist and Combative Current] - they are the ones who concentrate on demands for proper social security payments. Far more militant are independent organisations such as CTA Anibal Verón, and Movimiento Teresa Rodrigues (both named after piqueteros murdered by cops during blockades), and the MTD (Unemployed Workers Movement). They see their struggle as a Latin American one, and identify with the anti-capitalist movement. They are active, highly politicised people, and probably number 10,000."

The middle class are 'avin it on the streets, pissed off with the banks cos they've lost their money

The Piqueteros

Rising unemployment in Argentina over the last few years has created the world's largest concentration of unemployed industrial workers. Many piqueteros are experienced workplace and union activists. With no tools to down or workplaces to picket, they use the tactic of blocking roads as a way of disrupting production, setting up camp right on the asphalt, putting up tents and cooking food. Women and children are a fundamental part of the movement, and always present. The piqueteros have stepped up

their activities in the last few months, paralysing the capital a number of times, most recently when the latest IMF delegation arrived to 'negotiate'. In February they blockaded oil refineries and depots throughout the country, demanding 50,000 jobs; new, shorter shifts to employ more workers; no petrol price rises and the re-nationalisation of the oil industry and all the privatised companies. They also usually demand food packages, the release of political prisoners, unemployment benefits and 'work plans' - a type of workfare scheme worth a meagre

Bourgeois Block

An email to Schnews describes bizarre scenes as the 'bourgeois block', gangs of enraged savers denied access to their money, strikes again:

"Tearing off the metal cladding, they invaded the bank lobbies and in full sight of the police, without a mask or black hoody to be seen, proceeded to destroy the cash machines. Women with perms, golden bracelets and high heels kicked at the windows, lipstick grins spreading as they watched the glass shatter. Every armoured security van the mob of 300 people came across was surrounded. Men in business suits proceeded to unscrew the wheel-nuts, while others prised open the bonnets, tearing out wires from the engines. Soccer mums jumped up and down on top of vans, smashing anything that could be broken, wing-mirrors, lights, number plates..."

The piqueteros' trademark tactic is the blocking of highways and bridges, in the provinces and around the capital

Popular, neighbourhood assemblies are held in parks and on street corners throughout Buenos Aires and in the provinces. All the assemblies of the capital meet weekly at Parque Centenario (above) for discussion and coordination

Popular Assemblies

Popular assemblies, also known as neighbourhood (barrio) assemblies, have mushroomed in Argentina since December. A recent survey by the newspaper Página 12 found that 33% of those questioned in the capital had participated in them. Assemblies are held on street corners or public spaces, and operate in the most transparent way, with what they call a 'horizontal' structure and no leaders or representatives. Born of the first cacerolazos, and the fertile coming together of neighbours on the streets in protest, the assemblies discuss and vote on issues ranging from non-payment of the external debt to the defence of local families in danger of eviction for non-payment of rent. They have organised collective food-buying, soup kitchens, support for local hospitals and schools and even alternative forms of healthcare. Every Sunday, all the Buenos Aires assemblies meet in Parque Centenario for the Interbarrial - the inter-neighbourhood mass assembly. Certain sections of mainstream politics are attempting to participate in or co-opt the assemblies - like one proposal made in Congress that the assemblies be given their own space and resources at the Congress building - but these proposals were vehemently rejected. Pressure from left-wing parties such as the Partido Obrero (workers' party), has been harder to resist. At an Interbarrial in Centenario, a motion was put that "the party militants stop coming along to assemblies to lay down party lines - that they take the assembly's position back to their parties instead." The sovereignty of each local assembly has been reiterated again and again at the Interbarrial and motions voted there, based on proposals from each assembly, are taken back to local assemblies to be ratified. Despite this, a controversial proposal for a Constituent Assembly - an assembly of delegates - which many felt was an unacceptable move back towards representative politics, was voted through at the Interbarrial of March 17th.

Despite their differences, one important similarity between the piqueteros and the 'vecinos auto-convocados' ('self-convened neighbours') of the popular assemblies is that both are organising outside the sphere of work. But the assemblies' refusal to negotiate with the government, under the slogan 'Que se vayan todos' - out with all politicians - clashes with some sections of the piqueteros, who are demanding work, dole and recognition from the government. Since the economy collapsed at the end of last year, the total of Argentinians living in poverty has risen to some 14 million (pop. 36 million), and the middle class has been destroyed and impoverished. But the piqueteros' struggle has been going on for years, with little support from the wider public, and those who participate in the cacerolazos and at bank protests have been accused of having acted only when their own pockets were finally rifled. Despite these contradictions, everyone sees the need to link their struggles together; and many of the piqueteros' demands, which seemed radical just a few months ago (non-payment of the national debt, for example) have become the battle cries of the newly-impoverished middle class too. On the 27th February, a march of some 5,000 piqueteros from the poor Buenos Aires suburb of La Matanza was met by a number of local assemblies, who provided breakfast and then joined the march to the Plaza de Mayo. The piqueteros were also cheered along the route by the people of Buenos Aires, who gave out food and drink, and some came out to bang pots and pans. A new slogan was born - 'Piquete y cacerola, la lucha es una sola' (pickets and pot-bangers, the struggle is one). Piquetero demands include things like the return of savers' deposits, while motions at popular assemblies almost always include support for the piqueteros. Both have strong links with the occupied factories under workers' control, which include Brukman textiles in the capital, Zanon ceramics in the province of Neuquen and Panificacion Cinco, a bakery in Munro, Buenos Aires.

Zanon ceramics factory - under workers' control

Since the end of December, cacerolazos - pot banging protests - have been a daily feature of life in Argentina.

One of the mothers of the disappeared is lost in the teargas clouding the Plaza de Mayo

Repression

Despite the unprecedented changes happening at street level, there's little new in mainstream politics and government. President Duhalde is an old political hand, and well known for corruption during his previous years in office. In his nine years as governor of Buenos Aires, he amassed support, contacts and experience that now stand him in good stead, including the use of violent thugs ('patoteros'), both paid and party political. At his swearing-in as president, hundreds of his supporters, said to have been paid to come, battled outside and inside Congress with protestors, and there are even rumours that some of the looters who precipitated the downfall of President De la Rúa were paid by the Peronist party. Duhalde has ordered the repression of at least one cacerolazo, on the 25th

January, since taking power, and is now making use of the thugs of his party apparatus (officially called the Justicialist Party, aka Peronism) to intimidate a population which still clearly remembers the fearsome repression, torture and murder of the military dictatorship (1976-1983), when 30,000 people 'disappeared'. In the Buenos Aires barrio of Merlo a few weeks ago, the assembly was attacked and one assembly has even been shot at. In the barrio of Avellaneda last Sunday the assembly, gathered to protest at corruption in the local administration, was prevented from reaching their destination by a gang of 300 thugs sent by the local municipal leader. Last Tuesday during one of the regular savers' protests at the Bank of Boston, a woman was beaten to the ground, kicked and handcuffed and had teargas sprayed in her eyes by police and many of the other protestors were beaten and arrested.

And Finally...

From the first night of the uprising, the Argentinian people have shown utter contempt for politicians, summed up in the slogan 'Que se vayan todos' - out with all politicians. But this disillusionment with representative politics is nothing new. In last October's general elections, more than 40% of the (compulsory) votes were blank or spoiled, with the majority of them going to a cartoon character, Clemente the cat politician, who has no hands so he cannot steal! So while politicians in the West denounce their own demonstrators as either foolish, indulgent or violent for having the cheek to fight for a better world, the mass media focuses on protests in Seattle and Genoa, while burying news of general strikes and mass protests in countries like Argentina. But we know that it will only be people around the world working together and linking up with international struggles, that can defeat capitalism. As one of the speakers at last year's National Assembly of piqueteros, put it, "Argentina is part of a world-wide crisis - all over the world, piqueteros are arising. And last week, 300,000 piqueteros invaded the city of Genoa to say 'no' to world-wide imperialism." Others have taken up the slogan 'Todos Somos Argentinos' - 'We Are All Argentinians' - because people know that what is happening now in Argentina will be happening in a country near you soon, if the IMF and their big business mates carry on destroying the planet in their never-ending search for profit. Unless, of course, we stop 'em.

Hired and party hoodlums have been organised to intimidate and repress assemblies. The picture above shows a group of thugs, who confronted and fought with protestors at Congress on the day of President Duhalde's swearing-in

'I didn't vote for him' - Duhalde's presidency is widely considered illegitimate But even before the uprising, in October's general elections, more than 40% of (compulsory) votes were blank or spoiled

Subscribe!

Keep SchNEWS FREE! Send 1st Class stamps (e.g. 10 for next 9 issues) or donations (payable to Justice?) Ask for "Originals" if you can make copies. Post *free* to all prisoners. SchNEWS, c/o on-the-fiddle, P.O. Box 2600, Brighton, East Sussex, BN2 0EF.
Tel/Autofax +44 (0)1273 685913 *Email* schnews@brighton.co.uk *Download a PDF of this issue or subscribe at* www.schnews.org.uk

AFTER ARGENTINA, WHO'LL BE NEXT TO GO?
A Post Script for the Global Anticapitalist Movement

"Argentina's crisis is fast emerging as a sort of economic Rorschach test, used by economists and theoreticians of all ideological persuasions to prove their point," says the Financial Times. **"Opponents of the 'Washington Consensus' say Argentina's experience shows the perils of following the recipes of the IMF. Supporters of free markets say Argentina's experience shows the danger of not opening up [the economy] enough."**

Argentina may well prove to be the crisis which irrevocably splits the ever-widening crack in the neo-liberal armour, especially if things continue to unravel in other parts of Latin America. Recent events in Venezuela, and the possibility of left wing gains in this year's Brazilian presidential elections, point to a shift away from the "Washington Consensus" across much of the region.

The last decade has seen the increasing delegitimazation of the neo liberal model, as a movement of movements has sprung up on every continent, challenging the seemingly unstoppable expansion of capital. From Chiapas to Genoa, Seattle to Porto Alegre, Bangalore to Soweto, people have occupied the streets, taken direct action, practiced models of self-organization, and celebrated a radical spirit of autonomy, diversity, and interdependence. The movements seemed unstoppable, as mass mobilizations got bigger, more diverse populations converged, and the World Bank, WTO, IMF, and G8 were forced to meet on mountain tops, protected by repressive regimes, or behind fences defended by thousands of riot police. Seeing them on the defensive, having to justify their existence, gave the movements an extraordinary sense of hope.

By identifying the underlying global problem as capitalism, and by developing extraordinary international networks of inspiration in very short amounts of time, it felt almost as though history were speeding up, that perhaps we could succeed in the next phase, the process of imagining and constructing worlds which exist beyond greed and competition. Then, history did what it does best, surprising us all on September 11th when the twin towers were brought down, and it seemed for a while that everything had changed.

Suddenly hope was replaced by the politics of despair and fear. Demonstrations were called off, funding was pulled, and mass backpedaling and distancing occurred within the movement itself. Commentators immediately declared anticapitalism dead. The editor of The Guardian wrote "since September 11th, there is no appetite for [anti-globalisation], no interest, and the issues that were all-consuming a few months ago seem irrelevant now." Others suggested that the movement was somehow linked to the terrorists. Clare Short, the UK development minister, stated that the movement's demands were very similar to those of Al-Qaida.

September the 11th forced a reappraisal among activists, particularly in the global north. It challenged us all to take a deep breath, put our rhetoric into practice, and think strategically, and fast. Then three months later, history seemed to resume its accelerated speed, when Argentina erupted, followed closely by the collapse of Enron. It seemed that despite the blindly nationalist, racist, and indefinite "war on terror" to distract the world, neoliberalism was continuing to disintegrate.

Perhaps the biggest challenge the global movements face now is to realize that the first round is over, and that the slogan first sprayed on a building in Seattle and last seen on a burning police van in Genoa, "We Are Winning," may actually be true. The "crisis of legitimacy" expands exponentially almost daily. Corporations and institutions such as the World Bank and the G8 are constantly trying to appease the growing global uprising, with empty promises of environmental sustainability and poverty reduction.

On May Day, 2002 a new book is being launched by academics who lament, "Today there is an anticapitalist orthodoxy that goes beyond a latent hostility to big business. Its a well-organized critique of capitalism." The book argues that we must "start standing up for capitalism" because it's "the best thing that

ever happened to the world," and that "if we want to change the world then we should do it through business," and treat capitalism as a "hero, not a villain." Perhaps a few hours on the streets of Argentina, or a chat with former employees of Enron would show them the true villainy and absurdity of capitalism.

With mainstream commentators falling over themselves to declare that capitalism is good for us and will save the world, it seems clear that the first round of this movement has been a victory. There has been a "...nearly complete collapse of the prevailing economic theory," according to economist James K. Galbraith. But the next round will be the hardest. It will involve applying our critiques and principles to our everyday lives; it will be a stage of working close to home. A stage where mass conflict on the streets is balanced (but not entirely replaced) with creating alternatives to capitalism in our neighborhoods, our towns and cities, our bio-regions. This is exactly where Argentina can show us an inspiring way to move forward.

The situation in Argentina contains many elements of the anti-capitalist movements: the practice of direct action, self-management and direct democracy; the belief in the power of diversity, decentralization, and solidarity; the convergence of radically different social sectors; the rejection of the state, multinational corporations, and financial institutions. Yet, what is most incredible is that the form of the uprising arose spontaneously, it was not imposed or suggested by activists, but rather, created by ordinary people from the ground up, resulting in a truly popular rebellion that is taking place every day, every week, and including every sort of person imaginable.

Argentina has become a living laboratory of struggle, a place where the popular politics of the future are being invented. In the face of poverty and economic meltdown, people have found enough hope to continue resisting, and have mustered sufficient creativity to begin building alternatives to the despair of capitalism. The global movements can learn much in this laboratory. In many ways it is comparable with the social revolutions of Spain in 1936, of France in May 1968, and more recently, in southern Mexico, with the 1994 uprising of the Zapatista Army of National Liberation (EZLN) - all rebellions which inspired, then and now, millions around the world. It was a spirit of innovative solidarity that sparked a transformation of the practice of politics, and led us into the first stage of this new evolution of people's movements. The Zapatistas sowed the seeds for creating "rebellions which listen" to local needs and demands, and which are therefore particular to each place, and activists from around the world responded, not only through traditional forms of international solidarity as practiced during the 1970-80s, particularly by Central American solidarity groups, but also through applying the spirit of Zapatismo by "listening" at home.

This network of listening that has occurred between many different cultures has been a cornerstone for the first round of this global movement, as it wove together its multiple differences, forming a powerful fabric of struggle. The second round needs to maintain these networks that nurture mutual inspiration flowing, because no revolution can succeed without hope. But the global anticapitalist movement also needs the reassurance of seeing its desires and aspirations being lived on a daily basis. The Zapatista autonomous municipalities in Chiapas are a kind of model, but are firmly rooted in indigenous culture, are small enclaves within a larger state, and are largely unexportable. Argentina, however, is an entire society undergoing transformation. It is a model that is much easier for the movements, especially those of the global North, to imagine occurring at home.

However, the movement in Argentina is in danger of isolation; without the security and the mutual inspiration of international solidarity, it will suffer greatly. The mainstream press has mostly ignored the situation since the December riots, and most people we met felt that the world was unaware of their plight. For once, no one was chanting "the whole world is watching," because of course, it is in the interest of capitalism's defense team to ensure that we don't get to watch, don't get to see what's really going on. Although many anticapitalists worldwide have said "Thank god for Argentina," as we've had our hopes rekindled in the dark days post 9-11, most of the people on the streets of Argentina have no idea that they've provided such widespread optimism.

If Chiapas was the place from which the seeds of the first round of this movement blew, then Argentina could well be where those seeds land, begin to sprout, and put down roots. We need to find creative ways to support and learn from the rebellion there as we did with the Zapatistas. Some solidarity actions have been taken - the Argentinean embassy in London was occupied and an anarchist flag hung out front, cacerolazos have taken place from Seattle to Sao Paolo, Rome to Nairobi. A chant directed against the World Economic Forum when they met in New York, proclaimed, "They are Enron, we are Argentina!" But much more could be done, more stories could be exchanged, actions coordinated, and visits to the laboratory undertaken.

There is a joke currently circulating the Japanese banking community, that goes: "What's the difference between Japan and Argentina?" "About eighteen months." These bankers well know that the economic situation in Argentina will occur elsewhere, and that it is inevitable that the tug of war between people's desires for a better life and the demands of global capital will result in explosions across the planet. A recent report (also published in this book) by the World Development Movement documents 77 separate incidents of civil unrest in 23 countries, all relating to IMF protests, and all occurring in the year 2001. From Angola to Nepal to Columbia to Turkey, the same cracks are appearing in the neoliberal "logic," and people are resisting. A dozen countries are poised to be the "next Argentina," and some of them may be a lot closer to home than we ever imagined. We need to be prepared, not only to resist, but to find ways to rebuild our societies when the economic crisis hits. If the popular rebellion in Argentina succeeds, it could show the world that people are able to live through severe economic crisis and come out the other side, not merely having survived, but stronger, and happier for struggling for new ways of living.

As this goes to print, the economic crisis in Argentina continues to spiral out of control. Having succeeded in winning legal battles against the government (setting legal precedent that ricochets around the globe) and recovering their savings from banks, thousands of depositors are withdrawing their money from the banking system as fast as they can. In recent days a judge has sent a police contingent and a locksmith to a branch of HSBC to recover a claimant's savings, while the vault of a branch of Banco Provincia was opened with the aid of a blowtorch. With the banking system about to go belly up, the government decided to close all banks for an "indefinite holiday." When the IMF refused again to loan more money and the Argentinean congress threw out a bill that proposed converting the frozen bank savings into IOU government bonds, the new minister of economy resigned. In an emergency press conference, Duhalde declared "Banks will have to open again and God knows what will happen then. Banks cannot be closed permanently. It would be absurd to think of a capitalist system without banks."

It may be absurd to think of a capitalist system without banks, but it is equally absurd to believe in the continuation of the present global system. Perhaps the most realistic thing to imagine at the beginning of this already war torn century, is a system free of capitalism one without banks, without poverty, without despair, a system whose currency is creativity and hope, a system that rewards cooperation rather than competition, a system that values the will of the people over the rule of the market. One day we may look back at the absurdity of the present and remember how the people of Argentina inspired us to demand the impossible, and invited us to build new worlds which spread outwards from our own neighborhoods.

John Jordan and Jennifer Whitney, May Day 200

April 18: The Colombia Solidarity Campaign attends the BP AGM London to remind everyone of the severe human rights abuses in Colombia the company commits. BP don't mind doing things like kicking 300 peasants off their land to build an oil pipeline and not offering any compensation. Pic: Richie Andrew

SchNEWS Issues 301-350 Index

NB this index refers to articles within the SchNEWS issues only, and the numbers given denote issue, not page. Numbers in bold indicate front page SchNEWS stories, the rest are on back pages.

SchNEWS Round
Issues 51-100: Reclaim the Streets... Squatters Estate Agents... 3rd Battle of Newbury... The Land Is Ours!... cartoons... and loads more (NB not many left)

SchNEWS Annual
Issues 101-150: Anarchy... Networks... Ecology... Campaigns... Information... Sabotage... Weird Shit... Comics...

SchNEWS Survival Handbook
Issues 151-200: GM crop trashings, streets get reclaimed & much more PLUS all-round how-to guides to everything DIY and direct action...

SchQUALL: Issues 201-250 of SchNEWS and the best of SQUALL magazine (NB not many left)
GM crops... June 18th... Privatisation... Seattle... DIY culture... Photos... Cartoons... Satirical grafix... Subverts...

SchNEWS & Squall Yearbook 2001
Issues 251-300 of SchNEWS and the best of SQUALL magazine: Winston Gets A Mohawk... Prague S26... Summit round-ups: Nice, Davos, Melbourne... Cartoons... Subverts... the IMF... the WTO... the WEF... the ERT... TABD... ECGs... SAPs... and the BBC... BB King... Matt Busby... Dig It... Dig It... Dig It...

Mark Thomas Bootleg Video £7
Limited edition video, live in Brighton. 2 hours of Mark in fine form the day after Balfour Beatty pulled out of the Ilisu Dam.

SchNUSIC Compilation CD
Linking conscious, unsellable, H/C, rootsy music and musicians with a Schnewsy SCRAP vibe. SCRAP is a Brighton based record label. www.dirtysquatters.com NB It is NOT available in shops. **£7 inc p&p**

Not This Time
Casualisation Kills - the story of the Simon Jones Memorial Campaign [2002 update] (pal)
People like Simon Jones get killed at work all the time and nothing is done about it. Not this time. The video tells the story of the direct action campaign to bring his killers to justice. Order now from Cultureshop.

Cultureshop www.cultureshop.org, Box 91, Greenleaf Books, 82 Colston St, Bristol, BS1 5BB.

NOT THIS TIME
Casualisation Kills

The story of the Simon Jones Memorial Campaign

Guerillavision Compilation
Three films together on one video tape (pal)
'Rattle in Seattle' - WTO Meltdown, Seattle 30-11-99; 'Capitals III - DK in DC' - IMF/WB protest, Washington DC 16-4-00; 'Crowd Bites Wolf' - mass demonstrations against IMF, Prague, 26-9-00. The trio of stylish, hard-hitting Guerillavision films documenting the campaigns against globalisation from behind the barricades. Available now from Cultureshop.

PRACTICALLY GIVING 'EM AWAY OFFER
Order all five books and pay £20 including p&p for the lot.

Name..

Address..

....

....

Cheques/postal orders payable to Justice?' c/o On the Fiddle, PO Box 2600, Brighton, East Sussex, BN2 0EF.

NB If you can't afford to buy the books then order them for your local library.

Razz us over the following books to put in the bog:

SchNEWS round ISBN: 0 9529748 0 0	Number of copies @ £3 plus £1.50 p+p each..........................
SchNEWS annual ISBN: 0 9529748 1 9	Number of copies @ £3 plus £1.50 p+p each..........................
SchNEWS Survival Guide ISBN: 0 9529748 2 7	Number of copies @ £4 plus £1.50 p+p each..........................
SchQUALL ISBN: 0 9529748 3 5	Number of copies @ £6 plus £1.50 p+p each..........................
SchNEWS & Squall Yearbook 2001 ISBN: 0 9529748 4 3	Number of copies @ £5 plus £1.50 p+p each..........................
	Total ....
Or - what the hell I'll have the 'practically giving 'em away offer' of five for £20:	Number of sets @ £20 inc. p+p..........................
	Total ....
Mark Thomas Bootleg Video	Number of copies @ £8 plus £0.80 p+p each..........................
SchNUSIC Compilation CD	Number of copies @ £7 (includes p+p) each..........................
	Total ....

— — — Photocopy to save cutting up yer book! — — —

Legal Warning

Section 6 Criminal law Act 1977
As amended by the
Crmininal Justice and Public Order Act 1994

TAKE NOTICE

THAT: *we live in this house,* it is our home and *we intend to stay here.*

THAT: *at all times there is at least one person in this house*

THAT: *any entry into this house without our permission* is a **CRIMINAL OFFENCE** as any of one of us who is in physical possession is opposed to any entry without their permission.

THAT: *if you attempt to enter by violence* or by threatening violence we **WILL PROSECUTE YOU**, you may receive a sentence of up to **SIX MONTHS IMPRISONMENT** and/or a **FINE** of up to **£5,000**

THAT: *if you want us to leave* you will have to take out a summons for possession In the County Court or in the High Court, or produce to us a written statement or Certificate in terms of S. 12a Criminal Law Act 1977 (as inserted by Criminal Justice And Public Order Act 1994.

THAT: it is an offence under S. 12 a (8) Criminal Law Act 1977, (as amended), to knowingly make a false statement to obtain a written statement for the purposes of S. 12a. A person guilty of such an offence may receive a sentence of up to **SIX MONTHS** imprisonment and/or a fine of up to **£5,000**.

The Occupiers

N.B. SIGNING THIS LEGAL WARNING IS OPTIONAL.
IT IS EQUALLY VALID WHETHER IT IS SIGNED OR NOT.

YELLOW PAGES

Don't just let your fingers do the walking

The SchNEWS Yellow Pages is information for action - a list of hundreds of groups and resources to inform and inspire you to put down this book and get up and do something positive. This contacts list is a selection - put into handy categories - of the full list of 800 odd entries (updated as of June 2002) which you'll find on our website. Hopefully this shortened, categorised vershun will be easier to use, though obviously some of these categories overlap. You can also use many of these names to put you in touch with more specific or localised groups. This list is constantly being updated — and is never 'complete' - so if you would like to see your group put in (or your contact details changed) please get in contact.

The categories are: **Anarchism / Animal Rights / Anti-Capitalism / Anti-Racism / Bookshops / Cafes & Clubs / Children & Parenting / Community Groups / Culture / Disability Rights & Action / Drugs / Economics / Education / Energy / Environment / Food & Farming / Forests & Woodlands / Gardening / Genetics / Health / Housing & Homelessness / Human Rights / Indigenous Peoples / Media / Networking Support / Peace / Prisoner Support / Refugees / Sexuality / Transport / Travellers / Women / Workers' Rights.**
The format of the entries are: **Name** Address. T phone number F fax number email@address www.website *Description*.

ANARCHISM

A-Infos www.ainfos.ca *Regular anarchist newsfeed over the internet in various languages.*

Actiunea Anarchista în România http://alter-ro.tripod.com *Romanian anarchist website.*

Anarchist FAQ www.anarchistfaq.org *Frequently Asked Questions about anarchism. Its aim is to present what anarchism really stands for and indicate why you should become an anarchist.*

Anarchist Federation c/o 84b Whitechapel High St, London, E1 7QX. T 07946 214590 anarchistfederation@bigfoot.com www.afed.org.uk *Class struggle anarchists aiming to abolish capitalism and all oppression to create a free and equal society. This is Anarchist Communism.*

Anarchist Federation (Ireland) PO Box 505, Belfast, BT12 6BQ. T 07951 079719 ireaf@yahoo.ie *Irish Anarchist Federation.*

Anarchist Teapot Mobile Kitchen (See entry under Food and Farming)

Azzjoni Pozittiva (M.A.M.) manarkikum@yahoo.com http://azzjonipozittiva.cjb.net *Anarchist movement in Malta.*

Black Flag *Comprehensive list of UK Anarchist groups.* (See entry under Media)

Class War Federation PO Box 467, London E8 3QX. T 07931 301901 classwaruk@hotmail.com www.classwaruk.org *Exists to promote class consciousness and working class control over our day to day lives. Publish Class War paper.*

Czechoslovak Anarchist Federation (CSAF) POBox 223, 111 21 Praha 1, Czech Republic. intersec@csaf.cz www.csaf.cz/english *Anarchist propaganda, street actions, publishing anarchist materials, ABC group.*

Federation Collective Rampenplan PO Box 780, 6130 At Sittard, The Netherlands T +31 46 452 4803 F +31 46 451 6460 ramp@antenna.nl www.antenna.nl/rampenplan *Federation based on basic democracy and anarchism. Includes a mobile vegetarian/vegan ecological kitchen, anarchist/environment book publisher and a video action newsgroup.*

Kate Sharpley Library *Archive of Anarchist and related material.* (See entry under Media)

News and Views www.newsviews.prv.pl/ *Information about eastern Europe with links to lots of eastern Europe anarchist groups.*

Radical Routes *Mutual aid network.* (See entry under Networking Support)

Solidarity Federation (SolFed) PO Box 469, Preston PR1 8XF. T 01772 739724 solfed@solfed.org.uk www.solfed.org.uk *Anarcho-syndicalist federation of groups (contact them for your local group). Dedicated to an anti-authoritarian future based on mutual aid and individual freedom.*

ANIMAL RIGHTS

Animal Contacts Directory Veggies, 245 Gladstone Street, Nottingham NG7 6HX:*T 0845 458 9595.*

acd@veggies.org.uk www.veggies.org.uk *The essential guide to thousands of animal welfare rights campaigns across the world available online or as a book from Veggies.*

Animal Liberation Front UK Supporters Group BM 1160, London WC1N 3XX. T 0870 1385037 F as phone info@alfsg.co.uk *Info about animal rights prisoners and defence funds plus articles/news in bi-monthly newsletter.*

Animal Liberation Press Office (See entry under Media)

Animal Rights Calendar c/o Veggies, 245 Gladstone Street, Nottingham NG7 6HX. T 0845 458 9595 Arc@veggies.org.uk www.veggies.org.uk/calender *Comprehensive, monthly diary of UK animal rights events. Also appears in ARC News*

ARCNEWS POBox 339, Wolverhampton, WV10 7BZ T 0845 458 0146 james@arcnews.co.uk www.arcnews.co.uk *Independent animal rights magazine aimed at grass-roots campaigning. Available on subscription of £10 per year or on line.*

British Union For The Abolition of Vivisection (BUAV) 16a Crane Grove, London, N7 8NN. T 020 7700 4888 F 020 7700 0196 campaigns@buav.org www.buav.org *Anti-vivisection organisation specialising in public campaigning, hard-hitting undercover investigations, political lobbying and legal/scientific expertise.*

Close Harlan UK PO Box 152, Crowborough, E. Sussex, TN6 2EP. T 07870 929384 www.freespeech.org/chuk *Demos, letter writing, phone calls and leafleting to close Harlan, the biggest supplier of animals to the vivisection industry.*

Compassion in World Farming Charles House,5A Charles Street, Petersfield, Hampshire GU32 3EH T 01730 264208/268863 F 01730 260791 compassion@ciwf.co.uk www.ciwf.co.uk *Campaigning to end the factory farming of animals and long distance transport through hard-hitting political lobbying, investigations and high profile campaigns.*

Greyhound Rescue UK jill@rigolo.f9.co.uk www.greyhoundrescue.co.uk *Donate free Internet presence to any non-profit making organisation or charity for greyhound rescue in the UK. List of local contacts.*

Hunt Saboteurs Association (H.S.A) PO Box 5254, Northampton, NN1 3ZA. T 0845 4500727 /Press office only: 0961 113084 F as phone - call first. info@huntsabs.org.uk www.huntsabs.org.uk *The H.S.A is dedicated to saving the lives of hunted animals directly, using non-violent direct action.*

National Anti-Hunt Campaign (NAHC) 27 Old Gloucester Street, London WC1N 3XX. T 01442 240 246 nahc@nahc.freeserve.co.uk *Peaceful campaigning against all hunting with hounds through petitioning, demonstrations, investigations, lobbying and civil disobedience. Info pack on request.*

National Anti-Vivisection Society 261 Goldhawk Rd, London, W12 9PE. T 020 8846 9777 F 020 8846 9712 info@navs.org.uk www.navs.org.uk *Campaigns against vivisection and on animal rights issues.*

National Federation of Badger Groups (NFBG) 15 Cloisters Business Centre, 8 Battersea Park Rd, London, SW8 4BG T 020 7498 3220/mobile: 0976 153389 F 020 7627 4212 www.badgers.org.uk/nfbg enquiries@nfbg.org.uk *Promote conservation & protection of badgers. Represent 85 local voluntary badger groups. Provide information & advice, membership system.*

Seriously Ill Against Vivisection (SIAV) (See entry under Disability Rights and Action)

Shoreham Protester, The c/o 7 Stoneham Rd, Hove, Sussex, BN3 5HJ T 01273 885750 F as phone shoreham-protestr@ntlworld.com www.shoreham-protester.org.uk *Fortnightly newspaper reporting local and national animal rights news, especially reports from demonstrations. Input welcomed.*

Stop Huntingdon Animal Cruelty (SHAC) PO Box 381, Cheltenham, Glos, GL50 1UF T 0845 4580630 info@shac.net www.shac.net *SHAC campaigns to close down the animal-testing lab Huntingdon Life Sciences, and target anyone connected with them.*

Uncaged Campaigns St Matthew's House, 45 Carver St, Sheffield S1 4FT. T 0114 272 2220 F 0114 272 2225 uncaged.anti-viv@dial.pipex.com www.uncaged.co.uk *Not for profit organisation dedicated to bringing about the abolition of vivisection by democratic means.*

Vegan Prisoners Support Group (VPSG) POBox 194, Enfield, EN1 3HD T 020 8292 8325 F as phone www.cares.demon.co.uk hvpc@vpsg.freeserve.co.uk *VPSG assists vegan animal rights prisoners either held in police custody or within the prison system.*

Vivisection Information Network (VIN) (See entry under Health)

World Animal Net 24 Barleyfields, Didcot, Oxon, OX11 0BJ. T 01235 210775 info@worldanimal.net www.worldanimal.net *The world's largest network of animal protection societies with over 1700 affiliates in more than 90 countries campaigning to improve the status and welfare of animals.*

ANTI-CAPITALISM
(also see Anarchism)

A SEED Europe PO Box 92066 1090 AB Amsterdam, The Netherlands. T +31 20 6682236 F +31 20 4682275 aseedeur@antenna.nl www.aseed.net *Action for Solidarity, Equality, Environment, and Diversity is a global organisation linking youth groups and individuals on all continents.*

Adbusters 1243 West 7th Av, Vancouver, BC, V6H 1B7, Canada. T 604 736 9401 F 604 737 6021 info@adbusters.org www.adbusters.org *A global network of artists, activists, writers, pranksters, educators and entrepreneurs who aim to launch the new social activist movement of the information age.*

Autonomous Centre of Edinburgh (ACE) 17 West Montgomery Place, Edinburgh, EH7 5HA T 0131 557 6242/Pager 07626 128984 ace@autonomous.org.uk www.autonomous.org.uk

Campaign base for social and ecological resistance with a view to bring about the revolutionary overthrow of capitalism.

Bilderberg www.bilderberg.org *Research into The Power Elite's secretive Bilderberg Conferences.*

Biotic Baking Brigade c/o Whispered Media, POB 40130, San Francisco, CA 94140. USA. Bbb@asis.com www.asis.com/~bbb/ *Pie-throwing is just one tool in the large toolbox of resistance.*

Buy Nothing Day 25 Gloucester Road, Littlehampton, West Sussex, BN17 7BT. T 07887 608609 info@buynothingday.co.uk www.buynothingday.co.uk *Buy Nothing Day is a simple idea, which challenges consumer culture by asking us to switch off from shopping for a day.*

ChiapasLink *Provides a link between the Zapatista struggles in Chiapas, Mexico and in the UK.* (See entry under Indigenous Peoples)

Cuba Solidarity Campaign Red Rose Club, 129 Seven Sisters Road, London N7 7QG. T 020-7263-6452 office@cuba-solidarity.org.uk www.cuba-solidarity.org.uk *Provide material aid to Cuba, fundraising and produce a magazine called Cuba Si*

Earth First! Action Update (EF! AU) *Has list of contacts of all UK Earth First! groups.* (see entry under Media)

Ejercito Zapatista de Liberacion Nacional (EZLN) www.ezln.org *The EZLN web provides reliable information on the Zapatista uprising and serves as the mouthpiece for the Zapatistas in cyberspace.*

Eurodusnie Postbox 2228, 2301 CE Leiden, The Netherlands T: + 71 5173019 info@eurodusnie.nl http://eurodusnie.nl *Dutch anti-authoritarian organisation fighting against economic globalisation. Dutch and international links.*

Fanclub mail@fanclubbers.org www.fanclubbers.org *Fusing art and activism to create culture-jams with a focus on surveillance and the excesses of consumer culture.*

Gloupgloup www.gloupgloup.com *A French site of pie flingers with pictures of top politicians and corporate bosses getting a faceful of pie.*

Green Socialist Network c/o 15 Linford Close, Harlow, Essex CM19 4LR. T 01279 435735 F as phone. pete@petebrown.fsnet.com *Campaigning group for green and left ideas - we believe that environmental protection and issues of social justice are inseparable.*

Industrial Workers of the World *Union for all run by its members.* (See entry under Worker's Rights)

McDonalds Workers Resistance (MWR) *We work for McDonalds and fuck shit up.* (See entry under Worker's Rights)

McLibel Support Campaign 5 Caledonian Rd, London, N1 9DX T 020 787131269 F as phone mclibel@globalnet.co.uk www.mcspotlight.org *Encouraging people everywhere to see the sordid reality behind corporate propaganda, and to fight back against McWorld.*

Movement Against the Monarchy (MA'M) PO Box 14672, London, E9 5UQ T 07931 301901 www.geocities.com/capitolhill/lobby/1793/index mam_london@hotmail.com *Local and national direct action against the parasitic, undemocratic Royals; preparing major anti-Golden Jubilee 2002 activity.*

Peoples' Global Action c/o Canadian Union of Postal Workers, 377 Bank Street, Ottawa, Ontario, Canada pga @ agp.org www.agp.org *A global instrument for communication and co-ordination for all those fighting against the destruction of humanity and the planet by the global market.*

Reclaim the Streets (London) PO Box 9656, London, N4 4JY T 020 7281 4621 rts@gn.apc.org www.reclaimthestreets.net *Direct-Action for global and local social-ecological revolution(s) to transcend hierarchical and authoritarian society, (capitalism included), and be home in time for tea.*

Red Star Research BCM Box 3328 London WC1N 3XX. T 07960 865601 info@red-star-research.org.uk www.red-star-research.org.uk *Information about the Labour Party's shift to the right wing of politics. Identifies the links and networks of wealth and power and helps you to uncover the connections.*

Revolutionary Communist Group (RCG) BCM Box 5909, London WC1N 3XX. T 020 7837 1688 F 020 7837 1743 rcgfrfi@easynet.co.uk www.revolutionarycommunist.com *Supports Cuba, the Palestinian people, and the fight against racism and against poverty pay. It publishes Fight Racism! Fight Imperialism!*

Rhythms of Resistance info@rhythmsofresistance.co.uk www.rhythmsofresistance.co.uk *Radical pink and silver samba band that uses percussion and carnival to mobilise and move people on demos/actions.*

Rock around the Blockade c/o FRFI, BCM Box 5909, London WC1N 3XX. T 020 7837 1688 boycott bacardiuk@yahoo.co.uk www.boycottbacardi.co.uk *Rock around the Blockade was founded in 1995 and is open to anyone who supports Cuba's socialist revolution.*

RTMark info@rtmark.com www.rtmark.com/ *RTMark supports the sabotage of corporate products, with no risk to the public investor.* Subvertise! *An archive of 100s of subverts, political art, cartoons and articles.* (See entry under Culture)

They Rule http://theyrule.orgo.org *web site about how the different companies that run the world are interconnected.*

Wombles (White Overalls Movement Building Libertarian Effective Struggles) wombles@hushmail.com www.wombles.org.uk *Promote anarchism, libertarian solidarity, autonomous self-organisation and humour... To join the discussion list send a blank email to: maydaywhiteoveralls-subscribe@yahoogroups.com*

World Socialist Web Site editor@wses.org www.wsws.org *Provides analysis of major world events, comments on political, cultural, historical and philosophical issues.*

Yes Men, The administrative@theyesmen.org www.theyesmen.org *The Yes Men are a genderless, loose-knit association of some three hundred impostors worldwide. Eg. Send spoof WTO delegates to conferences.*

ANTI-RACISM

AntiFa.net www.antifa.net *Portal to anti-fascism and anti-racism on the web. Offer secure web hosting to anti-fascists.*

Campaign Against Racism & Fascism (CARF) BM Box 8784, London, WC1N 3XX. T 020 7837 1450 F 0870 052 5899 info@carf.demon.co.uk www.carf.demon.co.uk *CARF magazine exposes racism in multicultural Britain. Details the European offensive against refugees and shows how the domestic fight against racism is shaped by international forces.*

Evil:Austria: raw@raw.at www.raw.at *Multilingual monthly newsletter providing information about the Austrian coalition government including the far right FPOe.*

Institute of Race Relations 2-6 Leeke Street , London WC1X 9HS. T 020 7278 0623 F 020 7278 0623 info@irr.org.uk www.irr.org.uk *The IRR carries our research into issues of racism, from the rise of racial violence to the plight of asylum seekers. The IRR publishes Race & Class and the European Race Bulletin.*

Minority Rights Group International 379 Brixton Rd, London, SW9 7DE T 020 7978 9498 F 020 7738 6265 minority.rights@mrgmail.org www.minorityrights.org *Work to secure rights for ethnic, religious and linguistic minorities world wide, and educating people about minority issues in order to counter racism and prejudice.*

National Assembly Against Racism (NAAR) 28 Commercial St, London, E1 6LS T/F 020 7247 9907 AA_R@compuserve.com http://ourworld.compuserve.com/homepages/aa_r/Index.html *Aims to initiate campaigns, set agendas and raise awareness on the whole range of anti-racist issues affecting British society.*

Newham Monitoring Project (NMP) 63 Broadway, Stratford, London, E15 4BQ T 020 8555 8151 F 020 8555 8163 nmp@gn.apc.org *Local grassroots anti-racist organisation, offers independent advice and casework support for victims of racial harassment, police harassment and civil injustice.*

No Platform Anti-Fascist Network BM Box 5827, London, WC1M 3XX. noplatform@antifa.net http://noplatform.antifa.net *Network of anti-fascist socialists, anarchists and anti-capitalists, united by a commitment to the policy of 'no platform' for fascism. Northern: 07970 398933; Midlands: 07940 305017; South East: c/o Brigthon ABC; London: 07960 771572.*

Notes From the Borderland BM Box 4769, London, WC1N 3XX Pager: 07669-175886 larry@borderland.co.uk www.borderland.co.uk *We publish cutting edge parapolitical research into the secret state, fascists, etc - material that is too sharp for Guardian/Red Pepper.*

The Monitoring Group (TMG) 14 Featherstone Rd, Southall, Middx, UB2 5AA. T 020 8843 2333 Emergency Helpline 0800 374618 www.monitoring-group.co.uk *Agency helping victims of racial harassment, police misconduct, domestic violence and immigration detention.*

BOOKSHOPS
(also See Media - Publishers & Distribution)

56a Infoshop 56 Crampton St, London, SE17. 56a@safetycat.org www.safetycat.org/56a *Books, tea, zines, info, empties, bikes, library, history, action, people.....sometimes cafes...sometimes otherthings...*

Avalon 73 Fawcett Rd, Southsea, Hants, PO4 0DB. T 02392 293673 F 02392 780444 info@avalonheadshop.co.uk *Portsmouth's only head shop. Stock Undercurrents; distribute SchNEWS as well as information on local, national and international campaigns.*

Blackcurrent Bookshop 4 Allen Rd, Abington, Northampton NN1 4NE. T 07833 17328 *Specialises in radical and independent books, comix, cards, badges, tapes and CDs.*

Freedom Book Company 73 Fawcett Rd, Southsea, Hants, PO4 0DB. T 023 92780600 F 023 92780444 www.freedombooks.co.uk info@freedombooks.co.uk *Massive range of informative drugs related books and magazines (cultivation, legality, effects etc), Undercurrents videos, radical magazines and periodicals.*

Housmans Bookshop 5 Caledonian Rd, King's Cross, London, N1 9DX. T 020 7837 4473 F 020 7178 0444 shop@housmans.idps.co.uk *London's oldest radical bookshop, home to the weird & the wonderful, publisher of annual Housmans Peace Diary.*

News From Nowhere Bookshop 96 Bold Street, Liverpool, L1 4HY T 0151 708 7270 www.newsfromnowhere.org.uk *Long established, busy radical community bookshop run by a women's co-operative. Books, magazines, world music CDs and more. Open Mon-Sat 10am-5.45pm.*

R.E.C.Y.C. 54 Upperthorpe Rd, Sheffield, S6 3EB. T 0114 263 4494 *Re-use and second hand, recycling, waste campaigns, newsletter.*

Reading International Solidarity Centre (RISC) *Shop selling fair trade products, books and teaching materials.* (See entry under Cafes)

Word Power Bookshop 43 West Nicholson St, Edinburgh, EH8 9DB. T 0131 6629112 F as phone books@word-power.co.uk www.word-power.co.uk *Scotland's radical bookshop and mail order. Organise Edinburgh Radical Book Fair in May each year.*

CAFES & CLUBS

1in12 Club 21-23 Albion St, Bradford, BD1 2LY. T 01274 734160 info@1in12.com www.1in12.go-legend.net *Members social club based on the principles of self-management.*

CASA Club 29, Hope St, Liverpool. T 0151 709 2148 dockers@gn.apc.org www.gn.apc.org/initfactory *Club run on co-operative principles, run by sacked Liverpool Dockers. Profits go toward an employment-training centre.*

Kebele Kulture Projekt 14 Robertson Rd, Eastville, Bristol, BS5 6JY T 0117 939 9469 kebele@marsbard.com www.marsbard.com/kebele *Anarchist collective run drop-in and meeting centre, vegan cafe, bike workshops, anarchist library, housing co-op, exhibitions, campaign catering, political activities and more.*

Okasional Café Dept.20, 22a Beswick Street, Manchester, M4 7HS. T 0161 2266814 Okasional-café @nematode.freeserve.co.uk *Occasional squat cafes & reclaimed autonomous spaces in Manchester.*

Reading International Solidarity Centre (RISC) 35-39 London St, Reading, RG1 4PS. T 0118 9586692/0118 9569800 F 0118 9594357 admin@risc.org.uk www.risc.org.uk *Development Education Centre with World Shop selling fair trade products, books and teaching materials, Global Café, community meeting space.*

Swansea Community Resource Centre 217 High Street, Swansea SA1 1NN. T 01792 642404 / 07974 892651 no217crc@yahoo.co.uk www.geocities.com/no217crc/ *Free space for all, including cybercafe, gallery space, stage, permaculture garden. Free workshops, meeting space, information and other stuff.*

CHILDREN & PARENTING

Baby Milk Action 23 St. Andrew's St, Cambridge, CB2 3AX. T 01223 464420 info@babymilkaction.org www.babymilkaction.org www.ibfan.org *Aims to save lives and to end the avoidable suffering caused by inappropriate infant feeding.*

Informed Parent, The PO Box 870, Harrow, Middlesex, HA3 7UW. T 020 8861 1022 F as phone www.informedparent.co.uk *Quarterly newsletter to help parents make a decision regarding vaccination based on knowledge, not fear.*

Real Nappy Project PO Box 3704, London SE26 4RX. www.realnappy.com *Central source of*

information and advice on all nappy-related issues, for local authorities, health professionals, the media and individuals.

Woodcraft Folk, The 13 Ritherdon Road, London, SW17 8QE. 13 Ritherdon Rd., London, SW17 8QE. T 020 8672 6031 info@woodcraft.org.uk www.woodcraft.org.uk *We aim to develop self-confidence in young people and aim to building a sustainable world based on equality, peace, social justice and co-operation.*

COMMUNITY GROUPS

1990 Trust, The Suite 12, Winchester House, 9 Cranmer Road, SW9 6EJ, T 020 7582 1990 F 0870 127 6657 blink1990@gn.apc.org www.blink.org.uk *A national Black (African, Asian & Caribbean) organisation to increase the capacities of the Black communities to combat racism.*

Cardiff Bothered 39 Conway Road, Cardiff CF11 9NU. T 029 2037 8734 / 01443 650347 ceri@cardiffbothered.net nasia@cardiffbothered .net www.cardiffbothered.net *Fundraising, putting on gigs and parties, addressing/raising social/political awareness.*

Cornerstone Housing Co-op *Have a resource centre open to local groups and individuals.* (See entry under Housing)

Diggers & Dreamers *"The Guide to Communal Living in Britain" (See entry under Media)*

Dropseven T 07949 913123 team@dropseven.co.uk www.dropseven.co.uk/ *Concerned with community led collective action and strives to develop active, sustainable solutions to community development, capacity building and regeneration.*

Haringey Solidarity Group (HSG) PO Box 2474 London N8. T 020 8374 5027 hsg@globalinternet.co.uk http://hsg.cupboard.org *Local working class group encouraging radical solidarity, co-operation, and mutual aid in our community, workplaces, and lives.*

London Action Resource Centre a.k.a. Fieldgate, 62 Fieldgate St, London E1. T 020 7377 9088. *Resource centre for London activists.*

Living Streets 31-33 Bondway, London, SW8 1SJ. T 020 7820 1010 F 020 7820 8208 info@livingstreets .org.uk www.livingstreets.org.uk *Help people improve the safety and condition of local streets and public spaces through information and local support.*

Newham Monitoring Project (NMP) *Local grassroots anti-racist organisation.* (See entry under Anti-Racism)

Spitalfields Market Under Threat (SMUT) T 020 7613 5897 smut@smut.org.uk www.smut.org.uk *Oppose the destruction of three-fifths of the historic old covered market to make way for yet another office development.*

Steward Wood Moretonhampstead, Newton Abbot, Devon TQ13 8SD. T 01647 440233 Mob 07050 674464 affinity@stewardwood.org www.stewardwood.org *Demonstrating positive sustainable alternatives - a vegan community based in a woodland in Dartmoor. Permaculture, renewable energy, organic growing, low impact living. Visitors welcome.*

Sumac Centre 245 Gladstone St., Nottingham, NG7 6HX. T 0845 458 9595 F phone first sumac@veggies.org.uk www.veggies.org.uk/sumac *Resource centre for local groups campaigning for human and animal rights, the environment, peace, etc.*

Swansea Community Resource Centre (See entry under Cafes)

Truth & Reconciliation Commission for Stonehenge (TRCS) 96 Church Road, Redfield, Bristol BS5 9LE. T 0117 9542273 george@greenleaf.demon.co.uk www.greenleaf.demon.co.uk (follow Stonehenge link) *Open forum for resolution of Stonehenge conflict by discussion with all people including officials.*

CULTURE

Art, music, festivals, etc.
(for film see Media – Film, Video & TV)

Banksy www.banksy.co.uk *Political graffiti artist.*

Banner Theatre Company The Friends Institute, 220 Moseley Rd, Highgate, Birmingham, B12 0DG. T 0121 440 0460 voices@btinternet.com *Promotes political change in support of disenfranchised sections of society, through the use of documentary, multi-media cultural productions rooted in radical experiences.*

Brighton Alliance of Sound Systems (BASS) 43 Park Crescent Road, Brighton, BN2 3HE. info@bass23.org http://bass23.org *BASS is about positive free party politics. BASS generates funds to pay for communal safety equipment and courses.*

Chumbawamba PO Box TR666, Armley, Leeds, LS12 3XJ. chumba@chumba.demon.co.uk www.chumba.com *We are a music combo, we don't do weddings and barmitvahs but we would dance at several people's funerals.*

Continental Drifts Hilton Grove Business Centre, London, E17 4QP T 020 8509 3353 F 020 8509 9531 chris@continentaldrifts.co.uk www.continentaldrifts.co.uk *Not for profit organisation representing the finest in UK underground performing arts from "outside the mainstream".*

Fanclub mail@fanclubbers.org www.fanclubbers.org *Fusing art and activism to create culture-jams with a focus on surveillance and the excesses of consumer culture.*

Festival Eye BCM 2002, London, WC1N 3XX. T 0870 737 1011 F 0870 7371010 subscriptions@festivaleye.com www.festivaleye.com *Published each May (£3 + SAE) with the most comprehensive listings of UK festivals side by side with beautiful artwork, photography and reviews.*

Festival Zone, The info@thefestivalzone.org www.thefestivalzone.com *Website listing rock festivals in Europe.*

Green Road Show Ham Mill's Yard, Bowlish, Shepton Mallet, Somerset BA4 5JH. T 01749 343953 Mobile 07831 405661 or 07778 765724 info@greenroadshow.demon.co.uk www.greenroadshow.co.uk *Environmental education and family entertainment based in, and around, the Worlds only Wind and Solar powered Circus Top.*

Guilfin PO Box 217, Guildford, Surrey GU1 1WS. T 0795 193195 moneypenny@mi5.uk.com www.guilfin.net *The essential alternative guide to what's going on in the South East's underground scene.*

Levellers 55 Canning Street, Brighton, BN2 0EF. T 01273 608887 otf@levellers.co.uk www.levellers.co.uk *Band. Produce a magazine, sell merchandise.*

Network 23 www.network23.org *Free party network*

New York Surveillance Camera Players *Situationist-inspired anti-surveillance camera group.* (See entry under Media)

Partyvibe collective, The www.partyvibe.com/freeparties.htm *Bringing together partygoers, musicians and artists. This site is dedicated to offering resources to the free party community.*

Positive Outlook Records PO Box 233 /! Peterborough / PE4 6UB mail@positiveoutlookrecords.com www.positiveoutlookrecords.com *A youth collective of punk-rock kids, run a DIY record label, put on punk-rock shows and help causes with distribution of material through their stall.*

Raise Your Banners 641 Ecclesall Road, Sheffield, S11 8PT. T 0114 249 5185 www.ryb.org.uk pete@ryb.org.uk *Biennial festival of political song.*

Rhythms of Resistance *Radical pink and silver samba band.* (See entry under Anti-Capitalism)

SCRAP Records PO Box 2023, Brighton, BN1 1AA. dirtysquatters@hotmail.com www.dirtysquatters.com *Hardcore underground label bringing music and culture for your hot, drowning planet.*

Stonehenge Campaign c/o 99 Torriano Av, London, NW5 2RX. T 07970 378572 stonehenge@stones.com www.phreak.co.uk/stonehenge/psb/stonecam.htm *Meet at Solstice and Equinox sunrises at Stonehenge, want more Free Festivals at Stonehenge, and free access into the Stones for all who come in peace.*

Subvertise! c/o PO Box 68, Headington, Oxford OX3 7YS. webmaster@subvertise.org www.subvertise.org *An archive of 100s of subverts, political art, cartoons and articles.*

Sw@rm swarm@subdimension.com www.subdimension.com/community/subversion/swarm *Mobile radical infospace and information for action! Send an email to: swarmlist-subscribe @yahoogroups.com to get regular updates.*

ThePartyParty.Org www.thepartyparty.org *Promoting the positive aspect of the party, its benefits to our society and our basic human right to celebrate our lives as we are moved.*

William Morris Society Kelmscott House, 26 Upper Mall, Hammersmith, London, W6 9TA T 020 8741 3735 F 020 8748 5207 william.morris@care4free.net www.morrissociety.org *To stimulate interest in the life and work of William Morris: Victorian designer, poet and socialist.*

Wolfs Head Press PO Box 77, Sunderland, SR1 1EB. wolfsheadpress@hotmail.com *Fanzine (Wearwolf), music (Frankenstein Sound Lab), mail art and other stuff with a home made slant.*

Zion Train (Universal Egg) PO Box 3, Whitland, Dyfed, SA34 OYU T 01994 419800 F 01994 419357 perch@wobblyweb.com http://wobblyweb.com *Dub musicians with a conscience. Check out the Wobbler newsletter on the web.*

DISABLITY RIGHTS & ACTION

Federation of Deaf People PO Box 11, Darwen, Lancs BB3 3GH. F 01254 708071 contact@fdp.org.uk www.fdp.org.uk *A voluntary organisation that campaigns for Deaf people's rights funded by donations and membership.*

Incapacity Action 104 Cornwallis Circle, Whitsable, Kent CT5 1DT. T 01227 276159 F as phone incapacityaction@onetel.net.uk *Campaign for rights to benefits, independent living/home care supprt, other resources and linking with anti-war struggle.*

Seriously Ill Against Vivisection (SIAV) PO Box 116, High Wycombe, Bucks, HP14 3WX. T 0845 4581720 info@siav.org www.siav.org *Campaigning for a ban on all vivisection. We want non-animal, scientific methods of research to establish cures for disease.*

WinVisible: Women with Visible and Invisible Disabilities Crossroads Women's Centre, 230A Kentish Town Rd, London, NW5 2AB. T 020 7482 2496 (voice and minicom) F 020 7209 4761 crossroadswomenscentre@compuserve.com http://womenstrike8m.server101.com *Multi-racial self-help network of women with visible and invisible disabilities. Want the caring work we do recognised and paid for.*

DRUGS

Avalon *Portsmouth's only head shop.* (See entry under Bookshops)

Chillout Collective, The c/o 28 Partington Close, Archway, London N19 3DZ. T 07956 450 267 thechilloutcollective@hotmail.com www.caffeinehit.com/clients/chill *A collective of drug and health workers, legal advisers, researchers and activists, who run chillout spaces at dance events promoting harm reduction practices.*

Drug Culture www.drugculture.net *A non profit making website to collect names and emails addresses of people who feel that cannabis should be totally de-criminalised.*

Freedom Book Company *Massive range of informative drugs related books and magazines* (See entry under Bookshops)

Green Party Drugs Group c/o 1a Waterlow Rd, London, N19 5NJ T 020 8671 5936 F phone first greenpartydrugsgroup@gn.apc.org www.greenparty.org.uk/drugs *Promote and sell ecstasy testing kits, part of core group for annual Cannabis March and Festival, info stalls & E-testing at clubs, provide speakers, change drug policy.*

Legalise Cannabis Alliance (LCA) PO Box 198, Norwich, NR2 2DH T 01603 442215 lca@lca-uk.org www.lca-uk.org *A political party dedicated to campaigning for the full legalisation and utilisation of cannabis (hemp) - standing candidates in elections.*

Release 388 Old St, London, EC1V 9LT T 020 7729 525524 F 020 7729 2599 24-hour Helpline: 020 7729 9904 Drugs In Schools Helpline: 0808 8000 800 Sex Workers & The Law Advice Line: 020 7729 9904 www.release.org.uk *24 hour drugs and legal helpline. Also produces publications, such as the bustcard and runs training programmes.*

Transform Easton Business Centre, Felix Road, Easton, Bristol, BS5 OHE. T 0117 9415810 F 0117 9415809 Mob 07980213943 www.transform-drugs.org.uk info@transform-drugs.org.uk *Campaign for a just and effective drug policy including the legalisation of all drugs.*

ECONOMICS

ATTAC London Flat 1A, Rose Court, 34 Woodside, London SW19 7AN. info@attac.org.uk http://attac.org.uk *ATTAC campaigns for economic reforms, in order to re-conquer space lost by democracy to the sphere of finance.*

Corporate Europe Observatory, Paulus Potterstraat 20, 1071 DA Amsterdam, The Netherlands. T +31 20 612 7023 ceo@corporateeurope.org www.xs4all.nl/~ceo *Targeting the threats to democracy, equity, social justice and the environment posed by the economic and political power of corporations and their lobby groups.*

Corporate Watch 16b Cherwell St, Oxford, OX4 1BG T 01865 791391 www.corporatewatch.org mail@corporatewatch.org www.corporatewatch.org.uk *Research organisation investigating and exposing corporate power. Website for anti-corporate campaigners. Publishes bi-monthly newsletter (sub. £5/year).*

CorpWatch India PO Box 29344, San Francisco, CA 94129, USA. T +1 415 5616472 F +1 415 5616493 india@corpwatch.org www.corpwatchindia.org *Exposes the social and environmental impacts of corporate investment in India.*

Ecology Building Society 18 Station Rd, Cross Hills, Keighley, BD20 7EH. T 0845 674 5566 F 01535 636166 www.ecology.co.uk info@ecology.co.uk *A mutual building society dedicated to improving the environment by promoting sustainable housing and sustainable communities.*

Ethical Consumer Unit 21, 41 Old Birley St, Manchester, M15 5RF. T 0161 226 2929 F 0161 226 6277 mail@ethicalconsumer.org www.ethicalconsumer.org *Alternative consumer organisation looking at the social and environmental records of the companies behind the brand names.*

Ethical Junction 1st Floor, Dale House, 35 Dale Street, Manchester, M1 2HF. T 0161 236 3637 info@ethical-junction.org www.ethical-junction.org *Ethical Junction is a one-stop shop for ethical organisations and ethical trading.*

Fairtrade Foundation, The Suite 204, 16 Baldwin's Gardens, London, EC1N 7RJ. T 020 7405 5942 F 020 7405 5943 mail@fairtrade.org.uk www.fairtrade.org.uk *Exists to ensure a better deal for marginalised and disadvantaged third world producers.*

Green Guide Publishing Ltd 271 Upper St, London, N1 2UQ. T 020 7354 2709 F 020 7226 1311 sales@greenguide.co.uk http://greenguide.co.uk *Covers environmental, ethical and fairtrade products and services and provides the latest news, reviews, stories and information.*

LETSlink UK 12 Southcote Road, London N19 5BJ. T 020 76077852 F 020 76097112 Mob 07966 216891 letslink@synergynet.co.uk letslinkuk.org *National Development Agency and support network for Local Exchange Trading Schemes and other forms of local currency in the UK.*

New Economics Foundation (NEF) Cinnamon House, 6-8 Cole St, London, SE1 4YH T 020 7089 2800 F 020 7407 6473 www.neweconomics.org info@neweconomics.org *NEF works to put people and the environment at the centre of economic thinking.*

Public Citizen's Global Trade Watch 1600 20th Street NW, Washington DC, 20009, USA. T +1 202 588 1000 www.tradewatch.org *Educates the American public about the enormous impact of international trade and economic globalization on jobs, the environment, health and democratic accountability.*

Shared Interest Society Limited 25 Collingwood St, Newcastle upon Tyne, NE1 1JE T 0191 2339101 F 0191 2339110 www.shared-interest.com post@shared-interest.com *Co-operative lending society, lending money on fair terms to enable Third World producer groups to pay for labour, materials and equipment.*

UpStart Services 1 Court Ash, Yeovil, Somerset, BA20 1HG. T 0845 4581473 F 01935 431222 upstart@co-op.org http://users.cooptel.net/upstart *Provide help for people starting or running co-operatives and non-profit businesses, especially those with ecological or social change objectives.*

Women's Development Service No.30 Galtota Mulla, Kandy Road, Yakkala, Sri Lanka. T +94 33 27962 janawomented@lanka.ccom.lk *Movement of poor mothers united together to develop themselves and their families, economically, socially and culturally. An alternative banking system for elevation out of poverty.*

World Development Movement (WDM) 25 Beehive Place, London, SW9 7QR T 020 72747630 F 020 72748232 www.wdm.org.uk wdm@wdm.org.uk *Campaigns to tackle the root causes of poverty. Are currently campaigning to rewrite global trade rules to put people before profits.*

EDUCATION

Education Otherwise PO Box 7420, London N9 9SG. enquiries@education-otherwise.org www.education-otherwise.org *UK-based membership organisation which provides support and information for families whose children are being educated outside school.*

Education Workers Network PO Box 29, Southwest PDO, Manchester, M15 5HW. T 07984 675 281 ewn@ewn.org.uk www.ewn.org.uk *Network of education workers who favour collective direct action for decent education. Contact EWN for free bulletins.*

Educational Heretics Press, 113 Arundel Drive, Bramcote Hills, Nottingham, NG9 3FQ. T 0115 9257261 http://edheretics.gn.apc.org *Questions the dogmas of schooling in particular, and education in general, and to develop the logistics of the next learning system.*

Emerson College Trust Ltd Forest Row, East Sussex, RH18 5JX. T 01342 822238 F 01342 826055 www.emerson.org.uk bmail@emerson.org.uk *An international centre for adult education, especially in the areas of Bio-dynamic Organic Agriculture and Steiner Waldorf Teacher Training.*

Free Range Education AskFredService@aol.com www.free-range-education.co.uk *Home education site - stacked with resources, links, information, qualified legal help and an e-mail support service called Ask FREd.*

Home Education Reading Opportunities (H.E.R.O Books) 58 Portland Rd, Hove, East Sussex, BN3 5DL T 01273 775560 F 01273 389382 *Home education books via mail order. For a catalogue and list of local newsletters send a large SAE. Free Range Education book on how to home educate £13.20 inc. postage.*

Human Scale Education Fairseat Farm, Chew Stoke, Bristol BS18 8XF. Info@hse.org.uk www.hse.org.uk *Promotes smaller structures in education and a more holistic approach to learning.*

Lifecycles PO Box 77, Totnes, Devon, TQ9 5UA. T 01803 840098 people@lifecycles.info www.lifecycles.info *A pedal powered cinema and outreach collective dedicated to the pursuit of sustainability and sequins.*

Scientists for Global Responsibility (SGR) PO Box 473, Folkestone, CT20 1GS. T 07771 883696 info@sgr.org.uk www.sgr.org.uk *Promotes the ethical practice and use of science and technology.*

SELFED Collective (SelfED) PO Box 1095, Sheffield, S2 4YR selfed@selfed.org.uk www.selfed.org.uk *For self-education ideas and practice, developing real alternatives to state-sponsored education. Courses, self-help materials, workshops, etc.*

Travellers' School Charity Hayne Farm, Morebath, Tiverton, Devon. EX16 9DA. Tel 01398 332347 / 0845 2818571 F 0870 7064782 info@tsct.co.uk www.tsct.co.uk www.travellers-school.org.uk *The Travellers' School Charity's aim is to support traveller families access opportunities, freedom and choice through education.*

Wild Things (Ecological Education Collective) c/o 15 The Square, Bestwwod Village, Nottm NG6 8TS. T 0845 458 4727 info@wildthings.org.uk www.wildthings.org.uk

Environmental education for primary & secondary school children through hands on projects.

ENERGY

Campaign for Real Events info@c-realevents.demon.co.uk www.c-realevents.demon.co.uk *Providing renewable energy support for art projects and producing free DIY plans for pedal generators and other renewable energy devices.*

Centre for Alternative Technology (C.A.T) Machynlleth, Powys, SY20 9AZ. T 01654 705950 F 01654 702782 info@cat.org.uk www.cat.org.uk *Environmental centre covering renewable energy, building, sewage and water and organic growing. Displays, publications, courses, mail-order, consultancy and free information service.*

Energy Efficiency Advice Centre T 0845 7277200 www.saveenergy.co.uk *An independent, government-funded body – advice on saving money on your electricity/gas bill. Free action pack*

Energy Saving Trust 21 Dartmouth St, London, SW1H 9BP T 020 7222 0101 F 0207 6542444 www.est.org.uk info@est.co.uk *Set up by the government to stimulate energy efficiency in UK households and create a market for clean fuel vehicles.*

Gaia Energy Center Delabole, North Cornwall, PL33 9DA T 01840 213321 F 01840 213428 support@gaiaenergy.co.uk www.gaiaenergy.co.uk *A centre for the promotion of, and education about, renewable and sustainable energy and energy conservation.*

Green Dragon Energy Ceredigion, Wales. T 01974 821564 dragonrg@talk21.com www.greendragonenergy.co.uk *Electricity from Sun, Wind & Water.*

Hemp Food Industries Association *Hemp food, fibre, fuel and more. (See entry under Farming and Food)*

UK Solar Energy Society, The c/o School of Engineering, Oxford Brookes University, Headington Campus, Gipsy Lane, Oxford OX3 0BP. T 01865 484367 F 01865 484263 uk-ises@brookes.ac.uk www.thesolarline.com *A forum for all those interested in the advancement of the utilisation of the sun's energy.*

unit[e] UK Freepost (SCE9229) Chippenham SN15 1UZ. T 0845 6011410 enquiries@unit-e.co.uk www.unit-e.co.uk *Provides renewable electricity services to domestic and corporate customers.*

World Information Service on Energy PO Box 59636, 1040 LC Amsterdam, Netherlands. T +31-20-6126368 F +31-20-6892179 www.antenna.nl/wise *Information and networking centre for citizens and environmental organisations concerned about nuclear power, radioactive waste, radiation, and sustainable energy issues*

ENVIRONMENT

A SEED Europe *Action for Solidarity, Equality, Environment, and Diversity. (See entry under Anti-capitalism)*

Black Environment Network (BEN) UK Office, 9 Llainwon Uchaf, Llanberis, Wales, LL55 4LL. T 01286 870715 F as phone ukoffice@ben-network.org.uk www.ben-network.co.uk *Established to promote equal opportunities, with respect to ethnic communities, in the preservation, protection and development of the environment.*

British Trust for Conservation Volunteers 36 St Mary's Street, Wallingford, Oxfordshire OX10 0EU. T 01491 821600 F 01491 839646 info@btcv.org.uk www.btcv.org.uk *Practical environmental conservation charity.*

Centre for Alternative Technology (C.A.T) (See entry under Energy)

Climate Independent Media Centre www.climateconference.org *The Climate Independent Media Center provides up-to-the-minute independent and honest coverage of the climate summit, the backgrounds, the corporate lobby and the actions.*

Common Ground Gold Hill House, 21 High Street, Shaftesbury, Dorset SP7 8JE. T 01747 850820 F 01747 850821 kate.ofarrell@commonground.org.uk www.commonground.org.uk *Common Ground offers ideas, information and inspiration to help us learn about, enjoy and take more responsibility for our own localities.*

Communities Against Toxics (CATS) (See entry under Health)

Council for the Protection of Rural England (CPRE) Warwick House, 25 Buckingham Palace Rd, London, SW1W 0PP T 020 7976 6433 F 020 7976 6373 info@cpre.org.uk www.cpre.org.uk *Promotes the beauty, tranquillity and diversity of rural England by encouraging the sustainable use of land and other natural resources in town and country.*

Earth Centre Denaby Main, Doncaster, DN12 4EA T 01709 513933 F01709 512010 www.earthcentre.org.uk *Exhibition centre aimed at developing understanding of sustainable development.*

Earth First! Action Update (EF! AU) *A monthly round-up of ecological and other direct action from around Britain. Has list of contacts of all UK Earth First groups. (See entry under Media)*

Earth First! Journal *Voice o f the radical environmental movement. (See entry under Media)*

Ecologist, The *Environmental magazine. (See entry under Media)*

Ecovillage Network UK (EVNUK) (See entry under Housing)

Envirolink support@envirolink.org www.envirolink.org *Links to Sustainable Business Network, Animal Rights Resource Site where to buy environmental books. Essential & extensive web directory.*

Environmental Rescue International (ERI). PO Box 894, Benin City, Nigeria. environmentalrescue@yahoo.co.uk eri@justice.com *ERI – local and internationally focus environmental, human rights and community development organisation. Organises research, training, conferences and direct actions regularly.*

Friends of the Earth 26-28 Underwood St, London N1 7JQ. T 020 7490 1555 F 020 7490 0881 info@foe.co.uk www.foe.co.uk *Friends of the Earth exists to inspire solutions to environmental problems, making life better for people.*

Friends of the Earth Scotland 72 Newhaven Rd, Edinburgh, EH6 5QG T 0131 554 9977 F 0131 554 8656 www.foe-scotland.org.uk *We stand for environmental justice. And we aim to make the right to a decent environment available to everyone in Scotland and around the globe.*

Greenpeace Canonbury Villas, London, N1 2PN T 020 7865 8100 Press office T 020 7865 8255 F 020 7865 8200 info@uk.greenpeace.org www.greenpeace.org *Independent non-profit global environmental campaigning organisation that uses non-violent, creative confrontation to promote solutions to environmental issues and bring about change.*

Green Socialist Network (See entry under Anti-Capitalism)

Groundwork 85-87 Cornwall St, Birmingham, B3 3BY T 0121 236 8565 F 0121 236 7356 www.Groundwork.org.uk *Environmental regeneration charity making sustainable development a reality in many of the UK's most disadvantaged communities*

How to Build a Protest Tunnel www.discodavestu nnelguide.co.uk *Online manual on how to dig your own protest tunnel.*

Low Level Radiation Campaign (See entry under Health)

Manchester Environmental Resource Centre initiative (MERCi) Bridge-5 Mill 22a Beswick Street, Ancoats, Manchester, M4 7HR T 0161 273 1736 F 0161 274 4598 merci@bridge5.org www.bridge5.org/merci.htm *Sustainable development innovator and the largest membership based environmental charity in Manchester.*

Marine Conservation Society 9 Gloucester Road, Ross-on-Wye, Herefordshire, HR9 5ZZ. T 01989 566017 F 01989 567815 www.mcsuk.org *Charity dedicated to protecting the marine environment and wildlife.*

Mines & Communities Roger Moody, c/o Partizans, 41 Thornhill Square, London, N1. T 20 7700 6189 F 20 7700 6189 info@minesandcommunities.org. www.minesandcommunities.org *Seeks to empower mining-affected communities so they can struggle successfully against damaging proposals and projects. Has links to many anti-mining campaigns.*

Multimap.Com http://uk8.multimap.com/map/ places.cgi *A complete interactive atlas on the web!*

Nine Ladies Anti-Quarry Campaign Bramble Dene, Stanton Lees, Matlock, Derbyshire DE4 2LQ. all@nineladies.uklinux.net www.nineladies.uklinux.n et *Opposing destruction of ancient landscape at the edge of National Park, endangering standing stones.*

Peat Alert c/o CRC, 16 Sholebroke Avenue, Leeds, LS7 3HB. T 0113 262 9365 info@peatalert.org.uk www.peatalert.org.uk *Information for action against peat mining on Thorne and Hatfield Moors, South Yorkshire.*

People & Planet (P&P) *UK student action on world poverty, human rights and the environment.* (See entry under Human Rights)

People Against Rio Tinto and Subsidiaries (PARTiZANS) 41a Thornhill Square, London N1 1BE T 0207 700 6189 F same as phone partizabs@gn.apc.org www.minesandcommunities.org/Aboutus/ partizans.htm *Partizans has been campaigning since 1978 against the damage wreaked by the world's most powerful mining company.*

Pesticide Action Network UK (See entry under Health)

R.E.C.Y.C. 54 Upperthorpe Rd, Sheffield, S6 3EB. T 0114 263 4494 *Re-use and second hand, recycling, waste campaigns, newsletter.*

Rainbow Keepers PO Box 52, Kasimov, 391330, Russia. T +7 09131 41514 rk@lavrik.ryazan.ru, rk2000@mail.ru www.chat.ru/~rk2000 *Russian radical ecological movement.*

Reclaim the Streets (London) (see entry under Anti-Capitalism)

Rising Tide 16b Cherwell Street, Oxford OX1 1BG. T 01865 241097 info@risingtide.org.uk www.risingtide.org.uk *A network of independent groups and individuals dedicated to taking local action and building a national movement against climate change.*

River Ocean Research & Education (RORE) info@rore.org.uk www.rore.org.uk *A charity dedicated to increasing awareness and encouraging care for our water environments - focussed in the fields of environmental education and research.*

Scottish Opencast Action Group c/o 42 Woollords, by West Calder, West Lothian, EH55 8LH soag.info@virgin.net *A network of people across Scotland opposed to opencast coal mining. Mainly information exchange & help with opposing planning applications.*

Sea Shepherd Conservation Society PO Box 6095, 4000 HB Tiel, Netherlands. T +31 0344 604130 F +31 344 604808 info@seashepherd.nl www.seashepherd.nl *Dedicated to the protection and conservation of marine ecosystems and biodiversity. Take direct action where authorities are unwilling to enforce conservation regulations.*

Surfers Against Sewage (See entry under Health)

Tourism Concern Stapleton House, 277-281 Holloway Rd, London, N7 8HN. T 020 7753 3330 F 020 7753 3331 info@tourismconcern.org.uk www.touri smconcern.org.uk *Tourism Concern is an educational charity promoting awareness of the impact of tourism on people and their environment.*

UK Rivers Network (UKRN) T 07092-335227 F 07092-335227 info@ukrivers.net www.ukrivers.net *Community action, information and networking to improve rivers and inland waters across the UK and Ireland.*

Voice of Irish Concern for the Environment 7 Upper Camden St., Dublin 2, Ireland. T +353 1 6618123 F +353 1 6618114 avoice@iol.ie www.voice.buz.org *Ireland's leading independent environmental organisation with members throughout the country. We are committed to promoting positive solutions to environmentally-destructive activities.*

Womens Environmental Network (W.E.N) PO Box 30626 London E1 1TZ. T 020 74819004 F 020 74819144 www.gn.apc.org/wen info@wen.org.uk *A national UK charity and membership organisation educating, informing and empowering women and men who care about the environment.*

FOOD & FARMING
(also see Gardening)

Anarchist Teapot Mobile Kitchen, PO Box 74 Brighton BN1 4ZQ. anarchistteapot@yahoo.co.uk *Catering collective based on volunteer labour to cook vegan, mostly organic food for events we care about. Can cook outside, inside, anywhere for up to 300 people.*

Banana Link 38 Exchange Street, Norwich, NR2 1AX T 01603 765670 F 01603 761645 blink@gn.apc.org www.bananalink.org.uk *Works towards environmentally, socially and economically sustainable banana production and trade through campaigns, awareness raising and lobbying.*

Emerson College Trust Ltd *Adult education in Biodynamic Organic Agriculture* (See entry under Education)

ETC Group (Action Group on Erosion, Technology and Concentration) 478 River Avenue, Suite 200, Winnipeg, MB R3L 0C8, Canada. T 204 453 5259 F 204 284 7871 www.etcgroup.org *Dedicated to the conservation and sustainable advancement of cultural and ecological diversity and human rights.*

Federation of City Farms and Community Gardens The Green House, Hereford St, Bedminster, Bristol, BS3 4NA T 0117 923 1800 www.farmgarden.org.uk admin@farmgarden.org.uk *Bringing together information on city farms and community gardens across the county.*

Foundation for Local Food Initiatives PO Box 1234, Bristol BS99 2PG. T 0845 4589525 F 0117 9260221 mail@localfood.org.uk www.localfood.org.uk *Independent not-for-profit co-operative company promoting and supporting the growth of healthy local food economies.*

Hemp Food Industries Association PO Box 204, Barnet, Herts, EN4 8ZQ T 07050 600418 F 07050 600419 hemp@hemp.co.uk www.hemp.co.uk

Hemp food, fibre, fuel, plastic, paper (+more) information for farmers, manufacturer's, retailers, consumers, press + you.

McLibel Support Campaign *Encouraging people everywhere to see the sordid reality behind corporate propaganda, and to fight back against McWorld.* (See entry under Anti-Capitalism)

National Association of Farmers' Markets South Vaults, Green Park Station, Green Park Road, Bath BA1 1JB. T 01225 787914 F 01225 460840 nafm@farmersmarkets.net www.farmersmarkets.net *Promoting and supporting farmers' markets across the UK.*

Permaculture Association (Britain) BCM Permaculture Association, London, WC1N 3XX. T 0845 4581805 F as phone office@permaculture.org.uk www.permaculture.org.uk *Support people and projects to learn about and use permaculture in their homes, gardens, schools, business, farms and communities.*

Primal Seeds 22a Beswick Street, Manchester M4 7HR. mail@primalseeds.org www.primalseeds.org *Information on industrial agriculture with a focus on seeds, and its alternatives.*

Single Step Co-Op 78A Penny St, Lancaster, LA1 1XN T 01524 847234 *Selling wholefoods and organics in a democratic, non-hierarchical, workers' co-op stylee. Also stock non-mainstream mags and journals.*

Soil Association Bristol House, 40-56 Victoria St, Bristol, BS1 6BY T 0117 929 0661 F 0117 925 2504 info@soilassociation.org www.soilassociation.org *Campaigning and certification organisation for organic food and farming.*

Sustain 94 White Lion Street, London N1 9PF. T 020 78371228 F 020 78371141 sustain@sustainweb.org www.sustainweb.org *Sustain advocates food and agriculture policies and practices, that promote equity and enrich society and culture.*

Tools For Solidarity (TFS) Unit 1B1, Edenberry Industrial Estate, 326 Crumlin Rd, Belfast, BT14 7EE T 028 9074 7473. *Refurbishes unwanted hand tools and sewing machines for skilled tradespeople in Africa. Committed to the equal distribution of power and resources.*

Vegan Society, The Donald Watson House, 7 Battle Rd, St. Leonards On Sea, E. Sussex, TN37 7AA T 01424 427393 F 01424 717064 www.vegansociety.com info@vegansociety.com *Educational charity promoting ways of living which avoid the use of animal products - for the benefit of people, animals and the environment.*

Vegetarian Society of the UK, The Parkdale, Dunham Rd, Altringham, Cheshire, WA14 4QG T 0161 925 2000 F 0161 926 9182 info@vegsoc.org www.vegsoc.org *Educational Charity dedicated to the promotion of the knowledge of vegetarianism.*

Veggies Catering Campaign 245 Gladstone Street, Nottingham NG7 6HX T 0845 458 9595 mobile: 0787 0861837 info@veggies.org.uk www.veggies.org.uk *Event catering (all-vegan) and support for human, animal rights & environmental campaigns.*

Viva! 12 Queen Square, Brighton, E. Sussex, BN1 3FD. T 01273 777688 F 01273 776755 info@viva.org.uk www.viva.org *Organisation campaigning to end the factory farming of animals and promote the vegetarian and vegan diets.*

Wholesome Food Association 1 Barton Cottages, Dartington Hall, Totnes, Devon. TQ9 6ED. T 01803 840427 info@wholesomefood.org.uk www.wholesomefood.org *Campaigning for smaller-*

scale, sustainable, local food production, with low cost labelling scheme.

World Wide Opportunities On Organic Farms (WWOOF) PO Box 2675, Lewes, E. Sussex BN7 1RB. T 01273 476286 F as phone fran@wwoof.org www.wwoof.org *Opportunities with vast variety of host organic farms & holdings. Accommodation and food provided in exchange for work.*

FORESTS & WOODLANDS

Agroforestry Research Trust 46 Hunters Moon, Dartington, Totnes, Devon, TQ9 6JT T 01803 840776. F 01803 840776. mail@agroforestry.co.uk www.agroforestry.co.uk *Charity, which researches temperate agroforestry and into all aspects of plant cropping. Produce several publications and a quarterly journal, and also sell plants and seeds*

Forest Stewardship Council (FSC) Unit D, Station Building, Llanidgoes, Powys, SY18 6EB T 01686 413916 F 01686 412176 www.fsc-uk.demon.co.uk fsc-uk@fsc-uk.demon.co.uk *Certifying forests managed to standards which protect people and the environment and identifying timber products from them with the FSC logo.*

Rainforest Action Network 221 Pine St., Suite 500, San Francisco, CA 94104 USA rainforest@ran.org www.ran.org *Working to protect tropical rainforests and the human rights of those living in and around those forests.*

Reforesting Scotland 62-66 Newhaven Rd, Edinburgh, EH6 5QB. T 0131 554 4321 F 0131 554 0088 info@reforestingscotland.org http://reforestingscotland.gn.apc.org *Promote awareness of the deforestation of Scotland and to facilitate ecological restoration and community development through reforestation.*

Taiga Resue Network (TRN) Box 116, Ajtte, S-962 23 Jokkmokk, Sweden. T +46 971 17039 F +46-971-55354 info@taigarescue.org www.taigarescue.org *The TRN is an international network of non-governmental organisations and indigenous peoples working for the protection and sustainable use of the world's boreal forests.*

Tree Council 51 Catherine Place, London, SW1E 6DY. T 020 7828 9928 F 020 7828 9060 info@treecouncil.org.uk www.treecouncil.org.uk *Promoting the improvement of the environment through the care and planting of trees.*

Trees For Life The Park, Findhorn Bay, Forres, Moray, IV36 3TZ. T 01309 691292 F 01309 691155 trees@findhorn.org www.treesforlife.org.uk *A Scottish conservation charity dedicated to the regeneration and restoration of the Caledonian Forest in the Highlands of Scotland.*

GARDENING
(also see Food & Farming)

Community Composting Network 67 Alexandra Road, Sheffield, S2 3EE. T 0114 2580483 ccn@gn.apc.org www.othas.org.uk/ccn *Help and support on all issues around involving your local community in managing its organic resources, through composting.*

Composting Association www.compost.org.uk *Information about composting and its benefits.*

Forest Garden Network A.R.T, 46 Hunters Moon Dartington, Totnes, Devon, TQ9 6JT. mail@agroforestry.co.uk www.agroforestry.co.uk *An informal network of people planning or already cultivating a forest garden, aiming to visit each other's gardens and share knowledge of temperate agroforestry.*

Future Foods Luckleigh Cottage, Hockworthy, Wellington, Somerset TA21 0NN. T 01398 361347 F 01398 361541 enquiries@futurefoods.com www.futurefoods.com *Small independent mail order supplier specialising in rare and unusual edible plants. (Seed company only - do not supply produce.)*

Henry Doubleday Research Association Ryton Organic Gardens, Coventry CV8 3LG. T 024 7630 3517 F 024 7663 9229 enquiry@hdra.org.uk www.hdra.org.uk *Europe's largest organic membership organisation. Dedicated to researching and promoting organic gardening, food, and farming.*

Naturewise 20 The Triangle, Cromartie Rd, London, N19 3RX. T 0845 4584697 naturewise1@hotmail.com *Promotion of: sustainable land use and lifestyles in cities growing food in cities, education through permaculture courses. Permaculture consultations given.*

Permanent Publications The Sustainability Centre, East Meon, Hants GU32 1HR. T 0845 4584150 F 01730 823322 info@permaculture.co.uk www.permaculture.co.uk *Publishers and distributors of Permaculture Magazine – solutions for sustainable living and hundreds of books and videos on all aspects of sustainable living.*

Plants For a Future Blagdon Cross, Ashwater, Beaworthy, Devon EX21 5DF. T 0845 458 4719 / 01208 872963 F 01208 872963 (ring first) webmaster@pfaf.org www.pfaf.org *Research and provide information on edible, medicinal and useful plants, woodland gardening and vegan-organic horticulture.*

Terre de Semences, Ripple Farm, Crundale, Canterbury, Kent, CT4 7EB T 01227 731815 comments@terredesemences.com www.terredesemences.com *Organic seed catalogue with many unusual varieties. Also online gardening advice.*

GENETICS
(also see Food & Farming)

A SEED Europe Action for Solidarity, Equality, Environment, and Diversity (See entry under Anti-Capitalism)

Bayer Hazard bayerhazard@lycos.com www.bayerhazard.com *Find out more about Bayer and GM crops, as well as its involvement with heroin, the holocaust, withdrawn pharmaceuticals and toxic chemicals.*

Genetic Engineering Network (GEN) Archway Resource Centre, 1a Waterlow Road, London N19 5NJ. T 020 7272 1586 F as phone (call first) genetics@gn.apc.org www.geneticsaction.org.uk *Providing information for action for the grassroots campaign against genetic engineering. Has list of local contacts and field trial sites.*

Genetic Food Alert (GFA) 4 Bertram House, Ticklemore St, Totnes, Devon. TQ9 5EJ T 01803 868523 coordinator@geneticfoodalert.org.uk www.geneticfoodalert.org.uk *GFA campaigns to keep the UK wholefood trade GM-free, ban GM food & crops and meanwhile introduce full labelling and liability.*

Genewatch The Mill House, Manchester Road, Tideswell, Buxton, Derbyshire SK17 8LN. T 01298 871898 F 01298 872531 mail@genewatch.org www.genewatch.org *Questions how, why and whether the use of genetic technologies should proceed and believes that the debate over genetic engineering is long overdue.*

Human Genetics Alert 22/24 Highbury Grove, 112 Aberdeen House, London N5 2EA T 020 7704 6100 F 020 7359 8426 info@hgalert.org www.hgalert.org *We are a watch-dog group for Human Genetics, providing information to the public on the developments and policies.*

Scottish Genetix Action T 0141 334 4355 F 0141 588 0664 scottishgenetix@ziplip.com www.scottishgenetix action.org *Campaigning for a GMO free Scotland.*

HEALTH

Bayer Hazard *Find out more about pharmaceutical giant Bayer.* (See entry under Genetics)

British Anti-Vivisection Association (BAVA) PO Box 73 Chesterfield S41 0YZ. Bava@esmail.net www.eurosolve.com/charity/bava *Organisation trying to expose the uselessness and counter-productiveness of animal experimentation in regards to human health.*

Communities Against Toxics (CATS) POBox 29, Ellesmere Port, CH66 3TX T 0151 339 5473 F as phone ralph.ryder@communities-against-toxics.org.uk www.communities-against-toxics.org.uk *Campaigns against unsafe methods of waste disposal, industrial processes and polluting industries. Produces Toxcat newsletter.*

Herb Society Sulgrave Manor, Sulgrave, Banbury OX17 2SD. T 01295 768899 F 01295 768069 email@herbsociety.co.uk www.herbsociety.co.uk *The Herb Society aims to increases the understanding, use and appreciation of herbs and the benefits to health.*

London Hazards Centre 213 Haverstock Hill, London NW3 4QP. T 020 7794 5999 F 020 7794 4702 mail@lhc.org.uk www.lhc.org.uk *Resource centre for Londoners fighting health and safety hazards in their workplace and community.*

Low Level Radiation Campaign The Knoll, Montpellier Park, Llndrindod, Powys, LD1 5LW T 01597 824771 bramhall@llrc.org www.llrc.org *Publicising the effects of radioactivity in the environment; lobbying for use of sound science in setting radiation protection standards for such exposures.*

Médecins Sans Frontières 124–132 Clerkenwell Road, London EC1R 5DJ. T 020 7713 5600 F 020 7713 5004 office@london.msf.org www.uk.msf.org *Independent humanitarian medical aid agency providing medical aid wherever needed and raising awareness of the plight of the people.*

National Gulf War Veterans and Families Association 4 Maspin Close, Kingswood, Kingston upon Hull HU8 8LU. T 01482 833812 F 01482 833816 flusem666@aol.com *Support network, proactive at looking into what veterans have been exposed to.*

National Pure Water Association 12 Dennington Lane, Wakefield WF4 3ET T 01924 254433 F 01924 242380 jane@npwa.freeserve.co.uk www.npwa.freeserve.co.uk *Campaign for safe drinking water. against the artificial fluoridation of water supplies. International contacts.*

Natural Death Centre, 6 Blackstock Mews, Blackstock Road, London N4 2BT, UK T 020 8 208 2853; F 020 8 452 6434 rhino@dial.pipex.com www.naturaldeath.org.uk *Aims to support those dying at home and their carers and to help them arrange funerals. It has as a more general aim that of helping improve 'the quality of dying'.*

Pesticide Action Network UK Eurolink Centre, 49 Effra Rd, London SW2 1BZ. T 020 7274 8895 F 020 7274 9084 admin@pan-uk.org www.pan-uk.org *A scientifically based charity concerned with the health, environmental and policy aspects of pesticide manufacture, trade and use.*

Plants For a Future *Information on medicinal plants.* (See entry under Gardening)

Surfers Against Sewage Wheal Kitty Workshops, St Agnes, Cornwall. England TR5 0RD.

www.sas.org.uk *Call for full non-chemical treatment of sewage discharged into our seas.*

Vaccination Awareness Network UK (VAN UK) 147 Bath Street, Ilkeston, Derbyshire DE7 8AS. T 0870 444 0894 F 08707 418 415 enquiries@van.org.uk www.van.org.uk *Information about vaccinations and their side effects. Support group, meetings, newsletter.*

Vivisection Information Network (VIN) PO Box 223, Camberley, Surrey, GU16 5ZU. vivisectionkills@hotmail.com (Recommended website www.vivisection-absurd.org.uk) *VIN provides information by post and email which proves vivisection is failed and enables ordinary people to prove this.*

What Doctors Don't Tell You (WDDTY) Satellite House, London SW19 4EZ. T 0870 444 9886 F 0870 444 9887 office@wddty.co.uk www.wddty.co.uk *Publishers of Newsletter giving information on alternative health treatments and challenging traditional views on health treatments.*

HOUSING & HOMELESSNESS

Advisory Service for Squatters (A.S.S) 2 St. Paul's Rd, London, N1 2QN T 020 73598814 F 020 73595185 advice@squat.freeserve.co.uk www.squat.freeserve.co.uk *We give legal and practical advice and support to squatters and other homeless people.*

Big Issue, The *Paper sold by homeless vendors.* (See entry under Media)

Confederation of Co-operative Housing (CCH) Unit 19, 41 Old Birley Street, Manchester, M15 5RF. T 0161 232 1588 F 0161 226 7307 info@cch-uk.org www.cch-uk.org *National representative body for co-operative housing, made up of volunteer co-op members from all over the country.*

Cornerstone Housing Co-op 16 Sholebroke Avenue, Leeds, LS7 3HB T 0113 262 9365 cornerstone@gn.apc.org www.cornerstone.ukf.net *Communal housing for people engaged in working for social change. We have a resource centre open to local groups and individuals.*

Defend Council Housing P.O Box33519, London, E8 4XW T 0207 9879989 www.defendcouncilhousing.org.uk info@defendcouncilhousing.org.uk *To oppose transfer of council houses to private landlords & to campaign for more and better council housing.*

Ecovillage Network UK (EVNUK) PO Box 1410, Bristol, BS99 3JP T 0117 3730346 evnuk@gaia.org www.ecovillages.org/uk/network *Sustainable settlement project information/advice service. Our focus is on ecovillages as a way out of cash-based living.*

Empty Homes Agency (EHA) 195-197 Victoria St, London, SW1E 5NE T 020 7828 6288 F 020 7828 7006 info@emptyhomes.com www.emptyhomes.com *Highlight the disgrace of empty, wasted and under used homes and property throughout England.*

Groundswell Elmfield House, 5 Stockwell Mews, London SW9 9GX. T 0207737 5500 F 020 7733 1305 info@groundswell.org.uk www.groundswell.org.uk *Supporting & promoting self help approaches to tackling homelessness and poverty. Info & advice, publications, grants, exchanges, training and networking events.*

Homeless International Queens House, 16 Queens Rd, Coventry, CV1 3DF. T 024 76632802 F 024 76632911 info@homeless-international.org www.homeless-international.org *Charity that supports community-led housing and infrastructure related development in partnership with local partner organisations in Asia, Africa and Latin America.*

Radical Routes *Network of radical housing co-ops.* (See entry under Networking Support)

Talamh Housing Co-Op (THC) ML11 0NJ T 01555 820400 F 01555 820400 talamh@lineone.net *Provide access to housing, land, and resources for low income and unemployed community activists and volunteers.*

UK Cohousing Network coordinator@cohousing.co.uk www.cohousing.co.uk *CoHousing Communities are mutually beneficial neighbourhoods where individual households are clustered around a Common house with shared facilities.*

HUMAN RIGHTS

Action for Southern Africa (ACTSA) 28 Penton Street, London N1 9SA T 020 7833 3133 F 020 7837 3001 actsa@actsa.org www.actsa.org *ACTSA campaigns for peace, democracy and development in Southern Africa and is the successor organisation to the Anti-Apartheid Movement.*

Amnesty International 99-119 Rosebery Avenue, London EC1R 4RE *T 020 7814 6200 F 020 7833 1510* info@amnesty.org.uk www.amnesty.org *International organisation promoting human rights. In particular, campaigning to free all prisoners of conscience; ensure fair and prompt trials for political prisoners; abolish the death penalty, torture and other cruel treatment of prisoners*

Anti-Slavery International Thomas Clarkson House, The Stableyard, Broomgrove Yard, London SE27 9LA. T 020 7501 8920 F 020 7738 4110 antislavery@antislavery.org www.antislavery.org *Anti-Slavery is committed to eliminating slavery: debt bondage, forced labour, forced marriage, the worst forms of child labour, human trafficking and traditional slavery.*

Burma Campaign UK, Third Floor, Bickerton House, 25-27 Bickerton Rd, London, N19 5JT. T 020 7281 7377F 020 7272 3559 info@burmacampaign.org.uk www.burmacampaign.org.uk *Campaigns for human rights and democracy in Burma. We campaign to improve government and commercial policy on Burma.*

Campaign Against Criminalising Communities (CACC) c/o Haldane Society, Conway Hall, Red Lion Square, London WC1. T 020 7586 5892 knklondon@gn.apc.org www.cacc.org.uk *The supposed war on terrorism is in reality a war on dissent and holds inherent dangers for everyone's civil liberties.*

Campaign for Freedom of Information Suite 102, 16 Baldwins Gardens, London EC1N 7RJ. T 020 7831 7477 F 020 7831 7461 admin@cfoi.demon.co.uk www.cfoi.org.uk *Campaigns against unnecessary secrecy and for a Freedom of Information Act.*

Christian Aid, PO Box 100, London, SE 1 7RT. info@christian-aid.org www.christian-aid.org.uk *Funds projects in some of the world's poorest countries. It helps people to improve their own lives and to tackle the causes of poverty and injustice.*

Environmental Rescue International (ERI) *Nigerian environmental, human rights and community development organisation.* (See entry under Environment)

Free Tibet Campaign (See entry under Indigenous Peoples)

Haiti Support Group PO Box 29623, London, E9 7XU. T 020 7525 0456 haitisupport@gn.apc.org www.gn.apc.org/haitisupport *Solidarity with the Haitian people's struggle for justice, real democracy and equitable development.*

Kurdish Human Rights Project (KHRP) 162-168 Regent St, Suite 319 Linen Hall, London, W1B 5TG T 020 72872772 F 020 77344927 www.khrp.org

khrp@khrp.demon.co.uk *KHRP is committed to the protection of the human rights of all persons within the Kurdish regions.*

Peace in Kurdistan (PIK) and Kurdistan Solidarity Committee (KSC) 44 Alnger Road, London NW3 3AT. T 020 7586 5892 F 020 7483 2531 knklondon@gn.apc.org *Campaigning for international recognition for the right of the Kurdish people to self-determination in collaboration with the Kurdish community in the UK and Europe.*

People & Planet (P&P) 51 Union St, Oxford, OX4 1JP. T 01865 245678 F 01865 791927 people@peopleandplanet.org www.peopleandplanet.org *UK student action on world poverty, human rights and the environment.*

Privacy International T 07960 523679 pi@privacy.org www.privacyinternational.org *International anti-surveillance organisation. Campaigns on Big Brother issues like data tracking, ID cards, CCTV, encryption, police surveillance, corporate biometrics.*

Project Underground 1916A MLK Jr. Way, Berkeley, CA 94704, USA. T +1 510 705 8981 F +1 510 705 8983 project_underground@moles.org www.moles.org *Supporting the human rights of communities resisting mining and oil exploitation.*

Scottish Human Rights Centre (SHRC) 146 Holland St, Glasgow, G2 4NG T 0141 332 5960 F 0141 332 5309 info@scottishhumanrightscentre.org.uk www.scottishhumanrightascentre.org.uk *Aims to promote human rights in Scotland through advice/information, research, scrutiny of legislation, monitoring international human rights treaties.*

TAPOL, The Indonesia Human Rights Campaign 111 Northwood Rd, Thornton Rd, Surrey, CR7 8HW T 020 8771 2904 F 020 8653 0322 tapol@gn.apc.org www.gn.apc.org/tapol *TAPOL - which means political prisoner in Indonesian - is an English language authority on the human rights situation in Indonesia and East Timor.*

Western Sahara Campaign *T* 0113 245 4786 www.arso.org *The struggle of the Sahrawi people for Self-determination – Western Sahara former Spanish colony is the last African colonised country still waiting for independence.*

INDIGENOUS PEOPLES

Amazon Alliance for Indigenous and Traditional Peoples of the Amazon Basin 1367 Connecticut Ave, N.W Suite 400, Washington DC 20036, USA. T 1-202-785-3334 F 1-202-785-3335 amazon@amazonalliance.org www.amazonalliance.org *Works to defend the rights, territories, and environment of indigenous and traditional peoples of the Amazon Basin.*

Bougainville Freedom Movement PO Box 134, Erskineville, NSW 2043, Australia. T +61 2 9558 2730 F +61 2 9804 7632 vikki@law.uts.edu.au www.eco-action.org/bougainville *To assist the Bougainville people in their struggle for peace and freedom. To educate the world about the Bougainville.*

Centre For World Indigenous Studies PMB 214, 1001 Cooper Point Rd, SW Suite 140, Olympia WA 98502-1107, USA. T +1 360 754 1990 www.cwis.org *Non-profit research and education organisation dedicated to wider understanding and appreciation of the ideas and knowledge of indigenous peoples.*

ChiapasLink PO Box 79, 82 Colston St, Bristol, BS1 5BB. chiapaslink@yahoo.com www.chiapasnews.ukgateway.net *Chiapslink hopes to provide a link between the Zapatista struggles in Chiapas, Mexico and in the UK.*

Dark Night Press *Voices from indigenous struggles world-wide.* (See entry under Media)

Ejercito Zapatista de Liberacion Nacional (EZLN) *Information on the Zapatista uprising (See entry under Anti-Capitalism)*

Free Tibet Campaign 1 Rosomon Place, London, EC1R 0JY T 020 7833 9958 F 020 7833 3838 mail@freetibet.org www.freetibet.org *An independent membership organisation campaigning in support of the rights of the Tibetan people to freedom and independence.*

OPM Support Group (Free Papua Movement) c/o 43 Gardner St, Brighton, BN1 1UN opmsg@eco-action.org www.eco-action.org/opm *Direct action network to support Papuan peoples struggle for freedom. Videos talks and publications available to help start new groups.*

Palestine Solidarity Campaign Box BM PSA, London WC1N 3XX. T 020 7700 6192 info@palestinecampaign.org www.palestinecampaign.org *Aim to build an effective mass campaign, organising protests, political lobbying and raising public awareness.*

Survival International 6 Charterhouse Buildings, London, EC1M 7ET T 020 7687 8700 F 020 7687 8701 www.survival-international.org info@survival-international.org *World-wide organisation supporting tribal peoples. It stands for their right to decide their own future and helps them protect their lives, lands and human rights.*

Tibet Foundation 1 St. James's Market, London SW1Y 4SB. T 020 7930 6001 F 020 7930 6002 enquiries@tibet-foundation.org www.tibet-foundation.org *Non-political organisation working to preserve Tibetan Culture, and assist the Tibetan People across the world.*

JUSTICE AND THE LAW
(also see Human Rights and Prisoner Support)

Anti-Corruption Network PO Box 187, Chesterfield, Derbyshire, S40 2DU. T 01246 555713 F as phone. *The title says it all.*

Bindman & Partners Solicitors 275 Gray's Inn Rd, London, WC1X 8QF T 020 7833 4433 F 020 7837 9792 info@Bindmans.com www.Bindmans.com *A solicitor's firm specialising in human rights – including criminal law, protest, civil actions against the police.*

Coalition Against the Terrorism Acts BM Box 563, London WC1N 3XX *T* 01273 298192 http://go.to/ta2000 *Information and campaigning against the Terrorism Act 2000 and the Anti-Terrorism, Crime and Security Act 2001.*

Criminal Cases Review Commission (CCRC) Alpha Tower, Suffolk St, Queensway, Birmingham, B1 1TT. T 0121 633 1800 F 0121 633 1804/1823 info@ccrc.gov.uk www.ccrc.gov.uk *An independent body responsible for investigating suspected miscarriages of criminal justice in England, Wales and Northern Ireland.*

Earthrights Solicitors Little Orchard, School Lane, Molehill Green, Takeley, Essex, CM22 6PS. T 01279 870391 F 01279 870391 pager - 07669 127601 earthrights@gn.apc.org www.earthrights.org.uk *Provide legal advice and assistance to the environment movement and landrights campaigners.*

Environmental Law Foundation Suite 309, 16 Baldwins Gardens, London, EC1N 7RJ. T 020 7404 1030 F 020 7404 1032 info@elflaw.org www.elflaw.org *National charity that secures environmental justice for communities and individuals through a network of legal and technical experts.*

Freedom To Be Yourself, The 13 C, Pioneer House, Adelaide Street, Coventry M 07788 557078 thehumanmind@yahoo.co.uk www.geocities.com/thehumanmind *The right to be unclothed in all*

public places. Human skin. Body visibility. The human race: Every body!

Index on Censorship (See entry under Media)

Injustice 020 7254 9701/07770 432 439 (evenings-w/ends) www.injusticefilm.co.uk *A film about the struggle for justice by the families of people that have died in police custody.*

Innocent Dept. 54, PO Box 282, Oldham OL1 3FY http://innocent.org.uk innocent@uk2.net *We are committed to fighting miscarriages of justice in general and campaigning on behalf of specific cases.*

INQUEST Ground Floor, Alexandra National House, 330 Seven Sisters Rd, London, N4 2PJ T 020 8802 7430 F 020 8802 7450 inquest@inquest.org www.inquest.org *Advice, campaigning and information for bereaved people facing Coroner's Inquests, especially those involving deaths in custody (Police, prison, detained patients).*

Irwin Mitchell Solicitors St. Peter's House, Hartshead, Sheffield, S1 2EL T 0114 276 7777/273 9011 F 0114 275 3306 www.imonline.co.uk *Produce Claiming Compensation For Police Misconduct- A Guide To Your Rights, a booklet of civil liberties when dealing with the police.*

Kellys Solicitors Premier House, 11 Marlborough House, Brighton, BN1 1UB. T 01273 608311 F 01273 674898 *Criminal defence solicitors with experience in defending protestors 24 hour helpline 0800 387463*

Legal Defence & Monitoring Group (LDMG) BM Haven, London, WC1N 3XX. T 020 8245 2930 ldmgmail@yahoo.co.uk www2.phreak.co.uk/ldmg/index.php *Legal monitoring at demos & advice for others doing so, plus advice on police tactics, prisoners & legal stuff.*

Liberty 21 Tabard St., London, SE1 4LA. T 020 74033888 F 020 74075354 info@liberty-human-rights.org.uk www.liberty-human-rights.org.uk *Lobbies Parliament on proposed legislation and takes test case litigation to domestic and European Courts.*

Miscarriages of Justice UK (MOJUK) Tardis Studios, 52-56 Turnmill St., London, EC1M 5QR T 0121 554 6947 F 0870 055 4570 www.mojuk.org.uk *Founded by Paddy Hill, one of the Birmingham 6, they fight for people who are wrongly imprisoned.*

Public Law Project (PLP) Birkbeck College, 14 Bloomsbury Square, London WC1A 2LP T 020 72690570 F 020 72690579 admin@plp.bbk.ac.uk www.publiclawproject.org *Undertakes specialist research, training and information, advice and representation in public law to access justice for poor and disadvantaged people.*

Roger Sylvester Justice Campaign PO Box 25908, London N18 1WU. T 07931 970442 rsjc@hotmail.com www.rsjc.org.uk *Campaigns to establish how Roger, a fit and healthy 30 year old man came to a horrific and premature death after being detained by the police.*

Statewatch POBox 1516, London, N16 0EW T 020 88021882 F 020 88801727 www.statewatch.org office@statewatch.org *Statewatch monitors the state and civil liberties in the UK and Europe.*

United Families and Friends Campaign (UFFC) c/o Inquest, Ground Floor, Alexandra National House, 330 Seven Sisters Rd., London N4 2PJ. kevin@copwatcher.org *Vocal campaigning coalition of families and friends of people who have died in police custody, prison or in psychiatric care.*

Walkers Solicitors 2 Bouverie Road, Stoke Newington, London N16 0AJ. T 020 8800 8855 F 020 8800 9955 info@walkerssolicitors.co.uk *Specialist advice & representation in animal rights, political defence, etc.*

LAND RIGHTS & PLANNING

Brighton Urban Design & Development (BUDD) PO Box 108, Brighton BN1 4XN. T 01273 681166 mail@BUDDbrighton.org www.BUDDbrighton.org *BUDD aims to stimulate, encourage and initiate sustainable urban design and development through an inclusive and participatory process.*

Chapter Seven The Potato Store, Flaxdrayton Farm, South Petherton, Somerset, TA13. T 01460 249204 F 01460 249204 chapter7@tlio.demon.co.uk www.oneworld.org/tlio/chapter7 *Chapter 7 provides planning assistance to people wanting to build low-impact eco-homes, smallholders and ecovillagers. Want to change the planning system to allow for low-impact homes and more sustainable land usage.*

Land Is Ours, The (T.L.I.O) 16B Cherwell St, Oxford, OX4 1BG. T 07961 460171 office@tlio.demon.co.uk www.tlio.org.uk *Campaigns peacefully for access to the land, its resources and the decision making processes affecting them, for everyone - irrespective of race, age, or gender.*

Mast Action UK 20 Outwood Road, Radcliffe, Gtr. Manchester M26 1AQ. webmaster@mastaction.org www.mastaction.org *Voluntary organisation dedicated to supporting, advising and actively aiding and representing local campaigns fighting the current mobile phone mast invasion that is sweeping the country.*

Open Spaces Society (OSS) 25A Bell St, Henley-On-Thames, Oxon, RG9 2BA T 01491 573535 F 01491 57305 hq@oss.org.uk www.oss.org.uk *Exists to protect common land and public rights of way.*

Opposition To Destruction of Open Green Spaces (OTDOGS) 6 Everthorpe Rd, London, SE15 4DA T 020 8693 9412 F as phone *Advising people on how to prevent food giants building on open green spaces.*

Ramblers' Association 2nd floor Camelford House, 87-90 Albert Embankment, London SE1 7TW. T 020 7339 8500 F 020 7339 8501 ramblers@london.r amblers.org.uk www.ramblers.org.uk *Encouraging walking, protecting rights of way, defending the beauty of the countryside and campaigning for freedom to roam over uncultivated open country.*

Royal Town Planning Institute (RTPI) 41 Botolph Lane, London, EC3 8DL T 020 79299494 online@rtpi.org.uk www.rtpi.org.uk *To provide free and independent town planning advice to groups and individuals that cannot afford professional fees.*

MEDIA
Distribution and Publishers
(also see Bookshops)

Active Distribution BM Active, London, WC1N 3XX jon@activedistribution.org www.activedistribution.org *Anarchist (DIY) distribution, mailorder, wholesale, stalls etc of a non-profit, Books, Mags, Music, Badges t-shirts etc. Send SAE for a catalogue.*

AK Distribution PO Box 12766, Edinburgh, EH8 9YE. T 0131 5555165 F 0131 5555215 ak@akedin.demon.co.uk www.akuk.com www.akpress.org *Co-operative who distribute & publish a wide range of radical politics: books, mags, audio & t-shirts. Send for free mail-order catalogue.*

Anarchy: A Journal of Desire Armed C.A.L. Press, PO Box 1446, Columbia, MO 65205-1446, USA. jmcquinn@coin.org www.anarchymag.org *Anti-ideological anarchist publishing (magazines & books).*

Diggers & Dreamers BCM Edge, London, WC1N 3XX. T 07000 780536 F 0870 163 4661 info@diggersanddreamers.org.uk www.diggersanddreamers.org.uk

.uk *"Diggers & Dreamers - the Guide to Communal Living in Britain"* and books on related subjects.

Eco-Logic Books 10-12 Picton St, Bristol, BS6 5QA. T 0117 9420165 F 0117 9420164 books@eco-logic.demon.co.uk www.eco-logicbooks.com *Publishes and sells mail order books on practical solutions to environmental problems, sustainability, permaculture, organic gardening, etc.*

Edge of Time Ltd, BCM Edge, London WC1N 3XX. T 07000 780536 F 0870 1634661 sales@edgeoftime.co.uk www.edgeoftime.co.uk *Distributes books on communal living and other items associated with cultural change.*

Enabler Publications 3 Russell House, Lym Close, Lyme Regis, Dorset, DT7 3DE. T 01297 445024 F as phone adearling@aol.com http://members.aol.com/adearling/enabler *Books about counter culture, Travellers, protest and creative work with young people.*

Factsheet 5 PO Box 4660 Arlington, VA 22204, USA. T 703-553-2945 F 703-553-0565 twbounds@pop.mail.rcn.net www.factsheet5.org *Comprehensive quarterly guide to zines/alternative publications. Each issue packed with reviews/contact/ordering info for hundreds of independent publications.*

Freedom Press, 84b Whitechapel High St, London, E1 7QX. T 020 7247 9249 F 020 7377 9526 freedom@ecn.org www.ecn.org/freedom *Anarchist publishers and propagandists since 1886, through our periodicals, books and pamphlets, available from our bookshop or by mail order. Contact us for free sample copy of 'Freedom'.*

Godhaven Ink Rooted Media, The Cardigan Centre, 145-149 Cardigan Rd, Leeds, LS6 1LJ. T 0113 278 8617 merrick@stones.com www.godhaven.org.uk *Publishers of cheap books and zines about direct action and other counter-cultural stuff. Promoting a feeling of well-being since 1994.*

Green Books Foxhole, Dartington, Totnes, Devon, TQ9 6EB. T 01803 863260 F 01803 863843 www.greenbooks.co.uk paul@greenbooks.co.uk *Publishers of a wide range of books on politics, ecology, economics, eco-philosophy, eco-building, renewable energy and the environment.*

INK - Independent News Collective 2nd Floor, The Shiatsu Place, 97-99 Seven Sisters Road, London N7 7QP. T 020 7561 0683 ink@pro-net.co.uk www.ink.uk.com *Umbrella organisation for the alternative press. Deals with marketing and publishing, but not editorial matters.*

Kate Sharpley Library (KSL), BM Hurricane, London, WC1N 3XX. *Or* PMB 820, 2425 Channing Way, Berkeley CA 94704, USA. kar98@dial.pipex.com www.katesharpleylibrary.org/index.htm *Archive of Anarchist and related material, reclaiming Anarchist history to inform current struggles. Write for details of our (many!) publications.*

National Small Press Centre, The BM Bozo, London, WC1N 3XX. *Publishes small press handbook with information on thousands of small presses world-wide.*

Photon Press 37 The Meadows, Berwick-Upon-Tweed, Northumberland, TD15 1NY. photon.press@virgin.net *Publish "Light's List" of 1500 independent press magazines world-wide printing fiction, poetry, art, reviews etc. £2.50 inc. postage.*

Pluto Press 345 Archway Rd, London, N6 5AA. T 020 8348 2724 F 020 8348 9133 pluto@plutobooks.com www.plutobooks.com *One of the UK's leading independent publishers. Committed to publishing the best in critical writing across the social sciences and humanities.*

Revolutions Per Minute BCM Box 3328, London

WC1N 3XX T 07967 886257 revopermin@ukonline.co.uk www.red-star-research.org.uk/rpmframe.html *A radical publishing project, which aims to help liberate the working class. Includes books on strikes, fox-hunting and anti-racism.*

Rural Media Company, The Sullivan House, 72-80 Widemarsh St, Hereford, HR4 9HG. T 01432 344039 F 01432 270539 info@ruralmedia.co.uk www.ruralmedia.co.uk *We are a National Media Communications Charity, we cover print, web publishing, video production and multimedia production.*

Zabalaza Books Postnet Suite 116, Private Bag X42, Braamfontein, 2017, Johannesburg, South Africa. zabalaza@union.org.za www.struggle.ws/africa/safrica/zababooks/HomePage.htm *Publishers of Anarchist writings/pamphlets on the various issues effecting the building of a free and equal non-statist society under workers self-management.*

Zed Books, 7 Cynthia St, London, N1 9JF. T 020 7837 4014 F 020 7833 3960 hosie@zedbooks.demon.co.uk www.zedbooks.demon.co.uk *Independent workers co-op publishing annually 50+ scholarly, critical books on international issues, politics, the environment, feminism and 'the third world'*

MEDIA
– Film, Video & TV

Beyond TV mick@beyondtv.org, anna@beyondtv.org www.beyondtv.org *A website hosting alternative news features - in an online database linking features to campaigns, upcoming events and current projects.*

Conscious Cinema, 110 Elmore St, London, N1 T 020 7359 2755 F as phone inbox@consciouscinema.co.uk www.consciouscinema.co.uk *Media arts collective turned production company. Broadcast standard equipment available for commercial work and projects creating greater value than money.*

Cultureshop.Org PO Box 29683, London E2 6XH. T 07950 699562 admin@cultureshop.org www.cultureshop.org *Online distribution to allow progressive film makers to sell there work, may be extended to other forms of media soon.*

Direct Action Media Network (DAMN) Video www.tao.ca/earth/damn *Multimedia direct action news service with live direct action footage on the web.*

Exploding Cinema, The c/o 26 Fairwall House, Peckham Road, London SE5 8QW. T 020 7708 3501/020 7732 8058 explodingcinema@hotmail.com www.explodingcinema.org *Open Access Screenings for Short Films.*

Fifth Sun Archive, The Mobile 07940 393671 5un@freeuk.com www.fifthsunarchive.org *The Fifth Sun Archive is a video library of social and environmental protest in the UK, established in 1994.*

Groovy Movie Picture House, The mail@grooviemovie.org www.groovymovie.org *Documenting alternative issues, lifestyles and arts using the latest in cutting edge digital technology and powered only with green energy.*

Guerillavision Box 91, Green Leaf Bookshop, 82 Colston St, Bristol BS1 5BB guerillavision@angelfire.com *Troublemakers with other people's dv cameras.*

I-Contact Video Network c/o 76 Mina Rd, St. Werburghs, Bristol, BS2 9TX. T 0117 9400636 I-contact@videonetwork.org www.VideoNetwork.org *A non-profit making initiative set up to provide support for those using video for positive change.*

New York Surveillance Camera Players [SCP-New York] POB 1115, NYC 10009-9998, USA. T 001 212 561 0106 notbored@panix.com www.notbored.org/the-scp.html *Situationist-*

inspired anti-surveillance camera group.

Organic Chaos Network PO Box 234, 2300 AE Leiden, Netherlands, T +31-6-12520674 ocn@antenna.nl www.antenna.nl/organicchaos *Video action news group, part of Federation Collective Rampenplan (See entry under Anarchy).*

Reclaim the Streets -The Film T 07092 044579 reclaim_streets_film@yahoo.com www.come.to/rtsfilm *Video clips, background info and ordering details for this essential documentary, taking a frantic look at RTS actions in the UK and abroad.*

SKA TV Suite 75 Trades Hall Carlton Vic 3053 Australia T 61 3 9663 6976 accessnews@skatv.org.au www.skatv.org.au *A grass-roots community organisation using TV and video as tools for social change; training, screenings, broadcast, distribution.*

Turn Off Your TV www.turnoffyourtv.com *Articles on issues such as the role of advertisers, corporate ownership of mass media, and the potential effects of images on children.*

TV Go Home tvgohome@tvgohome.com www.tvgohome.com *Send up of the Radio Times Emailed*

Undercurrents alternative video news 16B Cherwell St, Oxford, OX4 1BG. 01865 203661/203662 underc@gn.apc.org www.undercurrents.org *Produce and distribute videos and CD-ROM on direct action. Organise BeyondTV video activist festival.*

Undercurrents foundation undercymru@joymail.com www.undercurrents.org *Train activists how to use video for social change.*

White Dot PO Box 2116, Hove BN3 3LR. info@whitedot.org www.whitedot.org *International campaign against television.*

MEDIA
– Internet News Services

A-Infos www.ainfos.ca *Regular anarchist newsfeed over the internet in various languages.*

Alternet www.alternet.org *San Fransisco alternative media site with hard-hitting news and investigations not covered in the mainstream press, fiery columns, insights into cultural trends.*

Anarcho-Syndicalism 101 www.anarchosyndicalism.org *A web archive of texts, articles, image and mp3 files, cultural items and outreach material (otherwise known as propaganda).*

GreenNet 33 Islington High Street, London N1 9LH. T 0845 055 4011 F 020 7837 5551 : info@gn.apc.org www.greennet.org.uk *GreenNet is an internet service provider that specialises in Internet services for organisations involved in Peace, The environment, Human Rights and Development.*

Indymedia www.indymedia.org *A collective of independent media organisations and hundreds of journalists offering grassroots, non-corporate coverage – links to Indymedia outlets around the world.*

Indymedia UK www.indymedia.org.uk reports@indymedia.org.uk *An evolving network of media professionals, artists, and DIY media activists committed to using technology to promote social and economic justice.*

Lobster www.lobster-magazine.co.uk/ *The journal of parapolitics, intelligence, and State Research.*

Monbiot, George www.monbiot.com *He's got a website about the corporate take-over of everything…*

Protest.Net rabble-rouser@protest.net www.protest.net *A site to help progressive activists by providing a central place where the times and locations of protests and meetings can be posted.*

Spunk Library, The spunk@spunk.org www.spunk.org *Collects and distributes literature* in electronic format, with an emphasis on anarchism and related issues.

SQUALL Magazine POBox 8959, London, N19 5HW mail@squall.co.uk www.squall.co.uk *Regularly updated online magazine presenting radical journalism, photography and culture with content.*

[Squat!net] squat@squat.net www.squat.net *An international internet magazine with main focus on squatted houses, car sites and other free spaces.*

Straight Goods www.straightgoods.com *Canada's independent on-line source of news*

URBAN 75 contact@urban75.com www.urban75.com *Serves up non-mainstream viewpoint on a wide range of issues including environmental action, rave culture and civil rights. Plus drug information, cartoons, short stories and useless games.*

MEDIA – Overseas

A4 Newsbot c/o L38 Squat Infoshop, Via Giuliotti, 8-00143 Roma, Italy. a4newsbot@paranoici.org www.tmcrew.org/laurentinokkupato/a4newsbot/ *A SchNEWS inspired quarterly A4 multi-language publication distributed on paper, e-mail, website and PDF about social, eco and anarchist issues.*

A-kontra POBox 223, 111 21 Praha 1, Czech Republic. a-kontra@csaf.cz http://a-kontra.csaf.cz *Czech anarchist magazine.*

Alternative Press Review PO Box 4710, Arlington, VA 22204, USA. T +1 703-553-2945 editors@altpr.org www.altpr.org *Your Guide Beyond the Mainstream! Each issue is packed with creative ideas, fresh perspectives, insightful analysis and pointed humour.*

An Phoblacht (Republican News) 58 Parnell Square, Dublin 1. T +353 1 873 3611 F +353 1 873 3839 aprn@irlnet.com www.irlnet.com/aprn *Ireland's biggest selling political weekly newspaper has been a source of uncensored news on world affairs and the Irish struggle for national self-determination for over 25 years.*

Dark Night Press PO Box 3629, Chicago, IL 60690-3629, USA. T +1 207 839 5794 darknight@igc.org www.darknightpress.org *Under-reported news and unheard voices from indigenous struggles worldwide.*

Earth First! Journal PO Box 3023, Tucson AZ 85702-3023, USA. T +1 520.620.6900 F 413.254.0057 collective@earthfirstjournal.org www.earthfirstjournal.org *Voice of the radical environmental movement containing direct action reports, articles on preservation of wild places, investigative articles, and discussions on monkeywrenching.*

Green Pepper CIA Office, Overtoom 301, 1054 HW Amsterdam, The Netherlands. T +31 20 665 7743 F +31 20 692 8757 greenpep@eyfa.org http://squat.net/cia/gp *An environmental and social justice magazine focussing on a different (anti-neoliberal/activist friendly) topic every edition.*

Kontrapunkt www.kontrapunkt-online.org *Serbo-Croation on-line magazine covering all aspects of libertarian thought, and it is open for all views which are in-support of liberating of human minds and lives.*

KUD Anarhiv Metelkova ulica 6, SI-1000 Ljubljana, Slovenia. T +386 1 434 03 45/+386 1 432 33 78 F +386 1 432 33 78 anarhiv@mail.ljudmila.org www.ljudmila.org/anarhiv *A resource centre for radical social change, also publish a magazine and organize events.*

Motkraft www.motkraft.net *The internet infocenter of the Swedish libertarian left. Publish news and information about actions, lectures, etc.*

No God-No Master PO Box 300, East Brunswick, Victoria 3057, Australia. anthropia@hotmail.com www.punk.gr/nogod-nomaster *Anarchist bulletin and publication of small Pamphlets in Greek.*

Paper, The PO Box 1733, Collingwood VIC 3066, Australia. info@thepaper.org.au www.thepaper.org.au *Fortnightly free independent paper from Melbourne - available online as PDF.*

Rocky Road Environmental Magazine Anne Ruimy, Mullagh, Co. Clare, Ireland. T +353 (0)65 708 7144 editor@rockyroadmagazine.com www.rockyroadmagazine.com *Publishing a bi-monthly magazine offering unbiased, investigative and science-based news, features and analyses on Irish and global environmental issues.*

Spacestation PO Box 209, Brunswick, Victoria 3056, Australia. T 03 9343 6593 spackids@myspinach.org http://spacestation.org.au *A media lab, a guerilla media node, a skill sharing network, melbourne indymedia centre.*

Tactical Media Crew c/o Radio Onda Rossa, Via dei Volsci, 56, Roma 00185, Italy. www.tmcrew.org tactical@tmcrew.org *A collective of media and political activists from the radical autonomous/ anarchist scene of Rome.*

Thrall PO Box 22-076 Christchurch, Aoteroa/New Zealand thrallnet@yahoo.com www.thrall.orcon.net.nz *Monthly anarchist magazine from NZ.*

Warhead PO Box 43, 15-662 Bialystok, Poland soja2@poczta.onet.pl *Anarchist news service for Poland.*

Z Magazine 18 Millfield Street, Woods Hole MA 02543, USA. T +1 508 5489063. sysop@zmag.org www.zmag.org *Z is an independent political magazine of critical thinking on political, cultural, social, and economic life in the United States, Z accepts no paid advertising.*

MEDIA – UK Based

Alan Lodge (Tash) T 0115 9113804 tash@gn.apc.org http://tash.gn.apc.org *Photographer (One Eye On The Road): travellers, festivals, raves, environmental direct actions and protest & police surveillance methods.*

Allsorts allsorts@gn.apc.org *UK based e-news for activists.*

Animal Liberation Press Office BM4400, London, WC1N 3XX. T 01623 746470 mobile: 07752 107515 F as phone *Media contact for the ALF and other radical animal rights groups. Supplies speakers for groups, rallies, etc.*

Aufheben POBox 2536, Rottingdean, Brighton, BN2 6LX http://lists.village.virginia.edu/~spoons/aut_html *Not an organisation, but a magazine dedicated to the theory and practice of revolutionary class struggle.*

Bellow Box 35, 82 Colston Street, Bristol, BS1 5BB. Bellow1@bigfoot.com *Radical women's newsletter, instigated by Women Speak Out – free, available for photocopying/ distribution - hardcopy or PDF*

Big Issue, The London, SW8 2LN T 020 75263200 F 020 75263302 news@bigissue.com www.bigissue.com *UK's biggest current affairs weekly, with 1.2 million readers. Campaigning for social justice. Sold by homeless vendors who keep 70p of each issue.*

Black Flag BM Hurricane, London WC1N 3XX blackflageds@hushmail.com http://flag.blackened.net/blackflag *Class struggle anarchist quarterly magazine with strong international coverage, recently revamped. Contact for subs info. Comprehensive list of UK Anarchist groups.*

Class War Paper *Promotes class consciousness and working class control over our day to day*

lives. (See entry under Anarchism)

Corner House, The, Station Rd, Sturminster Newton, Dorset DT10 1YJ. T 01258 473795 F 01258 473748 cornerhouse@gn.apc.org www.thecornerhouse.org.uk *Research, advocacy and solidarity work on social & environmental justice issues. Publish regular briefing papers. Free via email.*

Counter Information c/o ACE, 17 West Montgomery Place, Edinburgh, EH7 5HA T 0131 557 6242 ci@counterinfo.org.uk www.counterinfo.org.uk *Free anarchist newssheet reporting on struggles from around the world.*

Direct Action Collective PO Box 29, SW PDO, Manchester. M15 5HW. T 07984 675281 da@direct-action.org.uk www.direct-action.org.uk *DA - magazine of the anarcho-syndicalist Solidarity Federation. No political parties or dogma. Packed with positive anti-authoritarian ideas, news, comment and actions.*

Do or Die c/o Prior House, 6 Tilbury Place, Brighton, East Sussex, BN2 2GY doordtp@yahoo.co.uk www.eco-action.org/dod *Voices from the Ecological Resistance - an annual magazine crammed with reports and analysis from the world-wide ecological frontlines.*

Earth First! Action Update (EF! AU) PO Box 487 Norwich, NR2 3AL T 01603 219811 efactionupdate @bigfoot.com www.eco-action.org/efau *A monthly round-up of ecological and other direct action from around Britain. Has list of contacts of all UK Earth First! groups.*

Ecologist, The 18 Chelsea Wharf, 15 Lots Rd, London, SW10 0QJ T 020 7351 3578 F 020 7351 3617 sally@theecologist.org www.theecologist.org *Investigative journalists, leading thinkers and campaigners are constantly rethinking the basic assumptions which underlie mankind's steady march towards self-destruction.*

Freedom anarchist fortnightly 84b Whitechapel High St, London, E1 7QX. T 020 8771 8317 F as phone FreedomCopy@aol.com *Carries news and views from a growing range of activists. All contributions welcome.*

(NB. There are now two 'Green Anarchists')

Green Anarchist Green Anarchist, BCM 1715, London WC1N 3XX. www.greenanarchist.org *UK's original and best (apparently) anarcho-primitivist paper – uncensored forum for direct action news and discussion.*

Green Anarchist 9 Ash Avenue, Galgate, Lancaster LA2 0NP, UK T 01524 752212 grandlaf@lineone.net http://website.lineone.net/~grandlaf/Sotiga.htm *Quarterly magazine reporting on environmental issues, anarchism, animal rights, community resistance. With emphasis on positive empowerment and improving our lives.*

Index on Censorship 33 Islington High St, London, N1 9LH. T 020 7278 2313 F 020 7278 1878 natasha@indexoncensorship.org www.indexoncensorship.org *Publish a magazine, run a website and organise events on free expression and censorship around the world.*

Inkthief Rm 304, Maryland House, Manbey Park Road , London E15 1EY. T 020 8223 6011 / 07984 875471 contact@inkthief.org.uk *Designers committed to social and environmental justice who formed a professional design agency for socially progressive organisations.*

Morgenmuffel PO Box 74, Brighton BN1 4ZQ. *Personal anarchist zine with cartoons and rants published irregularly. Send three stamps for an issue.*

New Internationalist Tower House, Lathkill St, Market Harborough, LE16 T 01858 438896 F 01858 461739 newint@subscription.co.uk www.newint.org *Monthly informative magazine reporting on issues of world poverty and inequal-*

ity; focusing attention on the unjust relationship between the powerful and the powerless.

Nonviolent Action (NVA) 5 Caledonian Rd, London, N1 9DY T 020 7713 nva@gn.apc.org *Magazine serving campaigners seeking positive social change through non-violent means with news of activists and activities - and a stimulus to thought and action.*

Peace News 5 Caledonian Rd, London, N1 9DY T 020 7278 3344 F 020 7278 0444 admin@peacenews.info www.peacenews.info *Radical, international, antimilitarist, quarterly magazine. For nonviolent revolution. Bringing activists and campaigners together worldwide, sharing ideas, theories, and tactics.*

Positive News 5 Bicton Enterprise Centre, Clun, Shropshire, SY7 8NF. T 01588 640022 F 01588 640033 office@positivenews.org.uk www.positivenews.org.uk *A free quarterly newspaper which publishes good news stories from around the world to do with peace, environment, health & education.*

Red Pepper 1b Waterlow Rd, London, N19 5NJ T 020 72817024 F 020 72639345 redpepper@red pepper.org.uk www.redpepper.org.uk *Green - left monthly magazine.*

Resurgence Ford House, Hartland, Bideford, Devon, EX39 6EE T 01237 441293 F 01237 441203 ed@resurgeence.org www.resurgence.org *Encompasses environmental, social, economic and cultural issues. Thought-provoking and informative, bringing articles which nourish all aspects of your life.*

Total Liberty Magazine Box EMAB, 88 Abbey Street, Derby DE22 3SQ. ain@ziplip.com www.ecn.org/freedom/totlib/index.html *Evolutionary Anarchist magazine promoting the ideas of a peaceful and evolutionary path to Anarchism. Subscription £8.00.*

YearZero (YZ) PO Box 26276, London, W3 7GQ. T 07752 358928 yearzero@flashmail.com www.yearzero.org *The disobedient current affairs quarterly.*

MEDIA – UK Local News

- find out what's happening in your area

ActionNet-North Staffs Mob 07748 883981 Webgimp@ActionNet-NorthStaffs.co.uk www.ActionNet-NorthStaffs.co.uk *Web-based resource for activists based in N. Staffordshire who are campaigning about various issues social, environmental and humanitarian.*

Bangor-Werdd http://groups.yahoo.com/group/bangor-werdd *North Wales email discussion network of non-violent direct action protesters including peace, environment and animal rights.*

Brighton Sucks! Scaramanga@brightonsucks.com www.brightonsucks.com *Keeping us in touch with what sucks about Brighton.*

Bristle Box 25, 82 Colston St. Bristol, BS1 5BB. editor@bristle.org.uk www.bristle.org.uk *Quarterly magazine for Bristol activism and anarchism treating all relevant subjects from news to campaigns.*

Bristol Indymedia http://bristol.indymedia.org *Bristol's own IndyMedia site with news from Bristol and beyond.*

Broughton Spurtle c/o Broughton Books, 2A Broughton Place, Edinburgh.T 0131 556 0903 F 0131 557 6752 Spurtle@tpuntis.demon.co.uk www.tpuntis.demon.co.uk *Publish monthly free paper for local area - publicise work of local action groups and generally stir things up.*

BuryGreen, richb@bradgate.u-net.com http://BuryGreen.org *A service and gateway to the various groups in and around Bury St Edmunds, Suffolk, dedicated to protecting and improving our environment.*

Cardiff Activists Network bozavine@yahoo.co.uk www.geocities.com/bozavine/can/index.html *For everyone interested in direct action based in Cardiff - allowing information about future actions to be advertised and planned.*

Cold Bath Times c/o Dave Hubble, 7 Ainsley Gardens, Eastleigh, Hants SO50 4NX. T 023 80611307 coldbathinfo@yahoo.co.uk *Multi-issue newsletter covering the Hampshire area plus wider issues, generally with an environmental theme. Follows no party or organisational line.*

Dan-Cymru http://groups.yahoo.com/group/dan-cymru *Direct action Cymru discussion group*

Direct Action Scotland http://groups.yahoo.com/group/directactionscotland *A discussion and information email list focusing on direct action and protest in Scotland.*

Elffinews PO Box 923, Luton, LU2 0YQ. T 01582-512184 F 01582 619218 M 07903 382228 elffinews@aol.com *Activist news letter for Luton and Dunstable. Scurrilous! A community based monthly newsletter, reporting on local activists' actions.*

Eroding Empire c/o 56a Crampton St. London. SE17 3AE. eroding@eroding.org.uk www.eroding.org.uk *Monthly listings for London area, diy, actions, centres, gigs.*

FutureManchester www.futuremanchester.org.uk *Site dedicated to sign-posting you to others working for positive change in Manchester*

Global Action Scotland www.egroups.com/invite/globalactionscotland *an email discussion group for global justice Visit the website to sign up.*

Hackney Indymedia http://uk.indymedia.org/index.php3?resist=front&stance=hackney *Gives an insight into the fourth poorest borough in Britain and to show how the council's and central government policy affects the local people.*

Interference FM Box 6, Green Leaf, 82 Colston St, Bristol, BS1 5BB. *Bristol's anarchist pirate radio station.*

Loombreaker, The c/o Manchester EF!, Dept.29, 22a Beswick St, Manchester, M4 7HS. T 0161 226 6814 editorial@loombreaker.org.uk www.loombreaker.org.uk *Monthly free Manchester direct action & campaigns round-up - Spreading news the mainstream media won't print.*

Norwich Anarchists PO Box 487, Norwich, NR2 3AL. T 07941 657485 *Produce a community based newspaper.*

Oxyacetylene 16b, Cherwell St, Oxford, OX4 1BG, T 07970 343486 http://come.to/oxyace *A newsletter for and about social and environmental action in Oxford and beyond. Reports every fortnight on the real issues affecting the people of Oxford.*

Pork-Bolter, The POBox 4144, Worthing, West Sussex, BN14 7NZ www.eco-action.org/porkbolter porkbolter@eco-action.org *Radical local newsletter with historically-vindicated pig obsession. Rages against CCTV, Big Business, councils, police etc. etc. Free with SAE.*

Radio 4A T 07980 168115 info@radio4a.org.uk www.radio4a.org.uk *Monthly pirate radio with a substantial speech output. Open access, non-profit and broadcasting live as well as creating programmes. 107.8FM in Brighton or webcast on www.piratetv.net*

Sheffield Mayday sheffieldmayday@ukf.net www.sheffieldmayday.ukf.net *News and information for activists in the Sheffield area, also e-mail discussion group*

Swan Net SwanNetwork@yahoogroups.com www.geocities.com/swan_net D*iary of events for Swansea.*

Think Globally Act Locally POBox 1TA, Newcastle, NE99 1TA. tapp@sandyford.techie.org.uk www.tapp.cjb.net *Newsletter that reports and informs campaigns and direct action in North East England.*

Underdog, The PO Box 35832, London E11 3WT. T 07810 288889 info@walthamstowanarchy.org.uk www.walthamstowanarchy.org.uk *Bi-monthly newsletter published by Walthamstow Anarchist Group.*

WARCRY c/o BM Makhno, London, WC1N 3XX war1921war@yahoo.co.uk *Monthly newsletter produced by West London Anarchists & Radicals*

NETWORKING SUPPORT

Blatant Incitement Project (BLINC) Dept.29, 22a Beswick Street,Manchester M4 7HS. T 0161-226 6814 doinit@nematode.freeserve.co.uk www.eco-action.org/blinc *Empower people to organise themselves without hierarchy, for radical action towards social ecological change, by sharing skills, knowledge, and inspiration.*

Confederation of Indian Organisations 5 Westminster Bridge, London, SE1 7XW T: 0207 928 9889 F: 0207 620 4025 cio@gn.apc.org www.cio.org.uk *Working with south Asian voluntary organisations in the UK.*

Cynefin y Werin Uned 2, gwasg Dwyfor, Stad Ddiwydiannol, Penygroes, Gwynedd LL545 6DB. T 01286 882359 Pager 07669 179015 benica@gn.apc.org *All Wales network for organisations working on international peace, solidarity and social justice.*

Edinburgh CITY (Change IT Yourselves) c/o ACE, 17 West Montgomery Place, Edinburgh EH7 5HA. info@edinburghcity.org.uk www.edinburghcity.org.uk *A new independent forum with no set agenda. Monthly discussion/social evening for people interested in social change.*

European Youth For Action (EYFA) Minahassatraat 1, 1090 GC Amsterdam, The Netherlands. T +31 20 665 7743 F +31 20 6928757 eyfa@eyfa.org www.eyfa.org *International network of grassroots groups and individuals working on environmental and social justice issues.*

LeftDirect www.leftdirect.co.uk *More than just a comprehensive directory of all left, radical and progressive organisations in the UK.*

Leicester Radical Alliance (LRA) c/o Dept Z, Littlethorn Books, Humberstone gate, Leicester T 07718 629 651 leicesterradical@hotmail.com http://radical.members.beeb.net *Monthly meetings and newsletetr to bring together all those who are now without a political home, disillusioned Labour supporters, and all others, who want to see radical changes in the social order.*

Networking Newsletter Project 6 Mount St, Manchester, M2 5NS T 0161 226 9321 info@networkingnewsletter.org.uk www.networkingnewsletter.org.uk *Network activists around Manchester who are working for positive change on issues of peace, development, environment, human rights, animal rights and other areas of social change.*

Radical Routes c/o Cornerstone Resource Centre, 16 Sholebroke Av, Leeds, LS7 3HB. T 0113 262 9365 cornerstone@ukf.net www.radicalroutes.org.uk *Mutual aid network of radical housing & worker co-ops and social centres. Support, advice & loans to member co-ops.*

Rebel Alliance *Brighton's (ir)regular get together of direct action groups and individuals, see SchNEWS for details.*

Seeds for Change Network 96 Church Street, Lancaster, LA1 1TD. T 0845 3307853 hello@seedsforchange.org.uk www.seedsforchange.org.uk *Free training + support on campaign planning,* tactics, non-hierarchical organising, consensus and facilitation plus advice on low cost computing and free software (linux).

PEACE

Abolition 2000 (A2000 UK) 601 Holloway Rd, London, N19 4DJ. T 020 7281 4281 A2000UK@an.www.gn.apc.org/ abolition2000uk *To achieve for the 21st century a global treaty to abolish nuclear weapons.*

Active Resistance to the Roots of War (ARROW) 162 Hollway Road, London, N7 8DQ. T 020 7607 2302 lrcndnvrn@supanet.com www.justicenotven egance.org *Nonviolent action affinity group.*

Aldermaston Women's Peace Camp c/o 157 Lyndhurst Rd, Worthing, W. Sussex BN11 2DG. T 0845 4588362 / 07904 450307 awpc@gmx.co.uk www.aldermastonwpc.gn.apc.org *Based around a monthly peace-camp at AWE Aldermaston - opposes Britain's nuclear weapons through campaigns and nonviolent direct action.*

Campaign for the Accountability of American Bases (CAAB) 8 Park Row, Otley, West Yorkshire LS21 1HQ. T 01943-466405 or 01482-702033 F 01482-702033 anniandlindis@caab.org.uk www.caab.org.uk *Working for accountability of American bases through the systems and structures available and taking direct action when these fail.*

Campaign Against Arms Trade (CAAT) 11 Goodwin St, London, N4 3HQ. T 020 7281 0297 F 020 7281 4369 enquries@caat.demon.co.uk www.caat.org.uk *Broad coalition of groups and individuals committed to an end to the international arms trade, together with progressive demilitarisation within arms-producing countries.*

Campaign for Nuclear Disarmament (CND) 162 Holloway Rd, London, N7 8DQ T 020 7700 2393 F 020 7700 2357 enquiries@cnduk.org www.cnduk.org *Campaigns non-violently to rid the world of nuclear weapons and other weapons of mass destruction and to create genuine security for future generations.*

Campaign to Free Vanunu & for a Nuclear Free Middle East 185 New Kent Rd, London, SE1 4AG T 020 7378 9324 F as phone www.vanunu.freeserve.co.uk campaign@vanunu.freeserve.co.uk *Campaign for the release of Vanunu, the Israeli nuclear whistleblower who, in 1986 was sentenced for 18 years imprisonment for revealing Israel's nuclear stockpiles.*

Conscience - The Peace Tax Campaign Archway Resource Centre, 1b Waterloo Rd, London, N19 5NJ. T 0870 777 3223 F 020 7281 6508 info@consc ienceonline.org.uk www.conscienceonline.org.uk *Campaigns for right of conscientious objectors to war to have the military part of their taxes spent on peacebuilding initiatives.*

Faslane Peace Camp A814, Shandon, Nr Helensburgh, Dumbartonshire, G84 8NT. T 01436 820901 faslanepeacecamp@hotmail.com www.faslanepeacecamp.org *Live across the road from Britain's nuclear arsenal, stop nuclear convoys and generally harass the MoD.*

Free Flyingdales Network www.freefylingdales network.co.uk *A small organisation that aim to stop America's "Son of Star Wars" Plans and, in particular, the use of RAF Fylingdales in North Yorkshire as part of this plan.*

Gush Shalom POB 3322 Tel-Aviv 61033 Israel. info@gush-shalom.org www.gush-shalom.org *Aims to influence Israeli public opinion and lead it towards peace and conciliation with the Palestinian people.*

Housmans Peace Resource Project (HPRP) 5 Caledonian Rd, Kings Cross, London, N1 T 020 7278 4474 F 020 7278 0444 worldpeace@gn.apc.org

Produces World Peace Database: 3500 organisations in 170 countries (includes major environmental & human rights groups) - abbreviated annual Directory appears in Housmans Peace Diary.

Non-Violent Resistance Network (NVRN) 162 Holloway Rd, London, N7 8DQ T 020 7607 2302 F 020 7700 2357 c/o cnd@gn.apc.org *Network nonviolent direct action activists in the UK and supply with information about NVDA events.*

Nonviolent Action *Magazine reporting nonviolent actions* (See entry under Media)

Other Israel, The PO Box 2542, Holon 58125, Israel. AICIPP@igc.org (North America) otherisr@actcom.co.il (Rest of World) http:// other_Israel.tripod.com *Bi-monthly peace movement magazine (hardcopy), for free sample send address.*

Peace Brigades International British Section (PBI) 1b Waterlow Rd, London, N19 5NJ. T 020 7281 5370 F 020 7272 9243 pbibritain@gn.apc.org www.igc.org/pbi *Send teams of international observers to provide protective accompaniment to local human rights defenders who are at risk as a result of their work for social justice.*

Peace Museum, The Office: Jacob's Well, Manchester Rd., Bradford, BD1 5RW. Visitor Gallery: 10 Piece Hall Yard, Bradford Centre, BD1 1PJ T 01274 754009 F 01274 752618 peacemuseum@bradfo rd.gov.uk www.peacemuseum.co.uk *Covers peace history, non-violence, conflict resolution. Four travelling exhibitions. Educational outreach. Open 11-3 Wed and Fri or by appointment.*

Peace News *Radical, international, antimilitarist, quarterly magazine.* (See entry under Media)

Scottish Campaign for Nuclear Disarmament (CND), 15 Barrland Street, Glasgow G41 1QH. T 0141 4231222 F 0141 4332821 scnd@banthebomb.org www.banthebomb.org *Largest Peace organisation in Scotland. Campaign against Trident at Faslane, coordinates the Coalition for Justice Not War. Supports direct action and political action.*

Trident Ploughshares 42-46 Bethel St, Norwich, Norfolk, NR2 1NR T 0845 4588366 F 0845 4588364 tp2000@gn.apc.org www.tridentploughs hares.org *Open, accountable & non-violent disarmament of the British nuclear Trident system.*

Voices in the Wilderness UK 16b Cherwell St, Oxford, OX4 1BG T 0845 4582564 voices@viwuk. freeserve.co.uk www.viwuk.freeserve.co.uk *Breaks sanctions by taking medical supplies to Iraq without export licences. Regular newsletter and briefings.*

WoMenwith Womyn's Peace Camp PO Box 105, Harrogate HG3 2FE. T 01943 466825 http:// cndyorks.gn.apc.org/mhs/index.htm *Camp against the world's largest spy base. Operated by the US government and based in the Yorkshire Moors.*

World Court Project UK 67 Summerheath Rd, Hailsham, Sussex BN27 3DR T 01323 844269 F 01323 844269 geowcpuk@gn.apc.org www.gn.apc.org/wcp *Working to have implemented the Advisory Opinion of the International Court of Justice that nuclear weapons are illegal.*

Youth & Student Campaign for Nuclear Disarmament (Y&SCND) 162 Holloway Rd, London, N7 8DQ T 0207 607 3616 F 0171 700 2357 youth_cnd@hotmail.com www.nonukes.org.uk *Campaigning to trash Trident through actions, demonstrations, awareness raising & letter writing. New volunteers are welcome.*

PRISONER SUPPORT

(also see Justice & the Law)

Anarchist Black Cross, Brighton PO Box 74, Brighton BN1 4ZQ. mail@brightonabc.org.uk

www.brightonabc.org.uk *Support group for anarchists, black liberation activists, anti-fascists and others we feel an affinity with who have ended up in prison.*

Anarchist Black Cross Network c/o Austin ABC, PO Box 19733, Austin, TX 78760-9733, USA. abc-help@anarchistblackcross.org www.anarchistbla ckcross.org *Network of ABC organisations, has list on website of all ABC groups.*

Animal Liberation Front UK Supporters Group *Info about animal rights prisoners and defence funds.* (See entry under Animal Rights)

Campaign to Free Vanunu & for a Nuclear Free Middle East *Israeli nuclear whistleblower sentenced in 1986 to 18 years.* (See entry under Peace)

Earth Liberation Prisoners BM Box 2407, London, WC1N 3XX. www.spiritoffreedom.org.uk *Supports people who have been arrested and imprisoned for acts of direct action in defence of animals and the earth.*

Eddie Gilfoyle Campaign c/o Susan Caddick PO Box 1845, Stoke on Trent ST7 4EG. T 0781 501 2372 Paul.Caddick@btinternet.com *Campaigning for the release of Eddie Gilfoyle who was wrongly convivted of murder in 1993.*

Free Satpal Ram Campaign PO Box 30091 London SE1 1WP. www.appleonline.net/satpal *Satpal Ram was given a life sentence for defending himself from a vicious racist attack. Self-defence is no offence.*

Haven Distribution 27 Old Gloucester St, London, WC1N 3XX. *Supplies free educational literature to prisoners in UK and Ireland. Donations make this possible.*

International Concerned Family & Friends of Mumia Abu-Jamal www.mumia.org *Information and networking to save this journalist/activist's life.*

Justice For Mark Barnsley PO Box 381, Huddersfield, HD1 4XX MarkBarnsley@ncadc.demon.co.uk www.freemarkbarnsley.com *Campaign supporting Mark an anarchist prisoner serving 12 years after getting beaten up by a group of students.*

Legal Defence & Monitoring Group (LDMG) (See entry under Justice and the Law)

Miscarriages of Justice UK (MOJUK) (See entry under Justice and the Law)

Mumia Must Live! BM Box 4771, London, WC1N 3XX mumia@callnet.uk.com www.callnetuk.com/home/ mumia *Mumia Abu-Jamal is a political Prisoner facing death row in the USA. This is a coalition fighting to free Mumia and end the racist death penalty.*

Vegan Prisoners Support Group (VPSG) (See entry under Animal Rights)

REFUGEES

Asylum Aid 28 Commercial St, London, E1 6LS. T 020 7377 5123 F 020 7247 7789 info@asylumaid.org.uk www.asylumaid.org.uk *Provides free legal advice and representation to refugees seeking safety in the UK from persecution and campaign for fair treatment of refugees in the UK.*

Asylum Support www.asylumsupport.info *Online information focusing on all matters that concern people seeking asylum, together with a directory of hundreds of online resources relating to asylum and refugees.*

Barbed Wire Britain T 01865 558145/726804, 01993 703994, 07767 414714, 01753 852853 F 01865 558145 barbedwirebritain@yahoogroups.co m www.barbedwirebritain.org.uk *Linking and helping to establish local campaigns outside places of detention, demos, lobbies, publications, working with detainees past and present*

Campaign to Close Campsfield c/o 111 Magdalen St, Oxford T 01865 558145/557282/378734 www.closecampsfield.org.uk info@closecampsfie ld.org.uk *Campaign for the closure of Campsfield House Immigration Detention Centre and for the* end of detention of refugees nation-wide.

Close Down Harmondsworth Campaign 10 Endsleigh Rd, Southall UB2 5QL. T 07960 309457 F 08701 643017 closedownharmondsworth@hotmail .com *Campaigning against imprisonment of asylum seekers and others in racist detention centre.*

International Federation of Iranian Refugees (IFIR) PO Box 27236, London N11 2ZF. T 07730 107337 F 0870 1394253 ifir@ukonline.co.uk www.hambastegi.org *Committed to organising the protests of Iranian refugees and asylum seekers in support of political and social campaigns.*

National Coalition of Anti-Deportation Campaigns (NCADC) 110 Hamstead Road, Handsworth, Birmingham B20 2QS. T 0121 554 6947 F 0121 554 7891 Ncadc@ncadc.org.uk www.ncadc.org.uk *Bringing together families and individuals fighting deportation.*

Refugee Council 3 Bondway, London SW8 1SJ. T 020 7820 3000 F 020 7582 9929 info@refugee council.org.uk www.refugeecouncil.org.uk *Largest organisation in the UK working with asylum seekers and refugees.*

SEXUALITY

Intercourse: talking sex c/o 17 West Montgomery Place, Edinburgh EH7 5HA. info@intercourse.org.uk www.intercourse.org.uk *Encourages comfortable and positive ways of thinking and talking about sex by organising discussions and events and producing literature.*

OutRage! POBox 17816, London, SW14 8WT T 020 8240 0222 outreach@OutRage.org.uk www.OutRage.org.uk *World's longest surviving queer rights direct action group, dedicated to fighting homophobia and achieving equal civil rights.*

Queeruption 56a Infoshop, 56 Crampton Street, London SE17 5AE. T 07949 976016 info@queeruption.com www.queeruption.com (Europe) www.queeruption.org (USA) *Radical queer network. Organising the queeruption gatherings, parties, actions, alternative pride, cabaret, street intervention, cafe, squat and generally being sexy!*

Sexual Freedom Coalition BM Box Lovely, London, WC1N 3XX info@sfc.org.uk www.sfc.org.uk *Coordinating the groups who campaign for the sexual freedom of consenting adults, providing a back-up force when problems occur.*

Stonewall Lobby Group ltd. 46-48 Grosvenor Gardens, London , SW1W 0EB. T 020 7881 9440 F 020 7881 9444 info@stonewall.org.uk www.stonewall.org.uk *Working towards the advancement of the civil, political, economic, social and cultural rights of lesbians and gay men.*

TRANSPORT

Campaign Against Tube Privatisation (CATP) T 07961 440868 publictube@aol.com www.catp.org *Founded in 1999 by London Underground workers so they could campaign together with the travelling public against the Blair government's planned privatisation of the tube.*

Car Busters Magazine and Resource Centre Kratka 26, 100 00 Praha 10, Czech Republic +420 2 7481 0849 F +420 2 7481 6727 carbusters@ecn.cz www.carbusters.ecn.cz *A quarterly multilingual magazine and resource centre for the international anti-car movement. To facilitate exchange & co-operation, inspire, reach out, and change the world.*

Environmental Transport Association Services ltd (ETA) 10 Church St, Weybridge KT13 8RS. T 01932 828882 www.eta.co.uk *The ETA is the only British provider of breakdown services that cam-*

paigns for environmentally sound transport.

EVUK editor@evuk.co.uk www.evuk.co.uk *Campaign for REAL, long-distance electric vehicles.*

Green Skies, c/o Aviation Environment Federation, Sir John Lyon House, 5 High Timber Street, London EC4V 3NS. T 020 7248 2223 F 020 7329 8160 info@greenskies.org www.greenskies.org *GreenSkies is a world-wide information network of environmental organisations concerned with aviation's environmental effects.*

Re-Cycle 60 High St, West Mersea, Essex, CO5 8JE. T/F 01206 382207 info@re-cycle.org www.re-cycle.org *Sends second hand bicycles to Less Developed Countries and teaches local people skills to maintain and repair them.*

RoadPeace PO Box 2579, London NW10 3PW. T 020 8838 5102/Support line: 020 8964 1021 F 020 8838 5103 info@roadpeace.org www.roadpeace.org *Supporting those bereaved or injured in a road crash. Working for Real Road Safety.*

Slower Speeds Initiative (SSI) PO Box 19, Hereford HR1 1XJ. T 0845 345 8459 info@slowerspeeds.org.uk www.slower-speeds.org.uk *Lower speeds make walking and cycling safer, provide alternatives to road-building, support local economies and reduce CO2 emissions.*

Sustrans 35 King Street, Bristol BS1 4DZ. T 0117 926 8893 F 0117 929 4173 www.sustrans.org.uk *Designs and builds traffic-free routes for cyclists, walkers and people with disabilities.*

Transport 2000 Impact Centre, 12-18 Hoxton St, London, N1 6NG. T 020 7613 0743 F 020 7613 5280 www.transport2000.org.uk *Campaigns & lobbies for a sustainable transport policy.*

TRAVELLERS

Enabler Publications *Books about counter culture, Travellers, protest and creative work with young people.* (See entry under Media)

Friends, Families & Travellers (FFT) Community Base, 113 Queens Rd, Brighton BN1 3XG. T 01273 234777/mobile: 07971 550328 F 01273 234778 fft@communitybase.org www.gypsy-tyraveller.org *Advice and Information Unit for Gypsies, Travellers, service providers etc, on issues such as evictions, sites, planning, discrimination. Also lobbying and campaigning on Travellers' rights.*

New Futures Association The Cottage, Glaneirw, Tan-y-groes, Ceredigion. T: 01239 811929 nfauk@hotmail.com *Established a resource centre for nomadic people to encourage training, education and self-help. Supports travellers by providing information and advice and through campaigning.*

Traveller Law Research Unit (TLRU) www.cf.ac.uk/claws/tlru *Research and publication of Traveller-related legal issues.*

Travellers' School Charity (See entry under Education)

WOMEN

Aldermaston Women's Peace Camp (See entry under Peace)

Crossroads Women'sCentre PO Box 287, London NW6 5QU. T 020 7482 2496 F 020 7209 4761 crossroadswomenscentre@compuserve.com http: //allwomencount.net *Lively, welcoming, anti-sexist anti-racist home of a number of organisations which highlight the needs and concerns of grassroots women especially.*

Feminist Library, The 5-5a Westminster Bridge Rd, London, SE1 7XW. T 020 7928 7789 feministlibrary@beeb.net *Largest lending and reference library of contemporary feminist material in*

the UK, both fiction and non-fiction.

International Wages for Housework Campaign (IWFHC) Crossroads Women's Centre, 230A Kentish Town Road, London, NW5 2AB T: 020 7482 2496 F: 020 7209 4761 crossroadswomenscent re@compuserve.com http://allwomencount.net *International multi-racial grassroots women's network campaigning for governments to recognise and pay wages for all women's unwaged work.*

Women Against Rape (WAR) PO Box 287, London NW6 5QU. T 020 7482 2496 F 020 7209 4761crossroadswomenscentre@compuserve.com www.womenagainstrape.net *Grassroots multi-racial women's organisation provides counselling, legal advocacy, and campaigns for justice, protection and compensation for survivors of sexual violence.*

WORKERS' RIGHTS

Education Workers Network *who favour collective direct action for decent education.* (See entry under Education)

Global Women's Strike Crossroads Women's Centre, 230A Kentish Town Road, London Postcode: NW5 2AB T (020) 7482 2496 F (020) 7209 4761 womenstrike8m@server101.ocm http://womens trike8m.server101.com *Women everywhere strike annually on 8 March, to value all women's work and against no pay, low pay and overwork.*

Industrial Workers of the World PO Box 4414, Poole Dorset, BH15 3YL, UK T 01202 257556 info@iww.org.uk www.iww.org.uk *Union for all run by its members. For the abolition of wage-slavery through global solidarity, direct action and industrial democracy.*

Institute of Employment Rights (IER) 177 Abbeville Rd, London, SW4 9RL T 020 7498 6919 F 020 7498 9080 www.ier.org.uk ier@gn.apc.org *A trade union supported think tank acting as a focal point for the spread of new ideas in the field of labour law.*

Iranian Workers News PO Box 23734, London SW5 9GB. editor@iranian-workers-news.net www.iranian-workers-news.net *Solidarity campaign with Iranian workers.*

LabourStart ericlee@labourstart.org www.labourstart.org *Online global labour news service and portal.*

London Hazards Centre (See entry under Health)

McDonalds Workers Resistance (MWR) PO Box 3828, Glasgow, G41 1YU. Info@mwr.org.uk www.mwr.org.uk *We work for McDonalds and fuck shit up. We encourage other Mcworkers to do the same.*

No Sweat, PO Box 36707, London, SW9 8YA. T(mob) 07904 431959 admin@nosweat.org.uk www.nosweat.org.uk *Campaigning against child and sweated labour at home and abroad through direct action, organisation and making practical solidarity.*

Simon Jones Memorial Campaign PO Box 2600, Brighton, BN2 0EF. T 01273 685913 F as phone action@simonjones.org.uk www.simonjones.org.uk *Campaigns for justice for Simon Jones, killed on his first day as a casual worker on a Shoreham dock, and to expose the dangers of casualisation.*

Tools For Solidarity (TFS) Unit 1B1, Edenberry Industrial Estate, 326 Crumlin Rd, Belfast, BT14 7EE T 028 9074 7473. *Refurbishes unwanted hand tools and sewing machines for skilled tradespeople in Africa. Committed to the equal distribution of power and resources.*

UNISON Dudley Group of Hospitals, Union Offices, Wordsley Hospital, Stourbridge, West Midlands, DY8 5QX. T 01384 244350 F 01384 244350 dghunison@ic24.net *We are a trade union branch with a proud tradition of fighting PFI privatisation.*

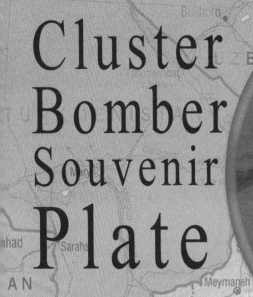